AMERICA'S
Favorite
INNS,
B&Bs
& SMALL HOTELS
Fifteenth Edition

The West Coast

States and Canadian Provinces Covered in This Edition

Alaska	WESTERN CANADA
California	Alberta
Hawaii	British Columbia
Oregon	Yukon
Washington	

Also in This Series

AMERICA'S
Favorite
INNS,
B&Bs
& SMALL HOTELS

Fifteenth Edition

The West Coast

Edited by Sandra W. Soule

Associate Editors:
Nancy P. Barker, Kathy Banak,
Carol Dinmore, Audrey S. Levine,
Amy Phillipps, Hilary Soule
Contributing Editors:
Mary Ann Boyle, Suzanne Carmichael,
Rose Ciccone, Gail Davis, Nancy Debevoise, Linda
Goldberg, Abby Humphrey, Betty Norman, Pam Phillips,
Joe Schmidt, Susan Schwemm, Diane Wolf
Editorial Assistants:
Meghan Morris, Sarah Phillipps

St. Martin's Griffin
New York

This book is dedicated to the people who take the time to write about the hotels and inns they've visited, and to my children—Hilary and Jeffrey—my husband, and my parents.

AMERICA'S FAVORITE INNS, B&BS & SMALL HOTELS, THE WEST COAST, FIFTEENTH EDITION. Copyright © 1997 by Sandra W. Soule. All rights reserved. Printed in the United States of America. No part of this book may be used or reproduced in any manner whatsoever without written permission except in the case of brief quotations embodied in critical articles or reviews. For information, address St. Martin's Press, 175 Fifth Avenue, New York, N.Y. 10010.

ISBN 0-312-16770-9

First St. Martin's Griffin Edition: December 1997

10 9 8 7 6 5 4 3 2 1

Maps by David Lindroth, © 1997, 1994, 1992, 1991, 1990, 1989, 1988, 1987 by St. Martin's Press.

Contents

Acknowledgments

I would like again to thank all the people who wrote in such helpful detail about the inns and hotels they visited. To them belong both the dedication and the acknowledgments, for without their support, this guide would not exist. If I have inadvertently misspelled or omitted anyone's name, please accept my sincerest apologies.

I would also like to thank my helpful and supportive editor, Anne Savarese; to my wonderful colleagues Nancy Barker, Kathy Banak, Audrey Levine, Amy Phillipps, Suzanne Carmichael, Rose Ciccone, Nancy Debevoise, Gail Davis, Linda Goldberg, Betty Norman, Pam Phillips, Susan Schwemm, and Diane Wolf; and to faithful respondents Heather Allen, Carolyn Alexander, Peg Bedini, Robert Boas, Donna Bocks, Judith Brannen, Sherrill Brown, James and Pamela Burr, Marjorie Cohen, Dianne Crawford, Lynne Derry, Gail DeSciose, Brian Donaldson, Sally Ducot, Lynn Edge, Ellie and Robert Freidus, Lynn Fullman, Kip Goldman, and Marty Wall, Gail Gunning, B. J. Hensley, Lisa Hering, Emily Hochemong, Tina Hom, Stephen Holman, Karen Hughes, Ruth Hurley, Linda Intaschi, Christopher Johnston, Keith Jurgens, Arleen Keele, Peggy Kontak, Bradley Lockner, Bill MacGowan, Myra Malkin, Celia McCullough, Mark Mendenhall, Michael and Dina Miller, Carol Moritz, Carolyn Myles, Eileen O'Reilly, Kathleen Lowe Owen, Marilyn Parker, Julie Phillips, Adam Platt, Penny Poirier, Lucia and Susan Rather, Jill Reeves, Stephanie Roberts, Glenn Roehrig, Duane Roller, Marion Ruben, Lori Sampson, Joe and Sheila Schmidt, B. J. and Larry Schwartzkopf, Robert Sfire, Fritz Shantz and Tara O'Neal, Nancy Sinclair, Mary Jane Skala, Ruth Tilsley, Susan Ulanoff, Wendi Van Exan, Hopie Welliver, Jim and Mary White, Tom Wilbanks, Beryl Williams, Rose Wolf, Karl Wiegers and Chris Zambito, Susan Woods, and the many others who went far beyond the call of duty in their assistance and support.

Introduction

Reading the Entries

Each entry generally has three parts: a description of the inn or hotel, quotes from guests who have stayed there, and relevant details about rooms, rates, location, and facilities. Please remember that the length of an entry is in no way a reflection of that inn or hotel's quality. Rather, it is an indication of the type of feedback we've received both from guests and from the innkeepers themselves.

Wherever a location is of particular tourist interest, we've tried to include some information about its attractions. In some areas the magnet is not a particular town but rather a compact, distinct region. Travelers choose one place to stay and use it as a base from which to explore the area. But because this guide is organized by town, not by region, the entries are scattered throughout the chapter. When this applies, you will see the name of the region noted under the "Location" heading; check back to the introduction for a description of the region involved. Cross-referencing is also provided to supplement the maps at the back of the book.

The names at the end of the quotations are those who have recommended the hotel or inn. Some writers have requested that we not use their names; you will see initials noted instead. *We never print the names of those who have sent us adverse reports, although their contributions are invaluable indeed.*

Although we have tried to make the listings as accurate and complete as possible, mistakes and inaccuracies invariably creep in. The most significant area of inaccuracy applies to the rates charged by each establishment. In preparing this guide, we asked all the hotels and inns to give us their 1998–1999 rates, ranging from the least expensive room in the off-season to the most expensive peak-season price. Some did so, while others just noted the current rate.

Some of the shorter entries are marked "**Information please**" or "**Also recommended.**" These tend to be establishments that are either too large or too small for a full entry, or about which we have insufficient information to complete a full entry.

Please remember that the process of writing and publishing a book takes nearly a year. *You should always double-check the rates when you make your reservations; please don't blame the inn or this guide if the prices are wrong.* On the other hand, given the current level of inflation, you should not encounter anything more than a 5% increase, unless there has been a substantial improvement in the amenities

1

offered or a change of ownership. Please let us know immediately if you find anything more than that!

If you find any errors of omission or commission in any part of the entries, we urgently request your help in correcting them. We recognize that it takes extra time and effort for readers to write us letters or fill in report forms, but this feedback is essential in keeping this publication totally responsive to consumer needs.

The Fifteen Commandments of Vacation Travel

We all know people who come back from a vacation feeling on top of the world, and others who seem vaguely disappointed. Here's how to put yourself in the first category, not the second.

1. Know yourself. A successful vacation is one that works for the person you are, not the person you think you should be. Confirmed couch potatoes who resent having to walk from the far end of the parking lot will not find true fulfillment on a trek through the Himalayas. If privacy is a top priority, a group tour or communal lodge will turn fantasy into frustration. Acknowledge your own comfort levels. How important is it for you to be independent and flexible? Structured and secure? How essential are the creature comforts when it comes to sleeping, eating, and bathing? Would you rather have one week of luxury travel or two weeks of budget food and accommodation? And remember that while your personality doesn't change, your needs do. The type of vacation you plan for a romantic getaway is totally different from a family reunion.

2. Know your travel companions. Adjust your plans to accommodate your travel partners. Whether you are traveling with friends, spouse, children, and/or parents, you'll need to take their age, attention span, agility, and interests into account. If you're traveling with the kids, balance a morning at an art museum with an afternoon at the zoo; if you're spending time with elderly parents, make sure that they can stroll a country lane while you go rock-climbing; if your group includes skiers and non-skiers, pick a resort that has appealing shops and other activities.

3. Plan ahead: anticipation is half the fun. Enjoy the process. The more you know about an area you're going to visit, the more fun you'll have. Skim a guidebook; get a calendar of events; write to the local chambers of commerce and tourist offices; read a novel set in the region; talk to friends (or friends of friends) who have been there recently.

4. Don't bite off more than you can chew. Keep your itinerary in line with the amount of time and money available. Focus on seeing a smaller area well, rather than trying to cover too much ground and seeing nothing but interstate highways. Don't overprogram; allow yourself the luxury of doing nothing.

5. Avoid one-night stands. Plan to stay a minimum of two nights everywhere you go. A vacation made up of one-nighters is a prescription for exhaustion. You will sleep poorly, spend most of your time in transit, and will get only the smallest glimpse of the place you're visiting. If it's worth seeing, it's worth spending a full day in one place.

6. Travel off-season. Unless your vacation dates are dictated by the school calendar, off-season travel offers many advantages: fewer crowds, greater flexibility, and a more relaxed atmosphere. Learn to pick the best dates for off-season travel; typically these are the weeks just before and after the rates change. Off-season travel offers big savings, too; for example, most ski areas are delightful places to visit in summer, and offer savings of 50% or more on accommodations.

7. Book well ahead for peak season travel. If you must travel during peak periods to popular destinations, make reservations well in advance for the key sites to avoid aggravation, extra phone calls, and additional driving time.

8. Take the road less traveled. Get off the beaten path to leave the crowds behind. Instead of booking a room in the heart of the action, find a quiet inn tucked in the hills or in a neighboring village. If you visit the Grand Canyon in August, at the height of the tourist season, stay at the North Rim, which attracts 90% fewer visitors than the South Rim.

9. Ditch the car. Sure you need a car to get where you're going. But once you're there, get out and walk. You'll see more, learn more, experience more at every level, while avoiding crowds even at the most popular destinations. We promise. Car travel is an isolating experience, even when you're in bumper-to-bumper traffic.

10. Hang loose. The unexpected is inevitable in travel, as in the rest of life. When your plans go astray (and they will), relax and let serendipity surprise you. And keep your sense of humor in good working order. If possible, travel without reservations or a set itinerary.

11. Carpe diem—seize the day. Don't be afraid to follow your impulses. If a special souvenir catches your eye, buy it; don't wait to see if you'll find it again later. If a hiking trail looks too inviting to pass up, don't; that museum will wait for a rainy day.

12. Don't suffer in silence. When things go wrong—an incompetent guide, car troubles, a noisy hotel room—speak up. Politely but firmly express your concern then and there; get your room changed, ask for a refund or discount, whatever. Most people in the travel business would rather have you go away happy than to leave grumbling.

13. Remember—being there is more than seeing there. People travel to see the sights—museums and mountains, shops and scenery—but it is making new friends that can make a trip memorable. Leave a door open to the people-to-people experiences that enrich travel immeasurably.

14. Don't leave home to find home. The quickest way to take the wind out of the sails of your trip is to compare things to the way they are at home. Enjoy different styles and cultures for what they are and avoid comparisons and snap judgments.

15. Give yourself permission to disregard all of the above. Nothing is immutable. If you find a pattern that works for you, enjoy it!

The Inngoer's Bill of Rights

Although nothing's perfect, as we all know, inngoers are entitled to certain reasonable standards. Of course, the higher the rates, the higher those standards should be. So, please use this Bill of Rights as a kind of checklist in deciding how you think a place stacks up on your own personal rating scale. And, whether an establishment fails, reaches, or exceeds these levels, be sure to let us know. We would also hope that innkeepers will use this list to help evaluate both the strong points and shortcomings of their own establishments, and are grateful to those who have already done so.

The right to suitable cleanliness: An establishment that looks, feels, and smells immaculate, with no musty, smoky, or animal odors.

The right to suitable room furnishings: A firm mattress, soft pillows, fresh linens, and ample blankets; bright lamps and night tables on each side of the bed; comfortable chairs with good reading lights; and adequate storage space.

The right to comfortable, attractive rooms: Guest rooms and common rooms that are as livable as they are attractive. Appealing places where you'd like to read, chat, relax.

The right to a decent bathroom: Cleanliness is essential, along with reliable plumbing, ample hot water, good lighting, an accessible electric outlet, space for toiletries, and thirsty towels.

The right to privacy and discretion: Privacy must be respected by the innkeeper and ensured by adequate sound-proofing. The right to discretion precludes questions about marital status or sexual preference. No display of proselytizing religious materials.

The right to good, healthful food: Fresh nutritious food, ample in quantity, high in quality, attractively presented, and graciously served in smoke-free surroundings.

The right to comfortable temperatures and noise levels: Rooms should be cool in summer and warm in winter, with windows that open, and quiet, efficient air-conditioning and heating. Double windows, drapes, and landscaping are essential if traffic noise is an issue.

The right to fair value: Prices should be in reasonable relation to the facilities offered and to the cost of equivalent local accommodation.

The right to genuine hospitality: Innkeepers who are glad you've come and who make it their business to make your stay pleasant and memorable; who are readily available without being intrusive.

The right to a caring environment: Welcoming arrivals with refreshments, making dinner reservations, providing information on activities, asking about pet allergies and dietary restrictions, and so on.

The right to personal safety: A location in a reasonably safe neighborhood, with adequate care given to building and parking security.

The right to professionalism: Brochure requests, room reservations, check-ins and -outs handled efficiently and responsibly.

The right to adequate common areas: At least one common room where guests can gather to read, chat, or relax, free of the obligation to buy anything.

The right of people traveling alone to have all the above rights: Singles usually pay just a few dollars less than couples, yet the welcome, services, and rooms they receive can be inferior.

The right to a reasonable cancellation policy: Penalties for a cancellation made fewer than 7-14 days before arrival are relatively standard. Most inns will refund deposits (minus a processing fee) after the deadline only if the room is rebooked.

The right to efficient maintenance: Burnt-out bulbs and worn-out smoke detector batteries are the responsibility of the innkeeper—not the guest. When things go wrong, guests have the right to an apology, a discount, or a refund.

Of course, there is no "perfect" inn or hotel, because people's tastes and needs vary so greatly. But one key phrase does pop up over and over again: "I felt right at home." This is not written in the literal sense— a commercial lodging, no matter how cozy or charming, is never the same as one's home. What is really meant is that guests felt as welcome, as relaxed, as comfortable, as they would in their own home.

What makes for a wonderful stay?

We've tried our best to make sure that all the inns listed in this guide are as special as our title promises. Inevitably, there will be some disappointments. Sometimes these will be caused by a change in ownership or management that has resulted in lowered standards. Other times unusual circumstances will lead to problems. Quite often, though, problems will occur because there's not a good "fit" between the inn and the guest. Decide what you're looking for, then find the place that suits your needs, whether you're looking for a casual environment or a dressy one, a romantic setting or a family-oriented one, a vacation spot or a business person's environment, an isolated country retreat or a convenient in-town location.

We've tried to give you as much information as possible on each property listed, and have taken care to indicate the atmosphere each innkeeper is trying to create. After you've read the listing, request a copy of the establishment's brochure, which will give you more information. Finally, feel free to call any inn or hotel where you're planning to stay, and ask as many questions as necessary.

Inn etiquette

A first-rate inn is a joy indeed, but as guests we need to do our part to respect its special qualities. For starters, you'll need to maintain a higher level of consideration for your fellow guests. Century-old Victorians are noted for their nostalgic charms, not their sound-proofing; if you come in late or get up early, remember that voices and footsteps echo off all those gleaming hardwood floors and doors. If you're going to pick a fight with your roommate, pull the covers up over your head or go out for a walk. If you're sharing a bath, don't dawdle, tidy up after yourself, and dry your hair back in your room. If you've admired the Oriental carpets, antique decor, handmade quilts, and the thick fluffy towels, don't leave wet glasses on the furniture, put suitcases on the bed, or use the towels for removing make-up or wiping the snow off your car. After all, innkeepers have rights too!

Hotels, inns ... resorts and motels

As the title indicates, this is a guide to exceptional inns, B&Bs, and small hotels. Generally, the inns have 5 to 25 rooms, although a few have only 2 rooms and some have over 100. The hotels are more often found in the cities and range in size from about 50 to 200 rooms.

The line between an inn or hotel and a resort is often a fine one. There are times when we all want the extra facilities a resort provides, so we've added a number of reader-recommended facilities. We've also listed a handful of motels. Although they don't strictly fall within the context of this book, we've included them because readers felt they were the best option in a specific situation.

Although we do not provide full coverage of hotel chains, we do want to point out that the Four Seasons and Ritz-Carlton hotels are almost impossible to beat at the luxury end of the spectrum. Readers consistently rave about their unbeatable combination of unparalleled service and plush accommodation; weekend rates make them an exceptional value.

What is a B&B anyway?

There are basically two kinds of B&Bs—the B&B homestay and the B&B inn. The homestay is typically the home of an empty nester, who has a few empty bedrooms to fill, gaining some extra income and pleasant company. B&B inns are run on a more professional basis, independently marketed and subject to state and local licensing. Guests typically have dedicated common areas for their use, and do not share the hosts' living quarters, as in a homestay. We list very few homestays in this guide. Full-service or country inns and lodges are similar to the B&B inn, except that they serve breakfast and dinner on a regular basis, and may be somewhat larger in size; dinner is often offered to the public as well as to house guests. The best of all of these are made special by resident owners bringing the warmth of their personalities to the total experience. A B&B is *not* a motel that serves breakfast.

Rooms

All guest rooms are not created equal. Although the rooms at a typical chain motel or hotel may be identical, the owners of most of the establishments described in this book pride themselves on the individuality of each guest room. Some, although not all, of these differences are reflected in the rates charged.

More importantly, it means that travelers need to express their needs clearly to the innkeepers when making reservations and again when checking in. Some rooms may be quite spacious but may have extremely small private baths or limited closet space. Some antique double beds have rather high footboards—beautiful to look at but torture for six-footers. Most inns are trading their double-size mattresses in for queens and kings; if you prefer an oversize bed, say so. If you want twin beds, be sure to specify this when making reservations and again when you check in; many smaller inns have only one twin-bedded room. If you must have a king-size bed, ask for details; sometimes two twin beds are just pushed together, made up with a king-size fitted sheet.

Some rooms may have gorgeous old bathrooms, with tubs the size of small swimming pools, but if you are a hard-core shower person, that room won't be right for you. More frequently, you'll find a shower but no bathtub, which may be disappointing if you love a long, luxurious soak. If you are traveling on business and simply must have a working-size desk with good lighting, an electric outlet, and a telephone jack for your modem, speak up. Some rooms look terrific inside but don't look out at anything much; others may have the view but not quite as special a decor. Often the largest rooms are at the front of the house, facing a busy highway. Decide what's important to you. Although the owners and staff of the hotels and inns listed here are incredibly hardworking and dedicated people, they can't read your mind. Let your needs be known, and, within the limits of availability, they will try to accommodate you.

Our most frequent complaints center around beds that are too soft and inadequate reading lights. If these are priorities for you (as they are for us), don't be shy about requesting bedboards or additional lamps to remedy the situation. Similarly, if there are other amenities your room is lacking—extra pillows, blankets, or even an easy chair—speak up. Most innkeepers would rather put in an extra five minutes of work than have an unhappy guest.

If you really don't like your room, ask for another as soon as possible, preferably before you've unpacked your bags. The sooner you voice your dissatisfaction, the sooner something can be done to improve the situation. If you don't like the food, ask for something else—since you're the guest, make sure you get treated like one. If things go terribly wrong, don't be shy about asking for your money back, and be *sure* to write us about any problems.

What is a single? A double? A suite? A cottage or cabin?

Unlike the proverbial rose, a single is not a single is not a single. Sometimes it is a room with one twin bed, which really can accommodate only one person. Quite often it is described as a room with a standard-size double bed, in contrast to a double, which has two twin beds. Other hotels call both of the preceding doubles, although doubles often have queen- or even king-size beds instead. Many times the only distinction is made by the number of guests occupying the room; a single will pay slightly less, but there's no difference in the room.

There's almost as much variation when it comes to suites. We define a suite as a bedroom with a separate living room area and often a small kitchen, as well. Unfortunately, the word has been stretched to cover other setups, too. Some so-called suites are only one large room, accommodating a table and separate seating area in addition to the bed, while others are two adjacent bedrooms which share a bath. If you require a suite that has two separate rooms with a door between them, specify this when you make reservations.

Quite a few of our entries have cabins or cottages in addition to rooms in the main building. In general, a cabin is understood to be a somewhat more rustic residence than a cottage, although there's no hard-and-fast rule. Be sure to inquire for details when making reservations.

Making reservations

Unless you are inquiring many months in advance of your visit, it's best to telephone when making reservations. This offers a number of advantages: You will know immediately if space is available on your requested dates; you can find out if that space is suitable to your specific needs. You will have a chance to discuss the pros and cons of the available rooms and will be able to find out about any changes made in recent months—new facilities, recently redecorated rooms, nonsmoking policies, even a change of ownership. It's also a good time to ask the innkeeper about other concerns—Is the neighborhood safe at night? Is there any renovation or construction in progress that might be disturbing? Will a wedding reception or bicycle touring group affect use of the common areas during your visit? If you're reserving a room at a plantation home that is available for public tours, get specifics about the check-in/out times; in many, rooms are not available before 5 P.M. and must be vacated by 9 A.M. sharp. The savvy traveler will always get the best value for his accommodation dollar.

If you expect to be checking in late at night, *be sure to say so;* many inns give doorkeys to their guests, then lock up by 10 P.M.; often special arrangements must be made for late check-ins, and a handful of inns won't accept them at all.

We're often asked about the need for making advance reservations. If you'll be traveling in peak periods, in prime tourist areas, and want to be sure of getting a first-rate room at the best-known inns, reserve at least three to six months ahead. This is especially true if you're traveling with friends or family and will need more than one room. On the other hand, if you like a bit of adventure, and don't want to be stuck with cancellation fees when you change your mind, by all means stick our books in the glove compartment and hit the road. If you're traveling in the off-season, or even midweek in season, you'll have a grand time. But look for a room by late afternoon; never wait until after dinner and expect to find something decent. Some inns offer a discount after 4:00 P.M. for last-minute bookings; it never hurts to ask.

Payment

The vast majority of inns now accept credit cards. A few accept credit cards for the initial deposit but prefer cash, traveler's checks, or personal checks for the balance; others offer the reverse policy. When no credit cards are accepted at all, you can settle your bill with a personal check, traveler's check, or even (!) cash.

When using your credit card to guarantee a reservation, be aware that most inns will charge your card for the full amount of the deposit, unlike motels and hotels which don't put through the charge until you've checked in. A few will put a "hold" on your card for the full amount of your entire stay, plus the cost of meals and incidentals that you may (or may not) spend. If you're using your card to reserve a fairly extended trip, you may find that you're well over your credit limit without actually having spent a nickel. We'd suggest inquiring; if the latter is the procedure, either send a check for the deposit or go elsewhere. If you have used American Express, Diners Club, MasterCard, or Visa to guarantee your reservation, these companies guarantee if a room is not available, the hotel is supposed to find you a free room in a comparable hotel, plus transportation and a free phone call.

Rates

All rates quoted are per room, unless otherwise noted as being per person. Rates quoted per person are usually based on double occupancy, unless otherwise stated.

"Room only" rates do not include any meals. In most cases two or three meals a day are served by the hotel restaurant, but are charged separately. Average meal prices are noted when available. In a very few cases no meals are served on the premises at all; rooms in these facilities are usually equipped with kitchenettes.

B&B rates include bed and breakfast. Breakfast can vary from a simple continental breakfast to a full breakfast. Afternoon tea and evening refreshments are sometimes included as well.

MAP (Modified American Plan) rates are often listed per person and include breakfast and dinner; *a 15% service charge is typically added to the total.* Full board rates include three squares a day, and are usually found only at old-fashioned resorts and isolated ranches.

State and local sales taxes are not included in the rates unless otherwise indicated; the percentage varies from state to state, city to city, and can reach 20% in a few urban centers, although 10–15% is more typical.

When inquiring about rates, always ask if any off-season or special package rates are available. Sometimes discounted rates are available *only* on request; seniors and AAA members often qualify for substantial discounts. During the week, when making reservations at city hotels or country inns, it's important to ask if any corporate rates are available. Depending on the establishment, you may or may not be asked for some proof of corporate affiliation (a business card is usually all that's needed), but it's well worth inquiring, since the effort can result in a saving of 15 to 20%, plus an upgrade to a substantially better room.

A number of companies specialize in booking hotel rooms in major cities at substantial discounts. Although you can ask for specific hotels by name, the largest savings are realized by letting the agency make the selection; they may be able to get you a discount of up to 65%. **Hotel Reservations Network** (8140 Walnut Hill Lane, Dallas, Texas 75231; 800–96–HOTEL) offers discount rates in over 20 U.S. cities plus London and Paris; **Quikbook** (381 Park Avenue South, New York, New York 10016; 800–789–9887) is a similar service with competitive rates.

Express Reservations (3800 Arapahoe, Boulder, Colorado 80303; 800–356–1123) specializes in properties in New York City and Los Angeles. For California, try **San Francisco Reservations** (22 Second Street, Fourth Floor, San Francisco, California 94105; 800–677–1500, or **California Reservations** (3 Sumner Street, 94103; 800–576–0003.

Another money-saving trick can be to look for inns in towns a bit off the beaten path. If you stay in a town that neighbors a famous resort or historic community, you will often find that rates are anywhere from $20 to $50 less per night for equivalent accommodation. If you're travelling without reservations, and arrive at a half-empty inn in late afternoon, don't hesitate to ask for a price reduction or free room upgrade. And of course, watch for our ₵ symbol, which indicates places which are a particularly good value.

If an establishment has a specific tipping policy, whether it is "no tipping" or the addition of a set service charge, it is noted under "Rates." When both breakfast and dinner are included in the rates, a 15% service charge against the total bill—not just the room—is standard; a few inns charge 18–20%. A number of B&Bs are also adding on a service charge, a practice which sits poorly with us. If you feel—as many of our readers do—that these fees are a sneaky way of making rates seem lower than they really are, let the innkeeper (and us) know how you feel. When no notation is made, it's generally expected that guests will leave $1–3 a night for the housekeeping staff and 15% for meal service. A number of inns have taken to leaving little cards or envelopes to remind guests to leave a tip for the housekeepers; most readers find this practice objectionable. If you welcome a no-tipping policy and object to solicitation, speak up.

While the vast majority of inns are fairly priced, there are a few whose rates have become exorbitant. Others fail to stay competitive, charging top weekend rates when a nearby luxury hotel is offering a beautiful suite at a lower price. No matter how lovely the breakfast, how thoughtful the innkeepers, there's a limit to the amount one will pay for a room without an in-room telephone, TV, or a full-size private bathroom. One B&B has the nerve to charge $125 for a room with shared bath, then asks you to bring your own pool towels during the summer (it's not listed here!).

Deposits and cancellations

Nearly all innkeepers print their deposit and cancellation policies clearly on their brochures. Deposits generally range from payment of the first night's stay to 50% of the cost of the entire stay. Some inns repeat the cancellation policy when confirming reservations. In general, guests canceling well in advance of the planned arrival (one to four weeks is typical) receive a full refund minus a cancellation fee. After that date, no refunds are offered unless the room is resold to someone else. A few will not refund *even if the room is resold,* so take careful note. If you're making a credit card booking over the phone, be sure to find out what the cancellation policy is. We are uncomfortable with overly strict refund policies, and wish that inns would give a gift certificate, good for a return visit, when guests are forced to cancel on short notice.

Sometimes the shoe may be on the other foot. Even if you were told earlier that the inn at which you really wanted to stay was full, it may be worthwhile to make a call to see if cancellations have opened up any last-minute vacancies.

Minimum stays

Two- and three-night minimum weekend and holiday stays are the rule at many inns during peak periods. We have noted these when possible, although we suspect that the policy may be more common than is always indicated in print. On the other hand, you may just be hitting a slow period, so it never hurts to call at the last minute to see if a one-night reservation would be accepted. Again, cancellations are always a possibility; you can try calling on a Friday or Saturday morning to see if something is available for that night.

Pets

Very few of the inns and hotels listed accept pets. When they do we've noted it under "Extras." On the other hand, most of the inns listed in this book have at least one dog or cat, sometimes more. These pets are usually found in the common areas, sometimes in guest rooms as well. *If you are allergic to animals, we strongly urge that you inquire for details before making reservations.*

Children

Some inns are family-style places and welcome children of all ages; we've marked them with our ♯ symbol. Others do not feel that they have facilities for the very young and only allow children over a certain age. Still others cultivate an "adults only" atmosphere and discourage anyone under the age of 16. We've noted age requirements under the heading "Restrictions." If special facilities are available to children, these are noted under "Facilities" and "Extras." If an inn does not exclude children yet does not offer any special amenities or rate reductions for them, we would suggest it only for the best-behaved youngsters.

Whatever the policy, you may want to remind your children to follow the same rules of courtesy toward others that we expect of adults. Be aware that the pitter-patter of little feet on an uncarpeted hardwood floor can sound like a herd of stampeding buffalo to those on the floor below. Children used to the indestructible plastics of contemporary homes will need to be reminded (more than once) to be gentle with antique furnishings. Most important, be sensitive to the fact that parents—not innkeepers—are responsible for supervising their children's behavior.

State laws governing discrimination by age are affecting policies at some inns. To our knowledge, both California and Michigan now have such laws on the books. Some inns get around age discrimination by limiting room occupancy to two adults. This discourages families by forcing them to pay for two rooms instead of one. Our own children were very clear on their preferences: although they'd been to many inns that don't encourage guests under the age of 12, they found them "really boring"; on the other hand, they loved every family-oriented place we visited.

Porterage and packing

Only the largest of our listings will have personnel whose sole job is to assist guests with baggage. In the casual atmosphere associated with many inns, it is simply assumed that guests will carry their own bags. If you do need assistance with your luggage, don't hesitate to ask.

If you're planning an extended trip to a number of small inns, we'd suggest packing as lightly as possible, using two small bags rather than one large suitcase. You'll know why if you've ever tried hauling a 50-pound oversize suitcase up a steep and narrow 18th-century staircase. On the other hand, don't forget about the local climate when assembling your wardrobe. In mountainous and desert regions, day- and nighttime temperatures can vary by as much as 40 degrees. Also, bear in mind that Easterners tend to dress more formally than Westerners, so pack accordingly.

Meals

If you have particular dietary restrictions—low-salt, vegetarian, or religious—or allergies—to caffeine, nuts, whatever—be sure to mention these when making reservations and *again* at check-in. If you're allergic to a common breakfast food or beverage, an evening reminder will ensure that you'll be able to enjoy the breakfast that's been prepared for you. Most innkeepers will do their best to accommodate your special needs, but be fair. Don't ask an innkeeper to prepare a special meal, and then, when it's being served, say: "I've decided to go off my diet today. Can I have the luscious peaches-and-cream French toast with bacon that everyone else is eating?"

In preparing each listing, we asked the owners to give us the cost of prix fixe and a la carte meals when available. An "alc dinner" price at the end of the "Rates" section is the figure we were given when we requested the average cost of a three-course dinner with a half bottle of house wine, including tax and tip. Prices listed for prix fixe meals do not include wine and service. Lunch prices, where noted, do not include the cost of any alcoholic beverage. Hotels and inns which serve meals to the public are noted with the l symbol.

Dinner and lunch reservations are always a courtesy and are often essential. Most B&B owners will offer to make reservations for you; this can be especially helpful in getting you a table at a popular restaurant in peak season and/or on weekends. Some of the establishments we list operate restaurants fully open to the public. Others serve dinner primarily to their overnight guests, but they also will serve meals to outsiders; reservations are essential at such inns, usually 24 hours in advance.

A few restaurants require jackets and ties for men at dinner, even in rather isolated areas. Of course, this is more often the case in traditional New England and the Old South than in the West. Unless you're going only to a very casual country lodge, we recommend that men bring these items along and that women have corresponding attire.

Breakfast: Breakfast is served at nearly every inn or hotel listed in this guide, and is usually included in the rates. Whenever possible we describe a typical breakfast, rather than using the terms "continental" or "full" breakfast.

Continental breakfast ranges from coffee and store-bought pastry to a lavish offering of fresh fruit and juices, yogurt and granola, cereals, even cheese and cold meats, homemade muffins and breads, and a choice of decaffeinated or regular coffee, herbal and regular tea. There's almost as much variety in the full breakfasts, which range from the traditional eggs, bacon, and toast, plus juice and coffee, to three-course gourmet extravaganzas.

We've received occasional complaints about breakfasts being too rich in eggs and cream, and too sweet, with no plain rolls or bread. A dietary splurge is fun for a weekend escape, but on a longer trip we'd advise requesting a "healthy breakfast" from your innkeeper. You can be sure that they don't eat their own breakfasts every day! Equally important to many guests are the timing and seating arrangements at breakfast. Some readers enjoy the friendly atmosphere of breakfast served family-style at a set time; this approach often enables innkeepers to serve quite spectacular three-course meals. Other readers much prefer the flexibility and privacy afforded by breakfasts served at tables for two over an extended time period.

Lunch: Very few of the inns and hotels listed here serve lunch. Those that do generally operate a full-service restaurant or are located in isolated mountain settings with no restaurants nearby. Many inns are happy to make up picnic lunches for an additional fee.

Dinner: Meals served at the inns listed here vary widely from simple home-style family cooking to gourmet cuisine. We are looking for food that is a good, honest example of the type of cooking involved. Ingredients should be fresh and homemade as far as is possible; service and presentation should be pleasant and straightforward. We have no interest in the school of "haute pretentious" where the hyperbolic descriptions found on the menu far exceed the chef's ability.

Drinks

With a very few exceptions (noted under "Restrictions" in each listing), alcoholic beverages may be enjoyed in moderation at all of the inns and hotels listed. Most establishments with a full-service restaurant serving the public as well as overnight guests are licensed to serve beer, wine, and liquor to their customers, although "brown-bagging" or BYOB (bring your own bottle) is occasionally permitted, especially in dry counties. Bed & breakfasts, and inns serving meals primarily to overnight guests, do not typically have liquor licenses, although most will provide guests with setups, i.e., glasses, ice, and mixers, at what is often called a BYO (bring your own) bar.

Overseas visitors will be amazed at the hodgepodge of regulations around the country. Liquor laws are determined in general by each state, but individual counties, or even towns, can prohibit or restrict the sale of alcoholic beverages, even beer.

Smoking

The vast majority of B&Bs and inns prohibit indoor smoking entirely, allowing it only on porches and verandas; a few don't allow smoking anywhere on the grounds. Larger inns and hotels usually do permit smoking, prohibiting it only in some guest rooms, and dining areas. Where prohibitions apply we have noted this under "Restrictions." We suggest that confirmed smokers be courteous or make reservations elsewhere. If there is no comment about smoking under "Restrictions," those allergic to smoke should inquire for details.

Physical limitations and wheelchair accessibility

We've used the well-known symbol ♿ to denote hotels and inns that are wheelchair accessible. Where available, additional information is noted under the "Extras" heading. Unfortunately, what is meant by this symbol varies dramatically. In the case of larger hotels and newer inns, it usually means full access; in historic buildings, access may be limited to the restaurant and public rest rooms only, or to a specific guest room but not the common areas. *Call the inn/hotel directly for full details and to discuss your needs.*

If you do not need a wheelchair but have difficulty with stairs, we urge you to mention this when making reservations; many inns and small hotels have one or two rooms on the ground floor, but very few have elevators. Similarly, if you are visually handicapped, do share this information so that you may be given a room with good lighting and no unexpected steps.

Air-conditioning

Heat is a relative condition, and the perceived need for air-conditioning varies tremendously from one individual to the next. If an inn or hotel has air-conditioning, you'll see this listed under "Rooms." If it's important to you, be sure to ask when making reservations. If air-conditioning is not available, check to see if fans are provided. Remember that top-floor rooms in most inns (usually a converted attic) can be uncomfortably warm even with air-conditioning.

Transportation

A car is more or less essential for visiting most of the inns and hotels listed here, as well as the surrounding sights of interest. Exceptions are those located in the major cities. In some historic towns, a car is the easiest way to get there, but once you've arrived, you'll want to find a place to park the car and forget about it.

If you are traveling by public transportation, check the "Extras" section at the end of each write-up. If the innkeepers are willing to pick you up from the nearest airport, bus, or train station, you'll see it noted here. This service is usually free or available at modest cost. If it's not listed, the innkeeper will direct you to a commercial facility that can help.

Parking

Although not a concern in most cases, parking is a problem in many cities, beach resorts, and historic towns. If you'll be traveling by car, ask the innkeeper for advice when making reservations. If parking is not on-site, stop at the hotel first to drop off your bags, then go park the car. In big cities, if "free parking" is included in the rates, this usually covers only one arrival and departure. Additional "ins and outs" incur substantial extra charges. Be sure to ask.

If on-site parking is available in areas where parking can be a problem, we've noted it under "Facilities." Since it's so rarely a problem in country inns, we haven't included that information in those listings. Regrettably, security has become an issue in most cities. Never leave anything visible inside the car; it's an invitation for break-in and theft.

Christmas travel

Many people love to travel to a country inn or hotel at Christmas. Quite a number of places do stay open through the holidays, but the extent to which the occasion is celebrated varies widely indeed. We know of many inns that decorate beautifully, serve a fabulous meal, and organize all kinds of traditional Christmas activities. But we also know of others, especially in ski areas, that do nothing more than throw a few token ornaments on a tree. Be sure to inquire.

Ranch vacations

Spending time on a ranch can give you a real feel for the West—far more than you could ever experience when driving from one tourist attraction to the next. Many families find a favorite ranch and return year after year, usually for the same week, and eventually become close friends with other guests who do the same. When booking a ranch vacation, it's wise to ask about the percentage of return guests, and to get the names and telephone numbers of some in your area. If the return percentage is low, or the telephone numbers of recent guests are "unavailable," try another ranch. When reading a glossy brochure, make sure that the pictures shown were taken on the ranch, and clearly show its cabins (both interior and exterior), horses, and other facilities, rather than generic Western pictures available anywhere.

While wonderful, ranch vacations are expensive, especially when you're budgeting for a family. When toting up the costs, remember to add on 10–15% for gratuities to the wranglers and staff—this is standard at almost every ranch but is not always mentioned in the rate information. Ranch vacations tend to be more expensive in northern Colorado, but they're also most accessible, since you can fly into Denver, rent a car and be on a horse within a few hours. Ranches in Idaho, Montana, and Wyoming tend to cost less for comparable facilities, but you may have to pay more to get there. When comparing prices, keep in mind that a ranch with a four-diamond AAA rating, gourmet cuisine, and resort facilities will not be in the same ballpark as a working ranch with comfortable but more basic food, accommodation, and activities. Finally, make sure that you pay for the things you want. A ranch with a full-fledged children's program is likely to cost more than one with a more casual approach. The cost of a ranch which includes unlimited riding will inevitably be higher than one that charges for riding by the hour. If you live and breathe horses, unlimited riding is clearly a better value. If one or two rides is all you have in mind, then the a la carte approach makes better sense. Read the fine print to be sure of exactly what is included. By the way, if you or another member of your family is not too keen on horses, look for a ranch that offers other activities—tennis, water sports, and hiking—or for a ranch that is near a major city or tourist center.

Is innkeeping for me?

Many of our readers fantasize about running their own inn; for some the fantasy will become a reality. Before taking the plunge, it's vital to find out as much as you can about this demanding business. Begin by reading *So You Want to Be an Innkeeper*, by Pat Hardy, Jo Ann Bell, and Mary Davies. Hardy and Bell are co-directors of the Professional Association of Innkeepers, International (PAII—pronounced "pie") which also publishes *Innkeeping Newsletter,* various materials for would-be innkeepers, and coordinates workshops for aspiring innkeepers. For details contact PAII, P.O. Box 90710, Santa Barbara, CA 93190; 805–569–1853, or visit their internet website at www.paii.org. Another good book is *How to Start and Run Your Own Bed & Breakfast Inn* by longtime innkeepers Ripley Hotch and Carl Glassman, covering everything from financing to marketing to day-to-day innkeeping responsibilities ($14.95; Stackpole Books, P.O. Box 1831, Harrisburg, PA 17105; 800–732–3669). Another excellent source, especially in the East, are consultants Bill Oates and Heide Bredfeldt. Contact them at P.O. Box 1162, Brattleboro, VT 05301; 802–254–5931 to find out when and where they'll be offering their next prospective innkeepers seminar. Bill and Heide are highly respected pros in this field and have worked with innkeepers facing a wide range of needs and problems; his newsletter, *Innquest,* is written for prospective innkeepers looking to buy property. An equally good alternative is Lodging Resources Workshops, 98 South Fletcher Avenue, Amelia Island, FL 32034; 888–201–7602. Director Dave Caples owns the Elizabeth Pointe Lodge in Amelia Island, and has been conducting workshops throughout the U.S. since 1992.

For more information

The best sources of travel information in this country and in Canada are absolutely free; in many cases, you don't even have to supply the cost of a stamp or telephone call. They are the state and provincial tourist offices.

For each state you'll be visiting, request a copy of the official state map, which will show you every little highway and byway and will make exploring much more fun; it will also have information on state parks and major attractions in concise form. Ask also for a calendar of events and for information on topics of particular interest, such as fishing or antiquing, vineyards or crafts; many states have published B&B directories, and some are quite informative. If you're going to an area of particular tourist interest, you might also want to ask the state office to give you the name of the regional tourist board for more detailed information. Most states have toll-free numbers; call 800–555–1212 to get the numbers you need. If there's no toll-free listing, call the information operators for the relevant states, and ask them to check for the number under the state's capital city. Many states have also established websites on the internet; use search engines to see what you can find.

You may also want to contact the local chamber of commerce for information on local sights and events of interest or even an area map. You can get the necessary addresses and telephone numbers from the inn or hotel where you'll be staying or from the state tourist office.

If you are one of those people who never travel with fewer than three guidebooks (which includes us), you will find the AAA Tour Guides to be especially helpful. The guides are distributed free on request to members, and cover hotels, restaurants, and sightseeing information. If you're not already an AAA member, *we'd strongly urge you join before your next trip;* in addition to their road service, they offer quality guidebooks and maps, and an excellent discount program at many hotels (including a number listed here).

Guidebooks are published only once every year or two; if you'd like to have a more frequent update, we'd suggest one of the following:

Country Inns/Bed & Breakfasts (P.O. Box 182, South Orange, NJ 07079; 800–877–5491), $23, 6 issues annually. You know what they say about a picture being worth a thousand words. A must for inngoers.

Easy Escapes (P.O. Box 120365, Boston, MA 02112–0365), $47, 10 issues annually, $6 single copy. Covers inns, hotels, and resorts in the U.S. and the world; exceptionally honest and forthright. Each issue usually covers one or two destinations in a breezy, informal style.

Harper's Hideaway Report (Box 300, Whitefish, MT 59937), $125, 12 issues annually. Covers the best (and most expensive) inns, hotels, resorts in the U.S. and abroad.

Yellow Brick Road (P.O. Box 1600, Julian, CA 92036–1600 or 800–79 Band B), $39, 12 issues annually, $5 single copy. Focuses on inns and special events in the western states and Hawaii.

The internet: Those of you with on-line access will want to check out the huge amount of travel information found on the World Wide Web. Start with our own website, at http://www.inns.com, where you'll find thousands of listings and photographs. From there, take a look at some of the other inn directories, as well as the many sites devoted to state and regional travel information. Of equal interest are the chat rooms and bulletin boards covering bed & breakfasts; you can find them on the internet as well as on the proprietary services like America on Line and Prodigy.

Where is my favorite inn?

In reading through this book, you may find that your favorite inn is not listed, or that a well-known inn has been omitted from this edition. Why? Two reasons, basically: In several cases, establishments have been dropped because our readers had unsatisfactory experiences. Feel free to contact us for details. Other establishments have been omitted because we've had little or no reader or innkeeper feedback. This may mean that readers visiting these hotels and inns had satisfactory experiences but were not sufficiently impressed to write about them, or that readers were pleased but just assumed that someone else would take the trouble. If the latter applies, please, please, do write and let us know of your experiences. We try to visit as many inns as possible ourselves, but it is impossible to visit every place, every year. So please, keep those cards, letters, and telephone calls coming! As an added incentive, we will be sending free copies of the next edition of this book to our most helpful respondents.

Little Inns of Horror

We try awfully hard to list only the most worthy establishments, but sometimes the best-laid plans of mice and travel writers do go astray. Please understand that whenever we receive a complaint about an entry in our guide we feel terrible, and do our best to investigate the situation. Readers occasionally send us complaints about establishments listed in *other* guidebooks; these are quite helpful as warning signals.

The most common complaints we receive—and the least forgivable—are on the issue of dirt. Scummy sinks and bathtubs, cobwebbed windows, littered porches, mildewed carpeting, water-stained ceilings, and grimy linens are all stars of this horror show.

Next in line are problems dealing with the lack of maintenance: peeling paint and wallpaper; sagging, soft, lumpy mattresses; radiators that don't get hot and those that make strange noises; windows that won't open, windows that won't close, windows with no screens, decayed or inoperable window shades; moldy shower curtains, rusty shower stalls, worn-out towels, fluctuating water temperatures, dripping faucets, and showers that only dribble, top the list.

Food complaints come next on this disaster lineup: poorly prepared canned or frozen food when fresh is readily available; meals served on paper, plastic, or worst of all, Styrofoam; and insensitivity to dietary needs. Some complaints are received about unhelpful, abrasive, or abusive innkeepers, with a few more about uncaring, inept, or invisible staff. Complaints are most common in full-service inns when the restaurant business preoccupies the owners' attention, leaving overnight guests to suffer. Last but not least are noise headaches: trucks and trains that sound like they're heading for your pillow, and being awakened by the sound of someone snoring—in the next room. More tricky are questions of taste—high Victorian might look elegant to you, funereal to me; my collectibles could be your Salvation Army thriftshop donation. In short, there are more than a few inns and hotels that give new meaning to the phrase "having reservations"; fortunately they're many times outnumbered by the many wonderful places listed in this guide.

Pet peeves

Although we may genuinely like an inn, minor failings can keep it from being truly wonderful. Heading our list of pet peeves is inadequate bedside reading lights and tables. We know that there is not always room for a second table, but a light can always be attached to the wall. For reasons of both safety and comfort, a lamp should be at every bedside. Another reader is irked by inadequate bathroom lighting: "I think it must be an innkeepers' conspiracy to keep me from ever getting my makeup on properly." *(SU)* Other readers object to overly friendly innkeepers: "The innkeeper chatted with us all during breakfast, and was disappointed that we didn't plan to go in to say good-bye after we loaded up the car. Innkeepers should remember that the guests are customers, not long-lost relatives." *(KW)* Another common gripe concerns clutter: "Although pretty and interesting, the many collectibles left us no space for our personal belongings." And: "Instructions were posted everywhere—how to operate door locks, showers, heat, air-conditioning, and more." Anything you'd like to add?

Glossary of Architectural and Decorating Terms

We are not architectural experts, and when we started writing *America's Favorite Inns, B&Bs & Small Hotels*, we didn't know a dentil from a dependency, a tester from a transom. We've learned a bit more since then, and hope that our primer of terms, prepared by associate editor Nancy Barker, will also be helpful to you.

Adam: building style (1780–1840) featuring a classic box design with a dominant front door and fanlight, accented by an elaborate surround or an entry porch; cornice with decorative moldings incorporating dentil, swag, garland, or stylized geometric design. Three-part Palladian-style windows are common.

antebellum: existing prior to the U.S. Civil War (1861–1865).

Arts and Crafts movement: considered the first phase of the Modern movement that led to the Prairie style (1900–20) of Frank Lloyd

Wright in Chicago, and the Craftsman style (1905–30) of the Greene brothers in Southern California. In the Arts and Crafts style, historical precedent for decoration and design was rejected and ornamentation was "modernized" to remove traces of its historic origins. It features low-pitched roofs, wide eave overhangs, and both symmetrical and asymmetrical front façades.

beaded board: simple ornamented board, with a smooth, flat surface alternating with a half-round, rod-like carving (bead) running the length of the board. Common wainscoting or panelling in Victorian-era homes.

carpenter Gothic: *see* country, folk Victorian.

chinoiserie: imitation of Chinese decorative motifs; i.e., simulated Oriental lacquer covering pine or maple furniture. See also Chinese Chippendale below.

Chippendale: named for English furniture designer, Thomas Chippendale, of the Queen Anne period (1750–1790); the style varies from the Queen Anne style in ornamentation, with more angular shapes and heavier carving of shells, leaves, scrolls. Chinese Chippendale furniture employs chiefly straight lines, bamboo turnings, and as decoration, fluting, and fretwork in a variety of lattice patterns.

Colonial Revival: building style (1880–1955) featuring a classic box design with a dominant front door elaborated with pilasters and either a pediment (Georgian-style) or a fanlight (Adam-style); double-hung windows symmetrically balanced.

corbel: an architectural member that projects from a wall to support a weight and is stepped outward and upward from the vertical surface.

Corinthian: column popular in Greek Revival style for support of porch roofs; the capitals are shaped like inverted bells and decorated with acanthus leaves.

cornice: projecting horizontal carving or molding that crowns a wall or roof.

country, folk Victorian: simple house form (1870–1910) with accents of Victorian (usually Queen Anne or Italianate) design in porch spindle-work and cornice details. Also known as carpenter Gothic.

Craftsman: building style (1905–1930) with low-pitched, gabled roof and wide, unenclosed eave overhang; decorative beams or braces added under gables; usually one-story; porches supported by tapered square columns.

dentil: exterior or interior molding characterized by a series of small rectangular blocks projecting like teeth.

dependencies: buildings that are subordinate to the main dwelling; i.e., a detached garage or barn. *See* also garçonniere.

Doric: column popular in Greek Revival style for support of porch roofs; the simplest of the three styles, with a fluted column, no base, and a square capital.

Eastlake: architectural detail on Victorian houses, commonly referred to as "gingerbread." Typically has lacy spandrels and knob-like beads, in exterior and interior design, patterned after the style of Charles Eastlake, an English furniture designer. Eastlake also promoted Gothic and Jacobean Revival styles with their strong rectangular lines; quality workmanship instead of machine manufacture; and the use of varnished oak, glazed tiles, and unharmonized color.

Eclectic movement: architectural tradition (1880–1940) which emphasized relatively pure copies of Early American, Mediterranean, or Native American homes.

eyebrow dormer: a semi-circular, narrow window over which the adjoining roofing flows in a continuous wave line; found on Shingle or Richardsonian Romanesque buildings.

faux: literally, French for "false." Refers commonly to woodwork painted to look like marble or another stone.

Federal: *See* Adam.

Franklin stove: metal heating stove which is set out into the room to conserve heat and better distribute it. Named after its inventor Benjamin Franklin; some designs resemble a fireplace when their front doors are open.

four-poster bed: variation on a tester bed but one in which the tall corner posts, of equal height, do not support a canopy. Carving of rice sheaves was a popular design in the Southern states, and signified prosperity.

gambrel roof: a two-slope, barn-style roof, with a lower steeper slope and a flatter upper one.

garçonniere: found on antebellum estates; a dependency housing unmarried male guests and family members.

Georgian: building style (1700–1830) featuring a classic box design with a dominant front door elaborated with pilasters and a pediment, usually with a row of small panes of glass beneath the crown or in a transom; cornices with decorative moldings, usually dentil.

Gothic Revival: building style (1840–1880) with a steeply pitched roof, steep gables with decorated vergeboards, and one-story porch supported by flattened Gothic arches. Windows commonly have pointed-arch shape.

Greek Revival: building style (1825–1860) having a gabled or hipped roof of low pitch; cornice line of main and porch roofs emphasized by a wide band of trim; porches supported by prominent columns (usually Doric).

half-tester bed: a bed with a low footboard and a canopy projecting from the posts at the head of the bed. Pronounced "half tee'stir."

Ionic: column popular in Greek Revival style for support of porch roofs; the caps of the column resemble the rolled ends of a scroll.

Italianate: building style (1840–1885) with two or three stories and a low-pitched roof with widely overhanging eaves supported by decorative brackets; tall, narrow windows arched or curved above with elaborate crowns. Many have a square cupola or tower.

keeping room: in a Colonial-era home, the equivalent of a modern family room; it was usually warm from proximity to kitchen, so infants and the ill were "kept" here.

kiva: stuccoed, corner beehive-shaped fireplace common in adobe homes in Southwestern U.S.

latillas: ceiling of unpeeled, rough sticks, supported by vigas (rough beams); seen in flat-roofed adobe homes.

Lincrusta (or Lincrusta-Walton): an embossed, linoleum-like wall-covering made with linseed oil, developed in 1877 in England by Frederick Walton.

lintel: horizontal beam, supported at both ends, that spans an opening.

mansard roof: having two slopes on all sides with the lower slope steeper than the upper one.

Mission: building style (1890–1920) with Spanish mission-style parapet; commonly with red tile roof, overhanging, open eaves, and smooth stucco finish. In furniture, the Mission style is best represented by the work of designer Gustav Stickley. Using machine manufacture, he utilized simple, rectangular lines and favored quarter-sawn white oak for the rich texture of the graining.

Palladian window: typically a central window with an arched or semicircular head.

Pueblo Revival: building style (1910 to present) with flat roof, parapet above; corners and edges blunted or rounded; projecting vigas, stepped back roof lines, and irregular stucco wall surfaces. Influenced by the flat-roofed Spanish Colonial buildings and Native American pueblos; popular in Arizona and New Mexico; common in Santa Fe and Albuquerque.

Pewabic (tile): glazed tiles made in the Detroit, Michigan, area, in the first half of the 1890s, whose unique manufacturing process has been lost.

pocket doors: doors that open by sliding into a recess (pocket) in the wall.

portal (or portale): in Spanish-style homes, the long, narrow porch that opens onto an internal courtyard; it functions as a sheltered passageway between rooms.

post and beam: building style based on the Medieval post-and-girder method, where upper loads are supported by heavy corner posts and cross timbers. In contemporary construction, the posts and beams are often left exposed on the interior.

Prairie: building style (1900–1920) with low-pitched roof and widely overhanging eaves; two stories with one-story wings or porches; façade detailing that emphasizes horizontal lines; massive, square porch supports.

Queen Anne: building style (1880–1910) with a steeply pitched roof of irregular shapes; an asymmetrical façade with one-story porch; patterned shingles, bay windows, single tower. In furniture design the Queen Anne style was prevalent from 1725 to 1750, characterized by a graceful, unadorned curve of the leg (known as cabriole) and repeated curve of the top crest and vase-form back (splat) of a chair.

quoin: wood, stone, or brick materials that form the exterior corner of a building and are distinguishable from the background surface because of texture, color, size, or material.

rice-carved bed: *See* four-poster bed.

Richardsonian Romanesque: building style (1880–1900) with massive masonry walls of rough, squared stonework and round-topped arches over windows, porch supports, or entrances; round tower with conical roof common.

Second Empire: building style (1855–1885) with mansard roof adorned with dormer windows on lower slope; molded cornices above and below lower roof, and decorative brackets beneath eaves.

Shaker: style of furniture which represents the Shaker belief in simplicity. The finely crafted pieces are functional, without ornamentation. Chairs have ladder backs, rush seats, and simple turned legs; tables and cabinets are angular, with smooth surfaces.

Sheraton: named for English furniture designer, Thomas Sheraton, of the Federal period (early 1800s); style marked by straight lines, delicate proportions, wood inlays, and spare use of carving; characteristically tapered legs.

Shingle: building style (1880–1900) with walls and roofing of continuous wood shingles; no decorative detailing at doors, windows, corners, or roof overhang. Irregular, steeply pitched roof line and extensive porches common.

shotgun: simple 19th century house form suited to narrow urban lots, featuring a single-story, front gable building one room wide. Rooms and doorways are in a direct line, front to back; theoretically, a bullet fired through the front door would travel through the house unobstructed.

spandrel: decorative trim that fits the top corners of doorways, porches, or gables; usually triangular in shape.

Santa Fe: *see* Pueblo Revival.

Spanish Colonial: building style (1600–1900) of thick masonry walls, with low pitched or flat roof, interior wooden shutters covering small window openings, and multiple doorways. Pitched roof style often has half-cylindrical tiles; flat style has massive horizontal beams embedded in walls to support heavy roof of earth or mortar. Internal courtyards or cantilevered second-story porches are common.

Stick: building style (1860–1890) with a steeply pitched, gabled roof, usually with decorative trusses at apex; shingle or board walls interrupted by patterns of boards (stickwork) raised from the surface for emphasis.

Territorial: a variation of the Spanish Colonial building style found in New Mexico, western Texas, and Arizona. The flat roof and single story are topped by a protective layer of fired brick to form a decorative crown.

tester bed: a bed with a full canopy (the tester), supported at all four corners by tall posts. Pronounced "tee'stir."

transom: usually refers to a window placed above a doorway.

trompe l'oeil: literally, French for "to trick the eye." Commonly refers to wall paintings that create an optical illusion.

Tudor: building style (1890–1940) with steeply pitched roof, usually cross-gabled; decorative half-timbering; tall, narrow, multi-paned windows; massive chimney crowned with decorative chimney pots.

vergeboard: decorative trim extending from the roof overhang of Tudor, Gothic Revival, or Queen Anne-style houses.

vernacular: style of architecture employing the commonest forms, materials, and decorations of a period or place.

viga(s): exposed (interior) and projecting (exterior) rough-hewn wooden roof beams common in adobe homes in Southwestern U.S.

wainscoting: most commonly, narrow wood paneling found on the lower half of a room's walls.

widow's walk: a railed observation platform built above the roof of a coastal house to permit unobstructed views of the sea. Name derives from the fate of many wives who paced the platform waiting for the return of their husbands from months (or years) at sea. Also called a "captain's walk."

Windsor: style of simple chair, with spindle back, turned legs, and usually a saddle seat. Considered a "country" design, it was popular in 18th and early 19th century towns and rural areas.

For more information:

A Field Guide to American Houses (Virginia and Lee McAlester, New York: Alfred A. Knopf, 1984; $19.95, paperback) was an invaluable source in preparing this glossary, and is highly recommended. Its 525 pages are lavishly illustrated with photographs and diagrams.

Clues to American Architecture (Marilyn W. Klein and David P. Fogle, Washington, D.C.: Starrhill Press, 1985; $7.95, paperback) is a handy, affordable 64-page pocket guide to over 30 architectural styles, from the Colonial period to contemporary construction. Each is clearly described in easy-to-understand language, and illustrated with numerous detailed sketches. Also in the same style and format is *Clues to American Furniture* (Jean Taylor Federico, Washington, D.C.: Starrhill Press, 1988; $7.95), covering design styles from Pilgrim to Chippendale, Eastlake to Art Deco. If your bookstore doesn't stock these titles, contact Starrhill directly at P.O. Box 32342, Washington, D.C. 20007; 202–387–9805.

Regional itineraries

Contributing editor Suzanne Carmichael has prepared these delightful itineraries to lead you from the best-known towns and cities through beautiful countryside, over less-traveled scenic highways to delightful towns and villages, to places where sights both natural and historic outnumber the modern ""attractions" that so often litter the contemporary landscape.

To get a rough idea of where each itinerary will lead you, take a look at the appropriate map at the back of this book. But to really see where you'll be heading, pull out a detailed full-size map or road atlas, and use a highlighter to chart your path. (If you're hopeless when it comes to reading maps, ask the AAA to help you plan the trip with one of their Triptiks.) Some of our routes are circular, others are meant to be followed from one end to another; some are fairly short, others cover hundreds of miles. They can be traveled in either direction, or for just a section of the suggested route. You can sample an itinerary for a weekend, a week, or even two, depending on your travel style and the time available. For information on what to see and do along the way, refer to our state and local introductions and to a good regional guidebook.

Northwest Mountain and River Route Most visitors to the Northwest head for the fabled Oregon coast, friendly but sophisticated Seattle, the Olympic Peninsula, or Washington's San Juan Islands. Our route introduces you to less-traveled areas in the Cascade Mountains, along the Columbia River—even through rarely visited ancient lava beds.

Start your route in Portland, heading south on I-5 through the Willamette Valley past Albany to Eugene. Stop in Eugene to picnic in one of the parks along the Willamette River; in spring, visit Hendricks Park Rhododendron Garden to see over 6000 plants in dazzling bloom. Head east on Route 126, which winds along the scenic McKenzie River. A few miles past the town of McKenzie Bridge, turn east on Route 242, which emerges from deep forest to pass miles of black lava set against a Cascade Mountain backdrop.

At Sisters, turn south on Route 20 to Bend, a small resort town near Mount Bachelor ski resort. Take a brief detour south 15 miles on Route 97 to see both the Lava River Cave and the Lava Cast Forest, two unique formations left by ancient volcanoes.

Continue north on Route 97 to Madras where you have your choice of two routes to the Columbia River. Either follow Route 97 through the almost-ghost town of Shaniko and up to Biggs, then west along the river on I-94 to Hood River, *or* follow Route 26 across the Warm Springs Indian Reservation to Timberline Lodge at the foot of Mt. Hood, and then take Route 35 to Hood River. If you choose Route 97, detour on Route 218 to see the unusual John Day Fossil Beds National Monument.

Oregon's apple and winter pear orchards surround Hood River, a pleasant river town. Cross over the Columbia here to Washington state where you can take a side trip north on Route 141 to Trout Lake, a jumping off point for Mt. Adams wilderness explorations. To continue on our route, follow Route 14 east along the Columbia River, stopping at Maryhill, a bizarre mansion built by Samuel Hill in 1907 and now housing an eclectic art collection (don't miss Hill's version of Stonehenge, one mile east).

Turn north on Route 97 through Goldendale, following it through Toppenish, stopping to visit the Yakima Indian Nation Museum, and proceeding to Yakima, gateway to Washington's wine country. Hop on I-82, exiting almost immediately on scenic Route 281. If you have the time, loop north from Ellensburg on Route 97 past Bavarianesque Leavenworth, to Chelan, at the base of skinny, 55-mile long Lake Chelan. Board an excursion boat to Stehekin at the tip of the lake, then return down Route 97, and go west on Route 970 to Cle Elum. If time is short, head west from Ellensburg on Route 10 through the Cascade foothills to Cle Elum.

I-90 west is your route to Seattle, passing towering Cascade Mountain peaks, and local ski areas near Snoqualmie Pass. Exit at North Bend to visit Snoqualmie (where the TV series *Twin Peaks* was filmed), or stop in Issaquah to see clusters of gift-shop malls. Our route ends in Seattle, but if you need to return to Portland, follow I-5 south, stopping to see what remains of Mount St. Helens and visiting the new National Volcanic Monument, just east of Castle Rock.

Northwest Ferry Tale You can't experience the essence of the Northwest without getting out *on* the water. Small forested islands, busy

Puget Sound ship traffic, and vistas of distant snowcapped peaks are all best sampled from a water vantage. Our route takes you on a series of ferries through some of the region's prettiest waterscapes and most imposing vistas. Before embarking, make sure you have sunglasses, binoculars (to spot whales and eagles), a sweater, and ferry schedules.

Begin in Seattle heading north on I-5 past Everett to Burlington. In spring, consider a side trip on Route 20 to Anacortes past fields of commercially grown daffodils and tulips. From Anacortes you can take a separate ferry trip to and through the San Juan Islands (see description in Washington state chapter). From Burlington take Route 11 north along the forested Puget Sound shoreline, which offers excellent views of the San Juan Islands. Route 11 ends in Bellingham, where you can stop by Fairhaven, a restored business district, or take a tiny ferry to Lummi Island, a quiet, pastoral isle once inhabited by local Native Americans.

Continue north on I-5 to Blaine, crossing point to British Columbia. Be aware that there's often a backup at customs, especially on holiday weekends. Across the border, go north on Route 99 to the city of Vancouver, which is worth several days of exploration itself. Tear yourself away, head south on Route 99, then take Route 17 to the Tsawwassen ferry terminal. From here huge ferries depart for Vancouver Island. Our suggestion? Make a reservation on one that stops midway (in the Strait of Georgia) at one of the quiet, forested Gulf Islands. Stay overnight on Mayne Island or hop to the other Gulf Islands on small, interisland ferries.

After visiting the Gulf Islands, ferry to Sidney, just north of Victoria. Give yourself at least a full day to explore very-British Victoria, then book passage on the ferry that crosses the Strait of Juan de Fuca to Port Angeles, Washington. Before heading east, drive up to Hurricane Ridge (directly south of Port Angeles) for impressive views of the Olympic Mountains' highest peaks.

Take Route 101 east to Sequim where we recommend you follow a side road north to Dungeness Spit, a wisp of sand that sticks out 7 miles into the Strait, the longest natural sandspit in the U.S. Return to Route 101, past scenic bays and quiet coves, then turn north on Route 20 to Port Townsend. Restored Victorian homes line the high bluff above tiny downtown Port Townsend, a lively artists' community.

Board your next ferry at Port Townsend for Keystone on Whidbey Island, Puget Sound's largest island. Turn northward first past Coupeville to Deception Pass State Park near the northern end of the island. After gaping at the Deception Pass chasm, head back south on Routes 20 and 525 through small island towns like Greenbank, Freeland, and Langley. Take one last ferry from Clinton to Mukilteo on the mainland, then follow I-5 south, back to Seattle.

You'll need to call the numbers listed below for ferry schedules and reservations:

Lummi Island: Private ferry, no reservations available. Hourly sailings. For schedule call 206–671–3990.

Vancouver to Vancouver Island or Vancouver to Vancouver Island

via Gulf Islands: Operated by BC Ferries. Reservations *not* available for Tsawwassen-Schwartz Bay (Vancouver Island); reservations *are required* for Tsawwassen-Gulf Islands (604–669–1211); reservations *not* available for inter-Gulf Island ferries. **Victoria to Port Angeles:** Operated by Black Ball Ferry. Reservations *not* available but call for schedule. Get to dock *hours* ahead of time during peak seasons (206–457–4491). **Port Townsend to Keystone; Clinton to Mukilteo; and Anacortes-San Juan Islands.** All operated by Washington State Ferries. No reservations available except from Anacortes to Sidney, BC. Clinton to Mukilteo route is very busy during commuter hours. Arrive at all three way ahead of scheduled sailing. (800–843–3779 in Washington state; 206–464–6400, out of state).

Sip-to-Shore Loop The only way to grasp California's multiple personalities is to plan individual trips to each of its distinct regions, or combine no more than two in a single sojurn. Anchored in San Francisco, our suggested loop takes you through the region's famous wine country, then whisks you down California's rugged north coast. Because there is so much for the palate and eyes to sample on this route, it could be tasted briefly in a long weekend or savored over two weeks.

Begin by crossing the San Francisco Bay Bridge north to Sausalito, an artists' enclave where studios vie for space with stylish boutiques and small outdoor cafés. From here follow Route 101 past Ignacio, then Route 37 east to Sears Point. Turn north toward California wine country on Route 121. Stop in Sonoma to visit local vineyards as well as excellent Sonoma State Historic Park. North on Route 121, just past Glen Ellen (Jack London's home), turn east on an unnumbered road to Oakville (ask locally for directions if necessary). One of the prettiest backroads in the area, this route winds through hills of vineyards, with occasional, sweeping glimpses of the entire Napa valley.

At Oakville turn south on Route 29 if you want to visit wineries in Yountville and Napa, or follow our suggested route north on Route 29, tippling your way through Rutherford to St. Helena and Calistoga. Take a dip in Calistoga's mineral springs, slather yourself with its "restorative" mud, visit local geysers, or soar the skies in a glider. Set your compass northwest now, following Route 128 through Geyserville, into southern redwood country at Boonville.

Route 128 ends at the Pacific Ocean. Turn north on Route 1, passing through Albion and Little River to Mendocino. Although popular with tourists, Mendocino's charm penetrates even crowded summer sidewalks. An optional side trip is to follow Route 1 north from Mendocino past Fort Bragg and Westport, then Route 101 deep into redwood forests. Turn west at Alton to Ferndale, known for its ""butterfat palaces" built by prosperous local dairymen. Return to Route 101 by following lightly traveled Route 211 through Capetown, Petrolia, and Bull Creek.

South from Mendocino, Route 1 hugs the northern coast, providing photogenic seascapes and sweeping panoramas; green hills, cut only by the highway, plunge directly into the sea. After passing through Elk, stop in Gualala to walk its nearby beaches, at Sea Ranch to view a planned community (West Coast–style), and at Ft. Ross to visit a one-time Russian toehold in America.

Return to San Francisco on Route 1, passing through Bodega Bay and Inverness, taking detours to Pt. Reyes Light Station (south of Inverness), Muir Woods National Monument, and Muir Beach. For a final adventure in your sip-to-shore loop, head to Point San Pedro to embark on an overnight adventure on a San Francisco Bay island.

Criteria for entries

Unlike many other guides, inns cannot pay to be listed in this book. All selections are made by the editors, based on guest recommendations and personal visits. Entries are written and compiled by the editors, not the inns. When we update a regional guide, inns that received full entries in the previous edition and that will also appear in the new edition are charged a processing fee to help defray our research costs. There is no fee for new entries, and no fee for listing in our *U.S.A & Canada* edition. If we receive significant complaints or insufficient recommendations about a particular property, we omit their listing. As always, what matters most to us is the feedback we get from you, our readers.

About our name

We've changed our name from *America's Wonderful Little Hotels & Inns* to *America's Favorite Inns, B&Bs & Small Hotels*. Why? First, we felt that it better reflects what we're all about. Properties listed here are *your* favorites—if you don't like them, we don't include them. Since the majority of our entries are inns and B&Bs, the new title better reflects their importance. Last but not least, reasons connected with the copyright were also a factor.

Key to Abbreviations and Symbols

For complete information and explanations, please see the Introduction.

¢ Affordable accommodations.

⋔ Families welcome. Most (but not all) have cribs, baby-sitting, games, play equipment, and reduced rates for children.

✕ Meals served to public; reservations recommended or required.

🎾 Tennis court and swimming pool and/or lake on grounds. Golf usually on grounds or nearby.

♿ Limited or full wheelchair access; call for details.

Rates: Range from least expensive room in low season to most expensive room in peak season.

Room only: No meals included; European Plan (EP).

B&B: Bed and breakfast; includes breakfast, sometimes afternoon/evening refreshment.

MAP: Modified American Plan; includes breakfast and dinner.

Full board: Three meals daily.

Alc lunch: A la carte lunch; average price of entree plus nonalcoholic drink, tax, tip.

Alc dinner: Average price of three-course dinner, including half bottle of house wine, tax, tip.

Prix fixe dinner: Three- to five-course set dinner, excluding wine, tax, tip unless otherwise noted.

Extras: Noted if available. Always confirm in advance. Pets are not permitted unless specified; if you are allergic, ask for details; *most innkeepers have pets.*

Free copy of INNroads newsletter

Want to stay up-to-date on our latest finds? Send a business-size, self-addressed, stamped envelope with 55 cents postage and we'll send you the latest issue, *free!* While you're at it, why not enclose a report on any inns you've recently visited? Use the forms at the back of the book or your own stationery.

We Want to Hear from You!

As you know, this book is effective only with your help. We really need to know about your experiences and discoveries. If you stayed at an inn or hotel listed here, we want to know how it was. Did it live up to our description? Exceed it? Was it what you expected? Did you like it? Were you disappointed? Delighted? Have you discovered new establishments that we should add to the next edition?

Tear out one of the report forms at the back of this book (or use your own stationery if you prefer) and write today. *Even if you write only "Fully endorse existing entry" you will have been most helpful.*

Thank You!

Important Note on Area Codes:

Telephone area codes are changing faster than a two-year-old's attention span. Although we've tried to incorporate all the new ones in our listings, many numbers were still in the "to be decided" stage at press time. *If you call a number listed here and get an announcement that it's not in service, we urge you to call the information operator and see if that region has been assigned a new area code.* Please forgive the inconvenience!

Alaska

Pearson's Pond Luxury Inn and Garden Spa, Juneau

Alaska is one of our most extraordinary states and a fantastic place to visit. Its size and scope are difficult to imagine: It encompasses an area one-fifth the size of the continental United States and has 3,000 rivers, 3 million lakes, 19 mountains higher than 14,000 feet, and more than 5,000 glaciers—one of which is larger than the state of Rhode Island.

Peak travel season to Alaska is during the summer months, when the weather is warmest and the days are the longest. Travelers are learning that the weather can be nearly as nice in the late spring and early fall, when the need for advance reservations is less pressing.

Alaska is the only state that Americans tend to visit by cruise ship and tour bus—as though it were some exotic foreign country. While it's true that old "Sourdoughs" refer to the U.S. as the "Lower 48" and anyplace outside of Alaska as "Outside," the fact remains that the state is easily accessible by air, road, and ferry. The people speak English, willingly accept U.S. dollars, and are extremely friendly and hospitable!

For more information, contact the Alaska Tourism Marketing Council (P.O. Box 110801, Juneau, AK 99811–0801; 907–465–2010), for a copy of the helpful "Alaska Official Vacation Planner." Both the state of Alaska and the province of British Columbia maintain extensive schedules on their modern, well-equipped ferries; contact them at Alaska Marine Highway, P.O. Box 25535, Juneau 99811 (907–465–3941 or 800–642–0066); and BC Ferries, 1112 Fort Street, Victoria, BC, V8V 4V2, Canada (604–386–3431). It's also worthwhile getting information on the AlaskaPass (P.O. Box 897, Haines, 99827; 907–766–3145 or 800–248–7598) offering unlimited travel within a specified time period on 10 Alaska surface transport companies, including Alaska and BC ferries and rail companies, as well as numerous bus routes. Whatever your route, early reservations are *essential* for peak season travel; cabins on the ferries are often fully booked before February for summer sailings, as are rooms in the most desirable inns and B&Bs in popular destinations.

In planning your Alaska trip, contact Pat Niven at **Alaska Northwest Travel Service** (3303 148th Street Southwest, Suite 2, Lynnwood, WA 98037; 425–787–9499 or 800–533–7381), who has specialized in individually planned itineraries of Alaska for years, and is very knowledgeable about its B&Bs. Another possibility is **Alaska Rainforest Tours** (369 South Franklin Street, Suite 200, Juneau 99801; 907–586–2959 or email at artour@alaska.net). Both companies specialize in individual travel, and can assist with B&B reservations, ferry bookings, airplane flights, wilderness trips, and more.

Reader tips: "Many Alaska B&Bs are simple homestays, not elegant inns. Be flexible, open-minded, adventurous and you'll have a wonderful time. On two-night stays our room and bath were untouched; we were told it was considered an intrusion. The hosts wait until after you leave. Don't forget to bring your rain gear. The Inland Passage is a coastal rain forest; expect changeable weather and frequent rain. Yes, the sun does come out and when it does, it is glorious." *(Kip Goldman & Marty Wall)* And: "Although the views were unsurpassed and the price was right, don't expect anything remotely resembling a cruise on the Alaska ferries. The facilities were spartan, sometimes old and frayed around the edges. Cleanliness could have been better, and often the staff was less than available. Omnipresent video games and average cafeteria food were typical. BC Ferries are far better maintained and appointed and the staff was friendlier." *(AP)*

ANCHORAGE

With nearly 250,000 inhabitants, Anchorage is Alaska's largest and most cosmopolitan city. Its modern skyscrapers contrast vividly with the surrounding miles of wilderness—it's not unheard of for a moose to take a wrong turn and come wandering into town. Anchorage is the gateway to South Central Alaska, and is a key stopover for anyone heading north to Denali and Fairbanks, the Arctic Circle, or south to the Kenai Peninsula.

Reader tips: "Anchorage has plenty of traffic, and diesel buses and trucks can endanger your sleep far more than the proverbial midnight sun. If you're a light sleeper, *insist* on an upper-floor room, away from the street, for any of the downtown hotels." *(DK)* "Good seafood at Simon & Seaforts, downtown; reservations necessary." *(Kip Goldman & Marty Wall)*

Information please: Built in 1916, the **Anchorage Hotel** (330 E Street, 99501; 907–272–4553 or 800–544–0988) was remodeled in 1993 with contemporary furnishings, done in muted shades of dusty green, pink, and taupe. The rates include a light continental breakfast and the morning paper, delivered to your door. B&B double rates for the 26 rooms range from $85–200.

The Glacier Bear B&B (4814 Malibu Road, 99517; 907–243–8818 or email gbear@alaska.net) is a 5,000 square-foot cedar-sided contemporary home, located 1.5 miles from the airport, 3 miles from downtown, and 3 blocks from floatplane departures on Lake Spenard. Rooms are highlighted with Victorian antiques and Oriental treasures; one has a pencil post canopy bed while another has a king-size bed and fireplace. B&B double rates for the five guest rooms (some with private bath) range from $60–95, including breakfasts of apricot-stuffed French toast with sausages; always-available coffee, tea, and cookies; plus use of the hot tub and airport pickups.

Located in the residential Bootlegger's Cove neighborhood, six blocks from downtown is **Two Morrow's Place** (1325 'O' Street, 99501; 907–277–9939). B&B double rates of $50–90 include breakfasts of home-baked scones, sourdough pancakes with reindeer sausage, or baked apple French toast. Guest rooms are equipped with queen- or twin-sized beds and bathrooms; both shared and private baths are available. Relax on the deck or in the guests' living room, equipped with cable TV, VCR, stereo, and a library; laundry facilities are also available. "Beautifully decorated room with private bath; delicious breakfasts." (*Kip Goldman & Marty Wall*)

For an additional area B&B, see **Chugiak,** just 20 miles north of Anchorage via the Glenn Highway, and **Wasilla,** 45 minutes to the north.

Swan House B&B Tel: 907–346–3033
6840 Crooked Tree Drive, 99516 800–921–1900
Fax: 907–346–3535
E-mail: 103164.466@compuserve.com

No expense was spared during the nearly two years it took to build the Swan House during the Alaskan oil boom of the 1980s, opened as a B&B in 1991 by Judy Swanson. A stunning contemporary home designed to resemble a swan in flight, it was constructed using heart redwood, and offers a bird's-eye view of the city of Anchorage, framed by Mt. McKinley in the distance. Each exterior beam has Arctic animal carved on the end. Light oak predominates inside, accented by designs in a swan motif. Over the entryway is a window made of semiprecious stones, showing a swan landing on a lake; above the fireplace mantel is an inlaid jade panel of swans. There are nearly 130 windows of different geometric shapes and 150 light fixtures of various types. In sensitive contrast are the 18th century English and Irish pine primitives pieces which furnish the dining rooms, and the turn-of-the century Victorian period pieces which decorate the living room. The Bavarian guest room has twin beds (can convert to king), signed and dated 1860 with inlaid rosewood, walnut and cherry; the American Country guest room has a queen-size antique pine replica bed. Breakfast is served at the dining room table from 7 A.M. to 8:30 A.M. and might include Belgian almond waffles with fresh fruit and, whipped cream, reindeer sausage, and fresh ground coffee.

"An absolutely stunning B&B; extraordinary design and decor." *(MW)* "Excellent Alaskan-style breakfast." *(Kevin Cuthbertson)* "Respect for privacy balanced with friendly service. Peaceful and relaxing, accommodating to business travelers. Flexible hostess." *(Brian Kossow)* "Wonderful views. Judy is a delightful, thoughtful hostess who prepares delicious breakfasts." *(Tomas P. Cuntin)*

Open All year.
Rooms 1 cabin, 2 doubles—all with private shower and/or bath, telephone with data port, clock/radio. 1 with desk, balcony/deck, kitchenette.
Facilities Dining/breakfast room, living room with fireplace, piano, TV/VCR, stereo, books; guest kitchen, deck. ½ acre with off-street parking. Golf, downhill, cross-country skiing, hiking nearby.
Location Hillside neighborhood; 20 min. to downtown; 15 min. to airport. Take O'Malley to Seward highway to town (call for directions).
Restrictions No smoking. No children.
Credit cards Amex, Discover, MC, Visa.
Rates B&B, $99–139 double, $89–119 single. 10% senior, AAA discount.
Extras Pets possible with prior approval.

Voyager Hotel ☏
501 K Street, 99501

Tel: 907–277–9501
800–247–9070
Fax: 907–274–0333
E-mail: rsvp@alaska.net

"This sturdy brick and concrete four-story building has a small but pleasant lobby with ample couches for comfortable seating, with coffee, tea, and cocoa available each morning. Most of the spacious guest rooms have two double beds, one set up much like a couch. There's a sturdy table to use for eating or as a desk. Each room has a kitchenette, with plates and cutlery free on request. The decor includes good lighting, firm beds, and sturdy, well-made furnishings. The showers offer strong water pressure, steady hot water (no fluctuations) in ample supply. Owner Stan Williams is often at the front desk, available to answer questions and chat. He bought the hotel in 1979, when it was a rundown boarding house, and each year has worked to upgrade some facet of the hotel. In 1996, he installed central air-conditioning, updated the bathrooms, and replaced the carpeting; in 1997, he replaced the bedspreads and drapes, and added additional electric outlets and phone jacks for computer use." *(SWS)*

"Stan is personable but not intrusive; the morning hostess is cheerful and gracious. The staff care about guests' comfort." *(Maria Rutigliano)* "Spotlessly clean and bright even in the dark of winter." *(D. Titus)* "The hotel's location is a plus—across the street from the well-known Captain Cook Hotel." *(Stephen Holman)* "Our nonsmoking room was impeccably clean, with lots of fluffy towels and plenty of hot water." *(Susan Prizio)* "Helpful, cheerful staff; high standards of cleanliness and comforts for a moderate price." *(Irving Carlisle)* "We used the Voyager as our home base. The attitude and efficiency of the reception desk made each return trip a positive experience; our luggage awaited us in our room and Stan greeted us like old friends." *(Bill & Liz Dingle)*

Open All year. Closed Christmas.
Rooms 38 doubles—all with full private bath, telephone with dataport, air-conditioning, radio, TV, desk, kitchenette, hair dryer, coffee maker (coffee supplied), ironing board (irons at front desk).
Facilities Restaurant, bar/lounge with TV, lobby, parking lot. Valet service. Parks, walking trails nearby.
Location City center. Junction K and 5th Sts., near Cook Inlet.
Restrictions No smoking in guest rooms.
Credit cards Amex, DC, Discover, MC, Visa.
Rates Room only (includes morning coffee), $79–159 double, $74–149 single. Extra person, $10. 10% senior discount. Off-season weekend specials.
Extras Crib.

CHUGIAK

Peters Creek B&B ♟ ♿   *Tel:* 907–688–3465
22626 Chambers Lane, 99567   888–688–3465
                                          Fax: 907–688–3466
                   E-mail: pcbnb@customcpu.com

Built by longtime Alaska residents, Lucy and Bob Moody in 1994, Peters Creek B&B was designed with the physically challenged in mind. Lucy is a watercolor artist, pianist, and craftsperson, while Bob, an experienced fisherman, is the captain of a commercial fishing vessel. Located on wooded terrain on the north shore of Peters Creek, the decor of this spacious home is highlighted by Victorian antique furnishings. The light and airy Violet Room abounds with flowers, while the Family Suite has a king-bedded room with a rose decor, and a second bedroom with a Noah's Ark motif. Breakfast, served 7:30–10 A.M. at the dining room table, includes cereal, fruit, yogurt, just-baked blueberry muffins, Alaskan berry jams and jellies, plus such dishes as strawberry crepes, sourdough pancakes with reindeer sausage, or omelets.

"Warm, welcoming hospitality; clean, comfortable accommodations. They welcomed our children and provided us with wonderful, home-cooked breakfasts. One evening, Lucy treated us to a tasty dessert when we returned. Our boys enjoyed exploring the nearby stream." *(Janice Sakoda)* "The charming rooms, great food, kindest hospitality, and location was exceptional." *(Mark Fox)* "The Alaska Room is big and airy, with a whale motif and paintings of this wonderful state; like the rest of the house it is furnished with every modern amenity. Delicious breakfasts, beautifully served." *(E.R. McBoyle)*

Open All year.
Rooms 1 suite, 3 doubles—all with private bath and/or shower, telephone, clock/radio, TV/VCR, ceiling fan, refrigerator. 2 with desk.
Facilities Dining room, living room with piano, fireplace; family room with wide-screen TV/VCR, stereo, books, games; guest laundry. 2½ acres with hot tub, children's swing set, lawn games, creek, fishing (gear available), kayaking, hiking, sled dog rides, cross-country skiing. 15 m to downhill skiing.
Location S central AK, 20 m N of Anchorage, 17 m N of airport, 8 m from Eagle River. ⁸⁄₁₀ m from Hwy. From Anchorage, go approx. 17 m N on Glenn Hwy to

Peters Creek Exit & go left of ramp. Take first road on left; pass restaurant, grocery etc. Where road curves to right, go left to B&B on left.

Restrictions No smoking.

Credit cards Amex, Discover, MC, Visa.

Rates B&B, $130–150 suite, $85 double, $75 single. Extra adult, $15; child under 12, $10.

Extras Wheelchair accessible; elevator, bathroom specially equipped. Crib. Spanish spoken.

DENALI NATIONAL PARK

Denali National Park covers 5.7 million acres of land and is home to 35 kinds of mammals, from grizzly bears to caribou and moose, plus a variety of bird and plant life. Mosquitoes are probably the most populous species in the park; fortunately they diminish by the latter part of the season. Private cars are discouraged in the park; shuttle buses bring guests to campgrounds and transport visitors to places of interest throughout the park. Area activities include hiking, canoeing, natural history and photography trips, rafting, bicycling, fishing, and panning for gold.

The park is 240 miles north of Anchorage, 120 miles southwest of Fairbanks.

Also recommended: A few miles past North Face Lodge (see below) is the **Kantishna Roadhouse** (P.O. Box 130, Denali National Park, 99755 or in winter, P.O. Box 80067, Fairbanks 99708; 800–942–7420 or 907–479–2436), offering daily guided hikes and horse-drawn wagon trips for sightseeing and gold panning; naturalists and photographers offer evening programs. The 27 cabins have private baths, plus there's a lodge with family-style dining room and saloon, and a sauna along the creek. Rates, including bus transportation for the 90-mile trip from Denali Depot, all meals and activities, are $550 per day for two people; it's open from early June to early September, and families are welcome. "A true wilderness experience; we spotted bear, moose, fox, and eagles. Our cabin had running water, electricity, comfortable bed, and a loft to accommodate two more. Delicious food." (*Kathleen Olson*)

Information please: The **Denali Riverview Inn** (Mile 238.5 Park Highway, P.O. Box 49, Denali National Park 99755; 907–683–2663 or in winter, 206–384–1078) is comprised of two-story timber buildings set among the evergreens; the balconies offer lovely views of the Nenana River and the National Park (though not of Mt. McKinley). The 12 motel rooms have soft blue fabrics complementing the natural birch and pine furnishings. Rates are $129, June through August, and $84 in September; children are welcome.

North Face Lodge/Camp Denali ♚

Denali National Park Wilderness Centers, Ltd.   *Tel:* 907–683–2290
P.O. Box 67, Denali National Park, 99755   *Fax:* 907–683–1568

Imagine waking from a good night's sleep, throwing back the covers of your handmade down-filled quilt, and stepping outside to watch the sun transform Mt. McKinley's 20,000 feet of majestic whiteness to a rosy pink. Then add a caribou grazing in the foreground to complete this idyllic picture, and you'll be on your way to understanding what it's like to stay at either the North Face Lodge or Camp Denali.

Longtime owners Wallace and Jerryne Cole have done an exceptional job of creating two havens from which to enjoy the wilderness, and are eager for their guests to appreciate the surrounding wilderness and its inhabitants. Their first effort, Camp Denali, consists of a central dining room, living room, and restroom/shower buildings along with the cabins, scattered along a high ridge. In 1987, the Coles renovated nearby North Face Lodge. An L-shaped building, the lodge consists of a spacious living/dining area, with a guest-room wing. A covered veranda provides an ideal place to relax and enjoy the view. Electricity to power everything from the reading lights to the pumps that supply hot water for your bath is produced by the inn's own generators. A hearty breakfast is served promptly at 7:30 A.M.; at 8:30 A.M., the lunch fixings are set out; at 6:30 P.M., the single-entree dinner is served.

"A handhewn log building with a central stove, large collection of books, telescopes, and audio-visual equipment serves as the main lodge at Camp Denali. Our cabin had bunks for the kids, a hot plate, woodstove, beautiful quilts, a writing table and a comfortable sofa. The kids were thrilled to ring the big triangle to announce the meals; the atmosphere is casual, with staff and guests mixed randomly at long tables." *(Chuck Darby)* "Our room at North Face had a down comforter and four pillows on the firm queen-size bed, and bedside lamps and tables on each side of bed. Soft shades of dusty pink and blue contrasted with the rustic pine paneling. The chairs on the porch outside our room were perfect for reading or chatting in the long evenings—sunset in mid-August came around 10:30. We breakfasted on French toast one day and eggs the next. We made lunch from a buffet of cheese, ham, and tuna spreads, homemade bread, sprouts, apples, oranges, cookies, plus plastic bottles to fill with water or lemonade. Dinner included halibut in sour cream sauce, rice, carrots and snow peas, and Waldorf salad, with strawberry rhubarb pie for dessert. The delightful staff mixed easily with guests, creating a warm, friendly, and knowledgeable atmosphere. The living room is handsomely furnished with plenty of comfortable couches, chairs, tables for games, and a stone fireplace." *(SWS)* "Our naturalist/driver made the long trip to the lodge an unforgettable experience." *(Janet & Howard Emery)* "Knowledgeable staff who are pleased to share their expertise with guests. Wonderful food with Alaskan specialties: salmon or halibut, local blueberries or lingonberries." *(Anne Clouser)* "The cabins are snug and attractive with quilted bed covers, photographs of Alaska, wood stoves and kerosene lamps." *(Catherine Cooper)*

Open Early June–early Sept.
Rooms North Face Lodge: 1 suite, 14 twins—all with full private bath. Camp Denali: 18 cabins—each with wood-burning stove, running water, gas hot plate, propane lights, outhouse. Shared shower facility.
Facilities Both lodge & cabins: Dining rooms, library/living rooms, natural history resource room, darkroom. Naturalist program in evenings. Greenhouse,

pond, hiking trails. Daypacks, fishing poles, rain gear, boots provided. Inquire about science, photography, environmental special sessions; academic credit available.

Location In center of park, 90 m W of Denali Station.

Restrictions No smoking. Alcoholic beverages permitted in cabin/room only. No fresh milk served. Children over 7 preferred.

Credit cards None accepted.

Rates Full board: North Face Lodge, $315 per person, double, $415 single; 2–3 night minimum stay. Camp Denali, $315 per person double, $415 single. Family, children's rates. 3–4 night minimum stay.

Extras Narrated safari and picnic from Denali Station included in rates. Crib. French, German spoken.

FAIRBANKS

When you consider the fact that Fairbanks is America's northernmost city, just 150 miles south of the Arctic Circle, it's not surprising that the local baseball team can play a midnight game on June 21 without the benefit of artificial light. Fairbanks was settled in 1901, and was first populated by gold miners. A second wave of growth came in 1968, with the discovery of gold in Prudhoe Bay and the building of the Alaska Pipeline. Sights of interest include the University of Alaska Museum, depicting the state's natural history; a 36,000-year-old preserved bison, killed by a lion, is the star attraction. Families will enjoy a visit to the pioneer theme park, Alaskaland, offering historic buildings, a sternwheeler, trains, and a salmon bake.

Reader tip: "Pike's Landing was superb for salmon; reservations needed." *(Kip Goldman & Marty Wall)*

Also recommended: The **Forget-Me-Not Lodge–The Aurora Express** (P.O. Box 80128; 99708; 907–474–0949) overlooks Fairbanks and the Tanana Valley, and offers excellent views of the Aurora Borealis. Three guest rooms are available in the contemporary lodge, while another six guest accommodations are await in the restored train cars. B&B double rates of $85–140 include a full breakfast served family-style at 8 A.M. Guests are welcome to relax in the TV lounge, the glassed-in living-dining area, or on the deck. "Susan and Mike Wilson are gracious hosts, helpful with advice on area sights. The lodge was immaculate and beautifully decorated. Breakfast was a fabulous spread in the dining room, with a great view. We stayed in the Golden Nellie Caboose, with gilded ceilings, burgundy velvet drapes, a queen-size bed, and private bath." *(Margaret Choa)*

Information please: Fifteen minutes from Fairbanks is **A Taste of Alaska Lodge** (551 Eberhardt Road, 99712; 907–488–7855), set on 200 acres originally homesteaded in 1947 by the Eberhardt family, who still own it today. Accommodations are available in the 7,000-square-foot log lodge, as well as two cottages, with rates ranging from $70–200. Each guest room has a queen-size bed, telephone, TV/VCR, and private entrance. Decor includes antiques and Alaska collectibles, and guests enjoy a buffet breakfast, use of the hot tub, and views of the Northern Lights over the Alaskan Range and Mt. McKinley.

Eight miles north of Fairbanks is the **Cranberry Ridge B&B** (705 Cranberry Ridge Drive, 99712; 907–457–4424), a log lodge built in 1994 by fifth generation Alaskans Mike and Floss Caskey, and decorated with Alaskan art. A family suite which sleeps four, plus a room for two are available for guests, at rates of $85 double, $150 suite, including a breakfast of strawberries Bonaparte, baked peach cobbler or perhaps lemon pecan sticky buns, with fresh fruit and juice, coffee or tea.

Seven Gables Inn ¢ &. *Tel:* 907–479–0751
4312 Birch Lane, P.O. Box 80488, 99708 *Fax:* 907–479–2229
E-mail: gables 7@alaska.net

Despite its name, the Seven Gables doesn't really have seven gables, but fourteen, seven along the front of this 7,000-square-foot Tudor-style house and another seven along the back. Custom-built by Paul and Leicha Welton in 1982, this B&B has many other unusual touches, including a flower-filled two-story atrium greenhouse, a foyer with a seven-foot rock waterfall and stained glass ceiling insets, and a living room with a cathedral ceiling 23 feet high. The Welton's home is simply furnished with contemporary decor. The well-equipped bedrooms are compact, and most have queen or twin-size beds with cheerful floral bedspreads and curtains.

"Set in a residential neighborhood, this B&B is private, secure, and homey, with a flower-filled greenhouse. Wonderful variety of breakfast." *(Lynn Watson)* "An enormous home, built for B&B, with excellent soundproofing between rooms. A full breakfast is served at 7:15; although a continental breakfast is available for late risers, early birds are well rewarded. The first morning we had a delicious meal of cheese-baked eggs with freshly baked apple muffins; the second we feasted on crepes stuffed with a cream cheese and pecan mixture, topped with peach sauce. The Weltons are friendly, hospitable innkeepers, eager to introduce visitors to Fairbanks." *(Pat Niven)* "Quiet, convenient, and clean. Leicha's breakfasts were so wonderful, that I bought a copy of her cookbook." *(TL)* Comments appreciated.

Open All year.
Rooms 4 suites, 4 doubles—all with full private Jacuzzi bath, refrigerator, deck, TV/VCR, telephone, clock/radio, desk, fan. 4 suites in annex.
Facilities Living room with piano, balcony, books; dining room, garden solarium, multipurpose room with fireplace, laundry privileges. Guitar, piano entertainment evenings. 1½ acres with canoes, kayaks, bicycles, children's play equipment. Off-street parking. Skiing, snowmobiling nearby.
Location From Parks Hwy., turn onto Geist Rd. Go right at Loftus Rd., left at Birch Lane to inn on left. Walking distance to U. of Alaska/Fairbanks.
Restrictions Smoking in 2 suites only.
Credit cards Amex, DC, Discover, MC, Visa.
Rates B&B, $75–130 suite, $50–120 double, $50–110 single. Extra person, $10. No tipping. Weekly, seasonal discounts.
Extras Crib. Spanish, German spoken.

GUSTAVUS

Gustavus is a small and isolated community on southeast Alaska's famed Inside Passage about 50 miles west of Juneau. Located on a large sandy plain created by receding glaciers, the area contrasts with the typical rocky wooded shoreline of southeast Alaska. There are no roads or ferry service—the only way to get here is by plane; the only paved surface in town is the landing strip.

The key attraction here is Glacier Bay National Park, a series of fjords and active tidewater glaciers extending over 65 miles. Activities include hiking in the rain forests of hemlock, spruce, and pine; cruising up the bay to watch for whales, bald eagles, black bear, deer, and 200 varieties of birds; or climbing into a kayak for a close-up look at the seals and porpoises that will accompany you. Fishermen will opt for deep-sea and river fishing for salmon, halibut, cutthroat and Dolly Varden trout, while winter visitors can add cross-country skiing to the recreation list. Another highlight is a bush plane flight-seeing tour of the park, revealing the bay's deep crevasses, enormous ice fields, jagged peaks, and breathtaking beauty. Berry-picking and picnicking on the beach are a delight for children of all ages.

Although outdoor activities are limitless, one thing the town does not have is a liquor store; if you enjoy a glass of wine with dinner, bring your own. Remember that the weather can be cool and damp even in summer, so bring along warm and waterproof clothing, including hat and gloves.

Reader tip: "Don't come to Glacier Bay for the weather; it's often cold and rainy, with low clouds obscuring the views. Bring warm clothes and foul weather gear."

Also recommended: "A truly rustic lodge with a beautiful setting overlooking Bartlett Cove and the Fairview Mountains is **The Glacier Bay Lodge** (P.O. Box 199, Glacier Bay National Park 99826; 907–697–2226). Rooms are spacious and comfortable, with high ceilings. Eat on the deck overlooking the cove and 'drink' in the scenery. Breakfast is a full, fixed price buffet. A courtesy shuttle to and from the Gustavus airport is convenient, as is the express check-in for departures on Alaska Air—an efficient and organized operation." (*Kip Goldman & Marty Wall*) A national park concessionaire, lodge rates for the 56 rooms, all with private bath, include complimentary morning coffee, and a nightly film presentation on Glacier Bay; the restaurant is open from 5:45 A.M. until 10 P.M. and offers a health-conscious menu. Double rates are $156 for the mid-May to mid-September season; also available are dorm beds for $28 per night.

Information please: Just completed in 1997 is **Glacier Bay's Bear Track Inn** (255 Rink Creek Road, 99826; 907–697–3017 or 888–697–2284 or email at Beartrac@aol.com), a log lodge with 14 spacious guest rooms with Alaskan decor, each with a private bath and two queen-size beds, down comforters and pillows, and oversize bath towels. Rates include breakfast and dinner at the lodge, with bag lunches for daytime excursions; salt and freshwater fishing packages are a speciality, in addition to glacier tours, whale watching, and kayaking.

Glacier Bay Country Inn/Whalesong Lodge 🛉   *Tel:* 907–697–2288
P.O. Box 5, 99826   800–628–0912
                                                   Fax: 907–697–2289

Glacier Bay Country Inn and Whalesong Lodge offer a wonderful way to experience the beauty of the Glacier Bay area, and have been owned by Sandi and Ponch Marchbanks since 1996.

"We were picked up from the airport in the inn's van. We bumped along dusty roads, going deep into the woods to the beautiful rustic inn, built of logs cut and milled on site. Arriving just in time for lunch, we enjoyed homemade soup and salmon salad sandwiches; the chef made up French bread pizzas for the kids. As we ate, we looked out through the windows to a sunny meadow, and watched a young black bear ambling through. After lunch, we were driven over to Glacier Bay National Park to take a ranger-led walk through the rain forest, then returned to the inn to explore and relax. At night, we dined on Dungeness crab and rice, just-picked salad greens, and delicious chocolate cake and raspberries for dessert. The next day we cruised in Glacier Bay, and were rewarded with sightings of calving, glaciers, seals, and whales." *(SWS)* "The inn is close to Adolphus Point, where endangered humpback whales come to feed in summer—they swam within 30 feet of our boat!" *(JMC)* "Food, facilities, service were outstanding. The owners' logistical skills ensured that all ran smoothly, whether guests need to get to the airport, a whale-watching trip, or a kayaking excursion." *(Nigel Franks)* "The staff was happy to serve the wine we had brought." *(Janet Emery)* "The inn has lots of nooks and crannies so that people can find a private corner, yet everyone gets together in friendly groups at mealtime." *(Shirley Holmgreen)* "For our afternoon whale-watching trip, we were given tasty bag lunches with halibut sandwiches, chips, potato salad, cookies, fruit, and soda. Our immaculate room overlooked the front gardens, and had a comfortable bed and a rocking chair." *(Susan Prizio)*

"Guests from the inn and lodge gathered for the evening meal. Our room at Whalesong Lodge was comfortable and clean with fresh towels daily." *(Suzee O'Brien)* "Accommodating staff; we were provided with jackets, gloves, and hats when needed." *(Ruth Fishman)* "Excellent food, gracious hospitality, relaxing atmosphere." *(Kurt Petrich)* "The owners and the entire staff were genuinely concerned about our welfare. Excellent meals, generous portions, attractively served." *(Helen Acton)* "My comfortable room balanced historic and modern charm." *(Rainer Klement)* "I felt welcome from the moment I stepped off the plane. The food is plentiful and delicious. The inn is small enough so that you are treated as an individual, not a number." *(Wayne Reynolds)* "Excellent housekeeping; friendly, outgoing, efficient staff." *(I.R. Gordon, also Cal Dunks)*

Open May–Sept.
Rooms GBCI: 3 cabins, 6 doubles—all with private shower and/or tub. Some with desk, fan. Whalesong: 5 doubles with private bath, 1 3-bedroom condo.
Facilities Dining rooms, living room with games, library. 160 acres with rain forest, gardens, bicycles, hiking trails, creeks. Deep sea fishing, fly-fishing, whale-watching, kayaking, flight-seeing, glacier trips available.

Location 6 miles from park headquarters. Take main road from airport, turn left at Tong Rd. & follow to end of dirt road.
Restrictions No smoking inside.
Credit cards Amex, Discover, MC, Visa.
Rates GBCI: Full board, $260 double, $160 single. Extra adult, $75; extra child under 12, $54. Lunch, $10; dinner, $24 (reservations required). Whalesong Lodge: Full board, $240 double. Room only, 3-bedroom condo, $300. Fishing packages.
Extras Airport/dock/Nat'l Park transfers. Crib.

HEALY

Information please: About twenty minutes from the Denali park entrance is the **Rock Creek Country Inn** (Milepost 261, George Parks Highway, H.C. 1, Box 3450, Healy 99743-9606; 907–683–2676), "a beautiful hand-built log house in the wilderness. Owners Wayne and Lolita Valcq are mushers and maintain a kennel of 25 sled dogs on the premises. We stayed in a basement apartment with a separate entrance. Alaskan decor is found throughout, reflecting Wayne's skill as a woodworker and Lolita's as an artist and taxidermist." *(Kip Goldman & Marty Wall)* Three guest rooms and three cabins (five with private bath), are available at B&B double rates of $75–100, including a full breakfast.

HOMER

Homer makes a delightful base for touring the beautiful Kenai Peninsula. Set on Kachemak Bay, it's about an hour south of Anchorage by plane or about a five-hour drive (225 miles on a paved road), following Cook Inlet much of the way to Homer. From Homer, intrepid adventurers can visit one of the wilderness lodges noted below, or can take the Alaska Marine Highway to Kodiak, home of the Alaskan brown bear.

Reader tips: "Homer is the halibut capital of the world; at the docks, we saw three 120-pound halibut, and were told that this was not unusual." *(Ann La Posta)* And: "Unless you're staying at a fly-in lodge, you'll need a car when you're in Homer." And: "Cafe Cups is a whimsical place with gourmet food." *(Kip Goldman & Marty Wall)*

For an additional area inn, see **Seldovia.**

Kachemak Kiana B&B ¢   *Tel:* 907–235–8824
Mile 5, East Road, 99603   *Fax:* 907–235–8349
Mailing address: P.O. Box 855, 99603

Longtime Alaska resident Amy Springer notes that if you drive as far west as you can on Alaska's highway system you'll end up in Homer; keep on going and you'll be at Kachemak Kiana B&B. Her B&B occupies the entire second floor of her handsome contemporary home, and offers beautiful views of the bay and mountains beyond. Amy notes that "wild game—moose, coyotes, and pheasant—often come into the yard, and sandhill cranes nest next to the cabin each summer." Winter visitors can drive onto the Homer Spit and see hundreds of bald eagles who congregate there to be fed by Jean Keane (the Eagle Lady). The breakfast of cereal, juices, fresh fruit, bagels, cream cheese, muffins, toast, jams and jellies, coffee, milk is available all morning, so guests can rise early or sleep in.

"Amy Springer is a gracious hostess, welcoming us by name as we walked in the door. We weren't surprised to learn that Kiana means 'welcome.' Our room, the Master Suite, had an incredible view of Kachemak Bay. It had a walk-in cedar closet, king-size bed with built-in reading lights, a small sitting area and a large bathroom with lots of towels and plenty of hot water. Breakfast each day was a feast of breads, muffins, fruits, cereals, juices, and coffee or tea. All the guests sit together at a long dining room table to share conversation and food. The inn is spanking clean and the common areas are comfortable. The kitchen is open for guests' use and is stocked with teas, coffee, hot chocolate, juices, and fruits." *(Susan Prizio)* "Amy had thought of every detail to make our cabin comfortable and homey, from the filled candy dish to the makings for coffee and tea. The hot tub was a treat after a day of fishing or sightseeing. Amy was like a personal guide, offering excellent information on sightseeing, restaurants, and shopping." *(Linda & Robert Pearson)* "Delightful home; Amy remains gracious even in trying conditions." *(E. Nickoloff)* "Hard to leave Amy's place without a smile on your face and a glow in your heart." *(Dennis Swing)* "Convenient, yet lovely country setting." *(Candee Noorda)*

Open All year.
Rooms 1 cabin, 3 doubles—all with private bath and/or shower, clock. Cabin with TV, refrigerator, balcony.
Facilities Living room with fireplace, den with fireplace, VCR/TV, books; deck. 3½ acres with hot tub. 8 m from boat harbor. Cross country skiing, hiking, fishing nearby.
Location 5 m E of town.
Restrictions No smoking. Children over 12.
Credit cards None accepted.
Rates B&B, $75–105 cabin, $85–95 double, $55–60 single. Extra person, $25.

JUNEAU

Set at the northern end of Southeast Alaska, Juneau is Alaska's capital city. It is the only state capital unreachable by road, and has the additional distinction of having a glacier (the Mendenhall) just 12 miles from town. The city dates to 1880, when gold was discovered by Joe Juneau and Dick Harris. Mining provided the underpinnings of the local economy for years; these days, government jobs provide most paychecks.

Reader tips: "Be sure to drive up to the site of the AJ Mine, either for the salmon bake or to picnic. You can pan for gold or hike one of the many trails. The setting is beautiful—steep forested hillsides and dozens of waterfalls." *(Lewis Bennett)* Also: "The Second Course restaurant on Front Street serves pan-Asian food, and is open only for lunch.

The Monday vegetarian buffet was excellent, with spicy tofu." *(Kip Goldman & Marty Wall)*

Also recommended: If you'd enjoy having your own place overlooking beautiful Auke Bay, call Carol and Charlie Smelcer at **Grandview B&B** (3324 Fritz Cove Road, P.O. Box 210705, Auke Bay 99821; 907–790–2648). Located just three miles from the Juneau airport and ferry terminal, this one-bedroom apartment is equipped with a kitchen, laundry, private bath, and TV/VCR, and the B&B double rates of $95–135 include breakfast makings. "Large picture windows and a deck maximize the wonderful views of water, whales, and wildlife. Decorated in country oak, with a generously stocked refrigerator. Extremely private. Carol and Charlie are friendly, kind, and full of Alaskan hospitality." *(Line & Bennie Weber)*

Information please: A hand-crafted 4,000-square-foot log home, **Blueberry Lodge** (9436 North Douglas Highway, 99801; 907–463–5886) is a ten-minute drive from downtown Juneau and offers views of the Gastineau Channel, the Mendenhall Wetlands State Game Refuge, and an active eagle's nest. A hearty breakfast is served in the main dining room; dinner is served by arrangement. Owners Judy and Jay Urquhart have five guest rooms with shared baths. B&B double rates range from $75–85, and include a full breakfast.

At the **Fireweed House B&B** (8530 North Douglas Highway, 99801; 907–586–3885 or 800–586–3885) you will receive a family welcome from owners Danith and Jeffrey Watts, their two young children, and their two yellow Labs. Located on Douglas Island, the B&B offers three guest rooms (two sharing a bath, one with private bath and Jacuzzi tub), a fully furnished two-bedroom cabin (with TV/VCR, woodstove, kitchen, laundry and gas grill), and a private apartment. Breakfasts include homemade breads, gourmet coffee, herbal teas, and fresh fruit; early morning coffee is available at 6 A.M. Double rates range from $75–110; the apartment rate is $85–125; and the cabin, for four persons, is $150–225.

Within walking distance of the historic downtown area, the **Mt. Juneau Inn** (1801 Old Glacier Highway, 99801; 907–463–5855) is surrounded by gardens, wetlands, and native-carved totem poles. Innkeepers Karen and Phil Greeney have named their seven guest rooms after animals in the native Tlingit culture; each room is decorated with Alaskan photographs and native art capturing each animal in its natural environment or depicting its mythical powers. They also offer a furnished one-bedroom cottage with a kitchen. Breakfast includes a hot entree, Karen's wild berry jams and fireweed honey, and possibly some of Phil's homemade sausage. Double B&B rates are $55–95; cottage rate is $115.

Pearson's Pond Luxury Inn and Garden Spa
4541 Sawa Circle, 99801–8723

Tel: 907–789–3772
Fax: 907–789–6722
E-mail: pearsons.pond@juneau.com

A contemporary home built in 1987, Pearson's Pond was opened as a B&B in 1991 by Diane and Steve Pearson. Highlights include the lovely setting, and the balance of warm hospitality with respect for guests' privacy. Diane can serve a breakfast of cereal, fruit, juice, yogurt, home-baked breads and jams between 8–10 A.M. in the great room; if you prefer, or would like to eat earlier or later, she keeps the guest kitchen stocked so guests can fix themselves a light meal at their own convenience, and enjoy it in their room or on the deck.

"Lovely, spacious, well-equipped room. Beautiful setting, with dramatic views of Mendenhall Glacier. Real Alaskan hospitality; inviting rooms with country decor." *(Linda Maybury, also Michael Young)* "We fixed ourselves a casual breakfast and ate it at the table in our room. Beautiful gardens, inviting hot tub." *(Kathy Halvorson)* "Unusually luxurious and well equipped for an Alaska B&B." *(MW)*

Open All year.
Rooms 3 suites—all with private shower bath, telephone, dataport, clock/radio, TV/VCR, desk, kitchenette, private entrance, deck, CD player; 2 with electric fireplace.
Facilities Great room with dining area, fireplace, TV/VCR, books, games, musical instruments; guest kitchens; deck with hot tub. 1 acre with gardens, fountains, barbecue/firepit, berry-picking; pond with dock, rowboat, kayak. Skis, bicycles, ice skates, portable gym, masseuse; health club privileges. River, ocean nearby. Hiking, fishing nearby.
Location SE AK. 10 m from downtown, 1 m from Mendenhall Glacier. Call for directions from ferry, airport, downtown.
Restrictions Absolutely no smoking. Children over 3.
Credit cards Amex, CB, DC, Discover, MC, Visa.
Rates B&B, $169–429 2–3 bedroom suite, $99–179 suite, $89–169 single.
Extras Limited wheelchair access. Car needed; no airport/ferry pickups.

KENNICOTT

Kennicott Glacier Lodge

P.O. Box 103940, Anchorage 99510
Tel: 907–258–2350
800–582–5128
Fax: 907–248–7975
E-mail: kgl@alaska.net

Wrangell-St. Elias National Park is vastness on a scale that's hard for non-Alaskans to grasp. Its acreage exceeds that of Connecticut, Massachusetts, and Rhode Island combined; the park contains nine of the 16 tallest peaks in the U.S., with glaciers each five times the size of Manhattan. In 1900, the Kennicott Mining Company began shipping huge quantities of copper ore by rail to ships waiting at Cordova. The high-grade ore was played out by the 1930s, and when the mining company moved out its 800 workers, Kennicott became a ghost town overnight.

Rich and Jody Kirkwood, who built the lodge in 1986, note that "Kennicott is a National Historic Landmark, located in the center of the Wrangell-St. Elias National Park. We offer guided glacier treks, historic tours of the ghost town, river rafting, nature hikes, flight seeing, photography, and more." They go on to explain that the park is reached by car with surprising ease in summer via the Glenn Highway from Anchorage or the Richardson Highway from Valdez. The road from Anchorage is paved up to the park entrance; the next 60 miles are a state-maintained gravel road. At the end of the road, near McCarthy, park your car, call the lodge on the "bush phone" and cross the Kennicott River on the footbridge. The lodge staff will pick you up in their shuttle van after you've crossed over.

"Along with commanding views of the Kennicott Glacier and the Wrangell Mountains, the lodge offers a comfortable oasis for recouping from the rigors of hiking mountain trails, glacier treks, and old mining camp rambles. Kennicott is early Alaska history, and the lodge illustrates life there from 1911 to 1938. The current lodge structure is a faithful reproduction of the housing for staff families of the Kennicott Copper Corporation (the original structure was destroyed by fire in 1983). Its walls are decorated with artifacts of mining life. A comfortable gathering area within the lodge opens onto a long porch with magnificent views. The porch also has benches, tables, and chairs for outdoor dining.

"Our lower level room was comfortable with a firm bed, a cold water sink, and an adequate clothing storage area. It opened out to the inner hall and outdoor porch. Across the hall from our room was an immaculate bathroom with toilet and hot and cold water sink; there are two hot showers at the end of the hall. A plus was Rich's considerable library of Kennicott and Wrangell/St. Elias books, pamphlets, and maps." (*Mr. & Mrs. John A. Lamb*) "Our cozy room was small but immaculate. Delicious meals were served family style—as much as you could eat. Those looking for luxury will be disappointed, but anyone looking for a new experience will be delighted. Rich and Jody were considerate, caring, and willing to make your stay special." (*Inger Ricci, also PN*) Reports appreciated.

Open May 15–Sept. 20.
Rooms 25 doubles share 6 shower rooms. 7 with deck.
Facilities Dining room, meeting room, living room with fireplace, books; porches. Hiking, rafting, games, picnic area, flight seeing.
Location S central AK. 320 m E of Anchorage (approx. 8 hrs.), 170 NE of Valdez.
Restrictions No smoking.
Credit cards Amex, Discover, MC, Visa.
Rates Room only, $169 double, $149 single. Extra person, $30. Full board, $240 double, $150 single. Extra person, $75. Children age 4–12 in parents' room, ½ price. Alc lunch, $10. Prix fixe dinner, $20.

KETCHIKAN

Reader tip: "Most shops and restaurants open and close according to cruise ship schedules, so plan accordingly. While the Five-Star Cafe closes at 6 P.M., it is terrific for breakfast and lunch; delicious Moroccan soup and turkey sandwiches." (*Kip Goldman & Marty Wall*)

Information please: One mile from the ferry terminal is **Hillberry's B&B** (Baker Street, P.O. Box 9578, 99901; 907–247–7111), a modern home surrounded by fruit trees and flower gardens, with views of the Tongass Narrows. The two guest rooms share a bath, and each has a queen-size bed; the B&B double rate, including a continental breakfast is $75; the entire house (sleeps six) may be rented for $175.

Millar Street B&B ¢ 👤
1430 Millar Street, 99901

Tel: 907–225–1258
800–287–1607
Fax: 907–225–1258
E-mail: bbkayak@ktn.net

Originally from Wales in Great Britain, innkeeper Kim Kirby arrived in Ketchikan by kayak in 1992 and never left; her partner Greg Thomas is an avid diver and musician, and enjoys playing songs of his native Australia on his guitar or didgeridoo. Their 1920s home, restored as a B&B in 1994, is located in a tree-lined cul-de-sac overlooking the waters of the scenic Tongass Narrows, marking the southernmost point of Southeast Alaska's Inside Passage. The B&B is within walking distance of shops, restaurants, and local attractions. Breakfast, served 7:30–9:30 A.M., includes homemade breads and muffins, fresh fruit, and cereals. It's served at a large pine table imported from an English farmhouse, and the meal is often highlighted by sightings of whales and bald eagles. Guest rooms have queen-size beds, private entrances, and simple but attractive contemporary decor.

"Extremely enjoyable stay at this exceptional B&B. Our room had a beautiful ocean view and a private deck. Kim and Greg were helpful with area information and set up the ultimate flightseeing trip for us. They really made our stay memorable." *(Jill Thomas)*

Open All year.
Rooms 2 doubles, 1 single—2 with private shower bath, 1 with maximum of 3 sharing bath. 2 with telephone, clock/radio, TV, desk. 1 with refrigerator, 1 with deck with barbecue.
Facilities Dining room, guest laundry, deck. Guided kayaking trips. Fishing, kayaking, swimming, boating, hiking nearby.
Location SE AK, Inside Passage. Historic district, ¾ m from town. From ferry terminal, take Airporter Bus to house, or take public transportation to Talbots and walk up hill.
Restrictions No smoking. Well behaved children welcome.
Credit cards MC, Visa.
Rates B&B, $65–85 double, $55–75 single. Extra person, $15. Children under 12 free. Senior discounts. Prix fixe dinner (by reservation), $45.
Extras Pets allowed outside. Cribs. Babysitting. French, Spanish, Australian spoken.

KODIAK

A Wintel's B&B ¢
1723 Mission Rd, P.O. Box 2812, 99615

Tel: 907–486–6935
Fax: 907–486–6935

Overlooking the water, and located within walking distance of Kodiak's famous fishing fleet, this contemporary home has been owned by Willie and Betty Heinrichs since 1989. Betty reports, "Our B&B attracts outdoor people. Favorite activities are fishing, hunting, hiking, photography, visiting archaeological digs, and watching bears, migrating birds, killer whales, and gray whales." Breakfast includes fresh fruit, juice, sourdough pancakes, eggs, sausage, ham, or bacon. For those in search of an authentic souvenir, the inn features gift items by Kodiak artisans: trading bead jewelry, hand-woven sea grass baskets, and Alaska fur articles.

"The charming hosts, Willie and Betty, have the ability to tell stories and draw everyone out. There is always a hot fresh drink of your choice with several choices of fresh baked goodies." *(Susan Stanford & Walt Cunningham)* "A home-cooked breakfast with delightful side order of local history! Relaxing atmosphere." *(Jeff Knights)* "The large, windowed living room offered a view of the ocean and several bald eagles could be seen soaring over nearby trees." *(Ron Scherzinger)* "Great breakfasts. Warm, inviting setting; clean rooms; helpful area information." *(Roger Lucas)* "Wonderful water views; delicious breakfasts of sourdough pancakes and cinnamon buns; Betty and Willie are welcoming, knowledgeable, and hospitable." *(MW)*

Open All year.
Rooms 1 suite with private bath, 2 doubles share 1 bath. All with telephone, radio, desk, fan.
Facilities Breakfast room, living room with fireplace, TV; family room with games, sun porch, gift shop, indoor Jacuzzi, sauna. Surf fishing, beach combing nearby.
Location S AK, NE Kodiak Island. ¾ m from town center, dock.
Restrictions No smoking. No drinking.
Credit cards MC, Visa.
Rates B&B, $90 suite, $55–70 double, $55 single. Extra person, $25.
Extras Airport pickup. German, Spanish spoken.

SELDOVIA

Swan House South   *Tel:* 907–234–8888
175 Augustine Avenue North, 99663   800–921–1900
Mailing address: 6840 Crooked Tree Drive,   *Fax:* 907–346–3535
Anchorage, AK 99516   *E-mail:* 103164.466@compuserve.com

Just across Kachemak Bay from Homer is Seldovia and the Swan House South, a contemporary home overlooking the water. Begun in 1980, it was purchased by Jerry and Judy Swanson in 1994 and completed in 1995 as a B&B; Doris Trotter is the manager. Expansive decks overlook the water; the tides rise and fall with a 25-foot difference from high to low. At low tide it is common to see bald eagles catching salmon; the high tides bring in ducks, birds, and sea otters. A short walk away is a salmon fishing hole, downtown shops, and the marina. Breakfast, served 8–10 A.M., may include sourdough blueberry pancakes, reindeer sausage, and freshly ground Costa Rican coffee.

"Incredible views; I caught a 200-pound halibut one day, and a 50-pound King Salmon the next." *(Leslie Habig)* "Quiet setting, excellent scenery. The Trotters and Swansons are great hosts. The inn is newly remodeled, clean, and modern. The town of Seldovia feels remote, but is easily accessible." *(Edward C. Faulk II)* "Views from every window; clean and modern with a relaxing atmosphere. Quaint shops, coffee shop, and a small town to explore." *(Jean Curtin)* "Exceptionally beautiful." *(Allen Hoffman)*

Open Memorial Day weekend–Labor Day weekend.
Rooms 5 doubles—3 with private bath and/or shower, 2 with maximum of 4 people sharing bath. All with clock.
Facilities Dining room, living room with stereo, books; sun room, decks. ½ acre with hot tub, berry picking. Ocean, river nearby for fishing, clamming, kayaking. Halibut, king salmon fishing charters.
Location S central AK, Kenai Peninsula; 16 m across Kachemak Bay from Homer via plane or boat. 110 miles S of Anchorage. 5 minute walk to downtown shops, marina. 10-minute walk from airport.
Restrictions No smoking. Children over 12 only.
Credit cards Amex, Discover, MC, Visa.
Rates B&B, $129 double, $109 single. Extra person $29. 10% senior, AAA discount.
Extras Free plane, boat pickups. Pets possible with prior approval.

SEWARD

Information please: Right at the water is the **Harborview B&B** (900 Third Street at "C" Street, 99664; 907–224–3217), with eight modern comfortable guest rooms plus two two-bedroom apartments. Each has a private bath, private entrance, TV, clock/radio, telephone, and queen-size bed(s). B&B double rates are approximately $85, and include a breakfast of fresh fruit, juice, muffins, yogurt and coffee, delivered to your room. Reports welcome.

SITKA

Along the western edge of the archipelago which dots the Inside Passage is the town of Sitka, known for its Russian and Tlingit heritage.

Reader tip: "Try the salmon burgers at the Westmark Shee Atika Hotel." *(Kip Goldman & Marty Wall)*

Information please: A contemporary home located in a quiet neighborhood just one block from the seashore and the Tongass National Forest, the **Alaska Ocean View B&B** (1101 Edgecumbe Drive, 99835; 907–747–8310 or 800–800–6870, #520) has three well-equipped guest rooms all with private bath, telephone, clock/radio, and TV. One can relax on the deck or in the hot tub, or admire the flower-filled courtyard. Tennis, boating, kayaking, and fishing charters are all nearby. The B&B double rates of $69–129 include a full breakfast, with fruit, fresh bread and muffins, coffee cake, and such entrees as crepes with strawberries, and bacon.

SKAGWAY

Information please: A restored B&B inn, the **Skagway Inn** (7th and Broadway, P.O. Box 500, 99840; 907–983–2289 or 800–478–2290 in AK) offers 12 handsome guest rooms, all with shared baths, plus a home-cooked breakfast included in the $78 double rate.

For a clean, comfortable motel accommodation, consider the **Gold Rush Lodge** (6th and Alaska Streets, P.O. Box 514, 99840; 907–983–2831). Coffee, juice, and rolls are set out in the lobby every morning for guests. Twelve units are available at rates of $80–95 double, depending on season. Reports please.

WASILLA

An ideal stopover between Anchorage and Denali, Fairbanks, or Valdez, Wasilla is located an hour north of Anchorage. It is the home of the International Iditarod Sled Dog Race, the Musk Ox Farm, the Reindeer Farm, and Matanuska and Knik Glaciers, and the Independence Gold Mine.

Information please: On the shores of Wasilla Lake is the eponymous **Wasilla Lake B&B** (961 North Shore Drive, 99654; 907–376–5985), a chalet-style home built in 1974, and opened as a B&B in 1987 by Arlene and LaVerne Gronewald. Three guest rooms in the main house share a bath; also available is a lower-level fully equipped two-bedroom apartment plus a lakeside cabin, ideal for families. B&B double rates of $75 double, $120–130 for the larger accommodations, include breakfasts of apple puff pancakes or eggs Lorraine. The innkeepers are avid gardeners, and the plants inside and gardens outside are exceptional. "Right on the lake. Beautiful backyard garden plus a boat dock. You can sit and watch the bush planes land on the lake and taxi up to the houses. Our basement apartment was comfortable and private, complete with kitchen and VCR." *(Kip Goldman)* Reports welcome.

Yukon Don's ¢ 🏃

2221 Yukon Circle,
1830 East Parks High-
    way, #386, 99654

Tel: 907–376–7472
800–478–7472
Fax: 907–376–6515
E-mail: 102737.3133@compuserve.com

Yukon Don is a real Alaskan character and his personality is evident in this B&B inn, a 10,000-square-foot converted farm building. The inn's longtime owners are Don Tanner, his wife Kristan, and their children. Guests can relax in the all-glass View Room on the second floor, with a 360° view of the Chugach and Talkeetna Mountain Ranges, or enjoy a variety of entertaining activities in the well-equipped Alaska Room. Each log-walled guest room has a sitting area and Alaskan decorations like bear skins, mounted salmon, moose racks, old tools, and even a dog sled. Most have a queen-size bed, plus a day bed with a trundle, ideal for families. Rates include a self-service expanded continental breakfast.

"Don entertained and astonished us with his Alaskan tales. Kristan was very helpful with area information and events. The well-stocked Alaska Room is relaxing for shooting pool, watching movies, and reading books. The hospitable Tanners accommodated our every need." *(Sharnee Epley)* "Exceptional views and hospitality; the accommodations just get better and better with each visit." *(Harry Porter)* "The owners have a wonderful grasp of Alaskan history and a well-stocked library." *(Stephen Swanson)* "Set in the valley at the edge of a bluff, with a spectacular view of the Matanuska Valley. Plenty of restaurants nearby." *(Linda Lockwood)* "Appreciated the breakfast flexibility." *(Wayne Krieger)* "Pleasant, quiet location; our hosts had a vast knowledge of Alaska." *(Jon & Penny Lyn Andreasen)* "Exceptional cleanliness, charm, decor, and friendliness." *(Bruce Williams)* "Each room has a different decorating theme, with charming antiques and intriguing Alaska collectibles. Wonderful mountain views. The breakfasts and coffee are excellent." *(Dr. Edward B. Evenson)*

Open All year.

Rooms 1 apartment, 2 suites, 4 doubles, 1 cabin; each with private bath. 4 double rooms share 2 baths. All with table, telephone. 2 with kitchen, 1 with laundry. Fan available.

Facilities View Room with fireplace, observation deck; Alaska Room with woodstove, pool table, snack bar, book/video library, TV/VCR; deck, sauna, exercise room. 2 acres with horseshoes, croquet, swing set.

Location Matanuska Valley. 60 min N of Anchorage. 5 m from Wasilla.

Restrictions Interior walls are not soundproof. No smoking.

Credit cards Amex, DC, Gold Dust, MC, Visa.

Rates B&B, $105–125 suite, apt. cabin; $85 double. Extra person, $10; children under 5 free. 10% weekly discount.

Extras Train pickups.

We Want to Hear from You!

As you know, this book is effective only with your help. We really need to know about your experiences and discoveries. If you stayed at an inn or hotel listed here, we want to know how it was. Did it live up to our description? Exceed it? Was it what you expected? Did you like it? Were you disappointed? Delighted? Have you discovered new establishments that we should add to the next edition?

Tear out one of the report forms at the back of this book (or use your own stationery if you prefer) and write today. *Even if you write only "Fully endorse existing entry" you will have been most helpful.*

Thank You!

California

The George Alexander House, Healdsburg

California is the nation's third largest state and the most populous. Its terrain is incredibly diverse, offering virtually every possible land- and seascape, much of it of great interest to tourists. Though the clock puts them three hours behind the East Coast, Californians tend to think of themselves as being ahead of the rest of the country. Many of the country's dominant trends got their start here and spread eastward across the country—not the least of them being the popularity of the small hotels and inns described in this guide. Small wonder then that this is our longest chapter.

There is one category for which we'd really like to request more recommendations: inns that actually *welcome* children! We're all in favor of romantic adult getaways, but there are regions of California—the Wine Country, for example—where there is hardly a place that will tolerate children, let alone welcome them. Perhaps as a reaction to this, a law was passed in California making it illegal for hotels and inns to discriminate on the basis of age. As a result, if we note under Restrictions "No children under 12," this has no legal bearing whatsoever. It is rather an indication given to us by the inns involved that they feel their property is more appropriate for older children.

In general, there's not too much seasonal variation in the rates of California's inns and hotels, although they do tend to be 10% to 20% higher on weekends in most areas. Exceptions are the North Coast region, where midweek rates are lower off-season (November to March), and the desert areas, where brutal summer heat cuts rates in half.

The California Office of Tourism divides the state into 12 distinct regions; we've noted them below, along with a few annotations and subdivisions of our own. At the end of each region, we list the towns with recommended inns and hotels, to help you in using this chapter. When reading the entries, you'll see the 12 regional divisions noted in the "Location" heading for each entry. Check back to these thumbnail sketches if you are liable to get Monterey mixed up with Mendocino.

Finally, please note that most of the greater Los Angeles area (excluding Orange County) is listed under Los Angeles, so you don't need to look through the entire chapter to find out what's available in this most sprawling of cities.

Shasta-Cascade   This relatively undiscovered region in north-central and northeast California offers a dramatic introduction to California's wilderness and geologic past. Best known is the Whiskeytown-Shasta-Trinity National Recreation Area, near 14,000-foot Mt. Shasta, where you can backpack or rent a houseboat on Lake Shasta. At Lassen Volcanic National Park, see the strange formations and caves left by wide-ranging volcanic activity. Even more unusual is Lava Beds National Monument, near the Oregon border, where the Modoc Indians made their last stand, using volcanic rubble for protection. This area fronts on Tule Lake, where over one million waterfowl visit each fall and huge populations of bald eagles spend the winter. At the southern edge of this region, take Route 70 through Quincy and the spectacular Feather River Canyon.

Shasta-Cascake towns with inns/hotels listed: Lake Almanor, McCloud, Mt. Shasta, O'Brien.

North Coast   This region has three distinct subregions. The **Wine Country** is located northeast of San Francisco, along Routes 29 and 12. In addition to over 200 wineries with free tours and tastings, there are rolling green hills, mud baths in Calistoga, gliding, and ballooning. Not to be missed is Petaluma Adobe, a restored 1840s headquarters of the Vallejo agricultural empire.

Not surprisingly, food is taken as seriously here as wine, and the area is noted for its many outstanding restaurants. *If you'll be visiting on a weekend, be sure to ask your host to make dinner reservations when you book your room.* Keep in mind that the Napa Valley, in particular, surpasses Disneyland in popularity with tourists; unless heavy traffic is your thing, avoid fall weekends when everyone goes wine-tasting!

The **Coast** area on Highway 1 north of San Francisco includes world-class scenery, shorelines, and accommodations. Near Jenner the road cuts through steep green slopes that sweep down to the sea. Close by is Fort Ross, an 1812 Russian trading post, complete with onion-domed Orthodox church. To the north are tiny towns and perfect beach combing shores near Sea Ranch and Gualala, Elk, Little River, and trendy Mendocino. The area then becomes more remote and wild as it passes through Westport. One recommended side trip for the experienced driver is the back road to Ferndale (from South Fork past Cape Mendocino), which winds up high bluffs with superb ocean views.

The **Redwood Empire** on Highway 101 stretches from Piercy to Crescent City. It's worth putting up with the cutesy tourist offerings to see the real scenery. Especially recommended are Avenue of the Giants near Pepperwood; Big Tree at Prairie City, north of Orick; and the Jedediah Smith area east of Crescent City.

North Coast towns with inns/hotels listed: Wine Country: Angwin, Boonville, Calistoga, Cazadero, Geyserville, Glen Ellen, Guerneville, Healdsburg, Lucerne, Napa, Occidental, Petaluma, St. Helena, Sonoma, Ukiah, Yountville. **Coast:** Albion, Elk, Ferndale, Fort Bragg, Gualala, Inverness, Leggett, Little River, Mendocino, Mill Valley, Muir Beach, Olema, Stinson Beach, Westport. **Redwood Empire:** Eureka, Garberville, Trinidad, Vichy Springs.

San Francisco Bay Area   Here and elsewhere along the coast, fog often shrouds the area in spring and early summer. To some this means unwanted cool weather only miles away from a sunny, warm interior. To others this underlines the special romance and mystery of the area. Although few cities can surpass San Francisco for culture, shopping, and sightseeing (see description in listings), there is more to the Bay Area. Across the Golden Gate Bridge are Sausalito and Tiburon, both artists' colonies with unusual homes clinging to the cliff sides. Nearby Muir Woods provides an easy introduction to the giant redwoods. The East Bay includes Berkeley with its hillside residential area, lively university district, and excellent botanical garden. To the south, stroll the pretty seaside boardwalk at Santa Cruz, and visit Año Nuevo State Reserve to see lolling elephant seals and rocks covered with fossilized seashells.

San Francisco Bay Area towns with inns/hotels listed: Alameda, Aptos, Berkeley, Capitola, Davenport, Half Moon Bay, Livermore, Montara, Moss Beach, Palo Alto, Pleasanton, Point Richmond, San Francisco, San Gregorio, San Jose, San Mateo, San Rafael, Santa Cruz, Sausalito, Soquel.

Central Valley   Extremely hot during the summer, this region offers comparatively little of interest to tourists. Extending south from Chico through the central portion of California to Bakersfield, this area has over 11 million acres of rich farmland, and produces an astonishing variety of fruits, nuts, and vegetables. Worth seeing: the Chinese temple in Oroville; Old Sacramento (take the walking tour); and Route 160 from Sacramento to Isleton, which winds along dikes, past almond and fruit groves, and through Locke, a bizarre, two-block, two-level town built in 1915 by Chinese workers. In the south, Bakersfield is near California's oil fields and is known as the state's country music center.

Central Valley towns with inns/hotels listed: Berry Creek, Chico, Coalinga, Hanford, Kernville, Lemon Cove, Livermore, Red Bluff, Redding, Sacramento, Springville.

Gold Country   Gold mining brought thousands of people to this region in the 1850s, but these days the only thing that is mined there are the tourists. Overcrowded with visitors in the summer, this area nevertheless has retained a genuine Old West flavor and should not be missed. Be sure to get off Route 49 to some of the smaller towns like

Murphys and Volcano; see nearby Grinding Rocks State Park where the Mi-Wok Indians lived for centuries, and the restored town of Columbia, now a state historical park. Don't avoid the unnumbered back roads that wind up hills and through picturesque farms. To the north, visit Downieville, which is tucked into the northern Sierras, then take passable dirt roads to Malakoff Diggings to see how hydraulic placer mining washed away a mountainside.

Gold Country towns with inns/hotels listed: Amador City, Berry Creek, Columbia, Grass Valley, Ione, Jackson, Murphys, Nevada City, Placerville, Plymouth, Quincy, Sonora, Sutter Creek, Volcano.

High Sierras   For 400 miles, the Sierra Nevada mountain range defines eastern California, from north of Lake Tahoe to the northern terminus of the desert region. Yosemite, Kings Canyon, and Sequoia national parks provide unlimited outdoor opportunities for everyone from car window sightseers to rugged backpackers. See 14,495-foot Mt. Whitney, giant sequoias and torrential waterfalls, or ski at one of 20 areas. Lake Tahoe provides resort offerings, with famous casinos, gambling, and glitzy shows nearby at Stateline Nevada. The crowning jewel here is Emerald Bay. For a bizarre foray into history, visit Donner Memorial Park, two miles west of Truckee, where an 1846 pioneer group, stranded by heavy winter snows, resorted to cannibalism.

High Sierra towns with inns/hotels listed: Bridgeport, Fish Camp, Groveland, Hope Valley, Kernville, Quincy, Springville, Tahoe City, Yosemite.

Central Coast   This photogenic region stretches from the Monterey Peninsula south to Santa Barbara. Inland, Pinnacles National Monument's volcanic spires, bluffs, and crags are worth a visit. On the coast, from Monterey (see description in listings), tour the peninsula via Seventeen-Mile Drive (a toll is charged) past Pebble Beach, wind-sculptured cypresses, cavorting otters, and on to Carmel. Highway 1 cuts through misty, ragged cliffs that rush into the sea. This is Big Sur—wild, beautiful, with almost no off-road access and too many crowds in the summer. To view the excesses of the rich, visit Hearst's San Simeon Castle (reservations required). To the south, Morro Bay marks the start of the renowned California beaches. Stop to see Solvang, a 1911 Danish settlement, and Santa Barbara, the heart of Spanish Mission country.

Central Coast towns with inns/hotels listed: Big Sur, Ballard, Baywood Park, Cambria, Carmel, Montecito, Monterey, Pacific Grove, San Luis Obispo, Santa Barbara, Solvang.

Greater Los Angeles   This city-region includes not only LA itself but the myriad surrounding cities, beaches, and islands. For relaxation, sail or fly to Santa Catalina Island, one of the top resort locations in the country. See listings for more information about the area.

Greater Los Angeles area towns with inns/hotels listed: Avalon, Los Angeles (also includes Beverly Hills, Hollywood, North Hollywood, Santa Monica), Seal Beach.

Orange County   Welcome to the California of commercials and legend. Here you can experience the mythic and somewhat crazed California beach life at Newport, Laguna, and Balboa. It's all here: sun, sand, surfers, theme parks (Disneyland, Knott's Berry Farm, Magic Mountain), nouveau everything, Super Hype. Your children will love it, but you may need a week on a desert island to recover.

Orange County towns with inns/hotels listed: Dana Point, Laguna Beach, Newport Beach, San Clemente, Seal Beach.

Inland Empire   From the San Gabriel Mountains in this region you can look down over Los Angeles. Route 2, east of Pasadena, twists through the mountains and past ski areas. East of San Bernardino, Route 18 is called the Rim of the World Drive. Although an overstatement, it is a pretty mountain road that leads to overdeveloped Lake Arrowhead and Big Bear Lake resort area. Southwest is Riverside, California's "citrus capital" and home of the famous Mission Inn, touted by Will Rogers.

Inland Empire towns with inns/hotels listed: Big Bear Lake, Lake Arrowhead, Orland, Redwood, Riverside.

San Diego County   Although San Diego (see description in listings) is the star of this region, there are several nearby areas in the county worth noting. La Jolla's natural caverns, formed by waves pounding against the sandstone cliffs, and the Mingei International Museum of prehistoric and contemporary crafts make for a special stop. I-8, which becomes Route 79, is a pretty drive to the old mining town of Julian. Farther on is the retirement community of Borrego Springs, with its superb Anza-Borrego Desert State Park. Stop at the headquarters for an excellent introduction to the varied plant and animal life of California's desert country.

San Diego County towns with inns/hotels listed: Borrego Springs, Cardiff-by-the-Sea, Del Mar, Julian, La Jolla, Rancho Santa Fe, San Diego, Temecula, Valley Center.

The Deserts   From posh Palm Springs to Nevada, from Mexico to Death Valley, this region is unlike anything else on earth. Since the desert area covers almost one-sixth of the state, it is important to plan your itinerary carefully. Unless you are a dedicated desert aficionado, it can get repetitive. South of Palm Springs, don't miss the enormous date groves near Thermal and Mecca, or the restaurants offering date milkshakes and date pecan pies. Just to the south, senior citizen communities dot the shoreline of Salton Sea, created in 1905 by human error during the construction of the Colorado River aqueduct. To the east are the Chocolate Mountains and the sprawling Sand Hills. North is Joshua Tree National Monument, best in spring when the cacti blossom. Finally there is Death Valley, a bewitching place of startling contrasts in altitude, colors, vegetation, formations, and texture. Close to the Nevada border is the equally fascinating but less well known Mojave National Preserve, established in 1994. Ranging in elevation from 1,000 to 8,000 feet, its 1.4 million acres include mountains, mesas, and more. Also of interest are ancient Indian rock art and abandoned mines. *A few reminders:* Try not to visit this region in the summer, always heed the warning to stay on the highway, and carry extra water in your car.

Desert Country towns with inns/hotels listed: Death Valley, Desert Hot Springs, Idyllwild, Nipton, Palm Springs.

ALAMEDA

Garratt Mansion   *Tel:* 510–521–4779
900 Union Street, 94501   *Fax:* 510–521–6796
                                E-mail: garrattm@pacbell.net

Although many people think of B&Bs only for weekend getaways, they're equally popular with business travelers who value the warm hospitality inns offer. The Garratt Mansion, built in 1893 and named for a turn-of-the-century industrialist, is just such a refuge. In 1977, after 50 years as a boarding house, Royce and Betty Gladden bought this Colonial Revival home, restoring it as a B&B in 1983. Betty notes that "we have lived in this area all our lives and have explored public transportation, theaters, restaurants, museums, parks and tourist attractions. Our day trip suggestions help guests maximize their time and enjoyment." Rooms are furnished primarily with period antiques, and the architectural detailing includes a carved oak stairway lined with beveled and stained glass windows. Breakfast is served at guests' convenience at the large dining room table, and might include freshly squeezed orange juice, sliced kiwi and mango, scalloped potatoes, banana bread, scrambled eggs with fresh chives and ham, or perhaps Dutch baby pancakes with sauteed apples.

"Hospitable hostess; room sunny and beautifully decorated. Thick towels, fresh flowers, homemade cookies and drinks always available, delicious breakfast, warm, friendly environment, helpful suggestions for local restaurants." *(SB)* "Great neighborhood for jogging, walking, exploring." *(P.J. Hoffer)* "Impeccably restored with original gas lights and stained glass." *(Lisa Gallagerh)* "Friendly, considerate hosts; delicious, varied breakfasts; clean, comfortable rooms. Fine, safe neighborhood, convenient to downtown Oakland." *(Robert Price)*

Open All year.
Rooms 1 suite, 6 doubles—5 with private bath and/or shower, 2 with maximum of 4 people sharing bath. All with radio, clock. 5 with telephone, desk; 3 with fan, 1 with fireplace.
Facilities Dining room, living room with books, stereo, games; Den with TV/VCR, guest pantry. Patio, porch, lawn swing. On-street parking. 2 blocks to park, tennis; 4 blocks to beach for wind-surfing, paved walking trail.
Location San Francisco Bay area. 15 m E of San Francisco; 12 m S of Berkeley. 8 blocks from center. Corner of Union & Clinton; call for directions.
Restrictions No smoking. Children over 6.
Credit cards Amex, DC, MC, Visa.
Rates B&B, $130 suite, $95 double, $85 single. Extra person, $15. 2-night minimum holidays, graduation.

ALBION

Albion is located on the Mendocino Coast, about 150 miles north of San Francisco, about six miles south of the town of Mendocino.

Also recommended: A stagecoach way station and tavern in the 1860s, the **Fensalden Inn** (33810 Navarro Ridge Road, P.O. Box 99, 95410; 707–937–4042 or 800–959–3850), is set amid acres of meadows and woods, with views of grazing deer and the rugged Pacific Coast. "An appealing, quiet spot. The lovely Mauve Suite in the main house has an ocean view, and a lovely big sitting area with a fireplace; spacious bathroom. We also enjoy the Captain's Walk room." (*Carolyn G. Alexander*) A full breakfast is included in the $100–155 double rates.

Information please: For a dramatic ocean view, call the **Albion River Inn** (Highway One, P.O. Box 100, 95410; 707–937–1919 or 800–479–7944) with 20 clifftop rooms on the edge of the Pacific, overlooking Albion Cove. All rooms have private garden entrances and private baths, many with a double whirlpool spa. A full breakfast is included in the $160–250 double rate. The inn is also home to a popular restaurant with an excellent reputation. "Superb dinner as usual." (*CA*) "Food much improved since our last visit." (*TW*)

AMADOR CITY

Also recommended: Just a few miles north of Sutter Creek, in Amador City, is the restored 1879 vintage **Imperial Hotel** (Route 49, P.O. Box 195, Amador City 95601; 209–267–9172 or 800–242–5594) offering six air-conditioned rooms with private bath (including hair dryers and heated towel racks) and a continental breakfast. "Though not as personal as a B&B, the small staff of five or six was friendly and helpful. Our room had lots of sunlight and wicker, a firm mattress, and a shower that worked. The restaurant, which is popular with both locals and tourists, had good food and good service. Amador City is much less developed than Sutter Creek." (*Kathleen Owen*) B&B double rates range from $80–100.

ANGWIN

For additional area inns, see **Calistoga** and **St. Helena**.

Forest Manor   *Tel:* 707–965–3538
415 Cold Springs Road, 94508   *Tel:* 800–788–0364
                                 Fax: 707–965–3303

Innkeepers Harold and Corlene Lambeth traveled throughout the world and lived for many years in Thailand before returning to California. They built Forest Manor, a large English Tudor-style home, in 1980, and furnished it with pieces they collected during their travels, including English antiques, Persian rugs, and Asian art. True to its name, Forest Manor is surrounded by woods and vineyards, making it an exceptionally peaceful retreat.

"The spacious Somerset Suite has a king-size bed with a carved headboard and a free-standing fireplace faced by two swivel armchairs with reading lights and a sheepskin rug. The dresser was actually a mirrored dining room buffet, and an armoire contained the makings for hot drinks for use with the coffee maker in the bathroom. The bath was done in inch-square brown tiles, and had a double shower with two shower heads, a massive counter with two sinks, and a double whirlpool bath backed by mirrors. Towels were lush and plentiful. We breakfasted in our room by the sunny five-sided bay window overlooking the pool and hot tub." *(SHW)* "Unlike most Napa Valley inns, Forest Manor is set on a meandering country road. The sumptuous breakfast typically consisted of juice, coffee, fresh fruit salad, fresh baked muffins, an egg dish or waffles, and carried us through to dinner. Our room was supplied with terrycloth robes, and a welcoming fruit basket; cookies or snacks were always available on a plate in the foyer." *(Michael Milne)* Comments appreciated.

Open All year.
Rooms 5 suites—all with private bath, air-conditioning, radio, clock, coffee maker, refrigerator. Telephone, TV on request. 3 with whirlpool tub, fireplace.
Facilities Dining room, living room with fireplace, piano, library; game room. 20 acres with swimming pool, hot tub, walking trail. Vineyard, forest adjacent. Tennis nearby. 20 min. to Lake Berryessa for fishing, boating.
Location North Coast, Napa Wine Country. 70 m N of San Francisco; 7 m NE of St. Helena; 27 m N of Napa. 5 m from Silverado Trail. N on Rte. 29 through St. Helena. Turn right at Deer Park Rd. Continue past blinking light 5½ m to Angwin. Go right on Cold Springs Rd. & go ¾ m to inn on left.
Restrictions No smoking. Children over 12.
Credit cards MC, Visa.
Rates B&B, $129–249 suite. Extra person, $25. 2–3 night weekend/holiday minimum.

APTOS

Aptos is located in the San Francisco Bay Area, 15 minutes east of Santa Cruz and 40 minutes north of Monterey. It's approximately 85 miles south of San Francisco. Set along the north side of Monterey Bay, it makes a convenient base for area explorations.

Mangels House　　　　　　　　　　　　　*Tel:* 408–688–7982
570 Aptos Creek Road, P.O. Box 302, 95001　　　800–320–7401

Mangels House is the house that beets built: in 1886, Claus Mangels, who co-founded California's sugar beet industry, built this country home in an eclectic, Greek Revival style. Owned by Jacqueline and Ron Fisher since 1979, and opened as an inn in 1985, the inn's high-ceilinged rooms are beautifully furnished with antiques and traditional pieces, complimented by rich but soothing colors and floral fabrics. Breakfast is served at 9 A.M. on weekdays, and 9:15 on weekends. Guests enjoy conversation over breakfasts of coffee and juice, fruit and yogurt, apple pancakes and sausage, or perhaps cheese-spinach soufflé, with fresh-from-the-oven scones, muffins, or French bread. Tea and cookies, cold drinks, and sherry or port are always available. Jacqueline describes her inn as a "peaceful escape from life's pressures." Guests spend their days hiking in the adjacent park or walking the nearby beaches at sunset.

"Gracious hostess; comfortable, airy guest rooms; generous, delicious breakfasts; lovely view and forest walking trails." *(Norma & Bob Simon)* "Striking setting at the edge of the Forest of Nisene Marks, a second-growth redwood preserve that offers extensive trails for hikers, joggers, and mountain bikers. The inn's grounds are absolutely gorgeous, beautifully planted with expansive lawns. The house has deep porches all the way around, an enormous and comfortable living room, and an elegant dining room. Although ours was the smallest guest room, it was charming, with a large bathroom." *(Susan Rather)* "Our spacious room was beautifully decorated, with an inviting fireplace. Our privacy was respected, yet we felt like family." *(Terry Fudenna)* "Worth a visit just to have breakfast with Jackie." *(Nancy Fitzhugh)*

Open All year. Closed 3 days at Christmas.
Rooms 6 doubles—all with private shower bath, clock, desk. 1 with fireplace, porch.
Facilities Dining room, living room with fireplace, piano; library, guest refrigerator; wraparound porches with swing. 4 acres with off-street parking, garden, fountain, lawn games, gazebo. Adjacent to 10,000-acre state park.
Location Santa Cruz County, 25 m S of San Jose, 60 m S of San Francisco. ½ m from village. Exit Hwy 1 at Seacliff / Aptos exit. Go N (away from water) on State Park Drive & turn right on Soquel Dr. Go left on Aptos Creek Rd. to inn on right.
Restrictions No smoking. Children over 12.
Credit cards Amex, MC, Visa.
Rates B&B, $115–150 double, $105–140 single. Extra person, $20. Tips appreciated. 10% senior, AAA midweek discount.
Extras Spanish, French spoken.

AVALON, SANTA CATALINA ISLAND

We can't think of Catalina without remembering these words from the old song, "26 miles across the sea, Santa Catalina is a-waiting for me..." Well, it's still waiting, and it remains a relatively unspoiled escape, easily accessible by ferry from San Pedro or Newport Beach. Most of the island is now owned by the Santa Catalina Conservancy, which keeps the terrain unchanged and uninhabited. William Wrigley, the chewing-gum magnate, purchased much of the island in 1919 and did quite an effective job of converting it into a California Riviera; be sure to visit the Wrigley Memorial and Botanical Garden, and the Casino, now a museum. Visitors today enjoy hiking and all water sports, especially fishing, scuba diving, and snorkeling, plus golf, tennis, horseback riding, and bicycling. Very few cars are permitted on the island, so most people get around on foot, bicycle, or golf cart.

Reader tips: "Avalon gets crowded on summer weekends; visit midweek for reduced hotel rates and to avoid the mob scene. November through April is off-season; ask about package rates for substantial savings." *(MA)* Also: "We thought the price was high for our small, simple room, but then, everything has to be shipped from the mainland." *(AMA)*

Information please: Listed in past editions, we need current reports on the well-known **Inn on Mt. Ada** (398 Wrigley Road, P.O. Box 2560, 90704; 310–510–2030 or 800–608–7669), a Georgian colonial mansion built by chewing-gum magnate William Wrigley, Jr. in 1921. If you've always wanted to stay in the home of a multimillionaire, this may be your best chance. Ocean views from the inn are spectacular, and the decor is lavish, with flowered chintzes coordinating comforters and draperies, overstuffed couches and easy chairs. The equally lavish double rates of $255–630, include a full breakfast, sandwich lunch, evening wine and hors d'oeuvres, dinner, and a shuttle to and from town; ask about midweek off-season rates for the best value.

Hotel Vista Del Mar
417 Crescent Avenue, P.O. Box 1979, 90704

Tel: 310–510–1452
Fax: 310–510–2917
E-mail: vista@catalina.com

Owners Jerry Dunn and Kelly Rowsey created this Mediterranean-style structure, originally built as the Hotel Campo Bravo, by gutting the interior and starting from scratch, reopening in 1988 as the Hotel Vista Del Mar. Rooms, which open onto a central plant-filled atrium (original to the 1930s structure), are decorated in soft pastels with wicker furnishings.

"Beautiful inside garden. Our ocean-view room was clean, comfortable, and well-equipped." *(Betty Davis)* "Excellent ambience, decor, cleanliness, and amenities. Delicious breakfast of coffee, tea, fresh-squeezed orange juice, and croissants with jam and butter, served on the patio." *(Dr. & Mrs. Shneidman)* "Conveniently located; everything within walking distance; the sound of the ocean lulls you to sleep." *(Philonise Williams)* "Excellent on all counts. The owner, front desk staff, and reservation people were friendly, helpful, accommodating, and genuine. Even the cleaning staff were professional and unobtrusive." *(Kathleen Evans)*

Open All year.

Rooms 2 suites with balcony, double Jacuzzi; 13 doubles—all with full private bath, telephone, radio, TV, desk, air-conditioning, hair dryer. Most with wet bar, refrigerator, fireplace.

Facilities Library, garden atrium, lobby. 10 steps from sandy ocean beach (towels and beach chairs provided).

Location Center of town; at foot of pier. 2 blocks from ferry.

Restrictions Smoking in lobby, courtyard only.

Credit cards Amex, Discover, MC, Visa.
Rates B&B, $195–275 suite, $65–165 double. Extra adult, $15. Off-season mid-week packages. 2-night weekend minimum.
Extras Crib, $5. Spanish spoken.

BALLARD

Ballard Inn ✗ ⅋   *Tel:* 805–688–7770
2436 Baseline Avenue, 93463   800–638–2466
                                               Fax: 805–688–9560

To experience the pleasures of 32 award-winning wineries, plus fine food and quality lodging, head to the uncrowded Santa Ynez Valley, an easy drive from Santa Barbara. Unlike the better-known Napa Valley vineyards, the Santa Ynez wineries are friendly, personal, and informal; tastings are free or modestly priced and typically include a souvenir wine glass. An excellent base for oenophilic explorations is the Ballard Inn, built by Larry Stone and Steve Hyslop; Kelly Robinson is the manager.

Guest rooms have queen- or king-size beds, highlighted with handmade quilts and antiques, reflecting the history of the Santa Ynez Valley and its residents. The individual decor varies from the spacious Vineyard room with its bent twig king-size headboard and chairs, to the country-style Farmhouse room, to the rustic Western charm of Davy Brown's room. Rates include a full breakfast, cooked to order from 8–10 A.M., and at 5 P.M., afternoon wine, tea, and hors d'oeuvres. The inn's Cafe Chardonnay serves creative wine country cuisine, with such entrees as lemon-herb roasted chicken, ahi tuna with snow pea and red onion salad, or grilled lamb in red wine and garlic sauce.

"Ballard is the place to be if you're into Pinot Noir. Our room had a lovely armoire; the sink was set into an antique bureau. Wonderful breakfast with fresh fruit and rolls, and your choice of such entrees as omelets or oatmeal pancakes. Evening wine and hors d'oeuvres are also included in the rates. Pleasant meal and good service in the Cafe Chardonnay." *(Ron & Betsy Kahan)* "Homey, informal atmosphere; lovely common areas; staff extremely friendly." *(Hugh Wilson Elliott)*

Open All year.
Rooms 15 doubles—all with private bath and/or shower, air-conditioning. 7 with wood-burning fireplace, 2 with balcony.
Facilities Living room with fireplace, dining room with fireplace, sitting room with TV, sun porch. Verandas with rockers. Bicycle rentals. Hiking, bicycling, horseback riding, fishing, boating nearby.
Location Santa Ynez Valley. 35 m N of Santa Barbara. 3½ m N of Solvang via Alamo Pintado Rd., 2 m S of Los Olivos.
Restrictions No smoking.
Credit cards Amex, MC, Visa.
Rates B&B, $150–220 double. 10% service. Alc dinner, $25.
Extras Wheelchair access; 1 room specially equipped.

BAYWOOD PARK

Also recommended: Twelve miles from San Luis Obispo and almost halfway between San Francisco and Los Angeles is the **Baywood B&B Inn** (1370 Second Street, 93402; 805–528–8888) overlooking beautiful Morro Bay. Each of the 15 guest rooms has an outside entrance, and individual decor ranging from the California Beach room, to the Santa Fe suite, to the Williamsburg room. Only a small tree-lined road separates the B&B and the bay; nearby are little shops and good seafood restaurants. Readers are delighted with the rooms' attractive decor, excellent lighting, plus such amenities as a fireplace, TV, phone, microwave, and refrigerator. B&B double rates of $90–150 include a full breakfast, brought to your room, with a choice of blueberry pancakes or perhaps quiche, and a 5 P.M. wine-and-cheese hour and room tour. Among the many compliments, readers mentioned that the staff was pleasant but that no innkeeper seemed to be in residence; that they would have preferred to breakfast in a dining room, with a proper table and the chance to meet other guests, and their two-bedroom suite lacked sound-proofing.

BEN LOMOND

Chateau des Fleurs	*Tel:* 408–336–8943
7995 Highway 9, 95005	800–596–1133, ext. 5679
	Fax: 408–336–2647 (call first)
	E-mail: ChateauBnB@aol.com

Built in the 1870s, and purchased at the turn-of-the-century by the Bartlett family of pear-growing fame, the Chateau des Fleurs has long been owned by Laura and Lee Jonas. Rates include a full breakfast, plus wine and hors d'oeuvres served in the Gallery from 5:30–6:30 P.M.

"A nicely restored farmhouse. We stayed in a cottage behind the main house, with a spacious bedroom and an ample sitting room. Guests in the main house were equally pleased with their accommodations. Laura is a good cook and her generous breakfasts left us with little need for more than a light midday snack. Each morning she served a fresh fruit cup (different each day), cinnamon muffins with a variety of fillings, a breakfast bread, and such entrees as eggs Benedict, cheese blintzes, or potato quiche; special dietary needs were easily accommodated, and recipes shared willingly. Breakfast is served at 9 A.M. at the dining room table in the handsome dining room, although earlier schedules are accommodated." *(Jim & Mary White)* "We found this to be a serene haven, an excellent alternative to busy Santa Cruz at the height of the summer tourist season." *(EB)*

Open All year.
Rooms 1 cottage, 3 doubles—all with private bath and/or shower. 2 with fireplace, 1 with deck.

Facilities Gallery common room with stereo, TV, darts, books, woodstove. Gardens, horseshoes. Hiking nearby.
Location 10 m N of Santa Cruz. From Santa Cruz, go N on Rte. 9 to inn on left, S of Ben Lomond.
Restrictions No smoking.
Credit cards Amex, Discover, MC, Visa.
Rates B&B, $100–130 double. Two night holiday/graduation minimum.

BERKELEY

Best known as the home of the University of California, Berkeley is the place to go to find out what the rest of the country will be doing three years hence. Gardeners will especially enjoy a visit here, from the university's Botanical Garden to the city's Rose Garden. **Reader tip:** "Probably a minority opinion, but we prefer Berkeley to San Francisco any day; it's a warmer, more hospitable, friendlier place; much less puffed up about itself than SFO." *(EDF)*

Information please: Across the street from the Berkeley campus is the **Bancroft Hotel** (2680 Bancroft Way, 94704; 510–549–1000 or 800–549–1002), a 1928 Arts and Crafts-style design building listed on the National Register of Historic Places. Renovated in 1993, it offers 22 guest rooms, at B&B double rates of $65–99.

Five buildings ringing a garden courtyard of lawns, flowers, and fruit trees make up **Gramma's Rose Garden Inn** (2740 Telegraph Avenue, 94705; 510–549–2145). Rooms in the two Victorian mansions are furnished with antiques; those in the newer buildings are larger, with scrubbed pine furnishings. B&B double rates for the 40 guest rooms range from $89–175, including a buffet breakfast, served in the light and airy Greenhouse, and afternoon coffee and cookies.

For an additional area entry, see **Alameda**.

BERRY CREEK

Lake Oroville B&B   ♿ ♙   *Tel:* 916–589–0700
240 Sunday Drive, 95916   800–455–5253
                                Fax: 916–589–5313
                E-mail: lakeinn@sunset.net

If you're looking for a secluded and quiet getaway, ideal for stargazing, birdwatching, or enjoying beautiful sunsets over the coastal mountain range, then call Ron and Cheryl Damberger, who built the Lake Oroville B&B in 1990. Covered porches wrap around the house, offering views of the oak-studded hillside, the lake below, the valley, and even Mount Diablo, a hundred miles distant. Inside are individually themed guest rooms, each with a queen- or king-size bed. The Rose Petal room has rose-patterned wallpaper with white Battenburg lace accents, while the Monet room is defined by its Impressionist prints; Max's Room features the colorful art of Maxfield Parrish. Breakfast, served 7–11 A.M. at individual tables, includes freshly squeezed orange juice, fresh fruit, muffins, and perhaps asparagus or crab quiche and apple fritters. "A long and winding gravel road leads up the hill to this beautiful yellow house. Ron and Cheryl showed us around the inn and let us pick the room we liked best. Sliding glass doors open to the wraparound porch where you can sit and enjoy the evening breeze or sip a cup of early morning coffee. The friendly cat and dog also helped us feel right at home. Our bathroom was supplied with bottles of lotion, shampoo, and soap, with lots of thick plush towels. Coffee and tea was set out at 7:30 A.M., with a breakfast of delicious apple cinnamon pancakes with fresh sliced peaches at 9:00 A.M. The innkeepers were kind and hospitable." *(Julie Phillips)* "We relaxed on the veranda drinking tea. Inside is an inviting living room, fully stocked game room, and sun room with marvelous sunset views. Lovely guest rooms, too. The delicious breakfasts—served with a warm smile—included apple pancakes, cherry crepes, and strawberry-filled French toast. One evening Cheryl provided wine glasses, plates, silverware, and even linen napkins so we could enjoy a romantic take-out meal in the sun room, listening to classical music and watching the sun slip behind the hills." *(Tracy Shearer)* "Wonderfully secluded and quiet setting, high up above the lake. Woods, birds, and fine views abound." *(Claudia Thompson)*

Open All year.

Rooms 6 doubles—all with full private bath, telephone, clock/radio/cassette player, desk, air-conditioning, ceiling fan, balcony/deck. 5 with whirlpool tub. TV/VCR on request.

Facilities Dining room, living room with stereo; game room with pool table, stereo, book/videotape library; wraparound porches, deck with barbecue. Occasional piano, fiddle music. 40 acres with patio, lawn games, hiking. Golf, marina nearby.

Location Butte Cty; 3 hrs NE of San Francisco, 1½ hrs. N of Sacramento, 15 m from Oroville. From Rte. 70, take Oroville Dam Blvd. (Rte. 162) & go E 1.7 m. Turn right at Olive Hwy. & continue for 13.5 m. Take left ¼ m after "End Route 162" sign onto Bell Ranch Rd., bearing right ⁹⁄₁₀ m to Sunday Drive. Go ¾ m to inn.

Restrictions No smoking.

Credit cards Amex, Discover, MC, Visa.

Rates B&B, $75–135 double. Extra person, $20. 10% senior, AAA discounts Sun–Thurs., except holidays.

Extras Wheelchair access; 1 room specially equipped. Pets with prior approval. Babysitting on request. Playroom, highchair. French, Spanish spoken.

BIG BEAR LAKE

Also recommended: On a quiet street one block from the lake and shopping village, **Janet Kay's B&B** (695 Paine Road, P.O. Box 3874, 92315; 909–866–6800 or 800–243–7031) offers 19 fully equipped guest rooms, many with double whirlpool tubs, gas fireplaces, TV/VCR, and decks. Each guest room has a different theme, from the king-size reproduction sleigh bed in the Victorian room to the mosquito netting draping the bed in the Jungle Room. The two suites on the top floor have lake views. B&B rates range from $59–199; midweek rates are an exceptional. "The Hunt Room was attractive and spacious, done in mauves and greens. Rates include continental breakfast, afternoon tea and cookies, and evening wine and cheese. Children are welcome in the suites; sound-proofing between units leaves room for improvement." *(RH)*

Ten cabins are available at the **Smoketree Resort** (40154 Big Bear Boulevard, P.O. Box 2801, 92315; 909– 866–2415 or 800–352–8581), located about a half-mile west of Big Bear village. Facilities include a swimming pool and hot tub, a playground, and lawn games; several restaurants are close by. Most cabins are good for kids and/or pets, and have equipped kitchens, microwave, TV, and a fireplace, and rates range from $69–150, depending on size and season. "Our cabin was cozy and comfortable with a queen-size brass bed and stone fireplace. Friendly, informative owners." *(Gail Davis)*

For additional area entries, see **Fawnskin.**

Eagle's Nest	*Tel:* 909–866–6465
41675 Big Bear Boulevard, P.O. Box 1003, 92315	*Fax:* 909–866–6025

Built in 1983, this Ponderosa-style log home has been owned by Diane and Don Johnson since 1996. Lodge rooms have queen-size beds with down comforters, and baths with clawfoot tubs or tiled showers, and are named for classic Western movies. Rates include a candlelit breakfast, served 7:30–9:30 A.M. at the dining room table, plus afternoon appetizers. A recent breakfast included homemade granola, eggs Florentine, melon, and blueberry banana walnut bread. Guests in the cottage suites have the option of having a breakfast basket delivered to their door at the time requested. The western-theme decor in the suites varies from the pine and plaid of Mountain Spirit, with Old West artifacts, a stone fireplace, and an in-room whirlpool, to the beaded paneling and antique metal bed with hand-painted roses of the Whispering Pines suite.

"The huge stone fireplace is the focal point of the cozy living room, furnished invitingly with antiques; we enjoyed watching a movie on the wide-screen TV. The ground-floor Rio Bravo room is done in burgundy and ivory, with an antique armoire." *(Gail Davis)* "Diane Johnson did an outstanding job decorating the common areas and guest rooms. From the welcome basket in the room, to the afternoon wine and cheese, to the tasty chocolates in our room, everything was perfect." *(Lynn Dargie)* "A charming log cabin in a beautiful setting." *(Bill & Lynn Conlan)* "In the winter you can walk to the slopes for skiing; we also enjoyed a horse-drawn sleigh ride." *(Phillip Ross)*

Open All year.

Rooms 5 cottage suites, 5 doubles—all with full private bath and/or shower. Suites with telephone, radio, clock, TV, fireplace, refrigerator, microwave, coffee maker, deck. 8 with ceiling fan, 4 with whirlpool tub, 1 with kitchen. Rooms in 3 buildings.

Facilities Living room with TV/VCR, stereo; library loft; guest refrigerator. 1

acre with off-street parking. Boating, fishing, swimming in Big Bear Lake. ½m to downhill skiing. 3–5 m to hiking, cross-country skiing.

Location Inland Empire. 30 m NE of San Bernardino. 1 m E of Big Bear Village on Hwy. 18. Take I-10 E, to Redlands to Rte. 30 to Rte. 330. At Running Springs 330 ends. Continue on Rte. 18 to Big Bear Lake. Stay on 18 (turn left before "the Village") until it becomes Big Bear Blvd. Inn is ½m past Middle School on right, 2nd driveway past Norwest Mortgage.

Restrictions No smoking. Occasional road noise possible in a few rooms.

Credit cards Amex, MC, Visa.

Rates Room only, $110–165 cottage. B&B, $135–185 cottage, $95–125 double.

Extras Local airport/station pickup. Pets allowed in one cottage suite.

BIG SUR

Novelist Henry Miller, Big Sur resident for 20 years, noted that "there being nothing to improve on in the surroundings, the tendency is to set about improving oneself." Unfortunately, news of Big Sur's breathtaking beauty is now well-known, and summer traffic jams often clog the hairpin turns of Highway One. Our advice is to travel off-season, or to leave the crowds behind by hiking the beautiful trails of Pfeiffer–Big Sur State Park, Julia Pfeiffer Burns State Park, and the Ventana Wilderness. May and October are probably the best times for minimal crowds and maximal weather.

Reader tip: "Dinner at Deetjen's was pricy but delicious; reservations essential. For breakfast, head up the road to Cafe Kevah or Nepenthe, both with a fabulous 20-mile coastal view."

Also recommended: Those interested in a taste of "old California" should try **Deetjen's Big Sur Inn** (Highway 1, 93920; 408–667–2377), a 20-room rustic retreat built in the early 1930s by Helmuth and Helen Deetjen, Norwegian immigrants. While not fancy, rooms rent for $44 (single) to $135 (double), and the restaurant has a good reputation. "A rustic hideaway built of rough-hewn dark wood, situated along the edges of a redwood-lined ravine on an isolated bend of scenic Highway 1. The Fireplace Room has a working fireplace, a firm bed with a warm comforter, and windows covered with calico curtains. The bath was across the hall. What it lacks in creature comforts, Deetjen's makes up in charm, romance, and isolation." *(Mark Mendenhall)* "Deetjen's is an acquired taste with its simple furnishings, non-existent sound-proofing, and 'funky style,' but is very popular because of its pretty setting by a babbling brook, historic appeal, and in-room guest journals. We paid $85, the weekend rate for a small double with shared bath and an electric heater; no meals included." *(LMS)* "Great food. Beautiful, but rustic and somewhat primitive; beautiful stone fireplaces." *(Doug Phillips)* "New innkeepers have done wonders to improve this old place." *(PH)*

If expense is no object, then try the ultra-chic, ultra-expensive **Post Ranch Inn**, (Highway One, P.O. Box 219, 93920; 408–667–2200 or 800–527–2200) just across Highway One from the Ventana. This "environmentally sensitive" luxury retreat will pamper you with magnificent cliffside ocean views, polished wood and natural stone decor, in-room slate-lined Jacuzzi tubs, designer robes, and fold-away massage tables, but you'll have to be "green" financially as well as ecologically: rates range from $285–545 for the 30 rooms, either set on stilts or burrowed into the hillside to minimize environmental impact. "Superb. On the ocean side of the Coast Highway and beautifully integrated into its bluff-top locale. The rooms have an unobtrusive, original and contemporary design, and are spacious and comfortable. Shockingly high prices, but both the food and views are marvelous, and not out of line for this pricey stretch of coastline. Take advantage of the complimentary guided hikes." *(Adam Platt)* "Pricey but beautiful; excellent food. Our room had a huge stone bath and lovely teak paneling." *(Doug Phillips)*

A longtime reader favorite, the **Ventana Inn** (Highway One, 93920; 408–667–2331 or 800–628–6500) has 60 guest rooms spread over 12 buildings on very ample grounds; 34 have ocean vistas, while the remainder overlook the mountains or forest. B&B double rates range from $215–395, with suites to $1050. The restaurant, one-eighth of a mile from the inn, has spectacular views of the Pacific and specializes in California cuisine, with an emphasis on fresh seafood, vegetables, and fruits; advance reservations are essential. Rates include breakfast, with fresh fruits and home-baked breads and pastries, brought to your room or available buffet-style in the lobby, and an afternoon wine and cheese buffet. Careful attention to detail in all areas—service, comfort, cuisine, and atmosphere—produces consistently positive reports from all sources: "Measures up to every super comment we've ever heard about it. Wooded setting with views. Spectacular food. Friendly staff provided help before we realized we needed it." *(Pat Hardy)*

Information please: A reasonable alternative in a pricy area, the **Big Sur Lodge** (Hwy. 1, P.O. Box 190, 93920; 408–667–3100 or 800–424–4787) is located in the center of Pfeiffer–Big Sur State Park, across from the ocean. The restaurant serves good food at reasonable prices. Depending on the season, rates for its simply furnished 61 units and condo-style cottages range from $80–180. A swimming pool, grocery store, and hiking trails make it a reasonable family choice. Another affordable option is the **Big Sur River Inn** (Highway One at Pheneger Creek, 93920; 408–667–2700 or 800–548–3610), with 20 motel units overlooking the river, restaurant, swimming pool, general store, and gift gallery. Rates range from $70–160, but the best deal is the midweek off-season package, starting at $99 for breakfast, dinner, and accommodations for two.

BOONVILLE

The Anderson Valley lies just 11 miles southeast of Mendocino, and offers quiet pleasures to travelers. Now reached by winding Highway 128, this valley was once so isolated that it developed its own dialect, called Boontling. Known primarily for its high-quality vineyards (sparkling wines a specialty), apple orchards, and sheep ranches, visitors will enjoy the low-key atmosphere of the wine-tasting rooms, road-side apple stands, and vistas of grazing sheep in this rural setting. Two good dining choices are found at the Boonville Hotel and the Floodgate Store and Grille.

Reader tip: "Lovely setting, a welcome relief from the glitz of high-priced Mendocino. Appealing wineries; lovely wildflowers dot the hill-sides in springtime." *(SWS)*

Information please: The spacious **Anderson Creek Inn** (12050 Anderson Valley Way, Boonville, 95415; 707–895–3091 or 800–LLAMA–02) offers four spacious guest rooms in a rambling contemporary room, each with full private bath and king-size bed. After a breakfast of organic juices, house-blend coffee, home-baked bread, and perhaps eggs Benedict or fruit-topped baked pancakes, guests follow the innkeepers outside to feed the inn's herd of llamas. The $95–175 double rates also include use of the inn's bicycles, swimming pool, and hot tub, plus afternoon hors d'oeuvres.

BORREGO SPRINGS

Reader tip: "Borrego Springs is located in the middle of the largest state park in California; the Anza-Borrego Desert State Park has a hugely varied, dramatic topography that is great for hiking and exploring. The town, population 3,000, is a throwback to easier times, with a few presentable restaurants and not much else—a great place to relax." *(Mark Mendenhall)*

The Palms at Indian Head ¢ ✗ ♿   Tel: 619–767–7788
2220 Hoberg Road, P.O. Box 525, 92004   800–519–2624
                                        Fax: 619–767–9717

Marilyn Monroe, Clark Gable, and Bing Crosby stayed at the Old Hoberg Resort in the 1950s, scenically perched above the Borrego Valley at the base of Indian Head Mountain. Built in 1947, the building burnt to the ground in 1958, and was rebuilt in its present Art Deco style. Later used as a nudist retreat, then a detention home, the resort was abandoned in 1978. In 1994, husband and wife David Leibert and Cynthia Wood pooled their respective experience in construction and hotel management, and began the inn's long-term rebuilding and restoration. Renaming it The Palms at Indian Head, the guest rooms have hand-crafted Southwestern lodgepole furnishings, with king- or queen-size canopy or four poster beds. Casual meals are served in the Krazy Coyote Saloon and Grille, while the fine dining Palm Restaurant will be opening in 1998. Rates include a full breakfast.

"A stark white low-slung two-story building. Some guest rooms have all-glass front walls to take advantage of the lovely desert-mountain vistas, with vertical blinds for privacy. Our room had a huge four-poster canopy bed constructed of smooth hand-hewn timbers bleached an antique white, and fitted with patterned linens and a maroon down comforter. Two large overstuffed chairs, bedside tables and lights, an oversized coffee table, and a TV rounded out the uncluttered room. The large bathroom had an excellent tub/shower. Breakfasts were served from 7–9 A.M., and were generous, leisurely, and healthy, and could be delivered to the room on a tray, served indoors in the breakfast room, or outside on the patio, and included fresh fruit, yogurt or cereal, muffins, croissants, and bagels, plus the San Diego newspaper. Cindy Wood and David Leibert were cheerful, friendly, and helpful. They have done the marvelous restoration themselves. Overall, a wonderfully relaxing, refreshing, and reasonably priced alternative to the famous Casa del Zorro." *(Mark Mendenhall)*

Open All year.
Rooms 3 suites, 7 doubles—all with full private bath, radio, clock, TV, air-conditioning.
Facilities Restaurant, breakfast room with fireplace, bar/lounge. 20 acres with bocce, swimming pool (under restoration; call to confirm availability). VCR/video rentals. Hiking, mt. bicycling, golf, tennis nearby.
Location San Diego County. 90 m E of San Diego, 1.5 hrs. S of Palm Springs. 1 m from park visitor center, at base of Indian Head Mt.; walking distance to Palm Canyon oasis.
Restrictions No smoking. Children over 5.
Credit cards DC, Discover, MC, Visa.
Rates B&B, $65–105 suite, double. Extra person, $15.
Extras Spanish spoken. Restaurant wheelchair accessible.

BRIDGEPORT

The Cain House
P.O. Box 454, 93517

Tel: 760–932–7040
Fax: 760–932–7419

Built in 1925, The Cain House was converted into an inn in 1989, by owner Marachal Gohlich. The guest rooms are individually furnished in wicker, oak, or white-washed pine, with some antiques. Breakfast menus change daily; freshly squeezed orange juice and melon is followed by lemon and blackberry pancakes, Tennessee sausage, and herbed oven fries one day, with breakfast burritos, pepper potatoes, and homemade salsa the next.

"Marachal greeted us warmly, and recommended the Bridgeport Inn for an excellent dinner. At 5 P.M. she served wine and cheese in the living room, as classical music played softly in the background. Our room was adequate in size, highlighted by an antique doll and a beautiful comforter. During the night, we heard cows mooing in a distant pasture, plus a coyote serenade. Breakfast is served between 8–10 A.M.; guests were asked upon arrival about their dislikes and dietary requirements. We enjoyed the quaintness of this little town (population 500), as well as its proximity to Bodie (a wonderful old ghost town), Mammoth Lakes, and Mono Lake." *(Patricia King)* "The well-equipped rooms are supplied with terry-cloth bathrobes and huge, fluffy towels. Marachal's wonderful breakfast started with freshly squeezed orange juice, accompanied by burritos filled with bacon, scrambled eggs, cheddar and jack cheese, chiles, and salsa; we never felt rushed or pressured." *(Jean Hembree)* "Friendly owner, immaculate room. After walking back from dinner, we settled in the living room in comfortable recliners and read. Tea, juice, and wine were available, but we enjoyed the hot chocolate. Excellent housekeeping; ideal bathroom lighting." *(Kathleen Owen)*

Open April 15–Nov. 15.
Rooms 7 doubles—all with full private bath, TV, fan, coffee/tea maker.
Facilities Living room with games, TV/VCR; breakfast room, deck. Lawn games, off-street parking. 100 yds. to tennis court. 10 m to cross-country skiing. Hiking, fishing nearby.
Location Eastern Sierras. 113 m S of Reno NV, via Hwy 395. 120 m NE of Yosemite Village. In center.
Restrictions No smoking.
Credit cards Amex, CB, DC, Discover, MC, Visa.
Rates B&B, $79–130 double. "No tipping necessary."
Extras Airport/station pickup, $10. Limited German, Spanish spoken.

CALISTOGA

Set in the North Coast's Wine Country, Calistoga is located at the northern end of the Napa Valley, about 75 miles north-northeast of San Francisco. Nestled in the foothills of Mt. St. Helena, it was founded in 1859 by Sam Brannan, a New Englander who moved west and started California's first newspaper. Brannan was familiar with New York State's Saratoga Springs, and his goal was to make the mineral springs of Calistoga equally well known. People still come for the spas—to sit and soak in tubs filled with volcanic-ash mud and naturally heated mineral water and in mineral-water whirlpools.

Other area attractions include the dozens of area wineries, many first-class restaurants and shops, a petrified forest, a lake for water sports, and a geyser, along with hot-air ballooning and a glider port, tennis, golf, hiking, bicycling, and outdoor summer concerts. The Sharpsteen Museum depicts Calistoga's early days. Summer and fall weekends are very busy; visit during the spring if possible. To reach Calistoga, take Route 29 (St. Helena Highway) north from Napa.

Worth noting: Route 29 is the major north/south route through the Napa Valley, and traffic can be heavy in peak periods. If you're staying at an inn on this road, be sure to ask if road noise is an issue. Route 29 is called Lincoln Avenue in Calistoga.

Reader tip: "Excellent dinner at All Seasons on Lincoln Avenue. Memorable duck with sour cherry sauce, and extensive wine list. Enjoyed the mud baths (the thin kind) at Lavender Hill. They have couples tubs and you have a little atrium to yourselves. At the end, the attendant gives you both a foot massage on the twin tables in the room." *(Barbara Ochiogrosso)* "Wonderful dinner at Catahoula, a Louisiana-style restaurant in the Mount View Hotel." *(SH, also SWS)*

Also recommended: The cheapest place to stay in Calistoga is the **Calistoga Inn** (1250 Lincoln Avenue, 94515; 707–942–4101) at the western edge of town. "Nothing fancy, but clean and reliable, with rooms around $50–65. The patio is a great place for lunch, with good food, little fountains, and sun filtering through the arbors. Some guest rooms get noise from the weekend bar crowd at night; others hear the kitchen crew in the morning, so ask for details." *(BO)*

In the heart of the spa district, amid the elms, is the **Cottage Grove Inn** (1711 Lincoln Avenue, 94515; 707–942–8400 or 800–799–2284) built in 1996. The 16 charming cottages are virtually identical, with a porch with two wicker rockers, a king- or queen-size bed, wood-burning fireplace, two overstuffed easy chairs set before the fire, hardwood floors, double Jacuzzi tub, cable TV/VCR, stereo system and wet bar. Although the cottages are quite close to each other, there are no windows at the sides, so privacy is preserved. Careful sound-proofing was used in construction and design to block traffic noise from Route 29. Each cottage has a different decorating theme, from botanical to nautical, fly fishing to Vintner, reflected in the fabrics, artwork, and furnishings. B&B double rates of $175–195 rates include a continental breakfast and afternoon wine and cheese, served in the compact guest lounge. "Comfortable, up-to-date, well-designed and decorated cottages." *(WVE)*

For a different experience, *Mark Mendenhall* suggests **Indian Springs** (1712 Lincoln Avenue, 94515; 707–942–4913), California's oldest continuously operating spa facility, with its own 120-by-600-foot steaming spring-fed mineral pool, using 100% volcanic ash in its mud baths. "Meticulously maintained facilities; courteous, efficient front desk service; white adobe cottages all in a row, plus a clay tennis court. The studio and 1-bedroom cottages have wide-board bleached wood floors, pale pink walls, and many built-in cabinets, with big brass beds and floral comforters." The rates for the cottages, ranging from a studio to a 2-bedroom unit, are $115–175 double occupancy; the midweek off-season rate includes free mud bath treatments. "The midweek, mid-winter deal here is terrific. A cool-weather dip in the thermally-heated waters of the enormous pool is a serene experience. Though spartan, the cottages are a good deal for families." *(Susan Rather)*

Information please: A Second Empire–style home built in 1871, **The Elms** (1300 Cedar Street, 94515; 707–942–9476 or 800–235–4316) is named for the seedlings which were planted when the home was built, now the largest elms in the Napa Valley. B&B double rates for the six guest rooms, each with private bath, queen- or king-size bed, TV, and air-conditioning range from $105–175, including in-room coffee, tea, port, and chocolates, plus a full breakfast and afternoon refreshments. The inn has an ideal location, convenient and quiet, next to a lovely park, just a block from Route 29.

A darling Tudor cottage tucked amid lush gardens, **La Chaumiere— A Country Inn** (1301 Cedar Street, 94515; 707–942–5139 or 800–474–6800) is just across the street from a small park and The Elms (see above), and just a half-block from Route 29. The inn has three guest rooms plus a cottage, with B&B double rates of $110–175, including afternoon wine and cheese, in-room glasses of port, and a full breakfast. "Welcoming innkeeper. Appealing redwood bungalow has two bedrooms, living room with a large fireplace, a well-equipped kitchen, and a wonderful patio; there's also a hot tub under a huge tree with a deck all around it. The house itself has a beautiful sitting room with lots of lovely fresh flowers." *(Barbara Ochiogrosso, also SWS)* Comments welcome.

For additional area inns, see **Angwin** and **St. Helena.**

Foothill House   *Tel:* 707–942–6933
3037 Foothill Boulevard, 94515   800–942–6933
                                            Fax: 707–942–5692

Foothill House was bought by Doris and Gus Beckert in 1992; this B&B is acclaimed for its comfortable, well-equipped rooms, excellent food, and attentive service. Rates include a breakfast of homemade breads and muffins, freshly squeezed orange juice, fresh fruit compote with raspberry sauce, French toast served with chicken turkey sausage and sun dried tomatoes or perhaps a Hungarian casserole and later, evening refreshments.

"Doris is warm, welcoming, mothering but not hovering, and makes a point of staying on top of guests' needs. Guest rooms are private and lovely, with maintenance and upgrading an ongoing process. Every room has a special feature, whether a fireplace and double Jacuzzi or a private deck with hot tub. Best of all is the spacious Quail's Nest Cottage, with a cathedral ceiling and a soothing decor of soft florals and shades of mauve, cream and gray, perfect for a romantic splurge." *(SWS)* "Amenities include clean, spacious rooms decorated with Laura Ashley fabrics, private entrances and patios, fireplaces, firm mattresses, reading lights, gourmet breakfast brought to your room, complimentary wine and hors d'oeuvres before dinner and off-street parking. Sherry, cookies along with other surprises await when you return from dinner." *(Jerralea & Hal Brown)*

"The guest rooms are on the ground level, with outside entrances, opening through sliding glass doors to a covered porch. Every amenity one could dream up: the fire ready-laid, bottled water in the room's refrigerator, coffee-maker, cloth-wrapped soaps, stationery, individual reading spotlights on each side of the bed in addition to nightstand lamps and lots of magazines." *(SHW)* "The Quail's Roost is elegantly furnished with a king-size bed and two-sided fireplace facing both the sitting area and the bathroom, which also had a shower for two facing a lighted outdoor waterfall." *(Sheri & Richard DeBro)* "Responsive to my requests for low-fat, vegetarian meals." *(Ann Bach)* "Elegant hot hors d'oeuvres and wine are served in the congenial sun room each night at 6 P.M. Doris is knowledgeable about dining all over Napa and Sonoma; Gus is familiar with the area wineries." *(Mary Lynch)* "Doris turns down the bed, dims the lights, sets soft music playing, and leaves an evening treat of cookies and sherry." *(Terry & Lisa Beth Howland)* "The grounds and garden are small but appealing with a waterfall, gazebo, and swing." *(Kathi Ann Brownl)*

And a word to the wise: "Watch carefully for the inn's sign if you're arriving after dark."

Open All year. Closed Dec. 23–26.
Rooms 1 cottage, 2 suites, 1 double—all with full private bath, telephone, TV, radio, desk, fireplace, air-conditioning, ceiling fan, refrigerator, CD player with discs, private entrance.

Facilities Dining/breakfast room with fireplace, sitting area, patio. 1½ acre with gardens, waterfall, picnic area. Swimming, tennis, golf, wineries nearby.
Location 1½m from center, on left past Petrified Forest Rd.
Restrictions No smoking. No children.
Credit cards Amex, MC, Visa.
Rates B&B, $275 cottage, 135–195 suite, double. Extra person, $35. 2-day weekend minimum.

Scarlett's Country Inn 👪 ♿

3918 Silverado Trail North, 94515

Tel: 707–942–6669
E-mail: Scarletts@aol.com

A turn-of-the-century farmhouse, Scarlett's Country Inn is built on the site of a Wappo Indian settlement; obsidian arrowheads can still be found on the grounds. Breakfast, served at your choice of times between 8–10 A.M., includes such menus as freshly squeezed orange juice, pineapple strawberry fruit platter, oatmeal banana buttermilk pancakes, chicken apple sausages.

"Reached by a winding lane off the main road. Our first view was of an inviting porch tucked amid the trees; the main house is set behind the guest cottage." *(Dr. & Mrs. Joseph Drugay)* "Scarlett is terrific with referrals for everything from restaurants to babysitters." *(Bill & Cheryl Shonborn)* "Secluded and charming. The Silverado Trail is a much quieter road, traffic-wise, for winetasting than Highway 29." *(JG)* "Scarlett couldn't have been nicer; excellent breakfast of Dutch babies with berry sauce, fresh fruit and juice; peaceful poolside area with patio and surrounding gardens. Our kids loved the swimming pool, the apple tree from which they could pick delicious apples, and the roaming rooster and hens." *(EL)* "Highlights are the lovely, peaceful country setting, yet convenient to all area attractions; the lovely grounds, inviting swimming pool, and old-fashioned rope tree swing; and Scarlett herself, a warm and welcoming innkeeper." *(SWS)*

Open All year.
Rooms 2 suites in guest cottage, 1 double in main house—all with private shower and/or bath, telephone, radio, TV, desk, air-conditioning, fan, refrigerator, microwave, private entrance. 2 with deck, 1 with fireplace.
Facilities Dining room, decks; play equipment, games. 1 acre with flower gardens, swimming pool.
Location From St. Helena, go N on Hwy. 29 to Bale Lane. Turn right on Bale, then left on Silverado Trail. Go ½m. Turn right on dirt road with sign "3918" on fence under tree. House is yellow 2-story farmhouse.
Restrictions No smoking.
Credit cards None accepted.
Rates B&B, $135–175 suite, $115 double, $105 single. Extra adult $20; extra child, no charge.
Extras Wheelchair access. Crib, babysitting. Spanish spoken.

Scott Courtyard

1443 Second Street, 94515

Tel: 707–942–0948
800–942–1515
Fax: 707–942–5102

If you'd like to combine the convenience of an in-town location with a quiet, lushly planted setting; if you enjoy the option of mingling with other guests without sacrificing privacy, then plan a visit to the Scott Courtyard, a cluster of 1940s bungalows restored in 1992 by Lauren and Joe Scott. Accommodations are offered in suites furnished with tropical-style Art Deco antiques and fascinating collectibles from the 1920s, 1930s, and 1940s. Rooms look in towards the courtyard's swimming pool, hot tub, and Mediterranean-style gardens. When in the mood to mingle, guests can gather by the stone fireplace in the vaulted social room. Calistoga's many spas and restaurants are just a short walk away.

Coffee is ready at 8 A.M.; from 9 to 10 A.M., guests help themselves to breakfasts of perhaps banana walnut pancakes or lemon poppyseed French toast, chicken apple sausage, fresh fruit, and cereal, eaten at guests' choice of bistro-style tables for two, a large harvest table in the common area, or by the pool. Complimentary wine, cheese, fruit, and hors d'oeuvres are offered from 4:30–6:30 P.M. Guests are always welcome to help themselves to soft drinks in the guest refrigerator.

"Charming, friendly, knowledgeable owners. Each cozy suite consists of two rooms, a sitting room and a bedroom with a queen-size bed, individually decorated with wonderful fabrics, a rich color palette, and eclectic charm. The inviting swimming pool was a perfect balance to a busy day of exploring; on chilly evenings the fireplace in the spacious common area was a perfect place to relax. Delicious breakfast of melon, scrambled eggs with mild chili peppers, black beans, salsa, and warm tortillas." *(SWS)*

Open All year.
Rooms 6 suites in 3 buildings—all with full private bath, clock, air-conditioning, ceiling fan, private entrance. Some with TV, desk, fireplace, kitchenette, porch.
Facilities Common room with fireplace, library, bistro dining area; guest refrigerator; TV/exercise room; art studio. ½ acre with courtyard garden, swimming pool, hot tub, gazebo.
Location Downtown historic district, 2 blocks from Hwy. 29. From Hwy. 29 N in Calistoga, turn right on Lincoln, left on Fairway, left on Second to inn at corner of Second & Fairway.
Restrictions No smoking. Children 7 and over preferred.
Credit cards Amex, MC, Visa.
Rates B&B, $110–165 cottage, suite. Extra person, $20.
Extras Crib.

CAMBRIA

Cambria is a good base from which to visit Hearst Castle in San Simeon six miles to the north and Morro Bay and San Luis Obispo to the south; it's located on the Central Coast, midway between Los Angeles and San Francisco. Winter visitors should take time to visit the town's seaside parks for a glimpse of sea otters and migrating gray whales. Take time to drive inland 25 miles to the Paso Robles wine country to visit the dozens of area wineries; you'll find enthusiastic vintners, uncrowded tasting rooms, and reasonable prices.

Reader tips: "The view from Moonstone Drive is exquisite. Trails follow the bluffs, and paths lead to the rock outcroppings and tidepools where you can watch the seals sun or frolic in the water. Surfers are a little farther away, and there's plenty of beachcombing to be done." *(Erika Holm)* "Don't miss driving along Route 46; it's what California beauty is all about." *(Diana Chang)* "We ate dinner at Ian's, probably the best place in town." *(Stephanie Roberts)* "Cambria is a good base for exploring Hearst Castle and for starting up a dramatic stretch of coastline. Although we did not care for the shops in town, we enjoyed the ocean views offered by our Moonstone Drive motel." *(SR)*

Also recommended: Moonstone Drive, just across the road from the ocean, is home to a number of motel-cum-inns which some readers adore, while others are left cold. While the architecture is basic motel, most have an appealing common area where breakfast and tea is served, and guest rooms done in French country decor—"Laura Ashleyfied to the max" as one correspondent put it. Typically, these properties are not owner-operated, but do have friendly, accommodating innkeepers and homemade breakfasts. The majority of guest rooms have canopy beds, ocean views, gas fireplaces, whirlpool tubs, refrigerators, telephones, and color cable television with VCRs—perfect for travelers who value modern conveniences over historic ambience. Here are some recommended choices for this type of lodging:

One excellent choice is the six-room **Blue Whale Inn** (6736 Moonstone Beach Drive, 93428; 805–927–4647). "Decorated in pink and mint green, Room #6 was immaculate. The homemade breakfast and hors d'oeuvres were fabulous, as were the friendly but unobtrusive innkeepers. Walk to the Sea Chest for fresh fish, or order in from Bamboo Moon, a Thai-Chinese restaurant which delivers." *(Janet Emery)* B&B double rates range from $155–195. Other possibilities include the **Fog Catcher Inn** (6400 Moonstone Beach Drive, 93428; 805–927–1400 or 800–425–4121) and the **Sand Pebbles Inn** (6252 Moonstone Beach Drive, 93428; 805–927–5600).

Olallieberry Inn ♿
2476 Main Street, 93428

Tel: 805–927–3222
Fax: 805–927–0202
E-mail: olallieinn@thegrid.net

"A darling Greek revival-style house built in 1873, the Olallieberry Inn is filled with Victorian antiques and country charm." *(Gail Davis)* "The marvelous back porch and yard with flower gardens and flowing stream is perfect for relaxing." *(Nancy Wood)* "Breathtaking gardens. The breakfast and late afternoon hors d'oeuvres were exquisitely prepared. Great location, within walking distance to quaint shops and almost everything you need—from medicine to a haircut." *(Bill & Leah Lipps)*

"The friendly owners, Peter and Carol Ann Irsfeld, are available to help with reservations or other information. Just a short walk to restaurants and shops. The sitting room has an antique sofa and chairs, and is a quiet place for reading. The bedrooms are beautifully furnished with antique beds, dressers, armoires, and chairs. The Harmony Room was fresh and immaculate with an English carved wooden double bed, rocking chair, armoire, and dresser. The bed had a peach-colored patchwork quilt, plenty of soft pillows, and rose-patterned cotton sheets. Fresh flowers in a vase and chocolates were set on the dresser. The bathroom had a clawfoot tub with shower and a pedestal sink. Breakfast is served family-style from 8–9 A.M., around the long wooden table in the kitchen." (*Wendy Kameda*)

"A warm and tranquil place; soft classical music sets the tone. The cordial, friendly staff provided helpful suggestions about restaurants, sights, and activities. Guests sit and chat during the evening cocktail hour, while sampling local wines and such homemade hors d'oeuvres as dilled salmon cream cheese, black bean and corn salsa, hot artichoke dip, crudités, and terrific brownies. Bowls of M&Ms and candies are always available. Carol Ann prepares a sumptuous breakfast of rich coffee, granola, ollalieberry jam, homemade muffins, and French toast or eggs. Special dietary needs were graciously met. The Room at the Top is small but comfortable and attractive, with a gas fireplace that lit with the flick of a switch. Robes and bubble bath were provided for our private bath across the hall." (*Diana Chang*) "We stayed in the romantic San Simeon room, overlooking a small garden. Lovely furnishings; clean, modern bath with sunken tub/shower." (*Stephanie Roberts*) "Lovely antiques, friendly staff, delicious apple crepes for breakfast, and tempting evening hors d'oeuvres and wine." (*Heather Ayer*)

Open All year.
Rooms 1 suite, 8 doubles—all with private bath and/or shower. 6 with gas fireplace. 3 rooms in cottage.
Facilities Dining room with fireplace, parlor, porch, deck. Guest refrigerator. ½ acre with lawn games, gardens, stream.
Location East Village. In Cambria, turn E on Main St. Go 1 m to inn on left (watch for redwood tree in front of inn).
Restrictions No smoking. "Not really suitable for children, over age 10 preferred."
Credit cards MC, Visa.
Rates B&B, $165 suite, $85–140 double. 10% senior discount.
Extras Wheelchair access; 1 room equipped for disabled.

The Squibb House
Tel: 805–927–9600
4063 Burton Drive, 93428

Built in 1877 in the Gothic Revival Italianate style, Squibb House was restored as a B&B in 1994 by Bruce Black. The house reflects the history of the area and its former occupants. Guest rooms are decorated with lovely hand-crafted pine furnishings and quilts from The Shop Next Door, built in 1889 as a carpentry business, and now a store offering ceramics, antiques, and hand-built furniture. Breakfast is served from 8 to 9:30 A.M., and can be enjoyed in the sitting room or brought to your room, and includes cheeses, homemade jam, fresh fruit, and bakery-fresh scones, crusty rolls, and brioches.

"Bruce has done an incredible job of restoring this beautiful old house. The Garden Room is our favorite, as are the gardens themselves. Tasty, light breakfasts." *(BJ Dolly)* "Bruce and his staff are gracious, hugable, and nurturing. Decorated with romantic, Victorian charm." *(M. Michele Manzella & Robert Rivero)*

Open All year.
Rooms 5 doubles—all with private shower bath. Some with fireplace.
Facilities Living room with fireplace, books; guest refrigerator, porch. Garden, courtyard, off-street parking.
Location Historic district. From Main St. turn W on Burton, S of village.
Restrictions Absolutely no smoking. Children over 12.
Credit cards MC, Visa.
Rates B&B, $95–140 double. Off-season senior discount.

CAPITOLA-BY-THE-SEA

Also recommended: A few miles southeast of Santa Cruz is Capitola, a popular beach resort on Monterey Bay. Two blocks from the ocean is **The Inn at Depot Hill** (250 Monterey Avenue, 95010; 408–462–DEPO or 800–572–2632), built in 1901 as a railroad depot, and transformed in 1990 into a luxurious, elegant, twelve-room inn. B&B double rates range from $165–265, and include a full breakfast, afternoon tea or wine, hors d'oeuvres, and after-dinner dessert. All rooms have a private bath, and most have a wood-burning fireplace, TV/VCR, stereo system, telephone with data port, king- or queen-size bed, and double Jacuzzi or soaking tub. "Good location; formal but pleasant lobby and living room; top-quality fabrics, linens, and furnishings; charming receptionist." *(SD)* "Our favorite California inn." *(Alanna Turco)*

CARDIFF-BY-THE-SEA

Information please: A rooftop terrace bedecked with rose gardens offers guests a panoramic view of the ocean and dramatic sunsets at **The Cardiff-by-the-Sea Lodge** (142 Chesterfield, 92007; 760–944–6474). Built in 1991, this lodge offers 17 rooms with private baths and queen-size beds; decor ranges from Victorian to country French to Southwestern. B&B double rates include a continental breakfast, and range from $105–350. Cardiff is located 25 minutes north of San Diego. "Courteous, accommodating staff. The Victorian room had lace sheer curtains, flowered wallpapers, and a beautiful cherry wood bed. The French Garden room overlooks a garden with a fountain, and is decorated in wicker with a soft green and mauve color scheme. Firm, comfortable beds. On the roof is a firepit to enjoy nightly, a spa, and lots of flowers." *(Ingrid Gain)* "Peaceful, romantic, relaxing, friendly atmosphere. Although the inn has no inside common area, we took our breakfast up to the roof garden and watched the ocean while eating." *(Judith & Michael Thommpson, MW)* Reports appreciated.

CARMEL

Carmel dates back to the early 1900s when it was an artists' colony and a popular summer resort for well-to-do San Franciscans. Opinion is divided on Carmel—most people think it's a charming seaside town filled with darling shops and beautiful art galleries; others find it a bit much. Whatever your opinion, there's no lack of suitable accommodations. Carmel probably has more attractive inns in its zip code than any other town in the country except Cape May, New Jersey! Most were built in the 1950s as motels and have since been renovated as inns, making for an interesting hybrid—the mood, decor, and amenities of an inn, added to the convenience and privacy found in a motel; inside common areas are generally limited or non-existent.

Location is important when booking an inn in Carmel. Parking in town is impossible, so be sure to book a place that's "within walking distance" of the places you want to see.

Other than shops and art galleries, Carmel's attractions include the historic Carmel Mission, golf and tennis, music festivals, and excursions to Big Sur, Monterey, and the Seventeen-Mile Drive. Both Carmel Beach and Point Lobos State Reserve are nice for walking, but the water is generally too cold for swimming, and the undertow is treacherous.

Carmel, also known as Carmel-by-the-Sea, is located just south of the Monterey Peninsula, 120 miles south of San Francisco. Most of Carmel is laid out in a grid pattern, with numbered avenues running east/west, starting at First in the north end of town and ascending as you go south. The exception is Ocean, the town's main east/west thoroughfare. Streets are named and run north/south; Junipero is the main drag. The center of town is Carmel Plaza, where Junipero and Ocean avenues meet. There is no numbering system for buildings.

Word to the wise: Most Carmel inns define a two-night weekend minimum as being either Thursday and Friday nights *or* Saturday and Sunday nights; some charge a premium for a Friday/Saturday combination. Call to double-check. Except for the occasional midweek, off-season bargain, room rates in Carmel range from expensive to astronomical, so plan accordingly.

Reader tips: "Carmel has a marvelous climate—cool, clean air encourages the lush growth of beautiful trees and abundant flowers. Rolling surf and clean white beaches where evenings find couples, families, and lone strollers." *(Dianne Evans)* "Recommend the Casanova for a lovely, romantic dinner." *(Stephanie Roberts)* "Although most Carmel visitors just stop at the beach in town, at the end of Ocean Drive, it's well worth the short drive to Point Lobos State Reserve for beautiful beaches, huge dunes, and hiking trails; you can watch for whales, seals, and sea lions, plus a wide range of sea birds. When I was there on a Saturday morning in July, the parking lot was almost empty, though the town was jammed full." *(SHW)*

Also recommended—resorts: Carmel has two outstanding luxury golf resorts, the **Quail Lodge** (8205 Valley Greens Drive, 93923; 408–624–1581 or 800–538–9516) and the **Carmel Valley Ranch Resort**

(1 Old Ranch Road, 93923; 408–625–9500 or 800–422–7635). Each has championship 18-hole golf courses, tennis courts, swimming pools, hot tubs, and fine dining, and each has about 100 guest rooms with rates starting about $250 double, with packages available.

For a special-occasion splurge, consider the recently redecorated suites at the **Highlands Inn** (Highway 1, P.O. Box 1700; 408–624–3801 or 800–682–4811): "Our suite had a double whirlpool tub, a fireplace, kitchen area, and patio with Pacific view. The restaurant perches on the cliff, 200 feet about the ocean's edge for a breathtaking vista." *(JM)* Ocean-view doubles start at $290; suites from $375 and *up.*

Also recommended—hotels: Originally built in 1904 as a private Spanish-style mansion is **La Playa Hotel** (Camino Real and 8th, P.O. Box 900, 93921; 408–624–6476 or 800–582–8900). The 75 guest rooms are done in soft colors, with good lighting and hand-carved Spanish mission-style furniture with the hotel's mermaid motif. Double rates range from $125–230; 5 cottages are also available, at rates of $230–495. "Delightful lunch on the terrace overlooking the beautiful gardens; excellent dinner, too." *(Tom Wilbanks)* "Quiet atmosphere; beautiful gardens, meticulously maintained; comfortable room with Spanish-style decor. Convenient location, an easy walk to the beach or shops." *(Susan Lane)*

Also recommended—inns: A flagship property of the Inns by the Sea group, the **Carriage House Inn** (Junipero at 7th & 8th, P.O. Box 1900, 93921; 408–625–2585 or 800–433–4732) offers 13 luxurious rooms, with rates ranging from $139–259, including a continental breakfast delivered to the room. "Our spacious suite had a fireplace, refrigerator, and double Jacuzzi tub. Charming and caring staff; delightful afternoon wine and hors d'oeuvres." *(Ruthie & Derek Tilsley)* Another good choice in this hotel group is the Dolphin Inn, with rates from $79–209.

Readers are delighted with the friendly staff, tasty food, and comfortable rooms at the **The Cobblestone Inn** (Junipero and Eighth Avenues, P.O. Box 3185, 93921; 408–625–5222 or 800–833–8836), a former motel, refaced with Tudor-style detailing and beautiful stonework. Each of the 24 guest rooms has a private entrance, opening to the walkway or second-floor balcony. B&B double rates of $95–175 include a generous buffet breakfast, afternoon wine and hors d'oeuvres, evening sherry and fresh-baked cookies, and always available soft drinks and fruit. "We had our choice of having breakfast in our room, in the cozy parlor by the fireplace, or at one of three tables in the beautiful garden patio. Lots of adorable teddy bears." *(Roxanne Mita, also JP)* "Excellent location for shops and restaurants." *(Derek & Ruthie Tilsley)*

Information please—inns: The **Happy Landing Inn** (Monte Verde between 5th & 6th, P.O. Box 2619; 408–624–7917) is just a block from Ocean Avenue, next door to an excellent restaurant. Built in 1925 in an early Comstock design, this B&B has seven guest rooms, with B&B double rates of $90–165, including a continental breakfast and afternoon tea or sherry. "A breakfast of coffee cake, quiche, fruit, juice, and a hot beverage is brought to your room any time after 8:30 A.M. Some rooms have cathedral ceilings, stained glass windows, and fireplaces and all are furnished with antiques." *(MK)*

Surrounded by lovely gardens, the **Normandy Inn** (Ocean at Monte

Verde, P.O. Box 1706, 93921; 408–624–3825 or in CA, 800–343–3825) has 48 guest rooms and suites, at rates ranging from $98–200, and three family cottages with rates of $250–350. "Convenient location, close to beach and shops. Light breakfast may be carried back to the room; sherry available in the evenings. Clean bright rooms, some with a fireplace; easy parking. Warm, friendly, pleasant staff; quiet rooms, except for a few at the front." *(George Outland)*

Cypress Inn
Lincoln & 7th, P.O. Box Y, 93921

Tel: 408–624–3871
800–443–7443
Fax: 408–624–8216
E-mail: hollace@cypress-inn

Noted for its Spanish-Mediterranean architecture facade, the Cypress Inn was built in 1929 and is located in the heart of Carmel, within walking distance of all shops, restaurants, galleries, and the beach. The spacious living room lobby and the garden courtyard are ideal for enjoying breakfast or an evening cocktail. Afternoon tea is served weekdays from 3–4 P.M.; the evening "Happy Hour is offered in the Library Lounge from 5–7 P.M. Rates include a continental breakfast, the daily paper, and an in-room decanter of sherry. Dog lovers will be pleased to know that guests are welcome to bring their pets.

"Friendly atmosphere and convenient location. Our spacious room had a large bathroom." *(Stephanie Blanc)* "Appealing architectural style, wonderful roof, flower-laden courtyard, and impressive portico. The public rooms are spacious, the decor elegant, the furnishings rich. Our enormous, well-appointed suite had a large dining alcove overlooking the street; a decanter of sherry and a basket of fruit were on the table. The continental breakfast could be taken outside to the courtyard to enjoy. We thought the best rooms were those on the second floor, overlooking the courtyard, with a balcony from which one could see the ocean." *(Hugh & Marjorie Smith)* "Our room was clean and beautiful, opening to the garden, with a gas fireplace. Light breakfast of coffee, juice, and a muffin." *(Joyce Rinehart)* "The best part was that our well-trained dog was also welcome. We were entertained watching the variety of pets and owners in the lobby." *(MW)*

Open All year.
Rooms 6 suites, 27 doubles—all with private bath and/or shower, telephone, TV. Some with gas fireplace, wet bar, veranda.
Facilities Bar/lounge, living room with fireplace, garden courtyard. Limited off-street parking.
Location Town center, 1 block S of Ocean Ave.
Credit cards Amex, MC, Visa.
Rates $174–265 suite, $88–165 double. Extra person, $15.
Extras Pets with permission: 1st pet, $17, 2nd, $10 (maximum 2 per room).

Mission Ranch ✕ ⟑ ⟨
26270 Dolores Street, Carmel 93923

Tel: 408–624–6436
800–538–8221
Fax: 408–626–4163

Although inns and movie stars usually mix about as well as oil and water, Clint Eastwood has once again proven to be the exception that proves the rule. Once a ranch and later a restaurant, bar, and dance barn, Eastwood frequented the bar at the Mission Ranch when stationed at nearby Fort Ord during the Korean War. When local developers were ready to bulldoze the property for condominiums in the 1980s, Eastwood, then mayor of Carmel, stepped in to preserve the property. Eleven acres were donated to the town as a nature preserve; the remainder was renovated, with accommodations in the original 1850s farmhouse, the bunkhouse, and in several newer buildings. Furnishings combine antiques and custom-designed ranch-style pieces; most of the newer rooms offer sunset views over the pastures to the ocean and Point Lobos beyond.

"The atmosphere is cozy and comfortable; check-in was courteous and friendly. Flowers abound throughout the grounds, and sheep graze in the fields. Our room had country decor, a distant ocean view, and a Jacuzzi tub with big thick towels and robes. Breakfast is served in the club room and was an attractive buffet of fresh fruits, bagels, sweet rolls, cereals and yogurt. At night, the piano bar was in full swing, with guests and locals belting out show tunes; the feeling was happy, friendly, and fun." *(Donna Pekkonen)* "Just as delightful on a return visit. The classic American cuisine in the restaurant was surprisingly good, the atmosphere delightful." *(DP)* "Turning in at the ranch, you are rewarded with a sight of grassy knolls, sprawling meadows, flower gardens, with mountains, Point Lobos, and the ocean in the distance. Our room had a king-size bed with a handmade quilt, matching bed skirt and shams, and mounds of pillows. The rough pine-paneled bathroom walls were painted in a warm honey beige; the tub was surrounded by tile and was spotlessly clean, as was the entire unit. Overall, a delightful oasis from the hustle and bustle of Carmel." *(Pat Lampasso)* "Though expensive, my spacious second-floor room in one of the ocean/meadow cottages was delightful. It had a vaulted ceiling, stone fireplace, king-size bed with wood and wrought iron, big tiled bathroom, and more. From my private deck, I could watch the stars at night, the water during the day. Beautiful grounds with lush grass and lots of flowers. Friendly, welcoming, unsnobby staff and fellow guests." *(Susan W. Schwemm)*

Open All year.

Rooms 31 suites, doubles—all with full private bath, coffee maker, Some with single or double Jacuzzi tub, gas fireplace, porch. Rooms in several buildings.

Facilities Restaurant with fireplace, piano bar, parlor, wraparound porch, club house. 6 tennis courts, putting green, exercise room, banquet/conference facilities.

Location 1 block from Carmel Mission, 8 blocks to village, 2.5 m to Point Lobos State Reserve. From Carmel, go S on Rte. 1 & go right (W) on Rio Rd., then left on Lasuen Dr. past Mission to ranch.

Restrictions Absolutely no smoking. Not all rooms have views; ask for details.

Credit cards MC, Visa.

Rates B&B, $85–225 suite, double.

Extras Bunkhouse wheelchair accessible; bathroom specially equipped.

Sandpiper Inn
2408 Bayview Avenue, 93923

Tel: 408–624–6433
800–633–6433
Fax: 408–624–5964

The closest inn to the beach in Carmel, the Sandpiper is located just 100 yards from Carmel's white sand beaches. Owned by Graeme Mackenzie since 1965, it's been managed by Michelle Higgins since 1995. The inn's early California architecture is complemented by floral fabrics, original paintings, and country antiques and reproductions in the individually decorated guest rooms. A buffet breakfast is served from 8 to 10 A.M. in the lounge, with its beamed cathedral ceiling, inviting library nook, and a fireplace built of Carmel stone; you can take a tray to the garden patio or to your room. The buffet includes fresh pastries or muffins, orange juice, fruit, and granola. Refreshments are served at 5 P.M.

"Our beautiful second-floor room—one of the inn's largest—had a king-sized bed with a view over the beach and ocean. Warm and welcoming innkeepers; ideal location; pleasant evening cocktail hour." *(Norma & Bob Simon)*

Open All year.
Rooms 3 cottages, 2 suites, 11 doubles—all with full private bath, clock/radio. 9 with desk, 3 with fireplace.
Facilities Living room with fireplace, dining room, library, guest refrigerator. Deck, patio, gardens, off-street parking. Beach nearby.
Location 1 mile to center of town. From Hwy. 1, go right (W) at Ocean Ave., through Carmel 1 m. Left at Scenic Rd. (S). Go ⁸⁄₁₀ m to end of beach at Martin Way (S).
Restrictions No smoking. Children over 12.
Credit cards Amex, MC, Visa.
Rates B&B, $150–185 suite, $95–160 double. Extra person, $20. Off-season AAA, senior discount.
Extras French, German spoken.

Sea View Inn ¢
Camino Real, between 11th and 12th Streets,
P.O. Box 4138, 93921

Tel: 408–624–8778
Fax: 408–625–5901

Marshall and Diane Hydorn have been welcoming guests to the Seaview since 1975. Guest rooms in this Victorian home are decorated with four-poster canopy beds and other antiques, Oriental rugs, fresh flowers, and whimsical toys. Rates include a weekday breakfast of juice, fresh fruit, yogurt, cereal, muffins, toast, and bagels, with a hot dish, such as quiche served on Sundays. Afternoons you'll find tea and coffee set out, and in the evening, sherry is enjoyed by the parlor fire.

"A convenient walk from both the beautiful waterfront and the heart of Carmel, on a quiet residential street. Our cozy room had a nice-sized bathroom with a clawfoot tub. Healthy breakfast served between 9 and 10 A.M. Cookies and tea in the afternoon, and sherry, wine, and cheese in the evening provided a nice touch. An excellent value in pricy Carmel." *(Karl Wiegers & Chris Zambito)* "Pleasant room; well-equipped, spacious bath. Lovely assortment of jams at breakfast. Excellent recommendations for an art show and restaurant for dinner." *(Ruth Tilsley)* "Our spacious room at the back of the house had a beautiful canopy bed, a window seat, and a sitting area in an alcove; tiny bathroom. We kept our windows open at night and could hear the waves crashing on the beach." *(Sherry Justiss)* "Marshall is an artist and his paintings adorn the walls; he and Diane made us feel that we left as friends." *(Patty Gibian)*

Open All year.
Rooms 8 doubles—6 with private bath and/or shower, 2 with a maximum of 4 people sharing bath. Some with desk.
Facilities Dining room, living room both with fireplace; library, porch. Garden, patio, picnic area. Deep sea fishing, whale watching, golf, tennis, kayaking nearby.
Location 120 m S of San Francisco. 5 blocks to center, 3 blocks to beach. From Hwy 1, Take Ocean Ave. W to Camino Real. Turn left, go S 5½ blocks to inn on left between 11th and 12th.
Restrictions No smoking. Prefer children over 12.
Credit cards Amex, MC, Visa.
Rates B&B, $85–140 double, $80–125 single. 2-night holiday/weekend minimum.
Extras Limited French spoken.

Vagabond's House   *Tel:* 408–624–7738
Fourth and Dolores Streets   800–262–1262
P.O. Box 2747, 93921   *Fax:* 408–626–1243

A brick half-timbered English Tudor country inn, the Vagabond's guest rooms are furnished with antiques, with decorating themes ranging from nautical American to English hunt. Under the same management is the **Lincoln Green Inn**, with a similar English theme to the architecture and decor of its steeply peaked cottages.

"Our brightly decorated room had freshly cut flowers, sherry, a fruit basket, books, coffee and teas. The bath was supplied with lavender soap and thick towels. At our request, our breakfast tray of coffee, hard-boiled eggs, fresh rolls, and the morning newspaper was served to us in the flower-filled courtyard." *(Mr. & Mrs. Paul Petrenk)* "On one visit we had a small but cozy room done in white wicker with yellow and blue accessories; on a return trip we had a large and airy corner room done in knotty pine." *(John & Sandra Nelipovich)* "The cooperative staff made dinner reservations and provided information." *(Pat & Peter Maschi)* "The flagstone courtyard is dominated by large oak trees, offering a shady place to read and relax." *(Laura Scott)* "Quiet location, yet close to shops and restaurants." *(Kathy & Roger Knieth)* Reports welcome.

Open All year.
Rooms 11 doubles—all with private bath and/or shower, telephone, radio, TV, desk, refrigerator, fireplace. Some with kitchen.
Facilities Parlor with fireplace. Courtyard with waterfall. Off-street parking. 8 blocks to beach.
Location 2 blocks from center. From Hwy. 1, turn W onto Ocean Ave., then turn right on Dolores.

Restrictions Some street noise in two rooms. No children under 12.
Credit cards Amex, MC, Visa.
Rates B&B, $79–150 double. Extra person, $20. 2-night weekend minimum. Midweek rates off-season.
Extras Pets by arrangement, $10 extra. Spanish, Korean spoken.

CAZADERO

Also recommended: If cost is not a concern, then you may find **Timberhill Ranch** (35755 Hauser Bridge Road, 95421; 707–847–3258) to be a restorative getaway. Double rates for the 15 cottages range from $365–385 (plus 12% service), including a continental breakfast, a six-course dinner, and use of the on-site swimming pool, hot tub, tennis courts, and hiking trails. A full breakfast and lunch are available at additional cost. "Our cedar cabin was decorated with comfortable country furniture; the private deck looked over the mountains. Breakfast was brought to our cabin every morning and included delicious breakfast breads with tea or coffee. We lunched on soup, salad, and fresh fruit by the pool. The path to the restaurant is landscaped beautifully." *(Tina Hom)* Cazadero is roughly halfway between Healdsburg and the coast.

CHICO

Information please: Close to downtown Chico, the university, the Chico Museum, and Bidwell Park, is **The Esplanade B&B** (620 The Esplanade, 95926; 916–345–8084), a historic California Craftsman bungalow. Each of the five guest rooms has a TV and a private bath. "A pretty place, comfortably restored with modern bathrooms. Natalie's room has a queen-size bed, Jacuzzi tub, and stained-glass window. Accommodating hostess; filling, creative breakfast." *(Emily Hoche-Mong, also Lisa Gallagher)* A full breakfast and evening refreshments are included in the $65–85 double rates.

Music Express Inn ♿   *Tel:* 916–345–8376
1091 El Monte Avenue, 95928   *Fax:* 916–893–8521
                               E-mail: icobeen@aol.com

Whether you're coming to Chico on business or to visit friends and family, you're assured of comfortable accommodations, tasty breakfasts, and warm hospitality when you visit Irene and Barney Cobeen, who have owned this contemporary 1977 home since 1981. As you might guess from its name, music plays an important role here; Irene teaches both piano and stringed instruments, from banjo to bass. Disabled travelers will find understanding hosts here; Barney uses a wheelchair and the Cobeens have made sure that the Music Express is fully accessible. Guest rooms are unusually spacious with queen- and king-size beds, comfortable sitting areas, good work areas with telephones, and excellent reading lights throughout. Puffy quilts top the beds, and color schemes range from white, light blue, and rose, to dark red and hunter green. Breakfast is served from 7–9:30 A.M. at guests' choice of a single large table or individual tables. Guests can help themselves from a buffet of breads and rolls, fresh fruit, juice, and coffee or tea; the entree of the day is prepared to order for each guest.

"A delightful respite on the long road trip; convenient to the highway and easy to find. Our room was fresh and clean, exceptionally well-equipped, with a most comfortable bed. Friendly, accommodating innkeepers." *(PH)* "Our lovely room was well supplied with everything from lots of towels to magazines and tea. Quiet, peaceful atmosphere. An ideal place to stay when visiting students at Chico State." *(Sally Valderrama)* "Barney's delicious breakfasts include omelets, fresh fruit, jams and breads. Sensitive to the needs of business travelers." *(Mary Kilpatrick)* "Irene's musical talent adds to the atmosphere. The Winter room has an inviting bed and sitting area. The decor combines a soft shade of blue with hearts and roses." *(Sylvia Schlosser, also Kathy Peter)* "Country-style home with a detached barn." *(Lisa Gallagher)* "Complete privacy, a warm welcome, and wonderful home-cooked breakfasts." *(Valerie Ryder)*

Open All year.

Rooms 1 suite, 8 doubles—all with private bath and/or shower, telephone, clock, TV, desk, air-conditioning, ceiling fan, refrigerator, microwave. 6 with deck, private entrance; 3 with whirlpool tub. Rooms in 3 buildings.

Facilities Dining room; living room with grand piano; cottage living room with fireplace, TV/VCR, books; family room; library; guest refrigerator; gift shop; deck/porch. 3 acres with lawn games, gazebos. Golf, rivers, lake nearby.

Location Central Valley. 1½ hour N of Sacramento. 4 m from center of town. From Sacramento, take Hwy 99 to Exit 32 & go right. Go past the 1st traffic light to El Monte Ave. Go left on El Monte & take an immediate left into first driveway.

Restrictions No smoking.

Credit cards Amex, Discover, MC, Visa.

Rates B&B, $85 suite, $75 double, $55–75 single. Extra person, $20.

Extras Fully wheelchair accessible; 1 room specially equipped. Station, airport pickup. Crib.

COALINGA

Information please: If you're looking for a break from the monotony of interstate 5, stop for lunch, dinner, or an overnight at the **The Inn at Harris Ranch** Route 1, Box 777, 93210; 24505 W. Dorris, Highway 198 and Interstate 5 (**Tel:** 209–935–0717 or 800–942–2333). Set in the heart of the San Joaquin Valley, halfway between San Francisco and Los Angeles, this resort hotel specializes in private label beef and farm fresh produce in its restaurant, with overnight accommodations in an early California setting. The architecture of the inn resembles a Spanish hacienda with adobe walls, red tile roofs and floors, and the main buildings center around a garden courtyard and swimming pool. The 123 guest rooms have high ceilings, double basin baths, pine furnishings, and floral print decor. Double rates range from $95–115; $225 for a suite.

COLUMBIA

City Hotel ¢ ✗
Main Street, Columbia Historic Park
P.O. Box 1870, 95310

Tel: 209–532–1479
800–532–1479
Fax: 209–532–7027
E-mail: info@cityhotel.com

A gold-rush town, founded in 1850, Columbia is now a historic park owned by the state of California and restored to its 1860s condition with authentic, museum-quality period antiques. Managed by Tom Bender, some staff members are hotel management students from Columbia College. The hotel is well known for its restaurant, open for dinners and Sunday brunch; a recent meal included portabella mushroom tart with tomato-basil salsa, rosemary smoked salmon with lentil ragout, and chocolate lava cake with creme fraiche and blackberry sauce.

"We had one of the balcony rooms overlooking the peaceful main street, which is closed to car traffic. The arrangement of a half-bath in our room and the shower at the far end of the parlor worked out fine— the hotel provides a basket with robe, slippers, towels, and Neutrogena soap and shampoo to carry back and forth." *(Linda Bair)* "Although the two best guestrooms are the ones at the front of the hotel, all are adequate. Ours had an elaborately carved headboard over six feet high; in the morning, we opened the French doors and stepped out onto our balcony, watching the early morning sun illuminate the silent streets. The simple breakfast buffet, set up in the spacious upstairs parlor, included orange juice, fruit cup, quiche, granola, yogurt, and freshly baked muffins and breads.

"Service at dinner was friendly yet professional. The prix fixe dinner was delicious and an excellent value, enhanced by a local wine, chosen from the first-rate wine list. In contrast to the formal atmosphere of the restaurant, the saloon is a completely casual local hangout." *(SWS, also Jerry Turney)* "Friendly, informative, and courteous staff; immaculate, charming facilities. First rate dining." *(Jill Mulcahy, also Shelly Baruch)* "Tasty quiche at breakfast." *(Connie Rice)*

Open All year. Closed Dec. 24 & 25, Jan. 1 through Jan. 7. Restaurant closed Mon. from Sept. through May.
Rooms 10 doubles—all with private half-bath; 2 showers in hall. All with desk, air-conditioning. 2 with balcony.
Facilities Restaurant, saloon, parlor with games, balcony. Tennis nearby. Lake, river nearby for boating, swimming.
Location Central Valley; Gold Country, Sierra foothills. 120 m E of San Francisco. 4 m N of Sonora, off Hwy. 49.
Restrictions Minimal interior soundproofing. No smoking.
Credit cards Amex, Discover, MC, Visa.
Rates B&B, $85–105 double, $80–100 single. Extra person, $10. Prix fixe dinner, $25–35. Theater, Victorian Christmas packages.
Extras Station/local airport pickup by prior arrangement. Crib.

DANA POINT

Information please: Perched on a cliff overlooking the harbor, the **Blue Lantern Inn** (34343 Street of the Blue Lantern, 92629; 714–661–1304 or 800–950–1236) is a small hotel with 29 guest rooms featuring traditional New England furnishings, original art, print wallpapers, and handmade quilts, complemented by the colors of the coast—seafoam green, lavender, periwinkle, sand. B&B double rates of $140–300 include a full buffet breakfast and afternoon wine and cheese.

DAVENPORT

New Davenport B&B ¢ ✗
31 Davenport Avenue (Highway 1)
Box J, 95017

Tel: 408–425–1818
408–426–4122
800–870–1817
Fax: 408–423–1160
E-mail: inn@swanton.com

After operating a pottery school for 15 years, Marcia and Bruce McDougal built the New Davenport Cash Store in 1977 as an outlet for their pottery and craft interests. They ended up with a mini-complex housing a B&B, a restaurant and bakery, and the Cash Store, a craft shop where African and Asian art is a specialty.

The McDougals describe the Davenport area as being a "rural-coastal environment in a rugged, outdoor area. There are endless beaches and mountain paths for hiking. It's eight miles to the Ano Nuevo State Elephant Seal Reserve, and you can see the whales migrating from January through May." The rates include a welcome drink from the restaurant bar, a $7 credit toward breakfast in the restaurant on weekdays, and on weekends a buffet breakfast of hard-boiled eggs, fresh granola, yogurt, fresh-baked pastry, fruit, juice, and coffee. Lunch favorites range from huevos rancheros to burgers to vegetarian lasagna, while dinner specialities include grilled salmon with salmon ravioli, rack of lamb with sun-dried cherry and port sauce, and penne with grilled chicken and vegetables; a selection from the list of local wines will complement your meal.

"The best rooms are above the restaurant and shop, most with ocean views. The Whale Watcher Room has lovely antique furniture, high stained-wood ceilings, skylights, and a modern bath. Breakfast choices included omelets, blueberry pancakes, and waffles. Although the inn is directly on Highway 1, I heard no traffic noise. Lovely, accommodating innkeeper." *(Gail Davis)* "Captain Davenport's Retreat is a corner room with two walls of floor-to-ceiling glass and a large sitting area. Comfortable chairs and coffee tables are arranged along the brick-walled porch making it a pleasant place to relax; a double-paned wall of glass cuts the ocean wind and most of the traffic noise, without obstructing the fantastic views of the cliffs and sea." *(Matt Joyce)* "I had an ample salad, fresh-baked bread, and delicious swordfish." *(Barbara Occhiogrosso)*

Open All year. Restaurant closed Christmas, Thanksgiving.
Rooms 1 suite (sleeps 4), 11 doubles—all with private shower and/or bath, telephone, desk. Some with fan, balcony, TV/VCR. 4 rooms in annex.
Facilities Restaurant, coffee bar, gallery, wraparound porch, common room with games, reading materials; patio. Ocean beach across street. Hiking, beachcombing, fishing, windsurfing, hang-gliding, bicycling nearby.
Location San Francisco Bay Area. 60 m S of San Francisco. 9 m N of Santa Cruz, halfway between San Francisco and Carmel. "Big brick building on Hwy. 1 in Davenport (only 2 blocks long)."
Restrictions No smoking. Traffic noise in some rooms. Some rooms equipped for families.
Credit cards Amex, MC, Visa.
Rates B&B, $75–125 double. Extra person, $10. Alc lunch, $6–9; alc dinner, $17–20. Picnic baskets available.
Extras Wheelchair access. Crib. Spanish, French, German spoken.

DEATH VALLEY

Furnace Creek Inn & Ranch Resort 🛏 ✕ 🏃   *Tel: 760–786–2345*
P.O. Box 1, 92328   *Fax: 760–786–2307*

Death Valley—the name still conjures up the hardships endured by America's pioneers. Travelers return today to explore this National Park and to learn about its geological and ecological wonders as well as its mining history, including 20-mule-team Borax wagons and famous Scotty's Castle. Although Death Valley is America's hottest place in the summer, the desert climate is inviting from October to early May.

The Furnace Creek Inn and Ranch Resort is owned and operated by AmFac Parks & Resorts Inc. Use the address and phone number above for information on the Ranch, a more casual, motel-like structure with 225 guest rooms. Although children are welcome at the inn, the ranch is perhaps a better choice.

Built in 1927, the inn is a Mission-style adobe villa overlooking Death Valley with a spectacular view of the valley and surrounding mountains. Extensively refurbished with Mission-style furnishings in late 1997 and 1998, the resort remains a luxurious one, set in an unlikely location. Guest rooms are furnished with twin or king-size beds.

"Hillside setting overlooking the valley, with fabulous sunset views of the desert. The building itself is a labyrinth of passageways and walkways built into the hillside. Lovely gardens step down the hillside; after dinner we enjoyed strolling past the little waterfalls and lush plantings to the big old swimming pool fed by a natural warm spring." *(JWM)* "The restaurant and grounds are outstanding. We were there for nearly a week, and the food was varied and consistently high in quality." *(Duane Roller)* "The breakfast special is a good deal and makes sense when there's so much to see." *(Kathleen Lowe Owen)*

Open All year.
Rooms 2 suites, 64 doubles—all with full private bath, telephone, TV, desk, air-conditioning.
Facilities Dining Room restaurant, Lobby lounge, sun deck. Service station.

85° naturally spring-fed swimming pool, waterfall, hot tub, lighted tennis courts, golf, hiking, trail rides.

Location Desert Country, SE CA. 120 m NW of Las Vegas, NV; 300 m NE of Los Angeles. From Los Angeles, take I-15 to Baker. From Baker, follow 127/190 to Furnace Creek. 1 m from National Park Visitor Center and Museum.

Restrictions Jacket suggested for dinner; tie optional.

Credit cards All major.

Rates Room only, $245–295 double. Extra adult, $50; extra child ages 5–12, $25; children under 5, free. Alc dinner, $20–40.

Extras Crib, $14.

DESERT HOT SPRINGS

Travellers Repose ¢   *Tel:* 760–329–9584
66920 First Street, P.O. Box 655, 92240

Built in 1986, Travellers Repose is a neo-Victorian home complete with gingerbread trim and fish-scale shingles. The interior decor includes ceiling fans, lace window treatments, iron and brass beds, and pull-chain toilets, complemented by country-floral wallpapers and hardwood floors. Innkeeper Marian Relkoff serves a breakfast of fresh fruit and juice, homemade granola, and a variety of home-baked muffins, plus afternoon tea.

"Marian is a warm, energetic, thoughtful, caring, creative, and well-organized person who maintains her inn meticulously. Enveloping calm; quiet, relaxing atmosphere. Individually decorated rooms have expansive views of mountains and desert, and truly evoke the feeling of being at home. Generous breakfasts with delicious made-from-scratch treats. While serving guests responsively, Marian also manages to facilitate congenial conversation among the guests." *(Yvonne & Melvin Morgan, also Mary Fiess)* "The charming Heart Room carries a heart motif in the quilts, pictures, and furniture; comfortable queen-size bed." *(George & Miriam Woodcock)* "Wonderful breakfasts of piping hot scones, homemade granola, fresh fruit, and tea." *(Ann Richey)* "Marian is attentive but not hovering. Our room had such thoughtful touches as a thermos of ice water and a dish of sweets on the dresser." *(Nancy McReynolds)* "Rooms are accented by bay windows, stained glass, and hand-crafted furniture." *(Toni Smith)* "Just a hop, skip and a jump from the freeway system, Palm Desert, and Palm Springs." *(Kimberley Klein)* "Serene setting away from the congestion and glitz of Palm Springs." *(Richard & Catherine McCarthy)* "Our room, Buttons & Bows, had lovely lace curtains, and a comfortable queen-size brass and iron bed. The house has a heart theme throughout; ask Marian to show you the heart-shaped shadow which forms each night on their walkway." *(Gail Davis)*

Open Sept. through June.

Rooms 3 doubles—all with full private bath, air-conditioning, ceiling fan, clock/radio.

Facilities Dining area, living room with games, books. Patio, swimming pool, hot tub, gardens.

Location Desert Country. 12 m N of Palm Springs, 3 blocks from town center. From I-10 take exit for Palm Dr., go N 5 m to Pierson Blvd, turn right. Go E 3 blocks, turn left on First St. to inn on right.
Restrictions No smoking. No children under 12.
Credit cards None accepted.
Rates B&B, $65–90 double, $60–80 single. No tipping. Weekly rates.

ELK

Elk is located just 15 miles south of Mendocino on the northern California coast. (See Mendocino for more information on area attractions.) This tiny hamlet developed as a logging town, and most of its inns were originally built of redwood by a local lumber company. It's 145 miles north of San Francisco, a 4½-hour drive by Highway 1, or just over three hours by way of Highway 101 to Cloverdale. From there take Route 128 to the coast, then 5 miles south on Highway 1 to Elk.

Information please: An excellent ocean view can be found at the **Griffin House at Greenwood Cove** (5910 South Highway One, P.O. Box 172, 95432; 707–877–3422), set high on the cliffs overlooking the sea. B&B double rates for the eight cottages range from $85–225, including a full breakfast delivered to your door each morning. The inn's pub serves dinner on weekends year-round and on most summer nights. "Amazing views from the private porch of our cottage. Dramatic sunsets followed later by moonlight reflecting off the water. Inside was a wood stove, queen-sized bed, good reading lights, and informal decor. Comfortable, clean, welcoming, and attractive; good value, too." *(Alan Reinach)* "Welcoming innkeeper with a knack for making guests feel comfortable. Simple furnishings. Wonderful place to relax and just 'be.' Great hamburger selection and delightful atmosphere at the inn's Irish Pub." *(PH)*

Elk Cove Inn   *Tel:* 707–877–3321
6300 South Highway 1, P.O. Box 367, 95432   800–275–2967
                                                    Fax: 707–877–1808
                                        E-mail: elkcoveinn@mcn.org

Formerly a Florida realtor, no one needed to remind Elaine Bryant about the old real estate adage, "location, location, location," when she decided to buy Elk Cove Inn in 1994. Although dozens of inns line Highway One on the Mendocino Coast, most of them offer views of the road, not the ocean. Not so with this 1878 mansard-roofed Victorian home, originally built by a local lumber company as an executive guest house. Perched on a bluff, the inn has easy access to the beach, views of the water and rock outcroppings, and trees—no cars, no buildings, or people. Guest rooms have down comforters, lots of pillows, comfy rocking chairs, and good reading lights; most have dramatic ocean views. Four ocean-front suites were completed in 1997 and are decorated in Arts and Crafts Mission style; each has a living room with balcony, window seat, fireplace, and wet bar, plus a bedroom with king-size bed. Breakfast seatings are at 8:30, 9:00, and 9:30 A.M.; the meal includes baked pears or perhaps a yogurt fruit parfait, followed by cheese souffle, corn pudding, and croissants.

"Wonderful views, lovely grounds, complete with an organic garden that provides the wonderful vegetables and herbs used in the mouth-watering breakfasts. Elaine's associate Jim Carr grows all the vegetables and maintains the lush grounds. Put that together with Elaine's flair for cooking and her sensitivity to dietary restrictions, and you get wonderful meals. Special touches include snowy white terry robes to don after a warm shower, plus choices of herbal tea, coffee, or chocolate." *(Carol Stoddard)* "The location perched above the beach, with direct access down a short trail, was wonderful. The second floor was added in 1990, so though the exterior has an older look, our second room had all modern amenities." *(James Burr, also PH)*

"The main house is at the end of a long driveway; the cabins are just past it. My quiet room was upstairs in the main house, with windows overlooking the trees and water. Spacious and elegantly furnished, it had fresh flowers and sherry to complement the blue wallpaper and natural wood wainscotting and trim. I had a chance to see the cabins, and found them rustic but comfortable, with equally wonderful water views. One has a floor-to-ceiling window in the hand-painted tile shower so you can wash and see the view at the same time." *(Linda Goldberg)* "Our cabin was large, yet cozy with picture windows facing the driftwood-strewn beach and ocean." *(David Maher)*

Open All year.

Rooms 4 cabins, 4 suites, 6 doubles—all with private bath and/or shower, clock/radio. 5 with whirlpool tub, fireplace, balcony, wet bar, microwave.

Facilities Breakfast room with fireplace, living room with fireplace; game room with TV/VCR, refrigerator, microwave; bar/lounge with TV; deck. 1½ acres with organic gardens, gazebo, picnic area, private beach access. Hiking, bicycling, creek and ocean for fishing, white-water kayaking, swimming nearby.

Location S end of town, on Hwy. 1.

Restrictions No smoking. Children 12 and over.

Credit cards Amex, Discover, MC, Visa.

Rates B&B, $228–298 suite; $88–198 double; $88–188 single. Extra person, $30. 2–3-night weekend/holiday minimum. 10% midweek, off-season, AAA, senior discount. Midweek winter specials.

Extras Limited wheelchair access. Spanish, French, Italian, some German spoken.

Harbor House—Inn by the Sea ✕ Tel: 707–877–3203
5600 South Highway 1, P.O. Box 369, 95432

Certainly no one would want to miss seeing a redwood forest on a trip to California, and a visit to the Craftsman-style Harbor House will give you a chance to see what a house built entirely of virgin redwood is like. As is the case with several other homes in the area, the Harbor House was originally built as an executive residence and guest house by a local lumber company. Now owned by Dean and Helen Turner, the inn has a footpath winding down the bluff to the beach below.

The innkeepers raise many of the inn's vegetables, and the rest of its food is purchased from local sources. Breakfast, served from 8:30 to 9:30 A.M., might include pears cooked in wine, eggs du bois, banana sesame bread, and freshly ground coffee or tea, while the dinner menu might entice you with Tuscan country bread and scallop bisque with julienned leeks and carrots; garden greens with citrus vinaigrette, roast chicken with polenta with gorgonzola, red pepper pesto, baby string beans, and roasted beets; concluded with cheese torta with strawberries in cassis.

"Set on a bluff with a breathtaking location overlooking the Pacific." *(Mary Steiss)* "Gracious, cordial owners; pleasant accommodations; gracious dining overlooking the water." *(Susan Schwemm)* "The guests are warm and friendly, the staff unobtrusive and professional." *(Mary Eleanor Haenggi)* "From our table in the dining room, we watched the waves crash against the giant rocks in the harbor. The Mountain View Room is on the land side of the inn, but is a large and lovely room with a stall shower painted with a meadow scene. The wonderful staff went out of their way to be helpful; the chef prepared a separate vegetarian dinner for us." *(Gail de Sciose)* "Delicious food, cordial owners. Beautiful gardens, secluded beach. Great views of the wind-and-water carved rocks." *(Betsy Immergut)*

Open All year.
Rooms 10 doubles, including 4 cottages—all with private bath and/or shower. 9 with fireplace, 5 with sun deck.
Facilities Dining room, living room with games, piano, guitar, record collection. 5 acres with extensive gardens, path to private beach. Fishing, tennis, golf, hiking, canoeing, white-water kayaking, galleries, wineries nearby.
Location North Coast. At N edge of Elk village.
Restrictions No smoking. Not recommended for children under 14. Minimal traffic noise; quiet after 10 P.M.
Credit cards None accepted.
Rates MAP, $185–275 double, $143–238 single. Extra person, $45. 2-night weekend minimum if Sat. included. Prix fixe dinner by reservation only, $26.

Sandpiper House Inn　　　　　　　　　　　　*Tel:* 707–877–3587
5520 South Highway 1, P.O. Box 149, 95432　　　　　800–894–9016
　　　　　　　　　　　　　　Fax: 707–937–2649 (call ahead)

Claire and Richard Melrose describe their inn as having a "serene location at the edge of rugged bluffs above Greenwood Cove, with magnificent views of off-shore rock formations, wave-hewn tunnels, and the Pacific. A cottage garden surrounds the house and continues to the edge of the cliffs, where a series of walkways and steps lead to a deck and down to a private beach in the cove below." The inn was built in 1916 by the Goodyear Redwood Lumber Company, and has been owned by the Melroses since 1987. Breakfast favorites include lemon pancakes with raspberry sauce, or an egg and cheese puff with sausage. Highlighted by ornate redwood paneling, the rooms are furnished with antiques, and beds are topped with down comforters.

"Exceptional breakfasts, myriad multicolored flowers, the warm glow of the fire on chilly evenings, a bouquet of roses at your bedside table, and falling asleep to the gentle sound of the sea." *(Carol Glen)* "Warm, inviting common areas, with wood-paneled walls and beamed ceilings. Guest rooms are spotless, thoughtfully equipped with fresh flowers, wine, and excellent lighting. At breakfast, guests are seated around a single large table, or at tables for two. We had orange-peach juice; then pureed strawberries with bananas, topped with a cinnamon sugar wafer; followed by baked Finnish pancakes, topped with apples sauteed in rum and accompanied by chicken-apple sausage. Claire uses low-calorie, low-cholesterol ingredients, though you would never know it. Afternoon tea is available with a variety of teas and homemade ginger cookies and lemon bars; homemade spiced pecans and sherry were also available. Exceptional hospitality." *(Linda Goldberg)* "Love the quiet charm of the garden with its playful cat." *(Emily & Paul Smith)* "Not a detail is overlooked in the Evergreen room, from the fine linens and luxurious towels to the discretely hidden refrigerator and the complimentary wine from a local vineyard. Home-baked cake or cookies are served on beautiful china." *(Leo Battaglia)*

Open All year.
Rooms 5 doubles—all with private bath and/or shower, with desk, refrigerator. 3 with fireplace, 2 with patio/balcony, 1 with double soaking tub.
Facilities Dining room, living room with fireplace, books; porch, deck. ½ acre with private beach. In house massage therapy by appointment.
Location In village center.
Restrictions No smoking. Not suitable for children under 12.
Credit cards Amex, Discover, MC, Visa.
Rates B&B, $120–225 double, $110–215 single. Extra person, $20. 2–3 night weekend/holiday minimum.

EUREKA

Visitors come to Eureka, still a major lumbering center and fishing port, to wander through its restored Old Town—once home to the area's many lumber barons—hike in the area's parks and forests, explore area beaches, and fish in Humboldt Bay. Eureka is located on the North Coast (Redwood Country), 250 miles (5 hours) north of San Francisco. To reach Eureka from the north or south, take Highway 101; from the east, follow Route 299 to 101. The town is laid out in a grid, with the numbered streets running north/south, parallel to the water, and the lettered streets running east/west.

   Information please: A Greek Revival home built in 1871 of virgin Redwood and Douglas fir, the **Old Town B&B Inn** (1521 Third Street, 95501; 707–445–3951 or 800–331–5098) has six guest rooms, most with private bath. A full breakfast, different each morning, is included in the $65–130 rates; dietary needs are accommodated with pleasure. "Friendly owners, Diane and Leigh Benson; generous, filling breakfast; good housekeeping and maintenance. The two guest rooms which share a bath are spacious and attractive, an excellent value." *(Sharon Bielski)*

Abigail's Elegant Victorian Mansion B&B   *Tel:* 707–444–3144
1406 C Street, 95501   *Fax:* 707–442–5594

This meticulously restored Queen Anne–influenced, Eastlake Victorian inn was built in 1888 for Eureka mayor and county commissioner William S. Clark. A National Historic Landmark, the inn has been owned by Doug and Lily Vieyra since 1989, who have made it into a showcase of authentic High Victorian decor. Doug describes the inn as a "living history house-museum of the Victorian experience." Rates include a "French gourmet" breakfast and a "horseless carriage" ride through town.

"Fascinating, authentic Victorian decor. Freshly squeezed orange juice, mango juice, and a wonderfully light almond cake began our breakfast." *(Jesse Ortel)* "Exceptional from the laundry service to the Belgian chocolate truffles, from the grand parlors to the elegant gourmet breakfast." *(Troy Sustarson)* "We had three bathrooms to choose from down the hall; bathrobes, thirsty towels, soaps and shampoo, hair dryer, were all supplied. One bathroom had a sauna and a shower for two; another had an old-fashioned tub. Doug and Lily joined us at breakfast to stimulate conversation—we started quietly, but had a hard time leaving the table. They also gave us a tour of the house, made sure that we knew where everything was, provided us with information about Eureka, and then left us to our wanderings." *(Nancy Male)*

"My immaculate bedroom had an antique bed with a firm queen-size mattress, two bedside reading lights, overstuffed chairs, and a desk. Our afternoon croquet game was followed by tea and delicious scones. Breakfast included fresh-ground coffee, Austrian apple strudel, eggs Benedict, fruit, and freshly baked muffins." *(Cindy Jansen)* "Doug and Lily provided us with a selection of menus from local restaurants and helped us make an excellent choice." *(Bernard & Catherine Bishop)* "Secure garaged parking protected our bicycles." *(Bill & Gail Smithman)* "The inn is in a modest residential district, a 10–12 block walk to restaurants." *(Heather Allen)* "Well-kept Victorian gardens." *(Lola & Philip Sherlock)* "Extensive collection of classic movies, plus a wide variety of reading material. Ample information on sightseeing and local restaurants." *(Virginia Sril)*

Open All year.
Rooms 1 suite, 3 doubles—1 with private bath, 3 sharing 3 baths. All with desk, air-conditioning.
Facilities Dining room, breakfast room with fireplace, living room with fireplace, books, TV/VCR, stereo; parlors, masseuse service, laundry service. Evening movies, chamber music weekly. Gazebo, Victorian flower garden, croquet, sauna, bicycles. Off-street garage parking. Tennis, health club nearby.
Location From Hwy. 101, go E on C St. to inn at 14th St.
Restrictions No smoking. No children under 15.
Credit cards MC, Visa.
Rates B&B, $125–165 suite, $95–135 double, $69–90 single. Midweek, off-season rate. Extra person in suite, $35.
Extras Station pickup; airport pickup, $15. Dutch, French, German spoken.

The Carter House Victorians ✕
301 L Street, 95501

Tel: 707–444–8062
800–404–1390
Fax: 707–444–8067
E-mail: Carter52@carterhouse.com

Long owned by Mark and Christ Carter, the Carter House Victorians is comprised of three Victorian buildings: the old Hotel Carter built in 1906; the original Carter House, a reproduction Victorian mansion built in 1982; and The Bell Cottage, a turn-of-the-century home built in 1996. Each is decorated with rich fabrics, antiques, and original local art; some have marble fireplaces and whirlpools with views of the marina; most have queen-size beds. Rooms at the Hotel Carter have country French pine antiques with Tuscan accents; those at Carter House have both Victorian accents; accommodations at Bell Cottage are furnished with European antiques. Open daily for dinner, Restaurant 301 in the Hotel Carter showcases herbs, greens, and vegetables from the inn's extensive gardens, as well as local delicacies. A recent menu included such entrees as tiger prawns with garlic, lemon and herbs; vegetable timbale with mushroom and cheese filling, pesto sauce and couscous; and grilled, marinated rack of lamb. Its wine list has been recognized for excellence by the *The Wine Spectator.*

"Mark and Christi and their staff were warm and attentive. The entire facility—from guest rooms to common areas—was beautifully maintained." *(Heidi Marie Claasen)* "Our room was lovely, the staff helpful and cordial; dinner at Restaurant 301 was impeccable." *(Ellen C. Larsen)* "Peaceful and relaxing." *(Kaye Ann Gallagher)* "Delightful stay, outstanding restaurant." *(Debbie King)* "Mark is enthusiastic and hospitable. He conducted us and other guests on a tour of the hotel, inn, garden and greenhouse. We had a delightful time with the other guests gathered around the wine and hors d'oeuvres; at 9 P.M., everyone returns for tea and cookies." *(Eileen O'Reilly)* "The food was healthy, hearty, homemade, and beautifully presented. The hotel's atmosphere was welcoming and comfortable, with classical music playing softly in the background, art and flowers set strategically around the rooms, and the fireplace burning." *(BA)*

Open All year.
Rooms 32 suites & doubles—all with full private bath, telephone, radio, TV, desk. Suites with double Jacuzzi, double shower, CD stereo, fireplace, mini-bar. Rooms in 3 buildings.
Facilities Restaurant, lobby with fireplace; wine shop. 3 parlors, 2 stocked guest kitchens. Charter fishing nearby.
Location N border of Old Town. From S, follow Hwy 101 through town; becomes 5th Street. Follow 5th for 13 blocks to L St. Turn left, go 2 blocks.
Restrictions No smoking in guest rooms. Street noise in some street-level rooms.
Credit cards Amex, CB, DC, Discover, MC, Visa.
Rates B&B, $145–290 suite, $105–175 double. Extra person, $20. Family, senior discounts; corporate rate midweek. Alc dinner, $35.
Extras Wheelchair access; elevator; 1 room equipped for disabled. Crib. Spanish spoken.

The Daly Inn
1125 H Street, 95501

Tel: 707–445–3638
800–321–9656
Fax: 707–444–3636
E-mail: dalyinn@humboldt1.com

This lovely white Colonial Revival home was built in 1905 by Cornelius Daly for his wife Annie and their five children. The Daly brothers owned and operated department stores throughout the North Coast of California for over a century. Restored as a B&B in 1990 by Sue and Gene Clinesmith, rooms are decorated with period antiques, from the French oak bedroom suite in the Annie Murphey room, to the English walnut antiques and Victorian reproduction wallpaper of the Garden View suite. Rooms have either twin or queen-size beds.

Served 8–9 A.M., breakfast can be enjoyed in the elegant dining room by the fireplace in cold weather, in the sunlit breakfast parlor, or on the garden patio. A typical menu includes a fruit juice smoothie, berry muffins, poached pears with raspberry puree and creme fraiche, vegetable quiche, and chicken and apple sausage. Wine and hors d'oeuvres are served at 5:30 P.M., and might include locally made wine and cheese, with fruit, crackers, and dip.

"Superbly decorated and immaculately kept, plenty of parking; quiet and peaceful. The innkeepers are wonderful and the food is fabulous." *(Karen Carroll)* "I love to curl up with a book in the window seat in the sunny breakfast room; breakfast favorite is the noodle kugel." *(Muriel Guzzi)* "Perfect for the business traveler, with creative and delicious breakfasts, and a lovely yard for sitting and doing paperwork. Sue keeps up with local activities, and is a gracious hostess." *(Diane McNall)* "Outstanding period decor. Just like having your own lovely Victorian home—without the work!" *(Mary Ann Thurmond)* "Warm and comfortable atmosphere in an opulent setting. Superb quality throughout." *(BI)*

Open All year.
Rooms 2 suites, 3 doubles—3 with full private bath, 2 with maximum of 4 people sharing bath. All with clock/radio. 1 with fireplace.
Facilities Dining room, breakfast parlor, living room, library—all with fireplaces; library with TV/VCR, video library, games. Guest refrigerator, laundry; porches. ½ acre with patio, off-street parking, lawn games, gardens, fish pond.
Location Historic residential neighborhood; walking distance to Old Town. Take Hwy. 101 to H St. & go E.
Restrictions No smoking. Children 12 and over.
Credit cards Amex, DC, Discover, MC, Visa.
Rates B&B, $120–150 suite, $100–125 double. Extra person, $20.

A Weaver's Inn ¢
1440 B Street, 95501

Tel: 707–443–8119
800–992–8119
Fax: 707–443–7923
E-mail: weavrinn@humboldt1.com

From time to time, we get letters from readers who sing an inn's praises, noting that "the only bad part about our stay was leaving." Lea Montgomery, a frequent guest of the Weaver's Inn solved that problem in

1997 by buying the inn, and becoming its full-time innkeeper, assisted by her mother and adult daughter, bringing three generations together. Lea also works with families who have children with special needs, and helps her daughter operate her own silk-screen business.

Built as a Queen Anne in 1883 and remodeled in 1907 with Colonial Revival elements, original 19th century elements include the faux graining in the entrance hall, wallpaper in one bedroom, and the oversize windows of hand-rolled glass brought around the Horn. Guest rooms have antique furnishings, down comforters, and fresh flowers. Breakfast is served between 8 and 10 A.M. at a time established by guest consensus. The menu varies daily, but might include white grape juice; fruit compote with mint marinade; chili cheese bake with fresh salsa, sour cream and tortillas, and corn muffins.

"The Pamela Suite includes a bedroom with queen-size bed, plus a sitting room with sofa bed and fireplace. Lovely antiques, linens, and fresh flowers throughout; careful attention to detail." (Barbara & David Engen) "Fresh and lovely furnishings, from the carefully selected throw pillows to the Oriental rugs. A croquet course was already set up, and the porch was an inviting spot for a glass of wine while we watched our kids play. Creative, delicious and healthy breakfasts served on fine china, with a convivial atmosphere around the dining table. A quiet neighborhood, so we could sleep with the windows wide open." (Dean & Kathi Johnson) "Attractive wood-panelled bathroom with a quaint but very effective shower." (Charles Walton) "Perfectly maintained, with a period decor. Fresh berries from Lea's garden highlighted our tasty breakfast. Good variety in the menu, too." (John & Marjie Washburn) "Loved sitting on the back porch in the crisp morning air, looking over the park-like garden. Our daughter loved the friendly outdoor pets. Yummy treats at bedtime." (Jennifer Walton) "Best of all was the friendly, interesting innkeeper, Lea, who was genuinely concerned for our comfort." (Janet Moos)

Open All year.
Rooms 1 suite, 3 doubles—2 with private bath and/or shower, 2 with maximum of 4 people sharing bath. All with radio, clock. 1 with desk, 2 with fireplace, 1 with double soaking tub.
Facilities Dining room, parlor with fireplace. Flower gardens, croquet. Limited off-street parking. Tennis, golf, fishing nearby.
Location 1 m from downtown. From Hwy. 101 take 14th St. or B St. to inn between 14th & 15th Sts.
Restrictions No smoking inside.
Credit cards Amex, DC, Discover, MC, Visa.
Rates $110 suite, $65–105 double, $55–95 single. Extra person, $20. $15, Children under 12. 10% service. Government, corporate, AARP rates.
Extras Airport/station pickup, $15. Pets by arrangement, $15.

FAWNSKIN

For additional area inns, see **Big Bear Lake.**

Windy Point Inn   *Tel:* 909–866–2746
39015 North Shore Drive, P.O. Box 375, 92333   *Fax:* 909–866–1593

When asked what we look for in a first-rate B&B, we typically reply with these criteria: location, hospitality, and comfort. The Windy Point Inn gets top marks on all three. First is its extraordinary location right on Windy Point, overlooking the lake, framed by mature pine trees and bordered by sandy beaches. Second is the warm and gracious hospitality extended by longtime innkeepers Val and Kent Kessler. Last are the exceedingly comfortable, well-equipped guest rooms. An award-winning custom design by David Zimmerman, the inn was built in 1990 and is owned by Denise Zimmerman; two luxury suites were added in 1997. Breakfast is served between 8 and 10:15A.M.; each room is served separately, with eggs Benedict, French toast with sauteed apples, and ginger pancakes with lemon sauce, among the favorite entrees. Rates also include afternoon hors d'oeuvres.

"A private, romantic escape in a breath-taking setting. The living room offers incredible views of the lake, complemented by tasteful carpeting and furnishings in shades of gray, soaring ceilings, wonderful modern architecture, and a beautiful assortment of paintings and sculpture from around the world. Val offered us hot drinks, and Kent helped with the bags. The Peaks, the master suite, is the ultimate in luxury. Every light was controlled by rheostat, enabling us to create the precise mood we desired. There was even one for the light illuminating a 200-year-old Ponderosa pine outside. Tall windows offered dramatic views of lake, mountain, and pine trees. We could see the stars through the skylight over our king-size bed, and listened to soft mellow music on the CD player. Only moonlight and the glow of the wood-burning fireplace illuminated our room as we drifted off to sleep. We awoke to a brilliant sunrise, birds singing in the pines outside our windows. I lounged in the Jacuzzi tub, enjoying the dramatic lake views. Breakfast was served privately in the cozy breakfast area, and was tailored to our dietary needs. Val and Kent were extremely warm and hospitable innkeepers, available when needed, but never intrusive. They were most helpful with advice about local ski areas and shared insightful local information. They told us about the adjacent preserve for bald eagles, and we were delighted to see one flying overhead. We were also able to see the smallest room, The Sands, which was equally elegant and comfortable." *(Gail Davis)* "Val and Kent are incredibly gracious hosts. Fresh-baked cookies in the afternoon and lovely homemade hors d'oeuvres in the evening." *(Janet Emery)*

Open All year.
Rooms 3 suites, 2 doubles—all with private shower/tub, clock/radio, VCR, ceiling fan, wood-burning fireplace, refrigerator, deck. 4 with whirlpool tub.
Facilities Living/dining area with CD player, books, videos, fireplace, grand piano; deck. ½ acre with off-street parking, hot tub, private boat dock, fishing. 15 min. to skiing, 5 min. to hiking.
Location San Bernadino Mts., approx. 100 m E of Los Angeles. From LA, take I-10 E to Redlands & take Exit for Hwy. 30/330. Continue 3 m to Hwy. 330, &

exit at Mt. Resort, Big Bear Lake exit. Go up mountain to lake. At dam, continue straight following signs to Fawnskin. Go 2.2 miles on to inn on right.
Restrictions No smoking. Children 5 and over preferred.
Credit cards Amex, Discover, MC, Visa.
Rates B&B, $185–225 suite, $125–165 double, $95–155 single. 2–3 night weekend/holiday minimum.

FERNDALE

Thought by many to be California's best-preserved Victorian village, the entire village of Ferndale is registered as a State Historic Landmark. The town has more than its share of pretty Victorian homes, originally called "butterfat palaces," since their owners made their money in the dairy industry. At the midpoint of Redwood Country, set off the tourist trail, Ferndale is a perfect town for an overnight stay. Although activities are planned year-round, a special effort is made for Christmas, highlighted (literally) by a 125-foot spruce, decorated with over 9,000 lights. Be sure to stop in at any shop for a free walking-tour brochure. Ferndale is located in the North Coast region (Redwood Country), 260 miles north of San Francisco, 15 miles south of Eureka, and five miles from Highway 101.

Reader tips: "During the late spring, Ferndale's rhododendrons are in bloom; each home seems to have huge bushes of gorgeous flowers." *(Erika Holm)* "Bibo's restaurant was superb." *(Margaret Sievers)* "Ferndale is lovely. We were pleased with our dinner at Curley's, with several vegetarian choices." *(Gail de Sciose)* "Be sure to visit Golden Gate Mercantile on Main Street, a fascinating old-time general store complete with every ointment and liniment that our grandparents used. Also unusual is the Museum of Kinetic Sculpture, home to several dozen vehicles, raced once a year. Entertaining for all ages." *(Christopher Hart Johnston, also Julie Phillips)* "A delightful array of Victorian buildings, well worth a detour. We took the long loop off Highway 101 on Highway 211 through Honeydew. Wild views and adventurous road, but fill up the gas tank before leaving 101." *(Carol Moritz)*

Information please: Built of redwood in 1854 by the founder of Ferndale, the **Shaw House Inn** (703 Main Street, P.O. Box 1125, 95536; 707–786–9958) is a gabled Carpenter Gothic house with elaborate gingerbread trim. Longtime owners Norma and Ken Bessingpass have furnished it with art, antiques, books, and memorabilia. B&B double rates for the six guest rooms, each with private bath, range from $75–135. "Charming home, convenient to historic downtown. We enjoyed a breakfast of Dutch pancakes at the lovely dining room table. Our first floor had a private porch overlooking the lovely gardens." *(BJ Hensley)*

If you prefer a small hotel setting, consider the **Victorian Inn** (400 Ocean Avenue, 95536; 707–786–4949 or 800–576–5949), in the heart of historic Ferndale. Built in 1890 as the town bank, it now offers a full service restaurant, open for lunch and dinner, plus twelve guest rooms, furnished with down comforters, oversized towels, and some antiques. B&B double rates range from $75–125, and include a full breakfast; children are welcome.

The Gingerbread Mansion *Tel:* 707–786–4000
400 Berding Street, P.O. Box 40, 95536 800–952–4136
Fax: 707–786–4381
E-mail: Kenn@humboldt1.com

Within seconds of your first glimpse of the Gingerbread Mansion, you'll know why longtime owner-innkeeper Ken Torbert chose that name and why this is the most photographed Victorian in northern California! Rates include breakfasts of fresh fruit and juice, local cheeses, homemade granola, just-baked coffee bundt cake, nut breads, and muffins, plus a daily entree, perhaps eggs Benedict with Hollandaise and baked polenta, plus afternoon tea and turndown service. Breakfast is served from 8 to 9:30 A.M.; guests are asked to request a seating time the night before.

"The Fountain Suite was spotless and well-equipped; the bathroom had side-by-side clawfoot tubs, a gas fireplace, and was equipped with ample towels and amenities. At 7:00 A.M., the innkeepers set up coffee and tea for early risers. During breakfast, the housekeeping staff makes the beds, replenishes towels, and opens the shutters in the guest rooms. Afternoon tea included such goodies as rum balls, petit fours, fresh fruit, chocolates, and more. The breakfast entree was stuffed cinnamon raisin French toast one day, a ham and egg soufflé the next." *(Julie Phillips)* "An immaculately detailed inn with elegant Victorian style. Ample common areas; one parlor had a table set up with a puzzle in progress. Breakfast consisted of fluffy, light pancakes served with real maple syrup; a wonderful apple, cinnamon, and raisin compote; and an assortment of sliced fresh fruit, local cheeses, and warm cranberry muffins." *(Joan Merrill)*

"The Heron Suite was beautifully done in dark wood and various shades of green, with a separate sitting room and a comfortable queen-size bed. Exquisite touches include the antique lamps, old photographs, and such thoughtful amenities as comfortable robes, bathroom night-lights, and magnifying mirrors. Delicious food and coffee at breakfast; the chef modified the menu for our vegetarian diet." *(Gail de Sciose)* "Lovely formal Victorian gardens." *(Gordon Green)* "This ornate gingerbread mansion is located off the main street in a quiet, well-lit residential neighborhood close to the well-preserved historic downtown area." *(Patrick & Gloria Smith)* "The Rose Suite has a fantastic mirrored bathroom, complete with an enormous claw-foot tub and shower." *(Jan & Barry Olsen)* "On a stroll through town you may pass a candy shop where you can watch the workers hand-dip chocolates; at night, you'll find these same delicious chocolates by your pillow." *(Erika Holm)* "Tea and bottled water always available in the kitchen." *(Barbara Ruppert)*

Open All year.
Rooms 5 suites, 5 doubles—all with private bath and/or shower. 4 with gas fireplace. Some with desk, twin claw-foot tubs.
Facilities 4 parlors with 2 fireplaces and library, dining room, porches. Guest pantry. Formal English gardens, fountain. Ocean, river, wilderness park nearby.
Location Take Ferndale exit off Hwy. 101, 5 m to Main St. Turn left at Bank of America; 1 block to inn.
Restrictions No smoking. Children over 10 preferred.
Credit cards Amex, MC, Visa.
Rates B&B, $150–350 suite, $140–180 double, $140–160 single. Extra person, $40. 2-night holiday/weekend minimum.

FISH CAMP

Thirty-five miles south of Yosemite Valley, Fish Camp sits just outside the southern entrance to Yosemite National Park on Route 41, one of three park access roads open year-round. A few miles north is one of the finest giant sequoia groves in the Sierras, the Mariposa Grove, with the Grizzly Giant (with a diameter of 30 feet) and the tunneled California Tree, so large that a car could drive through.

Also recommended: Just two miles from Yosemite's South entrance is the **Tenaya Lodge** (1122 Highway 41, P.O. Box 159, 93623; 209–683–6555 or 800–635–5807), a 242-room hotel with a full range of resort activities, including three restaurants, a children's program, fitness center, swimming pools, and more. Double rates range from $69–239, with lowest rates available midweek, off-season; ask about special promotions and AAA rates. "Great location, near the park, but with modern touches some of the park rooms lack. Ask for a room that's been refurnished recently." *(RH)*

Information please: Readers are delighted with the dinners at **The Narrow Gauge Inn** (48571 Highway 41, Fish Camp 93623; 209–683–7720), a 26-room motel combining western-style architecture with Victorian decor, most of the latter obtained from the now-defunct Pony Express Museum; double rates from $85–130. "We ate in the restaurant every night, enjoying the well prepared food, the friendly service, and the views of the moonlight on the mountains through the large windows." *(Carol Dinmore)* "Our room was furnished in "basic motel" but the view of the Sierra National Forest from our balcony made up for it. The nicely landscaped grounds and swimming pool provided an inviting setting. Not to be missed is a ride on the Narrow Gauge Railroad through the forest into the canyon." *(Glenn Roehrig)*

The **Apple Tree Inn** (1110 Highway 41, P.O. Box 41, 93623; 209–683–5111) a collection of six 50-year-old cottages, was closed for renovation when we went to press with this edition. Recommended by many readers for its comfort, privacy, and charming setting in the Sierra National Forest, current reports are requested.

FORT BRAGG

Located on the North Coast, Fort Bragg is eight miles north of Mendocino and approximately 160 miles northwest of San Francisco. The town's best-known tourist attraction is the scenic "Skunk Train" through the redwood forest to Willits; its name came from the smell of its original gas-powered engines. Also of interest in Fort Bragg are the miles of trails in the Mendocino Coast Botanical Gardens, where flowers frame ocean views nearly year-round; and in March, the Whale Festival, celebrating the migration of the California grey whale. Other activities include fishing and whale watching trips, horseback rides on the beach, and even a repertory theater company. Several of its B&Bs are on Main Street (Highway One), so expect *significant* traffic noise in front rooms; some B&Bs have rooms with ocean views, but it's a distant one—there's an industrial area between the residential section and the water.

Reader tips: "Fort Bragg is an honest working town, complete with a Georgia Pacific sawmill in its center. Be sure to follow the Noyo River road and explore the harbor, complete with seals, working fishing boats, funky shops, and casual waterside restaurants." *(SWS)* "Fort Bragg has nooks and crannies to explore, including a neighborhood of 1903s shingled arts-and-crafts style homes. Many Mendocino galleries have moved here due to lower rents." *(CB)* "The Wharf restaurant is a great place to view the boats coming in and out of the harbor." *(Carol Moritz)*

Also recommended: A short block from the main drag, the **Avalon House** (561 Stewart Street, 95437; 707–964–5555 or 800–964–5556) is a restored 1905 Craftsman home, carefully sound-proofed, with modern bathrooms and antique decor. Anne Sorrells is the longtime owner. "Quiet, convenient location, just a block from Highway One. Handsome house with blue-green shingles, attractively landscaped. While all the rooms are pleasant, the best room is the Yellow Room, with a canopy bed made from willow tree branches, good reading lights, a gas fireplace, a double whirlpool bath right in the room, and a large deck looking out to the ocean in the distance." *(SWS, also KLO)* B&B double rates for the six guest rooms range from $70–135.

Information please: Overlooking the harbor is the **Lodge at Noyo River** (500 Casa del Noyo Drive, 95437; 707–964–8045 or 800–628–1126). B&B rates for the 17 rooms are $95–150, with the most expensive accommodations offering water views, fireplaces, soaking tubs and private decks. Weather permitting, breakfast and the evening social hour are offered on the sheltered decks overlooking the river. "Terrific location, down by the river, far from the highway, with great views of the river, harbor, boats, and lots of seals and sea lions. Quiet, private, and relaxing; close to ramshackle galleries, fishing shacks, and seafood places along the water. When we visited, the furnishings appeared to need sprucing up, so ask if any redecorating has been done recently. Apparently a staff-run inn." *(SWS)*

For additional area inns, see **Little River, Mendocino**, and for an affordable country escape, see **Westport**.

The Grey Whale Inn ¢ ♿   *Tel:* 707–964–0640
615 North Main Street, 95437   800–382–7244
                                     Fax: 707–964–4408
                         E-mail: gwhale@mcn.org

The Grey Whale Inn, a Mendocino Coast landmark since 1915, has been handsomely restored by longtime owners John and Colette Bailey. Once the town hospital, it now looks as though it has always been an inn, and is furnished with pleasantly eclectic decor, featuring country quilts, antiques, local art, and reproductions. The breakfast buffet changes daily and includes such favorite as Greek frittata, zucchini pie, or poached eggs and spinach with Hollandaise sauce, plus fresh fruit and juices, hot and cold cereals, home-baked coffee cakes, toasting bread, sliced cheeses, homemade jams, house-blend coffee, teas, and hot chocolate.

"Guest rooms, hallways, and common areas are exceptionally spacious at the Grey Whale, allowing guests a degree of privacy unknown at many other inns. Built as a hospital, the only remaining clue to the inn's origins are the ramps which lead from floor to floor, making the inn especially welcoming to the disabled. Colette is a warm and caring innkeeper, knowledgeable about Fort Bragg and area activities." *(SWS, also Julie Phillips)*

"The hallways and entrance are decorated with fine prints, paintings, and old photographs of logging days and of the great whales. Helpful, candid, guest critique book of local restaurants." *(Donald Hook)* "Coffee is ready at 7 A.M., and breakfast is served buffet-style from 7:30 to 10 A.M. Four tables await guests, but you can easily take breakfast to your room. After breakfast, we walked along the cliffs and down the walking path. Colette is knowledgeable about area activities and the inn's history. The Sunrise Suite features a king-size bed with hand-embroidered pillows and a matching quilt, comfortable chairs for reading, a table and chairs, an armoire, and a space heater for chilly fog-bound evenings, and ample bedside reading lights. The bathroom has a huge whirlpool tub and separate shower. Large windows look out onto a private deck with patio furniture and views of town and the ocean. Although slightly smaller, the Sunset is also popular because of its ocean views and dramatic sunset vistas." *(Matthew Joyce)* "Colette assisted me with local contacts, and made me a special low-cholesterol breakfast each morning." *(Thomas Layton)*

Open All year.
Rooms 14 suites, doubles—all with private bath and/or shower, telephone, clock radio. 10 with TV; 3 with fireplace; 1 with whirlpool tub. 3 with balcony or patio.
Facilities Parlor, breakfast room, lounge with fireplace, guest refrigerator, recreation room with pool table, conference room, TV/VCR room, fax/copier. Garden, lawns. 4 blocks to ocean.
Location North Coast. On Hwy. 1.

Restrictions Street noise in some rooms might disturb light sleepers. No smoking. "Facilities for children very limited."
Credit cards Amex, Discover, JCB, MC, Visa.
Rates B&B, $95–190 suite, double, $75–175 single. Extra person, $25. 2–4 night weekend/holiday minimum. Winter midweek rate. Corporate rate.
Extras Wheelchair access; 1 room equipped for disabled. Building has ramps throughout. German, Spanish spoken.

GARBERVILLE

Also recommended: Just ten minutes south of the Avenue of the Giants, the **Benbow Inn** (445 Lake Benbow Drive, 95542; 707–923–2124 or 800–355–3301) is a longtime reader favorite, and a National Historic Landmark. Double rates of $115–215 for the 55 guest rooms include in-room coffee and sherry, afternoon tea and scones, and evening hors d'oeuvres. "A real find near the Avenue of the Giants. Rooms in the main inn feel like you are back in the Old West. Lobby full of puzzles and games. Restaurant terrific both for dinner and breakfast and very good value." *(Frank Reeder)* "Tudor-style 1920s hotel, with period charm and modern conveniences. Superb setting along the Eel River and Benbow Lake, excellent meals, inviting lobby with a welcoming fireplace, lots of puzzles and games." *(Diane Bean)* "Enchanting cottage, accommodating staff. A truly special place." *(Dianne Crawford)*

GEYSERVILLE

People go to the Sonoma Valley to explore the area wineries, visit the Russian River resorts, and enjoy the area's inns and restaurants. In general, the pace here is quieter and slower than in the neighboring Napa Valley.

Geyserville is located in the North Coast region, in the center of Sonoma County Wine Country, Alexander, and Dry Creek Valleys. It's 75 miles north of San Francisco and eight miles north of Healdsburg.

Information please: Two historic houses, just across the street from each other, the **Hope-Bosworth House** and **Hope-Merrill House** (21238 & 21253 Geyserville Avenue, P.O. Box 42, 95441; 707–857–3356 or 800–825–4BED), are a Queen Anne–style and an Eastlake Stick–style Victorian home, decorated with period furnishings, Bradbury & Bradbury wallpapers, and antique light fixtures. All 12 guest rooms have queen-size beds and private baths (three with whirlpool tub), and the double rate of $111–147 includes a full country breakfast. The inn was purchased in 1997 by Ron and Cosette Scheiber.

Campbell Ranch Inn 🏃
1475 Canyon Road, 95441

Tel: 707–857–3476
800–959–3878
Fax: 707–857–3239

Located in the heart of the Sonoma County wine country, the Campbell Ranch Inn is a large, comfortable home, set on a hilltop surrounded by gardens, terrace, and deck. The rooms all have comfortable king-size beds, quality linens, fresh fruit and flowers.

"Especially comfortable beds in the spacious, private guest rooms. Ample common areas, both for quiet reading or watching the huge TV. Easy highway access, yet a completely quiet setting." *(Sue Lippman)* "Highlights include the splendid panoramas, the music of the frogs, the flowers, the comfort, and the delicious food. Pleasant fellow guests. Mary Jane and Jerry are superb innkeepers—organized, hard-working, and capable, with genuine warmth and humor." *(Bob Davis)* "Terrific facilities, from tennis to bicycles. The helpful hosts have a telephone set up to speed dial favorite local restaurants. The Campbells also have a wonderful dog who makes you feel as if you are the most important person in the world. Soft and luxurious linens; wonderful scenery overlooking the vineyards." *(Lydia Terrill)* "The fireplace was ready to light; a basket of fresh fruit and assorted beverages were at our fingertips. Our spacious cottage had a spectacular view of the vineyards. After dinner, enjoyed dessert with our hosts; Mary Jane had baked delicious peach pie and chocolate cake." *(Betsy Buckwald)*

"Breakfast includes a choice of fruits and cereals, omelets, fried eggs, or an egg puff with chilies or mushrooms, plus homemade jam, muffins and breads, served at guests' convenience from 8–10 A.M." *(Phyllis & Walt Reichle)* "The second-story bedrooms have balconies, and the tree-shaded terrace is equally inviting." *(Stephen & Judy Gray)* "The good-sized rooms are quiet and well-insulated, with good temperature control. Great recommendations for touring, restaurants, and local wineries. Breakfasts are outstanding, with such treats as homemade salsa and raspberry jam. The breakfast table is set for ten; guests may eat together or take their food to individual tables on the deck or around the pool. My favorite rooms were #4 for privacy and #2 for the larger bathroom and the views." *(SHW)*

Open All year.
Rooms 1 2-bedroom cottage, 4 doubles—all with private bath and/or shower, air-conditioning. Cottage with cassette player, fireplace, hot tub on deck; 4 with desk, balcony.
Facilities Living room with fireplace, family room with fireplace, games, TV/VCR; dining room, terrace. 35 acres with flower gardens, heated swimming pool, hot tub, tennis court, aviary. Ping-Pong, horseshoes, bicycles, model trains. 3 m to Lake Sonoma for boating, swimming, fishing; 3 m to Russian River for fishing, canoeing.
Location 2 m from town. Take Canyon Rd. exit off Hwy. 101, go 1.6 m W to inn.
Restrictions No smoking. Young children not encouraged.
Credit cards Amex, MC, Visa.
Rates B&B, $225 cottage, $100–145 double, $90–135 single. Extra person, $25. 2–3 night weekend/holiday minimum.
Extras Local airport/station pickup.

GLEN ELLEN

A quiet base for tours of the Sonoma and Napa Valleys, Glen Ellen's main claim to fame—other than its vineyards and wineries—is the Jack

London State Historic Park, comprising the author's home and ranch, with a museum of his papers, personal belongings, and mementos. Its 800 acres also offer ample opportunities for walking, hiking, and riding. Glen Ellen is located in the Wine Country area of the North Coast, 55 miles north of San Francisco and 15 minutes north of Sonoma. From San Francisco, take Highway 101 north. Before Novato, take Highway 37 to Highway 121 toward Sonoma. Then take Highway 116 for a short distance and go right (north) on Arnold Drive to Glen Ellen.

Gaige House　　　　　　　　　　　　　*Tel:* 707–935–0237
13540 Arnold Drive, 95442　　　　　　　　　800–935–0237
　　　　　　　　　　　　　　　　　　　Fax: 707–935–6411
　　　　　　　　　　　　　E-mail: gaige@sprynet.com

Set in a wooded hamlet convenient for wine touring, Gaige House Inn is an 1890 Queen Anne/Italianate style building. Restored as an inn in 1980, it was purchased and refurbished by Ken Burnet and Greg Nemrow in 1996. The inn's decor is a stylish, subdued mix of plantation, Victorian and Polo style—no frilly lace curtains or teacup collections here! Chef Diane Peck prepares breakfasts of freshly-squeezed orange juice, and such entrees as crispy cornmeal waffles with fruit compote and lemon chicken sausage; creole eggs in spicy tomato sauce with turkey andouille sausage; chocolate chip pancakes with banana compote and turkey bacon; or spinach and feta cheese frittata with skillet potatoes, served to guests at their individual table. Local wine is poured in the evening, and complimentary cookies, fruit, and drinks are always available.

"We honeymooned in the idyllic Gaige Suite, with a soothing ivory and taupe color scheme, a twelve-foot ceiling, three walls of windows, king-size lace canopy bed, private deck, and huge whirlpool tub. Amazing scones at breakfast. Beautifully kept grounds with flowering trees and gardens. The staff are friendly, helpful, and professional." (*Camille Gage*) "Ken, Greg, and Sue were extremely warm, friendly, and eager to make sure that everything was perfect—and it was." (*Pat & Chuck Irek*) "Guest rooms are spacious and distinctive, with king- or queen-size beds; common areas are comfortable and inviting. The backyard has an inviting pool and well-shaded hammocks. Super breakfasts. You could park your car on arrival and never leave except to try one of the excellent restaurants nearby." (*Michael Dautel*) "I enjoyed reading the *New York Times* over a cup of delicious Peet's brand coffee before breakfast. Diane was kind enough to share her delicious recipes. Ideal location, away from the tourist crush but convenient to all the sights. The inn is super clean, extra quiet, and handsomely decorated. Cordial and warm hosts." (*Lynn & Bernard Grossman*)

Open All year.
Rooms 1 suite, 10 doubles—all with private bath and/or shower, telephone, radio, clock, air-conditioning. Some with desk, ceiling-fan. 7 with balcony/deck; 5 with fireplace, 2 with whirlpool tub. 3 rooms in carriage house. TV on request.
Facilities Parlor with fireplace, books; TV/game room; guest refreshment room; breakfast room; sun deck. 1¼ acres with lawns, garden, heated swimming pool, picnic deck overlooking creek, hammock, off-street parking.

CALIFORNIA

Location 45 m from Golden Gate Bridge. 6 m from Sonoma Plaza. From San Francisco, take Rte. 101 N to Rte. 37. Take Rte. 121; follow road as it turns into Rte. 116. Take Arnold Drive/Glen Ellen Exit off Rte. 116. Follow road approx. 10 m into Glen Ellen. Inn is 0.3 m from center of town on left.
Restrictions No smoking. Children over 12. Stairs required for most rooms. Two rooms face road.
Credit cards Amex, Discover, MC, Visa.
Rates B&B, $230–255 suite, $155–225 double. Extra person, $25. 2-night weekend minimum April–Oct. Winter specials usually available.

Glenelly Inn 👫
5131 Warm Springs Road, 95442

Tel: 707–996–6720
Fax: 707–996–5227

This southern-style house, encircled by verandas on both the first and second floors, was built as an inn in 1916; in those days guests arrived via the Southern Pacific Railroad. Completely renovated in 1985, it has been owned since 1990 by Kristi Hallamore and her husband Carl Jeppesen. Their young children Karl Christian and Frederick Hans welcome well-behaved children to the inn, where they can enjoy the kid-friendly play area. Orange tom cat Mungojerrie and calico cat Nutmeg are also on the guest greeting committee. Guest rooms open to a veranda or deck, and all have Scandinavian down comforters and terrycloth robes; most have queen-size beds and clawfoot tubs with showers. Guests enjoy relaxing on the verandas, and in the extensive gardens with benches for quiet times under the fruit trees. Breakfast always includes freshly squeezed orange juice, followed by fruit compote, leek-chevre tart, and strawberry bread; or perhaps baked bananas, nutmeg muffins, and quiche Florentine. The common room cookie jar is always filled with sugar or chocolate chip cookies; lemonade, iced tea, and hot beverages are always available.

"The grounds are lovely and each room opens to the veranda with chairs and tables. Kristi was helpful about local restaurants; menus are available in the common room." *(Nancy Cohn)* "The cozy little Glen Ellen room has an amusing selection of hats hanging on some antlers. An 'I forgot it' basket of toiletries was thoughtfully provided. Enjoyed the hot tub and the refrigerator stocked with iced tea and lemonade. Tasty breakfast of baked bananas, lemon-yogurt muffins, and Mexican salsa soufflé." *(Karl Wiegers & Chris Zambito)* "Our peaceful room had a garden view and was charmingly furnished with a wicker settee, small rocker, queen-size brass bed, an old oak washstand as a dresser and an antique armoire as a closet." *(Lynne Derry)* "Guests gather in the common room to enjoy wine, cheese and crackers, or sherry and tea; the buffet breakfast is also served here." *(Eileen O'Reilly)* "Kristi is friendly yet not intrusive. Our super breakfast included melon, fig walnut bread, smoked chicken and apple sausage, and peach raspberry cobbler with vanilla yogurt. Each guest room has a private outside entrance, lamps on both sides of the bed, luggage racks, thick white towels, and bathrobes. " *(Susan W. Schwemm)*

Open All year.
Rooms 3 suites, 5 doubles—all with full private bath, ceiling fan, balcony, private entrance. 2 with fireplace. 2 rooms in annex.

Facilities Common room with dining area, fireplace, books, games, verandas; children's play area; guest refrigerator. 1 acre with Jacuzzi, fruit trees, rose gardens. Golf, tennis, hot-air ballooning, wineries nearby.

Location 2 blocks from center. Go N on Arnold Rd., then turn left at Warm Springs Rd. to inn ½ m on right.

Restrictions No smoking. Children welcome by prior arrangement. Daytime traffic noise in some rooms.

Credit cards MC, Visa.

Rates B&B, $150 suite, $115–125 double. 2-night holiday/weekend minimum. 10% discount for 4-night stay. Off-season discount.

Extras Norwegian spoken.

GRASS VALLEY

Once the richest gold-mining town in the state, Grass Valley is located in the heart of the Gold Country, 60 miles northeast of Sacramento, and five miles south of Nevada City. Be sure to visit Empire Mine State Historic Park, with restored mine buildings, a look into the mines, and miles of hiking trails.

Information please: For a taste of old California, visit the **Holbrooke** (212 W. Main, 95945; 916–273–1353 or 800–933–7077) established in 1851. The hotel offers the Golden Gate Saloon, a restaurant, and 28 guest rooms. The B&B double rate of $55–106 includes a light continental buffet breakfast. "Great Western atmosphere in the saloon; guest rooms contrast period antiques and reproductions with original brick walls and flowered wallpapers." *(SWS)* Reports needed.

The **Peacock Inn** (439 South Auburn Street, 95945; 916–477–2179) is a petite Queen Anne Victorian built in 1866, and charmingly restored as a B&B in 1994 by Tom and Nancy McCoy. B&B double rates for the four guest rooms, each with private bath, range from $75–95, including a full breakfast and evening refreshments. Guests can relax on the front porch swing or read under the apple tree on the brick patio in the backyard while listening to the water fountain.

Elam Briggs B&B
220 Colfax Avenue, 95945

*Tel:*916–477–0906

When prosperous merchant Elam Biggs built a Queen Anne–style home for his family in 1892, he claimed that it was "the most modern and scientific of its time." Restored by Peter and Barbara Franchino in 1995, guests appreciate the modern conveniences we now take for granted, as well as the old-fashioned charms inngoers enjoy, from antique furnishings to home-cooked food. Breakfast, served 9–10 A.M. at the dining room table, includes fresh fruit and juice, home-baked muffins and breads, and such entrees as strawberry French toast, baked eggs with cheese and chili peppers, and Dutch Baby pancakes.

"The spacious Victorian-style rooms were decorated with beautiful antiques, quilted bed coverings, pillows, and charming collectibles. Convenient parking, lovely side yard." *(Greg Klein)* "Barbara and Peter were gracious hosts who made us feel as though we were visiting friends. Spotlessly clean; tasty breakfasts." *(Bob & Patty Tams)* "Warm, family feeling; the Franchinos were there to answer questions but were never intrusive." *(James Paul)* "Quiet rooms; no sounds from the other guests or plumbing." *(Vee Ward)* "Impeccable housekeeping; charming decor. Delicious breakfasts, different each morning, enhanced by Barbara and Peter's wonderful stories. The inn is surrounded by shade trees and a rose-covered picket fence. A short stroll to historic downtown, and convenient to area explorations." *(Linda & Kirk Ridgeway)*

Open All year.
Rooms 5 doubles—all with full private bath, clock/radio, desk, air-conditioning, fan.
Facilities Dining room, living room with books, guest kitchen, porch, guest refrigerator. Books available in common area. Parlor magic for evening entertainment. ¼ acre with off-street parking. Golf, tennis nearby.
Location 4 blocks to Main St. From Hwy. 49, take Colfax Hwy. Exit/Rte. 174. Go straight; at 2nd stop sign, go right to inn, 1½ blocks on left.
Restrictions No smoking.
Credit cards MC, Visa.
Rates B&B, $75–110 double, $70–105 single. Extra person, $20.

Murphy's Inn
318 Neal Street, Grass Valley 95945

Tel: 916–273–6873
800–895–2488

At Murphy's Inn, the first thing you'll notice is the ivy. Thick "columns" of ivy accent the veranda, punctuated by hanging ivy topiary baskets. Sketches of the building from 1882 show the same plantings in an earlier stage of growth. Built in 1866 as the home of Edward Coleman, gold-baron owner of the North Star and Idaho mines, the inn has been owned by Ted and Nancy Daus since 1995, assisted by longtime innkeeper Linda Jones. Rooms are furnished with pine, oak, and mahogany antiques. Breakfast is served at individual tables, and might include eggs Benedict, country French toast or Belgian waffles with sausage, plus muffins and coffee cake.

"Spotlessly clean, well-decorated, and cozy, with Victorian decor and modern comfort. Parking is adequate, the location quiet, and the breakfast excellent." *(Kathleen Thurman, also Julie Phillips)* "Gracious innkeeper. The comfortable parlor is done in mauve tones, with period furnishings. The breakfast room has attractively set tables. Soft drinks are available, as are homemade chocolate chip cookies. Most guest rooms have queen- or king-size beds, antique furnishings, and floral wallpapers, with good bedside lighting. Cozy Karina's Room is a good value, with a skylight, white wicker chairs and headboard, and floral accents, while the Hanson Suite in the Donation Day House has more space, including an appealing bathroom with an antique vanity and a tiled double shower." *(Linda Goldberg)*

Open All year.
Rooms 3 suites, 4 doubles—all with private shower and/or bath, TV. 3 suites with queen-size sofas, air-conditioning. 4 with fireplace or gas stove; 1 with refrigerator and stove.
Facilities Breakfast room, 2 parlors, veranda, deck. Golf, fishing, swimming nearby. Off-street parking.

Location 2 blocks from center. From Hwy. 20/49, take Colfax 174 exit. Left on S Auburn, left on Neal.
Restrictions No smoking. Children by arrangement.
Credit cards Amex, MC, Visa.
Rates B&B, $95–145 suite; $75–100 double. Extra person, $20. 2-night weekend/holiday minimum.

GROVELAND

The Groveland Hotel ¢ ✕ ♿
18767 Main Street, P.O. Box 289, 95321

Tel: 209–962–4000
800–273–3314
Fax: 209–962–6674
E-mail: peggy@groveland.com

Groveland, once known as Savage's Diggings, experienced two building booms, one with the Gold Rush and a second when the Hetch Hetchy Valley to the east was dammed to create a reservoir for the city of San Francisco. Now a popular stop en route to Yosemite, the town has a historic main street that reflects these important periods in its existence. The Groveland Hotel was built of adobe (with walls 18 inches thick) in 1849, and its 1914 wood-frame annex was constructed with Queen Anne styling. Owner Peggy Mosley restored the inn in 1992. The guest rooms have coordinating floral fabrics and wallpapers, antique beds (most queen-size or twins), down comforters and robes. Lyle's Room is a favorite of guests, not just because of its decor, but because of its resident ghost, the eponymous Lyle, a gold prospector who died (of natural causes) in this room in 1927.

Rates include continental breakfast, with brunch offered on Sundays. The restaurant features seasonal California cuisine, with such seafood and pasta favorites as mushroom and black pepper linguine in cheddar sauce, or mahi mahi with pineapples in black bean sauce.

"Friendly, helpful innkeepers; charming rooms with teddy bears on the beds." *(Alexa Parliyan)* "Our spotless room was decorated with period furniture, with an individual thermostat. Groveland is also home to California's oldest saloon, the Iron Door—great old-west atmosphere." *(E.R. Taft)* "Good location, with Yosemite close by and several restaurants within walking distance." *(Steve Talton)* "Friendly owners and staff, excellent restaurant." *(Burma Workman)* "Fine attention to detail, from the large, fluffy towels and bathrobes to the extra thick curtains to darken the rooms." *(Jean Wobbe)*

Open All year.
Rooms 3 suites, 14 doubles—all with private bath and/or shower, telephone, radio, air-conditioning, ceiling fan, balcony. TV on request. Suites with fireplace, Jacuzzi. 13 rooms in annex.
Facilities Restaurant/saloon with weekend entertainment, parlor with fireplace, laundry, porch, deck. Conference facilities, fitness center. ½ acre, hot tub, gazebo, courtyard. Mt. Lake, Tuolumne River for water sports & rafting; golf nearby.
Location High Sierras, 145 m E of San Francisco Bay area, 23 m W of Yosemite Park, on Rte. 120.
Restrictions Traffic noise in front rooms. No smoking.

Credit cards Most major credit cards.
Rates B&B, $175 suite; $95–115 double. Extra person, $25. MAP, full board rates. Golf package. Alc dinner, $25.
Extras Limited wheelchair access. Free Pine Mt. Lake Airport pickup. Pets by arrangement. Crib.

GUALALA

Pronounced "wa-*la*-la" (in case you were wondering), the unusual name of this town is derived, some people think, from an Indian word meaning "water coming down place"; others think the name originated with the early German and Spanish settlers, who may have thought this area resembled heaven, or Valhalla.

Gualala is located in the Mendocino area of California's North Coast, three hours north of San Francisco and two hours west of the Napa Valley. To reach Gualala, take Highway 101 to Petaluma and proceed west through Two Rock and Valley Ford to Bodega Bay. Follow Highway 1 north to Gualala.

The "banana belt" climate here is mild and mostly free of coastal fog. Golf, tennis, hiking, fishing, swimming, and diving are all popular activities. For more information on area attractions, please see the chapter introduction.

Reader tips: "Great area for R&R, but not if you want to be constantly on the go. Many art galleries in the area, most open Thursday through Monday." *(AR)* And: "Despite rave reviews, we were disappointed in our dinner at St. Orres. Great atmosphere, pretentious service, so-so food at high prices. Another night we ate at the Top of the Cliff restaurant. Utilitarian atmosphere, but excellent service and great food. Expensive but a wonderful meal." *(RV, also DB)* "Had a fabulous lunch at Oceansong, next door to The Breakers Inn." *(Carol Moritz)*

Also recommended: One of the area's most elegant—and expensive—inns, the **Whale Watch Inn** (35100 Highway 1, 95445; 707–884–3667 or 800–WHALE–42) is located on the water side of the highway, and is composed of five contemporary wooden buildings containing 18 luxurious guest rooms, most with spectacular ocean views. B&B double rates range from $170–265, including a full breakfast; the inn is owned by Jim and Kazuko Popplewell. Readers are delighted with the comfortable, airy rooms; dramatic ocean views and sounds of the crashing surf below; excellent housekeeping and maintenance; and private, romantic atmosphere. *Note:* This inn has not responded to any of our requests for information since 1992, so we felt that a full writeup would no longer be appropriate; it was however, a winner of the America's Favorite Inns awards in 1997.

Information please: Listed in many past editions, we need current reports on the **St. Orres** (36601 South Highway 1, P.O. Box 523, 95445; 707–884–3303 or 707–884–3335). Marked by the influence of Russian settlers, the inn's onion-dome architecture is unusual. The main building houses the inn's well-known restaurant and eight guest rooms (with shared baths); the remaining accommodations are in ten cottages scattered throughout the property and hidden in the redwood forest. Although all offer access to the sun deck, sauna, and hot tub, the simplest cottage has a woodstove and an outdoor hot-water shower; the most luxurious has a fireplace, full bath, and wet bar. Rates are $60–270.

North Coast Country Inn
34591 South Highway 1, 95445

Tel: 707–884–4537
800–959–4537

The North Coast Country Inn is composed of several weathered buildings set on a redwood-forested hillside, and has been owned by Loren and Nancy Flanagan since 1984. In 1997, the Flanagans expanded the inn, adding a common room in which guests can enjoy breakfast and afternoon sherry, as well as two wood-paneled penthouse rooms, with high ceilings, picture windows, fireplaces, whirlpool tubs, king-size beds, and private decks.

"Guest rooms are large, clean, and comfortable, with country antiques, braided rugs, handmade quilts, and unusual pictures and books. Private decks allow for quiet afternoons of reading and relaxing. Attractive landscaping with lots of flowers." *(Alice Boyer & Jim Martin)* "The Gallery room has a four-poster queen-size bed with handmade quilt. French doors open from a private deck into a fresh, bright sitting room/bedroom with a fireplace and mini-kitchen. A short walk through the trees along a softly lit path leads to a private open-air hot tub; the sound of barking sea lions drifts through the redwoods." *(Ginny Anderson)* "My favorite rooms are the Aquitaine Room with its French antiques and Oriental rugs, and the Quilt Room, with its country flavor. Nearly all the guest rooms have high, exposed beam ceilings." *(Linda Goldberg)* "Careful attention to detail, from the well-stocked kitchen, to the large closet with two luggage racks and ample hangers, to the extra heaters in the bedroom." *(Emmett & Carol Cooke)* "Nancy and Loren are attentive while respecting guests' privacy." *(Mark Steisel)* "Well-equipped room; wonderful sense of privacy. Excellent breakfast of sliced oranges with cinnamon, baked eggs, cinnamon rolls, and coffee, served right on time. Inn cats Sam and Sally were friendly, but knew their boundaries." *(Karl Wiegers & Chris Zambito)*

Open All year.
Rooms 6 doubles—all with private shower, fireplace, deck, kitchenette. 1 with skylight. 2 with double whirlpool tub.
Facilities Common room with fireplace, TV/VCR, books, games. Antique shop. 1 acre with garden, gazebo, hot tub, picnic table.
Location 4 m N of Gualala on Hwy 1. at Fish Rock Rd. ¼m N of Anchor Bay.
Restrictions No smoking. No children under 13.
Credit cards Amex, MC, Visa.
Rates B&B, $135–175 double. 2–3 night weekend, holiday minimum.
Extras Local airport pickup.

GUERNEVILLE

Guerneville is located in Sonoma County, 1½ hours north of San Francisco. From Highway 101 go north to Guerneville/River Road exit, then go west to town.

For an additional area inn, see **Occidental.**

Applewood Inn and Restaurant ✗   *Tel:* 707–869–9093
13555 Highway 116, Pocket Canyon Area, 95446   800–555–8509
                                           Fax: 707–869–9170
                         E-mail: stay@applewoodinn.com

Built in Guerneville's glory days in the 1920s, Applewood was bought by Darryl Notter and Jim Caron in 1985 and transformed into an elegant, yet comfortable inn. Before a roaring fire in the river-rock fireplace, guests sink into the down-filled cushions of the living room chairs and couches, or gather in the verdant solarium. Served from 9–10 A.M., a typical breakfast might include Grand Marnier French toast with strawberries, bacon or sausages, orange juice and dark French roast coffee. Rates also include a sunset wine hour, and evening turndown service with chocolates. Six guest rooms are in the historic Belden House, with seven luxurious suites in the Mission-style carriage house, built in 1996.

Dinner alone is worth the trip, with a set menu and a choice of three entrees. Menus change daily, and recent ones included linguine with vodka and herb sauce, Bibb lettuce salad with balsamic Roquefort dressing, salmon with mustard dill glaze, and apple walnut cream tarts; or shrimp and fennel risotto, corn and tomato salad, grilled pork chops, wasabi mashed potatoes, and lemon buttermilk tart.

"Romantic getaway. Peaceful setting in the redwoods, yet equally convenient to the Sonoma coast and to Wine Country. Fabulous dinners. Although the new suites are luxurious, we love the charm of the old manor." *(Shawnee Scharen)* "Careful attention to detail: roses in our room, fine chocolates at night, newspaper at our breakfast table." *(Pam & Steve Levine)* "After an early dip in the swimming pool, Jim brought us Mimosas, coffee, and the morning paper. Terrific breakfasts of eggs Florentine, local berries, and fresh-baked bread. Wonderful dinners, especially the baked salmon with tomato and basil beurre blanc, and a strawberry cream cake with brandy sabayon." *(Melissa Hultgruen)* "Wonderful hillside setting; well-maintained grounds. The inn is immaculate, and service is friendly, efficient and professional. The atmosphere is quiet and private." *(H. Leon Anderson)*

Open All year. Restaurant open Tues.–Sat.
Rooms 16 doubles—all with private bath, telephone, TV. Some with desk, private entrance, patio or balcony. 7 rooms in carriage house with air-conditioning, fireplace; 2 with jacuzzi.
Facilities Dining room, living room with fireplace, library, solarium with fireplace, stereo, breakfast room. 6 acres with redwood groves, vineyard, heated

swimming pool, hot tub, herb/vegetable gardens. Tennis, golf, horseback riding nearby. Fishing, canoeing in Russian River nearby.

Location North Coast, Sonoma wine country. In town, turn left on Rte. 116 & continue to inn.

Restrictions No smoking. No children.

Credit cards Amex, Discover, MC, Visa.

Rates B&B, $125–225 double. 2–3 night weekend/holiday minimum. Prix fixe dinner, $30–40.

Extras Wheelchair access; rooms equipped for the disabled. Local airport pickup.

GILROY

Information please: About 25 miles south of San Jose and east of Santa Cruz is the **Country Rose Inn** (455 Fitzgerald Avenue #E, San Martin 95046; mailing address, P.O. Box 1804, Gilroy, 95021-1804; 408–842–0441), close to Gilroy, the "Garlic Capitol of the U.S." A renovated 1920s Dutch Colonial home set in a grove of eucalyptus, oak, and pine, the guest rooms have a rose motif extending from the fresh flowers to the decor, and are comfortably furnished with some antiques and family memorabilia. A typical breakfast includes orange juice, baked apple pancake, fresh fruit, and cream biscuits. B&B double rates for the five guest rooms range from $129–189. "Although the locale is OK, innkeeper Rose Hernandez makes this a special place. She spoils her guests with delicious breakfasts, beautiful furnishings, fresh flowers, bath gels, and all the right touches." *(Pam Haddad)*

HALF MOON BAY

Less than an hour south of San Francisco, this 50-mile section of coast—from Half Moon Bay to Santa Cruz—is rarely visited by travelers rushing down to Monterey and Carmel. Towns here still retain much of their character as sleepy fishing villages, but people are beginning to discover the area's nine state beaches (horseback riding is allowed at some), elephant seals (at Ano Nuevo), and whale-watching tours. Bicyclists will enjoy following the horse trail for miles along the bluffs to Moss Beach. Half Moon Bay—called the Cape Cod of California by some—is located in the San Francisco Bay Area, 28 miles south of San Francisco. Take Highway 1 south, or Highway 280 to Highway 92 west to Half Moon Bay.

Reader tip: "Exceptional meal, reasonably priced at the Chateau des Fleurs." *(Tom Wilbanks)*

Information please: Just completed in 1997 is the **Beach House Inn** (4100 North Cabrillo Highway, P.O. Box 129, 94019; 650–712–0220 or 800–315–9366), overlooking the Pacific at Pillar Point Harbor, three miles from Half Moon Bay. A three-story Nantucket-style shingled hotel, it has 54 waterview lofts, each with king-size bed, wood-burning fireplace, wet bar or kitchenette, stereo, two TVs, and four phones with data ports, king-size bed, queen-size sleeper sofa, and bath with soaking tubs and double sinks. Guests can swim in the lap pool, relax in the hot tub, and walk on the beach. B&B double rates of $145–245 include continental breakfast and afternoon wine tasting.

If you love flowers and country Victorian decor, you'll be delighted with the **Mill Rose Inn** (615 Mill Street, 94019; 650–726–9794 or 800–900–ROSE), set among extensive rose gardens. B&B double rates for the six guest rooms range from $165–285, including a full breakfast brought to your room or enjoyed in the dining room; afternoon wine, hors d'oeuvres, and desserts; and evening turndown service with chocolates. Rooms are decorated with French and English antiques, floral motifs, and have king- or queen-sized beds, fireplaces, TV/VCRs, and stocked refrigerators. "Owner Terry Baldwin couldn't have been nicer or more helpful. Our charming room had many Victorian collectibles to enjoy." *(Tom Wilbanks)*

For additional area inns, see **Moss Beach, Montara,** and **San Gregorio**.

Cypress Inn on Miramar Beach   ♿   *Tel:* 650–726–6002
407 Mirada Road, 94019   In CA: 800–83–BEACH
                                       Fax: 650–712–0380
                E-mail: lodging@cypressinn.com

Set right on Miramar Beach, each individually decorated room at the Cypress Inn (built in 1989) has a deck with ocean view. The California Spanish–style decor features Mexican tiled floors, counters and showers; wicker and scrubbed wood furnishings with wonderful colors; whimsical Mexican carved animals and primitive paintings; and king-, queen-, or twin-size beds. The Beach House was added in 1996, with four rooms, each named for a local beach; most luxurious is Dunes Beach, with a terrific view, large deck, and an in-room whirlpool tub in front of the fireplace. Breakfast entrees include omelets with Brie and roasted red peppers, Belgian waffles, or peaches and cream French toast, accompanied by fresh fruit and homemade breads, plus afternoon tea, wine, and hors d'oeuvres.

"The inn is situated across the street from the ocean with undisturbed views. Sturdy construction with beautiful thick, exposed beams. The main house has a ground-floor living room with a high ceiling and comfortable seating around the fireplace. One third-floor room has windows running along the entire ocean-view side, with a queen-size bed, and a comfortable couch. The understated decor features a relaxing color scheme of beige and cream which effectively complements the wonderful view. The adjacent building has delightful murals painted throughout, including brightly painted underwater scenes." *(Abby Humphrey)* "Our spectacular room in the Beach House had a king-size bed, Jacuzzi, fireplace, little balcony and limited water view. Lovely spread at cocktail hour; phenomenal breakfast. The manager, Leigh, is a charming gentleman and was most helpful." *(Norma and Bob Simon)*

"Situated right on the Pacific, with unparalleled ocean views. We stayed in La Luna, on the first floor, with a tiled floor (with cozy radiant heating). Shuttered walls of windows face the ocean, with a clever latch that allows one to leave the shuttered glass door open just a crack to let in the sound and smell of the ocean, while retaining security and temperature. The inn is more modern and less frilly than many we've visited, a distinction I appreciate." *(Randy Delucchi)* "The sound of sea and surf put you at ease the moment you arrive. The fireplace is perfect for foggy days. Each room is painted a soft warm color to go with its Spanish name. The living room has an open-beam ceiling and giant skylight. Clean, uncluttered, and quiet." *(Matt Joyce)* "Our favorite activity was taking long walks on the beach." *(Marion Richardson)*

Open All year.
Rooms 1 penthouse suite, 11 doubles—all with private full bath, telephone, radio, desk, gas fireplace, deck. Some with whirlpool tub, TV; 1 with refrigerator. 4 rooms in Beach House with double whirlpool tub, gas fireplace, stereo, TV/VCR.
Facilities Dining room, living room with fireplace, laundry, masseuse. Water sports, whale watching, horseback riding, golf, wine tasting nearby.
Location From Hwy. 1, turn toward ocean on Medio St. Inn is on left.
Restrictions No smoking. 2 people per room.
Credit cards Amex, MC, Visa.
Rates B&B, $275 suite, $165–195 double. AAA discount.
Extras Wheelchair access; some bathrooms specially equipped.

Old Thyme Inn
779 Main Street, 94019

Tel: 650–726–1616
Fax: 650–726–6394
E-mail: oldthyme@coastside.net

The Old Thyme Inn is a Queen Anne home built in 1899 of redwood and hauled to this location by oxen; in 1986, it was completely renovated as a B&B, and was purchased by George and Marcia Dempsey in 1992. A typical breakfast might include fresh-squeezed orange juice, fresh fruit, yogurt, and such baked treats as lemon-thyme pound cake, frittata, or croissants baked with cheese and turkey.

"This meticulously kept inn is right in the heart of this pristine seaside town, a short drive and half a world away from San Francisco. The cozy rooms are furnished with well-cared-for wooden furniture, flowered wallpapers and fabrics. Our room had a queen-size bed with a firm mattress and four huge pillows; the bathroom had a gorgeous polished wooden floor and clawfoot bathtub. Breakfast is served at an antique table; couches and overstuffed armchairs invite guests to curl up with a cup of tea and a novel. George recommended a wonderful Italian restaurant for dinner which we would never have found on our own." *(Karl Sikkenga)*

"The well-maintained rooms (each with a resident teddy bear) vary considerably in size, and a few have the bathtub in the bedroom. The smaller rooms are cozy in feeling and are an excellent value, while the larger rooms, each with a fireplace, hardwood floors, and antique armoire and dressing table are elegant and comfortable. All rooms have freshly cut flowers, sherry, and lace curtains." *(MJ)* "We were greeted warmly and assisted with dinner reservations. Sherry, wine, and snacks were served in the early evening. Delicious bagels, scones, crumpets, muffins at breakfast." *(James & Elizabeth Smith)* "The honeymoon suite is lovely, with a canopy bed and sitting area all done in soft rose and cream." *(Irene Kolbisen)* "George gave me a tour of his herb garden and gave me a few cuttings to take home. The beach, interesting shops, and good restaurants nearby." *(Ruth Moran)* "Tasty homemade buttermilk-raisin scones and strawberries." *(Robert Nguyen)*

Open All year.
Rooms 1 suite, 6 doubles—all with full private bath. 3 with whirlpool bath, fireplace, 1 with refrigerator, TV/VCR, tape deck.
Facilities Living/breakfast room; herb garden. Video library.
Location Inn is 6 blocks S of Hwy. 92, 4 blocks E of Hwy. 1. 1 m from ocean.
Restrictions No smoking.
Credit cards Amex, MC, Visa.
Rates B&B, $165–220 suite, $75–150 double. 2-night holiday weekend minimum.
Extras French, Spanish spoken.

HANFORD

Information please: Four impeccably restored, turn-of-the century Victorian homes and surrounding tree-shaded lawns create the **Irwin Street Inn** (522 North Irwin Street, 93230; 209–583–8000 or 888–583–8080). Featuring leaded glass, gabled roofs, wood detailing, and period artifacts, each of the 30 guest rooms have a private bath, telephone, TV, and balcony, providing business travelers with old-fashioned charm and modern conveniences. B&B double rates range from $69–92, including breakfast. The inn's restaurant is open for lunch and dinner, and specializes in seafood. Hanford is located 30 miles south of Fresno.

HEALDSBURG

Taking a break from the serious business of wine tasting, visitors to Healdsburg enjoy swimming, fishing, boating, and canoeing in the Russian River and Lake Sonoma, plus hot-air ballooning, hiking, bicycling, tennis, and golf. Five wine-tasting rooms are right in town, with 50 more within an easy drive.

Located in the Sonoma Valley, along the Russian River Wine Road in California's North Coast region, Healdsburg is 70 miles north of San Francisco, and 13 miles north of Santa Rosa, on Highway 101.

Reader tips: "In the past decade Healdsburg has gone from a sleepy little nothing to a real destination with wonderful wineries and restaurants, yet is still relatively undiscovered. Room rates are relatively reasonable, too." *(Katherine Owen, also SWS)*

Camellia Inn ¢ &.
211 North Street, 95448

Tel: 707–433–8182
800–727–8182
Fax: 707–433–8130
E-mail: info@camelliainn.com

Ray and Del Lewand opened this B&B in 1981 after a careful restoration of their 1869 Italianate Victorian home. Antiques and Oriental rugs complemented by soft shades of salmon and peach create a warm and soothing atmosphere. The Lewands also own an inn in Puerto Vallarta, Mexico; in the winter, you may find them there, while their daughter Lucy hosts guests in California. Rates include a buffet breakfast, served 8:30–10 A.M. at the dining room table, plus afternoon refreshments.

"The inn is painted a lovely shade of soft apricot, surrounded by camellia trees—all blooming when I visited. Inside, the double parlors are warm and inviting, a lovely place for guests to relax. Lucy is a delightful innkeeper, warm and friendly, sensitive to guests' needs." *(SWS)* "Ray graciously hosted the wine and cheese hour; he put everyone at their ease and we were soon talking freely of our wine country experiences. We were delighted with the wonderfully light and airy Memento room with a queen-size brass bed. The buffet breakfast was ample and tasty. A thoughtful touch is the refrigerator on the back porch for guests to use to chill wine and store picnic supplies." *(Jim & Mary White)* "Impeccable housekeeping and maintenance; warm, hospitable, well-informed innkeepers; handsome decor." *(Jan & Fred Thrasher)*

"The Royalty Room had a huge, comfortable maple tester bed from a castle in Scotland." *(Caroline & Jim Lloyd)* "Our room had antique lamps and fixtures, fresh flowers, and a bathroom which was once a sunporch. Breakfasts include homemade jams and preserves, excellent sourdough bread for toasting, fresh fruit, yogurt, granola, cereals, juice, and a main dish, such as quiche or huevos rancheros. Complimentary beverages, cheese, and crackers are served in the early evening at the pool; the Lewands really know how to bring people together for informal conversation." *(Maria Castrulla)* "Quiet neighborhood, with colorful grounds. Our hosts were friendly, helpful, and knowledgeable about the wine industry." *(Ruth & Joe Cochrane)* "The inn is within walking distance of six or seven wine tasting rooms—no need to be concerned about designating drivers." *(DCB)* "The pool is a real plus on a 95° August day." *(Brooke Abercrombie)*

Open All year.
Rooms 9 doubles—all with private bath and/or shower, air-conditioning. Some with gas fireplace, whirlpool tub for 2, ceiling fan, private entrance.
Facilities Double parlor with 2 fireplaces, books, games; dining room; guest refrigerator. ½ acre with 50 varieties of camellias, swimming pool. Off-street parking.
Location 2 blocks from main plaza. Exit Hwy. 101N at central Healdsburg exit. Go N for 4 lights, turn right on North St. Go 2½ blocks to inn on left; parking in rear.
Restrictions No smoking. Infants and children over 10 preferred.
Credit cards Amex, MC, Visa.

Rates B&B, $75–145 double. 2-night weekend/holiday minimum.
Extras Public rooms have wheelchair access; 1 guest room equipped for disabled.

George Alexander House ¢
423 Matheson Street, 95448

Tel: 707–433–1358
800–310–1358
Fax: 707–433–1367

Readers are always delighted to discover a smaller B&B like the George Alexander House, owned by Phyllis and Christian Baldenhofer, that offers high-quality accommodations with the personal touch found only at an owner-operated inn. This exuberantly ornamented 1905 Victorian home, which was built for the son of the area's first settler, has been furnished with antiques and custom-made furniture, accented by stained glass and quatrefoil windows. Phyllis and Christian bought the inn in 1991, and describe themselves as "San Francisco expatriates, with past experience in the coffee roasting business." Guests report that the inn's best features include the interesting collections of art and Oriental rugs, the comfortable beds, the tasty breakfasts and quality coffee, the relaxing atmosphere, and the convenient location.

"Guest room decor varies from lovely antiques to soothing contemporary, but all are extremely well-equipped and mercifully uncluttered. The inviting parlor at the front of the house is beautifully done in Eastlake Victorian pieces." *(SWS)* "Beautifully renovated with lovely stained glass windows. Great location, an easy walk to restaurants, wine tasting, and antique stores. Our delightful room had two reading lights, plus two comfy easy chairs with their own lamps. Even the parlor has ample comfy chairs and sofas with good lighting. The innkeeper keeps a small fridge in the kitchen stocked with various bottled waters; there's an electric teakettle on the counter, a cupboard of teas to choose from, and a tempting lemon poppy seed bundt cake waiting on the counter for afternoon or evening snacks. Congenial breakfast of tasty polenta with scrambled eggs, served at 9 A.M." *(Kathleen Owen)* "Our room, the Back Porch, had a private entrance, a large sitting area, a wood-burning stove, a wonderful bathroom with a double Jacuzzi, and a ceramic tile floor with radiant heating." *(Randy Delucchi)* "Just the right classical music in the background, plenty of books on the shelves and comfortable places to sit." *(Steve & Juel Craig)* "The inn's smallest room, the darling Butler's Room, has a comfortable queen-size bed and is a great value." *(MW)*

Open All year.
Rooms 4 doubles—all with private bath and/or shower, air-conditioning. 2 with fireplace/wood-burning stove, 1 with Jacuzzi, deck.
Facilities 2 parlors (1 with fireplace), dining room, guest refrigerator, porch. Laundry privileges. Patio, gardens, off-street parking. Near Russian River for water sports.
Location 3 blocks from town center. From Healdsburg Ave. drive 3 blocks east on Matheson to inn on left.
Restrictions No smoking.
Credit cards MC, Visa.

Rates B&B, $80–170 double, $70–160 single. No tipping. Babies free. 2-night weekend/holiday minimum.
Extras Local airport/station pickup. Crib; babysitting by arrangement.

Grape Leaf Inn
539 Johnson Street, 95448

Tel: 707–433–8140
Fax: 707–433–3140
E-mail: sweet@sonic.net

A Queen Anne Victorian home built in 1900, the Grape Leaf Inn has been owned since 1981 by Karen and Terry Sweet. Named after different varieties of grapes, guest rooms are furnished with period antiques; those on the first floor have high ceilings and old-fashioned charm; those on the second are tucked under the eaves with skylight roof windows. Each evening, the Sweets hold a wine-tasting from 5–7 P.M., with a minimum of six wines, plus locally made cheese and bread. Breakfasts include vegetable and cheese frittatas, blueberry-pecan pancakes, or cinnamon raisin-walnut French toast, plus home-baked breads and muffins, with fresh fruit.

"Great location on a quiet, tree-lined street. Karen always has a smile for her guests. Returning guests are treated like family, and newcomers are welcomed equally warmly. At the evening social hour, everyone talked about the great wines they had tasted that day. On Saturday night, the owner of a local winery came to the inn and led us through a tasting of his wines. As we tried each one, he explained what made it special. Karen's breakfasts were different each day—we enjoyed French toast, quiche, and an egg speciality, garnished with potatoes, fruit and other goodies." *(Sue & Tom Nardi)* "Karen and Terry are warm, friendly people who welcome you to their home. Great restaurant advice and help with reservations. Our favorite rooms are Merlot and Zinfandel on the second floor, with skylights above the double Jacuzzi tubs, so you can see the stars overhead. Merlot has a beautiful king-size bed, set in the middle of the peaked roof line, a stained glass window, and a pale lavender color scheme. Done in blue, Zinfandel has the same appealing sloped ceiling. Excellent showers. Delicious breakfasts; vegetarians accommodated with advance notice." *(Vicki & Paul Helbig)* "Karen is a charming innkeeper—warm, energetic and friendly." *(SWS)* "Our favorite rooms have skylights which allow the fresh evening air to flow into the room. Karen and Terry are fun to be around. They care about their guests and do all they can to make your vacations what you want it to be. They are knowledgeable about area wineries, and will plan tours. The family atmosphere continues during the generous breakfasts, with chatter about dinner the night before, and plans for the coming day." *(Peg Fenton)*

Open All year.
Rooms 1 suite, 6 doubles—all with private bath and/or shower, air-conditioning. 5 with double whirlpool tub.
Facilities Dining room, living room with fireplace, parlor, porch. Shaded lot with seating, off-street parking.
Location 4 blocks from town square. From Hwy. 101 N, take "Central Healdsburg" exit. Go ¾ m to Grant St., turn right. Go 2 blocks to inn on right.

Restrictions No smoking. Children over 10.
Credit cards Discover, MC, Visa.
Rates B&B, $150 suite, $90–140 double, $60–110 single. Extra person, $35. 10% weekly discount in winter. 2-night minimum some weekends.

Healdsburg Inn on the Plaza ♿

110/116 Matheson Street
P.O. Box 1196, 95448

Tel: 707–433–6991
Fax: 707–433–9513

Set in a turn-of-the-century structure, originally housing doctors, dentists, and a Wells Fargo office, the Healdsburg Inn has been owned by Genny Jenkins since 1981. Rates include a full breakfast served at 9 A.M. (continental breakfast available at 7:30 on weekdays), round-the-clock coffee and a never-empty cookie jar, plus afternoon snacks, popcorn, and wine. Afternoon tea is served on weekends.

"In the heart of Healdsburg. Most guest rooms and the common areas are on the second floor, with a beautiful, spacious breakfast solarium. Good-sized guest rooms, freshly decorated. Those at the front overlook the Plaza; some at the back open to a balcony." *(SWS)* "Song of the Rose is a spectacular room, with a bay window overlooking the plaza. This grand, high-ceilinged space is decorated in pale yellow, green, and soft gray-white, with a working fireplace. There was ample space for a queen-size brass and iron bed; a small draped table with chairs; a large wardrobe; velvet-covered settee; a tastefully concealed TV; and a working pump organ. A small hallway with a stained glass window led to the large bathroom with an old-fashioned tub and a separate shower." *(Susan Rather)*

"Overlooking the plaza, a small park with trees, grass, fountain and gazebo. The entrance to the inn is a storefront, with arts and crafts exhibits for sale around the reception area. Breakfast was excellent— orange juice and champagne, croissants, muffins, toast, fruit and a wonderful quiche. Staff were pleasant and helpful." *(Hugh & Marjorie Smith)* "Decorated in pastel Victorian style, the guest rooms have comfortable queen- or king-size beds and ample seating. The bathrooms have large clawfoot tubs, showers, fluffy towels, lovely soaps and lotions, and whimsical rubber ducks. The main hall has comfortable seating for reading and jigsaw puzzle working." *(Alan & Irma Judkins)*

Open All year.
Rooms 10 doubles—all with private bath and/or shower, telephone, TV/VCR, air-conditioning. Some with fireplace, double Jacuzzi, balcony.
Facilities Lounge with games, books; solarium breakfast room; lobby with art gallery, gift shop. Off-street parking ½ block away. 1 m to Russian River.
Location Center of old town.
Restrictions No smoking. Children by arrangement. "The ground-floor guest room has little natural light."
Credit cards MC, Visa.
Rates B&B, $135–250 double. Extra person, $35. Off-season rates in early Dec., Jan. 2-night holiday weekend minimum. Senior, AAA, off-season, midweek, corporate rates. Discount for extended stays.
Extras 1 room wheelchair accessible.

The Honor Mansion   *Tel:* 707–433–4277
14891 Grove Street, 95448   800–554–4667
Fax: 707–431–7173
E-mail: Cathi@honormansion.com

An Italianate Victorian mansion, the Honor Mansion was built in 1884, and was owned by the Honor family until 1992. Cathi Fowler restored it as a B&B in 1994, furnishing it with antiques, feather beds, and European linens. Breakfast menus change daily, but might include ginger spice pancakes, sausages, and baked grapefruit scones, or Mexican crepes with ham, raspberry-lemon muffins, and baked pears. Rates also include evening refreshments.

"A beautifully restored mansion, carefully painted in shades of gray, black, and white to highlight the lovely trim. Inside is an inviting, spacious living room, and a dining room with tables for two and four. Breakfast was served at 9 A.M. sharp and included broiled grapefruit halves, freshly squeezed orange juice, baked peach blintzes with sausages, cranberry cream scones to die for, and excellent coffee, both regular and decaf. Afternoon sherry and cookies are also available. An unusual feature, in a little alcove off the dining room, is the cappucino maker—just push the button and it makes you a perfect cup (hi-test or regular). A refrigerator and glasses are available to guests who would like to chill and serve their own wine. The guest rooms are lavishly decorated with the highest quality linens and fabrics in beautiful shades of soft pink, apple green, and other appealing colors. Each has good lights at bedside and in the bathroom. Our room on the first floor at the back had a comfortable queen-size bed and its own private porch, a perfect spot for sampling some of the day's purchases." *(SWS)*

Open All year.
Rooms 1 cottage, 5 doubles—all with private bath and/or shower, radio, clock, desk, air-conditioning, fan. 2 with TV/VCR, fireplace, refrigerator, porch/deck.
Facilities Dining room, living room with fireplace, piano, TV, stereo, books; family room, guest refrigerator. 1 acre with off-street parking, swimming pool, gardens, koi pond with waterfall, lawn games.
Location 1 m walk from town center. From San Francisco, take Hwy. 101 N to Healdsburg. Take Dry Creek Rd. exit; go right onto Dry Creek. Take 1st right onto Grove St. & watch for inn's white picket fence on right.
Restrictions No smoking. Children over 16.
Credit cards Discover, MC, Visa.
Rates B&B, $120–220 cottage, double. Tips encouraged for housekeepers.
Extras Spanish.

Madrona Manor ✕ ऴ   *Tel:* 707–433–4231
1001 Westside Road, P.O. Box 818, 95448   800–258–4003
Fax: 707–433–0703
E-mail: madronaman@aol.com

Originally built in 1881 by a wealthy San Francisco banker, Madrona Manor sits on a high knoll overlooking the town of Healdsburg and nearby vineyards. In 1983 it was bought by John and Carol Muir, who have turned it into an elegant country inn. Most of the space on the first floor of the main building is devoted to dining rooms, although the front parlor has a five-piece Victorian suite with carved griffin arms. Guest rooms in the main house are very large, and those on the first and second floors have furnishings original to the house; those in the Carriage House are luxuriously furnished with more modern decor. The Manor is a busy place in season, and reservations are essential for both the rooms and restaurant, especially on weekends.

Todd Muir is the executive chef, and a recent dinner included sea scallops with artichoke puree, rack of lamb with potato terrine, and cappucino pots de creme with fresh fruit and cookies. Be sure to save room for the breakfast buffet of juice, fresh fruit, and granola; a selection of European hams and local and imported cheeses; and vegetable frittata with salsa; toast, homemade raspberry jam, and bread pudding.

"Lovely hotel. Excellent dinner on the outside patio." *(Pat & Doug Phillips)* "Our dinners were prepared by an outstanding Italian guest chef; excellent service by knowledgeable, intelligent wait staff. Highlights included the lobster quenelles, veal filet with spinach, frozen mascarpone with blueberries." *(SWS)* "We relaxed by the fire, had a wonderful dinner, and woke up to a great breakfast. The reception staff was gracious, helpful, and knowledgeable with good recommendations on wineries and antique shops." *(Edwin Jones)* "The gardens were appropriate to Victorian era, beautifully maintained with a fountain, flowers, herbs and vegetables." *(Helen Nicholas)* "Through the French doors on either side of the 10-foot-high carved headboard in our bedroom was a terrace from which we could see across the valley to the mountains." *(Virginia Severs)*

Open All year.
Rooms 3 suites, 15 doubles—all with full private bath, telephone, radio, desk, air-conditioning, fan. 18 rooms with fireplace (gas or Duraflame), 5 with balcony. 9 rooms in main house, 9 in Carriage House, 3 in 2 cottages.
Facilities 3 dining rooms, music room, lobby, terrace. 8 acres with gardens, fountain, orchard, walking trails, swimming pool. Golf, tennis, swimming, canoeing, horseback riding nearby.
Location ¾m from town. From Central Healdsburg exit of Hwy. 101, go left on Mill St., which becomes Westside Rd.
Restrictions Occasional traffic noise midweek. No smoking.
Credit cards Amex, DC, MC, Visa.
Rates B&B, $200–250 suite, $155–210 double. Extra person, $30. Alc dinner, $37–45.
Extras Wheelchair access. Local airport pickup, $25. Pets by arrangement. Crib, babysitting. Spanish spoken.

Raford House   *Tel: 707–887–9573*
10630 Wohler Road, 95448   *800–887–9503*
                                     Fax: 707–887–9597

If you'd prefer a quiet country location, surrounded by vineyards, visit the Raford House, built as a summer home in the 1880s, and owned by Carole and Jack Vore since 1993. Set on a prominent knoll, the house is surrounded by towering palm trees and old-fashioned flower gardens. The dozens of rose bushes are home to hummingbirds, orioles, and swallows. A wonderful porch stretches the length of the house, with wicker chairs and tables, perfect for reading a book or enjoying an afternoon wine and cheese. Breakfast, served 9–9:30 A.M. at guests' choice of small or large tables, might include broiled grapefruit or perhaps poached pears, stuffed French toast or potato cheese pie, and croissants or biscuits. Rates also include afternoon wine and cheese, and evening chocolates and sherry.

"Friendly, helpful, unobtrusive innkeepers; good restaurant information. Delicious food and drink, from the local berries used in the breakfast pancakes and muffins, to the wines served before dinner. Striking location, on a hill above the Sonoma vineyards. Far from any noise; well-insulated walls. Great sunporch. Convenient to restaurants and wineries. Well-cared-for antiques in common areas and guest rooms." *(T. Rosenal)* "Beautiful setting in Russian River Wine Country. Charming B&B, lovely hosts. Delicious breakfasts, enjoyable wine tasting." *(Margaret Moss)*

Open All year. Closed Christmas.
Rooms 1 suite, 5 doubles—all with private bath and/or shower, clock/radio, ceiling-fan. 2 with wood-burning fireplace, 2 with porch, 1 with desk, private entrance.
Facilities Dining room with fireplace, sitting room with books, stereos; porch. 4½ acres with lawn games, off-street parking. 10 m from public beach of Russian River for swimming, boating, fishing.
Location Halfway between Santa Rosa & Healdsburg. From Hwy 101 N, take River Rd. Exit 3 m N of Santa Rosa, & go W 7.5 m on River Rd. Turn right on Wohler Rd., & watch for inn on right, between Eastside Rd. & Westside Rd. From Healdsburg, go S on 101. Go right on Eastside Rd., right on Wohler Rd. to inn on right.
Restrictions No smoking. Children not encouraged.
Credit cards Amex, Discover, MC, Visa.
Rates B&B, $180–220 suite (sleeps 4), $100–155 double. Extra person, $30. 2-night weekend minimum April–Oct. Winter rates, Nov.–March.

HOPE VALLEY

Sorensen's Resort ♦ ✕   *Tel:* 916–694–2203
14255 Highway 88, 96120   800–423–9949

Dating back to 1906, Sorensen's Resort was opened as an inn in 1982 by John and Patty Brissenden. The restaurant serves three meals daily. Breakfast includes quiche, waffles, and ham-and-cheese croissants; the lunch menu lists sandwiches and beef or chicken stew; and filet mignon, pesto pasta, and fresh fish with vegetables are among the dinner entrees.

"Warm hospitality in summer and winter. Well-appointed cabins, beautiful setting. Helpful staff, lots of area activities if you feel the need to do more than enjoy the lovely surroundings." *(Pat O'Brien)* "The Chapel cabin was originally built for Santa's Village, near Santa Cruz. When the village was torn down, Sorensen's had the opportunity to acquire several buildings, which were then rebuilt—log by log—at

Sorensen's. The Chapel is delightful, with a high vaulted log ceiling with a double glazed clerestory window giving lots of space and light. The cozy loft bedroom is reached by a spiral staircase. Added pluses are the warm hospitality of John and Patty Brissenden, the hearty food at the cafe, plus beautiful surroundings and great skiing at Kirkwood." *(Craig Fusaro)* "The brook trickling by the front door of our cabin, Rock Creek, provided a calming lullaby each night." *(Barbara Gault)* "Friendly, smiling staff and management. Excellent meals, quality wines, and homemade desserts served in the cozy atmosphere of the dining room, with a fireplace and soft, live music in the background." *(Kay Danielson)* "Immaculate housekeeping, careful attention to detail, tasty meals." *(GR)*

Open All year. Restaurant closed Christmas Day.
Rooms 30 cabins with private bath and/or shower. Most with kitchen, porch. 18 with fireplace/woodstove. 2 B&B rooms share 1 bath. 1 with whirlpool bathtub.
Facilities Restaurant, porch, gift shop. 165 acres with fishing pond & stream, swimming holes, swing set, gazebo, hiking; cross-country ski center with rentals, tours, instruction. 14 m to downhill skiing at Kirkwood. Tennis, golf, hot springs, kayaking, bicycling, horseback riding nearby.
Location Sierra Nevada, 20 m S of Lake Tahoe. 1½ m S. Reno airport.
Restrictions Traffic noise in some rooms. No smoking: $250 fine.
Credit cards Amex, MC, Visa.
Rates Room only, $65–350 cabin. B&B, $80–120 double. Extra person, $15–20. Tipping encouraged. No charge for children under 7. 2–4 night weekend/holiday minimum for advance reservations. Sleeping bags in dorm accommodations. Alc breakfast, $6; lunch, $6; alc dinner, $20. Midweek Kirkwood ski packages.
Extras 1 cabin wheelchair accessible; bathroom specially equipped. Pets in 3 cabins with approval. Cribs, babysitting by arrangement.

IDYLLWILD

Set at an elevation of 5,500 feet, Idyllwild is a quiet resort village in the San Jacinto Mountains. Surrounded by thousands of acres of national forest, it's an ideal spot for fishing, hiking, and horseback riding. It's also the base of the Idyllwild School of Music and the Arts, which sponsors musical theater productions through the summer. Located at the edge of Desert Country, Idyllwild is approximately one hour west of Palm Springs and two hours east of Los Angeles. From I-10, go south on Route 243 to Idyllwild. From Hemet or Palm Desert, take Route 74 to Mountain Center and go north on Route 243 to Idyllwild.

Reader tip: "This mountain retreat just east of San Bernardino makes a great stop between Los Angeles and Las Vegas, or is an alternative to Palm Springs. It's quiet, full of pines, and excellent for hiking. The town also has three or four good restaurants." *(Lon Bailey)*

Information please: Tucked into the pines, we need current reports on the **Strawberry Creek Inn** (26370 Highway 243, P.O. Box 1818, 92549; 909–659–3202 or 800–262–8969) set among the pines, beside the stream that is its namesake. Longtime owners Jim Goff and Diana Dugan welcome guests to this rambling shingled home, decorated with antiques and handmade quilts. B&B double rates for the nine guest rooms range from $85–105; the cottage is $135.

INVERNESS

Although Point Reyes almost became as developed as the rest of Marin County, it was saved by the environmental movement in the 1970s and was declared a National Seashore. Only an hour northwest of San Francisco, the area offers magnificent beaches, hiking trails in the forests, and Inverness Ridge with abundant wildlife including deer, fox, rabbits, and birds. Other activities include fishing, whale-watching, tennis, golf, kayaking, horseback riding, birdwatching, and attending theater at the Point Reyes Dance Palace.

Inverness is located in the southernmost part of the North Coast area, in west Marin County. Visitors frequently make Inverness their base for explorations of the Point Reyes National Seashore.

Also recommended: Established in 1906, the **Hotel Inverness** (25 Park Avenue, P.O. Box 780, 94937–0790; 415–669–7393) offers guest rooms with queen-size beds, private baths, and decks, at B&B double rates of $100–160. "Upstairs are the simply furnished but immaculate guest rooms, painted in bold colors with original artwork. Breakfast of fresh fruit and juice, with tasty muffins, is served on a tray to your room or on the downstairs deck. Extremely quiet, even though all rooms were full; no TV or radio in our smallish room. No common room, although future plans call for adding one. Friendly, helpful innkeepers." (GD)

For additional area inns, see **Olema, Point Reyes Station** and **Stinson Beach.**

Sandy Cove Inn   *Tel:* 415–669–2683
12990 Sir Francis Drake Boulevard,   800–759–2683
P.O. Box, 869, 94937   *Fax:* 415–669–7511
                        E-mail: Innkeeper@sandycove.com

Bigger is not necessarily better when it comes to B&Bs, as you'll appreciate after a visit to the Sandy Cove Inn, a shingled Cape Cod–style home owned by Kathy and Gerry Coles since 1979. The uncluttered guest rooms are beautifully decorated with queen-size beds, pine and wicker furniture, comfortable sitting areas, original art, and Turkish kilim rugs on the tile and hardwood floors. Careful attention to detail ensures that each room is equipped with every imaginable amenity, from a backpack and walking stick for hiking, to a library of books and CDs for the stereo, to a refrigerator stocked with wine and cheese. Breakfast is served at a time convenient to guests (within reason), at individual tables on the breakfast solarium, or can be brought to guests' rooms. Made with the organic produce from their own gardens, plus locally produced and preservative-free ingredients, a typical midweek menu includes fresh fruit, warm gingerbread with lemon curd, creme fraiche, and apple sauce, and soft cooked eggs. A weekend meal might consist of pumpkin-pecan pancakes, chicken and wild mushroom sausages, and grilled pears and fresh sage. "Guests' dietary restrictions are meticulously respected," note the Coles, who also report that they make every effort to use natural fibers and products, free of herbicides and chemicals.

"A short walk to the beach at Tomales Bay, and a quick drive to Point Reyes National Seashore. You enter through a locked gate—they send you the combination with your confirmation. Exceptional breakfasts." *(Michael Stulbarg)* "Peaceful garden setting. Romantic room supplied with area guidebooks, robes, slippers, and more." *(Gerry & Clare Ann Hayes)* "Clean, attractive, and quiet; easy access to beach and water. The thoughtful owners suggested local activities." *(Lee Miller)* "Plentiful, delicious breakfast delivered to our room at the desired time. Charming, comfortable, immaculate room. Exceptionally helpful innkeepers." *(Monte Frankel)* "Remote location, yet just an hour from the Golden Gate Bridge. Great location near the beach; saw wild deer grazing, and visited Truffles the pony in the barn." *(J. Ward, also MW)* "Wonderful homemade croissants and freshly squeezed orange juice." *(Jennifer Brogan)* "A private, romantic getaway. The two rooms I saw were on the second floor, one with a nautical, the other with an equestrian theme, with vaulted ceilings and skylights to let in the bright morning sunlight. The outstanding breakfast included baked eggs with roasted potato and Canadian bacon, cranberry scones, fresh-ground nutmeg muffins, cornbread muffins with sage." *(Susan W. Schwemm)*

Open All year.
Rooms 3 doubles—all with private shower and/or tub, telephone, clock/radio, CD player, books, wood-burning or gas fireplace, refrigerator, coffee maker, terry robes, hair dryer, private entrance, balcony/deck. 1 with desk. 2 rooms in separate building.
Facilities Breakfast solarium. 5 acres with picnic area, swimming pool, lawn games, gardens, barn with farm animals, hiking trails. Trail to beach on Tomales Bay; kayak rentals.
Location 35 miles from San Francisco. 1 m W of town (going toward lighthouse) on the right.
Restrictions Absolutely no smoking. Infants, children 12 and over midweek. Slippers provided to wear in house.
Credit cards Amex, DC, Discover, JCBC, MC, Visa.
Rates Room only, $120–225 double. B&B, $130–250 double. Extra person, $50. AARP, AAA discount.
Extras Spanish, German, Italian, some French spoken.

Ten Inverness Way　　　　　　　　　　　*Tel:* 415–669–1648
10 Inverness Way, 94937　　　　　　　　　*Fax:* 415–669–7403
　　　　　　　　　　　　　　　　　　　E-mail: tiw@nbn.com

Innkeeper Mary Davies writes that "guests come to enjoy the three nearby parks—seashore, bay, and redwoods—and gather around the stone fireplace in the evenings to talk, read, or play the piano and guitar." The inn was built in 1904 and is decorated with comfortable antiques; guest rooms are simply furnished with shiplap siding and quilt-topped queen-size beds.

"A perfectly run inn. The innkeepers are gracious, helpful, yet unobtrusive. Though not large, the rooms are extremely comfortable, with excellent mattresses and pillows, luxurious towels, and beautiful quilts. Delicious breakfasts, not too sweet. Just-baked cookies await you after a long afternoon hike. A charming garden to enjoy, full of English lavender and brightly colored flowers. Lovely floral bouquets in the rooms, too." *(Joan Simon)* "On stormy days, a fire is always going in the living room, accompanied by hot tea and cookies. Ample reading lights in common areas and guest rooms. The tasty breakfasts are tailored to the needs of cholesterol-conscious people if desired." *(Rena Ziegler)* "Quiet, relaxing, scrupulously clean. I loved watching the stars from our skylight." *(Rosemarie Engel)* "Woodsy seclusion. Our room had a high window running the length of the room with a view of the back gardens. Breakfast was a hot croque monsieur sandwich with white sauce, fresh fruit, juice and coffee." *(Diane Schwemm)* "The living room was exceptionally homey and warm, with a beautiful stone fireplace, Oriental rugs, a piano, and plump sofas." *(Linda Goldberg)* "They mapped out excellent paths for us to hike, along ocean shores teeming with wildlife." *(Heide Bredfeldt)*

Open All year.

Rooms 1 suite, 4 doubles—all with private bath and/or shower, clock/radio, fan/heater. Suite with kitchen, private garden.

Facilities Sun-room with wood stove, living room with fireplace, piano, library. ¼ acre with garden, hot tub.

Location From San Francisco, take Hwy 101 N to San Anselmo–Sir Francis Drake Blvd exit. Follow Drake Blvd. to Olema. Turn right onto Hwy. 1, then left at Bear Valley Rd. Go 3 m to stop sign, go left again, and continue 4 m to Inverness. In village, turn left at 2nd Inverness Way to house on immediate right.

Restrictions No smoking. Small closets in most rooms.

Credit cards MC, Visa.

Rates B&B, $110–160 double, $100–150 single. Extra person, $15, 2-night weekend minimum.

Extras A little French spoken.

IONE

The Heirloom ¢ & *Tel:* 209–274–4468
214 Shakeley Lane, P.O. Box 322, 95640

One of the earliest settlers of the Gold Country built the Heirloom in the 1850s; Melisande Hubbs and Patricia Cross are its longtime owners. The inn's good-sized rooms are furnished with antiques and quilts, including many family heirlooms. A typical breakfast might include freshly squeezed orange juice, popovers, broiled grapefruit, and spiced apple blintzes; or perhaps cranberry coffee cake, zucchini muffins, baked pears, and cheddar cheese soufflé. It's served in your room, on your veranda, in the garden, or in the fireside dining room.

"Manicured grounds with blooming roses, azaleas and many other flowers. We napped in the hammock and enjoyed an evening glass of wine on the veranda. Our room was cool and fresh-smelling, with furnishings that complemented the age of the house perfectly. Charming, attentive, friendly, unobtrusive innkeepers. The inviting living room had comfortable couches and easy chairs, soft music, fresh flowers, plus games, books, and magazines." *(Nancy Stella)* "Beautiful bedrooms and two inviting cottages, with a king- or queen-size bed." *(Julie Phillips)* "Exceptional breakfast, excellent value." *(Henry Aaron)* "The friendly owners will direct you to excellent local wineries, impressive underground caves, melodrama theater, antique stores galore, and beautiful outdoor recreational areas." *(Jennifer & Jerry Wilhelm)* "The cottage has adobe walls and a sod roof. Comfortable chairs, good lighting, and plenty of reading material made for a pleasant evening. The bath had a large tiled shower, a stained glass window and plenty of thick towels." *(Mary Moses)*

"A cool glass of lemonade awaits you on a warm summer afternoon or a glass of wine by the living room fire on a cold fall day. Tasty hors d'oeuvres tempt guests before dinner. Sandy and Pat stay current on local restaurants and have never steered us wrong; advance dinner reservations are made with pleasure. Breakfasts are delicious, and carefully planned to avoid repeats for returning guests. Incredible Christmas decorations." *(Bob & Kim Stetson)*

Open All year. Closed Thanksgiving, Dec. 24, 25.
Rooms 6 doubles—4 with private bath and/or shower, 2 with maximum of 4 sharing bath. All with desk, fan; some with fireplace, balcony; 5 with air-conditioning. 2 rooms in cottage, each with woodstove.
Facilities Living room with fireplace, piano; dining room with fireplace. Verandas. 1½ acres with swings, hammocks, croquet. Walking distance to golf course; tennis, wineries, antiquing, historical sights nearby. Lakes, rivers nearby for boating, fishing, swimming.
Location Gold Country. 45 min. SE of Sacramento. Ione is at the intersection of Rtes. 104 & 124.
Restrictions No smoking. No children under 10.
Credit cards Amex, MC, Visa.
Rates B&B, $80–98 suite, $65–98 double, $60–90 single. Extra person, $15. 2-night holiday, weekend minimum.
Extras Limited wheelchair access. Airport pickup. Portuguese spoken.

JACKSON

Jackson is located in Amador County, in the Gold Country; it's about one hour southeast of Sacramento via Route 16. Jackson Gate Road is a largely residential road, running roughly parallel with Highway 49 from Jackson partway to Sutter Creek.

Also recommended: Listed on the National Register of Historic Places, **The Gate House** (1330 Jackson Gate Road, 95642; 209–223–3500 or 800–841–1072) is a turn-of-the-century Victorian home. It offers five guest rooms, at B&B double rates of $95–135, including a full breakfast served at 9 A.M. After a busy day of exploring, guests enjoy cooling off in the inn's swimming pool. "Helpful innkeeper; spacious, comfortable well-maintained rooms decorated with period antiques; excellent breakfasts; lush gardens with fragrant flowers." *(Jacqueline Steven)* "Cordial innkeepers, Keith and Gail Sweet; careful attention to detail; welcome refreshments. Beautiful original oak parquet floors with mahogany inlays." *(Doris Levy)*

For additional area inns, see **Ione** and **Sutter Creek.**

The Wedgewood Inn
11941 Narcissus Road, 95642

Tel: 209–296–4300
800–933–4393
Fax: 209–296–4301
E-mail: vic@wedgewoodinn.com

Take the best of old and new, and blend it well with warmth and hospitality, and you have the recipe for the Wedgewood Inn, built by Vic and Jeannine Beltz in 1987. "By building an Eastlake-style Victorian replica farmhouse," notes Jeannine, "we were able to select a quiet, secluded setting with all modern conveniences." The inn is beautifully furnished with family heirlooms, antiques, collectibles, stained glass, and needlecraft. Rates include a full breakfast, served at the dining room table at 9:00 A.M., and afternoon refreshments, set out from 3–6 P.M.

"A fascinating living museum with four generations of family memorabilia. The spacious Victorian Rose room has a view of the lovely rose garden, a doll collection, and a queen-size English carved bed and tapestry chairs. A Christian grace was said before the serving of a delicious breakfast of raspberry sorbet, almond cake, and blintzes with turkey sausage and fruit." *(BZ)* "Our favorite room is the Wedgewood Cameo with a blue and white color scheme, Wedgwood pieces and a cameo collection, and English and French carved furniture. Another favorite is Granny's Attic, a warm, cozy third-floor room, with a skylight, a window seat overlooking the garden, and a display of antique nightgowns." *(Will & Elaine Small)* "Although the inn and its setting are lovely, best of all are innkeepers Vic and Jeannine." *(Pam Raffaelli)* "Superb breakfasts start with dessert; my favorite entree is eggs Wedgewood—eggs scrambled, layered, and baked with bacon, scallions, sour cream, mushrooms, and cheese. Beautifully set table with flowers, candles and fine china. Equally delicious afternoon refreshments. Firm queen-size mattresses; ample hot water. We relaxed in a hammock in the beautiful garden, and watched the stars come out. Exceptionally clean, even the collectibles." *(Glynis Evans)* "Jeannine and Vic welcome us like family. Our favorite room is Country Pine, with a queen-size antique iron bed, German pine armoire, and a green and peach decor." *(Jo Ann Carey)* "The innkeepers provided a multitude of special touches, from an early morning cup of coffee delivered to our door to chocolate truffles placed on the bed in the evening." *(Julie Phillips)*

Open All year.
Rooms 1 cottage suite, 5 doubles—all with private bath and/or shower, clock/radio, desk, air-conditioning. 4 with fireplace, 3 with ceiling fan, 2 with balcony/deck. Suite with double whirlpool tub, telephone, refrigerator, microwave.

Facilities Dining room, parlor with piano; guest refrigerator, porch; gift shop. 5 acres with terraced gardens, hammocks, fountains, croquet lawn, gazebo, lawn games. Golf nearby.

Location Take Hwy. 88 E from Jackson 6.5 m to 2,000-foot elevation. Turn right onto Irishtown Rd.; *immediately* go right onto Clinton Rd. Drive ¾ m to Narcissus Rd. Go left ¼ m to inn on left.

Restrictions No smoking. Children over 12.

Credit cards Amex, Discover, MC, Visa.

Rates B&B, $155–175 suite, $90–130 double, $80–120 single. Extra person, $20 in suite only. 10% AAA discount midweek.

JAMESTOWN

Founded as a mining camp during the 1848 gold rush, Jamestown looks much like a Western movie set—or should that be the other way around? That the town keeps this atmosphere owes much to the fact that it's bypassed by Highway 49—the main north/south route. Appealing shops invite you to browse, and crossing the street is not a life-endangering experience. Unlike the original miners, today's residents extract their gold quite painlessly from travelers who come to experience Jamestown's history and picturesque setting. Jamestown is located 2½ hours east of San Francisco and south of Sacramento. Visitors also enjoy the Railtown Museum and steam train rides.

Information please: For the flavor of an old-fashioned Western hotel, *Ronald Byledbal* suggests the **Jamestown Hotel** (Main Street, 95327; 209–984–3902), with "lots of character, a good restaurant, and a pleasant place to stay." Downstairs is a pub, restaurant, and a dining patio in back; upstairs are eleven guest rooms named for famous women of the Old West (the newest rooms have whirlpool tubs and TVs). The B&B double rates are $75–135.

For additional area inns, see **Sonora.**

Palm Hotel   ♿   *Tel:* 209–984–3429
10382 Willow Street, 95327   *Toll-free:* 888–551–1851
                                    Fax: 209–984–4929
                                    E-mail: palmbb@sonnet.com

Built in 1890, the Palm Hotel has been owned by Rick and Sandy Allen since 1994. Most guest rooms are simply furnished, some with patchwork quilts and homemade afghans; Room 5 has twin old-fashioned corner sinks and twin clawfoot tubs. The Grand Suite has a king-size bed, double-headed marble shower, arched windows and private balcony, and the Victoria Suite has a cozy queen-size bed, vaulted ceiling and sunny sitting alcove. Breakfast, served 8–10 A.M. at the old marble soda fountain bar, includes fresh fruit and juice, muffins, breads and breakfast meats, and perhaps apple crisp, egg dishes, stuffed French toast, or pancakes.

"Cheery, immaculate rooms with comfortable antique furnishings. Pleasant atmosphere, comfortable beds, friendly innkeepers, and a convenient but quiet location. Delicious breakfast of fresh fruit, eggs, sausages, fried potatoes, warm apple crisp, muffins, and blueberry pound cake. Just a block away are the antique shops, boutiques, and restaurants of Main Street." *(Russ & Dottie Wilson)* Reports appreciated.

Open All year.
Rooms 2 suites, 6 doubles—all with private shower or tub, TV, air-conditioning. some with desk, balcony, refrigerator. Clock on request.
Facilities Dining room, parlor, porches. Off-street parking, garden with pergola, lawn games.
Location 1½ blocks from Main St. From Hwy 108 E, bear right on Main St. Take 3rd left onto Willow St. to inn on left. From Hwy. 108 W, go left on 5th Ave., then right on Willow St. to inn on right.
Restrictions No smoking.
Credit cards Amex, MC, Visa.
Rates B&B, $145 suite, $95–115 double. Extra person, $10.
Extras Wheelchair access; 1 room specially equipped.

JULIAN

Julian is an old mining town founded by Mike Julian, a Confederate soldier; gold was discovered here in 1868. It's located in San Diego County, 60 miles northeast of San Diego, and 160 miles southeast of Los Angeles. Area activities include fishing, hiking, and horseback riding. The 4,000-foot elevation makes it ideal for fruit trees, and the area has many apple and pear orchards.

Reader tip: "They roll up the sidewalks early each night in Julian, so do your shopping early and don't plan to dine late." *(MW)*

Information please: About 15 miles west of Julian, overlooking Lake Sutherland and the Cleveland National Forest, is the **Lake Sutherland Lodge B&B** (24901 Dam Oaks Drive, Ramona 92065; 760–789–6483 or 800–789–6483). This contemporary lodge has sweeping views from most of its rooms and the expansive deck. Inside is a great room with a cathedral ceiling, two-story stone fireplace, and comfortable, contemporary furnishings. B&B double rates for the four guest rooms (including a luxurious honeymoon suite), range from $110–185, including a creative full breakfast and evening dessert.

Julian Gold Rush Hotel ¢
2032 Main Street, P.O. Box 1856, 92036

Tel: 760–765–0201
In CA: 800–734–5854
Fax: 760–765–0327

In the 1880s Albert and Margaret Robinson, two freed slaves from Georgia, arrived and started a restaurant. Their reputation for good food grew, and in 1897 they decided to build a hotel. The Julian is now Southern California's oldest continuously operating hotel and is listed on the National Register of Historic Places. In 1976 it was purchased by Steve and Gig Ballinger, who furnished the rooms with authentic antiques and period wallpapers. A typical breakfast includes fresh fruit and juice, oatmeal and granola, eggs Florentine, and date nut bread. Rates also include afternoon tea.

"Accommodating staff, delicious breakfast of eggs Florentine. Enjoyed the challenging puzzles in the parlor. Charming, quiet town." *(Maria Dangel)* "Relaxing, renewing, and romantic. Cheerful, obliging staff; excellent food at breakfast and afternoon tea." *(Anne Bingley)* "The staff is knowledgeable about the town and glad to make reservations and inquire about schedules." *(Jock Crook)* "We stayed in the 'Honeymoon Cottage,' cozy and quaint with fireplace and clawfoot tub." *(Robert & Barbara Pavick)* "Clean and safe, delicious breakfast." *(Alice Chandler)*

Open All year.
Rooms 2 cottages (1 with fireplace), 12 doubles—all with private bath.
Facilities Lobby with books, games, woodstove, parlor, dining room, deck, patios. Fishing, boating, cross-country skiing nearby.
Location At intersection of Hwys. 78 & 79.
Credit cards Amex, MC, Visa
Rates B&B, $110–160 cottage, $72–110 double. 2-night weekend minimum. 15% senior discount midweek.

The Julian White House B&B

Tel: 760–765–1764
P.O. Box 824, 3014 Blue Jay Drive, 92036
800–WHT–HOUSE
E-mail: marvin@electiciti.com

A Southern plantation–style home, the Julian White House was built in 1976, and has been owned by Alan and Mary Marvin since 1984. The spacious guest rooms have antique furnishings, queen-size beds, floral wallpapers, plush carpeting, ample storage, and good bedside lamps and tables. One favorite room has a white iron and brass bed, deep blue-patterned comforter, and a soft blue-and-white patterned wallpaper. Breakfast is served at 9:00 A.M., and includes such fruit dishes as baked grapefruit, orange ambrosia, or pears with blue cheese and pecans; followed by eggs Benedict, gingerbread waffles, oatmeal pancakes, or perhaps peach souffle; accompanied by chicken sausage and herbed potatoes. Rates also include evening tea and cookies.

"Peaceful, quiet atmosphere; beautiful decor; private and secluded. Cozy fireplace in the living room, with classical music playing softly in the background. Delicious breakfast served at the dining room table, beautifully set with silver, linens, and candles. Excellent service; immaculate housekeeping; welcoming ambiance." *(Claudine Natelborg)* "The delightful package gave us a great feel for Julian and included lodging, dinners, lunch, a horse-drawn carriage ride, and a gift basket." *(Jacqueline Stroh)* "Cordial innkeepers, homey atmosphere, wonderful meals and snacks." *(Chris Johnson)*

Open All year. Closed Dec. 24, 25.
Rooms 1 suite, 3 doubles—all with private shower and/or tub, clock, air-conditioning, ceiling fan. 2 with fireplace, 1 with double shower.
Facilities Dining room, living room with fireplace, stereo, books; guest refrigerator, porch/deck. 1 acre with rose garden, hot tub. Walking distance to Pine Hills Dinner Theater; 2 m from William Hiese Park for hiking, riding.

Location 3 m from Historic District. From San Diego, take Hwy 78 E toward Julian. 6 m after Santa Ysabel, watch for Methodist Church on left & go right Pine Hills Rd. Go 2 m & go right on Blue Jay Rd. to inn at end.
Restrictions No smoking. Children 12 and over.
Credit cards MC, Visa.
Rates B&B, $135 suite, $90–135 double. Extra person, $25. 10% senior, AAA discount. 2-night weekend minimum.

Orchard Hill Country Inn ✕ &
2502 Washington Street, P.O. Box 425, 92036

Tel: 760–765–1700
800–716–7242
Fax: 760–765–1700

Set on a hill overlooking the town of Julian and the surrounding apple orchards is the Orchard Hill Country Inn, built in 1994 by Darrell and Pat Straube. Occupying three California Craftsman–style cottages and a main lodge, the guest rooms have town or mountain views, and are furnished with handmade quilts, antiques, and traditional and Mission-style pieces. All have queen- or king-size beds, and many of the individually decorated suites—named for apple varieties—also have two-sided fireplaces and double Jacuzzi tubs. The inviting great room has lots of comfortable seating, beautiful fabrics, an Oriental rug on the tile floor, and a dramatic rock fireplace which rises to the vaulted ceiling above. The accommodations are sufficiently luxurious to have earned the inn a four-diamond rating from AAA.

Breakfast, served 8–10 A.M., includes fresh fruit and juice, cereal, just-baked muffins, and a hot entree. Rates also include afternoon hors d'oeuvres, fresh-baked cookies, and hot or cold drinks. Prix fixe dinners are served in the Julian Room, decorated with hand-painted murals of Julian's history. A recent menu included cream of zucchini soup, salad, beef tenderloin, herbed potatoes, asparagus, and bread pudding; or cream of asparagus soup, salad, rack of lamb with Dijon mustard crust, sugar snap peas, herbed wild rice, and coffee ice cream with coffee sauce.

"Set atop a hill, surrounded by woods and gardens. Brilliant stars at night. Upon arrival the staff bought us snacks, an ice bucket, and cold drinks. The spacious Jonathan Suite had an attractive yellow and blue color scheme, and a two-sided fireplace. The adjacent room, The Cortland, is done in blue toile with antique furnishings, and has a huge Jacuzzi tub, and French doors opening to an outside private patio; there were books to read and games to play. We explored the walking trails, and relaxed in the hammocks. Breakfast included a buffet of cereal, fruit, and breads; an egg entree was brought to the table with juice; seating was inside the main lodge or out on the second-floor balcony." *(Ruth Hurley)*

Open All year. Restaurant closed Sun.; some weekdays off-season.
Rooms 12 suites, 10 doubles—all with full private bath, clock/radio, TV/VCR, Desk, air-conditioning, ceiling fan. Some with telephone, double whirlpool tub, fireplace, wet bar, refrigerator, deck/balcony. Rooms in 4 buildings.
Facilities Restaurant, bar/lounge, great room with fireplace, player piano; balconies. 4 acres with gardens, off-street parking. Hiking, fishing nearby.
Location Historic district. Take Hwy. 78 or 79 E to Julian. Name becomes Wash-

ington St. in town. Inn is 1 block past Main St. on left. From Hwy. 78 or 79 W, road becomes Main St. in town. Go right on Washington St. to inn on left.
Restrictions No smoking. Children 12 & over.
Credit cards Amex, MC, Visa.
Rates B&B, $140–195 suite; $120–155 double. Extra person, $25. Prix fixe dinner, $30.
Extras Wheelchair access; 2 rooms specially equipped. German, Hungarian, Spanish spoken.

KERNVILLE

Kern River Inn ¢ ♿.
119 Kern River Drive, P.O. Box 1725, 93238

Tel: 760–376–6750
800–986–4382
Fax: 760–376–6643
E-mail: kribb@kernvalley.com

The area around Kernville and the Kern River is rugged territory, bordered by Sequoia National Forest and the foothills of the Sierra Nevada Mountains. Built in 1991, the Inn is patterned after a Victorian ranch house. Guest rooms are accented with paintings and curios from local artists; some rooms have a handsome river rock fireplace, others feature a whirlpool tub; all have a king-or queen-size bed. Breakfast entrees change daily, but might include giant cinnamon rolls, egg casseroles, homemade granola, juice, fresh fruit compote, and coffee or tea. Rates also include afternoon refreshments.

The area provides a wide range of activities year-round, starting with whitewater rafting, kayaking, and fishing in the Kern River which runs in front of the inn; hiking, rock climbing, and the giant Sequoias are nearby, as is Isabella Lake for all water sports. The less energetic can just enjoy the river from the swing on the veranda, and stroll to restaurants, shops, and the museum in town.

"Carita and Jack are so friendly, and more than eager to listen to the umpteenth river rafting story. The inn is quaint, spotlessly clean, and the food is incredible. Delicious breakfast, tempting afternoon snacks." *(Tami Jacoby)* "Friendly, outgoing hosts; excellent service." *(Bobby & Betsy Butler)* "Terrific half-way stop between Death Valley and the San Francisco area." *(Kathleen Lowe Owen)*

Open All year.
Rooms 6 doubles—all with private bath, radio, air-conditioning. 3 with fireplace, 2 with whirlpool tub.
Facilities Dining room, living room with fireplace, stereo, TV/VCR, movies, books, games; wraparound veranda with swing. Flower garden, off-street parking. On Kern River for whitewater rafting, kayaking, water skiing, wave-riding, wind surfing, fishing. Hiking, bicycling, golf, rock climbing, nearby; 14 m to downhill, cross-country skiing.
Location S Sierra Nevada. 55 m NE of Bakersfield, in S section of Sequoia National Forest. From Bakersfield, take Hwy 178 E. 45m to Hwy. 155. Go N 10m to Kernville. After "Welcome to Kernville" sign, take 1st right onto Kern Drive to Inn. Walking distance to restaurants, shops, museum.
Restrictions No smoking.

Credit cards Amex, MC, Visa.
Rates B&B, $79–99 double, $69–89 single. Extra person, $15.
Extras Wheelchair access; 1 room equipped for disabled. Local airport pickup.

LAGUNA BEACH

Laguna became popular as a resort at the turn of the century and was established as an art colony in the 1930s. It provides both beautiful beaches and year-round sun, but life here isn't entirely without pressure—there are parking meters by the tennis courts to indicate remaining court time. Laguna offers theater and ballet as well as a number of arts and crafts festivals and plenty of shops. Of course, water sports, from surfing to scuba diving, are very popular.

Laguna Beach is located on the Orange County coast 11 miles south of Newport Beach, about 38 miles south of Los Angeles and about 60 miles north of San Diego on Coast Highway 1. From Los Angeles take Route 5 south to Irvine and then west on Route 133 to the coast. From San Diego, take Route 5 north to Capistrano Beach and continue north about 8 miles on Coast Highway 1.

Information please: Two blocks from the beach, **Laguna House** (539 Catalina Street, 92651; 714–497–9061) is described as having a "beach cottage" atmosphere, with nine suites, each furnished with bleached pine, wicker, and fresh print fabrics. An efficiency kitchen accompanies each suite; most surround a brick courtyard. Accommodations also include a two-bedroom cottage with beamed ceilings and a woodburning fireplace, and The Catalina Suite, with its own private rooftop deck with a view of Main Beach. Rates range from $95–185. Weekly rates are also available.

Listed in past editions, we need current reports on **Eiler's Inn** (741 South Pacific Coast Highway, 92651; 714–494–3004), located in the heart of Laguna Beach. Two guest rooms have water views; the other ten open to a charming interior courtyard garden with a fountain. B&B double rates of $85–195 include a breakfast of fresh-baked breads, fresh fruit and juice, boiled eggs, and Viennese coffee; always available coffee and tea; and evening wine and cheese.

Inn at Laguna Beach   🛏 ♿   *Tel:* 714–497–9722
211 North Coast Highway, 92651   800–544–4479
     Fax: 714–497–9972

The Inn at Laguna Beach is where you'd expect it to be—its white stucco buildings climb the bluff overlooking the main beach and village. Guest rooms have large windows, crisply dressed with wooden blinds, Spanish-style accents in wrought iron and wood, and soothing colors of gray, blue, and soft peach. Fifth-floor rooms (the "Coastal Level") have feather beds and duvets, a more extensive breakfast, and other amenities. Rates include a light breakfast of coffee, juice, and pastry, brought to guest rooms each morning with the newspaper.

"Great location, just a short walk to the beach, and a bit further to dozens of shops and restaurants. Friendly staff, from check-in desk to housekeeping to management." *(John P. Sullivan)* "The lovely rooms are large, clean, and tastefully appointed, and most face the beach. Many have private patios with table and chairs. The Jacuzzi and swimming pool are on a bluff overlooking the sea. The public rooms are light, airy, and well maintained." *(William Frick)* "At sunset, head for the rooftop deck for a drink and a wonderful view." *(MW)*

Open All year.

Rooms 70 doubles—all with private bath and/or shower, telephone, radio, TV/VCR, air-conditioning, mini-bar, refrigerator, hair dryer. Some with desk, balcony. Fifth-floor rooms also with CD players/CDs, make-up mirrors, coffee makers, books.

Facilities Lobby, roof top solarium/sun deck, Jacuzzi. 1 acre with heated swimming pool, hot tub, fitness spa. On ocean beach for water sports. Underground parking. Tennis, golf nearby.

Location 1 block N of town center.

Credit cards Amex, CB, DC, MC, Visa.

Rates B&B, $99–399 double. Extra person, $20. 10% senior, AAA discount. 2-night minimum stay weekends.

Extras Wheelchair access; rooms equipped for disabled. Crib. French, German, Spanish spoken.

LA JOLLA

La Jolla (pronounced "La Hoya") is a suburb of San Diego, about a 20-minute drive north of downtown. Not just a bedroom community, this sophisticated village on the Pacific Ocean has a number of attractions, including the Museum of Contemporary Art, the Scripps Institute of Oceanography, and U.C. San Diego, along with over 30 restaurants and 120 shops, which range from trendy to traditional. Cove Beach, a marine-life preserve, is a favorite for snorkeling. The Torrey Pines Golf Course and the Del Mar Racetrack are a short drive away to the north. La Jolla is located 89 miles south of Los Angeles and 12 miles north of San Diego.

Also recommended: Built in 1926 of pink stucco and red tile, **La Valencia Hotel** (1132 Prospect Street, 92037; 619–454–0771 or 800–451–0772) overlooks Cove Beach and Scripps Park and is surrounded by some of La Jolla's finest boutiques and art galleries. Rooms are traditionally decorated, and most have ocean views. "In the heart of the village, steps from all attractions." *(Sally Ducot)* "Incredibly romantic, incredibly beautiful. In my next life, I'd like to live here." *(BNS)* "Exceptionally friendly staff; wonderful food. Careful attention to detail, from the Crabtree and Evelyn soaps and lotions, to the thick terry-cloth robes and slippers for trips to the hot tub. Our partial ocean view room was picturesque, overlooking the ocean and seaside park." *(Debbie Bergstrom)* Rates for the 90 double rooms range from $180–395; the 10 suites cost $450–750.

Information please: The **Bed & Breakfast Inn at La Jolla** (7753 Draper Avenue, 92037; 619–456–2066 or 800–582–2466) is a beige stucco home built in 1913 and one of the first examples of Irving Gill's "Cubist" architecture. Conveniently located within two blocks of restaurants and shops, it is across a grassy park from the cliffside cove path. Rooms are beautifully decorated in Laura Ashley fabrics, although some are quite small. B&B double rates of $85–225 include a home-baked continental breakfast and afternoon wine tasting.

In the heart of the village, at the corner of Fay and Silverado, is the **Empress Hotel** (7766 Fay Avenue, 93027; 619–454–3001 or 888–369–9900), offering a garden patio with fountain, a sundeck, hot tub and exercise room, plus valet parking. B&B rates for the 73 guest rooms range from $110–130, suites $250–325, each with private bath, hair dryer, and in-room refrigerator; some have ocean views, kitchenettes, and whirlpool tubs.

Prospect Park Inn
1110 Prospect Street, 92037

Tel: 619–454–0133
800–433–1609
Fax: 619–454–2056

Overlooking La Jolla Cove, the Prospect Park Inn was built in 1945. Purchased in 1995 by Joseph Witzman, the manager is John Heichman. Rates include a continental breakfast, enjoyed in the room or on the ocean-view sundeck, plus afternoon refreshments. Coffee and tea are available throughout the day.

"An excellent value; well-run European-style hotel. Great location near the ocean and steps from stores and scores of restaurants. While not large, our second-story room (#15) had a balcony and a kitchen. It was spacious enough to accommodate a queen-size bed and still leave room for an arm chair and space to walk around. The room was tastefully decorated in beige and peach tones with ample reading lights, closet and drawer space. You can breakfast in your room or on the sun deck, overlooking the Pacific. Just call down when you're ready and the tray—complete with daily newspaper—is delivered promptly. We stayed for a week and found a different basket of goodies each day— fresh orange juice, croissants, fruit scones, muffins, or other delicious pastries. The inn is squeaky clean. Our bathroom was well-lit and we appreciated the oversize bath towels and extra shelf space to hold toiletries." (*Carolyn Myles & Colburn Aker*) "Cordial staff made every effort to be helpful." (*ABK*)

Open All year.
Rooms 2 suites, 22 doubles—all with full private bath, telephone, radio, clock, TV, air-conditioning, fan, coffee maker, hair dryer. 8 with refrigerator, 12 with balcony.
Facilities Lobby/library, sun deck. Free indoor parking in garage across street; off-street parking. 1 block to ocean, park.
Location Center of village.
Restrictions Traffic, restaurant noise in front rooms (until 11 P.M.). No smoking.
Credit cards Amex, DC, Discover, MC, Visa.
Rates B&B, $250–300 suite, $100–165 double. Senior, AAA discount. Weekly, corporate rates.

LAKE ALMANOR

Lake Almanor is located in Plumas County, 1½ hours northeast of Chico, two hours west of Reno Nevada, and about 40 miles south of Mt. Lassen National Park. Area activities include the lake for water sports, hiking, riding, bicycling, snowmobiling, and cross-country skiing.

Information please: For a downhome mountain getaway, consider the **Lake Almanor Inn** (3965 Highway A-13, 96137; 916–596–3910), a rustic log lodge, built from foot-thick timbers in 1963, and owned by Les and Margo Olinger since 1995. Downstairs is a coffee shop, dining room, lounge with a rock fireplace, pool table, antique piano, and arcade-style video games, plus five guest rooms with shared baths ($59); upstairs is another guest room with king-size bed and private bath ($85); also available is a cabin on the river ($115). Rates include a full breakfast in the coffee shop; omelets are a speciality. "Located on Hamilton Branch Creek, with great hiking trails. Clean, spacious rooms; exceptionally clean shared baths. Tasty meals, great omelets. Friendly, accommodating service." *(Susan Little)*

LAKE ARROWHEAD

Lake Arrowhead is a popular all-season resort with Los Angelenos, with lake fishing, the scenic 40-mile Rim-of-the-World drive (at 5,000 plus feet with spectacular vistas), and nearby San Bernardino National Forest for winter activities, including downhill and cross-country skiing. It's located in the San Bernadino Mountains in the Inland Empire region of southwest California, 90 minutes from Los Angeles. From I-10, go north on I-15E to Route 30 E to State Highway 18. Go north, then east on Highway 18.

The Carriage House B&B ¢
472 Emerald Drive, P.O. Box 982, 92352

Tel: 909–336–1400
800–562–5070
Fax: 909–336–6092

Tucked in the pines just a stone's throw from Lake Arrowhead, the Carriage House welcomes visitors with its country decor, rich oak woodwork and floors, and leaded glass windows. Lee and Johan Karstens, owners since 1989, invite guests to snuggle under plump European down comforters at night; the morning brings breakfasts of fresh fruit, baked goods, coffee and tea, and Belgian waffles with raspberry sauce, eggs Florentine, or Dutch Babies.

"Ideally located next to the lake and a beautiful lakeside path to the village, full of shops and restaurants. From the lovely Surrey Room you can step out on your own private balcony for a majestic view of the lake. In the morning, we enjoyed a delicious breakfast with fellow guests; in the evening, a special treat was coming home to a turned-down featherbed and a homemade treat." *(Renee & William Fremgen)* "Exceptionally clean; great warmth and hospitality." *(Angela Heidfeld)* "Johan and

Lee make you feel as if the house were your own. Every day at 5 P.M. we sat in front of the fire with a glass of wine and a snack, chatting with the other guests, sharing the day's events or the plans for the evening ahead. Friendly inn dog, Deke." *(Haven Show)* "The Karstens are there to chat if you like, but give you space and freedom if preferred. Lee is pleased to make reservations and provide information on area activities. Guest rooms are clean, well equipped, with invitingly plump duvets and feather beds." *(Harriet Bailey)* "It's worth a trip just for Lee's Dutch Baby pancakes." *(GR)*

Open All year.
Rooms 3 doubles—all with private bath and/or shower, radio, clock, TV, fan. 1 with VCR, fireplace, balcony.
Facilities Dining room, living room with fireplace, stereo, books; sun room with TV/VCR, stereo, games, CD/video library; deck with hammock. Near lake for water sports; lakeside walking path.
Location 2 m from Lake Arrowhead Village. On Emerald Drive, off Rte. 173.
Restrictions No smoking. Children over 13.
Credit cards Amex, Discover, MC, Visa.
Rates B&B, $95–135 double. Extra person, $15. 10% discount seniors, also midweek, 2-night stays. 2–3 night weekend, holiday minimum.
Extras Dutch spoken.

Eagle's Landing *Tel:* 909–336–2642
27406 Cedarwood, 92317 800–825–5085
Mailing address: Box 1510, Blue Jay, 92317 *Fax:* 909–336–2910

Dorothy and Jack Stone built and operate Eagle's Landing in a spacious contemporary house, nestled into the wooded hillside. Rooms are large, amply lighted, and comfortably furnished with accents from the owners' collection of folk art, antique farm implements, and travel remembrances. Rates include a full breakfast (brunch on Sunday), and afternoon wine hour.

"An attractively designed house with multilevel decks, balconies and tower in a setting of pine and spruce. Our suite had a private balcony and fireplace. Dorothy served us a delicious breakfast in the top of the tower." *(Judith Powell)* "The Lake View suite has over 900 square feet of space with a woodburning fireplace, queen-size bed, huge sofabed, refrigerator, and a large covered patio. Delicious 'Eagle's Nest' for breakfast—hot fruit with cinnamon-spiced sauce and topped with vanilla yogurt, accompanied by muffins and cheese." *(Jan Peverill)* "Dorothy and Jack must have written the book on hospitality and graciousness." *(Shirley Barlow)* "Excellent hosts; most pleasant visit. Excellent advice on area restaurants and sights." *(D.A.)*

Open All year.
Rooms 1 suite, 3 doubles—all with private bath and/or shower, radio, fan. Suite with fireplace, TV/VCR, stereo, wet bar, deck.
Facilities Breakfast room, living/family room with TV, games, stereo; decks. ½ acre with picnic area, hammock.
Location 20 m N of San Bernardino, 2 m W of Lake Arrowhead. From Hwy. 18, follow signs to Blue Jay. At fork in road in Blue Jay, go left on North Bay Rd. Inn on left at corner of North Bay and Cedarwood Rd.

Restrictions No smoking. "Not appropriate for children."
Credit cards Discover, MC, Visa.
Rates B&B, $185 suite; $95–125 double. Extra person, $25. 10% senior discount midweek. 2–3 night weekend/holiday minimum.

LASSEN VOLCANIC NATIONAL PARK

Also recommended: The only accommodations inside the park is the **Drakesbad Guest Ranch** (in-season: End of Warner Valley Road, Lassen Volcanic National Park, Chester, 96020; off-season: 2150 North Main Street, Suite 5, Red Bluff 96080; telephone, Drakesbad #2 via Susanville 916 operator or 916–529–1512). Named for the warm water baths and swimming pool filled by the nearby hot springs, the ranch has been providing bed and board for over a century; kerosene lamps are provided to light the rustic cabins. You can hike or take a guided horseback ride to Boiling Springs Lake, the Devil's Kitchen, Terminal Geyser, and other colorfully named geological wonders. The clang of the dinner bell announces each meal; food is simple but ample, and sack lunches are available for day-long hikes or rides. Drakesbad is accessible only via the road from Chester. "A charming unusual place, like a lodge of 50 years ago. Quiet and unassuming; seems to cater to families—quiet ones! There is minimal electricity in the dining room and the 5 lodge rooms. Food is good—a large buffet and a hot dish at breakfast, cold cuts, salads, and breads at lunch; and a single entree at dinner. Lots of fun." *(Duane Roller)* Rates include three meals daily, and range from $185–210 double, plus service, with weekly rates and children's discounts available. The ranch is open from early June to mid October.

For additional area entries, see **Almanor, Red Bluff,** and **Redding.**

LEMON COVE

Information please: Halfway between Visalia and Sequoia National Park is the **Mesa Verde Plantation B&B** (33038 Sierra Highway 198, 93244; 209–597–2555 or 800–240–1466), previously known as the Lemon Cove B&B. Set in the foothills of the Sierras, guests can pick oranges or avocados, swim in the heated pool or soak in the spa. Built in 1968, it was purchased by Scott and Marie Munger in 1996; rooms are named for characters in *Gone with the Wind.* B&B double rates for the eight guest rooms, most with private bath, range form $70–125, including a full home-cooked breakfast.

LITTLE RIVER

Little River is located two miles south of the Victorian town of Mendocino. You can easily visit all of Mendocino's boutiques and restaurants during the day and then escape the evening noise and bustle by staying in Little River. Located on the North Coast, it's 155 miles north of San Francisco. The area was originally settled in the 1850s as a major source of redwood lumber for San Francisco. (Redwood, being pitch-free, was found to be more fire-resistant than other woods.) Logs were floated down the river to the coast, then taken by schooner to San Francisco.

Worth noting: If an unobstructed, panoramic ocean view is a priority for you, be sure to ask for details; many inns claim a "water view," but all you get is a glimpse of blue in the distance. If you care about proximity to the ocean, ask if you can *hear* the waves. Many inns are on Highway 1, so be sure to ask about traffic noise if you're a light sleeper.

Also recommended: The **Heritage House** (5200 North Highway 1, 95456; 707–937–5885 or 800–235–5885) gets our vote for the most beautifully situated inn in northern California. Except for a few units, the inn is located west of Highway 1, so all you see from your room is green lawns, beautiful flowers, dramatic cliffs, crashing waves, and endless ocean. The beautiful restaurant and bar offer equally gorgeous views from huge windows. Guest rooms are comfortable, with double rates ranging from $95–285, depending on room, view, and season. Breakfast is extra, and new chef Lance Dean Velasquez offers an a la carte menu of contemporary American cuisine. "We were pleased with our spacious room, Deerfield #7, with a nice deck and ocean views. The accommodations, views, and grounds continue to be exceptional." *(Tom Wilbanks)* Reports on the food and especially the service are appreciated.

For unobstructed ocean views and reasonable rates in this expensive area, it's hard to beat the **Little River Inn** (Little River, 95456; 707–937–5942 or 888–INN–LOVE). This family-owned facility offers satisfactory motel rooms with spectacular vistas in the moderate $85–115 price range, as well as luxury cottages with fireplaces and whirlpool tubs ($180–255); with the exception of a couple units, rooms are not affected by traffic noise. Facilities include a modest but fun nine-hole golf course, and a tennis court. "Pleasant staff, good restaurant, convenient location. Well-kept grounds with beautiful flowers blooming everywhere; walking distance to Van Damme State Park with a beach and hiking trails into Fern Canyon. The food was quite good, highlighted by the Swedish pancakes at breakfast and the ollalieberry cobbler at dinner." *(SWS)* "Our favorite is the Coombs Cottage across the street on the ocean side. This private little cottage is perfect for romance and privacy, with a Jacuzzi tub and a wonderful stone fireplace, beautiful French doors looking out to spectacular ocean views, and a private sundeck." *(Linda Haakenson)*

A short walk to the ocean and beautiful Van Damme State Park is **Glendeven** (8221 North Highway 1, 95456; 707–937–0083), a Maine-style farmhouse built in 1867, and owned by Jan and Janet deVries since 1977; the decor effectively combines antique quilts and country furnishings with contemporary arts and crafts. Additional rooms are located in Stevenscroft, a relatively new building modeled after the original Victorian one. "The Gallery at Glendeven" occupies the ground floor of the Barn; it features Jan's handmade seating in addition to other fine contemporary art and crafts; the second floor suite is ideal for families. B&B double rates for the 10 doubles are $90–160; the suite costs $185–200; some rooms have a distant bay view.

For additional area entries, see **Albion, Fort Bragg,** and **Mendocino**.

LIVERMORE

Information please: Just 50 minutes or less east of the San Francisco, Oakland, and San Jose airports is Livermore's first B&B resort, **The Purple Orchid Inn** (4549 Cross Road, 94550; 510–606–8855 or 800–353–4549), completed in 1997. Set on a working olive ranch, this log building has nine guest rooms with double Jacuzzi tubs and fireplaces. Facilities include spa services, a tennis court, swimming pool with hot tub and waterfall, exercise room and sauna, golf cages and a chipping bunker. One of the oldest wine-making regions in the state, the area is home to 16 wineries as well as seven golf courses. B&B rates range from $150–250, including a full breakfast (selected from a menu the night before), and afternoon wine and refreshments.

For an additional area inn, see **Pleasanton.**

LODI

Also recommended: About 30 miles south of Sacramento and 15 miles north of Stockton is the **Wine & Roses Country Inn** (2505 West Turner Road, 95242; 209–334–6988) with a restaurant and ten guest rooms, built as a farmhouse in 1901. B&B double rates range from $99–150; rooms have private baths, telephones, and TVs, as well as charming country Victorian decor, making them popular for business midweek, romance on the weekends. "Lovely garden setting. The entire staff took the extra step to make us comfortable, welcome, and happy. Even their pet chicken Dumpling was polite. The rooms we saw were tidy, nicely decorated, and had reading lights on both sides of the bed. Dinner was very good, and the service was attentive but not intrusive. A delightful experience we can't wait to repeat. " *(Kathleen Owen)*

LOS ANGELES

Larger than Rhode Island and Delaware combined, Los Angeles is both linked and separated by an amazing maze of freeways. In fact, if the people of Detroit could have dreamed up the perfect town, they would have invented Los Angeles, where it is impossible to get anywhere without a car.

Los Angeles is a hodgepodge of different ethnic groups—you can visit different restaurants and shops for a taste of countries from Hungary to Thailand, from Polynesia to Ethiopia. Large Mexican, Japanese, Chinese and Southeast Asian neighborhoods are intrinsic parts of Los Angeles. There's really a lot to see in Los Angeles—not just the TV and movie industry tours but other kinds of cultural and historic sights as well, including a number of outstanding art museums.

To make things a little easier, we've grouped most of our suggestions for the Los Angeles area in this section, so you won't have to check through the whole California chapter to find Beverly Hills or Santa Monica. Before you make reservations, it's a good idea to look at a map and identify the areas where you'll be spending most of your time; then book your room in that area of the city. Los Angeles is so spread out and the traffic so heavy (the afternoon rush hour starts at 3 p.m.) that you could easily spend your entire day in the car (and a car you must have). If you're traveling with the family and will mainly be doing the theme-park circuit, you'll be better off staying in Orange County to the southeast.

LA is a four area code town: downtown remains 213; to the north it's 818; and the area south and west of downtown has become 310 and 562. Los Angeles is located in Southern California, about 400 miles south of San Francisco and 125 miles north of San Diego.

To save money on many Los Angeles area hotels, call **Express Hotel Reservations** at 800–356–1123 or 303–440–8481. They offer discounts of 20–50% off rack rates, and since they receive a commission from the hotels, there's no charge to you. Don't feel you have to get stuck with a chain property—the Los Angeles area has many hotels of style and distinction worth checking out.

Reader tip: "The Huntington Library, Museum and Gardens in Pasadena is well worth a visit; stay for a delicious lunch or a bounteous tea. Tea lovers will also enjoy a visit to the Chado Tea Room (213–655–2056) in Los Angeles, with dozens of teas to sample. Delightful French-Mediterranean dinner at Cafe Pierre in Manhattan Beach." *(Emily Hoche-Mong)*

Also recommended: A classic on Sunset Strip **The Argyle** (8358 Sunset Boulevard, West Hollywood 90069; 213–654–7100 or 800–225–2637) is a 1929 Art Deco classic tower. Double rates for its 64 beautifully furnished guest rooms cost around $225, and the hotel restaurant, Fenix, is one of the city's best. The rooftop deck and swimming pool offers wonderful sunset and city views. "Stunning. We felt just like movie stars of the 1930s. Rooms were authentically furnished and comfortable. Staff was friendly and accommodating. We ate breakfast on the deck with an awesome skyline view. Fenix is an outstanding restaurant with imaginative flair." *(Ginny Watkins)*

Glowing superlatives seem to be the operative mode when it comes to describing the **Hotel Bel-Air** (701 Stone Canyon Road, Los Angeles, 90077; 310–472–1211 or 800–648–4097)—it receives top honors in nearly every hotel ranking survey. Rates for the 91 guest rooms are $325–450 for doubles, with suites starting at $525, although promotional rates are sometimes available. "A classic pink stucco building in a spectacular setting—a wooded, secluded canyon close to the Bel-Air Country Club. Beautifully landscaped grounds, with a fabulous swimming pool. The lobby is cozy and well appointed, with a fireplace. The luxurious rooms are individually done in pastel colors with down comforters. The restaurant is excellent, and the bar is the former haunt of Humphrey Bogart and other movie stars of the 1940s." *(Linda & Paul Duttenhaver)* "We couldn't afford to stay overnight, but came for lunch and relished every moment and every bite." *(MA)*

Two good choices directly on the beach are the **Malibu Beach Inn** (22878 Pacific Coast Highway, Malibu 90265; 310–456–6445 or 800–4–MALIBU), a three-story, Mediterranean-style building offering 47 guest rooms, some with gas fireplace and balcony with ocean view (B&B $205–295 double); and **Shutters on the Beach** (1 Pico Boulevard, Santa Monica 90405; 310–458–0030 or 800–334–9000), highly recommended for "its distinctive style, beautifully designed public areas, well-equipped, handsome guest rooms with huge, comfortable beds, highest quality electronics, luxurious bathrooms, attentive service, lovely swimming pool, and excellent food in two restaurants." *(Mark Tattersall)* Double rates for the 198 guest rooms range from $300–500.

If you've always dreamed of having your own beach house at Malibu, you can come close at **Bed, Breakfast, & Beyond** (310–456–8124), a beautiful hilltop home overlooking the coastline, with a secluded ocean-view swimming pool. B&B double rates for the two guest rooms range from $85–135, available September through June. "Simple but elegant decor, spectacular ocean views from every room. Charming hostess." *(CB)*

Information please: The Kimco Hotel chain, well-known for its boutique hotels in San Francisco, operates the **Beverly Prescott Hotel** (1224 South Beverwil Drive at Pico Boulevard, P.O. Box 3065, Beverly Hills, 90212; 310–277–2800 or 800–421–3212). Most of the 140 luxurious guest rooms have balconies, plush overstuffed furnishings in florals and stripes, two telephones, terry robes, and more at rates of $205–250 double. There's even a swimming pool for a cooling dip. Ask for a high-floor room facing the hills to avoid traffic noise.

An elegant option in South Pasadena is **The Bissell House** (201 Orange Grove Avenue, South Pasadena 91030; 818–441–3535 or 800–441–3530), built on Millionaire's Row in 1887. B&B double rates for the five beautifully decorated guest rooms, each with private bath, include a generous continental breakfast on weekdays, a full one on weekends, and range from $125–200.

Listed in many past editions, we'd like current reports on **La Maida House** (1150 La Maida Street, North Hollywood, 91601; 818–769–3857), long owned by Megan Timothy, who created many of its paintings, sculptures, and stained glass. Rates include continental breakfast and afternoon aperitifs; no animal products are served. Six guest rooms are available in three nearby bungalows, with B&B rates ranging from $85–210. Although Megan has sold the La Maida mansion, she notes that one of the houses has a "cute new dining room with a beamed ceiling and fireplace, also a small living room with skylights."

In the heart of the Long Beach downtown historic district, within walking distance of the convention center is **The Turret House** (556 Chestnut Avenue, Long Beach 90802; 562–983–9812 or 888–4–TURRET), a 1906 Queen Anne Victorian home restored as a B&B in 1996. B&B double rates of $90–125 include a full breakfast and evening refreshments; each of the five guest rooms have a private bath, and king-, queen-, or twin-size beds.

A few blocks from the beaches of Venice and Marina del Rey, only fifteen minutes from the airport (LAX), is **The Mansion Inn** (327 Washington Boulevard, Marina del Rey 90291; 310–821–2557 or 800–828–0688), with 43 hotel rooms, each furnished in French-country decor. B&B double rates of $89–99 (suites to $145), include a continental buffet breakfast.

Just one building away from the beach and within walking distance of numerous restaurants is the Craftsman-style **Venice Beach House** (15 Thirtieth Avenue, Venice, 90291; 310–823–1966), built in 1911. The four rooms with shared baths cost $85–95; the other five with private bath range from $120–165. Rates include a buffet breakfast of fresh fruit and juice, and home-baked goods. "Fresh flowers everywhere, delicious breakfast, friendly, relaxed staff; classical music in background; lovely backyard." *(Susanne Wright)*

For an additional area inn, see **Seal Beach.**

The Artists' Inn B&B   *Tel:* 818–799–5668
1038 Magnolia Street, South Pasadena 91030   888–799–5668
Fax: 818–799–3678
E-mail: artistinn@aol.com

If all you know of Pasadena is the Rose Bowl, or perhaps an old song by the Beach Boys, then you're in for a pleasant surprise at the Artists' Inn. Starting in 1991, Janet Marangi began restoring an 1895 Victorian farmhouse, originally built by Indiana native C.R. Johnson as a home base for his chicken farm. She opened the inn in 1993; Lean Roberts is the manager. Janet notes that the inn is convenient for business travelers midweek, while vacationers will enjoy the Huntington Library and Gardens, the Norton Simon Museum of Art, the Pan Asia Museum, the Gamble House, Dodger stadium, and more. Breakfast is served at separate tables at guests' choice of time, between 7:30–9:30 weekdays, and 8–10:00 A.M. weekends. The menu includes guests' choice of tea and coffee (including espresso and cappucino), fresh fruit and juice, cereal, home-baked muffins and bread, and such entrees as baked apple pancakes or stuffed French toast.

The common areas include the spacious front porch, with its graceful arches and inviting white wicker rockers and loungers, and the equally appealing living room, with its deep green walls, Oriental rugs, floral fabric accents, and more white wicker. Each guest room was inspired by a different artist or artistic period, from the soft colors and queen-size brass bed in the Impressionist room to the king-size canopy bed, rose-patterned wall coverings, and reproductions of works by Gainsborough, Reynolds, and Constable in the Eighteenth Century English Room. The Van Gogh Room is designed to replicate the artist's depiction of his own bedroom; sunflowers painted on the bathroom walls evoke another of his most famous works.

"Beautifully decorated, charming in spirit and ambiance; romantic setting. Superb baked apple puff for breakfast." *(Donald Blosser)* "Accommodating, friendly, helpful innkeepers who were pleased to make dinner reservations for us. Quiet, very clean, cleverly decorated old farmhouse, close to museums and shops. Wonderful sitting porch. Great books; thoughtful attention to detail." *(Maureen Boren)* "Pleasant, relaxing surroundings and accommodations. Wonderful garden. Inventive delicious breakfast." *(Carol Moore)* "Lovely people who understand the true meaning of hospitality." *(Susan Wilson)* "Wonderful roses in every color. The 100% cotton sheets made for a luxurious night's sleep. Beautifully maintained inn." *(Emilie & Ruedi Vest)*

Open All year.

Rooms 1 suite, 4 doubles—all with full private bath, clock/radio, TV (on request), air-conditioning. Some with desk, ceiling fan.

Facilities Dining room, living room with fireplace, TV, stereo, books; guest refrigerator, porch. Off-street parking, flower gardens, lawn games. Tennis, golf, fishing nearby.

Location 10 m E of downtown LA. Mission West district, 2 block to historic district, 4 blocks to center of town. 10 min. to Rose Bowl, five min. to Old Town Pasadena. From Los Angeles, take Freeway 110 N to Orange Grove exit. Go right at end of ramp, and take immediate left onto Grevalia. Cross Prospect Meridian. Go right on Fairview to inn at end of block, at corner of Magnolia & Fairview.

Restrictions No smoking. "More appropriate for adults."

Credit cards Amex, Discover, MC, Visa

Rates B&B, $120 suite, $105–$130 double. Extra person, $20. Special request dinner, $35–40 per person.

Channel Road Inn   ♿   *Tel:* 310–459–1920
219 West Channel Road, Santa Monica 90402   *Fax:* 310–454–9920
E-mail: ChannelInn@aol.com

A shingle-clad Colonial Revival home, the Channel Road Inn was built for Thomas McCall in 1910. The house was moved to Santa Monica Canyon in the 1970s and then abandoned after reconstruction plans fell through; fortunately, it was rescued from demolition and restored as a B&B in 1988 by Susan Zolla. During the renovation process the walls were stuffed with insulation and the windows double-glazed. One guest room has an elaborate Victorian bedroom set, while another has a pencil-post canopied bed framed with feather-light sheers; most have ocean views. Rates include a breakfast of home-baked breads and muffins, an egg dish, and fresh fruit plus afternoon wine and cheese, tea and cookies. "Friendly, helpful staff. At my advance request, a special breakfast was prepared to accommodate my allergies. The food was plentiful and inventive; the dining tables, spread through the bay-windowed library and into a lovely sitting room, were set with white linen and fresh flowers from the rose garden." *(Jeanette Van Doren)* "Location is perfect for people who want to be close to LA but like the beach; it's a five-minute walk to the ocean with a bike path that runs to Malibu in one direction—the Santa Monica pier in the other. Lovely rooms; genuine Turkish towel bathrobes, plenty of hot water. Unobtrusive innkeepers who are pleased to suggest activities. An international mix of guests." *(Nancy Granese)* "The neighborhood affords wonderful seaside walks along the concrete paths or along the sand itself. First-rate service." *(Elwy & Lila Yost)* "Wonderful breakfasts; scones to die for." *(Brandon Lowitz)*

"Four or five good restaurants are within easy walking distance." *(Sally Ducot)* "Welcoming owner Susan Zolla and innkeeper Kathy Jensen were helpful with dinner reservations, and were sensitive to our dietary needs." *(Sharene Walsh)* "Exquisite wood panel work; the living room is warm, colorful, spacious, and well appointed." *(LJ)* "The well-appointed Honeymoon Suite has a sitting room with a French door leading to a porch, as well as a deck spa with Pacific views." *(Sylvia Barkley)* "Kathy assisted with my luggage, and offered me a refreshing drink. Small touches made for a homey feeling—a welcoming note, just-picked roses, freshly baked chocolate chip cookies, plush terry-cloth robe, huge bath sheets, a wicker basket filled with toiletries, and a magnifying mirror in the bathroom." *(Gail Davis)*

Open All year.
Rooms 2 suites, 12 doubles—all with private bath and/or shower, telephone, TV/VCR, radio, fan. 12 with desk.
Facilities Breakfast room, living room with fireplace, library with books, videotapes; patio. ½ acre with garden, hot tub, off-street parking. Beach towels, bicycles. 1 block to beach. 30-mile bike path parallels beach. Horseback riding, tennis nearby. Fax, secretarial, conference services.
Location Los Angeles area, Santa Monica Canyon. 25 min N of downtown Los Angeles. From Pacific Coast Hwy., exit at W. Channel Rd. From San Diego Freeway (Hwy. 405) take Wilshire W. exit & go to 7th St. (becomes Channel Rd.). Map mailed/faxed with confirmation.
Restrictions Traffic noise in front rooms. No smoking.
Credit cards Amex, MC, Visa.
Rates B&B, $95–225 suite or double. Extra person, $10. Crib, $10.
Extras Wheelchair access; 1 room equipped for the disabled. Crib, babysitting. French, Spanish, Italian spoken.

Inn at Playa del Rey ₵ 🏃 ♿ *Tel:* 310–574–1920
435 Culver Boulevard, Playa Del Rey, 90293 *Fax:* 310–574–9920
E-mail: Channelinn@aol.com

To rephrase a saying by Abraham Lincoln, "you can't please all the people all the time," but at the Inn at Playa del Rey, owner Susan Zolla has sure come close with the Cape Cod–style inn she built in 1995. (For a description of her other inn, see the Channel Road Inn above). Although its convenient location on a major road close to Los Angeles International Airport does have drawbacks, readers rave about every other aspect of the inn: the gracious hospitality of Susan, manager Donna Donnelly, and the staff; the beautiful decor; the well equipped rooms, ideal for business or romance; the delicious food; and the lovely setting overlooking the Ballona Wetlands bird sanctuary. Guest rooms are individually decorated, with a subdued and restful color scheme. Most rooms have a queen- or king-size bed, some with a canopy, others with a sleigh bed; some have a country accent, others are elegantly traditional. Breakfast, served at tables for two from 7:30 to 10 A.M., includes a buffet of fresh fruit, juice, cereal, granola, muffins, breads, or scones and the entree of the day—perhaps artichoke soufflé or peach French toast. Rates also include tea and cookies, and afternoon wine and cheese.

"A sanctuary for humans overlooking an equally lovely one for birds." *(MW)* "We were buzzed in at the front door, took the elevator up to the first floor reception area, and were suddenly in a 'country inn.' The air was scented with fresh-baked scones and chocolate cookies; the innkeeper welcomed us warmly and showed us around. The inn's style is consistent throughout—uncluttered, light, and airy, with a Cape Cod accent. The decor and artwork reflect the inn's setting, overlooking wetlands and a marina. The living room is an inviting space with lots of comfortable seating and a marble fireplace. French doors open to the deck. Delicious breakfast, with a sinfully rich entree." *(Abby Humphrey)* "Although our room was one of the least expensive, it had a real working desk with good lighting and a modem connection, bedside tables and lights on both sides of the bed, couch, and ample storage space. The excellent bathroom had luxurious and plentiful towels, and an extendable, lighted magnifying mirror. Delightful innkeeper, fluent in Japanese. Attentive, helpful staff. Spacious, airy common areas, neither cluttered nor overdone, with interesting books and magazines as well as the usual tourist materials. Plentiful decks with binoculars supplied for bird-watching. Breakfast served on beautiful Spode china. Gorgeous suites are an excellent value, too." *(Emily Hoche-Mong)* "Understated elegance; relaxing, welcoming atmosphere. Love the flexibility in breakfast times." *(Elizabeth McIlwain)*

Open All year.
Rooms 2 suites, 19 doubles—all with full private bath, telephone with voice mail, data port, clock/radio, TV, desk, air-conditioning. some with single/whirlpool tub, fireplace, refrigerator, balcony/deck.
Facilities Breakfast room, living room with fireplace, TV/VCR, books, stereo, games. Off-street parking, swimming pool, hot tub, garden, bicycles. Overlooks Ballona Wetlands bird sanctuary. Beach, bike path, fishing jetty nearby.
Location 18 m W of downtown LA, 4 m N of airport. 3 blocks from beach; walking distance to restaurants. From LAX, take Sepulveda Blvd N to Lincoln Blvd (Rte. 1) N (stay in left lanes). Go N on Lincoln 2.5 m to light at Jefferson Blvd. Go left on Jefferson & go almost 1 m W to end of Jefferson to Culver Blvd. Go left on Culver & go ½ m to inn on right. From I-405, exit on #90 Freeway W to Marina del Rey. Freeway ends at Culver Blvd. Go left onto Culver, 2 m to inn.
Restrictions Air-conditioning, double-glazed windows block traffic/airport noise. No smoking.
Credit cards MC, Visa.
Rates B&B, $95–250, suite, double. Extra person, $15.
Extras Wheelchair access; some rooms specially equipped. Crib, babysitting. Japanese, French, Spanish spoken.

LUCERNE

Also recommended: The **Kristalberg B&B** (P.O. Box 1629, 95458; 707–274–8009) was built as a B&B in 1987, and offers panoramic views of Clear Lake, known for its excellent fishing. It's located 50 miles north of Calistoga, and 40 miles east of Ukiah. The living room and three guest rooms are decorated with Victorian and European furnishings, and the B&B double rates range from $60–150. "Calming, inspiring view. Friendly, intelligent, knowledgeable host." *(Lucy Daggett)* "Surrounded by fields of grass and trees with deer visible in early morning and evening. Early American decor, careful attention to detail, beautiful paintings and flower arrangements. Welcoming host, delicious breakfasts." *(Joyce Hodgkinson)* "Magnificent sunsets and views of Mount Konocti. Host Merv Meyers is a retired German professor who also speaks Spanish. I enjoyed exploring the treasures he collected over years of travel, and his suggestions for area restaurants and sights." *(Harriet Beckett)*

McCLOUD

McCloud B&B Hotel ✕   *Tel:* 916–964–2822
408 Main Street, P.O. Box 730, 96057   800–964–2823
            Fax: 916–964–2844
         E-mail: mchotel@telis.org

McCloud dates back to the 1890s, when the McCloud River Lumber Company built this company town to house its workers, constructing the McCloud River Railroad to deliver supplies, and take the lumber to market. The McCloud Hotel was built in 1915 to replace an earlier hotel that had burned down. Housing mill workers, teachers, and visitors, it had 93 tiny rooms with hall baths. Abandoned in the 1980s, the hotel was scheduled for demolition when it was purchased and restored by Lee and Marilyn Ogden in 1995. Lee used his extensive experience as an architect and construction manager to reduce the number of rooms, expand them in size, and add private baths. Now listed on the National Historic Register, the hotel's guest rooms have ample closet space, coordinated decorator fabrics, queen- or twin-size beds, antique trunks used as tables and benches, and restored furniture from the original hotel; some rooms have canopy or high four-poster beds. The spacious lobby contains the original registration desk with cubby holes for mail, plus ample comfortable seating, with original pine paneling, and overstuffed chairs and couches from the 1930s. Juanita Rushton is the manager.

Breakfast, served 8–9 A.M. at individual tables, includes fresh fruit, muffins and breads, and a hot entree. Afternoon tea and scones are served at 3:30 P.M. The hotel's restaurants, in adjacent buildings, include the Dining Room, with a selection of beef, chicken, and seafood dishes, and North Yard, specializing in barbecue.

For additional area inns, see **Mount Shasta** and **O'Brien.**

"Extensively renovated, with spacious rooms, new baths, excellent restoration. The lighting over the sink was better than average and they even supplied a night light. Marilyn and Lee were friendly and more than helpful. Delicious breakfasts, including a tasty egg and tomato on toast entree." *(Kathleen Lowe Owen)* "Just as friendly and welcoming on a return trip." *(KLO)* "Even the hotel's least expensive room was clean and comfortable. Friendly, helpful staff." *(Dorothy Huggett)* "Extremely clean. Fine wood trim and furniture sparkles with careful polishing. Lots of hot water in the bathrooms great after a day of skiing." *(Gwen Knaebel)* "A wonderfully wild and totally uncrowded part of California." *(MW)*

Open All year.
Rooms 4 suites, 13 doubles—all with full private bath, ceiling fan. Some with whirlpool tub, desk, balcony.
Facilities 2 restaurants, lobby with fireplace, books, games; parlor with fireplace, porches. ¾ acre with off-street parking, lawn games. Fishing, boating, hiking, downhill/cross-country skiing nearby. Across street from Shasta Sunset Dinner Train.
Location N CA, Shasta-Cascade. 50 m S of OR border, 65 m NE of Redding, at foot of Mt. Shasta. Historic district. From I-5 at Mt. Shasta, exit E on Hwy 89. Go 9 m to McCloud. Follow signs to Historic District and Main St.
Restrictions No smoking. "Limited facilities for children."
Credit cards Discover, MC, Visa.
Rates B&B, $120–130 suite, $68–88 double, $61–80 single. Extra person, $10. 20% discount if driving a pre–WWII car. 10% senior, AAA discount. Alc lunch, $6; dinner, $17. Dinner train packages.
Extras Wheelchair access; room specially equipped.

MENDOCINO

Originally founded by Maine sea captains, Mendocino still looks a bit like a New England fishing village, and has even been used many times as a set for movies meant to be taking place on the East Coast.

Aside from looking into the many craft shops and art galleries and discovering the area restaurants and vineyards, take the time to explore the shore and the redwood forests, accessible in the area's five state parks. Canoeing, trail rides along the beach, river and ocean fishing, whale watching, tennis and golf are all favorites. For more information on area attractions, please see the "North Coast" section of the chapter introduction, plus the listings for Fort Bragg and Little River.

Mendocino is located about 150 miles north of San Francisco, in the center of the Mendocino coast. From San Francisco, take Highway 101 through Santa Rosa to Cloverdale. Then take Route 128 to Highway 1 north to Mendocino. From Eureka, take Highway 101 south to Leggett, and follow Highway 1 through Fort Bragg to Mendocino.

Rates in the Mendocino area are *high*, with no difference between weekday and weekend rates from July through October; 2-night weekend minimums are the rule. Winter rates are in effect from November through March, with the best values available midweek. Your biggest decision in selecting a room is the question of a view. Some inns have dramatic water views, with the sound of the waves to lull you to sleep, while others offer a only a glimpse, through the trees, of a relatively distant bay or shoreline. If there's any question in your mind, be sure to ask for specifics, and *don't* pay a premium for a water view unless you'll really get one. Inns located right in the village or on the east side of Highway One are *least likely* to offer unobstructed ocean views. Of course, if the fog rolls in, all views are obliterated, so factor that in as well. If you're traveling on a budget, our advice would be to book a no-view room on a waterfront property; if the weather is clear, you can enjoy the views from the gardens without breaking the bank.

Reader tips: "Book early if you're planning to visit on the weekend, and make dinner reservations ahead. The Mendocino Botanical Gardens are a must." *(Nancy Cohn)* "The fog may not lift until noon in summer—sometimes it stays all day." *(Ron Kahan)* "Although it's crowded in summer, the village was charming for strolling during our October weekend visit. Delightful hiking in Russian Gulch State Park, up through the redwoods to a lovely waterfall." *(RSS)* "Visit the wonderful store called Out of This World, where you can look through fifteen telescopes pointed at the ocean." *(Christopher Hart Johnson)*

For additional area entries, see listings for **Little River**, just 2 miles away, **Albion**, six miles south, **Elk**, 15 miles south, or **Fort Bragg**, 8 miles north.

Information please: The **Joshua Grindle Inn** (44800 Little Lake Road at Highway One, P.O. Box 647, 95460; 707–937–4143 or 800–GRINDLE), a Victorian farmhouse, was built by Joshua Grindle in 1879, and 100 years later became a country inn. The ten guest rooms (in the main house, Saltbox cottage and Historic Watertower) are light, airy, and furnished with antiques; five have fully renovated bathrooms with whirlpool or soaking tubs. The inn offers views of the village, the bay, and the ocean; all of Mendocino's attractions are a short walk away. The $95–185 double rates include a breakfast of fresh fruit and juice, home-baked breads and muffins, a hot egg dish or casserole, coffee and tea.

Built in 1990, the contemporary **Reed Manor** (Palette Drive, P.O. Box 127, 95460; 707–937–5446) provides five luxurious rooms, equipped with every amenity, including a king-size bed, gas fireplace, whirlpool tub, a small refrigerator, and a telephone with answering machine. A deck with a telescope and a secluded garden area with patio might also accompany the room. Rates, including an in-room breakfast of fruit, yogurt, and mini-muffins, range from $175–350. "A good choice if you want privacy, luxury, and romance; less so if you're looking for guest interaction or hearty meals." *(SWS)*

Agate Cove Inn
11201 Lansing Street, P.O. Box 1150
95460

Tel: 707–937–0551
800–527–3111
Fax: 707–937–0550
E-mail: agate_cove@juno.com

The main structure of this 1860s farmhouse was built by Mathias Brinzing, Mendocino's first brewer. The exterior of the building appears

153

much as it did at the turn of the century; the candlestick fence still graces the entry garden. In 1994, the inn was purchased by Scott and Betsy Buckwald; the inn was handsomely redecorated in 1996 by a noted interior designer, and combines country-style furnishings with lavish use of designer fabrics. The family-style breakfasts, prepared on an antique woodstove, include home-baked bread or scones, fresh fruit and juice, jams and jellies, coffee and tea, plus an entree of omelets, cheese frittata, or French toast, with country sausage or baked ham. Rates also include in-room sherry and the morning newspaper.

"Gets my vote for the best situated inn in Mendocino, on a quiet street, yet an easy walk from town. Breathtaking views of ocean and cliffs from the lovely gardens and breakfast room. Appealing guest and common rooms." *(SWS, also Mary Jane Campbell)* "In the afternoon, we relaxed on the front lawn in Adirondack chairs, looking out across the water, enjoying an excellent bottle of Anderson Valley wine, and strolling through the stunning gardens. Betsy is a superb host, providing just the right amount of assistance." *(Phill Emmert)* "Having our own bottled water dispenser was a thoughtful touch. Friendly breakfast gatherings with other guests." *(Gloria Laffey)* "The secluded Topaz cottage features a canopy bed, double shower, large deck with sea view, and a Franklin fireplace." *(Linda Goldberg)* "Meticulously maintained gardens and cottages. Our room had a four-poster bed, country decor, antiques and a wood-burning Franklin stove. The sherry decanter was replenished daily. The breakfast room has panoramic water views. Our first morning began with baked apples stuffed with cranberries and walnuts topped with vanilla yogurt, followed by hot quiche and homefries, garnished with an edible flower." *(Merrily Basham)*

Open All year.
Rooms 2 doubles in main house, 8 cottages—all with private bath and/or shower, writing table, TV/VCR, fireplace, deck. 1 with radio.
Facilities Dining room, living room with fireplace, games; guest pantry. 1½ acres with gardens, off-street parking.
Location Take Lansing St. exit off Hwy. 1. ½ m N of town center.
Restrictions No smoking. No children under 12.
Credit cards MC, Visa.
Rates B&B, $90–250 double. Extra person, $25. 2-night weekend minimum.
Extras Airport/station pickup.

Captain's Cove Inn　　　　　　　　　　*Tel: 707–937–5150*
44781 Main Street, P.O. Box 803, 95460　　　　800–780–7905
　　　　　　　　　　　　　　　　　　　Fax: 707–937–5151

Built in 1861 by a local sea captain, the Captain's Cove Inn was purchased by Robert, Linda, and Wendy Blum in 1995. Decorated in a mix of contemporary and antique pieces known as "California Coastal" decor, the rooms have charming handmade quilts on the bed and walls. One room has a king-size bed; the others have queens. The sitting room has strong seafaring accents, with extensive woodwork, nautical pillows, and a table built from a ship's wheel. Breakfast is served at individual tables at 9 A.M., and includes fresh fruit and juice, applesauce muffins, just-baked bread, and such entrees as pancakes, French toast, and quiche.

"Linda is very attentive to food allergies, serving a different breakfast each day despite dietary limitations, and going out of her way to be kind. The quaint dining room faces the ocean. Enjoyed jogging on the Headlands each morning, then coming home to a hearty breakfast. The spacious Captain's Suite had a fireplace that kept us cozy and warm. Marvelous decor." *(Joyce Pope)*

Open All year.
Rooms 1 carriage house suite, 2 cottages, 2 doubles—all with private bath and/or shower, clock/radio, fireplace, refrigerator/wet bar, microwave, sun deck/balcony, private entrance. Some with desk, fan.
Facilities Breakfast room, living room with fireplace, piano, books; deck, porch. ¾ acre with gardens, cedar swing, hot tub, off-street parking. Path to beach on Mendocino Bay, hiking nearby.
Location Take Hwy. 101 N to Hwy 128 W at Cloverdale. At coast, go N on Hwy. 1 for approx. 10 m to Mendocino. After crossing bridge, turn left at 1st entrance to village. Inn is 200 yds. on left.
Restrictions No smoking. Children 16 and over.
Credit cards MC, Visa.
Rates B&B, $165–197 suite, $145–173 double. Extra person, $20.
Extras Local airport pickups.

Headlands Inn ♿   *Tel: 707–937–4431*
Corner of Howard and Albion Streets   800–354–4431
Mailing address: P.O. Box 132, 95460   *Fax: 707–937–0421*

The Headlands Inn began life in 1868 as a one-story barber shop on Main Street; a second story was added in 1873 to provide living quarters for the barber's family. In 1893 the house was moved from its original location on Main Street to its current one, transported by horses pulling the house over rolling logs. David and Sharon Hyman, owners since 1992, are interior designers, and have added many antiques and handcrafted furnishings to the decor, in addition to queen- and king-size featherbeds in all rooms. Breakfasts, served on a tray in each guest's room, includes fruit dishes garnished with edible flowers and perhaps bacon quiche, tomato shells with baked Gruyère-topped eggs, or peach Amaretto crepes.

"The Wilson Room had its own long balcony, where I had breakfast and spent some quiet time reading in the Adirondack chairs. Generous breakfasts; afternoon tea is served in the cozy upstairs parlor where cold drinks are always available. The innkeeper made advance dinner reservations for me and was concerned for my comfort." *(Nancy Cohn)* "Our room's little sitting area was the perfect place to enjoy breakfast, delivered directly to the room at 9 A.M. Our large private deck provided a view of the stars at night, the village during the day." *(Maria Valls)* "My favorite room is the Bessie Straus, with a bay window offering views of the inn's garden and the bay beyond." *(Linda Goldberg)* "Professional, welcoming, knowledgeable innkeeper. Enjoyed the privacy this inn affords." *(MW, also SWS)*

Open All year.
Rooms 1 cottage, 6 doubles—all with full private bath, fireplace, clock. 1 with parlor stove, balcony. Cottage with TV/VCR.
Facilities Second-floor parlor with games, books, guest refrigerator. Front porch, decks, gardens. 2 blocks to Big River Beach.
Location Historic District, 2 blocks from center. Going N on Hwy. 1, turn left to business district; pass church, then right on Howard St. Inn is 1½ blocks on left.
Restrictions No smoking. Street noise in some rooms.
Credit cards All major cards.
Rates B&B, $130–195 double, cottage. 2–4 night weekend/holiday minimum. Reserve 1 to 3 months in advance for weekends, in summer.
Extras Cottage has wheelchair access. Limited Spanish spoken.

John Dougherty House
571 Ukiah Street, P.O. Box 817, 95460

Tel: 707–937–5266
800–486–2104
E-mail: jdhbmw@mcn.org

Marion and David Wells welcome guests to their 1867 farmhouse overlooking the village and bay. Accommodations include a guest suite in a historic water tower (with an 18-foot beamed ceiling) and a separate cabin, to supplement the "Port" and "Starboard" cottages in the garden.

"We stayed in the Captain's Room, with a private veranda overlooking the village and the water beyond. The bathroom had a fine array of soaps, perfumes, shampoos, lotions, and big, fluffy towels. We also enjoyed a bountiful breakfast and nice chat in front of the fire with our hosts." *(Joan & Larry Martens)* "The First Mate room has a view of the village, walls stenciled with blue flowers, and a carved headboard depicting a whale swallowing a woman. The local Mendocino chocolates on the dresser, fresh flowers, bottled water dispenser, and complimentary wine in the room's small refrigerator added a nice touch. A mellow inn cat named Tristan shared my room. David and Marion helped me with dinner reservations, and provided area pamphlets and magazines. Breakfast was a standout—fresh fruit, hot currant scones, chicken-sausage rolls, banana nut bread, juice, tea, or coffee." *(LG)* "Pleasant setting right in the village, with a good-sized backyard sloping down to street behind inn. The common area is appealingly decorated with simple Colonial-style charm and wonderful folk art. The water tower room is delightful, with lots of character and a good value in this pricy town, ample compensation for the lack of a view." *(SWS)*

Open All year.
Rooms 4 cottages/suites, 2 doubles—all with private bath and/or shower. Most with veranda, fireplace, refrigerator, TV.
Facilities Living/dining room with fireplace, keeping room, porch, garden. Ocean, boating, horseback riding nearby.
Location Village center.
Restrictions No smoking. Not recommended for children under 13. Sidewalk close to some rooms.
Credit cards MC, Visa.
Rates B&B, $95–185 cottage/suite, double. Extra person, $20. 2-night weekend minimum. 3 nights for price of 2, midweek, off-season.
Extras Free local airport pickup.

Sea Rock B&B Inn ♀ ♿
11101 Lansing Street, 95460

Tel: 707–937–0926
800–906–0926
E-mail: searock@mcn.org

"You've come a long way, baby," proclaimed an ad campaign of the 1980s, and the same can be said of Sea Rock, built in the 1960s as a cluster of motor court cottages. Purchased in 1994 by Andy and Suzanne Plocher, these once-modest units have been fully renovated and refurbished; one building has been demolished, replaced in 1997 with a four-unit structure housing four luxury suites with fireplaces and dramatic ocean views. In fact, the only thing the Plochers haven't changed is the one thing that didn't need improvement—the dramatic view of the Pacific and the rocky cliffs of the Mendocino Headlands. Most rooms have simple country-style furnishings, with quilts or flowered comforters, featherbeds on the queen-size beds, and wood-burning Franklin stoves. The breakfast buffet is available from 8 to 10 A.M., and includes fresh fruit, juices, yogurt, breakfast cakes, muffins, bagels.

"Friendly, hard-working owners have transformed the Sea Rock into a delightful getaway. The larger units, with kitchen, are ideal for an extended stay or a family; the least expensive ones have only a glimpse of ocean from the room, but a fine view from their decks, and are an excellent value. The location is ideal: spectacular setting, convenient to town, and quiet, except for the sound of the surf." *(SWS)* "Clean, comfortable room; cordial owners; delicious banana bread for breakfast." *(Tina Hom)*

Open All year.
Rooms 6 cottages, 8 suites—all with private shower and/or tub, clock/radio, TV/VCR, deck. 13 with fireplace; some with whirlpool tub, desk, refrigerator. 2 2-bedrooms units.
Facilities Dining room, deck. Gardens, off-street parking.
Location After crossing the bridge on Hwy 1 into Mendocino, turn left at the traffic light on Hwy 1, onto Little Lake Rd. Go 1 block to Lansing St. & turn right. Inn is ½ m N of town.
Restrictions No smoking. Well-supervised children welcome.
Credit cards Amex, Discover, MC, Visa.
Rates B&B, $95–225 cottage, suite. Extra person, $20.
Extras Wheelchair access; 1 bathroom specially equipped. Spanish spoken.

Stanford Inn by the Sea/Big River Lodge ♀ ♿
44850 Comptche-Ukiah Road and Highway 1
P.O. Box 1487, 95460

Tel: 707–937–5615
800–331–8884
Fax: 707–937–0305

Originally built as a motel, the Stanford Inn was bought in 1980 by Joan and Jeff Stanford, who have upgraded their property into a quality bed & breakfast inn. Their other endeavors include raising their two children, operating a canoe livery service, breeding llamas, and growing organic produce. Breakfast consists of fresh fruits and juices, champagne, coffee, tea, hot chocolate, granola, porridge, quiche, and pastries. Afternoon wine and hors d'oeuvres are also served in the recently expanded common room, furnished with antiques and collectibles.

"Enjoyed the canoe ride and bicycling along the river path. Welcoming staff, excellent housekeeping." *(AJK)* "Beautifully landscaped hillside overlooking the ocean and the town. Plumbing is modern, with good water pressure; quality soaps and toiletries were supplied. The staff assisted us with restaurant advice and reservations." *(Timothy & Cynthia Egan)* "While not large, my room was amply furnished with a four-poster king-size bed, great reading lamps, remote-control TV, and a sofa. The radio was playing, the fireplace was ready to light, there were chocolates, crackers with herb cheese dip, fresh flowers, and crystal decanter of red wine and two crystal wineglasses ready on the coffee table." *(Linda Goldberg)* "The indoor swimming pool is also a giant conservatory with flowering shrubs and trees, and translucent walls." *(Hugh & Marjorie Smith)* "We took our breakfast tray to our room to eat in privacy. At night, we left our window open and one of the friendly inn cats came to pay a welcome visit." *(MW)* "The inn's terraced grounds have organic vegetable and flower gardens, suppliers to many of Mendocino's best restaurants." *(SWS)*

Open All year.
Rooms 5 2-bedroom suites, 4 1-bedroom suites, 1 cottage, 22 doubles—all with private bath and/or shower, telephone, radio, TV/VCR, desk, wood-burning fireplace, refrigerator, deck. Some with kitchen.
Facilities Reception area, common room with fireplace, deck; videotape library; gift shop; dining room. 10 acres with enclosed heated greenhouse, swimming pool, sauna, hot tub; flower and vegetable gardens, horses, ducks, llamas. Mountain bicycles, fishing; canoe, kayak, outrigger rentals. Beaches, dock nearby.
Location ¼ m S of village, at corner of Hwy. 1 & Comptche-Ukiah Rd.
Restrictions No smoking in common areas.
Credit cards Amex, CB, DC, Discover, Enroute, MC, Optima, Visa.
Rates B&B, $225–560 suite, $190–245 double. Extra person, $15. 2–3 night weekend/holiday minimum. Gardening seminars, March–Oct.
Extras Wheelchair access; bathroom equipped for disabled. Airport/station pickup. Pets permitted by arrangement. Crib. French, German, Spanish spoken.

Whitegate Inn   *Tel:* 707–937–4892
499 Howard Street, P.O. Box 150, 95460   800–531–7282
Fax: 707–937–1131

When the Whitegate was built in 1883, a newspaper article described it as "one of the most elegant and best appointed residences in town." Under the ownership of Carol and George Bechtloff, who bought the inn in 1991, this description applies equally today. Rates include a full breakfast, afternoon cookies, pre-dinner refreshments, and bedtime chocolates.

"I was warmly greeted by Carol and George. One of the inn cats has become the official greeter who runs to the door to welcome guests, then 'shows them to their rooms.' The elegant dining and living rooms have coordinating Oriental carpets, hand-painted wallpaper borders, and beautifully upholstered Victorian furniture, in a soothing color scheme of seafoam green and rosy peach. The dining room has collections of cut glass and porcelain figurines, with a crystal chandelier, silver tea service, and Victorian artwork. Rich floral fabrics and wallpaper borders add elegance to the guest rooms without clutter; plush towels and bath rugs, luxurious linens and curtains add comfort. The flower-filled backyard offers a distant view of the sea from the gazebo. Breakfasts include artichoke potatoes, eggs Florentine, shrimp soufflé, caramel-apple French toast, or waffles, with fresh fruit salad or a granola parfait, fresh-squeezed juices, and cinnamon rounds. Light hors d'oeuvres and wine are offered at 5 P.M." *(Linda Goldberg)* "The inn is extremely clean, well maintained, quiet and private with plenty of parking along the street." *(Terri Ann Flores)* "Cordial innkeeper. Common areas elegant, formal, handsome, elaborate; pretty gardens at back. Guest rooms fresh and pretty, in excellent condition." *(SWS)*

Open All year.
Rooms 1 cottage, 5 doubles—all with private bath and/or shower, clock, fireplace/woodstove. 2 with TV, refrigerator, 1 with deck.
Facilities Dining room, living room with piano, deck/gazebo. ½ acre with off-street parking, lawn games. 1 block from ocean.
Location In village historic district. Turn W of Hwy 1 into Mendocino at Little Lake Rd. (only stoplight). Go W 2 blocks, turn left on Howard St., & go S 1 block to inn on corner of Howard & Ukiah.
Restrictions Absolutely no smoking inside. No hard liquor. Children over 12.
Credit cards Amex, MC, Visa.
Rates B&B, $189 cottage, $115–189 double. Extra person, $25. $20 midweek off-season AAA, senior discounts. 2-3 night weekend/holiday minimum.
Extras Airport/station pickups.

MILL VALLEY

Mill Valley is located 12 miles north of San Francisco, on the slopes of Mt. Tamalpais (known as Mt. Tam), surrounded by redwoods. The town offers galleries, shops, theaters, cafes and restaurants. Muir Woods and Mt. Tam State Park are close by for great hiking.

The **Mill Valley Inn** (165 Throckmorton Avenue, 94941; 415–389–6608 or 800–595–2100) offers 16 guest rooms and two cottages, at B&B double rates of $135–250, including continental breakfast and espresso bar, morning newspaper, and covered guest parking. This in-town hotel has guest rooms elegantly decorated with the work of California artisans, many with Franklin stoves and balconies with views of Mt. Tam and the redwoods. "Close to many appealing restaurants; ask for a quiet room to avoid traffic noise." *(MA)*

The **Mountain Home Inn** (810 Panoramic Highway, 94941; 415–381–9000) overlooks Mill Valley 1000 feet below, and San Francisco Bay beyond. The inn offers a bar, restaurant, and dining patio, plus ten guest rooms, many with balconies, fireplaces, and bay views, at B&B double rates of $133–249. Forty miles of hiking trails can be accessed from the inn's door to Mt. Tam and Muir Woods. "Friendly innkeepers, great terrace overlooking the bay; large room with fireplace and balcony; tasty breakfast." *(Pat & Doug Phillips)*

For an additional area inn, see **Muir Beach.**

MONTARA

"Tiny Montara boasts a wide clean beach, a Victorian lighthouse, and hiking trails on Mount Montara." *(EHM)*

For additional area inns, see **Half Moon Bay** and **Moss Beach**.

The Goose & Turrets B&B ¢   *Tel:* 650–728–5451
835 George Street, P.O. Box 370937, 94037-0937   *Fax:* 650–728–0141
E-mail: goose_and_turrets@montara.com

The Goose and Turrets is a Northern Italian villa–style home built in 1908, restored as a B&B in 1986 by Raymond and Emily Hoche-Mong. Rooms are eclectically decorated with antique and contemporary furnishings, original paintings, and wood carvings. Breakfast is served at 9 A.M., and might feature smoked salmon and herbed cream cheese on bagels, Tennessee sausages and Southern spoonbread with sourwood honey, or Southwest corn-pepper pancakes served with sour cream and salsa, plus freshly ground coffees, imported teas, and fresh fruits and berries.

"Careful attention to detail throughout; house and garden are beautifully maintained; quiet location. Gracious, helpful, attentive hosts." *(Amelia Kaplan)* "Spotless, quiet, and comfortable. Excellent and unobtrusive service, convenient and abundant parking. Lovely yard, faultless plumbing, plenty of good reading material. Friendly atmosphere; marvelous multicourse breakfasts." *(Frank Mayer, Jr.)* "Lovely drive south from San Francisco. We were delighted with the Lascaux room, with a firm double-size canopy bed with a down comforter. The bathroom night light and towel warmer were typically thoughtful details." *(Katherine Fedor)* "Delightful afternoon tea, beautiful gardens. Friendly, hospitable, well-traveled innkeepers." *(Leda Dederich)* "Ample off-street parking; quiet street." *(Ellen Belliveau)*

"Three adorable if pesky 'guard' geese live in the inn's beautiful gardens. Our little room had a dressing room with an armoire, a desk with a welcome note and delectable chocolate truffles with evening turndown service." *(Cindy Banks)* "We met the other guests over afternoon tea, highlighted by a delicious berry tart. Emily and Raymond were always on hand, but did not hover." *(Monique Noah)* "Hummingbird is the largest room, colored in blue and gray, with a woodburning stove and extra large bathroom. Super lighting for reading in bed and putting on makeup. Responding to my request for a strictly vegetarian meal, I was served a delicious Egyptian dish of fava beans and onions with pita bread, followed by strawberry sorbet." *(Gail Davis)*

Open All year.
Rooms 5 doubles—all with private bath and/or shower. All with desk.
Facilities Breakfast area, living room with woodstove, books, audio tapes,games, piano. 1 acre with swing, hammock, bocce ball court, garden, fountain. ½m to beach for water sports.
Location San Francisco Bay area. 25 m S of S.F; 20 min. to SF airport. 8 m N of Half Moon ld), $20. Midweek, senior discounts. Weekly rates.
Extras Local airport pickup. French spoken.

MONTEREY

Originally built up around the sardine fishing and canning business (which collapsed about 40 years ago), Monterey was first made famous by John Steinbeck's novel *Cannery Row*. The old cannery buildings have long been renovated and now house art galleries, antique shops, restaurants, and inns. Its newest attraction is the Monterey Bay Aquarium, an imaginatively designed building, that is now home to over 500 species of ocean life. Unfortunately, only a few of the side streets retain any real character; the rest is all for "show."

For more information on the Monterey peninsula, see the Central Coast section of the introduction to this chapter; for additional area entries, see **Pacific Grove.**

On scenic Highway 1, Monterey is located about 120 miles south of San Francisco and 320 miles north of Los Angeles, on California's central coast. From Los Angeles, drive up Highway 101 to Salinas, then west on Route 66. If you have more time, take exit 101 at San Luis Obispo and stay on Highway 1 to Monterey. From San Francisco, take Highway 101 to Route 156 to Highway 1, or stay on Highway 1 the whole way.

Reader tips: "Be warned that Cannery Row is wall-to-wall tee-shirt shops and junk food carry-outs, and that there are long lines to get into the aquarium on weekend afternoons in summer; ask your innkeeper about obtaining tickets." *(SHW)*

Also recommended: In Carmel Hill, halfway between Carmel and Monterey, is the **Bay Park Hotel** (1425 Munras Avenue, Monterey 93940; 408–649–1020 or 800–338–3564), an 80-room hotel built in 1968, offering views of the bay and wooded hillside. Facilities include a bar, restaurant, heated swimming pool, and hot tub. B&B double rates for the well-equipped rooms range from $79–169 including a continental breakfast. "Just a mile from Monterey; convenient highway access. Friendly, helpful, courteous staff, with little turnover. Guest rooms area clean, comfortable, and attractively decorated. Longtime owner Kurt Lang is constantly upgrading some part of the hotel." *(Phillip Garcia)*

Graceful adobe architecture and lush gardens highlight the **Hotel Pacific** (300 Pacific Street, 93940; 408–373–5700 or 800–554–5542). The 105 guest rooms are furnished with original art, goose-down featherbeds, hardwood floors, and wet bars; the double rates of $169–279 include a continental breakfast, afternoon tea, and nightly turndown. The hotel is one of the "Inns of Monterey"; readers who like being in the heart of the action can also use the 800 number above to contact the Spindrift Inn on Cannery Row. "Walking distance to the historic center of Monterey and Fisherman's Wharf. A fine California mission-style structure built around courtyard gardens. Our handsome junior suite had a kitchen, bedroom, and sitting areas, plus a fireplace. Generous breakfast buffet of pastries, cereal, fruit, yogurt, fresh orange juice, and more. Some traffic and airplane noise, but nothing significant." *(Duane Roller)*

Information please: Named for the Lewis Carroll poem, the **Jabberwock** (598 Laine Street, 93940; 408–372–4777) carries its theme from the names of the rooms to the breakfast creations. The five guest rooms overlook with bay or the gardens. B&B double rates of $105–190 include breakfast, afternoon hors d'oeuvres and sherry, and evening milk and cookies. The inn was purchased in 1996 by John and Joan Kiliany. "Friendly, helpful owners. Delicious breakfast of croissants followed by bread pudding with raspberry sauce." *(Julie Phillips)* "Good location, an easy walk to the aquarium; most rooms have bay views. Beautiful gardens, charming theme, comfortable bed with down pillows and comforter." *(Emily Hoche-Mong)* Reports appreciated.

Old Monterey Inn　　　　　　　　　　*Tel:* 408–375–8284
500 Martin Street, 93940　　　　　　　　　800–350–2344
　　　　　　　　　　　　　　　　　　Fax: 408–375–6730
　　　　　　　　　　　E-mail: omi@oldmontereyinn.com

A consistent reader favorite, The Old Monterey Inn is a half-timbered Tudor-style residence built in 1929. It was bought in the 1960s by Ann and Gene Swett as their private home; as their six children grew up and moved out, their rooms were gradually redone as guest rooms. The inn is decorated with stained glass windows and skylights, period furniture, and family antiques; guests stay cozy with European goose-down comforters and featherbeds. "Attention to detail is the hallmark of this inn, from the gorgeous gardens to the impeccable interior. Gene, Ann, and their staff welcome you warmly, and strive to make your stay special. Guests can choose to have the delicious breakfast served in the dining room by the roaring fireplace, delivered to their room, or enjoyed in the rose garden." *(Patricia & Charlie Bell)* "The Brightstone room is small but cozy, with charming French country decor. I relaxed on the chaise with a good book and a glass of wine. The armoire had a few nice surprises—old books, a writing desk, and thoughtful amenities. The little bathroom was fully stocked, and the corner window offered a pretty view through the trees to the garden. The first morning we had breakfast outside: orange juice with slices of banana, fruit compote, and baked crunchy French toast with orange marmalade sauce. After a day of exploring, it was pleasant to return to the inn and help ourselves to hors d'oeuvres and wine. The second morning was cooler, so we had breakfast in the lovely dining room: baked pear with mandarin oranges, and baked apple pancakes. When we return, we'll request the Library room, with a patio, fireplace, and bookshelves. Another nice touch is the stocked refrigerator on the second floor." *(Lynne Derry)* "Staff attentive to every detail. The wonderful garden enhances the sense of space and privacy. Our room had a luxurious featherbed, plenty of hot water and a magnifying mirror in the bath. Casement windows, stained glass and a Dutch door allowed us to enjoy the cool air. Social hour between 5–7 P.M.; hot and cold beverages always available." *(Sherry & Clif Daniel)*

"Cozy, well decorated rooms with fireplaces that were easy to light. Scrupulously clean." *(Nan Decker)* "The fountain edged with carnations was a prelude to the beautiful gardens." *(Tom Wilbanks)* "The lavish breakfasts can be packed in a basket for those leaving before 9 A.M." *(Ellin Spitzer)* "The innkeepers prepare helpful newsletters with tips on picnicking, restaurants, and shopping." *(Jane & Rick Mattoon)* "The Garden Cottage has a sitting room furnished with a white wicker settee and rocking chair facing a fireplace, a huge skylight, and Dutch door with a stained glass window." *(Richard & Sheri DeBro)* "Walking distance to everything." *(Ray Farris)*

Open All year. Closed Dec. 25.
Rooms 1 suite, 8 doubles, 1 cottage—all with private bath and/or shower, radio. 9 with fireplace. Guest refrigerator, deck. 3 rooms with private entrance, whirlpool tub.
Facilities Dining room, living room both with fireplace. 1 acre, flower gardens, sitting areas, hammocks, picnic area. Near Monterey Bay & Aquarium.
Location 4 blocks from center. From Hwy. 1 S, take Soledad-Munras Ave. exit. Cross Munras Ave., then go right on Pacific St. Go ½ m to Martin St. on left. From Hwy. 1 N, take Munras Ave. exit. Take immediate left on Soledad Dr., then right on Pacific St. Go ½ m to Martin St.
Restrictions No smoking.
Credit cards MC, Visa.
Rates B&B, $280 suite & cottage, $200–260 double. Extra person (in suite only), $50. 2–3 night weekend/holiday minimum.

MOSS BEACH

Reader tips: "Dinner at the Moss Beach Distillery is a must!" *(Debbie Sorich).* "The Fitzgerald Marine Reserve offers ranger-led tours of the finest tide pools south of Mendocino. Hiking along the bluffs down to Princeton will allow views of Maverick's, a surfing spot renowned for its waves, danger, and difficulty." *(Emily Hoche-Mong)*

For additional area inns, see **Half Moon Bay** and **Montara**.

Seal Cove Inn 🏨 ♿   *Tel:* 650–728–4114
221 Cypress Avenue, 94038   *Fax:* 650–728–4116
E-mail: sealcove@coastside.net

Guidebook author Karen Brown, along with her husband, Rick Herbert, took their years of travel experience and built an inn of their own, overlooking a field of wildflowers, with the ocean in the distance. Constructed in 1991, the inn has handsomely decorated guest rooms, in a variety of styles from English country to French Provençal to American Amish.

"Karen and Rick built the inn with the goal of including all the things they like about other inns—fresh flowers everywhere, fruit, refrigerators stocked with complimentary wine, snacks, and soft drinks, heated towel racks, even movies and popcorn. The Carl Larsson Room was decorated with 18 of his famous illustrations, furniture, and fabrics, in keeping with the Scandinavian theme. Delicious breakfast of freshly squeezed orange juice, fruit, waffles or French toast. Wine and appetizers served at 5 P.M." *(JO, also Tom Wilbanks)*

"Careful attention to detail throughout. Our room had a king-size bed, a loveseat in front of the ready-to-light fireplace, high ceilings, large windows, thick carpeting, a VCR, and a double Jacuzzi tub which filled in a minute. Instead of a mint on the pillow, an entire bowl of Hershey's Almond kisses. Coffee and the San Francisco newspaper are left on your doorstep each morning. The sumptuous breakfast featured strawberry-blueberry pancakes, and generous snacks are served in the afternoon." *(Abigail Humphrey & Karl Sikkenga)* "We breakfasted on Monte Cristo sandwiches with raspberry preserves." *(Kim Schoknecht)* "We enjoyed walking to the beach and its tide pools or up to the bluff overlooking the ocean for spectacular sunsets." *(Cliff & Elizabeth Wright)* "I spent an evening settled in my room, wrapped in a fluffy terry robe, enjoying the fireplace. The next morning I sipped coffee and read the newspaper waiting outside my door. Over afternoon tea, Karen chatted with me about the coastal area, giving a personal touch to my day of touring." *(Mary Kathryn Newberry)*

Open All year.

Rooms 2 suites, 8 doubles—all with full private bath, telephone, radio, TV/VCR, fan, wood-burning fireplace, refrigerator, hair dryer, deck/patio/balcony. Some with desk. 2 with whirlpool tub.

Facilities Living room with fireplace, video library, books; dining room, conference room. 1½ acres adjoining 20 acre marine reserve. 5 min. walk to beach for whale-watching, fishing, surfing.

Location 17 m S of San Francisco, 6 m N of Half Moon Bay. From Hwy. 1 turn W on Cypress Ave. to inn on right.

Restrictions No smoking. Children in garden level rooms only.

Credit cards Amex, Discover, MC, Visa.

Rates B&B, $250 suite, $180–195 double. Extra person, $25. 2-night holiday weekend minimum.

Extras Wheelchair access; 1 room equipped for disabled. Crib. French, German, Spanish spoken.

MOUNT SHASTA

At the foot of 14,000-foot Mount Shasta, the little town of the same name is the gateway to hundreds of miles of wilderness in the Shasta-Trinity National Forest. Summer activities include hiking, fishing, whitewater rafting, mountain biking, and golf, plus all water sports at nearby Lake Siskyou; downhill, cross-country skiing, and snowmobiling will keep you busy in winter. It also makes a delightful and convenient stopover point if you're driving between California and Oregon, since it's just off Interstate 5. As the area is relatively undiscovered, you'll find the reasonable rates to be a delightful surprise. **Also recommended:** For peaceful getaway, *Carolyn Alexander* recommends **Ward's Big Foot Ranch** (P.O. Box 585, 96067; 916–926–5170 or 800–926–1272). "Warm and friendly hosts, retired educators from Saratoga, California. Quiet setting, with a magnificent view of Mt. Shasta. The main house has two guest rooms; one has a king-size bed with a bath en suite; the other has a queen-size bed with a private bath across the hall. Lovely breakfasts of fresh fruit, juice, eggs, sausage, abelskivers, waffles, good coffee, and lots of warm, friendly conversation with Phil and Barbara Ward.

The ranch has a donkey, two llamas, and two golden retrievers. Next door is an ostrich ranch." B&B double rates range from $65–76.

The **Mount Shasta Ranch** (1008 W. A. Garr Road, 96067; 916–926–3870) was built in 1923 as a thoroughbred horse ranch, and has long been owned by Bill and Mary Larsen. Twelve guest rooms are available in the main house, carriage house and cottage, and B&B double rates range from $55–95, including a full breakfast (except in the cottage), afternoon snacks, and use of the game room and hot springs spa. Most rooms have queen-size beds and shared baths; those in the main house have enormous private baths. "Comfortable, well-equipped, casually furnished two-bedroom cottage; great for families. Friendly owners; delightful dog and parrot. Rustic decor; delicious breakfasts with blackberry crepes one morning, and omelets with ham, salsa, and avocados the second." (*Julie Phillips*)

Information please: Located in "downtown" Mt. Shasta is the **Dream Inn** (326 Chestnut Street, 96067; 916–926–1536), built in 1904; it's owned by Lonna Smith and run by David Ream since 1993. B&B double rates for the five guest rooms are $70 for the shared bath rooms, and $90 for the one with a private bath, including a full breakfast, served at guests' convenience throughout the morning.

For additional area inns, see **McCloud** and **O'Brien**.

MUIR BEACH

Information please: When the fog rolls in and you need a cozy haven, consider the **Pelican Inn** (10 Pacific Way, 94965–9729; 415–383–6000), a Tudor replica built in 1979 and managed by R. Barry Stock since 1986. Rates include a traditional English breakfast, while lunch favorites are cottage pie, bangers and mash, and fish 'n chips; dinner entrees range from mixed grill to Pacific snapper and roast beef. "English country antique furnishings, with damask curtains surrounding the high bed. Breakfast was served in a dark, cozy candlelit room." (*Joanne Ashton*) "Just like being in a real English country inn, but with modern plumbing and soft towels; bedside lighting a bit too authentically dim." (*SB*) Muir Beach is in Marin County, 30 minutes north of San Francisco. B&B double rates for the seven guest rooms range from $155–175.

For additional area inns, see **Mill Valley.**

MURPHYS

The sleepy village of Murphys is in the heart of Gold Country's southern Mother Lode, one of the best preserved of the Calaveras County mining towns. The town has a community park, swimming pool, and tennis courts open to visitors. There are state parks nearby for hiking and fishing, and visitors enjoy gold panning and visiting caves and wineries (six major ones within two miles), golf and skiing. While here, don't miss the enormous sequoias at Calaveras Big Trees State Park.

Murphys is located in the foothills of the Sierras, 2½ hours east of San Francisco, just east of Angel's Camp on State Route 4.

Reader tip: "Excellent dinner at the historic Murphys Hotel on Main Street." *(Jim & Mary White)*

Information please: Built in 1995, **The Redbud Inn** (402 Main Street, 95247; 209–728–8533 or 800–827–8533) has a convenient location on Murphy's historic Main Street, and offers 14 individually themed guest rooms, decorated with antiques, family heirlooms, and artwork, many with fireplaces, woodstoves, balconies, window seats, or whirlpool tubs. B&B double rates range from $90–225, including a full breakfast and afternoon wine and hors d'oeuvres. "Pleasant, staff-run inn. Good lighting; modern bathroom. Couldn't find anyone to check us in when we arrived; later we met a young, enthusiastic, attentive innkeeper; never met the owners." *(MW)*

Dunbar House, 1880   *Tel:* 209–728–2897
271 Jones Street, P.O. Box 1375, 95247   800–692–6006
                                           Fax: 209–728–1451
                      E-mail: dunbarhs@goldrush.com

Dunbar House is an Italianate Victorian home, bought by Bob and Barbara Costa in 1987; Felice Cizmick is the manager. From 8:30–9:30 A.M., guests are served breakfast in the dining room, the garden, or in their rooms; a typical menu might include artichoke bacon frittata, rosemary potatoes, lemon scones, fresh fruit with Amaretto sauce, and orange juice spritzers.

"Vases of fresh beautiful flowers everywhere. Delicious breakfast of crabmeat with melted cheese on English muffins, sauteed tomatoes with pine nuts and basil, fresh fruit, and apple bread. Afternoon hors d'oeuvres included smoked salmon and asparagus, and at night, our bed was turned down with homemade chocolates. Classical music played in the background; lots of books to read, puzzles to do. Snacks and candies are always available, along with hot water for fixing coffee and tea." *(Julie Phillips)* "Cozy room with lots of charming Victoriana; competent staff, lots of extras." *(JMW)* "Complimentary local wine provided in the in-room refrigerator. Cozy quilts and afghans." *(Corrine Ruokangas)*

"The inn was built in 1880 and has been painstakingly restored and elaborately furnished with antiques and collectibles." *(Jim & Sybilla Elrod)* "We were greeted with an afternoon buffet of fruit, cheese and crackers, then escorted to our room. Fascinating pictures, books, magazines, and memorabilia found throughout the inn. The comfortable Ponderosa Room is medium-sized with a sink in the room and a small bath with a claw-footed shower/tub combination. Family-style breakfast served at the large dining room table." *(JTD)* "The cozy parlor fire and gentle music, or the welcome breeze on the veranda, create a relaxing atmosphere." *(Robert Reagan)* "Inviting verandas and tree-shaded grounds." *(L.L. Rowell)* "Delightful small touches—the flowers, the lemon drops, bath amenities, potpourri, magazines." *(Elaine Rex)*

Open All year.

Rooms 2 suites, 2 doubles—all with full private bath, clock/radio, TV/VCR, desk, air-conditioning, fan, woodstove/fireplace, refrigerator, hair dryer, robes. 1 with double whirlpool tub.

Facilities Dining room with fireplace, parlor with fireplace, piano, stereo, games, books, VCR/videotape library; veranda. 1 acre with off-street parking, gazebo, gardens, lawn games, hammock.

Location Turn W off Main St. at Monument. 2 blocks from historic district.

Restrictions No smoking. Children over 10.

Credit cards Amex, MC, Visa.

Rates B&B, $125–175 suite, double. Extra person, $20. 2-night weekend minimum. Carriage winery tour/picnics. Ski packages.

NAPA

Although Napa's founding about 100 years ago was due to the gold rush, today's gold flows from the wine industry and the extensive tourism industry that has developed along with it. The town is a popular base for wine touring—perhaps overly so during fall harvest weekends. Napa is located in the North Coast region, in Napa Valley Wine Country, just one hour north of San Francisco.

Reader tip: "If you have any money left after visiting the local wineries, the Napa Factory Outlet will be happy to slenderize your wallet further." *(MW)*

Information please: A beautifully restored Victorian mansion, **The Blue Violet Mansion** (443 Brown Street, 94559; 707–253–BLUE) is an 1886 Queen Anne home. Guests can relax in the inn's parlors, on the veranda or deck, or in the gazebo. Each of the 15 guest rooms has a queen- or king-size bed and private bath; some have a balcony, gas fireplace, and whirlpool tub. B&B double rates of $145–285 include a full breakfast, afternoon tea or wine, and late night dessert. Expensive but worth it, or just expensive? Your comments please.

The **Tall Timber Chalets** (1012 Darms Lane, Napa Valley 94558; 707–252–7810) consists of "seven white cottages with green trim in the redwoods just south of Yountville on Route 29. The delightful innkeeper is delighted to share the secrets of wine country. Decorated country style, our cottage had a large living room with sofa and chairs, a separate kitchen, large bedroom, and small bath. Sitting at a table in the morning sun, we enjoyed our breakfast muffins and juice on the homey front patio, surrounded by flowers." *(Mark Mendenhall)* B&B double rates are $105–150.

Beazley House ⚲
1910 First Street, 94559

Tel: 707–257–1649
800–559–1649
Fax: 707–257–1518
E-mail: JBeaz@aol.com

A Napa landmark since 1902, Beazley House was Napa's first B&B when Carol and Jim Beazley opened it in 1981. Their son, Scott, who grew up in the inn, has also joined the innkeeping staff. Guest rooms are furnished with antiques and country flair, and have either king- or queen-size beds. Recent breakfast menus included orange juice, sliced fresh fruit with yogurt, pumpkin bread, and artichoke swiss cheese quiche; or perhaps strawberry shortcake muffins with a chili-cheese puff.

"Jim and Carol are full of information and recommendations about wineries; their inn is beautifully furnished." *(Nancy Banfield)* "Our loft room in the Carriage House was peaceful, quiet, and airy, done in floral prints, overlooking the well-kept gardens. Scrumptious muffins, freshly squeezed orange juice, baked French toast, and fresh fruit." *(Fred Hinners)* "Bed of Roses is a spacious room with a vaulted ceiling, gorgeous queen-size brass bed, antique dresser with a tray of bottled water and chocolate kisses, and comfortable chairs with a reading lamp. We really enjoyed the whirlpool tub with the fireplace blazing. The bathroom had excellent light for makeup plus a shower stall. Upstairs, the West Loft has a huge Palladian window framed with a colorful stained glass design of grapevines. Fran was most helpful with dinner suggestions, and referred us to an excellent Mexican restaurant." *(Gail Davis, also SWS)* "Excellent combination of inn charm and business convenience." *(GR)* "The Beazleys spend time with their guests and are genuinely warm and hospitable." *(Bill Doomey)*

Open All year.
Rooms 5 suites, 6 doubles—all with private bath and/or shower, telephone (on request), clock/radio, air-conditioning. Some with desks, gas fireplace, refrigerator, patio. TV on request. 5 rooms in carriage house with double whirlpool tubs, fireplaces.
Facilities Dining room, living room, library, porch. ⁹⁄₁₀ acre with off-street parking, garden with fountain, swing.
Location Historic district. From Hwy. 29 N, take Central Napa 1st St. Exit & follow around to right until 2nd St. Go left on 2nd, left on Warren to inn at corner of 1st & Warren.
Restrictions No smoking.
Credit cards Amex, MC, Visa.
Rates B&B, $200–225 suite, $115–160 double, $102–148 single. Extra person, $25. 10% senior, AAA discount. 2-night weekend minimum. Off-season midweek rates; ballooning, wine train, golf, fitness center packages.
Extras Wheelchair access; 1 room specially equipped. Babysitting. Spanish spoken.

Churchill Manor ¢ ♿   *Tel: 707–253–7733*
485 Brown Street, 94559   *Fax: 707–253–8836*

Churchill Manor is a magnificent three-story mansion built in 1889, now listed on the National Register of Historic Places, and restored as a B&B in 1987 by Joanna Guidotti and Brian Jensen. The manor encompasses 10,000 square feet, with seven fireplaces and 12-foot carved redwood ceilings and columns, and is decorated primarily with European antiques, Oriental rugs, and brass and crystal chandeliers. Breakfast includes omelets or perhaps French toast, afternoon fresh-baked cookies, and evening Napa varietal wines and cheeses.

"Gorgeous mansion, with charming, energetic innkeepers who are constantly working to improve their inn. Brian and Joanna are friendly, hospitable, energetic, and gregarious innkeepers. Lots of common space, inside and out, for guests to relax in privacy or with the other guests. Despite the scale of this impressive mansion, the atmosphere is warm and friendly, not stiff and formal. The guest rooms are spacious, attractive and well equipped. My favorite was Victoria's Room (#2), done in soft shades of pink and cream, with exuberant floral wallpaper, a king-size bed, exquisite original tiling. There's an oversize clawfoot tub in the corner of the room, in addition to the private bath and shower. The less expensive rooms are one of the best buys in expensive Wine Country." *(SWS)* "Enjoyable stay; wonderful antiques throughout this beautiful home. Charming Christmas decorations. Cookies are set out during the day, and lovely cheese and wine are served in the afternoon." *(Carolyn Alexander)*

"The huge grounds were lovely, and the common areas brought us back to an earlier era. The breakfast room is sunny and cheerful with individual tables. We were served fresh fruit, juice, muffins, croissants and a choice of French toast or an omelet." *(DG)* "Friendly cats." *(MW)*

Open All year.
Rooms 10 doubles—all with private bath and/or shower, telephone, radio, desk, air-conditioning. 1 with Jacuzzi, 3 with fireplace.
Facilities 3 living rooms with fireplace, games (1 with TV/VCR); music room with grand piano, fireplace; garden breakfast room, veranda. 1 acre near river. Off-street parking. Tandem bicycles, croquet. Tennis, golf, health spa, mud baths, balloon rides nearby.
Location Historic section, 4 blocks from center. From Hwy. 29, take Imola Ave. exit; go E to Jefferson; turn left & go ¾ m to Oak; turn right & go 7 blocks to Brown. Manor on right corner.
Restrictions No smoking. Children over 12.
Credit cards Amex, Discover, MC, Visa.
Rates B&B, $135–165 suite, $85–165 double. Extra person, $15. 2-night minimum with Sat. stay.
Extras Wheelchair access; bathroom specially equipped. Local airport pickups.

La Residence

4066 St. Helena Highway, 94558

Tel: 707–253–0337
Fax: 707–253–0382

Just north of Napa, where the town ends and vineyards begin, is La Residence, a luxury inn set among heritage oaks and redwoods. Owned by Craig Claussen and David Jackson since 1987, the inn consists of The Mansion, a Gothic Revival Victorian home built in the 1890s, and a recently built French-style barn called Cabernet Hall. The two structures are linked by a lovely gazebo-like structure, as well as the beautifully landscaped swimming pool and spa. Guest rooms are furnished with careful attention to detail, combining quality antiques and reproductions, designer fabrics and top-notch linens to create a comfortable yet elegant setting—lush but not fussy; most have a queen- or king-size bed. Breakfast, served 8:30–10 A.M. at individual tables, includes fresh fruit, juice, and perhaps homemade croissants with whipped eggs and cream cheese. Rates also include afternoon wine and hors d'oeuvres, hosted by the innkeepers, served by the fire or outdoors by the pool.

"La Res offers country atmosphere, yet one can still walk to dinner. Our room had an extremely comfortable bed, and a cozy fireplace. Delicious, leisurely breakfast; sociable wine hour. Appreciated the assistance with our luggage. Relaxing soak in the hot water of the spa, welcoming during our February visit; pretty setting." *(Brian & Maureen Tramontana)*

Open Closed Christmas day.
Rooms 3 suites, 17 doubles—all with private bath and/or shower, telephone, radio, clock, air-conditioning. Most with fireplace, veranda/patio. 10 with desk. TV on request. Rooms in 2 buildings.
Facilities Breakfast room with piano, fireplace; library, honor bar, meeting room with fireplace, decks. Wine hour. 2 acres with off-street parking, swimming pool, hot tub, gazebo, garden, mini-vineyard. Golf, tennis nearby.
Location Just N of town, on Hwy. 29. Carneros wine region.
Restrictions No smoking. Traffic noise possible in a few rooms.
Credit cards Amex, MC, DC, Visa.
Rates B&B, $200–235 suite, $165–235 double. 10% senior discount Nov.–March.
Extras Wheelchair access; 2 rooms specially equipped. Dutch, German, French, Spanish spoken.

NEVADA CITY

Founded in the heat of the gold rush, Nevada City remains one of the most picturesque towns along the Mother Lode. Victorian homes, white frame churches, and covered sidewalks still line the hilly streets, in spite of two fires that ravaged the town in the 1800s. Excellent restaurants and charming shops invite strolling and browsing. Nevada City is located in the Sierra foothills, approximately 50 minutes northeast of Sacramento, and 3 hours northeast of San Francisco. Nearby are golf, tennis, swimming, hiking, fishing, downhill and cross-country skiing, river rafting, and horseback riding, as well as a winery and brewery.

Ten miles north of Nevada City are the Malakoff Diggins, the site of the world's largest hydraulic gold mining operation where miners directed high-powered streams of water onto the hillsides. Effective as the practice was, entire mountainsides were washed away before some of the earliest environmental legislation stopped the destruction.

Also recommended: A Queen Anne Victorian home built in 1860, the **Deer Creek Inn** (116 Nevada Street, 95959; 916–265–0363 or 800–655–0363) has been by owned by Elaine and Chuck Matroni since 1993. B&B double rates for the five guest rooms, each with private bath, range from $90–150 ($215–245 for the suite) including lavish breakfasts and afternoon treats. Rooms have queen- or king-size canopy beds and private verandas overlooking the creek or town. Guests can relax in the lovely creekside gardens, or even try their hand at panning for gold. "Guest-pleasing details, from homemade brownies and cookies throughout the day to bubble bath and a rubber ducky for your tub.

Lounge chairs alongside the creek provide a spot for reading or napping. Delicious breakfast that tempts you to have seconds; the menu changes daily." *(Kimber Harvey)*

Convenient to all Nevada City attractions is the charming **Grandmere's Inn** (449 Broad Street, 95959; 916–265–4660), dating back to 1856 and decorated country-style with antique pine, silk flower arrangements, baskets, crafts, and quilts. B&B double rates for the seven guest rooms range from $110–175. "Superbly decorated and immaculately kept. Quiet and peaceful with a beautiful garden." *(Karen Carroll)* "Our room was spacious yet cozy with a great bathroom, large shower, and antique vanity. French doors opened to the second floor veranda. Extremely comfortable bed. Delicious, sinfully rich breakfast. Terrific innkeepers." *(Heather Allen)*

Information please: Set on two secluded acres just two blocks from downtown is the 1860s-era **Kendall House** (534 Spring Street, 95959; 919–265–0405) which balances pre-Victorian architecture with modern amenities. All five guest rooms have a private bath, and the B&B double rate ranges from $98–115; the cottage costs $150; a full breakfast is included, as is use of the inn's inviting swimming pool.

Emma Nevada House
528 East Broad Street, 95959

Tel: 916–265–4415
800–916–EMMA
Fax: 916–265–4416
E-mail: emmanev@oro.net

Although dozens of B&Bs are named for the men who played roles in their history, we must admit to a special pleasure in describing a delightful B&B named for a woman of distinction. When Ruth Ann Riese restored this 1856 Victorian cottage in 1994, she named it for Emma Nevada, a world-renowned coloratura soprano, who lived in this house as a child. Although her maiden name was Wixom, Emma choose Nevada as her stage name in honor of her native city and the state of Nevada, where she grew up.

Although it appears small from the street, the inn is surprisingly spacious, with a formal parlor and an inviting sun room with floor-to-ceiling windows on six sides. Each guest room has a queen-size bed; the decor varies from the cheerful Mignon's Boudoir, done in blue and white with yellow accents to the elegant Nightingale's Bower, with Italian bedding and a sitting area in the bay window. Breakfast is served at 9 A.M. at several large tables; one morning Ruth Ann might serve pink grapefruit juice, sliced tropical fruit, garden quiche, cranberry-almond scones, and baked pears with vanilla yogurt; the next day might bring cranberry-raspberry juice, fresh fruit salad, pumpkin waffles with pure maple or boysenberry syrup, sausages, and mountain berry cobbler.

"Beautifully decorated for Christmas. Ideal location, within easy walking distance of shops and restaurants. Ruth Ann is a gracious and meticulous innkeeper." *(Helen Krause)* "Warm welcome, careful attention to detail from this very organized, creative, friendly innkeeper. Ruth Ann suggested restaurants and made advance dinner reservations for our weekend stay. The Empress Chamber has an exquisite armoire, luxurious imported linens, plush towels and robes, even passion fruit-scented soap. Delicious breakfast; tempting afternoon tea and cookies." *(Elliott & Arlene Shapero)* "Gracious, homey atmosphere." *(Grace & Steve Fabula)*

Open All year

Rooms 6 doubles—all with full private bath, clock, air-conditioning. Some with double whirlpool tub, desk, fireplace, TV. Telephone on request.

Facilities Dining room, living room with fireplace; game room with TV, books, games, antique slot machine; sun room, porches. ⅓ acre with rose garden, off-street parking.

Location 2 blocks from historic district. From Sacramento, take I-80 N to Auburn, then Hwy. 49/20 E to Broad St. Exit in Nevada City. Go left on Broad up to "Y" and veer right to inn on right.

Restrictions No smoking. Children over 10.

Credit cards Amex, DC, MC, Visa.

Rates B&B, $110–160 double. Extra person, $20. 20% discount midweek.

Flume's End
317 South Pine, 95959

Tel: 916–265–9665
800–991–8118

Built in 1863, Flume's End B&B was bought by Steve Wilson and Ter-rianne Straw in 1990. "Flume's End appears to be an unprepossessing Victorian cottage, set right on the street. In back, the inn descends a steep hillside, overlooking spring-fed, fast-flowing Gold Run Creek. Al-though the common areas are basic, its bedrooms are appealing with country Victorian floral fabrics and wallcoverings, and modern baths. Our favorite was the Creekside Room, cantilevered over the creek—you look through floor-to-ceiling windows to the rushing waters below. Several levels of terraces overlook the stream and shaded hillside. It's hard to believe that town is just a short walk across the scenic Pine Street Bridge." *(SWS)* Breakfasts, served on the terrace deck, might include smoked salmon and dill tart, spicy browned potatoes and locally made sausage. Homemade fudge, brownies, and cookies are put out each evening for guests to savor.

"We enjoyed chatting with Steve and Terrianne about their experi-ences as innkeepers." *(DCB)* "The Garden Room has its own little deck right above a waterfall. Although both the room and bed were small, we loved it because of the sound of the water, plus the Jacuzzi tub. Out-side our room was a little living room with a woodstove and a stocked guest refrigerator. Excellent breakfast of cheese-baked potatoes, home-made granola, baked apple sauce, eggs Florentine, bread, and French roast coffee." *(Lisa Gallagher, also JTD)*

Open All year.

Rooms 1 cottage, 5 doubles—all with private shower and/or bath, radio, air-conditioning. 2 with balcony, Jacuzzi; cottage with kitchenette, stove, deck.

Facilities Dining room, living room with fireplace, piano, banjo, flute. Family room with TV, refrigerator, wet bar. 3½ acres with terraces, creek. 15 min. to cross-country skiing; 45 min. to downhill.

Location 2 blocks from town.

Restrictions No smoking.
Credit cards MC, Visa.
Rates B&B, $75–135. 2-night weekend minimum.

The Red Castle Inn   *Tel:* 916–265–5135
109 Prospect Street, 95959   800–761–4766

On a steep hillside overlooking Nevada City sits this dramatic four-story Gothic Revival red brick mansion, dripping white icicle trim with elaborately carved balconies. Longtime owners Mary Louise and Conley Weaver have furnished this 1860 mansion with period antiques, historic memorabilia and family heirlooms. A special feature is the horse-drawn carriage ride through the historic district every Saturday morning; on special occasions, "Mark Twain" or "Lola Montez" will join guests for tea. Breakfast is served between 8–10 A.M. on weekends, and at 9:00 A.M. on other days; coffee is ready at 7:30.

"Mary Louise has a talent for decorating with comfortable and inviting antiques. Scrumptious breakfasts enjoyed on our private balcony, with specially blended coffee, fresh fruit, freshly baked breads, granola, and delicious egg dishes. In the afternoon, tempting sweets and a special ginger ale punch were served. Our well-maintained room was furnished in period, with a four-poster bed, dresser, and marble-top washstand. It's a comfortable walk down the lighted path to the main shopping and historic district, and two fine restaurants are just down a short walk away. The delightful garden has lots of areas to sit and chat with the other guests or to read in a secluded, fragrant corner." *(Darlene Harper)* "The gardens and walkways enhanced the quiet, beautiful, and restful atmosphere. The 'conversation with Mark Twain' was a highlight." *(Anne & George Derfer)* "Mary Louise has a wealth of wonderful knowledge about the house, its history, and furnishings. She has created a comfortable but authentic Victorian ambiance with lovely shawls draped over antique chairs and knickknacks. The grounds were lovely, with little ponds, beautiful plants, and Victorian gazing balls." *(Sarah & Jan Williams)* "Delicious grilled grapefruit with ginger at breakfast. Owners friendly and knowledgeable but not cloying." *(David Kobosa)*

"Thoughtful details included ice brought to our room, lovely background music, and books on the Gold Country everywhere." *(Susan Payne)* "Tasty breakfast with breakfast breads, rice pudding, orange compote, and a wonderful quiche." *(Lois Revlock)* "The Garret West was small but cozy, with a great view of the town. We enjoyed Mary Louise's stories about the Inn and its ghost (we didn't see her)." *(Sharon Bielski)* "The Rose Room opens onto a large hall where a delicious breakfast buffet was set out at 9:00 A.M., including an unusual cheese-tomato-egg dish, toast, yogurt breakfast cake, and berry cobbler." *(Joyce Rinehart)* "We were welcomed by Mary Louise, then shown to our room, with a handsome canopied bed and love seat. Across the hall in the living room, guests gathered for tea, a delicious whipped-cream cake, and chocolate nut cookies. In the morning, it was too chilly to eat outside, so we took our breakfast tray into the living room." *(SWS)*

Open All year.
Rooms 3 suites, 4 doubles—all with private shower and/or bath, ceiling fan. 4 with desk, air-conditioning. 2 with radio. Most with private balcony.
Facilities Parlor with pump organ. 1½ acres with terraced English rose gardens, three fountains, fish pond, footpaths, arbors, trellises, croquet, swing. Off-street parking.
Location Historic district, walking distance to downtown. From Hwy. 49, take Sacramento St. exit and turn right just past Chevron station. Turn left on Prospect St.
Restrictions No smoking. "Children must be carefully supervised." No candles in rooms.
Credit cards MC, Visa.
Rates B&B, $100–140 suite, $70–135 double, $65–130 single. Extra person, $20. 2-night holiday/weekend minimum April–Dec. Corporate rates. Christmas Dinner with entertainment.
Extras Airport/Amtrak connector pickup.

NEWPORT BEACH

Although a noisy mob scene in spring and summer, Newport's wide beaches are ideal for long quiet walks, jogs, or bike rides off-season; stroll down to Balboa to explore its appealing shops or to catch the hydrofoil to Catalina. Weekend rates here are high; come midweek and ask for a corporate rate.

Information please: The **Doryman's Inn** (2102 West Ocean Front, 92663; 714–675–7300) is located on a busy corner right on the beach with glorious views. On the first floor is a popular seafood restaurant; on the second floor, reached through a separate entrance, is the inn. Rooms are lavishly decorated with European antiques, floral fabrics and lace curtains, reproduction Victorian wallpapers, and sunken marble bathtubs. The buffet breakfast of pastries and breads, brown eggs, cheeses and yogurt, fresh fruit and juices, tea and coffee can be enjoyed in the parlor or on the flower-filled terrace. B&B double rates for the ten guest rooms range from $140–275.

NIPTON

Hotel Nipton &
107355 Nipton Road, HCI Box 357, 92364

Tel: 760–856–2335
Fax: 760–856–2352
E-mail: Seeniptonc@aol.com

If you want to get away from it all—really far away—go to the desert town of Nipton, the last stop on I-15 before Nevada. Built between 1904 and 1910, the hotel was restored with Southwestern flair in 1986 by owners Gerald and Roxanne Freeman. The Freemans also own the rest of the town, including the Nipton Trading Post—a gift shop and convenience store, and the Nipton Town Hall—a cafe and bar. Experienced desert dwellers, they are pleased to help guests enjoy the Mojave National Preserve, established in 1994, a rugged desert wilderness. Guest rooms have been named for local personalities (silent film star Clara Bow was a frequent guest), and are decorated with old photographs, personal mementos, original documents, and antiques.

"Charming and clean, with intelligent hosts who enjoy their guests and appreciate the surroundings." *(Denise Terry)* "An amazing place, located in a remote desert area. We celebrated our honeymoon in a hot tub on the porch, watching falling stars in the Milky Way. A living piece of railroad frontier history yet just minutes from the interstate. Incredibly clean, tastefully decorated; wonderfully romantic, too." *(Julia Alkema)* "Beautiful sunset, loved the trains." *(Marilyn Andrews)* "Warm, friendly, unpretentious, genuine. The hotel's historical significance is well researched and verified." *(HL)* "Originally a railroad depot, the tiny desert town of Nipton seems like another world, but the owners of the hotel are definitely aware of today's travelers' need for service and privacy. The sitting room has terrific old pictures, and the scenery is astounding, with desert and mountains that seem to go on forever. Breakfast is served in the parlor, and included good coffee, orange juice, fruit and huge blueberry muffins." *(Sherrill Brown)*

Open All year.
Rooms 4 doubles share 2 baths. All with air-conditioning.
Facilities Parlor with books, radio. Cactus garden. Hiking, mt. biking, fishing, boating nearby.
Location Mojave National Preserve. 300 m E of Los Angeles, 55 m SW of Las Vegas, between Grand Canyon & Death Valley. 10 m off I-15. From Las Vegas, take I-15 S 55 m to Nipton Rd off-ramp. Go E on Nipton Rd, 10 m to Nipton.
Restrictions No smoking. Train noise possible.
Credit cards DC, MC, Visa.
Rates B&B, $55 double. Extra person, $8.
Extras Limited wheelchair access.

OAKHURST

Also recommended: Fifteen miles south of Yosemite's South Entrance is **The Estate by the Elderberries** (48688 Victoria Lane, P.O. Box 577, Oakhurst 93644; 209–683–6860), constructed to resemble a manor house from the south of France, complete with stucco facade and tile roof, and previously called the Chateau du Sureau. The ten luxuriously appointed rooms are complete with stereo/CD system, imported linens, woodburning fireplace, and marble bathrooms; one is wheelchair accessible. Open for lunch, brunch, and dinner, the restaurant, Erna's Elderberry House, is well-regarded for its innovative and elegant cuisine. Double rates of $310–410 include a European-style breakfast with cold meats, cheeses, fruit, freshly baked breads, and coffee. "The six-course dinner is an outstanding value. Wonderful hospitality; immaculate, beautifully furnished rooms with all amenities. Delicious breakfast is served on the patio." *(Tina Hom)* "Spectacular dinner, makes any occasion special." *(ACR)*

O'BRIEN

O'Brien Mountain Inn Bed and Breakfast   *Tel:* 530–238–8026
18026 O'Brien Inlet Road   *Fax:* 530–238–8026
P.O. Box 27, 96070   *E-mail:* obrienmt@snowcrest.net

Whether you're passing through on I-5, or spending some time exploring the beauty of the Shasta National Recreation Area, you'll have a relaxing stay at the O'Brien Mountain Inn. A contemporary-style home built in 1963, and renovated as a B&B by Greg and Teresa Ramsey in 1996, the area offers endless opportunities for the outdoor enthusiast, from a visit to Shasta Dam to Shasta Lake for all water sports, from tours of Shasta Caverns to a hike to the top of Castle Crag.

A musical motif accents the decor with old and new instruments; each guest room is named for a different style of music. Teresa once worked for Warner Brothers Music, and Greg played with a bluegrass band. As Greg and Teresa put it, "if you enjoy conversation, microwbrews, wine, and good music, you'll find a haven at our B&B." Breakfast, served 8–9 A.M. at guests' choice of a small or large table, includes fresh fruit and juice, home-baked breads, and such entrees as stuffed French toast, banana pancakes, or Tex-Mex potato pancakes with black bean puree and guacamole. Welcome refreshments are served on arrival.

"Though just minutes from the interstate, you wouldn't know it from the quiet, peaceful forest setting, with millions of stars visible in the evening sky. The comfortable, uncluttered decor combines contemporary, reproduction, and antique pieces. Each bedroom has French doors opening onto the landscaped yard. The musical theme is appealing but not overpowering, and can been seen in the clever use of CD jewelcases as doorplates, the instruments on display in the library, and the keyboard lampstand in one guest room. Best of all are the vegetarian breakfasts, served at our private little table across from a crackling fire, overlooking the forested hillside. The first day we had home-baked banana nut bread and bananas-strawberry-lemon juice, followed by fresh fruit salad, then grilled vegetables, eggplant on toast, and roasted new potatoes. Each day the table setting, juice, bread, fruit salad, and entree were different, but equally flavorful, memorable, and delicious. Greg and Teresa made our stay special with their pleasant company and warm hospitality." *(Joy Matsura)*

Open All year.
Rooms 4 doubles—all with private bath and/or shower, radio, clock, air-conditioning, fan, private entrance.
Facilities Dining room, living room with fireplace, books; gameroom with piano, stereo; library with fireplace, guest refrigerator; patios. 47 acres with gardens, lawn games, hiking. 1 m to Shasta Lake for all water sports. Golf, Shasta Caverns, river rafting, cross-country skiing, snowshoeing nearby.
Location Shasta Cty, 15 m N of Redding. From Redding, go N on I-5. Take exit for O'Brien/Shasta Caverns Rd. Turn left (W) & go ¼ m to inn.

Restrictions No smoking.
Credit cards Amex, DC, Discover, MC, Visa.
Rates B&B, $95–125 double. Extra person, $15.

OCCIDENTAL

For additional area inns, see **Guerneville.**

The Inn at Occidental ♿
3657 Church Street, 95465

Tel: 707–874–1047
800–522–6324
Fax: 707–874–1078
E-mail: innkeeper@innatoccidental.com

A clapboard and brick homestead built in 1877, The Inn at Occidental has been owned by Jack Bullard since 1994. Set on a hillside studded with redwood trees, the inn overlooks the little town of Occidental, set midway between the dramatic ocean vistas of the Sonoma coast, and the vineyards and wineries of the Alexander Valley, Dry Creek, and the Russian River. The inn's original fir floors, wainscotted hallways, and covered porches are enhanced by handsome antiques and quality reproductions. Each guest room features a display cabinet with an exceptional collection of cut or patterned glass, silver, ivory, quilts, or even antique marbles. Coffee is ready at 7 A.M., and breakfast, served 8–10 A.M. at the dining room table, might include fresh blueberries, homemade granola, yogurt, Belgian waffles, or perhaps orange thyme pancakes. Rates also include afternoon wine.

"An elegant inn, wonderfully furnished with beautiful antiques. Jack welcomed us warmly, offering wine and chatting amiably before the living room fireplace. At breakfast, we helped ourselves to juice, homemade granola, yogurt, and fruit, and then were served blueberry waffles and cinnamon rolls. In warm weather, the meal is served on the porch that wraps around two sides of the inn, overlooking the beautiful courtyard." *(Marilyn Parker)* "Fabulous English garden with exquisite begonias, trumpet vines, hydrangeas, and more. The veranda is a welcoming place to enjoy a glass of wine or a private breakfast on a warm morning. The living room has handsome English antiques and Oriental carpets, and the glassed-in dining room is lovely; a gathering room is downstairs at ground level with a massive stone fireplace, wall-size wine rack, and a collection of Lundberg art lamps. Jack's beautiful hand-stenciling is found throughout the inn, as are fresh flowers. Each guest room has a king- or queen-size bed with a puffy feather bed, and is decorated around a different theme; all were quite spacious, and even the smallest had ample room for a queen-size four poster bed, bedside tables and lamps on both sides, a small table, and comfortable chairs. The Ivory Suite has antique twin beds reconfigured as a king-size bed, and is named for its Japanese netsukes—miniature antique ivory carvings. A favorite is the Tiffany Suite, with Battenburg lace on the queen-size canopy mahogany Charleston bed, an antique fireplace, private balcony, and Tiffany silver pieces. The Quilt Room has bathroom louver doors which fold back, allowing you to enjoy the fireplace from the double Jacuzzi tub. Jack's careful attention to detail extended to the marvelous bathrobes, numerous amenities, and designer-decorated tiled bathrooms. Exceptional breakfast with freshly squeezed orange juice, a melon and berry medley, and poached eggs with cheese, spinach and croissants." *(Susan Waller Schwemm)* "As a cat lover, I was delighted to meet the inn's three resident felines." *(MW)*

Open All year.

Rooms 2 suites, 6 doubles—all with private bath and/or shower, telephone, clock/radio. Some with double Jacuzzi or hot tub, balcony/patio, fireplace. TV on request.

Facilities Dining room, living room, gathering room with fireplace, games, piano, wine cellar; verandas. ½ acre with courtyard garden with fountain, off-street parking.

Location 1 hr. N of San Francisco. 10 m W of Santa Rosa, 5 m E of ocean. Take Hwy 101 N to exit for Rohnert Park/Sebastopol–116 W & follow signs to Sebastopol. In Sebastopol turn left at light to Bodega Bay for 6.4 m. Turn right at sign to Freestone & Occidental, on Bohemian Hwy. Go 3.7 m to stop sign in Occidental. Turn right up hill to inn.

Restrictions No smoking. Children 10 and over.

Credit cards Amex, MC, Visa.

Rates B&B, $135–245 suite, double. Tips appreciated. Senior, AAA discount. Fri. & Sat. Occasional Sunday dinners by reservation.

Extras Wheelchair access; 1 room specially equipped.

OLEMA

Olema is located 35 miles north of San Francisco, in Marin County, with Point Reyes National Seashore to the west, and Golden Gate National Recreation Area to the east. Giant redwoods can be seen in Samuel Taylor State Park.

Information please: A recently built country lodge, the **Point Reyes Seashore Lodge** (10021 Coastal Highway One, P.O. Box 39, 94950; 415–663–9000 or in CA, 800–404–5634) offers 21 guest rooms with simple but comfortable furnishings. Some have whirlpool tubs, others have an upstairs sleeping loft, plus a sofa bed by the fireplace. B&B double rates range from $85–195, and include a breakfast of juice, coffee, sweet rolls, muffins, cheeses, and cereals.

The **Roundstone Farm** (9940 Sir Francis Drake Boulevard, P.O. Box 217, Olema 94950; 415–663–1020), was designed as a B&B by solar architect Jim Campe to take full advantage of the surrounding natural beauty. "Comfortable bed, English antiques, and expansive views of the hills surrounding Point Reyes and Tomales Bay. A telescope for viewing the stars added to the pleasant surroundings. Ample skylights, windows, and privacy." *(Carol Van Horn)* Each of the five guest rooms has a private bath and fireplace, and the B&B double rate of $120–140 includes a full breakfast.

For additional area inns, see **Inverness, Point Reyes Station,** and **Stinson Beach.**

ORLAND

The Inn at Shallow Creek Farm ¢   *Tel:* 530–865–4093
4712 County Road DD, 95963   800–865–4093

"A quiet location, close enough to the freeway so as not to get lost, but far enough away not to hear it" *(Norma & Mike McClintock)* summarizes the initial appeal of this inn's location near Interstate 5, roughly a halfway point for those traveling between California and southern Oregon. Kurt and Mary Glaeseman have owned the farm since 1982, and in addition to the care and feeding of their guests, tend to citrus orchards and poultry flock. "Kurt and Mary welcome you with smiles and warmth. Family-style breakfast with home-made marmalade from their own oranges, fresh custard made from their own eggs, and juice made from their own tangerines." *(Dionne Clabaugh)* "When you turn into the shade of the tree-lined front yard, ducks, geese, and guinea hens will come to greet you. Surrounding the inn are groves of citrus trees, which give the air a glorious scent when in bloom." *(Geralynn Myrah)* "Kurt recommended historic sites, a quiet lakeside spot, and a nearby restaurant." *(Collin Batey)* "Great location for birdwatching and wildlife viewing. Though sensitive to our privacy, Mary and Kurt were delightful hosts and we enjoyed their conversations, excellent advice, and directions." *(Glenn Lustig)* "Peaceful setting; comfortable accommodations and common areas; graciously served breakfast with homemade jams and jellies." *(Barbara Green)* "Like a visit to grandmother's house. Charming, interesting owners. From our bedroom window, we watched deer wander though the citrus orchard." *(Alice Homes)* "Charming country farmhouse, with ducks and geese wandering the grounds. Genuine hospitality." *(Heather & Jerry Allen)*

Open All year.
Rooms 1 cottage, 1 suite, 2 doubles—2 with private bath and/or shower, 2 with maximum of 4 sharing bath. All with telephone, air-conditioning. 2 with desk. Cottage with wood-burning stove.
Facilities Dining room, living room with fireplace, piano, TV, stereo. Sun porch with books, games, refrigerator. 3 acres with citrus orchards. 5 m to lake for boating, swimming, fishing, hiking.
Location Central Valley. N. Sacramento Valley, Glenn County. 100 m N of Sacramento, 20 m W of Chico, 2½ m W of I-5. Take Black Butte/Orland/Chico exit and go W 2½ m on Newville Rd. Turn right at Rd. DD (watch carefully; can be hard to see at night). Go ½ m, cross small concrete bridge, and turn right down the 1st country lane.
Restrictions No smoking.

Credit cards MC, Visa.
Rates B&B, $75 cottage, $65 suite, $55 double. Extra person, $15. Includes tax and service.
Extras Airport/station pickup. French, German, Spanish spoken.

PACIFIC GROVE

Set on the Monterey Peninsula, bordering the town of Monterey, Pacific Grove begins at the Monterey Bay Aquarium on Cannery Row and extends along the bay to the beginning of the Seventeen-Mile Drive. Many think this is the peninsula's best town for bicycling and shore-walking. The town was founded by Methodists in 1875 as a "Christian seaside resort"; most of its Victorian inns were built during this period. Its rather stodgy character lingered on—until the late '60s, liquor could be bought in Pacific Grove only with a doctor's prescription. The town is filled with flowers in the spring, but its most famous site is "Butterfly Park" (George Washington Park), where thousands of monarch butterflies winter from October to March.

Pacific Grove is located about 120 miles south of San Francisco. For more information on the Monterey Peninsula, see listings for Monterey and Carmel (three miles away) as well as the Central Coast section of the introduction to this chapter.

Also recommended: Built in 1888, the **Green Gables** (104 Fifth Street, 93950; 408–375–2095 or 800–722–1774) is a half-timbered, many-gabled Queen Anne Victorian mansion with beautiful stained glass and leaded small-paned windows. Most of the eleven guest rooms have private baths, and are decorated with antiques, ruffled curtains, and wall-to-wall carpets. B&B double rates of $110–160 include a full breakfast; afternoon tea, wine, and hors d'oeuvres; a stocked refrigerator; and evening turndown service with chocolates. "Room #7 in the carriage house was spacious and well equipped; we could see the water, and hear the waves all night. Wonderful breakfasts." *(Julie Phillips)* "Helpful concierge service. Guests have the option of eating at tables for two, four, or six. An exceptionally well-run inn." *(Jim & Mary White)*

Information please: Listed in past editions, we need current reports on **The Centrella** (612 Central Avenue, 93950; 408–372–3372 or 800–233–3372), built in the 1880s, and extensively restored a century later by longtime owner Dr. Joseph Megna. The decor includes lots of wicker, some antiques, and Laura Ashley fabrics. A total of 25 guest rooms and cottages are available, at B&B double rates of $135–195, including the morning paper, an extensive breakfast buffet, and evening sherry and hors d'oeuvres.

A light and airy Victorian house, the **Gatehouse Inn** (225 Central Ave., 93950; 408–649–8436 or 800–753–1881) offers a view of Monterey Bay. "Terrific location, two blocks from the ocean and three blocks from the Aquarium. Careful attention to detail throughout. The common areas are lavishly decorated with stunning stained-glass windows, elaborate Victorian reproduction wallpaper on the walls and ceilings, and period antiques. Stuffed animals are scattered throughout the inn and can be 'adopted' at the end of your stay."(*Diana Chang*) Each of the eight guest rooms has a private bath, and a generous buffet breakfast is included in the double rates of $120–160.

The Martine Inn ♿

255 Oceanview Boulevard, 93950

Tel: 408–373–3388
800–852–5588
Fax: 408–373–3896

Although built in 1899 as a Victorian cottage, the Martine Inn was remodeled over the years as a pink-stuccoed Mediterranean mansion. The inn was bought by the Martine family in 1972 and was opened as an inn by Marion and Don Martine in 1984. It has been fully restored and decorated in period, from authentic wall coverings to museum-quality antique furnishings. Breakfast is served from 8:30 to 10:00 A.M.; wine and hors d'oeuvres are offered from 6 to 8:00 P.M.

"Beautiful location overlooking the cliffs and the Pacific. The light, creative breakfast was nicely served, as were the evening refreshments. Lovely antiques throughout the Inn. Comfortable, well-lit rooms with windows that opened to enjoy the sea breeze. Pleasant staff." (*Sandy Truitt*)

"Perfect location within walking distance of the aquarium, Cannery Row, and the Wharf. Right on the ocean with a jogging trail that goes along the shore for miles." (*F. T. McQuilkin*) "From the parlor, you get a magnificent view of the rocky coastline, while enjoying wine and hors d'oeuvres. Breakfast included fresh fruit, homemade muffins, a hot entree, and piping hot coffee." (*Mrs. Donald Hamilton*) "Elegant, romantic ambiance. Spectacular oceanfront setting, high above the street below. Don proudly showed us his collection of classic MGs which he restores and races. Incomparable water views. Lace-curtained French doors separated the bedroom and bath. Bedside lights made reading in bed a pleasure. A vase of roses and bowl of fresh fruit was set on our dresser. At night, our bed was turned down, a chocolate placed on each pillow. We fell asleep to the sounds of the gently pounding surf. The large dining room also has picture windows, with binoculars set on the windowsills to enhance viewing." (*Gail Davis*)

Open All year.

Rooms 19 doubles—all with private bath and/or shower, telephone, desk, refrigerator. Many with fireplace.

Facilities Dining room, parlor with fireplace, piano entertainment nightly; library with fireplace, conference room with TV/VCR, game room with pool table, 2 sitting rooms. Courtyard with fountain, garden, gazebo, hot tub. Fishing, jogging, bicycling, tennis, golf nearby. Limited on-site parking.

Location ¾m from center, directly on Monterey Bay. 4 blocks to aquarium.

Restrictions Smoking permitted in guest rooms with fireplace only. "Children discouraged."

Credit cards Amex, Discover, MC, Visa.

Rates B&B, $135–245 double. Extra person, $35. 2–3 night weekend/holiday minimum. Picnic lunches on request.

Extras Wheelchair access; 1 room equipped for disabled. Airport/station pickup, $16.

Seven Gables Inn & Grand View Inn   *Tel:* 408–372–4341
555 & 557 Oceanview Boulevard, 93950

Built in 1886, Seven Gables is a grand Victorian home situated on a rocky point at the edge of Monterey Bay. The inn features ocean views from all guest rooms, and contains an exceptional collection of Victorian antiques, including Tiffany stained glass windows, crystal chandeliers, Oriental rugs, inlaid furniture, and queen-size canopy beds. The inn is owned and operated by the Flatley family, who have been in the B&B and antique collecting businesses since 1958. Rates include a full breakfast, served from 8–10 A.M., and afternoon tea from 4 to 5 P.M.

"We stayed in the least expensive room, yet still had a fine view and comfortable accommodations. Gorgeous gardens. Breakfast included an egg dish, breads, fresh fruit, yogurt, and fresh-squeezed orange juice." *(James & Janice Utt)* "Meticulously clean; beautiful decor; friendly, efficient staff." *(Adele & Paul Britton)* "The location is convenient to everything in Monterey." *(Lonnie Felker)* "Rooms are fastidiously clean, beautifully furnished, light and airy." *(JP)*

In 1994, the Flatleys purchased the mansion next door, completely renovating it and naming it the **Grand View Inn,** offering equally elegant rooms with queen-size beds, antique furnishings, and the same outstanding water views. "The innkeeper welcomed us warmly, showed us to our room, and made dinner reservations at a restaurant nearby. The second-floor Seal Rocks room was elegantly decorated with rich fabrics, and had a spectacular second-floor ocean view. We fell asleep to the sound of the waves lapping at the shore, and awoke to the sound of seals calling to their mates. Family-style breakfast, with excellent muffins." *(Randi Rubin)*

Open All year.
Rooms 21 doubles, 3 cottages—all with private shower and/or bath, desk. Double rooms in 2 adjacent buildings.
Facilities 2 parlors, 2 dining rooms, family room, breakfast area, porches. Gardens with patios, off-street parking.
Location On ocean, 2 blocks from beach. 1 block to downtown. From Hwy. 1, take Pacific Grove exit (Rte. 68W) to Pacific Grove. Continue on Forest Ave. to Oceanview Blvd., then right 2 blocks to Fountain Ave. & inn.
Restrictions No smoking. "Well-behaved, older children are welcome."
Credit cards MC, Visa.
Rates B&B, $125–225 double. 2-night weekend minimum.
Extras German, Italian, Spanish spoken.

PALM SPRINGS

Located in California's Desert Country, Palm Springs is 115 miles east of Los Angeles, 26 miles east of Joshua Tree National Monument. Palm Springs is famous for its warm and dry winter climate and its championship golf courses. For instant air-conditioning, the tramway to the top of the San Jacinto Mountains is also a favorite; you can even cross-country ski there in winter. Hiking in nearby Palm Canyon, home to trees over a thousand years old, is also popular. Because summer is very definitely off-season here, rates drop considerably during the hottest months. Palm Canyon Drive (Highway 111) is the main street in town, and most directions use it as a point of reference.

Reader tips: "Be aware of the college 'spring break'; Palm Springs gets a bit noisy when overrun with students, motorcycles, and police." Also: "Be aware that the desert can be windy."

Information please: A Mediterranean-style villa, the **Korakia Pensione** (257 South Patencio Road, 92262; 619–864–6411) offers twelve lovely guest rooms surrounding a Mediterranean courtyard. Most rooms have full kitchens; some have fireplaces. Continental breakfast is served in the garden, where fruit trees surround tiled Moroccan fountains and a swimming pool. B&B double rates range from $79–169.

Built in 1949 as a luxury hotel for celebrities, **Le Palmier Inn** (200 West Arenas, 92264; 619–320–8860 or 888–862–8866) is located one block from the shops and restaurants on Palm Canyon, and is equally convenient to the mountains. B&B double rates for the 25 well-quipped guest rooms range from $65–150, including a continental breakfast. This small hotel's landscaped grounds include a heated swimming pool.

For a complete change of pace, **Sakura** (1677 North Via Miraleste, 92262; 619–327–0705), a Japanese-style B&B, awaits your discovery. Guests can relax in Japanese kimonos and slippers; in the morning, you'll have a choice of an American or a Japanese breakfast. "American George Cebra and his wife Fumiko have lovingly designed a simple, yet elegant Japanese-type B&B. The three guest rooms are furnished in traditional Japanese decor, complete with tatami mats on the floor, handmade futon beds, rice-paper windows and lamps, sliding shoji doors leading out to the swimming pool, Buddha statues, and other beautiful Japanese decorations." *(Gail Davis)* B&B double rates range from $45–125.

Casa Cody B&B Country Inn ¢
175 South Cahuilla Road, 92262

Tel: 760–320–9346
800–231–2639
Fax: 760–325–8610

Casa Cody was founded in the 1920s by Hollywood pioneers Harriet Cody and her husband Bill—cousin to the original "Buffalo Bill." After years of decline, Frank Tysen and Therese Hayes purchased the inn in 1986, and spent a full year restoring its early California adobe hacienda-style architecture; Elissa Goforth is the manager. Decorated in Santa Fe style, guest rooms have tiled floors, hand-woven rugs, hand-painted furniture, rattan chairs, and textured walls. Breakfast is available from 8–10 A.M., and includes juice, muffins, cereal, and fresh fruit.

"Peaceful little oasis; friendly, helpful staff; welcoming atmosphere; ample breakfasts; clean and well maintained. The flower-filled gardens and the tiny white lights in the trees create a wonderful atmosphere." *(Andrea Huntley)* "A great place to visit with a pet. Our clean, comfortable room (the only one then available in a recently acquired building) had a king-size bed, saltillo tile floors, full kitchen, cathedral ceiling, well-equipped bathroom with thick towels, and French doors opening to a private fenced yard. The lush landscaping and the inn's location at the base of the mountains were spectacular. There's a kidney-shaped pool for lounging, and a rectangular one for swimming laps. Owners Frank and Alissa were charming; she introduced us to her four cats, and Frank told us about the inn's history." *(Gail Davis)* "Just a block to the main drag. Spacious rooms, simply furnished." *(Ruth Tilsley)*

Open All year.

Rooms 8 1-2 bedroom suites, 13 doubles, 2 cottages—all with private shower and/or tub, telephone, TV, desk, air-conditioning, refrigerator. Some with ceiling fan, patio, wood-burning fireplace, VCR, kitchen. Rooms in 4 buildings.

Facilities 3 acres with 2 heated swimming pools, hot tub, croquet, gardens. Hiking from property in San Jacinto Mts.

Location From Los Angeles, take I-10 to Hwy. 111 to Palm Springs. Becomes Palm Canyon Dr. in town. Go right on Tahquitz Canyon Way. Take second left on Cahuilla to inn on right.

Restrictions "Light smoking OK."

Credit cards Amex, Carte Blanche, DC, Discover, MC, Visa.

Rates B&B, $89–189 suite, $49–129 double. Extra person, $10. Children "usually free during low/shoulder season." AAA rate.

Extras Wheelchair access; 1 bathroom has grab bars. Crib. French, Dutch & some German, Spanish spoken. Pets allowed.

The Willows Historic Palm Springs Inn   *Tel:* 760–320–0771
412 West Tahquitz Canyon Way, 92262

Albert Einstein slept here, and so did Carole Lombard and Clark Gable, and while owners Tracy Conrad and Paul Marut, and manager Diane Bailey can't promise you either brilliance or beauty, they can assure you of comfortable accommodations in a lovely setting, good food, welcoming hospitality, and excellent service. The Willows was built in 1927 as the private winter getaway of New York attorney and human rights activist Sam Untermeyer, and was later owned by Marion Davies, life-long mistress of newspaper magnate William Randolph Hearst. When Tracy and Paul—both emergency room physicians—first saw the mansion in 1995, it needed emergency attention as well. Abused and neglected, the mansion required huge transfusions of cash and careful renovation to restore its original elegance. Tracy supervised the work personally, overseeing the restoration of the mahogany beams of the Great Hall, the frescoed ceiling of the dining room, and much more, complementing these fine architectural details with elegant fabrics and antique furnishings.

Breakfast, served 8–10 A.M. at individual tables, varies daily, but might include puffed pancakes, baked eggs with white truffles and Parmesan, praline bacon, and apple sausages. Rates also include evening wine and hors d'oeuvres, served 4–7 P.M. Guests have the option of having lunch or dinner from Le Vallauris—an excellent French restaurant located across the street—served to them at the inn.

"Comfortable and luxurious, yet low-key and unpretentious. Breakfast is served in the beautiful and comfortable dining room with an entire glass wall just a few feet from a dramatic 50-foot waterfall that flows over the rocky hillside." *(John Gartland)* "Delicious wine and hors d'oeuvres served in a lovely homey atmosphere before a fireplace glowing with real logs." *(Raquel Ross)* "In the evening, we followed a path up the hill behind the inn to a sitting area where we enjoyed the cool night air and the city lights below. The inn's lap pool and hot tub are supplied with lots of large fluffy towels." *(Mary Seward)* "Quiet setting, just a block from Palm Springs' main street. Luxurious antique furniture, hardwood floors, armoires, four-poster beds, wood panelling, rich rugs, and French doors, in a 1920s and 30s atmosphere. Comfortable beds, luxurious linens. Our bathroom had a spacious shower; the water poured straight down from above, like a warm rainstorm. The house is built with the stone, stucco, and tile roof of desert architecture, surrounded by palm trees, bougainvillea, desert flowers, and citrus trees. Immaculate throughout, with friendly, efficient staff." *(Lee Hubbard)* "Careful attention to detail; sensitive to guests' needs for privacy; responsive to social interaction." *(Ellen Palo)*

Open All year. "Abbreviated hours July/Aug."

Rooms 8 doubles—all with private bath and/or shower, telephone, clock/radio, TV, desk, air-conditioning, ceiling fan. 4 with fireplace, refrigerator; 2 with balcony/deck.

Facilities Dining room with fireplace, living room with fireplace, piano, library; porch, veranda. Pianist in evening. 1 acre with heated pool, hot tub, gazebo, locked off-street parking.

Location From Los Angeles, take I-10 to Hwy. 111 to Palm Springs. Becomes Palm Canyon Dr. in town. Go right on Tahquitz Canyon Way to inn on right. Adjacent to Desert Museum.

Restrictions *Absolutely no smoking whatsoever.* Children over 16.

Credit cards Amex, CB, DC, Discover, MC, Visa.

Rates B&B, $175–550 double. 10% AAA discount. Alc lunch, $15; dinner, $50 (at La Valluris).

Extras Airport/station pickup. French, Spanish spoken.

PALO ALTO

Palo Alto, meaning "tall tree," was named for a landmark redwood tree, which appears today on the seal of Stanford University. You can get an overview of the city, located at the southern end of San Francisco Bay, 30 miles south of San Francisco, from the top of the Hoover Tower, on campus. Also recommended is a visit to the Leland Stanford Museum to see the extensive collection of Rodin sculptures; the museum is also home to the original Golden Spike, driven in 1869 to signal the completion of the transcontinental railroad.

Also recommended: The European-style **Garden Court Hotel** (520 Cowper Street, 94301; 415–322–9000 or 800–824–9028) has 61 spacious, elegant guest rooms, with flower-bedecked balconies overlooking an interior courtyard. The hotel's Northern Italian restaurant, Il Fornaio, serves meats and poultry from the wood-fired rotisserie, and all pasta, bread, and desserts are made on the premises. B&B double rates range from $210–265, with weekend and corporate rates available. "Excellent location within walking distance of numerous restaurants, shops, and the Stanford campus. Friendly atmosphere, fine service." *(Matt Joyce)* "The feel of an Italian villa. Our room included a small but very pleasant balcony overlooking a central courtyard. The room itself was very comfortable with two double beds and an attractive color scheme." *(Robert A. Boas)*

Unpretentious and straightforward, **The Hotel California** (2431 Ash Street, 94306; 415–322–7666) offers 20 guest rooms, all with telephone, clock, TV, air-conditioning, and a ceiling fan; the simple decor includes eclectic antiques, colorful comforters, and fresh flowers. B&B double rates of $60–68 include a continental breakfast, available at the Palo Alto bakery downstairs from 6 A.M. to noontime. The guest rooms ring the perimeter of the building, while inside is a courtyard, pleasant for relaxing. "Well maintained and clean. Close to public transpiration serving the Bay area." *(Clay Curtiss)* "Close to Stanford University, shops and restaurants; ideal for visiting the area without transportation worries. Some rooms have been enlarged, others are small; double-glazed windows cut down on traffic noise. Pluses include the relaxed atmosphere; guest kitchen and laundry; and reasonable rates." *(Kathleen Kerry)*

Information please: Occupying a century-old home, the **Cowper Inn** (705 Cowper Street, 94301; 415–327–4475) is located on a quiet road, just two blocks from Palo Alto's main street. "Spacious rooms, with a good collection of books; individual phones with voice mail a real plus. Light continental breakfast with grapefruit, corn flakes, and bagels." *(CF)* B&B double rates range from $65–120.

PETALUMA

Cavanagh Inn ¢   *Tel:* 707–765–4657
10 Keller Street, 94952   888–765–4658
                               Fax: 707–769–0466

Sonoma County's southernmost town, Petaluma's downtown area overlooks the Petaluma River; its collection of Victorian homes and iron-front commercial buildings have earned it a listing on the National Register of Historic Places. You can also make it your home base for tours of nearby Point Reyes National Seashore and the Sonoma Valley wineries. If you stay at the Cavanagh Inn, you can count on comfortable accommodations, warm hospitality, and a breakfast that will keep you going through a day of antiquing, wine-touring, or hiking. The inn consists of a Colonial Revival home built by John Cavanaugh in 1902, plus an adjacent Western Stick-style Craftsman cottage, and has been owned by Ray and Jeanne Farris since l995. An accomplished cook, Jeanne's creative breakfasts are served at two large tables at 8:30 A.M. weekdays, 9:30 A.M. weekends. The menu changes daily, but might include pears with butterscotch sauce, oatmeal raisin muffins, persimmon or pumpkin bread, scrambled eggs with crab and seafood sauce, or perhaps a baked layered dish of potatoes, eggs, cheese, spinach, and sausage, topped with pie crust. Local wines are served daily at 5:30 P.M.

"Completely meets my four basic B&B criteria: comfortable bed, feather pillow, modern shower, and ample, imaginative breakfast. Beautifully restored house with a heart redwood interior; ample common areas. Our spacious room had a good desk and effective lighting. Lovely yard; easy walk to restaurants, shops, and galleries. Helpful, knowledgeable owners; we were pleasantly pampered." *(Emily Hoche-Mong)* "We were delighted with our cozy, affordable room in the cottage; charming second-floor hall mural with faux drapes, balcony, and plants." *(MW)* "When I called to make a reservation, Ray was friendly and informative; he promptly mailed me a helpful packet of material. Upon arrival, we were greeted with smiles all around. Ray and Jeanne gave us a wine touring map which guided us along beautiful roads to great local wineries; they also recommended an excellent Italian restaurant for dinner. Jeanne's breakfasts are wonderful, and she's pleased to accommodate special diets." *(Deb & Mark Olszewski)* "Ray and Jeanne create a friendly atmosphere among the guests. Inviting parlor area, with books to read. Delightful crepes and quiches at breakfast; excellent afternoon wines." *(Jeanette Johnson)*

Open All year.
Rooms 7 doubles—5 with private bath and/or shower, 2 with maximum of 4 sharing bath. All with clock/radio, ceiling fan. 3 with desk. Rooms in 2 buildings.
Facilities Dining room, 2 living rooms with TV/VCR, fireplace, books; piano; porch. ⅓ acre; off- and on-street parking.
Location Sonoma Cty. 32 m N of Golden Gate Bridge; ½ hr. E of Pt. Reyes Nat'l. Seashore. From Hwy. 101, take Washington St. exit in Petaluma. Go W to center of historic downtown. Cross Petaluma Blvd. & Kentucky St. & go left onto Keller St., to inn on the left after Western Ave.
Restrictions Absolutely no smoking. Children over 12.
Credit cards Amex, MC, Visa.
Rates B&B, $70–125 double.
Extras Bus station pickup. Spanish spoken.

PLACERVILLE

Information please: For a lovely country setting, consider the charming, rustic, log cabins of **Shadowridge Ranch & Lodge** (3500 Fort Jim Road, 95667; 916–295–1000), a historic homestead surrounded by beautiful flower gardens. Restored by Carlotta and Jim Davies, the ranch was built by the owner's grandparents, and B&B double rates for the three cottages range from $80–125, including a full breakfast and afternoon wine and hors d'oeuvres.

The Chichester-McKee House
800 Spring Street, 95667-4424

Tel: 916–626–1882
800–831–4008
Fax: 916–626–1882 (call first)
E-mail: inn@innercite.com

An 1892 issue of the *Mountain Democrat* reported that the "Chichester House is the finest home built in Placerville"; indoor plumbing was its claim to fame; equally attention-getting was the discovery of tunneling for a defunct gold mine under the dining room floor. Restored as a B&B in 1984, this Queen Anne–style Victorian home has been owned by Bill and Doreen Thornhill since 1990. Period furnishings and an antique doll collection accent the original stained glass and intricate wooden fretwork; the guest rooms have queen-size beds. Breakfast is served at the dining room table between 8 and 9 A.M., and includes fresh juice and fruit, crepes, quiche or perhaps eggs Benedict, muffins and coffee cake. Doreen's acclaimed caramel brownies are served in the evening. Assistant innkeeper Heidi, a miniature Dachshund, greets guests and shows them to their rooms.

"Charming innkeepers, very knowledgeable about their house. I loved getting a tour on arrival and hearing all about its history." *(Mimi Valenti)* "I had business appointments and they were pleased to serve me early breakfasts, accompanied by entertaining conversation. The house is beautifully appointed and was warmly lit for my return each evening; I was welcomed with brownies and tea. Although the inn is on a well-traveled street, I was not disturbed by traffic noise." *(Kara Brimhall)* "We relaxed in the parlor reading and playing cards. Our delightful room had a queen-size canopy bed and a single sleigh bed in one corner. The lavatory had a Pullman train sink that you tipped to make the water run out. The bathroom was down the hall, with a claw-foot tub, thick towels, and scented soaps. At breakfast, my son was enchanted by their tiny dachshund doing her counting tricks." *(Mary Jane Skala)* "Bill Thornhill was happy to help us bring our luggage up the stairs from the parking lot." *(MW)*

Open All year.
Rooms 1 suite, 3 doubles—2 with private bath, 2 with maximum of 4 people sharing bath. All with clock, air-conditioning. 1 with balcony, fireplace.
Facilities Dining room, living room with fireplace; library with books, games, fireplace; porch. ¾ acre with off-street parking. Golf, tennis nearby.
Location Gold Country. 45 min. E of Sacramento. 1½ block from downtown. From Sacramento, take Hwy. 50 N to Placerville. Go left at Spring St. exit (Hwy 49). Take next three right turns on Coloma, High, Wood Sts. to parking lot.
Restrictions No smoking. Storm windows, air-conditioning block traffic noise.
Credit cards Amex, DC, MC, Visa.
Rates B&B, $125 suite, $90–125 double, $80–105 single. Extra person, $25.
Extras Local airport/bus station pickup, free.

PLEASANTON

For an additional area inn, see **Livermore**.

Evergreen Bed & Breakfast
9104 Longview Drive, 94588

Tel: 510–426–0901
Fax: 510–426–9568

Not every B&B is a century-old Victorian mansion in a well-known tourist destination. Evergreen, for one, is a delightful exception. Set into the lush, green hillside, this California contemporary home built of natural cedar and oak has numerous decks, balconies, skylights, and patios. It's convenient to businesses in the East Bay area, the wineries of the Livermore Valley, and hiking in the adjacent nature preserves. Of course, if you book the romantic Grand View room—with king-size bed, double Jacuzzi tub, and fireplace— you may never leave the house at all. In 1995, innkeepers Jane and Clay Cameron took the home they had originally built in 1988 for their family of seven, and renovated it as a luxury B&B. Breakfast is served until 9:30 A.M., and includes fresh fruit and juice, homemade granola, coffee cakes, bagels, and perhaps French toast, omelets, or scrambled eggs. Rates also include wine and cheese, and freshly baked cookies.

"Clay and Jane greet you warmly and make you feel at home. While they spend lots of time with their guests, they also respect their privacy. The inn is so quiet, I thought I was the only guest." *(Dan Rosenbledt)* "Accommodating, pleasant hosts; romantic, rustic, warm and comfortable inn." *(Phyllis Enea)* "Gracious hospitality. The well-maintained rooms are elegantly decorated with both antiques and contemporary pieces, queen- or king-size beds, and fresh flowers." *(Madonna Eddy-Brown, also MW)* "Breakfast is served in a bright setting, looking out at the beautiful oak trees." *(Carol Lind)* "Excellent breakfast. The lounge area has an inviting window seat with lots of pillows, perfect for reading." *(Rebecca Schmidt)* "Highlights included the fresh flowers in my bedroom and bath, the freshly squeezed orange juice, fresh fruit, and home-baked treats for breakfast." *(Kathleen Marlon)* "The inn is located on a picturesque ridge that connects to hiking trails in a protected park. Light, clean, and airy, with hardwood floors in the public areas. The Grandview room has a corner fireplace, king-size sleigh bed positioned in the center of the room in front of glass patio doors that overlook a grove of trees and the Pleasanton Valley for beautiful sunrise views. The rustic tiled bathroom had a large Jacuzzi, double sinks, and a large double-headed tiled shower. Plush towels were replaced daily. Plenty of interesting reading material. Breakfast included fruit, bagels, cereal, coffee and juice; bacon and eggs were offered. Several morning papers awaited my perusal." *(HRT)*

Open All year.
Rooms 4 doubles—all with private bath and/or shower, telephone, clock/radio, TV, air-conditioning, ceiling-fan, refrigerator, robe. 2 with deck, whirlpool tub; 1 with desk, fireplace, private entrance.
Facilities Dining room; living room with fireplace, stereo, books; workout room with TV, treadmill, weight bench; guest refrigerator, guest laundry; balcony. 1¼ acres with hot tub, off-street parking. DelValle Reservoir nearby. Adjacent to Augustin Bernal Park, Pleasanton Ridgeland for hiking, bicycling. Golf, tennis, horseback riding nearby.
Location East Bay; Livermore Valley Wine Region. 40 m SE of San Francisco.

5 min to historic district. From San Francisco, take Rte. 580E to Hwy. 680 S. Take to Bernal Ave. West exit. Turn left on Foothill Rd. Go ¼ m. Turn right onto Longview Dr. to inn on left.

Restrictions No smoking. Children 10 and over.

Credit cards Amex, MC, Visa.

Rates B&B, $135–225 double. Extra person, $20.

Extras German spoken.

PLYMOUTH

Information please: In the Gold Country, about halfway between Placerville and Sutter Creek is the **Indian Creek B&B** (21950 Highway 49, 95669; 209–245–4648). A mountain lodge built in 1932 by Hollywood millionaire, producer, and playboy Arthur Hamburger, the great room has a log interior, cathedral-beamed ceiling, two-story stone fireplace, and a balcony leading to the four guest rooms. The inn is known as the John Wayne House, since he was a frequent guest of the original owner. The inn is surrounded by mature oaks, pines and cottonwood trees; its ten acres include a swimming pool, hiking trails, and a creek. B&B double rates of $90–120 include a full breakfast, afternoon hors d'oeuvres, and bedtime cookies.

POINT REYES STATION

Reader tip: "Point Reyes Station is in Marin County, about one hour north of San Francisco. It's a good base from which to explore Point Reyes National Seashore, as well as the small towns in the area. Be sure to spend time at the Point Reyes Lighthouse, a popular place for whale watching in January, when the gray whales make their migration from Alaska to Baja. Be sure to visit the Gordon Frost Folk Art Collection for wonderful textiles and art objects, and the Station Cafe, a great place to eat. I'll bet you can't eat just one basket of their whole wheat sourdough bread." *(Marty Goldman & Kip Wall)*

Also recommended: Built in 1991, the **Carriage House** (325 Mesa Road, 94956; 415–663–8627 or 800–613–8351) offers three spacious well-equipped guest rooms at B&B double rates of $90–160, including a kitchen stocked with breakfast makings. "Attractively furnished suite with local art and framed pictures. Spacious bathroom with shower. Large cozy room with fireplace, comfortable seating and a small table and chairs for meals." *(Kip Goldman & Marty Wall)*

The **Holly Tree Inn** (3 Silver Hills Road, Inverness; mailing address: Box 642, Point Reyes Station, 94956; 415–663–1554), set amongst the trees, offers hospitality, firm beds, and a relaxing, quiet environment. In addition to the four guest rooms and cottage at the main location, the innkeepers also have a one-bedroom cottage with a fireside living room, and solarium set on pilings out in Tomales Bay. B&B double rates rooms range from $125–145, with the cottages at $175–230. "Beautifully situated house tucked up against a wooded area by Point Reyes National Seashore. Immaculate throughout. Delicious breakfasts with spinach quiche and raspberry scones; fruit and freshly baked cookies were always available. Fresh flowers everywhere. The informative innkeepers were respectful of our privacy. The Cottage in the Woods is small but luxurious and private, with a beautiful pine-framed king-size bed, a spacious bathroom, and a small kitchenette. There is a hot tub on the property, reserved for private use with a changing room." *(Suzanne Perry)*

For additional area inns, see **Inverness, Point Reyes Station,** and **Stinson Beach.**

POINT RICHMOND

Also recommended: If you love the sound of a foghorn, and have always dreamed of living in a lighthouse, then the **East Brother Light Station** (117 Park Place, Point Richmond 94801; 510–233–2385) offers an unforgettable experience with incredible views. Overnight accommodations are available Thursday through Sunday in the 1874 Victorian-style frame lighthouse that marks the straits separating San Pablo and San Francisco bays. Restored and owned by a local preservationist group, the inn has four simply furnished guest rooms, with queen-size beds and private and shared baths (the island's only source of water is a cistern; showers are not available). The rates of $295 double includes evening wine and cheese, a four-course dinner with wine, a full breakfast, and the boat ride to and from the San Pablo Yacht Harbor; part of the cost goes to maintaining the lighthouse. "We stayed in the San Francisco room, with a view south to the city. The fog horn amazingly caused no interruption to an excellent night's sleep. Relaxing and peaceful, with tugs and sailboats passing on all sides." *(Mark Mendenhall)*

QUINCY

An old gold mining town on the gentle slopes of the Sierra Nevadas, Quincy is close to several state and national parks for hiking and fishing, and is set at the eastern end of the stunning and precipitous Feather River Canyon; 25 miles to the east is skiing near the ghost town of Johnsville. Quincy is 75 miles northwest of Reno, Nevada, 146 miles north of Sacramento, and 230 miles northeast of San Francisco via Highway 70.

Reader tip: "The area around Quincy is beautiful in September, with lots of color, warm days, crisp nights." *(SR)*

The Feather Bed ¢   *Tel:* 530–283–0102
542 Jackson Street   800–696–8624
P.O. Box 3200, 95971

The Feather Bed was built in 1893 in the Queen Anne style, and was restored as an inn in 1980; it's been owned by Bob and Jan Hanowski since 1992. The rooms are comfortably decorated with antiques and period wallpaper. Breakfast is served at tables for two, four, and six, from 8:30–10:00 A.M., although early meals are available midweek for business travelers. Breakfast starts with a fruit smoothie, followed by fresh or baked fruit, then such entrees as blueberry buttermilk pancakes, salmon quiche, or tomato basil frittata, and concludes with raspberry almond muffins or perhaps lemon coffee cake.

"The spacious Guest House cottage has a comfortable queen-size bed, ample seating, a day bed, and a large bathroom. Though not as large, Barrett's room was similarly well equipped; like all the guest rooms in the main house, it has a private entrance, accessed via an outside staircase. The family room was well supplied with area maps and information; hot water was always available with the fixings for coffee and tea, plus jars of cookies and fudge. For breakfast, we had blackberry smoothies, hot apple crisp, chili egg puff with salsa, hickory smoked sausage, and sherry coffee cake. The second morning we had equally delicious raspberry smoothies, baked pears in wine sauce, spinach omelets, sausage, skillet fried potatoes, and gingerbread muffins. Recipes happily shared. Jan and Bob were kind and helpful." *(Julie Phillips)* "Our room was light, airy, and attractive. The well furnished front porch was inviting in the warm evening. The excellent breakfast started with signature fruit smoothies, made from their own just-picked berries; they'll make it without yogurt for the lactose intolerant." *(Jim & Mary White)*

Open All year.
Rooms 1 suite, 5 doubles, 2 cottages—all with private bath and/or shower, telephone, clock/radio, desk, ceiling fan. 4 with air-conditioning, 3 with TV, gas fireplace/woodstove, balcony, private entrance.
Facilities Dining room; living room with fireplace, stereo, books; family room with TV, books, games; porch. 2 acres with off-street parking, lawn games, hiking. Lakes, rivers, streams nearby for swimming, fishing, boating. 10 min. to cross-country skiing.
Location Plumas Cty. Historic district. From Sacramento, take Hwy. 70/89 N to Quincy. From Reno, take Hwy. 395 N to Hwy. 70/89 to Quincy. Road becomes W. Main St. in town; turn at courthouse onto Jackson. Inn at corner of Court & Jackson Sts.
Restrictions No smoking. No toddlers in upstairs rooms.
Credit cards Amex, DC, Discover, MC, Visa.
Rates B&B, $120 cottage, $85–88 suite, $75–88 double, $70–82 single. Extra person, $12. Business rate midweek.
Extras 1 cottage meets ADA requirements. Local airport pickup.

RANCHO SANTA FE

Information please: The well-known **Inn at Rancho Santa Fe** (5951 Linea del Cielo at Paseo Delicias, P.O. Box 869, 92067; 619–756–1131 or 800–654–2928) was originally developed by the Santa Fe Railroad. B&B double rates for the 90 guest rooms (most in cottages spread over the 20-acre grounds) range from $100–520, depending on size, amenities, and location; meals are extra, and AAA discounts are available. In addition to its beautiful gardens, facilities include a championship croquet course, 3 tennis courts, a heated swimming pool, 20 miles of walking trails, and a beach cottage at Del Mar for ocean swimming. Three 18-hole golf courses are nearby. "Immaculate, with updated furnishings. Our room was in a garden cottage, built in the mid-1950s. Blissful peace and quiet. The patio outside our door was the perfect setting for breakfast. Service was courteous, efficient, and reasonably priced. The Saturday night band specialized in 1940s swing music. When dining, ask for a table in the cozy book-lined library." *(Janet Emery)*

An even more luxurious resort is the **Rancho Valencia** (5921 Valencia Circle, P.O. Box 9126; 619–756–1123 or 800–548–3664), with 43 lavishly decorated suites, at double rates of $360–970. Built in California hacienda style, the rooms are decorated in Santa Fe style, and have fireplaces, saunas, and whirlpool tubs; facilities include outstanding tennis on 18 courts, excellent dining, and outstanding service. Reports welcome.

RED BLUFF

For additional area inns, see **Orland** and **Redding.**

Also recommended: Built in 1890, the Queen Anne–style **The Faulkner House** (1029 Jefferson Street, 96080; 916–529–0520 or 800–549–6171) is decorated with period antiques by longtime owners Mary and Harvey Klingler. B&B double rates for the four guest rooms, each with private bath, range from $65–85 including a full breakfast. Train whistles from nearby tracks evoke nostalgic feelings in some readers. "Lovely tree-lined street with lots of beautiful Victorian homes. A great jumping-off point for visits to Lassen Volcanic National Park." *(Frank Reeder)*

REDDING

For an additional area inn, see **O'Brien.**

Information please: A Victorian hilltop home with panoramic views of the Mt. Lassen range, **Tiffany House** (1510 Barbara Road, 96003; 916–244–3225) has three guest rooms with private baths. Guests can relax in the Victorian parlor or music room, or outside on the deck or in the swimming pool. B&B double rates of $75–125 include a full breakfast and afternoon refreshments.

Palisades Paradise B&B ¢   *Tel:* 916–223–5305
1200 Palisades Avenue, 96003

A contemporary home built in 1977, the Palisades Paradise was opened as a B&B in 1986 by Gail Goetz. Breakfasts include cereal, fresh fruit, and pastry.

"Gail had the city's first B&B, and lobbied for a year for permission to open. The view from the deck of the Sacramento River and mountains beyond is outstanding." *(Shirley Dittloff, also Joan Reiss)* "The hot tub is right on the edge of the bluffs overlooking the river—gorgeous at sunset." *(Patricia Pantaleoni)* "Outstanding personal attention and flexibility regarding guests' needs and schedules. Good information on surrounding area." *(Stephen Aronow)* "We enjoyed a relaxing evening, watching the river and city lights below. Gail's gift of hospitality makes you feel like you are visiting an old friend. Her warmth and kindness added to the pleasure of our weekend, yet never intruded on our privacy." *(Patricia Wheeler)* "Charming home, immaculately clean. Gail went above and beyond the call of duty when we had car trouble." *(Ted & Fran Larsen)* "Delicious and ample breakfasts." *(Sandra Ferguson McPhee)*

Open All year.
Rooms 2 doubles share 1 ½ bath. All with radio, clock, TV, air-conditioning, fan.
Facilities Dining room, living room with fireplace, piano, TV/VCR, guest refrigerator, patio. ½ acre with off-street parking, hot tub, tree swing, lawn games. River rafting, fishing, boating, swimming nearby.
Location Halfway between Sacramento & OR border. Center of town.
Restrictions No smoking. Children over 8 unless both rooms taken.
Credit cards Amex, MC, Visa.
Rates B&B, $60–95. Extra person, $15.

RIVERSIDE

Also recommended: The extraordinary **Mission Inn** (3649 Seventh Street, 92501; 909–784–0300 or 800–843–7755), a famous California landmark, re-opened in 1992 after a $40 million renovation. Many of the 240 rooms have such architectural features as domed ceilings, wrought iron balconies, tiled floors, leaded and stained-glass windows, gargoyles, and carved pillars. The architectural style is Mission Revival, with touches of Spanish, Moorish, Italian, and Chinese. Double rates range from $120–230, with suites to $600. "Our comfortable, spacious, attractive room had a king-size bed, chaise, tables and chairs. We took a tour of the inn ($6 per person), which was very interesting and worthwhile." *(Carolyn Alexander)*

SACRAMENTO

Sacramento was founded by John Sutter, who is best known as the man on whose property gold was discovered in 1848, precipitating the great California Gold Rush of 1849. The town grew into a key supply source for the northern Mother Lode country and was named the state capital in 1854. It remains a major transportation hub to this day. It has a few sights of interest—the State Capitol, Sutter's Fort, Old Sacramento, and the California State Railroad Museum—but most Sacramento visitors come for the business of government or the business of business. Those who want to get out of town enjoy swimming, fishing, and rafting in the nearby Sacramento and American rivers.

Sacramento is located in Gold Country, 90 miles northeast of San Francisco and 90 miles southwest of Lake Tahoe. The center city is laid out in a grid pattern of numbered and lettered streets, with the former running east/west and the latter running north/south.

Information please: Overlooking Southside Park, in the heart of town is the **Inn at Parkside** (2116 Sixth Street, 95818; 916–658–1818 or 800–995–7275), a beautiful Spanish-style mansion, built in 1936 as the office residence of the Nationalist Chinese ambassador. Rates for the seven guest rooms range from $70–185, and include a continental breakfast and access to the guest kitchen. Antique decor is combined with such modern conveniences as a private bath, telephone, and TV/VCR.

For an additional area inn, see **Lodi.**

Abigail's	*Tel:* 916–441–5007
2120 G Street, 95816	800–858–1568
	Fax: 916–441–0621

Susanne and Ken Ventura, describe their inn as being "especially good for the business traveler. We have all the little things people tend to forget—an iron or hair dryer, aspirin, razors, and so on. Our guests also enjoy the extra touches—beds turned down, evening tea and hot chocolate, a refrigerator stocked with cold drinks, and extra-soft towels. Our building is a 1912 Colonial Revival mansion; the rooms are large and airy, with lots of windows." Breakfast specialties include fresh fruit, zucchini waffles, and home-baked coffee cake.

"An imposing white house with tall columns framing the front door. We were shown to our rooms, given a tour of the house, and were soon relaxing in the outdoor hot tub amid a flower-filled garden." *(Sandy Holmes)* "The well-lit guest rooms are supplied with books and bedtime sherry; the beds were firm and comfortable and the plumbing efficient. The living room is huge with an eclectic assortment of cushy sofas and chairs, perfect for curling up with a good book. Abigail's is located on a tree-lined street in a quiet neighborhood close to shops and good restaurants." *(JoAnn & Richard Mlnarik)* "The light-filled solarium room has a lovely deck and a private bath across the hall. Excellent cookies and hot chocolate awaited us at night; tea and coffee are always available." *(Jennifer Ball)* "Friendly cat, Fiona. A fainting couch, plus a desk and chair, provided good spots for reading or working in my room. Fun political chats over breakfast." *(DCB)* "Anne's room is spacious, with a king-size poster bed. Susanne and Ken were helpful and pleasant." *(Les Lewis)*

Open All year.
Rooms 5 doubles—all with private bath and/or shower, radio, desk, air-conditioning, telephone, TV, refrigerator. 1 with deck.
Facilities Living room with fireplace, dining room, sitting room with piano, games; guest pantry. Hot tub, garden with patio. Limited off-street parking.
Location Walking distance to downtown. From Business 80 Loop, exit at H St. (E) or E St. (W), to G St. (at 22nd St.). From I-5, take "Downtown—J St. Exit." Proceed on J St. to 22nd St., turn left. Go to G St., turn left.
Restrictions No smoking.
Credit cards Amex, DC, MC, Visa.
Rates B&B, $99–165 double. 2–3 night holiday minimum.

Amber House B&B	*Tel:* 916–444–8085
1315 22nd Street, 95816	800–755–6526
	Fax: 916–552–6529
	E-mail: InnKeeper@AmberHouse.com

Amber House, a brown Craftsman-style home from the early 1900s, has been owned by Jane and Michael Richardson since 1987. The inn has the original stained glass windows and distinctive woodwork of the period, and is furnished with Oriental rugs, velvet wingback chairs, antiques, and collectibles. Guest rooms have antique beds and patterned wallpapers; fresh flowers accent the colorful glass in the windows. The renovated 1913 bungalow next door offers marble-tiled bathrooms with Jacuzzi tubs for two. Rates include early morning coffee and a full breakfast served in the dining room, on the veranda, or in your room.

"The spacious Renoir Room has a comfortable king-size bed, TV/VCR in an armoire, and the best lighting we've encountered in our B&B travels; the tiled bathroom had a large Jacuzzi. Coffee and newspaper were at our door at 7 A.M., followed by scrumptious breakfasts with freshly baked croissants; bedtime cookies are brought to your room." *(Happy Copley)* "The library is stocked with books and local restaurant menus, and sherry is always available. At 5 P.M., Michael joined us for wine in the living room and we chatted about area attractions and restaurants." *(JoAnn Davis)* "Accented by blue stained glass windows, the dining room was a perfect setting for Michael's hearty breakfast of melon with poppy seed dressing, followed by fluffy scrambled eggs with scallions and cream cheese, potatoes sauteed in lemon pepper, and a ham-and-cheese croissant. The inn's residential location is quiet and convenient, a medium walk or an easy drive downtown." *(SWS)* "The Lord Byron Room had a marvelous marble bath and Jacuzzi. Hospitable, genuinely caring hosts, excellent breakfasts." *(MR)* "Spotless; careful attention to detail. Friendly staff, excellent service; easy parking." *(Carrie Hagerty)*

Open All year.
Rooms 9 doubles—all with full private bath, robes, telephone with voice mail, radio/cassette players. TV, desk, air-conditioning. 8 with double Jacuzzi tub, VCR; 1 with fireplace. 4 in annex.
Facilities 2 living rooms with fireplace, 2 dining rooms, library, veranda, patio, meeting room. Bicycles.
Location Midtown. 7 blocks E of Capitol building, between Capitol Ave. and N St. 8 blocks to convention center.
Restrictions No smoking.
Credit cards All major.
Rates B&B, $99–225 double, $89–149 single. Extra person, $20. Corporate rates.

ST. HELENA

St. Helena is located 60 miles north of San Francisco, in the Napa Wine Valley region of the North Coast. Although there are many things to do in the area, the main activity is visiting wineries—there are nine in St. Helena alone. Keep in mind that this area is extremely popular from June through October, especially on weekends. Try November, April, and May for good weather and smaller crowds.

For more information, see the North Coast section of the chapter introduction and the listings for Calistoga.

Reader tip: "While our B&B was perfectly adequate, we didn't think it was a good value at $165 a night; on the other hand, a motel wasn't much less, and didn't include breakfast and afternoon treats."

Also recommended: For an elegant small resort, suitable both for families or romantic escapes, the **Meadowood Resort** (900 Meadowood Lane, 94574; 707–963–3646 or 800–458–8080) may be a good choice. Although reminiscent of an old-style Adirondack lodge or Newport cottage, Meadowood was originally built as a private country club in the 1960s, and was expanded into a full-scale luxury resort in the 1980s. Guest rooms are clustered in gabled cottages scattered around the grounds, while the main lodge is home to an elegant restaurant and a more casual grill. In addition to a heated swimming pool, 7 tennis courts, a 9-hole golf course, hiking trails, a fitness center, and a playground, Meadowood has two championship croquet courts, with a resident teaching pro. Double rates for the 85 guest rooms range from $295–525, suites to $825, with packages available. "Quiet country setting just off the Silverado trail; charming Craftsman-style bungalows scattered in the wooded hillside house the restaurants, meeting rooms, and 100 guest rooms. Guest rooms are spacious and handsome, equipped with all amenities, as you would expect in this price range." *(SWS)*

A sister property to Meadowood, the **Inn at Southbridge** (1020 Main Street, Highway 29, 94574; 707–967–9400 or 800–520–6800) takes its inspiration from the small town squares of Europe, and is located in town. The 21 guest rooms are designed with vaulted ceilings and fireplaces; French doors open onto private balconies with views of the courtyard and the vineyards. A short walk away is the noted restaurant, Tra Vigne. Guests may take advantage of all of Meadowood's facilities, few miles away. B&B double rates range from $195–415, including a continental breakfast.

We also need reports on the well-known **Auberge du Soleil** (180 Rutherford Hill Road, Rutherford 94573; 707–963–1211 or 800–348–5406), about five miles south of St. Helena. Its restaurant is famous for creative California cuisine, and the 48 luxurious guest rooms occupy a series of elegant cottages with stunning views of the Napa Valley, plus such amenities as fridges stocked with champagne and juices, a wet bar with coffeemaker, whirlpool baths, lounging robes, and fireplaces. The 33 acres offer a heated swimming pool, hot tub, 3 tennis courts, health spa, bicycles, and hot air ballooning. B&B double room rates range from $375–800.

A 1904 brown shingled Craftsman-style bungalow, **The Cinnamon Bear** (1407 Kearney Street, 94574; 707–963–4653 or 888–963–4600) is located in a residential neighborhood two blocks from St. Helena's main street, across the street from a grade school. B&B double rates for the three guest rooms, each with private bath, range from $90–155. "Port, sherry, sodas, and delicious homemade chocolate chip cookies were available in the inviting common rooms, with beautiful woodwork. My room had a queen-size bed, and several silk flower arrangements. The bathroom had lots of thick towels, and a clawfoot tub; a pitcher was provided for rinsing hair. The morning light and Sunday church bells ringing ensured that I was ready for the delicious breakfast of blue corn blueberry pancakes with blueberry honey. Innkeeper Cathye Raneri is friendly and helpful, knowledgeable about the area." *(SHW)*

The **Shady Oaks Country Inn** (399 Zinfandel Lane, 94574; 707–963–1190) has four guest rooms with private baths and queen-size beds; B&B double rates of $135–195 (less midweek off-season) include a full breakfast, served on the garden patio, in the dining room, or in your room, plus afternoon wine and cheese. "Charming little inn; cozy, cheerful guest rooms, simply decorated with ruffled curtains, flowered fabrics, and quilts. Lovely setting in the trees, surrounded by vineyards and mustard fields. Guest rooms are in the Craftsman-style bungalow and the adjacent 1880s winery building." *(SWS)*

For ample space and modern conveniences, a good choice may be the **Vineyard Country Inn** (201 Main Street, 94574; 707–963–1000), a 21-suite hotel, located between Napa and St. Helena on Highway 29. Rooms have king- or queen-size four poster beds with full private baths, and a sitting area before the fireplace. B&B double rates of $140–195 include breakfast and use of the swimming pool and hot tub.

For more information, see the North Coast section of the chapter introduction. For additional area inns, see **Angwin, Calistoga, Napa,** and **Yountville**.

SAN CLEMENTE

Information please: Built in 1990 at the San Clemente Pier is the **Casa Tropicana B&B** (610 Avenida Victoria, 92672; 714–492–1234), a five-story Spanish-style inn. B&B double rates for the nine guest rooms range from $85–350, including a full breakfast and use of beach chairs and umbrellas. Rooms, each with a different tropical theme, have fireplaces and double Jacuzzi tubs. San Clemente is halfway between Los Angeles and San Diego. "Very romantic, exotic decor." (*David & Melissa King*)

SAN DIEGO

San Diego is located in southernmost coastal California, 127 miles south of Los Angeles and about 20 miles north of Tijuana, Mexico. For many years a sleepy coastal town, San Diego didn't really start to grow until World War II, when the U.S. Navy moved its headquarters from Honolulu to San Diego. Since then, the city has grown to become California's second largest. San Diego's climate is arguably one of the best in America—very little rain, with an average winter temperature in the mid-60s and summer in the mid-70s. Major sights of interest include Balboa Park's many museums, the world-famous zoo, Old Town San Diego, Cabrillo National Monument, Sea World, the Maritime Museum, and trips on the Tijuana Trolley to Mexico.

To make sure you're getting the best rate available, it's worth calling **San Diego Hotel Reservations** (619–627–9300 or 800–SAVE–CASH), offering discounted rates at over 250 hotels throughout San Diego County, including several recommended here.

Reader tips: "We enjoyed dinners at Cafe Bacco, close to the U.S. Grant Hotel, at Croce's in the Gaslight District, and at Poehe's on Coronado Island, about a block from the ferry landing." (*KLH*) "The Gaslight District is a lively scene. We had a wonderful dinner at an Italian restaurant called Fio's. The district is quite safe and heavily patrolled, but not far away are some rough neighborhoods, so stay within the tourist area." (*JMW*) "We were told that air-conditioning is not necessary here, but during our August visit, they had an atypical heat wave, and the un-conditioned air in our room was uncomfortably warm." (*RW*) "Due to the airport and military bases, airplane noise is fairly common." (*MW*)

Also recommended: Readers are pleased with the **Horton Grand Hotel** (311 Island Avenue, 92101; 619–544–1886 or 800–542–1886), a 134-room complex of three re-created Victorian-era hotels in the redeveloped Gaslight district, once San Diego's skid row. The queen-size beds are modern, with draped antique headboards; the marble fireplaces are antique as well, but they frame gas-log fireplaces, and the mirror above each mantel hides a remote control TV. Double rates range from $119–209, with off-peak weekend rates starting at $79. "Our comfortable, quiet room overlooked a courtyard and opened onto a foyer decorated with attractive antiques. Attractive decor, efficient valet parking. Reasonable rate through San Diego Reservations." (*Jim & Mary White*)

Located in the Gaslight quarter, the **U.S. Grant Hotel** (311 Island Avenue; 619–232–3121 or 800–237–5029) dates back to 1910. "Elegant old hotel, terrific location; free airport pickup. Our air-conditioned room was tastefully decorated and immaculate; the good-sized bathroom had quality soaps and other amenities. Good breakfasts were served in the lobby restaurant; off the lobby was a quality coffee and ice cream place and a bagel restaurant." *(KLH)* Double rates for the 220 guest rooms and 60 suites are $165–185 (suites start at $245); ask about weekend and promotional rates.

Within walking distance of Old Town's quaint shops and Mexican restaurants is the **Vacation Inn** (3900 Old Town Avenue, 92110; 619–299–7400 or 800–451–9846). B&B double rates for the 125 guest rooms range from $79–165, and include an in-room coffee maker, refrigerator, and microwave, continental breakfast, afternoon refreshments, free underground parking and airport shuttle, and use of the swimming pool and hot tub; ask for the AAA rate. "A two-story, tile-roofed Mexican-style motel with a lovely flower-drenched courtyard, where we enjoyed breakfast each morning. The swimming pool at one end of the courtyard is concealed behind a brick wall and shrubbery. Attractively furnished rooms with armoires and floral bedspreads. Friendly, efficient staff always eager to assist. A lovely little oasis, yet just a block from I-5, and minutes from major attractions." *(Mary Jane Skala)*

Information please: In Pacific Beach, just a few miles north of downtown, is the **Crystal Pier Hotel** (4500 Ocean Boulevard, 92109; 619–483–6983 or 800–748–5894), which consists of bungalows built atop the 350-foot pier. "Spacious, light, and airy. Each bungalow has a kitchenette complete with microwave and coffeemaker. The pier is open to the public during daylight hours, so when you make your reservation, decide whether you want the new bungalows with private decks, or enjoy the camaraderie of others (the older ones have patio areas along the outer walkway)." *(Mary Louise Rogers)* Double rates range from $95–225, with weekly rates available. Book well ahead, especially for weekends, even off-season.

For more information on San Diego area accommodations, see **Cardiff-by-the-Sea,** La Jolla, and **Rancho Santa Fe.**

Balboa Park Inn ¢ ⅔.
3402 Park Boulevard, 92103

Tel: 619–298–0823
800–938–8181
Fax: 619–294–8070

Dating back to 1915, The Balboa Park Inn is a complex of four pale pink Spanish Colonial-style buildings with a variety of individually furnished rooms, each with queen-, king-, or twin-size beds and a sitting area. The decor ranges from Spanish to Southwestern, Victorian to country. The breakfast of fresh fruit and juice, and pastries or cereal, can be delivered to your door, the sun terrace, or the courtyard between 7:30–10:00 A.M. Rates also include in-room coffee and the daily paper. In addition to its pleasant ambience and reasonable rates, the inn's key advantage is its convenient location across the street from Balboa Park. Balboa Park is the cultural hub of San Diego and offers a full range of sport and cultural activities, including seven museums, the famous San Diego Zoo, and the Old Globe Theater.

"Perfect location, pleasant service, adequate accommodations, tasty breakfast simply served, with a delicious cinnamon roll." *(Joanne Ashton)* "Most enjoyable, with an ideal location. Outstanding value; though we had one of the less expensive accommodations, it had two rooms and a balcony." *(Duane Roller)*

Open All year.
Rooms 19 suites, 7 doubles—all with full private bath, telephone, TV, refrigerator. Some with kitchen, microwave, wet bar, wood-burning fireplace, Jacuzzi, deck/patio.
Facilities Courtyard, terrace, balconies, garden with fountain. On-street parking; security provided. Balboa Park for golf, tennis, Olympic-size swimming pool.
Location N edge of Balboa Park. Walk to San Diego Zoo, etc. 10 min. to airport, train, bus stations. From I-5, exit at Hwy 163 & go N. Turn right at Richmond, right at Upas to inn at corner of Upas & Park Blvd.
Credit cards All major.
Rates B&B, $95–200 suite, $80–105 double. Extra person, $8; children under 12, free. 3-night holiday minimum.
Extras Wheelchair access; bathroom specially equipped. Crib, babysitting. Spanish spoken.

Heritage Park Inn ♿
2470 Heritage Park Row, 92110

Tel: 619–299–6832
800–995–2470
Fax: 619–299–9465
E-mail: innkeeper@heritageparkinn.com

Heritage Park is a seven-acre site, home to seven classic period structures from the 1800s. The buildings, originally located on Third Avenue in San Diego, were saved from the wrecker's ball and moved here in 1978. The B&B is an 1889 Queen Anne mansion, adorned with a variety of chimneys, shingles, a corner tower, and encircling veranda. In 1992, the inn was bought by longtime San Diego residents Nancy and Charles Helsper. Rooms are furnished with 19th-century antiques, and rates include breakfast, afternoon social hour, and a classic film shown in the parlor, evenings at 7 P.M. Breakfast is served by candlelight in the dining room at 8:30 A.M., and a typical menu might include Victorian French toast with apple cider syrup and sour cream-peach coffee cake; plus homemade granola, yogurt, fruit, juice, coffee, and herbal teas. A light continental breakfast is available for those leaving earlier.

"Afternoon tea (with lovely finger sandwiches) was a delight, as was meeting the other guests and sharing stories. Conversation continued at breakfast, as we lingered over fresh fruit, orange juice, apple crepes." *(Joanne & Chuck Edmondson)* "Beautifully coordinated wallpapering and stenciling throughout the house." *(Anne Mietzel)* "Loved the crab soufflé and raspberry almond scones." *(Jeannie Bell)* "Quiet location, yet convenient to highways and an easy stroll downhill to Old Town, the trolley, sight-seeing, and dining. The accommodating owners and staff were happy to help with restaurant and concert reservations. Comfortable wicker furniture on the veranda, perfect for afternoon tea, reading, and enjoying the view." *(Peggy Kontak)* "Nancy and Charles go out of their way to accommodate business travelers. Fax lines have been placed in all the rooms; and desks or tables provide working space for laptops. Attention to detail includes ironed sheets and pillowcases; robes, bath salts, and shampoo; plus fruit, cookies, tea and coffee always available. The inn feels safe and secure; parking is convenient and well lighted." *(Linda Jones)*

Open All year.

Rooms 1 family suite, 10 doubles—all with private bath and/or shower, radio, clock, telephone, desk. 3 with fan or fireplace. Suite with double Jacuzzi. Suite in adjacent building.

Facilities Parlor with fireplace, TV/VCR; dining room, guest refrigerator, veranda. Meeting room. Croquet. In 7-acre Victorian park. Off-street parking.

Location 1 block to Old Town. 2 m from downtown. Follow I-5 to Old Town Ave. exit. Turn left on San Diego Ave., right on Harney to Heritage Park to inn on right.

Restrictions No smoking.

Credit cards MC, Visa.

Rates B&B, $225 suite, $90–150 double, single. 15% senior, AAA discounts. 2-night weekend minimum. Candlelight dinner, $105 per couple plus 15% service. Special occasion packages.

Extras First-floor wheelchair accessible; bathroom specially equipped. Spanish, French, German spoken.

SAN FRANCISCO

Romanticized in song, hyped in commercials, featured in movies and sitcoms, San Francisco is everything promised and more. Compact, ethnically diverse, culturally rich, filled with wonderful stores, cable cars, and restaurants, it's what every city should aspire to be. The weather is best in late summer and early fall, but you don't come here to get a tan, so what does it matter? Bring your walking shoes and a sweater (even summer can be cool), and explore everything. Less well known but worth visiting are the exquisite Japanese Tea Garden and Asian Art Museum in Golden Gate Park and the museums and bookstores at North Beach. Watch the sea lions from Cliff House near Point Lobos Avenue.

For discount rates of 10 to 60% at many San Francisco hotels and B&Bs, including several listed here, call **San Francisco Reservations** (22 Second Street, 4th floor, 94105; 415–227–1500 or 800–677–1500) or **California Reservations** (3 Sumner Street, 94103; 415–252–1107 or 800–576–0003). California Reservations also handles properties in the Wine Country, Carmel area, and other cities.

Reader tips: "San Francisco has excellent public transportation, even by East Coast standards, and it's a very economical and practical alternative. Parking costs $10–20 a day, and in some areas, on-street parking requires you to move your car every two hours 8 A.M. to 9 P.M." *(Adam Platt)* Also: "San Francisco is noisy at all hours. If you're a light sleeper, be sure to let the innkeeper know when making reservations!"

(SHW) "Even in San Francisco's newly renovated hotels, all rooms are *not* created equal. If you are shown a room that is too small, noisy, musty-smelling or whatever, politely note that it simply won't do and ask to be shown another." *(BI)* "North Beach is a great multicultural neighborhood, with buses and cable cars nearby for convenient transportation. Fantastic Italian and Chinese restaurants abound, and there are many bars with music on the weekend." *(KMC)*

If you'd prefer having your own apartment, contact **B&B California** (P.O. Box 282910, 94128-2910; 415–696–1690 or 800–872–4500). "We stayed at **Molly's B&B** on Russian Hill just one block from Lombard and ½ block from the cable car. For $175, we had a spacious two bedroom second-floor apartment for the four of us. The innkeepers live upstairs. Molly's an artist and stenciled all the walls beautifully." *(Penny Poirer)*

Important note: Space limitations simply do not permit us to include full write-ups on San Francisco's many wonderful hotels and inns. The abbreviated recommendations which follow are no reflection of their quality—we just don't have the room to describe each place in full—but we still need your reports! Listings are alphabetical, divided by price range.

Also recommended—budget: For a friendly B&B experience, visit **Carol's Cow Hollow Inn** (2821 Steiner Street, 94123; 415–775–8295 or 800–400–8295), located in the Pacific Heights/Cow Hollow residential area, within walking distance of Union Street and the Palace of Fine Arts. Built in 1908, the house has three well-equipped guest rooms; B&B double rates of $95–135 include a full breakfast, prepared at guests' requested time. "Delightful experience. Carol was raised in San Francisco, and can tell you what to do, see, and eat. Her husband Sasha is an artist, and his work fills the house. Two rooms have views of the harbor, Alcatraz, and the Golden Gate Bridge; the suite has a fireplace and can sleep four." *(Carol Blodgett)*

The Cartwright (524 Sutter Street, 94102; 415–421–2865 or 800–227–3844), a favorite of many readers, is now a Kimco Hotel. Unusual in a budget-priced hotel are the triple-sheeted beds, oversized reading pillows, terry-cloth robes, evening mints, and fresh flowers supplied daily to guest rooms. Some rooms are small, some bathrooms are tiny, but the location is excellent, close to the cable car, buses, and Union Square shops. Double rates for the 110 guest rooms range from $119–299, including breakfast.

Travelers come back to the **Golden Gate** (775 Bush Street, 94108; 415–392–3702 or 800–835–1118) for the personal attention its resident owner/operators provide, its pleasant atmosphere and convenient location. Its 23 rooms (with private and shared baths) rent for a reasonable $65–99; while Spartan in size and decor, the mattresses are top quality, and the hot croissants are outstanding. "Afternoon tea and cookies are an added plus." *(Dianne Crawford)* "Rooms on the higher floors are brighter, lighter, and quieter. If the sitting room is crowded at breakfast, ask for a tray to take up to your room." *(Lynne Derry)* "Many restaurants within a five-minute walk. The best rooms are at the back of the inn (for quiet), and a bay window (for light)." *(BZ)*

One of San Francisco's best values is the **Marina Inn** (3110 Octavia at Lombard; 94123; 415–928–1000 or 800–274–1420), in the Marina District close to Fisherman's Wharf. Each of the 40 guest rooms has a queen-size bed, private bath, telephone and color TV; B&B double rates of $55–120 include a continental breakfast, afternoon tea and sherry, and evening turndown service with chocolates. "Excellent value. Giant breakfast Danish; trays enable you to breakfast in your room. Marina Green is just down the street, with excellent views of the bay; residential area. Courteous staff. Charming room with floral wallpaper, bay windows, pine furnishings; minuscule bathroom. Ask for a room away from the street." *(RM)*

The **Monticello Inn** (127 Ellis Street, 94102; 415–392–8800 or 800–669–7777) has patterned its decor after its namesake, with Colonial reproduction furnishings and Williamsburg colors. B&B double rates for the 91 guest rooms range from $129–209. In addition to valet parking, the inn offers free morning transportation to the financial district. "Room charming and spotless; luxurious bath. Inviting public spaces with two fireplaces. The breakfast buffet nicely set up with juice, coffee, breads and cold cereals plus an ample supply of morning papers." *(Ruth Tilsley)* "Small, pretty, and quiet yet just a block from tons of activity." *(Randi Rubin)*

Perhaps the most affordable hotel in San Francisco is the **San Remo Hotel** (2237 Mason Street, 94133; 415–776–8688 or 800–352–REMO), built in 1906 as a boarding house. Restored to showcase its redwood wainscotting, stained glass skylights, and antique furnishings, its 63 guest rooms have brass or iron beds and oak or pine armoires; some have a pedestal sink in the room. The inn is in North Beach, close to Fisherman's Wharf and the cable car turnaround. "Quiet residential block in the old Italian district. The small, spare rooms share scrupulously clean hall baths. Set on the roof is the penthouse, with redwood paneling, windows all around, a queen-size bed, small private bathroom, and a fenced-in area with outdoor furniture and views of the city all around—you can just see the Golden Gate Bridge." *(Susan Rather)* Double rates range from $60–70; the penthouse rents for $100. The inn is popular with Europeans, and smoking is permitted.

Built as a hotel in 1902, the **Stanyan Park Hotel** (750 Stanyan Street, 94117; 415–751–1000) is located right across the street from Golden Gate Park, and many of its 36 well-equipped, traditionally furnished guest rooms have park views. B&B double rates of $85–99, suites $109–189, include a continental breakfast. "Wonderful staff—friendly, efficient, and helpful. Splendid breakfast in a nice little dining room plus afternoon tea." *(Ruth Emerson)*

Ten minutes walk from Union Square is the 96-room **York Hotel** (940 Sutter Street, 94109; 415–885–6800), made famous in Alfred Hitchcock's *Vertigo*. Continental breakfast, a morning newspaper, and a wine hour are included in the double rates of $109–139. "Renovated rooms decorated in soft tones of peach and green, floral rugs and bedspreads. Rooms ending in twelve on each floor a little larger than others, with a sitting area and king-size bed. All have a coffee-maker and walk-in closet with a safe. Rooms in the back of the hotel tend to be more quiet. Famous cabaret, The Plush Room."*(Wendi Van Exan)*

Also recommended—moderate: Appealing decor and location are strong points at **The Bed & Breakfast Inn** (4 Charlton Court, 94123; 415–921–9784), located on a quiet mews just off bustling Union Street. The inn is composed of two adjoining buildings, furnished with a mixture of contemporary and antique pieces. "Great location; attractively decorated two-room suite, supplied with sherry, tea, good books, and current magazines, at $135 nightly. Parking is an extra $10 at a garage nearby. Uninspired continental breakfast in the room or dining room; no other common areas." *(JMW)* B&B rates for the 11 guest accommodations range from $115–250.

Renovated at a cost of $24 million in 1995 by the Kimpton Group is the **Hotel Monaco** (501 Geary Street, 94102; 415–292–0100 or 800–214–4220), a 1910 Beaux Arts–style hotel. The 210 guest rooms have playful, creative, eclectic decor, with lavish use of fabric. Facilities include a fitness center, spa, restaurant, meeting room and parking garage. Rates of $165–395 include morning coffee, evening wine tasting and preferred seating in the restaurant. Convenient location, just two blocks from Union Square.

The Inn San Francisco (943 South Van Ness Avenue, 94110; 415–641–0188 or 800–359–0913) is an Italianate Victorian B&B, painted pink, green, and gold, located in a residential area 12 blocks from the Civic Center. The interior has marble fireplaces, ornate woodwork, and authentic period decor, accented with Oriental rugs, polished brass fixtures, and fresh flowers. "The rooftop sun deck offers a panoramic view of the city, and the garden hot tub is perfect after a day of sightseeing." *(Dale & Virginia Wright)* "Room #45 in the adjacent building had a light and airy country feeling, unlike the darker Victorian-style rooms in the main house. Pluses include the individually controlled heat, marble fireplace, private balcony, skylight, comfortable queen-size featherbed, and bathrobe. " *(Gail Davis)* B&B double rates for the 22 guest rooms range from $85–225.

"The **Inn at Union Square** (440 Post Street, 94102; 415–397–3510 or 800–AT–THE–INN) is small and secure, with 30 rooms and suites. Positive attributes include its location, half a block from Union Square, the wonderfully furnished and individually decorated rooms; the continental breakfast, afternoon tea, and evening wine and cheese; and a friendly, welcoming, knowledgeable staff." *(Hugh & Marjorie Smith)* B&B rates are $145–350; no tipping.

Built in 1924, and renovated as a hotel in 1983, the **Kensington Park Hotel** (450 Post Street at Union Square, 94102; 415–788–6400 or 800–553–1900) has 96 guest rooms with B&B double rates of $125. "Great location, a safe choice for women traveling alone. The hotel is small and cozy, with continental breakfast set out on each floor in the mornings, plus tea and cookies from 4–6 P.M. My good-sized room was very quiet, with a great bed, not-so-great pillows, and a good shower; local calls are 75 cents each. Outstanding staff." *(DC)*

An eccentric but entertaining choice is the **Mansion Hotel** (220 Sacramento Street, 94115; 415–929–9444), decorated with antiques and an extraordinary collection of objects d'art and not so d'art. "Wonderful breakfast; nice, quiet location, with bus stop across the street." *(Carol*

Blodgett) Double and suite rates range $129–350, including breakfast, flowers, nightly concerts, a performing ghost, a magic parlor, and more.

The Warwick Regis Hotel (490 Geary Street, 94102; 415–928–7900 or 800–827–3447) is located across the street from the Clift, two blocks west of Union Square. It has 80 guest rooms with European antique furnishings. B&B double rates of $105–210 include a continental breakfast, morning newspaper, and evening turndown service. "Great location; comfortable, clean rooms, on the small side. Excellent bathrooms, recently remodeled. Breakfast included muffins and croissant, but no low-fat options. Would definitely return." *(KLH)*

The **Washington Square Inn** (1660 Stockton Street, 94133; 415–981–4220 or 800–388–0220) is located in the Italian District of North Beach, almost midway between Fisherman's Wharf and Union Square. The 15 guest rooms are decorated with English and French antiques, and the B&B double rates of $120–185 include breakfast, afternoon tea, wine and hors d'oeuvres. "Just as delightful on a return visit—one of my favorite inns. My second-floor room had a window seat with a view of Coit Tower. Inner rooms are quieter, but lack the view; front rooms may be noisy." *(KMC)*

In the Union Square area, most readers are delighted with the **White Swan Inn** (845 Bush Street, 94108; 415–775–1755 or 800–999–9570), decorated with an English country theme. B&B double rates for the 26 guest rooms range from $145–260, and include breakfast, afternoon tea and cookies, wine and hors d'oeuvres. "Our room was extremely quiet, large, and lovely." *(Susan Rather)* Under the same ownership is the nearby **Petite Auberge** (863 Bush Street, 94108; 415–928–6000 or 800–365–3004), decorated in the style of a French country inn, with soft colors, antiques, floral wallpapers, and fresh flowers. Double rates are $110–230.

Also recommended—luxury: The **Archbishop's Mansion Inn** (1000 Fulton Street, 94117; 415–563–7872 or 800–543–5820) was built for the archbishop of San Francisco in 1904, and has been restored as a small luxury hotel. Rooms are formally decorated with an operatic theme, with Victorian antiques, flower-painted ceilings, canopy beds, embroidered linens, Oriental rugs, marble fireplaces, and crystal chandeliers. Rates include a light breakfast of croissants, scones, or pastry, juice, and a beverage of choice, delivered to your room or served in the dining room; in the afternoon, wine is served in the parlor. B&B rates for the 15 rooms range from $129–385. "Helpful staff; breakfast tasty, though not homemade. Best to have a car for this location; the inn has a private parking lot." *(RH)*

The famous **Clift Hotel** (495 Geary Street at Taylor 94102; 415–775–4700 or 800–332–3442), built right after the 1906 earthquake and fire, offers elegant guest rooms and common areas. Located at the bottom of Nob Hill, its convenience to Union Square and the attentiveness of its staff make it most appealing. "Booked through San Francisco Reservations and got a great rate, and were even upgraded to a gorgeous suite. Wonderful bar, great atmosphere." *(Donna Pekkonen)* Double rates range from $215–365.

The luxurious **Huntington** (1075 California Street, 94108; 415–474–5400 or 800–227–4683) sits at the crest of Nob Hill with its impressive views of the Bay Bridge and Huntington Park. Family-owned since 1924, the lobby is hushed and intimate, while the 144 spacious guest rooms are decorated in soft colors with Asian accents. Double rates of $190–240 (suites to $600) include limousine service. "Spacious rooms, gorgeous views, careful attention to detail." *(SHW)*

If you're ready for that special-occasion splurge of all splurges, **The Sherman House** (2160 Green Street, 94123; 415–563–3600 or 800–424–5777) is probably the place to go. This gleaming white Victorian palazzo, built in 1876, is decorated in exquisite detail with period antiques, imported chandeliers, Belgian tapestries, and the finest fabrics and furnishings; service is equally indulgent. "A jewel. We had one of the least expensive rooms, and found it small but lovely, with a draped canopy bed, a wood-burning fireplace, comfortable reading chairs, and more. The room looked out on the pretty inside courtyard garden. Breakfasts in the solarium are wonderful. The windows overlook the Golden Gate Bridge and San Francisco Bay, and the food is marvelous—delicious muffins and pastries, perfect fruit, French toast, and other entrees." *(EL)* B&B double rates for the 13 guest rooms and suites range from $295–850, and also include evening hors d'oeuvres and wine.

For additional San Francisco area entries, see **Alameda, Berkeley, Livermore, Mill Valley, Montara, Moss Beach, Muir Beach, Pleasanton, Point Richmond, San Mateo, San Rafael, Sausalito.**

Auberge Des Artistes ¢
829 Fillmore Street, 94117

Tel: 415–776–2530
Fax: 415–441–8242
E-mail: LAKPersons@aol.com

If you book a room at a San Francisco hotel you may glimpse the creativity that makes this city a special place, but if you stay at the Auberge des Artistes you can experience it first hand. This spacious Edwardian home was built in 1901, and was restored and opened as a B&B in 1996 by David and Laura Ann Novick. As they describe it: "Although the Auberge welcomes all guests, we are especially geared to artists, food lovers, and those who are interested in a real San Francisco experience. With cooking classes, photographic darkroom, spontaneous drawing/painting sessions, and our endless list of recommendations, we appeal especially to free-spirited, creative, and adventurous travelers."

The individually furnished accommodations include the Floral Fantasy Suite, with a bright wicker-furnished sitting room with garden views, and a bedroom with queen-size bed with flowers, frills, and tiny gilt-framed mirrors. The other guest rooms are equally spacious and bright, with Art Deco, Arts & Crafts, or Art Nouveau accents, plus paintings done by Laura and other local artists. Breakfast, served 8–10 A.M. at the dining room table, includes such entrees as crepes, eggs with caviar, huevos rancheros, Southwestern-style tofu, or dim sum, accompanied by dishes ranging from polenta with sun dried tomatoes to ham and cheese turnovers, chocolate-banana-apricot cake to carrot muffins. Guests are always welcome to fix themselves a cup of espresso or a latte—instructions gladly provided.

"A fun, funky inn, convenient to just about everything. We walked or took public transportation everywhere. Our comfortable room had huge windows facing the flower-filled backyard. Soft bath towels were supplied in abundance and changed every day. Best of all was the enthusiasm, warmth, helpfulness, and accommodating style of innkeepers Laura and David. Innovative, multicourse breakfasts, with stand-out gravlax, and bottomless cups of marvelous coffee." *(Naomi Sadowsky)* "David and Laura have personally renovated and decorated the building and are pleased to share their experience with anyone interested. The results are beautiful, both inside and out. The Auberge sits on a small street, on a hill, in the middle of a row of quaint old homes overlooking the city. A convenient bus line runs right in front of the building. Breakfasts were extraordinary; both innkeepers have been chefs and restaurant critics and their experience shows. Exceptional housekeeping and cleanliness, too." *(Kent Micho)* "My mouth still waters at the memory of their French toast." *(Gisela Soliman)*

"The Arts & Crafts Suite overlooks the gorgeous terraced garden of wildflowers and herbs, and has a beautiful bathroom with a double Jacuzzi tub. David and Laura gave us their list of favorite restaurants; after trying their first recommendation we looked no further and followed their knowledgeable suggestions." *(Jackie Ross & Rob Fisher)* "From the living room window, I watched the fog roll in, and heard the fog horn at night." *(Cathy Lockwood)* "Warm hospitality, yet complete respect for our privacy. Course upon course of sumptuous breakfast fare. The innkeepers make an exceptional effort to make each guest comfortable." *(Larry & Bobbie Liebenbaum)* "This beautifully decorated house showcases Laura Ann's murals and tile work." *(Rita & Paul Marth)* "Laura Ann painted a beautiful reproduction of a Gustav Klimt Tree of Life mural in the sitting/breakfast room." *(Pamela Barras)*

Open All year.

Rooms 2 suites, 3 doubles—3 with full private bath, 2 with maximum of 4 people sharing bath. All with clock/radio. 1 with telephone, whirlpool tub, kitchen, laundry; 3 with fireplace, 2 with porch.

Facilities Living/dining room, library, darkroom; guest kitchen & laundry. Patio, garden. 2 off-street parking spaces; unmetered on-street parking.

Location Alamo Square Historic District. 7 blocks to Civic Center. Hwy. 101 N to 9th St. Take 9th to Hayes, Hayes to Fillmore.

Restrictions Absolutely no smoking. Children over 14 welcome. "Back bedrooms on garden are very quiet."

Credit cards Amex, Discover, JCB, MC, Visa.

Rates B&B, $100 suite, $85 double, $75 single. Extra person in suite, $15. Cooking seminars. Lunch ($12), dinner ($25) by advance reservation.

Extras Spanish, French spoken.

Hotel Vintage Court ¢ ♁ ✗ ♿
650 Bush Street, 94108

Tel: 415–392–4666
800–654–1100
Fax: 415–433–4065

A reader favorite, this appealing little hotel is located a few blocks from Union Square, just off the Powell Street cable-car line. Included in the rates are day-long coffee and tea service and afternoon wine-tasting. For dinner, guests may want to try Masa's, one of the city's top French restaurants, with possibly the largest selection of California wines.

"Our spacious twin room was decorated in an appealing dark flowered chintz and had good reading lights, a comfortable chair, and ample closet space." *(CM)* "Our room was small but comfortable and charming. Accommodating staff, excellent location. We enjoyed sipping wine by the fire and meeting the other guests." *(Nancy Sinclair)* "Pretty lobby with lighted fireplace and gracious staff; quick and courteous check-in. Our spacious eighth-floor room had a lovely window seat and adequately sized bathroom. We could hear the pleasant, not-too-distant clang of the passing cable cars." *(Gail Davis)* "Safe, convenient, appealing neighborhood. Lovely lobby where wine was served each afternoon. Our recently redecorated room was delightful, done in vibrant pink and green florals." *(Betsy Immergut)* "Friendly and personable employees. This hotel does all the little things without being asked." *(Philip Houser)* "Comfortable room, excellent staff, convenient location." *(D.L. Watson)*

Worth noting: We have also had positive reports on other hotels in the Kimpton Group, including the **Bedford**, the **Monticello**, and the **Prescott**.

Open All year. Restaurant closed Sun., Mon., also Dec. 25 through 2nd week of Jan.

Rooms 1 suite, 106 doubles, singles—all with private bath and/or shower, telephone with voice mail, clock/radio, TV, iron & board, desk, air-conditioning, mini-bar, cable TV, pay-per-view movies, hairdryer, irons/ironing boards. Suite with fireplace, Jacuzzi.

Facilities Lobby with fireplace; restaurant; meeting room. Room service (through outside service) 11 a.m. to midnight. Valet, laundry services. Health club facilities nearby. Parking garage ½ block away, $16.

Location Nob Hill/Union Square. 1½ blocks N of Union Sq., between Powell & Stockton. 10-min. walk to financial district; 5 min. to Chinatown.

Restrictions Smoking in designated areas only. Double-glazed windows in street side rooms.

Credit cards All major cards.

Rates Room only, $275 suite, $129–169 double. Extra person, $10. AARP discount. Corporate rates. Prix fixe dinner, $70 & $75. Continental breakfast, $8.

Extras Wheelchair access; some rooms equipped for the disabled. Crib, babysitting. Spanish, Tagalog, Chinese spoken. Member, Kimpton Group.

Inn at the Opera   🛏 ✕ ♿   *Tel:* 415–863–8400
333 Fulton Street, 94102   800–325–2708
                                         Fax: 415–861–0821

Built more than a half century ago to cater to opera stars, the Inn at the Opera has been transformed into a luxury hotel for artists and fans alike. The European-style rooms are handsomely decorated with muted colors and quality reproductions; amenities include terry robes and night-time chocolates. The lounge and restaurant, Act IV, has an "English club" look, with dark wood paneling and leather chairs. In 1997, the inn was purchased by the Shell Hospitality Group, and is managed by Mary Ann Serpa.

"Friendly, helpful, attentive staff; reasonably priced and comfortable rooms; good food; extremely well managed. Special attention to returning guests." *(Timothy Heartt)* "Quiet location, convenient to Brooks Hall." *(Peter Francis)* "Act IV is a delightful restaurant, popular with the opera/ballet crowd." *(William Rothe)* "The suites are well worth the extra cost. Delicious breakfast of fruits and baked goodies, served in the English pub. Nice amenities in the bathrooms, everything clean and neat. Parking can usually be found on the street." *(Carol Blodgett)* "The Opera Package is a great way to get good opera seats, pleasant accommodations, and a wonderful dinner in one stroke." *(Barbara Mahler)* "The lobby has the ambiance of a friend's parlor. My room was comfortable, with plenty of shelves in both the bath and closet, lots of pillows and towels." *(Cindy Schonhaut)* "Personal care provided by entire staff; ideal for business travelers." *(WH)* Reports welcome.

Open All year.
Rooms 18 suites, 30 doubles—all with full private bath; 2-line telephone with data ports, voice mail; radio, TV, desk, refrigerator, wet bar, microwave.
Facilities Lobby, restaurant, bar/lounge with fireplace, nightly pianist. Concierge, room service. Valet parking, $19.
Location 1 block W of City Hall. On Fulton, between Franklin & Gough Sts.; 1½ blocks from Van Ness. "About 90 feet from the Opera House, Davies Symphony Hall and Ballet."
Restrictions Prefer children over 10.
Credit cards Amex, DC, MC, Visa.
Rates B&B, $220–275 suite; $150–200 double. Extra person, $15. Alc lunch, $18–25, alc dinner, $25–60. Special packages.
Extras Wheelchair access; some rooms equipped for disabled. Crib, babysitting. Weekday transportation to Financial District, Union Square.

The Spencer House
1080 Haight Street, 94117

Tel: 415–626–9205
Fax: 415–626–9230

Like many San Francisco B&Bs, the 1887 Spencer House was built to the highest standards of its day. Then it slipped to the lowest standards before its rescue in 1984 by Jack and Barbara Chambers. After two years of restoration and vast expense, they opened Spencer House as an elegant inn, furnished in period and highlighted by antiques, lace curtains, wall coverings, and linens, all purchased in England by Barbara. The beds have feather mattresses, down duvets, and pillows. The exterior of the house has a classic "painted lady" look, artfully combining five shades of soft gray, ivory and mauve. Breakfast, served 8–10:00 A.M. at the dining room table, is different each day, with such entrees as baked apple pancakes, Belgian waffles, eggs Benedict, or perhaps polenta and eggs.

"A magnificent house, remarkably restored and furnished by the Chambers. Fans of Victorian wall and ceiling treatments will swoon at the Bradbury & Bradbury creations. The furnishings gave one the feeling of Victorian wealth and comfort. We received the royal treatment from owners and staff." *(James & Pamela Burr)* "After a busy day of sightseeing, we came home to this island of serenity to be pampered by the staff." *(Daniel Graham)* "Our room was exquisitely decorated and I appreciated the in-room thermostat." *(Debra Garrard)*

"Great attention to detail, both the obvious and the subtle. In making our reservation, we enjoyed talking with Barbara and learning about each guest room in order to make our selection. We weren't disappointed in our choice, with a view in the distance of the Golden Gate Bridge through the huge windows; heavy velvet curtains could be drawn to keep out the light and sound. Our room was spotless, with plenty of towels, extra blankets, a huge king-size bed, and a gorgeous chandelier. At breakfast we had juice and blueberry pancakes served on exquisite china and silver. Overall, we felt comfortable, secure, and pampered." *(John & Kris Paulson)*

Open All year.
Rooms 6 doubles—all with private shower bath, telephone, clock. 3 with desk, 1 with TV.
Facilities Dining room, living room with fireplace, piano, books. 3 off-street parking spaces; on-street parking.
Location 20 blocks from downtown. From Hwy. 101, take Fell St. exit & continue to Baker St., then turn left. Go 3 blocks to Haight St. Turn left to inn.
Restrictions No smoking. Adults preferred.
Credit cards Amex, MC, Visa.
Rates B&B $115–165 double.
Extras $25 airport pickup. Spanish, some German, French, Russian spoken.

SAN GREGORIO

Reader tips: "San Gregorio has a fine beach and a quaint town a mile inland. A group of 19th-century buildings make this a popular spot for filming old-time movies; in the famous San Gregorio store, one can find kerosene lanterns, new age music, and surprisingly serious books." *(Emily Hoche-Mong)* "Duarte's Tavern in nearby Pescadero offers superior food in a rural atmosphere. Lots of locals at the bar. Fresh fish and wonderful pies at reasonable prices, open for lunch and dinner." *(Ruthie Tilsley)*

Rancho San Gregorio ¢ 🏃
5086 LaHonda Road, Rte. 1 Box 54, 94074

Tel: 415–747–0810
Fax: 415–747–0184
E-mail: Rsgleebud@aol.com

Set in the pine-covered hills overlooking San Gregorio Valley, this Spanish Mission–style home has heavy redwood beams, terra cotta floors, and carved oak antiques. Innkeepers Bud and Lee Raynor built the house in 1971 and have been extending their hospitality to B&B guests since 1986. Lee notes that "we grow apples, pears, plums, berries, kiwi, cactus pears, zucchini, artichokes, and more, so our breakfasts depend on what's in season." The menu is different each day, perhaps grapefruit and strawberries, chili egg puff with homemade salsa, kielbasa sausage, hash-brown potatoes, and corn bread muffins; followed the next day by tropical fruit compote, apple–cream cheese crepes, turkey ham slices, banana bread with ollalieberry jam, and cinnamon-nut rolls.

"An excellent value, and our favorite B&B of the trip. The Corte Madera room has a private balcony with a great view, wood-burning stove, and old-fashioned bathtub. Wonderful breakfast of oven-baked omelets, ham, biscuits with homemade jam, and blueberry muffins. We watched a movie from their video collection, and helped ourselves to complimentary soda and bottled water, popcorn and candy." *(Lori Murray Sampson)* "Lee and Bud do everything possible to make your stay enjoyable. Amazing breakfasts, with light and tasty pancakes; wonderful breads and cookies. Spacious, charming guest rooms and common areas." *(Derek & Ruthie Tilsley)* "Charming, rustic setting in the coastal ranchlands. A creek meandering alongside the orchard contributes to the quiet, relaxed setting." *(Lynne & Mike Fritz)*

"Bud and Lee provide you with area maps and helpful recommendations." *(Andrew Rateaver)* "This area extends from redwood forests of the Santa Cruz Mountains, down through lush foothills to the coast. The Raynors' property has a history reaching back to the Spanish ranchers, and Bud shares colorful stories of the artifacts he's found." *(Ginny Babbitt)* "The orchards, quiet hills, and creeks were pleasant for private, relaxing walks." *(Charles Moorman)* "Bud and Lee's breakfasts were great fuel for the bicycling we did along quiet roads with views of the ocean beyond." *(Timothy Leermont)* "During breakfast, we were introduced to the other guests and helped with plans for a day of sightseeing along the coast. The inn dog Sancho plays a mean game of ball." *(Alan & Sharon Leaf)*

Open All year.

Rooms 1 suite, 3 doubles—all with private bath and/or shower, radio, desk, deck, robes. 3 with woodburning stove, 2 with refrigerator.

Facilities Dining room with organ, woodstove; living room with woodstove, TV/VCR, videotape library, stereo.

Location San Mateo County. 45 m S of San Francisco; 45 m N of Santa Cruz. 10 m SE of Half Moon Bay; 25 m W of Redwood City/Palo Alto. 5 m inland from coastal Hwy. 1 on Hwy. 84.

Restrictions No smoking.

Credit cards Amex, Discover, MC, Visa.

Rates B&B, $145 suite, $85–115 double. Extra person, $15. 10% 4-night discount.

Extras Airport pickup with prior notice. Crib.

SAN JOSE

Reader tip: "San Jose deserves the award as the most undiscovered major city in the U.S. After a successful redevelopment program in the 1980s, it now has a world class performing arts center, a gem of an art museum, and unparalleled technological innovation museum, and a first-rate convention center." *(Gene Altshuler)*

Information please: Dating back to 1884 is the **The Hensley House** (456 North Third Street, 95112; 408–298–3537), combining historic ambiance with amenities that suit the needs of Silicon Valley business travelers. A Queen Anne Victorian home built of redwood, a portion of the interior was remodeled in the Craftsman or Tudor style about 1906. Each of the six guest rooms has hand-stenciled wallpaper motifs and crystal chandeliers. B&B double rates of $115–175 include breakfast and afternoon tea.

A restored Art Deco building, the **Hotel De Anza** (233 West Santa Clara Street, 95113; 408–286–1000 or 800–843–3700), just three miles south of the San Jose Airport, offers small, elegant, full-service accommodations combining the cachet of the 1930s and the amenities of the 1990s at rates of $105–220; ask about weekend packages. Each of the 110 rooms has a working desk and electronic hookup to accommodate the business traveler; its restaurant, La Pastaia, offers California with an Italian accent.

Although larger with 170 rooms, the **Hyatt Sainte Claire** (302 South Market Street, 95113; 408–295–2000 or 800–824–6835) retains a small scale elegance. The restored 1926 building has been refurbished with handsome exposed beams, custom furnishings, and handsome wool carpets. Double rates are $85–210.

SAN LUIS OBISPO

In California's central coast region, San Luis Obispo is 200 miles north of Los Angeles and 200 miles south of San Francisco. Affectionately known as "SLO," this town of 50,000 is surrounded by mountains, and some 35 wineries within an easy drive. Pismo, Avila, and Grover beaches are nearby, as is Hearst Castle.

For an additional area inn, see **Baywood Park**, 12 miles west of San Luis Obispo.

Information please: Although the owners no longer appear to be in residence, readers are generally pleased with the **Garden Street Inn** (1212 Garden Street, 93401; 805–545–9802), an Italianate Queen Anne home built in 1887. The guest rooms have antique furnishings, queen- or king-size beds, and decorating motifs which range from Irish to Western, butterflies to sports memorabilia. B&B double rates for the 13 guest rooms range from $90–130 for doubles, $140–170 for suites, including a full breakfast and pre-dinner wine and cheese. "Clean, comfortable, convenient with a hearty breakfast and beautifully decorated rooms. Great place to stop on the way up or down the California coast." (*Ivana Buric*)

Known for being wonderfully tacky, the **Madonna Inn** (100 Madonna Road, 93405; 805–543–3000 or 800–543–9666) has theme rooms such as the Cave Man room, carved from solid rock. The Madonna's color scheme is equally memorable—although some rooms are done in lime green or bordello red, what you'll find throughout is bright pink, from the napkins to the toilets, from the matches to the dining room banquets. Double rates for the 109 guest rooms range from $99–198.

SAN MATEO

Also recommended: Alan and Marian Brooks are the hospitable owners of the **Palm House B&B** (1216 Palm Avenue, San Mateo, 94402–2438; 650–573–PALM), a Craftsman-style home built in 1907, centrally located between San Jose and San Francisco. "Delightful from the welcome drink served in fine crystal to healthy breakfasts served on lovely china. Pure cotton, sun-dried sheets and towels. This turn-of-the-century home has leaded windows, dark wood paneling and beams, a huge porch, a balcony, and solarium." *(Katherine Madden)* "Delightful stay; super innkeepers helped us feel right at home. Delicious breakfasts, different each day." *(Gwen & Bob Vaughan)* The B&B double rate for the three guest rooms (with private and share baths) range from $65–70, including a home-cooked breakfast and afternoon refreshments.

SAN RAFAEL

Gerstle Park Inn
34 Grove Street, 94901

Tel: 415–721–7611
800–726–7611
Fax: 415–721–7600
E-mail: gerstle@pacbell.net

Lovely antiques, rich colors and fabrics, fine art and comfortable furnishings, plus all the modern conveniences and business amenities—that's not exactly what comes to mind when century-old servants' quarters are mentioned. But that's just what Jim and Judy Dowling have worked hard to create at The Gerstle Park Inn. Originally built in 1895 to house workers at the Louis Sloss Estate, the Dowlings restored the run-down building as an inn in 1995, along with an adjacent 1880 Carriage House, and named it for Gerstle Park, which adjoins the property. (The original mansion burned down in 1953). Breakfast, served 7:30–10 A.M., includes such specialities as omelets and five-grain pancakes. Rates also include in-room sherry and candy.

"The inn sits high on a hill on a suburban street. On arrival, Jim greeted us warmly, offered us a glass of wine, and a tour of the inn. The decor is an elegant mix of antiques and modern amenities. The living room has an Oriental theme, the dining room is sunny and warm, and the sparkling kitchen is available anytime for drinks or snacks. Our room, the Sloss Suite, was one of eight on the main floor, and I liked the comfortable queen-size bed, plush carpeting, dark wood furniture, and especially the little terrace with wrought iron chairs off the sitting area; I read there in the morning sun. The bathroom was new and clean, with a pedestal sink. Though the rooms were equally attractive, most with queen- or king-size beds, our favorite aspect of the inn were the Dowlings themselves. Jim and Judy invited us to pick plums from their tree, suggested a wonderful place for dinner, and made the reservations.

They were friendly but unobtrusive. The next morning, breakfast was served at individual tables, which we prefer, and included fresh-squeezed orange juice and eggs scrambled with five different kinds of cheese. The inn is equally inviting for a romantic getaway, a business trip, or a family visit." *(Randi Rubin)*

Open All year.
Rooms 2 cottages, 4 suites, 6 doubles—all with private bath, dual-line telephone with voice mail & data port, clock/radio, TV/VCR, desk, balcony/deck, hair dryer, robes, iron. Some with whirlpool tub, ceiling fan, kitchen. 2 suites in Carriage House.
Facilities Dining room, living room with fireplace, books; guest kitchen; decks. 1 ½ acres with gardens, redwood grove, orchard, off-street parking. Park adjacent with tennis courts, walking paths. Fishing nearby.
Location 10 m NE of San Francisco. Exit Highway 101 at San Rafael Central Exit. Go E on 4th St., left on D St. Right on San Rafael Ave., left on Grove St. 10 min. walk to village.
Restrictions No smoking.
Credit cards Amex, MC, Visa.
Rates B&B, $169–189 suite, $129–169 double. Extraperson, $15. 10% senior discount, AAA discount.
Extras Free pickups from airport shuttle bus.

SANTA BARBARA

With its crystal-clear skies and steady 65-degree temperatures, Santa Barbara has been a popular winter seaside resort for over 50 years. The rest of the year has always been just as nice, with summer temperatures rarely exceeding the 70s, but people have only recently begun to discover Santa Barbara's year-round appeal. Most activities here are connected with the ocean—the beautiful beaches are ideal for swimming, surfing, diving, sailing, as well as whale and seal watching—but the city is also becoming known as an arts center, with several museums and galleries of interest. In addition to lots of lovely shops, Santa Barbara is the place to go for some of California's best food. Of course, there's no shortage of golf courses or tennis courts either.

The city's appearance is generally Spanish—adobe walls and red-tiled roofs abound. Part of this is because of the city's Spanish heritage—it was ruled by Spain for over 60 years—but a 1925 earthquake, which leveled much of the town, is also responsible. When rebuilding began, the local Architectural Board determined that Spanish, not Victorian, style would prevail.

Santa Barbara is located at the southern end of California's Central Coast, 91 miles north of Los Angeles, via Highway 101, and 335 miles south of San Francisco. Weekend traffic coming up from LA can be heavy.

Worth noting: Santa Barbara is an expensive town; $100–150 per night gets you adequate, not luxurious, accommodations. If you'll be in Santa Barbara during the week on business, don't make a reservation without inquiring about corporate rates; nearly every establishment offers them. Rates also tend to be 10 to 20 percent lower from October to May.

Reader tip: "Fun, excellent lunch at Matte's Tavern in Los Olivos; superior dinner at the Montecito Inn Cafe." *(Ruthie Tilsley)*

Also recommended: Just across from the Montecito Inn is the **Coast Village Inn** (1188 Coast Village Road, Montecito 93108; 805–969–3266 or 800–257–5131), a 25-room motel with a heated swimming pool, beautifully landscaped grounds, and guest rooms with country pine decor; some have ocean views, wet bars, or kitchens. B&B double rates range from $95–165, and include a continental breakfast; kids stay free and advantageous AAA rates are available midweek. "One of the few places we found in Santa Barbara that would take a Saturday night only reservation; adequate accommodations, reasonably priced." *(RT)*

The **Bath Street Inn** (1720 Bath Street, 93101; 805–682–9680 or 800–788–BATH) has a homey, welcoming ambience. This Queen Anne Victorian cottage was built over 100 years ago, and is decorated with period wallpapers, handmade quilts and English antiques. Double rates of $95–175 include a full breakfast with egg dishes, French toast, or pancakes, and afternoon refreshments.

The **Montecito Inn** (1295 Coast Village Road, 93108; 805–969–7854 or 800–843–2017), built in 1928 by Charlie Chaplin and Fatty Arbuckle, was a favorite getaway for the movie stars of the day. It features wrought-iron balconies, white stucco walls, classic red Spanish tiles, and graceful arches. The 53 guest rooms are decorated with French country furniture, overhead fans, and tiled baths. "Convenient location on Montecito's main street, though some rooms can be noisy. Small but appealing swimming pool and hot tub." *(SWS)* "Spacious, comfortable suite; excellent, reasonably priced restaurant. Used the hotel's free bicycles to ride along the ocean path." *(EL)* B&B double rates range from $185–225, with suites from $350–625.

Five miles south of Santa Barbara is the famous **San Ysidro Ranch** (900 San Ysidro Lane, Montecito 93108; 805–969–5046 or 800–368–6788), a beautifully groomed and furnished luxury resort. Many famous people have stayed here—presidents, kings, and prime ministers—yet the atmosphere remains California casual. Some of the 43 suites and cottages are spacious and elegant, with beautiful mountain and distant ocean views, others are considerably more modest—be sure to get one that's been refurbished recently. Rates range from $225–750, exclusive of any meals, refreshments, snacks, and most activities. "A wonderful, if expensive place for dinner. The Stonehouse Restaurant is truly serene, with roughly textured taupe-colored walls, well-worm and deep hued Oriental carpets, and warm lighting. Outstanding, well-priced prix fixe menu, including a vegetarian meal. Exemplary service, solicitous without being pretentious or overweening." *(Susan Rather)*

The **Tiffany Inn** (1323 De la Vina Street, 93101; 805–963–2283 or 800–999–5672) is a Victorian gem, built in 1898. The seven guest rooms, all with queen-sized beds and telephones, are furnished with antiques and other period pieces; some have a double whirlpool tub, wood-burning fireplace, and TV/VCR. The B&B double rate ranges from

$125–225, including a full breakfast, served in the dining room or veranda, and refreshments in the afternoon and evening. "Goldie, the innkeeper, cares for the inn as if it were her own. Lots of repeat guests, including ourselves. Exceptional antiques, beautifully maintained." *(Sandy Truitt)*

For an additional area inn, see **Summerland.**

The Cheshire Cat Inn
36 West Valerio Street, 93101

Tel: 805–569–1610
Fax: 805–682–1876
E-mail: cheshire@cheshirecat.com

In 1984 Christine Dunstan restored two of Santa Barbara's oldest adjoining homes, opening them as a B&B. Named for characters in *Alice in Wonderland*, most have Laura Ashley–style fabrics and sitting areas highlighted with English antiques. Breakfast is served in the dining room or on the shaded patio, and might include freshly squeezed orange juice, baked apples with yogurt, just-baked breads, pastries, an egg casserole or quiche; locally made chocolates and imported cordials are placed in each guest room as a welcome gift.

"Appealing guest rooms done in upscale country decor. My favorite rooms are the romantic and private Tweedledee and Tweedledum, in the Coach House. The beautiful courtyard has a gazebo enclosing a spa. In addition to the delicious breakfast, they also provide little extras like freshly baked cookies, tea, and lemonade in the afternoon, and a wine and cheese reception on Saturday nights. The staff aims to please—they make dinner reservations for you, and will even arrange for an in-room massage. Convenient location, within walking distance of the shops and restaurants of State Street." *(Marsha Houston)* "Delightful. My large, lovely, beautifully decorated suite had a Jacuzzi tub on a platform in a window alcove in the bedroom." *(Leigh Robinson)*

"The Mock Turtle room has four huge windows overlooking the front garden, and was beautifully decorated, immaculate, and quiet. The grounds were glorious, with flowers everywhere, and a wonderful Jacuzzi in the gazebo, with white lights twinkling in the trees and hanging potted plants and flowers." *(Cynthia Grylov & Thomas Pinto)* "Lovely guest rooms, many with beautifully tiled Jacuzzi tubs. Some rooms have a summer look with soft blues, pinks and greens while others have deeper maroons and navy color schemes." *(SWS)*

Open All year.
Rooms 8 suites, 6 doubles—all with private bath and/or shower, telephone, fan. Some with TV, fireplace, Jacuzzi, microwave, refrigerator, patio or balcony, kitchen. 2 rooms in Coach House.
Facilities Dining room, parlor, lounge, all with fireplace. TV/game room. ½ acre with patio, swing, rose garden, gazebo with hot tub, bicycles, lawn games. Off-street parking.
Location 3 blocks to theater, restaurants, shops. Take State St. to Valerio St.
Restrictions Noise in 3 rooms might disturb light sleepers. No smoking.
Credit cards MC, Visa.
Rates B&B, $190–270 suite, $140–180 double. 2-night weekend minimum. Corporate rate midweek, $89 single. 2-night weekend minimum.

Glenborough Inn
1327 Bath Street, 93101

Tel: 805–966–0589
800–962–0589
Fax: 805–564–8610
E-mail: glenbboro@silcom.com

Travelers who steer clear of B&Bs because the enforced early-morning camaraderie is not their cup of tea—or coffee—will enjoy the Glenborough. The innkeepers maintain guests' privacy by bringing breakfast to each room at 8:30, 9:00, or 9:30 A.M.; the meal includes a hot entree, freshly baked bread, fresh fruit, and juice. Owned by Michael Diaz and Steve Ryan since 1992, the inn comprises a 1906 Craftsman-style building with beveled glass windows and cross-cut oak beams, a 1912 Craftsman farm-style home, and an 1885 Victorian summer cottage. Guest rooms are comfortably furnished with some antiques, most with queen-size brass, iron, or canopy beds, and floral fabrics. Guests enjoy gathering for wine and hors d'oeuvres from 5–6 P.M.; tea and cookies are available later in the evening. A refreshment center stocked with coffee, tea, and cocoa, instant hot water, an ice maker, and refrigerator is always available to guests.

"We splurged on the luxurious Nouveau Suite, with a private gated entrance, garden, and hot tub. The spacious rooms had Art Nouveau decor and a firm, queen-size bed. Sunlight streamed in through the bay windows. Charming bathroom with wood paneling and a clawfoot tub and shower. Everything was spotless. Michael recommended an appealing restaurant nearby, and we learned that they offered free desserts to Glenborough guests. Promptly the next morning, an adorable picnic basket was delivered to our door, complete with a vase of flowers, place mats, fruit, quiche, and muffins, allowing us to have breakfast in bed or at the table and chairs in our room. A friendly kitty even invited herself in to say hello. Later, Michael gave us a driving itinerary for sightseeing in the area. The grounds are beautiful with gorgeous flowers. A wonderful getaway for privacy and romance." *(Randi Rubin)*

"Great innkeepers, delicious breakfast, lovely rooms. Highlights include the whirlpool baths, plush towels, flowers, soft music, and desserts." *(Maureen McTeague)* "Quiet, safe location; short walk to downtown." *(Gary Kuenzli)* "Michael and Steve really care about their guests, and keep abreast of restaurants, events, and activities." *(Barbara Harris)* "Close to the shuttle, so you don't need a car." *(Darlene Jordan)*

Open All year.

Rooms 4 suites, 7 doubles in 3 buildings—all with private bath and/or shower, telephone, clock/radio, fan, robes, coffee maker. Many with private entrance, fireplace, refrigerator; some with desk, Jacuzzi tub, hot tub, patio.

Facilities Parlor with fireplace, games, books; stocked guest pantry; porch, bicycles. Gardens, hot tub, lawn games. Off-street parking.

Location Downtown residential area; 3 blocks to restaurants, shops, museums. On Bath St. between Victorian & Sola. From Hwy. 101, go E on Carrillo, N on Bath.

Restrictions No smoking.

Credit cards Amex, DC, Discover, MC, Visa.

Rates B&B, $170–225 suite, $100–225 double. Extra person, $30. Tips appreci-

ated. Senior, AAA, corporate rate midweek, Oct.–May. 2–3 weekend/holiday minimum.
Extras Spanish spoken.

Secret Garden Inn and Cottages
1908 Bath Street, 93101

Tel: 805–687–2300
800–676–1622
Fax: 805–687–4576
E-mail: garden@cheshirecat.com

Picture a California-style bungalow and four cottages with lush green gardens, secluded behind high hedges and you will understand why this B&B is called the Secret Garden Inn. Each guest room is decorated with antiques and country furnishings, and four have a secluded hot tub, available only to the occupants of that room. The full breakfast is served in the garden or in the privacy of your own room. Rates also include afternoon wine and cheese, and evening cider and sweets. The inn is owned by Jack Greenwald and Christine Dunstan (owner of the Cheshire Cat).

"Our cottage in the back garden was very quiet, with an exceptionally comfortable bed equipped with excellent pillows. Several lamps made the sitting room very cozy. The garden is quite beautiful and equipped with tables for breakfast. We met Jack Greenwald who was refreshingly opinioned on local restaurants." *(Susan Rather)* "The gardens were lovely, the cottages charming, clean, quiet, and well maintained." *(Sabella Haverland)* "We were welcomed with cheese, wine and juice; when we returned from dinner, cookies and hot chocolate were waiting." *(Deborah Magee)* "Simple but charming rooms, a refreshing change from the clutter of many other inns." *(SWS)*

Open All year.
Rooms 3 suites, 8 doubles—all with private bath/shower, radio. Some with TV, refrigerator, ceiling fan. Rooms in 4 cottages and main house. 4 with hot tub. Most with private entrance.
Facilities Dining room, living room with TV, guest refrigerator. Gardens, patios, bicycles.
Location ½ m from downtown. From Hwy. 101, go NE at Mission. Turn right on Castillo St., left onto Pedregosa St., left onto Bath St. to inn.
Restrictions No smoking. Children welcome in some cottages.
Credit cards Amex, MC, Visa.
Rates B&B, $145–195 suite, $110–180 double. Extra person, $20. 2-night holiday/weekend minimum. Off-season, midweek rates.

Simpson House Inn &
121 East Arrellega Street, 93101

Tel: 805–963–7067
800–676–1280
Fax: 805–564–4811
E-mail: SimpsonHouse@compuserve.com

Owned by Glyn and Linda Davies since 1976, Simpson House consists of a beautifully restored 1874 Eastlake Victorian home, a renovated 1878 barn, and three garden cottages. Dixie Budke is the innkeeper. Served between 8:30–9:30 A.M., a typical breakfast might include baked pears with whipped cream, eggs with garden herbs, scones with lemon curd and raspberry preserves. The extensive evening wine and Mediterranean hors d'oeuvres buffet offers such temptations as marinated mushrooms, focaccia with pesto and sun-dried tomatoes, baked Brie, olive tapenade with sourdough toast, and vegetable antipasto. Rates also include a free 90-minute trolley pass, and evening turndown service with chocolate truffles.

"Dixie and the staff greet us with a smile, and are ready to accommodate any special requests. There is always a warm or cool drink to enjoy and some delicious treat awaiting us. Although our favorite cottage is Abbeywood, we have also enjoyed the beautiful Hayloft with its pitch-beamed ceiling and lovely view of the garden. The rooms and baths are always impeccably clean, the beds piled high with pillows and down comforters. The fire needs only a match to start, wonderful tapes are there for our favorite music, and warm robes wait in the closet. One can walk, bike or take the State Street trolley to shops and restaurants." *(Geoff & Carole Gillie)* "Each cottage is secluded behind a veil of lush flowers, plants and assorted hedges; the gurgle of running water mixes with the subtle sounds of classical music. We enjoy the whirlpool bubble bath, and sip complimentary glasses of wine from a local vineyard. Requests to the staff are handled immediately, restaurant reservations made, and directions provided. Breakfasts are fresh and creative, hors d'oeuvres unique and plentiful. The evening often ends sipping a glass of port on the rear veranda. " *(Jeffrey Weber)*

"Huge living and dining room with beautiful Oriental rugs. Guest rooms in the main house are decorated with lovely antiques; the handsome barn suites have king-size beds and a rustic country look, accented with antique farm equipment." *(SWS)* "A magnificent breakfast of freshly squeezed orange juice and blintzes topped with luscious strawberries was delivered to the private patio of our cottage at the time specified." *(Ron Kahan)* "Attentive staff. A light bulb over our vanity was changed within minutes. Fresh orchids in every room." *(Jill Hennes)* "A minor plumbing problem was fixed within the hour, and a bottle of wine was sent to us as an apology for the inconvenience. Wonderful thick, fluffy towels changed twice daily." *(Yvonne Stoner)*

Open All year.

Rooms 3 cottages, 4 suites, 7 doubles—all with private bath and/or shower, desk, telephone, air-conditioning. 4 suites in restored barn—all with telephone, TV/VCR, wetbar, fireplace, deck. Cottages with fireplace, stereo, hair dryer, Jacuzzi tub, TV/VCR, patio with fountain.

Facilities Dining room, living room with fireplace, library; porch. 1 acre, garden, sitting areas, croquet, picnic area. Bicycles, beach equipment. On-site spa services; gym, pool, health club nearby. Golf, tennis nearby.

Location 5 blocks from center. From Hwy. 101 N take Garden St. exit. Go right 13 blocks then left on Arrellega St. From Hwy. 101 S take Mission St. exit. Go left on State St., left on Arrellaga St.

Restrictions No smoking.

Credit cards Amex, Discover, MC, Visa.

Rates B&B, $250–350 cottage, $250–300 suite, $150–250 double. Extra person, $25. 2–3 night weekend/holiday minimum.

Extras Wheelchair access. French, Danish, Spanish spoken.

SANTA CRUZ

Santa Cruz is a classic old beach resort, complete with a boardwalk and amusement park. The area's white sand beaches—fun for both swimming and fishing—have been a playground for San Franciscans for over 100 years. The municipal pier is lined with seafood restaurants and souvenir shops, while the local sea lion population frolics in the water below. Other nearby attractions include the redwood forests, golf, tennis, hiking, fishing, and, of course, shopping. Santa Cruz is also home to 20 wineries, seven with tasting rooms. Summer is peak season here; many, although not all, establishments lower their room rates from November through February. Located on Monterey Bay, on the Central Coast, Santa Cruz is 75 miles south of San Francisco, 35 miles south of San Jose, and 40 miles north of Carmel/Monterey.

Reader tips: "The drive to Santa Cruz (Spanish for holy cross) takes about 40 minutes from the San Jose Airport on a winding road over redwood-covered mountains. As you descend, you see the town nestled in the coastal plain with Monterey Bay as a backdrop. The best view is from the University of California Santa Cruz campus in the northwest part of town, and it's just as lovely at night as during the daytime." *(Michael Salkind)* Also: "The best time to visit is in the spring or fall when the days are warm and summer fog and tourists are absent." *(Matt Joyce)*

For additional area inns, see **Aptos, Ben Lomond, Capitola, Davenport,** and **Soquel**.

Information please: Under new ownership in 1997 is the **Babbling Brook Inn** (1025 Laurel Street, 95060; 408–427–2437 or 800–866–1131), a B&B since 1981. Once a favorite fishing spot of the Ohlone Indians, it later housed a gristmill, then a tannery, and was even used as a set for silent movies. Four of the 12 guest rooms are in the original historic buildings, with the remainder in chalet-style buildings; the decor is French country. B&B double rates range from $85–165. Reports welcome.

SANTA ROSA

Located 50 miles north of San Francisco, Santa Rosa is a small city (population 113,000) and a convenient base for touring the Sonoma and Napa Wine Country. Gardening enthusiasts will want to visit the Luther Burbank Home and Gardens to learn more about the horticulturist who developed hundreds of new varieties, while history buffs will prefer the walking tour of the historic Railroad Square district.]

For additional area inns, see **Glen Ellen, Occidental,** and **Petaluma.**

Information please: A Queen Anne Victorian home built in 1880, the **Pygmalion House** (331 Orange Street, 95401; 707–526–3407) was named to reflect the inn's painstaking transformation from dilapidation to restoration. Its furnishings include antiques from the collection of the famous stripper, Gypsy Rose Lee, and the famous madam and past

Sausalito mayor, Sally Stanford; the six guest rooms have either queen or king-size beds. B&B rates of $65–115 include a full breakfast. "Quiet, convenient location on a dead-end street three blocks from downtown. My cozy room was small, clean, tastefully decorated and inviting. Bountiful breakfast; extremely affordable place to stay in an expensive area." *(DC)*

Vintners Inn ✗
4350 Barnes Road, 95403

Tel: 707–575–7350
800–421–2584
Fax: 707–575–1426

The Vintners Inn was built in 1984 by John and Cindy Duffy, who also operate the vineyards which surround the inn. Located at the crossroads of the Sonoma Wine Country, the inn is ideal for touring in the nearby Sonoma, Russian River, Dry Creek and Alexander Valleys. The furnishings include French Country decor and antique European pine furniture. A buffet breakfast is available from 7–10 A.M.; guests help themselves to home-baked bread and pastries, waffles, fruit, juice and cereal, to be enjoyed at individual tables. The inn complex includes John Ash & Co, one of Sonoma's premier restaurants. A recent dinner menu included corn and fennel chowder, Dungeness crab cakes with parsnip rosemary puree, and such tempting desserts at chocolate Gomorah— a flourless brownie-truffle dumpling under fallen walls of chocolate. Comments appreciated.

Open All year.
Rooms 5 suites, 41 doubles—all with full private bath, telephone, modem jack, radio, clock, TV, desk, air-conditioning, refrigerator, balcony/patio. 23 with fireplace. Rooms in 3 buildings.
Facilities Restaurant, cafe/bar, breakfast room, library. 45 acres with courtyard gardens, hot tub, off-street parking, vineyards. Swimming, tennis, golf nearby.
Location 3 m from town. From Hwy. 101, take River Rd exit & go W on River Rd. Take 1st left, Barnes Rd. to inn on left. Vineyards border Hwy 101.
Restrictions No smoking.
Credit cards Amex, MC, Visa.
Rates B&B, $200–225 suite, $158–198 double. Extra person, $20. 10% AARP discount. Alc lunch, $15; alc dinner, $45.
Extras Wheelchair access; bathroom specially equipped. Crib; babysitting by arrangement. Spanish spoken.

SAUSALITO

Just across the Golden Gate Bridge from San Francisco, Sausalito perches precariously on steep hillsides dropping to the bay below. Originally developed in the mid-1800s with elegant Victorian mansions, its nature became more bawdy and commercial when the town became the railway and ferry terminus at the century's end. Sausalito's waterfront was again active during World War II, when it became a center for Liberty ships, with the shipyards in operation round-the-clock. The town has been known as a center for artists and craftspeople since the '50s and has been popular as a tourist center since ferry service was resumed in 1970. Although many visitors make Sausalito their San Francisco base, area activities also include boat and fishing charters, kayaking, whale-watching, bicycling, and hiking.

To reach Sausalito by car from San Francisco, cross the Golden Gate Bridge and exit at Alexander Avenue. Follow Alexander until it becomes Bridgeway, Sausalito's main street. From Highway 101 south, take Marin City/Sausalito exit and follow signs to downtown Sausalito. Ferry service is available daily to Fisherman's Wharf and the San Francisco Ferry building.

Information please: Built in 1915 in the Mission Revival style, the **Hotel Sausalito** (16 El Portal, 94965; 415–332–0700 or 888–442–0700) was rumored to be a bordello in the 1920s; Baby Face Nelson was said to be a regular guest. During the permissive 1960s and 1970s, such artistic types as the writer Sterling Hayden lived at the hotel. Completely renovated in 1996, the hotel has 16 guest accommodations decorated in French Riviera style, with park or harbor views. The decor includes custom-made furniture, decorative and wall painting, faux finishes, mosaic mirrors, Impressionist reproduction oil paintings, and wrought iron king- and queen-size beds. B&B rates of $155–245 include a breakfast of pastry and coffee.

The Casa Madrona Hotel   ♁ ✕ ♿   *Tel:* 415–332–0502
801 Bridgeway, 94965   800–415–567–9524
                               Fax: 415–332–2537
                     E-mail: casa@nbn.com

Owned since 1976 by John Mays, the Casa Madrona consists of an 1885 Victorian mansion with a new section completed in 1983; the two structures are linked by suites and rooms winding down the hillside. The old rooms are furnished with antiques, while many of the newer ones have Mediterranean touches; each is unique, so be sure to ask for details. American West Coast cuisine is served at the hotel's Mikayla restaurant, with such entrees as Ahi tuna with shiso, chili and lime; scallops with snap peas, jalapeno, and bacon; and chicken with potato puree and mushrooms.

"Overlooks the bay, past marinas filled with beautiful sailboats and yachts, to Angel Island, the Bay Bridge, and more. Welcoming staff. Colorful landscaping of blooming flowers. The stairway to the mansion and restaurant is lined with star jasmine, orange trees, roses and plants, as well as a beautiful water stairway that ends in a fountain at the restaurant's entrance. The hotel is well maintained and updated; rooms have been decorated by local designers and take their name from the decor. The Renoir room has a claw-footed tub, a step up from the bedroom area; the wall behind the tub has a hand-painted garden scene. The Artist Loft is near the elevator, with a large glassed-in shower, an easel and paints; guests are encouraged to do a canvas of whatever they wish. Rooms are supplied with plenty of large towels and toiletries; the lighting is on dimmer switches, with bedside lights for reading in bed. In-room coffee makers are stocked with Starbucks coffee. Beds are turned down at night and often home-baked cookies or fresh flowers are left on your pillow." *(Mrs. J. Lawrence Guthrie)* "From my first visit, I was hooked by the loveliness of the walkway next to the cascading water, by the hillside setting, by the charm of the individualized rooms. And the food is superb. Best of all is the kind and caring staff, who go out of their way to accommodate guests with everything from an emergency umbrella to a toothbrush." *(Alfred Jacobs)* "Loved both the hotel and the location. Excellent housekeeping. No need for the car—everything in Sausalito is within easy walking distance and the ferry to San Francisco is just across the street." *(Peggy Vaughn)* "Tucked into the hills above the bay, up a flight of stairs from the main boardwalk. Most rooms have a private deck with a bay view. Several waterside restaurants are within walking distance." *(Christine Adkins)* "Breakfast consists of juice, coffee, fruit, and muffins." *(AW)* "Fantastic water views in the dining room." *(HBS)*

Open All year.

Rooms 3 suites, 24 doubles, 5 cottages—all with full private shower and/or bath, telephone, radio, TV, desk, hairdryer, coffee maker.

Facilities Parlor, restaurant. Gardens, hot tub. Massage therapy. Tennis, golf nearby. Valet parking, $7.

Location San Francisco Bay Area, Marin County. 15 min. drive, 30-min. ferry from San Francisco. On main street, 350 yds. to ferry. From San Francisco, cross Golden Gate Bridge; exit at Alexander Ave. Follow Alexander to Bridgeway. From Hwy. 101 S, take Marin City/Sausalito exit; follow signs to downtown Sausalito. Follow Bridgeway for approx. 2½ m.

Restrictions Smoking restricted.

Credit cards Amex, DC, Discover, MC, Visa.

Rates B&B, $225–300 suite, $138–205 double. Extra person, $20. 2-night weekend minimum. Alc lunch, $15; alc dinner, $30–40. Sunday brunch, theme dinners, tastings. Ask about MAP rates.

Extras 1 room wheelchair accessible. Crib, babysitting. German, Spanish, French, Vietnamese, Chinese spoken.

The Inn Above Tide 🏃

30 El Portal, 94965

Tel: 415–332–9535
800–893–8433
Fax: 415–332–6714
E-mail: inntide@ix.netcom.com

If you were much closer to the water than the rooms at the Inn Above Tide you'd be wet. Built in 1962, this contemporary wood-shingled building rests on pilings in the bay, and was renovated as an inn in 1995 by William H. McDevitt; Verena Zurcher is the innkeeper. Along with the morning paper, breakfast is delivered to guest rooms between 7 and 10 A.M., and includes fruit, pastries, croissants, rolls, granola, and freshly squeezed orange juice. A sunset wine and cheese reception is offered each evening in the common room. Echoing the colors of the bay outside, guest room decor includes traditional furnishings done in soothing neutral tones of white, ivory, and pearl gray, accented with various shades of blue. The rooms have queen- or king-size beds; several have canopy beds. Binoculars are provided to focus on the sweeping views of San Francisco Bay, including the Bay Bridge, Alcatraz, and the San Francisco skyline. Several waterfront restaurants are within a block or two, and the staff is happy to make reservations.

"Convenient, clean, and quiet, with unbelievable views. Excellent base for business or vacation. Pleasant breakfast, enjoyable wine and cheese hour; friendly atmosphere." *(Dr. T. A. Lasky, also James Hensley)* "After an exhausting conference in the city, we treated ourselves to a night at this waterside hideaway. Although it was foggy at night when we arrived, we awoke to a glorious sunny morning and the incredible view. We took breakfast out to the deck, and left reluctantly when checkout time inexorably arrived. Nearby are the shops, galleries, and restaurants of picturesque (and pricy) Sausalito." *(MW)*

Open All year.

Rooms 2 suites, 28 doubles—all with full private bath, 2-line telephone, data port, clock/radio, TV/VCR, desk, air-conditioning, refrigerator, robes, binoculars. Most with deck, gas fireplace. 5 with double whirlpool tub.

Facilities Drawing room, courtyard sundeck. Off-street valet parking.

Location From bridge, follow Alexander Ave. until it becomes Bridgeway. Go right on El Portal toward water, ½ block to inn. From Hwy. 101 S, take 1st turnoff into Sausalito to Bridgeway. Turn right. Go 1 m to El Portal; turn left toward water. Adjacent to ferry dock; 25 min. by boat to Fisherman's Wharf, financial district; $2–6 per person.

Restrictions No smoking.

Credit cards Amex, MC, Visa.

Rates B&B, $300–425 suite, $195–265 doubles. Extra person, $15. Tips appreciated. Children under 12 free.

Extras Wheelchair access; bathroom specially equipped. Crib, babysitting. Spanish, German, French spoken.

SEAL BEACH

Just east of Long Beach, and 25 miles from Los Angeles is Seal Beach, a sleepy beach town, little changed from the 1950s. Main Street offers a few antique shops, and ends at the Seal Beach Pier, one of the longest in Southern California.

Information please: Built in 1922, the **Seal Beach Inn & Gardens** (212 Fifth Street, 90740; 562–493–2416 or 800–HIDEAWAY) has long been owned by Marjorie and Harty Schmaehl. It has seven well-equipped suites, and the B&B rates of $120–255 include a generous buffet breakfast of waffles, quiche, fresh fruit and juice, granola, and Danish, as well as evening hors d'oeuvres. Guests are welcome to relax in the courtyard, surrounded by a profusion of flowers, in the swimming pool, or take a short walk to the beach or town. "Quiet, romantic atmosphere; polite, accommodating staff; elaborate Victorian decor; lush garden setting; delicious food." *(Joe & Vicki Carpenter, also MW)*

SOLVANG

Solvang was founded in 1911 by Midwesterners of Danish heritage, who wanted to start a traditional Danish folk school and ended up with an entire Danish-style town. Danish customs still prevail, and many come to Solvang for the "European atmosphere," shops, bakeries, and outdoor theater.

Solvang is located in the Central Coast region, 135 miles north of Los Angeles in the Santa Ynez Valley Wine Country. It's 30 miles from Santa Barbara and about 15 minutes from the beach.

Information please: Listed in past editions, we need current reports on the **Alisal Guest Ranch** (1054 Alisal Road, 93463; 805–688–6411 or 800–4–ALISAL). Families who've despaired of ever finding a welcome for their children among California's inns will find an oasis at the Alisal; it's enjoyed equally by adult travelers as well, especially when school is in session. Dating back to an 1803 land grant, the ranch was used primarily for raising cattle until 1946; at that time it was purchased by the Jackson family who started taking in guests. Activities range from trail rides, square dancing, cookouts, and hay rides to golf, tennis and fly fishing. Double rates for the 63 guest accommodations range from $325–3600, and include breakfast and dinner; activities are extra in summer, but are included in the rate off-season.

The **Chimney Sweep Inn** (1554 Copenhagen Drive, 93463; 805–688–2111 or 800–824–6444) has a courtyard garden, gazebo-covered hot tub, and 28 country-style rooms with four-poster or canopy beds, and in-room coffee. Lodge rates range from $70–150; cottage rates from $145–260. "Nice garden and cottages. Rooms in the main building are generic but nicely decorated, and the entire place has a kind of fairy-tale appeal. Breakfast consisted of sweet rolls, canned apple juice, and coffee. We opted for a more authentic Danish buffet down the street." *(DR)*

The **Peterson Village Inn** (1576 Mission Drive, 93463; 805–688–3121 or 800–321–8985) is a modern facility constructed in the style of old Denmark; it shares its building with the 24 shops and cafes of Petersen Village. The 40 guest rooms are luxuriously decorated with canopy beds and love seats; TVs are hidden in armoires. A Danish buffet breakfast of fresh fruit and juice, cereals, boiled eggs, ham, cheese, and bakery-fresh pastry and rolls, plus afternoon wine are included in the $95–195 double room rates.

For an additional area entry, see **Ballard.**

SONOMA

Sonoma is California's oldest mission, founded in 1823. Today people come to this charming old Spanish town to visit the area wineries; California's first vineyard was planted here in 1855 by a Hungarian nobleman by the name of Haraszthy. Visitors also enjoy touring its historic buildings, playing golf and tennis, and going horseback riding or ballooning.

Sonoma is located in the North Coast region, in the Sonoma Wine Country, about 40 miles north of San Francisco. From San Francisco, take Highway 101 to 37 east, then 121 north to Highway 12, which runs right through the town.

Reader tips: "We never begin an afternoon of wine tasting in Sonoma without first having lunch at the Sonoma Cheese Factory. Wonderful dinner at the Sonoma Hotel." *(Nancy Sinclair)* "Eating in the wine bar at Babette was an excellent and economic way to enjoy their justly famous cuisine." *(Ruthie & Derek Tilsley)*

Also recommended: Right on the plaza is the **El Dorado Hotel** (405 First Street West, 95476; 707–996–3030 or 800–289–3031), dating from 1843, with 27 guest rooms redone with elegant simplicity. Rates range from $100–170, including continental breakfast and complimentary wine. "Our spacious room overlooked a vine-covered courtyard, and the heated swimming pool was a real plus." *(Joanne Kronauer)* "Nicely located on the square. Rooms are simply but attractively decorated. Pleasant lounge." *(Ruthie & Derek Tilsley)* "Romantic and gracious. Our room had a balcony with chairs and a table overlooking the park, a wonderful place to sit and enjoy the split of wine provided in our room." *(Nancy Sinclair)*

The **Sonoma Mission Inn** (Highway 12, P.O. Box 1447, 95476; 707–938–9000 or 800–862–4945) offers natural hot springs, full spa services, an excellent restaurant and 170 luxurious guest rooms. Double rates range from $140–380, with suites to $670. "A charming Wine Country inn, with a spacious lobby and handsome Spanish Colonial antiques. Excellent restaurant and spa facilities. Our comfortable room had a king-size bed and a more than adequate bathroom. Pleasant and knowledgeable staff. We enjoyed taking a hike in the hills above the inn early one morning. Convenient location for visiting area wineries." *(Robert Boas)*

Information please: About four miles from Sonoma Plaza is **Morningsong Country Lodging** (21725 Hyde Road, 95476; 707–939–8616), with two guest rooms in the main house ($100), and a separate cottage ($135). Surrounded by orchards, vineyards, and berry bushes, guests are welcome to pick apples, pears, and blackberries in season; owners Dan and Ann Begin are pleased to provide advice on area wine touring. Rates include a breakfast of fresh fruit, juice, cereal, and croissants.

A half-block west of the Plaza is the **Thistle Dew Inn** (171 West Spain Street, 95476; 707–938–2909 or 800–382–7895), owned by Larry and Norma Barnett. The inn occupies two adjacent turn-of-the-century homes, surrounded by lush gardens. The six guest rooms are decorated with Arts and Crafts furnishings, Oriental carpets, and handmade quilts; each has a queen-size bed and private bath, and some have private entrances, gas fireplaces, and double whirlpool tubs. B&B double rates of $100–180 include a creative full breakfast, afternoon hors d'oeuvres, and use of the inn's bicycles and garden hot tub.

On Highway 12 just north of town is the **Trojan Horse Inn** (19455 Sonoma Highway, 954476; 707–996–2430 or 800–899–1925), built in 1887 and decorated with period antiques. B&B double rates of $110–145 include breakfasts of fresh fruit salad, sourdough waffles, and lemon chicken sausage, plus afternoon wine and cheese. Each of the six guest rooms has a private bath.

For additional area inns, see **Glen Ellen.**

Victorian Garden Inn
316 East Napa Street, 95476

Tel: 707–996–5339
800–543–5339
Fax: 707–996–1689
E-mail: gardeninn@aol.com

A Greek Revival farmhouse built in 1870, the Victorian Garden Inn is furnished with period antiques, surrounded by authentic Victorian gardens, complete with mazes and secret corners. Breakfast can be enjoyed in the dining room or taken on a bed tray to your room or your patio; rates also include evening wine or sherry, served by the parlor fireplace or on the creekside patio.

"Within walking distance of downtown Sonoma, this Victorian home sits off the street and is shielded by the trees and beautiful garden. Brick walks allow you to meander through the rose and perennial beds, where I sat on an ornate Victorian-style iron patio chair and read in seclusion, to the sound of the garden fountain. The Tower Room, in the old water tower adjacent to the house, is small, done simply in blue and white, with a double bed. Donna was pleasant and helpful in getting me settled and arranging restaurant reservations. Tasty breakfast of cherry juice, granola, fresh fruit plate, muffins and pastry, and hard boiled eggs; I let Donna know the night before that I wanted to take a breakfast tray outside. The guests had an enjoyable conversation, gaining lots of tips for the day's travel." *(Joanne Ashton)*

"The Garden Room is decorated in Laura Ashley rose and white, with a queen-size white cast iron bed, a sitting area, dressing area with large mirror, and a bathroom with a claw-foot tub, supplied with bubble bath and soaps." *(Lisa & Mark Gallagher)* "Peaceful garden, where breakfast is served; inviting pool, too." *(Roberta Maguire)*

Open All year.
Rooms 5 doubles—4 with private bath, 1 with shared bath. 3 with private entrance, 2 with gas fireplace. 2 rooms in cottage.
Facilities Dining room, living room with fireplace. Gardens, swimming pool, therapeutic spa.
Location Between E. 3rd and E. 4th St. 3 blocks E of Plaza.
Restrictions Smoking restricted.
Credit cards Amex, Enroute, JCB, MC, Visa.
Rates B&B, $159 cottage, $89–149 double. Extra person, $20. 2–3 night weekend/holiday minimum.

SONORA

The seat of Tuolumne County, Sonora was named by Mexican miners after their home state. Sonora's handsome Victorian homes date from gold rush days when it was the site of the richest gold mine in the Mother Lode. Summer activities include sightseeing and spelunking in the nearby caves, along with golf, and several lakes and rivers for water sports. Winter offers skiing at Bear Valley and Dodge Ridge. Sonora is located 120 miles east of San Francisco, 70 miles west of Yosemite.

Also recommended: The **Lavender Hill Inn** (683 South Barretta Street, 95370; 209–532–9024) was built in 1900 and is eclectically furnished with antiques and reproductions. There is a porch swing for relaxing on summer evenings and a fire in the woodstove for winter chills. B&B rates for the four guest rooms, each with private bath, range from $75–95, including a full breakfast. "We stayed in the air-conditioned Lavender Room with a king-size bed and lamps on both sides, sitting area, and clawfoot tub in the bath. We relaxed on the big, comfortable porch, cooled by an evening breeze. Owner Charlie Marinelli prepares great breakfasts, and his wife Jean prepared home-baked cookies and unbelievably good apricot iced tea each afternoon. They're warm, gracious, friendly, but not pushy—ideal innkeepers. They're relatively new to the area, but are learning about it quickly." *(Kathleen Owen)*

Information please: For a peaceful Gold Country getaway, consider **Serenity** (15305 Bear Cub Drive, 95370; 209–533–1441 or 800–426–1441), a B&B, not just a state of mind. Recently built in the style of a Victorian farmhouse, it offers four handsome guest rooms with antique furnishings and handmade needlework, each with private bath and sitting area. The B&B double rate of $85–125 includes a full breakfast and evening refreshments.

For additional area inns, see **Jamestown.**

SOQUEL

Blue Spruce Inn	*Tel:* 408–464–1137
2815 South Main Street, Soquel, 95073	800–559–1137
	Fax: 408–475–0608
	E-mail: pobrien@BlueSpruce.com

Soquel makes a fine base for visits to the Santa Cruz mountain wineries, the Capitola and Santa Cruz beaches, and nearby state forests for hiking. The Blue Spruce is composed of two adjacent homes, built in 1875 and 1891, restored by Pat and Tom O'Brien in 1989. Guest rooms are charmingly decorated with brass and iron beds, graced with Amish quilts; walls are hung with original local art. Rates include breakfast (served at guests' convenience) and afternoon cookies; the morning menu might offer raspberries with vanilla yogurt, applesauce cake, granola, spinach-feta cheese strata, and smoked chicken-apple sausage; or fresh fruit, almond scones with lemon curd, hot oatmeal, and sourdough Belgian waffles. The O'Briens also own the **Bayview Hotel** (8041 Soquel Drive, Aptos 95003; 408–688–8654 or 800–422–9843), ten minutes from Santa Cruz. This three-story Italianate hotel, totally renovated and refurbished, has eleven guest rooms with private baths, featherbeds, robes, and comfortable sitting areas; some have oversized soaking tubs. Their other property is **Marvista** (212 Martin Drive, Rio del Mar, 95003; 408–684–9311), an Arts and Crafts–style home with two luxury guest rooms overlooking Monterey Bay.

"Once you park your car, you can forget it for the weekend. A white picket fence and beautiful garden surrounds the inn. Coffee is available early each morning before Pat's scrumptious family-style breakfasts; Pat and Tom generally join the morning talk around the table. Although each room has its own personality, they all have fluffy feather beds, plenty of towels, robes, antiques, and fresh flowers. Summer Afternoon, our favorite, is located at the back of the inn, and has a sitting area and a separate alcove for the bed; Gazebo is our second choice. Both have always been squeaky clean, with reading lights on each side of the bed. When we're out to dinner, the bed is turned down, accompanied by chocolates and a carafe of fruit wine. At the back of the inn is a patio for all to enjoy, with ample seating, a hot tub, and a bubbling pond. Last but not least are gracious innkeepers Pat and Tom, who seem to know when people want company, and when privacy is preferred. They have a great knowledge of the area, and are always willing to suggest places to go and things to see." (*John & Kathy Griffin*)

"Ideal location within walking distance of the beach, local wineries, antique shops, and restaurants. Lots of little extras, including homemade cookies in the parlor, wonderful wine barrel hot tub, real sense of security, wine glasses at the ready, welcoming dog to greet you with a lick and a wagging tail." *Sandy Brook* "Delightful wine and cheese in the arbor by the spa." (*Charlene Enoch*)

Open All year.

Rooms 6 doubles—all with private bath and/or shower, clock, telephone. 5 with balcony/deck, gas fireplace; some with radio, TV/VCR, desk, whirlpool tub. 3 guest rooms in carriage house.

Facilities Living/dining room with fireplace, books, guest refrigerator, deck. ⅓ acre with garden hot tub, off-street parking. Swimming, golf, tennis, beaches, boating, fishing, hiking, mountain bicycling nearby.

Location 4 m S of Santa Cruz, 60 m S of San Francisco, 30 m SW of San Jose, 20 m N of Monterey. Historic area, 2 blocks from downtown. 1 m from Capitola beaches. From Hwy. 1, take Capitola/Soquel exit. From N, turn left from exit & go under freeway to 2nd signal at Main St., then go right to inn on left. From S, turn right at exit & right again onto Main.

Restrictions No smoking.

Credit cards Amex, MC, Visa.

Rates B&B $85–150 double, $80–145 single, Extra person, $20. 10% midweek discount Oct.–April. 2-night weekend minimum. Midweek packages.

Extras Airport/station pickup, $40. Spanish spoken.

SPRINGVILLE

Also recommended: In the foothills of the Sierras, 75 miles northeast of Bakersfield and about 50 miles south of Kings Canyon/Sequoia National Park is **Annie's B&B** (33024 Globe Drive, 93265; 209–539–3827) built in 1906 and restored as a B&B in 1990 by Annie and John Bozanich. The B&B rate for the three guest rooms, each with private bath, is $95, includes a full breakfast, served at guests' convenience. Guests can relax by the antique stove in the parlor, in the swimming pool or hot tub, or watch Annie's pet pot-bellied pigs do tricks for treats. "Annie has the good sense to know when to talk and make you feel part of the family and when to leave you alone. Her husband is a nationally known horseman and has a corral where he breaks horses, plus his own custom saddle and golf club shop." *(Phyllis Wikoff)* Area activities include an 18-hole championship golf course, as well as fishing, boating on Lake Success, tennis, hiking, and swimming.

STINSON BEACH

Information please: Avid gardeners will want to make a beeline for the incredible flower gardens at the **Casa del Mar** (37 Belvedere Avenue, P.O. Box 238, 94970; 415–868–2124 or 800–552–2124). Located 35 minutes north of San Francisco, the inn rests at the base of Mt. Tamalpais, close to Point Reyes National Park. The six guest rooms, each with private bath, have views of the Pacific or Mt. Tam, and cost between $100 and $225. Owner Rick Klein is noted for his breakfasts of freshly squeezed orange juice, fresh fruit, and black bean ginger pancakes, huevos rancheros, or cheese omelets, plus blueberry poppy seed cake or lemon walnut bread. Reports appreciated.

SUMMERLAND

Also recommended: Five miles south of Santa Barbara is the **Inn on Summer Hill** (2520 Lillie Avenue, Summerland 93067; 805–969–9998 or 800–845–5566), a rambling Craftsman-style bungalow constructed in 1989. Guest rooms are decorated in a fantasy of European country-style fabrics and patterns, billowing curtains and ruffled cushions, most with a king-size canopy bed. Floral paintings and antique trunks provide accents, along with Tiffany-style lamps and fresh flowers; all rooms have ocean views, private baths with whirlpool tub, telephone, TV/VCR, stereo, refrigerator, air-conditioning, instant hot water for tea and coffee, and gas fireplace. Although right on Highway 101 and the train tracks, double-glazed windows close to keep noise to a minimum. Rates include a creative full breakfast, afternoon refreshments, and after-dinner dessert. Terry robes are tucked into the armoire to wear to the gazebo-covered hot tub. B&B double rates for the 16 guest rooms range from $170–200, $325 for the suite. "Extravagant decor with uncounted yards of fabrics and rolls of wallpaper; excellent lighting and sound-proofing; experienced, professional staff; deliciously rich, creative food; peaceful village." *(Janet Emery, and others)*

SUTTER CREEK

Sutter Creek is located in Gold Country, in Amador County, about 45 minutes west of Stockton and Sacramento and 2½ hours from San Francisco. In addition to gold panning, visitors look for gold of another sort in the liquid found at the many area wineries. Area activities include boating, fishing, and hiking.

Reader tip: "Stop for afternoon tea at Somewhere in Time, a combined antique and tea shop." *(Julie Phillips)*

Also recommended: About a mile from town is the **Gold Quartz Inn** (15 Bryson Drive, 95685; 209–267–9155 or 800–752–8738), in a residential/commercial area just off Highway 49. Built in 1988 in a neo-Victorian style, this 24 guest-room inn has beautifully furnished common areas, and an inviting porch which wraps around the back of the inn. The spacious guest rooms are furnished in Queen Anne reproductions, with handmade quilts on the queen- and king-size beds, and well-equipped modern baths. "Tea time was great with crackers and cheese, cakes and cookies, tea and juice. Breakfast, served at individual tables, included chili Relleno, oven-baked potato wedges, hot spiced apricots, scones, poppy seed muffins, bagels, English muffins, jam, fruit, cereal, and more. Hot drinks and cookies are always available. Beautiful, spacious, comfortable rooms with many little extras. Excellent staff-run inn." *(Julie & Doug Phillips, also MB)* B&B double rates range from $85–155.

For additional area inns, see **Amador City, Ione,** and **Plymouth.**

The Foxes in Sutter Creek	*Tel:* 209–267–5882
77 Main Street, P.O. Box 159, 95685	800–987–3344
	Fax: 209–267–0712
	E-mail: foxes@cdepot.net

Pete and Min Fox purchased this house, dating back to 1857, in 1980; in 1986, they constructed a carriage house behind the original Victorian structure. The spacious guest rooms are luxuriously furnished with antiques and quality reproductions. Breakfast might include grapefruit juice, pear cranberry compote, Swedish pancakes with fresh berries, and Black Forest ham.

"Top marks for ambiance, food, and attention to detail." *(Mrs. James Hallbeck)* "Beautifully decorated rooms, clean as a whistle. Pete and Min welcomed us warmly, and could not have been nicer or more helpful. Pete's excellent breakfast, plus Min's strawberries in Grand Marnier sauce was brought to our room or the patio, as we preferred." *(Beverly Weller)* "Each guest room has a table with two chairs, where your breakfast is brought at the time requested on gleaming silver tea service. Our favorite was the Garden Room, on the second floor of the carriage house. Two comfortable upholstered chairs are set before the fireplace, while the breakfast table overlooks the branches of a lovely shade tree. Even the compact gardens surrounding the house have tables for two, screened with greenery for privacy, where you can also relax or enjoy breakfast." *(SWS)* "Pete and Min suggested an excellent restaurant for dinner. The location was perfect for exploring this delightful Gold Rush town." *(JTD)* "Welcoming innkeepers, lovely shaded grounds. We especially like the Garden and the Blue rooms." *(Julie Phillips)*

Open All year.
Rooms 7 doubles—all with private bath and/or shower, radio, air-conditioning. Some with fireplace, TV. 3 rooms in annex.
Facilities Dining room, living room. Gardens with gazebo, patio. Tennis, golf nearby. Covered off-street parking.
Location Gold Country. On Main St. (Hwy. 49) in center of town.
Restrictions No smoking. "Inn not appropriate for children."
Credit cards Discover, MC, Visa.
Rates B&B, $100–155 double, $105–160 single. 2-night Sat., holiday minimum.
Extras Local airport pickup by arrangement.

Grey Gables Inn
161 Hanford Street, 95685

Tel: 209–267–1039
800–GREY–GAB
Fax: 209–267–0998

Grey Gables brings a touch of the English countryside to Gold Country. Built in 1897, Roger and Sue Garlick restored their home as a B&B in 1994. Named for English poets such as Byron, Browning, Shelley, and Wordsworth, guest rooms are decorated with antiques, with a color scheme using different shades of pink, green, and ivory, with floral fabrics and wallcoverings.Rates include coffee at 8:00 A.M., breakfast at 9:00 A.M., afternoon tea in the parlor, and evening hors d'oeuvres. Breakfast is served at individual tables in the dining room, though guests have the option of a private meal in their room.

"Beautiful both inside and outside with lovely gardens. Sue greeted us warmly, introduced herself, and showed us around the inn. We stayed in the Byron room, with crisp white trim and a white chair rail separating the dark rose walls above from the forest green floral wallpaper below, forest green wall-to-wall carpet. Furnishings included a comfortable queen-size bed, ample seating and a small table, a large armoire, and a beautiful dresser. Extras included a heart-shaped 'Do Not Disturb' sign, books of Lord Byron's poems, and a basket of magazines. The bathroom had a clawfoot foot tub with shower, plenty of thick white towels, and a night light. After settling in, we were invited to the parlor for iced tea, cranberry scones, whipped cream and jam. Sue then sat down and chatted with us and the other guests. Between 6:00 and 7:00, Sue and Roger served wine and cheese. They were pleased to make dinner reservations and are delightful, attentive, accommodating innkeepers. At 8:00 A.M. the next morning, coffee was ready in the dining room, so you could enjoy a steaming cup and read the paper in the parlor while waiting for breakfast. Breakfast was served at beautifully set tables. The delicious meal included orange or grapefruit juice, lemon nut bread, fresh fruit with granola, and a bacon and egg quiche with grilled tomato." *(Julie & Doug Phillips)*

233

Open All year.

Rooms 8 doubles—all with private bath and/or shower, clock/radio, air-conditioning, desk, ceiling fan, gas fireplace, hair dryer.

Facilities Dining room, living room, lounge, porch. ⅓ acre with terraced English garden with fountain, off-street parking.

Location On Hwy 49, 1 block N of downtown.

Restrictions No smoking. Children over 12. Traffic noise in one room.

Credit cards Amex, Discover, MC, Visa.

Rates B&B, $90–150 double, $85–145 single. Extra person, $20.

Extras Wheelchair access; 1 room fully equipped.

TAHOE CITY

Located on the quiet, less developed west shore of Lake Tahoe, Tahoe City makes an appealing base for all water sports, plus bicycling, golf, riding, and hiking in summer. Winter-time bring cross-country and downhill skiing at Squaw Valley, Alpine Meadows or Homewood.

Also recommended: Dating back to 1938—built in the old Tahoe knotty pine style—is the **Cottage Inn** (1690 West Lake Boulevard, P.O. Box 66, 96145; 916–581–4073 or 800–581–4073), with 15 guest rooms in five rustic, charming cottages, set in the pines. Each has a private bath and fireplace, and some have a whirlpool bath, TV/VCR and/or kitchen; decorating themes range Native American to Western, fishing to skiing; a favorite is the Enchanted Cottage with an indoor tree and a lodge pole pine bed. Guests gather in the original residence for a full breakfast, afternoon cookies, or a glass of lemonade or wine. B&B double rates range from $140–210. "Beautiful setting on the lake, with a dock and beautiful beach. Charming theme decor; generous breakfasts." *(JP, also POB)*

A stone-and-shingle home built in 1932, the **Mayfield House** (236 Grove Street, P.O. Box 5999, 96145; 916–583–1001) is a fine example of old Tahoe architecture. Its six bedrooms, each with private bath, have down comforters and pillows, lots of books, fresh flowers, and queen- or king-size beds. The B&B double rate of $85–150 includes a full breakfast and evening wine and cheese. "We enjoyed The Study, downstairs, a spacious room with a comfortable king-size bed. Delicious breakfast of Portuguese waffles with hot peach sauce." *(Mark Mendenhall)*

Information please: On the banks of the Truckee River, next to the Alpine Meadows ski area is the **River Ranch Lodge** (Highway 89 & Alpine Meadows Road, P.O. Box 197, 96145; 916–583–4264 or, in CA, 800–535–9900). This casual, rustic lodge has 18 guest rooms, some with balconies overlooking the river, and simple Victorian-style decor. B&B rates of $50–135 include a continental breakfast. The inn also has a popular bar and restaurant, with such favorites as salmon, trout, portobello mushroom Napoleon, rack of lamb, and baby back ribs.

Two miles south of the casino center, right across the street from the lakeside bike path is **The Inn by the Lake** (3300 Lake Tahoe Boulevard, South Lake Tahoe 96150; 916–542–0330 or 800–877–1466). The attractively landscaped grounds offer a swimming pool, hot tub, and rental bikes, while the double rates for the 99 guest rooms (some with kitchens and whirlpool tubs) are $84–148.

Chaney House
4725 West Lake Road, P.O. Box 7852, 96145

Tel: 916–525–7333
Fax: 916–525–4413

Built in 1928 by Italian stone masons, and set amid massive pines, the Chaney House has 18-inch thick stone walls, Gothic arches, a massive stone fireplace in the living room that reaches to the top of the cathedral ceiling, exposed wooden beams, and pine paneling throughout. Gary and Lori Chaney purchased it as a private home in 1974 and opened Chaney House to B&B guests in 1989. Rooms are traditionally furnished with some antiques; most have queen- or king-size beds topped with fluffy quilts. Breakfast is served at the dining room table at guests' convenience, or in good weather, on the patio overlooking the lake. A typical menu might include oven-baked French toast with homemade blackberry sauce and creme fraiche, fresh fruit parfaits, and homemade coffee cake. "On the quiet west side of Lake Tahoe. Delicious breakfast served in the attractive dining room." *(AS)* "Panoramic view of the lake from the great room, where wine and cheese is served each evening. Lori and Gary create a welcoming atmosphere which encourages full use of their home and grounds." *(Gretchen & Jim Hinerman)* "A lovely inn with beautiful lake and mountain views from the dock." *(Julie Phillips)*

Open All year.
Rooms 1 apartment with kitchen over garage; 2 suites, 1 double—all with private bath, telephone, clock; 2 with radio. 1 with TV.
Facilities Dining room, living room with fireplace, TV, stereo; patio. 1 acre with off-street parking; lakefront with private beach, pier; bicycle, paddle boat rentals. Bicycling, hiking, boating, fishing, windsurfing, golf, tennis, downhill/cross-country skiing (18 ski areas) nearby.
Location High Sierras; near CA/NV border. 50 m W of Reno; 5 miles S of town. West shore. From I-80, go S on Hwy. 89 (Lake Tahoe Blvd.) to Tahoe City. Go right on W Lake Blvd. (Hwy. 89) for 5 m. Inn on left just after Cherry St., N of Homewood.
Restrictions No smoking. Children over 10.
Credit cards MC, Visa.
Rates B&B, $110–150. Extra person, $20. 2-night weekend minimum.

The Shore House at Lake Tahoe
7170 North Lake Boulevard, Tahoe Vista 96148

Tel: 916–546–7270
800–207–5160
Fax: 916–546–7130
E-mail: shorehse@inntahoe.com

After a day of swimming, canoeing, kayaking, skiing or whatever activity you prefer, come "home" to the Shore House where you can relax on the lawn or deck, or inside by the river rock fireplace in the lakefront dining room, munching on just-baked cookies. Built in 1950, this contemporary lakeside lodge was restored as a B&B in 1994 by Marty and Barb Cohen. Breakfast is served in the dining room at individual tables with seatings at 8, 9, and 10:00 A.M. In addition to freshly ground coffee, herbal and black teas, the menu might include granola fruit parfait or baked apples, followed by eggs Benedict, stuffed French toast with chicken-apple sausage, or chili strata and scones. Rates also include evening wine and hors d'oeuvres. Guest rooms have knotty pine walls and custom-built log furniture, including queen- or king-size beds topped with down comforters and featherbeds; several have lovely hand-painted walls in the bathroom or even the ceiling.

"Charming rooms with wonderful decor, cozy comforters, and thoughtful amenities. Impeccable grounds with a great dock and beach. Great French toast." (*Jennifer Campbell*) "The feather beds are a real treat. Homemade goodies are left in your room each day." (*Don & Joan Rooten*) "Helpful, well-informed, sincere innkeepers. Convenient location; delicious, creative breakfasts." (*Trent & Anna Riding*)

Open All year.
Rooms 2 cottages, 7 doubles—each with private bath and/or shower, clock/radio, refrigerator, balcony, outdoor entrance. 1 with whirlpool tub, 2 with kitchen.
Facilities Dining room with fireplace, stereo, books; decks. ⅓ acre on lake with lawns, gardens, swimming, boating, fishing, private pier, sandy beach, off-street parking.
Location In Tahoe Vista, 8 m N of Tahoe City, 30 m W of Reno, NV. Take Reno or Sacramento, take I-80 to Hwy. 267 S. At end, go right on North Lake Blvd. to inn on left (lakeside).
Restrictions No smoking.
Credit cards Discover, MC, Visa.
Rates B&B, $125–165 double. Extra person, $20.
Extras Babysitting by arrangement.

TEMECULA

Loma Vista B&B
33350 La Serena Way, 92591

Tel: 909–676–7047
Fax: 909–676–0077 (call first)

If you're lamenting the fact that your Southern California trip won't allow you to visit wine country, just alter your Los Angeles–San Diego routing slightly and overnight at Loma Vista, with a hilltop setting overlooking acres of vineyards. Thirteen wineries open for tasting are minutes away. A Mission-style home, Loma Vista's guest rooms are named for locally grown grapes, and are furnished with queen- and king-size beds in a variety of styles—white wicker, Art Deco, Southwestern, and country oak. A typical breakfast includes strawberries with vanilla yogurt and granola, huevos rancheros with avocado, cornbread muffins, and champagne; or perhaps a low-fat version of eggs Benedict, and strawberries with yogurt sauce.

"Betty and Dick Ryan designed and built Loma Vista as a B&B in 1987. The rooms are beautifully decorated and furnished, the atmosphere is restful and quiet, the hilltop view is spectacular, and the food is delicious and abundant. Betty and Dick create a relaxing ambience, demonstrated by the easy camaraderie of the guests who gathered on

Saturday evening for the 6 o'clock wine and cheese get-together on the patio, and again the next morning for the delectable breakfast cooked and served by the Ryans. The Sauvignon Blanc room was done in Southwestern style, with a comfortable four-poster peeled pine bed and inviting sitting area. Our balcony offered a lovely view of the valley lights and distant town. We had a wonderful Italian dinner at the Bailey Wine Country Cafe, and a fun taste of country music at the Stampede in Old Town Temecula." *(Toni & Lee Marteney)*

Open Closed Jan. 1, Thanksgiving, Dec. 25.
Rooms 6 doubles—all with private bath and/or shower, radio, air-conditioning. 4 with balcony. Some with desk, fan.
Facilities Dining room, living room with fireplace, TV, games, library. Patios with fire pit, hot tub. 5 acres with gardens, vineyards. 5 m to Lake Skinner for boating, fishing. Golf nearby.
Location San Diego area. 61 m N of San Diego, 75 m S of LA, 60 m E of Orange County. 4 m to town. Take I-15 to Rancho California Rd. Go E 4½ m and look for Callaway Winery on left. Inn is located on first dirt road past winery.
Restrictions No smoking. "Only 2 people allowed in a room, so parents must split up to sleep with child in separate room."
Credit cards Discover, MC, Visa.
Rates B&B, $95–135 double. Extra person, $25. 2-night weekend minimum for patio rooms. Midweek rates.
Extras Spanish spoken.

TRINIDAD

Trinidad is a little fishing village located on the North Coast, 25 miles north of Eureka, 300 miles north of San Francisco. Visitors enjoy hunting for agates on the beach at Patrick's Point State Park, hiking in the redwood forests just a short drive to the north, or exploring the waterfalls of Fern Canyon. The town was used as a port by gold miners in the 1850s and was a whaling station in the 1920s. Today's visitors come to view the migrating whales and to enjoy fishing for salmon, cod, crab, and clams.

Reader tip: "Redwood National Park is a short drive away, and hikes in Fern Canyon and the Lady Bird Johnson Grove are not to be missed." *(EL)*

Also recommended: A simple Cape Cod–style home, the **Trinidad Bay B&B** (560 Edwards Street, P.O. Box 849, 95570; 707–677–0840) has been owned by Paul and Carol Kirk since 1984. B&B double rates for the four guest rooms ranges from $125–155. "Carol is warm and friendly; rooms are attractive, comfortable and well-equipped. Our room had a private entrance, wonderful ocean views, and was equipped with a fireplace, microwave (popcorn supplied), and refrigerator. Breakfast, delivered to our door, included baked apples, fresh fruit with yogurt, freshly baked muffins, and wonderful blackberry preserves. Pricy but quite delightful." *(AGC)*

A recently constructed oceanfront B&B, the **Turtle Rocks Inn** (3392 Patrick's Point Drive, 95570; 707–677–3707) is set on a bluff overlooking the Pacific, and has four spacious guest rooms, each with ocean view, deck, king-size bed, private bath, contemporary decor, telephone and TV. B&B double rates of $120–170 includes early-bird coffee, full breakfast buffet, and afternoon tea and desserts. "Our room had a sliding glass door to a balcony, with wonderful views of the Pacific, dramatic rock formations, and huge seals basking on the rocks. Easy wheelchair access to the dining room and glassed-in balcony; I thought the wheelchair accessible guest room was the inn's nicest. Tasty apple pie and chocolate chip cookies on arrival." *(Pam Haddad)*

The Lost Whale Inn 🕴

3452 Patrick's Point Drive, 95570

Tel: 707–677–3425
800–677–7859
Fax: 707–677–0284
E-mail: 1miller@lost-whale-inn.com

The Lost Whale is a Cape Cod–style B&B, built in 1989 and designed with families in mind; Susanne Lakin and Lee Miller are the innkeepers. The enclosed yard has a playhouse and berry patches. A scenic wooded trail leads to a private beach with tide pools to explore. Rates include a breakfast buffet with such treats as oatmeal currant pancakes, breakfast pudding with rum sauce, blueberry buttermilk tarts, spinach pie, or apple Dutch babies. Rates also include afternoon wine and sherry, pastries and fruit, coffee and tea.

"Wonderful coastal setting; Trinidad is a nice, nontouristy village. Our second-floor room had a balcony, sleeping loft, and queen-size bed; it had a comfortable chair for gazing out to sea, and good bedside reading lights. Stunning honey-colored Douglas fir floors and woodwork throughout. Well-kept grounds. Tasty, attractively presented food at the breakfast buffet. The back deck was a wonderful, peaceful place to read, contemplate the ocean, and relax." *(Judy Dawson)* "Airy, spacious rooms. Outside is a wonderful fire pit at edge of the cliff with ocean views. Outstanding beach access trail with strategically placed benches so one can sit and enjoy the view. Great hot tub to relax in on a cool evening." *(Dan & Sherry Wentland)*

"Five of the eight guest rooms have beautiful ocean views, complete with the sounds of sea lions barking and waves crashing. The cozy sitting area has large ocean-view windows, comfy chairs, and a table with a jigsaw puzzle in progress." *(Dan & Sherry Wentland)* "Guest rooms are immaculate, light and airy, simply furnished with lace curtains billowing in the fresh air, sea shells, and whale artwork." *(Patricia Kuhn)* "The family-style breakfast included delicious eggs scrambled with fresh salmon, potatoes, blackberry coffee cake, or on another occasion, wild rice pancakes and egg frittata." *(Pat Fink)* "The appealing great room adjoins a large inviting deck, and one can look out at the woods and ocean below. Our daughter loved the sleeping loft, the friendship she developed with the innkeepers' daughter, the friendly farm animals, and the rugged beach." *(EL)*

Open All year.
Rooms 8 suites with private bath and/or shower. 2 with balcony, 2 with sleeping loft.

Facilities Living room with books, games, puzzles, woodstove; dining room, deck with hot tub; 4 acres with gardens, playhouse, farm animals. Trail to private beach. Adjoins Patrick's Point State Park.

Location 1 m from Hwy. 101. From the South, take Seawood Dr. Exit off Hwy. 101; go left under highway, right on Patrick's Pt. Dr. 1.8 m N to inn on left. From Hwy. 101 S, take Patrick's Point Dr. Exit S 1 m to inn.

Restrictions No smoking. Strict 7-day cancellation policy.

Credit cards Amex, Discover, MC, Visa.

Rates B&B, $90–160 suite, $80–130 single. Extra adult, $20; extra child (age 3–16), $15.

Extras Crib, highchair.

UKIAH

Vichy Hot Springs Resort and Inn   ⅏   *Tel:* 707–462–9515
2605 Vichy Springs Road, 95482   *Fax:* 707–462–9516

Named for the famous French mineral springs, Vichy Hot Springs' water is naturally warm and effervescent. Reversing years of neglect, Gilbert and Marjorie Ashoff opened a water bottling plant here in 1978, and re-opened the resort in 1990, after nine years of renovation. A California State Historic Landmark, the buildings maintain their historic charm and are surrounded by the serene and beautiful grounds. Rates include breakfast, use of the mineral baths and swimming pool; guests are welcome to hike the ranches' 700 acres, including the old Cinnabar Mine shaft, the Falls where the water keeps the ferns green, and the forest around Little Grizzly Creek, perfect for a picnic.

"In its glory days, visitors included Robert Louis Stevenson, Jack London, Mark Twain and three U.S. presidents. The redwood buildings housing most of the guest rooms date from the 1860s. A comfortable porch runs their length, affording views of the oak-covered hills." *(William MacGowan)* "Guest rooms are small and pleasant, with white walls, clear fir floors, attractive floral print decor, and the original bathrooms. Breakfast was excellent—a buffet of granola, fruits, breads and pastries, juices, coffee, and hard-boiled eggs. Take thongs for the rough stone path to the mineral baths, most of which are in an enclosed building. The century-old, ochre-colored troughs, when filled to the brim with 90°, naturally carbonated mineral water, made for a peaceful soak. We swam in the cold, clear mineral water of the 80-foot-long pool, and took a midnight dip in the Jacuzzi with a view of the starlit sky. Take a hike along the small river into the cool, shaded woods. For wine-tasting and local artwork, the nearby Parducci Winery is worthwhile." *(Mark Mendenhall)* "A wonderfully relaxing experience; the carbonated "champagne" bath was superb." *(Robert Pritikin)* "Rooms are clean, light, and pleasant. Excellent massage and mineral baths. Tasty breakfast, nicely presented." *(Frank Riggs)*

Open All year.

Rooms 3 cottages, 17 doubles—all with private bath, telephone, radio, desk, air-conditioning. Cottages with fireplace, kitchen.

Facilities Dining room, porch, therapeutic massage building, hot water pool, indoor/outdoor mineral bath tubs, mineral water swimming pool. 700 acres for hiking, bicycling, children's play equipment. RV parking. Tennis, golf, water-skiing, wineries, redwoods nearby.

Location North Coast/Redwood Empire. 2 hrs. N of San Francisco. Follow Hwy. 101 N to Ukiah. Go E on Vichy Springs Rd. & follow Historical Landmark signs approx. 3 m to resort.

Restrictions No smoking. "Soundproofing between guest rooms was minimal."

Credit cards Amex, CB, DC, Discover, JCB, MC, Visa.

Rates B&B, $185 cottage (for 2 people), $135–150 double, $95 single. Extra person, $30. 2-night holiday minimum. Day use rates for mineral baths.

Extras Wheelchair access. Station/airport pickup. Babysitting. Spanish spoken. Station pickups, $10. Crib. Spanish, French, Farsi spoken.

VOLCANO

Saint George Hotel ¢ ✕
16104 Pine-Volcano Grove Road
P.O. Box 9, 95689

Tel: 209–296–4458
Fax: 209–296–4458

The Saint George, built in 1862 and listed on the National Register of Historic Places, was once the tallest and most elegant hotel in the Mother Lode. Marlene and Chuck Inman have owned it since 1975. "The rooms are filled with interesting and unusual antiques; the beds have pretty crocheted spreads. If you like authenticity, choose one of the original rooms facing the front in the main hotel. Volcano had 10,000 people in the 1860s; now the population is 102. Modern life has passed it by—all the better to wander the tiny streets and have conversations with the past." *(SC)* "One can enjoy a 'Moose Milk' or add a business card and dollar bill to those covering the ceiling. Marlene and Chuck are active innkeepers, providing the atmosphere for people to meet one another." *(Ruth Ann & Terry Lane)* "Love the out-of-the-way location and unchanged atmosphere of the hotel. Food is always first rate, and the wine list features local vintages. Rooms are clean and comfortable, if a bit Spartan." *(William Vendice)* "Our favorite spot for relaxing is the porch." *(Laura Hartman)*

Open Mid-Feb. through Dec. Closed Mon., Tues.

Rooms 18 doubles, 2 singles—5 with private shower, 1 with full private bath, 14 rooms with 4–8 people sharing bath. 6 rooms in annex.

Facilities Dining room, bar, lounge with fireplace. 1 acre with horseshoes, hammock. Fishing, swimming hole 1 block away. Tennis, golf nearby.

Location Gold Country. 61 m E of Sacramento. From Jackson, take Hwy. 88 NE to Pine Grove; from Pine Grove, follow road N to Volcano.

Restrictions No smoking in guest rooms. No children under 12 in main house; OK in annex.

Credit cards Amex, MC, Visa.

Rates B&B (Weds.–Thurs.), $78–88 double. MAP (Fri.–Sun.), $120–136, includes tax. Prix fixe dinner, $15–20 (by reservation only).

Extras Babysitting.

WESTPORT

Travelers come to Westport for total "R&R": to hike in the surrounding mountains and wander the deserted beaches. "Set on a high bluff overlooking the ocean, Westport is one of the smallest, most peaceful places we've ever visited. As if time had passed it by, you can walk down almost-deserted streets, and in the middle of town horses graze in fields overlooking the ocean. Even in December there were flowers blooming and crickets chirping." *(SC)*

Westport is located on the North Coast, in the Mendocino area, 180 miles north of San Francisco, 15 miles north of Fort Bragg.

Howard Creek Ranch ¢   *Tel: 707–964–6725*
40501 North Highway 1, P.O. Box 121, 95488   *Fax: 707–964–1603*

The Howard Creek Ranch was first settled in the 1860s, when it included 2,000 acres for raising sheep and cattle, plus a sawmill, blacksmith shop, and stagecoach shop. Many of these buildings, all constructed of virgin redwood, have survived. The inn is the original Howard homestead, and owners Charles (Sonny) and Sally Grigg have furnished it with collectibles and Victorian antiques. The hearty breakfasts are prepared on the original wood stoves, and might include baked apples with granola; omelets with tomatoes, green onions, and cheese; strawberry banana hot cakes with real maple syrup; plus locally made sausages, fresh orange juice, strong coffee, black or herbal teas, hot chocolate with whipped cream, sliced fruit with edible flowers, or pears poached in apple cider.

"Just as wonderful on a return visit. Sally and Sonny continue to improve their wonderful inn. Lucy's Room is small and quaint, with a double bed and balcony. The romantic Garden Room has a king-size canopy bed, and a private porch which opens to the garden. The Boat Cabin is on the river bank, so at night you are lulled to sleep by the sound of the water rushing by. This redwood cabin is built around a real boat, and has a kitchenette, so you can bring your own dinner makings and avoid the drive to Fort Bragg. The hot tub on the hill (along with the sauna and open-air showers) is unsurpassed. At breakfast, Sally seats people in groups to make for good table conversation." *(Barbara Ochiogrosso)*

"The ranch is tucked into a wooded valley along a section of pristine coastline. Wooded, gently rolling hills surround the property and the sound of the surf lulls guests to sleep at night; the fresh sea air mingles with lush forest scents. We stayed in the spotless, inviting two-level Redwood Suite, in the restored barn. The bedroom is on the upper level and over the king-size bed are large skylights, while to the west are high windows, which open to the sound and sight of the surf as it breaks on the beach. The woodstove keeps you warm in chilly weather, and the refrigerator and microwave are perfect for snacks. Sally and Sonny are always informative, helpful, and accommodating." *(Linda Lou Ellard)* "Lots of animals, from cats and llamas to cows and sheep to wild deer and elk." *(MW)* "The Beach House is a redwood cabin with charming decor and ocean views. It has a king-size bed, skylights, Jacuzzi, and more. Amazing breakfast with homemade blueberry muffins and soufflé. Sally went out of her way to make us feel welcome." *(Stephanie Sheedlo & Kelly Fuchino)* "The rooms are finished in redwood cut and milled on the property by the owner; Sonny is a craftsman and perfectionist. Superb breakfasts, whether you're eating fat-free or want to indulge." *(Larry Sample)* "Wonderful fresh flowers everywhere."*(Lavon Delp)* "Lace curtains, books, and homey accents create a relaxing, comfortable atmosphere." *(Linda Riley)*

Open All year.
Rooms 3 suites, 4 doubles, 3 cottages—all with full private bath. Some with radio, desk, deck, woodstove, wet bar, refrigerator, microwave, balcony, Jacuzzi, private entrance.
Facilities Parlor with fireplace, dining room, music room. 40 acres with gardens, hot tub, sauna, swimming pond, massage room; farm animals. 300 feet to ocean. Hiking, beachcombing, whale watching, horseback riding, deep-sea fishing, bicycling nearby.
Location North Coast. 3 m N of village. From Westport, look on right for a large state sign, "Vista Point/One Mile." Turn into the next driveway after sign (milepost 80.49)—gate is marked. From the N, 2½ m after reaching ocean, cross Howard Creek Bridge and take 1st driveway on left.
Restrictions Smoking restricted. Children by prior arrangement.
Credit cards Amex, MC, Visa.
Rates B&B, $55–145 suite, $55–115 double. Extra person, $15. 2-night minimum some weekends.
Extras Spanish, Italian, German spoken. Pets by arrangement.

WILLITS

Also recommended: If you're looking for an affordable alternative to high-priced coastal accommodations, or need a break when driving Highway 101, consider the **Baechtel Creek Inn** (101 Gregory Lane, Willits, 95490; 707–459–9063 or 800–459–9911), just off 101, 35 miles east of Fort Bragg via Route 20. "Jane and Robert Rodriguez run this attractive motel like a Swiss watch. Excellent housekeeping, hospitality; tasty continental breakfast." *(Frank Byrnes, also KLO)* The 46 guest rooms have private bath, TV, and telephone; B&B double rates are $65–105. Although the inn is just behind McDonald's and Taco Bell, it has an attractive swimming pool and a pleasant creekside location.

YOSEMITE

Yosemite's proximity to California's major cities make it one of the country's most popular national parks. Recent statistics indicate that well over 4 million visitors come to Yosemite annually, *with over 500,000 arriving in July alone.* January visitors number closer to 100,000, most of them day-trippers not competing for scarce beds at prime hotels. So, if you can, go off-season, and bring along snowshoes or cross-country skis, and explore the deserted trails in peace—and remember that Yosemite is far more congested than Yosemite Valley.

Reader tip: "Keep in mind that Yosemite is an extremely large park, and slow-moving traffic makes for sluggish travel. In September, it took us one hour to get from Fish Camp to Yosemite Village, and 2½ hours to reach Tuolumne Meadows at the park's eastern end. Overall, this is a difficult, crowded park to visit in season, with expensive, disappointing accommodations and food." *(Adam Platt)* "Although car travel in this park can be slow and frustrating, the scenery is unmatched. Park your car (come early to find a space), then take shuttles, ride bikes, and hike around the valley." *(JTD)*

Also recommended: Everyone knows the adage: the three most important rules about real estate are location, location, and location. The Ahwahnee proves that these rules apply equally to inns as well. Built in 1927, **The Ahwahnee** (Yosemite National Park, 95389; Yosemite Reservations, 5410 East Home Avenue, Fresno, 93727; 209–252–4848) is a massive seven-story structure with three wings, faced with native granite and concrete stained to look like redwood. The 123 guest rooms and common areas are decorated with Yosemite Indian motifs, including original craft and art work; A two-year, $1.5 million renovation of all common areas and guest rooms was completed in 1997; soft goods and furnishings have been replaced or restored. Immensely popular despite rates of $207–230 (no meals), summer and holiday reservations are recommended one year ahead. A regular contributor who visited on a nonholiday winter trip reports that the service was friendly but inexperienced, the housekeeping satisfactory, and the dining room experience such a lengthy ordeal that they resorted to room service as the only way to obtain adequate meals in a timely manner. Although her room in the main hotel was quiet, sound-proofing between the rooms in the cottage buildings is apparently inadequate. Nevertheless, despite inefficiency and other annoyances, she noted that "there's so much tradition, and the public rooms are so inspiring that we plan to return anyway." *(SD)* More comments welcome.

Information please: At the South Entrance to Yosemite, about 45 minutes south of Yosemite Valley is the **Wawona Hotel** (State Route 41, 95389; 209–252–4848), a classic Victorian hotel, with a double-storied balcony, ideal for relaxing after a day of hiking. Despite lovely sunset views from the hotel's restaurant, reports have been mixed: "The double rooms with private bath are attractively decorated and moderately priced." *(Adam Platt)* "The best place to stay in the southern part of the park. Breakfast was the best meal, with long serving hours, and tasty pancakes and waffles." *(Bob Freidus)* Less positively: "Our dingy room did not appear to have been updated since it was built. Noisy heating system; little soundproofing. Check-in was long and tedious, the meals worse." *(JB)* Double rates for the 104 rooms (50 with private bath) are $71–98. Reports please.

Information please: About 35 miles west of the western and southern entrances to Yosemite is the **Little Valley Inn** (3483 Brooks Road,

Mariposa 95338; 209–742–6204 or 800–889–5444) a contemporary guest house built in 1994, with one suite and two double rooms, each with a TV, clock/radio, air-conditioning, refrigerator, private entrance, and deck. B&B rates of $85–110 include a breakfast of fresh fruit, and juice, yogurt, cereal, bagels, and home-baked muffins, plus a free gold-panning lesson in the inn's creek. Innkeeper Kay Hewitt's house is adjacent to the inn.

For additional area inns, see **Fish Camp, Groveland,** and **Oakhurst.**

YOUNTVILLE

Yountville is located in the North Coast, Napa Valley Wine Country, 8 miles north of the town of Napa and 55 miles north of San Francisco off Route 29.

Vintage Inn–Napa Valley 🛏 ✕ 🐾 ♿   *Tel:* 707–944–1112
6541 Washington Street, 94599   800–351–1133
                                            Fax: 707–944–1617

Constructed in the 1970s by Kipp Stewart, designer of the Ventana Inn in Big Sur, the Vintage Inn is a cluster of small buildings, linked by walkways and a flowing fountain and stream meant to cool the air and camouflage traffic noises. Rooms have natural wood, handcrafted furnishings, and ivory and beige fabrics hand-painted in mauves, plums, and burgundies. Numerous specialty stores and fine restaurants are within walking distance; dozens of wineries are just a short bike ride or drive.

"The staff was helpful, patient, and courteous. The lovely lobby has a baby grand piano, plush sofas, huge fireplace, and wooden floors. Our immaculate room had a vaulted ceiling with fan and track lighting, fireplace with logs, king-size bed with accent pillows, French doors opening onto a balcony overlooking the vineyards, terry-cloth robes, and a complimentary bottle of the inn's wine. The delicious breakfast included fresh fruit, cheese, bagels, croissants, sweet rolls, muffins, egg salad, cereal, yogurt, coffee, tea, milk, fresh-squeezed orange juice, and champagne, all beautifully presented on silver serving pieces." *(Karen Gruska)* "Though the inn was full, privacy was maintained. The grounds were meticulously kept, reflecting the lushness of the valley." *(Barbara Hattem)* "Combines hotel convenience with inn charm." *(DD, also Hugh & Marjorie Smith)*

Open All year.
Rooms 80 doubles—all with full private bath, telephone, radio, TV, air-conditioning, fan, fireplace, refrigerator, coffee maker, porch or patio. Most with desk. 8 with wet bar. Rooms in clusters of 4 to 12 units; 4 rooms in individual villas.
Facilities Lobby with fireplace, piano, bar; conference rooms. 3 acres with fountain, gardens, heated swimming pool, hot tub, 2 tennis courts, biking, jogging trail, hot air balloon (weather permitting). Bicycle rentals. Concierge, room service. Golf and fitness facilities nearby.

Location In center of village, on Hwy. 29.
Restrictions Traffic noise in rooms near Hwy. 29. Guests may request inner court room locations to avoid highway noise. No smoking in most guest rooms.
Credit cards Amex, CB, DC, MC, Visa.
Rates B&B, $175–325 double. Extra person, $30. 10% senior discount. Mid-week packages off-season. 2-night weekend minimum Mar. 1–Nov. 30.
Extras Wheelchair access; 4 rooms equipped for the disabled. Pets permitted; $30 one-time charge. Crib, babysitting. Spanish spoken.

Free copy of INNroads newsletter

Want to stay up-to-date on our latest finds? Send a business-size, self-addressed, stamped envelope with 55 cents postage and we'll send you the latest issue, *free!* While you're at it, why not enclose a report on any inns you've recently visited? Use the forms at the back of the book or your own stationery.

The Shipman House B&B, Hilo, Hawaii (The Big Island)

In planning your Hawaii vacation, you may want to consider the "Seven Wonders of Hawaii," as compiled by readers of the *Honolulu Star-Bulletin:* Kilauea in Hawaii Volcanoes National Park and 420-foot Akaka Falls on the Hamakua Coast on the Big Island of Hawaii; the cliffs of the Na Pali Coast and Waimea Canyon on Kauai; the 10,000-foot-high Haleakala Crater on Maui; and Hanauma Bay, a marine preserve, and Diamond Head on Oahu. And remember, to leave crowds and stress behind, hike the trails and walk the beaches whenever you can.

Remember that each island has two weather zones: the leeward side, to the south and west, where the weather is sunny and dry; and the windward side, to the east and north, which is rainier but has the lush vegetation one associates with Hawaii. On the Big Island, for example, monthly precipitation is typically two inches on the leeward side, ten on the windward. Check the map and plan in accordance with your preferences.

Note: With the exception of the island of Hawaii, a restaurant license is required for B&Bs to serve a hot (or full) breakfast, so most serve expanded continental.

Homestay B&Bs have become quite popular throughout the islands, and are typically booked through a reservation service; rates are often very reasonable. **Hawaii's Best Bed & Breakfasts** (P.O. Box 563, Kamuela 96743; 808–885–4550; or in continental U.S., 800–262–9912) is the brainchild of Barbara Campbell. After years with one of the big resorts, Barbara has not only her own B&B cottage in Waimea near the Parker Ranch, but also represents many others throughout the islands.

Hawaiian tips: "As far as we can tell, a *lanai* (la-NIE) is used interchangeably in Hawaii to mean a balcony, porch, or deck." And: "Speaking of Hawaiian words, although there are only twelve letters in the

Hawaiian alphabet, it seems like thirteen of them are vowels. When trying to say a Hawaiian word, pronounce every vowel separately. Thus *Pu'upehe,* Sweetheart Rock, is said poo'-oo-peh'-heh. Got it?"

Entries are listed alphabetically, first by island, then by town.

HAWAII—THE BIG ISLAND

More than twice the size of any other Hawaiian island, The Big Island offers the greatest variety of scenery, with the drama of active volcanoes, stark lava flows, black sand beaches, and great hiking.

HILO, HAWAII

Hilo (pronounced Hee'-low) was the headquarters of King Kamehameha I, who used it as a base to conquer all the islands by 1810. It later became a center for Christian missionaries, sugar plantations, and a thriving port. Devastated by tsunamis in 1946 and 1960, the town slowly decayed until a restoration program began in 1985. Since then there's been a turnaround, with many of its historic buildings handsomely restored. Don't forget an umbrella—Hilo has 120 inches of warm rain annually, making for lush vegetation and lots of rainbows.

Information please: A modern home on the bluff facing the ocean, **Hale Kai** (111 Honolii Pali, 96720; 808–935–6330) has four guest rooms with water views and private baths. Guests can relax in the swimming pool, Jacuzzi, or patio, or take advantage of the common rooms. B&B double rates range from $85–105. Reports welcome.

Ten minutes from downtown Hilo is **The Inn at Kulaniapia** (P.O. Box 204, Kurtistown 96760; 808–966–6373), offering views of Hilo, the ocean, and Mauna Kea. The inn's 22 acres include orchards of macadamia nuts and tropical fruits, as well as several dramatic waterfalls. Built as a B&B, the inn's spacious rooms have private baths and balconies with views of the waterfall or ocean. B&B double rates of $136–165, include a breakfast of fresh fruits and just baked breads, and well-behaved children are welcome.

The Shipman House Bed & Breakfast	*Tel:* 808–934–8002
131 Ka'iulani Street, 96720	800–627–8447
	Fax: 808–935–1032
	E-mail: bighouse@bigisland.com

Hawaii has a rich and fascinating history, and at the Shipman House, you can learn about it first hand. The home of the Shipman family for 80 years, Barbara Shipman Anderson spent much of her childhood at this house, and is delighted to share her knowledge of area, with its fascinating anecdotes and legends. Jack London, author of *Call of the Wild* stayed here, as did Hawaii's last queen, Lili'uokalani, who enjoyed playing the grand piano in the parlor and enjoying a cigar with her friend, Mary Shipman.

Known locally as "The Castle," the 9,000-square-foot Shipman House was completed in 1900, and is one of the few remaining Victorian mansions in the state of Hawaii. This Queen Anne–style house features a striking three-story rounded tower with a conical roof, accented by a circular veranda, and four curved bay windows on both the first and second floors. Around 1930, the Shipmans installed Hilo's first residential elevator, still in use today. The house has been restored to its former elegance by the Shipman's great-granddaughter and her husband, Barbara Ann and Gary Andersen, who purchased it in 1994.

A breakfast buffet, served 7:30–9A.M. on the lanai, includes cereal, fresh local fruit and juice, Kona coffee, teas, yogurt, homemade fruit bread, muffins, or popovers, and pancakes, waffles, or French toast, and local sausage. Dietary Restrictions accommodated with notice. Rates also include afternoon lemonade, iced tea, and cookies on the enclosed lanai.

"The mansion sits prominently on a hill with a view of Hilo's harbor and is a short drive to famous Rainbow Falls and the Boiling Pots. Barbara's restoration combines historic authenticity with the Shipman tradition of gracious, unpretentious hospitality; she has used the original antique furnishings, carpets, and books. The first-floor guest room has antique koa twin beds with mosquito nets; upstairs are rooms with queen-size beds. Extensive tropical gardens, lawns, and palm trees surround the mansion and historic cottage. Barbara is a delightful hostess and is a wealth of information." *(Linda Goldberg)* "Antique koa furniture and Hawaiian-style print fabrics; beautiful dark-grained woods. Lovely ginger fragrance throughout the house. Guests can pick their own pineapples and harvest their own coffee. Beautiful location, yet an easy walk to town." *(Sasha Duerr)*

Open All year.

Rooms 5 doubles—all with full private bath, clock/radio, desk, refrigerator. 3 with ceiling fan. TV on request. 2 rooms in 1910 cottage; shared screened porch.

Facilities Double parlor with fireplace, piano; library with fireplace, books; screened porch, wraparound verandas. 5.5 acres with off-street parking, gardens, orchards, croquet.

Location 5 blocks from downtown. From Kona take Hwy 19 to Hilo. Turn left up Waianuenue Ave. (Hwy 200) at 1st light in Hilo. Go through 3 more lights; turn right at Ka'iulani St. Go 1 block, then cross wooden bridge onto Reed's Island & inn on left. From Hilo airport go right at light onto Hwy 11, then left at next light onto Hwy 19. When road splits after bridge, stay left. Go left at 2nd light after split onto Waianuenue Ave (Hwy 200). Follow directions above.

Restrictions No smoking. BYOB. Children over 15.

Credit cards Amex, MC, Visa.

Rates B&B, $140 double. Extra person, $25. 10% AAA discount. 2–3 night minimum some holidays/festivals.

Extras Some French spoken.

HOLUALOA, HAWAII

Information please: An elegant option in the mountains above Kailua-Kona is the **Holualoa Inn** (P.O. Box 222-A, Holualoa 96725; 808–324–1121 or 800–392–1812), a B&B inn on a private estate overlooking the Kona Coast. Set among pastures and coffee groves, the inn's four guest rooms each have a private bath; the decor includes contemporary Scandinavian furnishings highlighted by Hawaiian and Indonesian art. Built of imported cedar in 1979, the inn overlooks the swimming pool and the ocean 1,200 feet below. B&B double rates range from $100–160.

HONOKAA, HAWAII

At the northern section of the Hamakua Coast is Honokaa, once a major center for sugar plantations and cattle ranching. Sights of interest include hiking in the Waipio Valley with its waterfalls and its black sand beach, the wonderful trails through the ohia forest in Kalopa State Park, and Akaka Falls State Park, ten miles north.

Also recommended: Close to Kalopa State Park is the **Kalopa Homestead Guest House** (P.O. Box 1614, Honokaa, 96727; 808–775–7167) with ocean views through the eucalyptus trees, a fully equipped two-bedroom cottage. Miles and Colette Hirata, the owners, raise goats and make their own goat milk soap in natural floral scents. A continental breakfast with farm fresh eggs is served. The rate for two people is $95, four people $125, with discounts for longer stays. Fresh pineapple, papaya, and just-laid eggs are provided for breakfast along with homemade taro bread, mango bread, guava marmalade, and locally grown coffee. "We awoke each morning to the sounds of bird songs and the smell of homemade baked breads. We loved the privacy and convenience of our charming cottage, complete with a kitchen, whirlpool tub, and washer/dryer." *(Debbie Nelson)*

The **Waipio Wayside B&B** (Highway 240, P.O. Box 840, 96727; 808–775–0275 or 800–833–8849) was built in 1938 as a sugar cane plantation home, and is owned by Jackie Horne. Furnished in old Hawaiian motifs with antiques, Chinese rugs, and rattan and wicker furnishings, the B&B has five guest rooms, at B&B rates of $70–110. "An attractive green-and-white house on the ocean side of the road, surrounded by trees and a white picket fence. Jackie was very helpful in suggesting activities and recommending local restaurants; she has two friendly cats. Fantastic breakfast of a fruit smoothie, crisp bacon, waffles, pesto eggs with organic tomatoes, fresh strawberries and pineapple, with freshly ground Kona coffee or a wide variety of tea. Clean, comfortable guest rooms with knotty pine walls and Oriental rugs. The large deck and gazebo, hammocks and chairs overlooking the surrounding trees and the ocean were great places to relax." *(Linda Goldberg)*

KAILUA-KONA, HAWAII

Also recommended: About 15 miles north of Kailua-Kona via Highway 19 is the well-known **Kona Village Resort** (P.O. Box 1299, Kaupulehu-Kona 96745; 808–325–5555 or 800–367–5290) built on the site of the ancient Hawaiian village of Kaupulehu. In 1801, when Mt. Hualalai erupted, this cove was the only one spared the massive lava flows that devastated the area. The village's 125 thatched *hales* (Polynesian-style bungalows) have been built among the actual stone platforms of the ancient Hawaiians, and are located around the lagoon, along the beach, and in a lava field along the ocean. Many have been recently renovated, and some have a private hot tub. Although its not for everyone (no TV, no AC), many feel that Kona Village Resort is still the best Polynesian resort on the island, and one of the finest tropical resorts in the world. Popular with both couples (excepting school vacations) and families alike, activities include pool and ocean swimming, tennis, snorkeling, sunfish sailing, canoeing, boat excursions, children's program, and a new fitness center. All this does not come cheap; all-inclusive double rates range from $425–710, plus 15% service. "I was warmly greeted, given a flower lei, rum punch or pineapple juice, and then driven on a golf cart to my thatched-roof Lava Tahitian hale, set on stilts overlooking a black pebble and rock lava beach. Open-air laundry rooms with complimentary washers, dryers, and laundry soap were greatly appreciated. The food was outstanding, chosen from a menu at breakfast and dinner, with a buffet set out at lunch—creative, imaginative, and delicious. I toured a renovated hale, and would highly recommend requesting one." *(Linda Goldberg)* Just down the beach from Kona Village is the **Four Seasons Resort Hualalai at Historic Ka'upulehu** (P.O. Box 1269, 96740; 808–325–8000 or 800–340–5662), just opened in 1996. This luxury hotel has 243 guest rooms and suites in 36 contemporary two-story Hawaiian-style villas with beautifully landscaped grounds and lush tropical gardens. Facilities include the swimming pools, and a lagoon for snorkling lessons, an 18-hole golf course, lighted tennis courts, a sports club and spa, shops, a Hawaiian Interpretative Center, an aquarium, and a Hawaiian art collection. "Excellent local, Asian, and Western dishes are served at the Pahuia beachside restaurant. Spacious guest rooms with all modern conveniences and amenities." *(LG)* Paradise doesn't come cheap: double rooms are $450–650, suites $750–3000 (meals extra).

Also recommended: The **Kailua Plantation House** (75–5948 Alii Drive, 96740; 808–329–3727), offers superb ocean views and relaxing accommodations. Built as a B&B, it faces the Pacific from atop a promontory of black rocks formed by ancient lava flows. Most rooms have tiled floors and sliding glass doors that lead out to balconies; furnishings are spare but elegant, mostly bamboo with soft Hawaiian print fabrics. Double rates for the five guest rooms range from $145–205, including a breakfast of breads, muffins, Hawaiian fruits, Kona coffee, tea, and juice, plus a hot entree such as Belgian waffles, French toast, or quiche, served from 7:30–9:30 A.M. "Beautiful setting, delicious breakfast. We watched dolphins playing in the surf, 100 yards from the lanai. Our comfortable room had a great bed and was well equipped with such extras as beach towels, a thermos, and coolers. Innkeeper Danielle Berger is the owners' daughter and is both charming and helpful." *(Mike & Cindy Wilkinson)*

Information please: In a peaceful setting ten minutes from Kailua Village is **Hale Maluhia B&B** (76-770 Hualalai Road, 96740; 808–329–5773 or 800–559–6627). This rambling shingled home was built on old coffee plantation land at an elevation of 900 feet. The interior combines open-beamed ceilings and natural woods with Hawaiian and Victorian furnishings. Breakfast is served on the lanai, and double rates for the four guest rooms are $75–110; the cottage is $145. "Laid-back atmosphere; warm, hospitable owners Ken and Ann Smith provided plush beach towels, snorkeling gear, underwater cameras, and detailed directions to Turtle Beach, where we swam with colorful tropical fish and huge sea turtles. Lavish buffet breakfast of tropical juices and fruit, plus scrumptious strawberry crepes. Our room was spacious and comfortable with simple Hawaiian furnishings." *(Gail Davis)*

KEALAKEKUA, HAWAII

Also recommended: Eighteen miles south of the Kailua-Kona airport is the **Kealakekua Bay B&B** (c/o Hawaii's Best B&Bs, P.O. Box 563, Kamuela, 96743; 808–885–4550 or 800–262–9912). This five-acre tropical estate consists of a luxurious two-story Mediterranean-style villa with three guest rooms, plus a two-bedroom cottage. "Overlooking Kealakekua Bay and the lush tropical gardens, the Ali'i Suite was decorated with warm colors of green and terra-cotta, with beamed ceilings, a ceiling fan above the king-size bed, a large walk-in closet, stereo system with CD player, and a two-person Jacuzzi tub in the bathroom. Delicious breakfast served on the upper dining lanai: mango smoothies, fresh pineapple, papaya with lime, homemade banana bread, cereal, and yogurt." *(Linda Goldberg)* B&B rates are $95–175. It's a three minute walk to snorkling at Kealakekua Bay; two other beaches are within walking distance.

Information please: Set among acres of tropical flowers and palm trees, the **Rainbow Plantation** (816327B Mamalahoa Highway, Kealakekua; mailing address, P.O. Box 122, Captain Cook 96704; 808–323–2393 or 800–494–2829) is located 17 miles south of the Kailua-Kona airport, between Kealakekua and Captain Cook, on Highway 11. This working macadamia nut and coffee plantation has been owned by Marianna and Reiner Schrepfer since 1982, and opened as a B&B in 1995. The four guest rooms, two located in main house, have private baths, clock/radio, TV, fan, and refrigerator; B&B double rates range from $65–85, and well-behaved children are welcome. One guest room is in a restored cabin cruiser on the lawn; another occupies a renovated water storage building. "Set well back from the road, the two-story main house is surrounded by tropical gardens and a small fish pond. Breakfast is served on the upstairs ocean-view terrace, and includes their own Kona coffee, plus home-grown organic fruit, and banana bread, croissants, or apple pancakes. Charming atmosphere." *(LG)* It's a short drive Kealakekua Bay, a marine sanctuary and snorkeling paradise, and gear is provided free to guests.

VOLCANO, HAWAII

Try to spend a couple of days exploring Hawaii Volcanoes National Park, one of only two national parks devoted to active volcanoes; the park is bigger than the island of Oahu, so allow ample time. The summit areas are in a sub-alpine tropical rain forest zone, with about 125 inches of rain annually, making for lush green forests. At an elevation over 3,500 feet, the weather is typically cool and rainy, so come prepared with warm, comfortable clothes, sturdy hiking shoes (an extra pair is good when the first pair gets wet), and rain gear; binoculars are recommended for birdwatching. Stop at the visitors' center for details on the drives around the Kilauea caldera or down the Chain of Craters road, and maps for the many exciting hiking trails; heli-tours are also a thrilling option. Area restaurants options are extremely limited, so ask your innkeeper about advance reservations. The park is about 25 miles southwest of Hilo on the "Big Island" of Hawaii.

Reader tips: "Cold, wet, and rainy throughout our visit. The wood and paper were too wet to light for a fire; our towels never dried. Bring warm clothes and ask if your room is heated!" *(MW)* "Kilauea is a very active volcano; ask a park ranger for safety advice and follow it!" *(WT)* "Visit the National Park Headquarters across the street from Volcano House. Check out the caldera view, enjoy the park, but eat and sleep at one of the B&Bs down the road." *(MR)*

Also recommended: If proximity to the Kilauea caldera is your paramount concern, make advance reservations for a crater-view room at the **Volcano House** (Box 53, Hawaii Volcanoes National Park, 96718; 808–967–7321). When Mark Twain stayed at the Volcano House in 1866, the building was made of grass and ohia poles; he thought the $5 nightly charge for room and board was a fair deal. Guests have been coming ever since, although the main building of today's Volcano House was built in 1941, with a wing added in 1963. The 42 guest rooms have standard hotel layouts; all were refurbished with handsome Koa wood furnishings and Hawaiian fabric comforters in 1991. Rates are $80–110 for nonview rooms; $135 for crater-view rooms. Be aware that the lobby and restaurant can be busy with tour groups; guest rooms facing the parking lot can be noisy with car and bus traffic. "The main lounge with its large stone fireplace—burning continuously since 1866—was a nice place to warm up. Awesome crater views from some rooms." *(Linda Goldberg)* "Only the view is impressive." *(MR)*

Chalet Kilauea—The Inn at Volcano ¢
Wright Road, Box 998, 96785

Tel: 808–967–7786
800–937–7786
Fax: 808–967–8660
E-mail: bchawaii@aol.com

The Chalet Kilauea has been owned by world travelers Lisha and Brian Crawford since 1990. The Crawfords have worked hard to make their inn a romantic, luxurious getaway, and are constantly improving it with such luxuries as marble baths with Jacuzzi tubs, and in-room fireplaces. Rates include a full breakfast, afternoon tea, fresh flowers, and bedtime chocolates. For those who prefer greater independence, privacy, or are traveling with families, a range of vacation homes are also available, from a cozy cottage to a six-bedroom house.

"Quiet, serene green forested setting, with exceptional landscaping. The luxurious TreeHouse Suite has a private entrance off the upstairs deck. Inside is a well-equipped kitchenette with a table and chairs; a spiral staircase leads to the cozy wood-paneled bedroom with its comfortable king-size bed and picture windows looking out over the treetops. The fantasy bathroom downstairs is done in soft green Italian marble, and has a fireplace, TV, double Jacuzzi tub, and separate shower. A door from the bathroom leads to a private covered deck surrounded by the fern forest. I was able to see the other rooms, and all are lovely, with fully remodeled marble baths, and decor ranging from the delicate pink-and-white Continental Lace suite to the rich earth tones of the Out of Africa suite. Breakfast is served on fine china and linen, and accompanied by classical music in the Art Deco–style dining room; both tables for two and larger tables are available. We started with fresh peaches topped with a mixture of whipped cream, sour cream, and yogurt; a juice combination of papaya, orange, and guava; followed by a delicious croute fromage—layered bread and cheese—with sliced tomato and chives." *(Linda Goldberg)* "Luxury plus warm hospitality. In the afternoon we enjoyed tea by the fireplace, listening to soft music." *(Francis McCabe)* "Tropical flowers scent the air. Highlights include the friendly greeting from their dog and cat; breakfasts with homemade Ohelo berry sauce; sipping Kona coffee liqueur in front of the fireplace; sharing a bottle of wine while watching the lava flow at night in the park, then returning for a late-night soak in the outdoor hot tub; then off to bed with chocolates waiting on our pillows." *(Michelle Robinson)* "Lush setting, careful attention to detail. Brian and Lisha Crawford are widely travelled, and have furnished their home with ebony sculptures from Africa, Art Deco from Northern Europe, and more. I lounged in the Jacuzzi, browsed through the extensive library, and dozed contentedly by the open fire." *(Saul Rollason)*

Open All year.
Rooms 6 vacation homes, 3 suites, 3 doubles—all with private bath and/or shower, robes, TV/VCR, private entrance. Some with double whirlpool tubs, telephone, stereo, fan, gas fireplace, refrigerator, deck. Suites with refrigerator, microwave, coffee maker.
Facilities Dining room, living room with fireplace, library, stereo, games. Gift

shop, cafe, deck, hot tub, laundry facility. Hiking, bicycling, golf, swimming, bird watching.

Location In village. From Rte. 11 turn on Wright Rd. (Rte. 148). Go ¾ m to Chalet Kilauea sign on right.

Restrictions No smoking. No shoes in house. Children welcome in vacation homes.

Credit cards Discover, MC, Visa.

Rates B&B, $195–395 suite, $135–175 double. $125–225 vacation homes. Extra person, $15. Honeymoon packages.

Extras French, Dutch, Spanish, Portuguese spoken.

Hale Ohia Cottages ¢ ♦ ⅍
Highway 11, P.O. Box 758, 96785

Tel: 808–967–7986
800–455–3803
Fax: 808–967–8610
E-mail: haleohia@bigisland.com

The historic Dillingham summer estate, Hale Ohia was built in 1931, and includes the main residence and several cottages. The gardens were developed over 30 years by a resident Japanese gardener; the natural volcanic terrain was gently groomed into a beautiful botanical garden.

"Beautiful landscaping around the main house and cottages, tucked back among many trees and beautiful flowers. Owner Michael Tuttle went out of his way to advise us on what to see and do; he takes pride in everything he does. Attractive, comfortable accommodations. Beautifully prepared continental breakfast. Great for couples or families." *(Brenda Stanko)* "Loved our rustic cottage, comfortable and mercifully free of lace and clutter." *(MW)*

Open All year.

Rooms 5 cottages, 3 suites—all with private bath and/or shower, lanai. 2 with fireplace, 2 with kitchenette.

Facilities 3 acres with gardens, gazebo, Japanese soaking tub.

Location 26 m from Hilo, 11 m from Volcano Village, 1 m from HI Volcanoes Nat'l. Park. From Hilo, take Hwy. 11 to Volcano. After passing Rte. 148 on right, watch for driveway for Hale Ohia on left.

Credit cards MC, Visa.

Rates B&B, $85–115 cottage, $75–95 double. Extra person, $15. Weekly rates.

Extras Wheelchair access.

Kilauea Lodge ♦ ✕ ⅍
P.O.Box 116, 96785
Email: k-lodge@aloha.net

Tel: 808–967–7366
Fax: 808–967–7367

Hawaii may not be the first place that comes to mind when "mountain country inns" are mentioned, but that's just what Kilauea Lodge is. Built in 1938 as a YMCA lodge, it was converted into an inn in 1987 by Albert and Lorna Jeyte. Lorna notes that "I was raised on the Big Island, and have decorated our inn with original Hawaiian art and furnishings made from local woods. Our menu combines local specialities with dishes reflecting Albert's European background." The inviting guest rooms are country comfortable with patchwork quilts, and breakfast is a hearty meal of bacon and eggs to order, pancakes, or Hawaiian-style French toast with fresh fruit.

"Our serene room featured a king-sized bed, a wood-beamed cathedral ceiling, and garden views. The inviting dining room is decorated with eye-catching local artwork and an imposing stone fireplace. Chef Albert accommodated our strict vegetarian diet with a special entree, and the staff served us breakfast before our early morning flight." *(Gail Davis)* "Blissfully quiet location, with wonderfully starry skies at night. Friendly but unobtrusive service, plus lots of pet dogs, cats, and birds." *(Jennifer Baker)* "Charming setting among tree ferns and cypress. Rooms are immaculate, with flowers and Hawaiian prints. Accommodating innkeepers; gentle, gracious staff." *(Carol Lied)*

"The common room has books and videotapes about Hawaii, comfortable seating, and a fireplace to take off the chill. Birds sang outside our window; a couch was placed in front of the fireplace, which needed only a match to light. Our room also had a comfortable king-size bed, and a double-headed shower." *(Pam Thatcher)* "Convenient parking, excellent restaurant, friendly helpful staff; insider books and area information in our room; pottery and pictures enhanced the decor of our spacious room. The fireplace was replenished daily, and the bathroom towels were heated by a warmer." *(George Vorhauer)* "Comfortable, spacious guest rooms; one of the best restaurants on the island." *(Joseph Lacey)* "Great tasting, creative dinner menu." *(Michelle Robinson)* "Heartily endorse existing entry." *(Allan & Judy Rachap)*

Open All year.
Rooms 3 cottages, 11 doubles—all with private bath and/or shower, clock. Some with fireplace, desk, balcony. Rooms in several buildings.
Facilities Restaurant with bar, books, fireplace; common area with games, books, fireplace. 10 acres with off-street parking, croquet, hiking trails.
Location From Hwy 11 S, exit at Wright Road & bear left on Old Volcano Hwy. to lodge on right. From Hwy 11 N, bear left after Visitors' Center to village. Approx. 1 m from park entrance.
Restrictions No smoking.
Credit cards Amex, MC, Visa.
Rates B&B, $95–135 cottage, $105–115 double, $95–105 single. Extra person, $15. No charge for children under 2. Tips welcome. Alc dinner $35.
Extras Wheelchair access. Cribs, babysitting. German, Spanish spoken.

My Island B&B ¢ **ħ**
P.O. Box 100, 96785

Tel: 808–967–7216
Fax: 808–967–7719
E-mail: myisland@ilhawaii.net

Built around 1886 by the Lyman missionary family, My Island B&B is the oldest house in the Volcano community. Originally a two-story building, it was later raised so that the existing living room and kitchen could be built underneath. The Lyman family lived here until 1941; the house was then used for storage until it was acquired by the Gordon and Joann Morse family in 1972. Rooms are furnished with Koa wood furniture, handcrafted quilts from Maine, and Joann's paintings; the guest rooms have no closets, the Morses note, because during the 1800s there was no need; people had so few clothes that a few hooks would suffice.

"This eclectic old missionary's house has almost as much character and history as its hosts—Joann, a local artist, and Gordon, a great storyteller who was born on Molokai. Ceilings are low, some floors are slightly slanted, and the fireplace has a fire going continuously, adding to the inviting "back in time feeling." Guests gather around the big dining room table for breakfast, and share their experiences. Gordon and Joann pride themselves on having different hot breakfast selections each morning, including waffles and French toast, as well as papaya, guava juice, and coffee (ready at 7 A.M. for early risers). Thanks to Gordon's suggestion, a real highlight (literally) for us included a hike at dusk to view the bubbling lava erupting into the ocean at the end of the Chain of Craters Road. Gordon provided us with a special map and flashlights that made the hike back after dark safe and easy." *(Jill Reeves)*

"Excellent breakfasts, beautifully landscaped grounds. Nice company, many international guests. Printed handouts of day trips and local hikes were exceptionally helpful." *(David Bindman)* "Helpful and friendly hosts; extended library of Hawaiiana; wonderful breakfasts with fresh papaya, pineapple, and macadamia nuts; tropical flower gardens; conveniently located near National Park entrance." *(Cathy Joslyn)*

Open All year.
Rooms 3 vacation homes, 3 apartments with private entrances, private baths, kitchen, TV; 3 doubles—4 with private bath, 2 with maximum of 4 sharing bath.
Facilities Dining room, living room with TV, library. Gardens.
Location In Village. From Hwy 11, turn onto Wright Rd., (Rte. 148). Take 1st right to inn on left.
Credit cards None accepted.
Rates Room only, $125 vacation house. B&B, $65–80 double, $40–65 single. Extra adult, $20; child 3–16, $15; under 3, $5.

WAIMEA/KAMUELA , HAWAII

Reader tip: "An excellent base for touring the northern half of the island, Waimea is a charming pastoral ranch community in the foothills of the Kohala Mountains. It's just eight miles east of the beautiful Kona and Kohala beaches, such as Mauna Kea or Hapuna, and 13 miles west of the scenic Hamakua coast and the Waipio Valley. Mauna Kea is more suitable for swimming and snorkeling, while Hapuna, with its big waves, and softer, whiter sand, is more suited to body surfing. I found myself strolling along Mauna Kea Beach within 20 minutes after leaving Waimea (limited beach parking; arrive early, especially on weekends). Waimea is a charming country town, with Western-style shopping centers, art galleries, and excellent restaurants, surrounded by the rolling hills of the Kohala Mountains, and the Parker Ranch with its grazing cattle and horses. With an elevation of 2,500 feet, the air is cooler and crisper, making it pleasant during the day and more comfortable to sleep at night." *(Linda Goldberg)*

Worth noting: Kamuela is the official name of the post office, but the town is Waimea. Brochures tend to have Kamuela on them, so it's confusing.

Also recommended: If you prefer a well-run motel, a good choice is the **Waimea Country Lodge** (P.O. Box 458, Kamuela 96743; 808–885–4100). The 21 rooms of this motel (5 with kitchenette) have two queens, doubles, or a king-size bed, rent for $80–100 double, and look out to the hills. Rooms in the single story building have vaulted ceilings. Josh and Janice Akana are the longtime managers; the motel is owned by Parker Ranch, and is operated by Hawaiian Pacific resorts.

For an excellent experience, contact Barbara Campbell at the **Waimea Gardens Cottage** (P.O. Box 563, Kamuela 96743; 808–885–4550 or 800–262–9912). "Two charming cottages just two miles from Waimea. The streamside Kohala Wing has a double swing on the tree outside the cottage, and a delightful flower garden. French doors lead out to a private brick deck. The sitting room had window seats and a small desk. The well-equipped country kitchen was fully supplied with breakfast makings, including just-laid eggs, and overlooked the stream and rolling hills. The bedroom had a queen-size bed with a pretty blue flowered comforter and fluffy pillows, a love seat, a TV and stereo, and a neatly set table and two chairs. The many little extras included an antique coffee grinder, afghan, umbrella, sewing kit, ironing board and iron, board games and books, telephone, clock/radio, fruit bowl, cottonballs and Q-tips, and more. The other cottage is equally appealing." *(Linda Goldberg)* The B&B rate is $110–125. For information on Barbara's B&B reservation service, Hawaii's Best B&Bs, see the chapter introduction.

KAUAI

Although hardly undiscovered (it's third among total visitors), Kauai has maintained its relaxed island pace despite increased traffic. Visitors will especially enjoy its challenging golf courses and spectacular scenery. Tropical vegetation doesn't last long without ample rain, so try the Poipu area for the best chances for sun.

Reader tips: "A drive to the north shore is a must, as it is the most picturesque and peaceful part of the island, with many beautiful white-sand beaches, high cliffs, lush foliage, and natural, rugged beauty. This side is the least crowded, with less traffic and many tiny villages. There are many interesting things to do on Kauai, other than lounge on the beach. Try a drive to Waimea Canyon, where you can also hike, or a helicopter tour, or an exciting boat trip to view the humpback whales and the impressive Na Pali cliffs." *(Linda Goldberg)* And: "Kauai's red earth stains shoes, clothes, carpets, and more. Many B&Bs ask that you leave your shoes outside, and provide slippers." *(JR)*

KAPAA, KAUAI

Information please: High above the lush Wailua River Valley near Opaekaa Falls on the east side of Kauai is **Mohala Ke Ola B&B Retreat** (5663 Ohelo Road 96746; 808–823–6398 or 888–GO–KAUAI) which means "shining with life." Rejuvenate yourself with a hike in the mountains, a swim in the pool, or relax in the Jacuzzi; acupuncture, shiatsu, and lomi-lomi are also available from owner Ed Stumpf. The four guest rooms have private baths, and the B&B double rates are $65–95.

KILAUEA, KAUAI

Information please: On Kauai's famous north shore is the **Hale Ho'o Maha** (P.O. Box 422, 96754; 808–828–1341 or 800–851–0291). Meaning "House of Rest," this split-level home is set on a cliff overlooking five acres of landscaped grounds. Breakfast features homemade granola with macadamia nuts, tropical fruits, juices, Kona coffee and tea. Within a 15-minute walk of two white sand beaches, this B&B is also minutes away from two world-class golf courses, shops, and restaurants. B&B rates for the four guest rooms range from $55–80 double. Comments welcome.

KOLOA/POIPU, KAUAI

Information please: Listed in many past editions, we'd appreciate reports on the **Poipu Bed & Breakfast Inn** (2720 Hoonani Road, Poipu Beach 96756; 808–742–1146 or 800–22–POIPU), a restored 1933 plantation house with four guest rooms. Under the same management is the nearby Oceanfront Inn; its five units have king-size beds, double whirlpool baths, and kitchenettes with microwave. B&B rates range of $125–185. Breakfast includes mangoes, papayas, pomegranates, and other edibles grown in the yard, plus cereal, breads, and pastries; rates also include afternoon tea. Snorkel and scuba access is right across the small road; it's a short walk to Poipu Beach.

For an additional area inn, see the next entry in **Lawai**.

Gloria's Spouting Horn B&B   *Tel:* 808–742–6995
4464 Lawai Beach Road, 96756   *Fax:* 808–742–6995

Extensive renovation is a normal part of innkeeping, but at Gloria's Spouting Horn B&B, Mother Nature took charge of the job; in 1992,

Hurricane Iniki swept Bob and Gloria Merkle's home out to sea. Plans to rebuild better than ever were drawn up, and sixteen months later, this custom-built cedar home was completed, securely anchored by deep pilings. Balconies stretch along the first and second floors of the house, overlooking the beach below and the ocean beyond. The three ocean-view rooms have queen-size beds; one has a dramatic curved willow branch canopy queen bed. Each room has a wet bar with a refrigerator stocked with cold drinks, lots of shuttered windows, and a balcony with spectacular coastal views. Bathrooms have deep soaking tubs, separate shower and dressing areas, and ample closet space. Breakfast, served 7–9 A.M., might include fresh tropical fruits, orange-guava juice, macadamia nut or raspberry-chocolate Kona coffee, and such entrees peach French toast with warm peach syrup, seafood frittata with salsa and bran muffins, spinach souffle with coffee cake, and perhaps home-baked crusty Cuban or Irish soda bread. Rates also include evening liqueurs and snacks

"Superb physical facilities, with large, private bedrooms which front directly on the Pacific. I'd bet there are cruise ship cabins further from the water than our room. Friendly gracious hospitality; fabulous breakfasts. Just as great on a return visit, too." *(Allan & Judy Rachap)* "We appreciated the option of having breakfast either in the living room or in our beautiful bedroom." *(Jerry & Judy McGrath)* "Married on the beach by Bob, Gloria's was the perfect honeymoon retreat. Convenient mini-kitchen in each room." *(R.J. Thiessen)* "Bob welcomed us to breakfast playing beautiful Hawaiian music on the guitar. We watched whales while feasting on walnut French toast with maple syrup and whipped cream. Helpful, charming innkeepers." *(Nancy & Mark Donatelli)* "An elegant and intimate seaside retreat combining Gloria's mouthwatering breakfasts with Bob's classical guitar serenades." *(Barbara & Jim Oilar)* "We woke to the sound of the surf crashing on the rocks below, and the sun streaming into our room. From our balcony we watched sea turtles graze. Rich Kauai coffee." *(Craig Swanson)* "Wonderful location—beautiful views, quiet and serene. Superb snorkeling and great restaurants nearby." *(Nancy Fengold)* "Our refrigerator was stocked with juice and chocolate macadamia nuts. Thoughtful extras included beach chairs and a cooler for day trips. An extensive collection of books, videos, and local guide books as well as snacks and liqueurs were readily available." *(Theresa Brink)*

Open All year.
Rooms 2 suites, 1 double—all with full private bath, telephone, ceiling fan, clock/radio, TV/VCR, desk, fan, wet bar with refrigerator, microwave, coffee maker; balcony.
Facilities Dining room, living room, library with books, lounge, guest kitchen, balcony. Occasional classical guitar music. ¼ acre on ocean; off-street parking, koi ponds.
Location Poipu Beach, 3 m from Koloa. From Lihue Airport, follow Hwy. 50 W to Koloa-Poipu turnoff at Hwy. 520 (Tree Tunnel) Go left (S) & continue to Koloa. Turn right at Kolua Rd. Go left at Poipu Rd. At "Welcome to Poipu" sign, take right fork on Lawai Rd. and proceed 1.5 miles to inn.
Restrictions No smoking. Children over 14.

Credit cards None accepted.
Rates B&B, $175–200 suite; $170–185 double. Extra person, $25; three-night minimum.

LAWAI, KAUAI

Victoria Place ¢ &.   *Tel:* 808–332–9300
3459 Lawai Loa Lane, P.O. Box 930, 96765   *Fax:* 808–332–9465

Edee Seymour is a Michigan native who adopted Kauai as a personal paradise, and enjoys sharing its beauty with her guests. Victoria Place is set high in lush hills, overlooking dense jungle, cane fields, and the Pacific. Three of the guest rooms have glass doors that open directly onto a swimming pool surrounded by flowers. Rates include a breakfast of Hawaiian coffee, homemade breads and muffins, and fresh fruit, usually served at poolside.

"You enter the house, set in a cul-de-sac in a small village, through a gate that leads you into a swimming pool area surrounded by flowering bushes and trees. Edee, a wonderful hostess with a great sense of humor, mixed with a dose of Norwegian good taste and practicality, provides guests with every amenity an eager visitor might need. Some appealing touches include the veranda with a great view—a reflective place for a delicious breakfast with local papayas and pineapples, an old-fashioned popcorn machine ready for guests' use, a rack of snorkeling gear, extra towels, and even extra shoes for guests to use when hiking, because of the intensely staining red soil. Our room was clean, comfortable, and tastefully decorated. Edee treats her guests well; she has a strong commitment to promoting the beauty of Kauai." *(Jill Reeves)* "Peaceful setting, immaculately clean, tasty breakfasts. The charming innkeeper offers helpful suggestions and provides everything from maps to snorkeling equipment." *(Lisa Grebo)*

Open All year.
Rooms 1 apt., 3 doubles—all with private bath and/or shower. Cottage with kitchen, laundry.
Facilities Living room with TV, books; balcony, deck, guest refrigerator/microwave. Swimming pool, garden with fountain. Beaches, golf, tennis nearby.
Location S Kauai, 2 min. from Hwy. 50. 20 min. from Lihue; 10 min. NW of Poipu. From Lihue airport, go straight through light to 2nd light & turn left. At next light, turn right on Hwy 50. Take Hwy 50 past Junction 520, approx. 10½ m from Lihue. Continue 3½ m to Junction 530 (Koloa Rd.). Turn left & continue for 1.2 m. Look for green & white striped pole on left across from Lanai Loa Lane. On right is bus stop sign and dead end sign, marking Lawai Loa Lane. Turn right & go to #3459. At night, watch for Lawai Loa between 2nd & 3rd street lights after 1 mile marker on Koloa Rd.
Restrictions No smoking. Children over 14.
Credit cards None accepted.
Rates B&B, $95–105 apt., $65–85 double, $55–65 single. Extra person, $10. $10 additional 1-night stay.
Extras Wheelchair access; 1 bathroom specially equipped.

PRINCEVILLE, KAUAI

Also recommended: Noted for its extraordinary setting and lushly landscaped grounds and cascading waterfalls is the **Hanalei Bay Resort and Suites** (5380 Honoiki Road, 96722; 808–826–6522 or 800–367–5004). Extensively renovated in 1995 after Hurricane Iniki, the hotel has 280 well-equipped guest rooms and suites, spread over 16 separate buildings; facilities include eight tennis courts and two swimming pools. Guest rooms and studios range from $150–240, with 1-3 bedroom suites from $275–500 suite, with many package rates available. "An exceptional setting, beautifully landscaped, amazing views, wonderful swimming lagoon, comfortably furnished rooms." *(Linda Goldberg)* "Although our room was one of the less expensive ones, it was large, well equipped, and clean. We made our own breakfast (utensils provided) and ate on our own lanai, with views of the mountains, pool, and gardens. Although popular with tour groups, we didn't see them or feel their presence." *(Michael & Dina Miller)*

Hale 'Aha B&B   *Tel:* 808–826–6733
P.O. Box 3370, 96722   800–826–6733
Fax: 808–826–9052
E-mail: kauai@pixi.com

"Princeville is a planned recreational community on the north coast of Kauai, consisting of championship golf courses, many beautiful condominium projects, exclusive homes, and the Hanalei Bay Resort. A 20-minute scenic drive will take you to the start of the Na Pali hiking trails, and some of the most beautiful beaches on the island are just a short car ride away. "Hale 'Aha, meaning 'house of gathering,' was built as a B&B in 1990 and is lovingly maintained by owners Herb and Ruth Bockelman. The house overlooks the golf course, with distant sea and mountain views. The decor is soothing, in shades of peach, blue, and beige, with houseplants and flowers. The 1,000-square-foot penthouse suite has open-beamed ceilings, and a deck with panoramic views of Bali Hai and the Kilauea lighthouse." *(Linda Goldberg)*

"I felt comfortable enough to stretch out on the couch with one of their delightful books on Kauai. We stayed in the least expensive room with a mountain view; it was sizable with a large closet and bathroom, and separate entrance. We enjoyed talking with Herb and Ruth each morning after breakfast. They are knowledgeable about the island's many attractions and helped us plan our activities." *(John Dearborn)*

"Spectacular drive to the inn, past the Hanalei Valley lookout, famed Lumahai Beach where South Pacific was filmed, the one-way bridges, the quaint green church in the town of Hanalei, the dry and wet caves, the State Park, streams, and craggy mountain peaks. The beautifully decorated honeymoon suite is comfortable, peaceful, and homey, with a well-equipped kitchenette, and a private entry leading to a deck overlooking the golf course. The bedroom has a king-size bed; the bathroom is done in pale peach tiles and has a large Jacuzzi tub and separate shower. The Penthouse Suite is even more special, but all the rooms are lovely. Breakfast was served at the dining room table, and included poppy seed muffins with guava butter, blueberry coffee cake, and steamed brown rice and raisins, topped with fresh pineapple, strawberries, brown sugar. Fruit smoothies were blended from guava, passion fruit, banana, orange juice, and strawberries." *(LG)*

Open All year.
Rooms 2 suites, 2 doubles—all with full private bath, private entrance, radio, TV, desk/table, deck, ceiling fan, refrigerator. Some with air-conditioning. Suites with whirlpool tub, kitchenettes. Penthouse suite with laundry, deck, gas grill.
Facilities Dining room, living room with fireplace, balconies. 1½ acres on golf course. Trail to secluded beach. Tennis, fitness center, horseback riding nearby.
Location N coast. From Lihue airport take main road N past Kapaa to Princeville. Turn right on Ka Haku at main entrance to Hanalei. Go past golf course, turn right on Kamehameha Rd. to inn on right.
Restrictions No smoking. No children. Sunday check-ins discouraged; by special arrangement only.
Credit cards MC, Visa.
Rates B&B, $150–220 suite, $85–90 double. Weekly discount. Extra person in suite, $15–20. 3-night minimum.

WAIMEA, KAUAI

Information please: A favorite of those searching for the old Hawaii, the **Waimea Plantation Cottages** (9600 Kaumualii Highway, #367, 96796; 808–338–1625 or 800–9–WAIMEA), consists primarily of early 1900s cottages, originally the homes of sugar plantation workers, now restored to combine simple period charm and modern amenities. Although guests may have a hard time leaving the resort's relaxing grounds, nearby activities include a walking tour of the historic village; to the northwest, the sandy beaches of Polihale at the road's end; and to the north, Waimea Canyon State Park, with magnificent vistas, beautiful hiking trails, and a 3,000-foot-deep gorge. Rates for the fifty cottages—each with private bath, telephone, TV, and lanai—range from $160 for a one-bedroom cottage off-season to $470 for a five-bedroom oceanfront cottage in season. There's a swimming pool and tennis court, plus the black sand beach for strolling and surf-casting (it's often too rough and muddy for swimming). Reports appreciated.

LANA'I

Once known for its pineapple—not its tourist—crop, Lana'i offers a minimum of crowds and beautiful beaches. Plan to rent a car to get around on Lanai; it may be worth it to pay the extra for four-wheel drive, since there are only 30 miles of paved road on the island.

Reader tips: "To get to Lana'i, try the ferry. It's cheaper than the plane, more reliable in poor weather, fun and a pretty ride, and you will likely see humpback whales." *(Carol Blodgett)* "Although once known as the 'Pineapple Island,' the only pineapples I saw were in a small field near the airport. The weather on Lana'i is much wetter at higher elevations; when I was at the Lodge at Koele for tea it rained buckets; Manele Bay stayed completely dry." *(LG)*

Also recommended: Opened in 1991, the 250-room **Manele Bay Hotel** (P.O. Box 774, Lanai City, 96763; 808–565–7700 or 800–321–4666) was designed to take full advantage of its spectacular location overlooking the beach on Hulopoe Bay, rugged coastline, and the blue Pacific Ocean beyond. "An elegant Mediterranean villa–style hotel, with an ornate lobby with high ceilings and walls decorated with massive Oriental murals. My exquisite oceanview suite had Oriental decorative accents, beautiful floral fabrics, and a bathroom with all possible amenities. Sliding glass doors opened to a patio overlooking the gardens and ocean. Inviting swimming pool and spa were especially private at night, as was sitting in the moonlight on the sugar-fine white sand beach. Dining options range from several reasonably priced, casual options to the acclaimed (and expensive) Ihilani Restaurant." *(LG)* Double rates range from $275–500, regular suites from $700–$750; meal plans available.

Information please: Dreams Come True on Lana'i (547 12th Street, P.O. Box 525, Lanai City 96763; 808–565–6961 or 800–566–6961) is a simple B&B, surrounded by banana, papaya, and passionfruit trees. Double rates are $75–85; also available is a three-bedroom house which rents for $125–190, and can sleep up to eight people. "A plantation-style home on a quiet residential street, about a five-minute walk from the center of town. Large, casual, homey living room, decorated with art and craft work which owners Michael and Susan Hunter have collected in Bali, Sri Lanka, and Thailand. There is a pleasant backyard and sheltered deck surrounded by tropical fruit trees. Breakfast includes passionfruit juice, island bread, and organic fruits and jams from the Hunter garden. Friendly and helpful owners; modest but comfortable rooms." *(Linda Goldberg)*

Hotel Lanai ¢ ✕	*Tel:* 808–565–7211
828 Lanai Avenue, 96763	800–795–7211
P.O. Box 520	*Fax:* 808–565–6450

Originally built by Jim Dole as a guest house for the Hawaiian Pineapple Company in 1923, you can still find a taste of old Hawaii (along with your fresh pineapple juice) on the verandas of the Hotel Lanai, shaded by towering Norfolk pines. Owned by the Lana'i Company, the hotel has been leased to chef/innkeeper Henry Clay Richardson since 1996. Guest rooms have natural wood floors, bleached pine furniture, patchwork quilts, and functional bathrooms with showers and pedestal sinks; a few have four-poster beds. Breakfast, served 7–9:30 A.M., includes cereals, pastries, juices, coffee and tea. Guests can enjoy cocktails and appetizers at the knotty pine bar or on the front lanai, and enjoy dinner in the hotel restaurant, Henry Clay's Rotisserie, specializing in spit-roasted meats and fish, Cajun and Creole-style dishes, pizza, and salad. Richardson is an experienced chef, having previously been the chef at the well-known Gerard's at the Plantation Inn in Lahaina, Maui.

"Inviting and unpretentious; marvelous pine-scented air. Evenings can be cool at this 1700-foot elevation, making the wood-burning fireplace in the dining room particularly inviting." *(Linda Goldberg)* "Helpful service; the staff are neat and tidy, with lovely smiles. Convenient location to the local shops plus the free shuttle bus to the other hotels makes it easy to get around without a car." *(Paul Russell)* "Relaxed but polite, friendly and helpful atmosphere, created by a combination of sincerely accommodating staff, a pleasant, quiet pineapple plantation setting, and an outstanding restaurant." *(Nat Lovell)* "Clean, comfortable rooms; quiet in the morning—good for sleeping in. Pleasant, helpful staff; delightful breakfast. Inviting front veranda for relaxing, with ceiling fans and white wicker furnishings." *(Judith Stanke)*

Open All year.
Rooms 1 cottage, 11 doubles—all with private bath and/or shower, telephone, clock/radio, desk. 4 with lanai with swings; 1 with TV.
Facilities Restaurant with fireplace, bar, library; lanais. 3 acres with off-street parking; bicycles. 15 min. to ocean, tennis, hiking, golf.
Location 2 min. from town. Free shuttle bus to Lodge at Koele or Manele Bay Hotel.
Restrictions No smoking in dining room, guest rooms. Children 8 and over.
Credit cards Amex, JCB, MC, Visa.
Rates B&B, $135 cottage, $95–105 double. Extra person, $10. Alc lunch, $12–15; alc dinner, $25–30.
Extras Wheelchair access to restaurant. Airport, ferry pickups. Crib. Spanish, Tagalog, Japanese, French spoken.

Lodge at Koele 🛏 ✕ 🎿
P.O. Box 310, Lana'i City 96763

Tel: 808–565–7300
800–321–4666
Fax: 808–565–4561

The don't-blink-or-you'll-miss-it town of Lana'i City will leave you totally unprepared for the luxurious experience offered by the Lodge at Koele. The Lodge sits on a 59,000-acre up-country estate, and both its architecture and decor evoke turn-of-the-century English manor elegance, from the Great Hall with two stone fireplaces to the Library and Trophy rooms, and outside to the croquet lawns and Orchid House. The decor is lightened with a mix of country antiques, folk art by local Lana'i artists, and Asian accent pieces. Guest rooms have dark bamboo furnishings and four-poster beds with pineapple finials, and luxuriously equipped bathrooms. The Lodge's restaurant offers an imaginative menu featuring such entrees as skillet chicken on field greens with chive onion rings; lamb shanks with polenta; and grilled fish with fennel citrus vinaigrette.

"Because of its 1,700-foot hillside elevation, the Lodge is sometimes shrouded in mist from nearby Lana'i Hale, the highest point on the island, but that only adds to its appeal. Upscale atmosphere, yet low-key and liveable." *(BN)* "Beautiful grounds, outstanding decor. Service is professional and helpful. You can use all the beach facilities at the sister resort, Manele Bay, where sometimes you can see spinner dolphins playing in Hulopoe Bay; there's free shuttle service for the 20-minute drive. Lanai is fascinating in a stark way. You really feel the old Hawaii on this island, with long stretches of uninhabited beaches." *(Carol Blodgett)* "The lodge is surrounded by acres of manicured lawns and pine trees, and a magnificent pond surrounded by flowering bushes; its golf course is among the world's most scenic and challenging. Rustic but elegant common rooms, with cozy fireplaces; spacious, well-appointed guest rooms, with oversized furniture and spacious ornate bathrooms with wonderful magnifying mirrors for make-up. Delightful 4:00 afternoon tea with a variety of teas, pastries, miniature cranberry scones, clotted cream, and lemon cream." *(Linda Goldberg)*

Open All year.
Rooms 14 suites, 88 doubles—all with private bath and/or shower.
Facilities Restaurants, lounge, lobby, gift shops. Orchid house, sporting clays course, golf, fitness center, swimming pool, Jacuzzi, tennis, croquet, lawn bowling, horseback riding, mountain biking. At Manele Bay: spa, beach, snorkeling, children's program. Scuba diving, sailing, fishing nearby.
Location Lana'i City.
Credit cards Amex, CB, DC, JCB, MC, Visa.
Rates Room only, $600–1,500 suite, $315–475 double. Extra person, $40; no charge for child under 15 in parents' room. MAP, add $90 per person. FAP, add $115 per person. Minimum stay Dec. 21–Jan. 4. Package rates. Picnic lunches by arrangement.
Extras Airport pickups by arrangement. Shuttle van between Koele, Manele Bay, Hulopoe Beach, Lanai City, Manele boat harbor.

MAUI

Years ago, we saw a corny bumper sticker which proclaimed: "Here today, gone to Maui." Unfortunately, millions of others have been so inspired, making Maui second only to Oahu in popularity. Don't expect isolation here, although you will find the full spectrum of accommodations, shopping, night life, water sports, beautiful beaches and dramatic scenery.

HAIKU, MAUI

For an additional area inn, see **Paia**.

Haikuleana ¢
555 Haiku Road, 96708

Tel: 808–575–2890
Fax: 808–575–9177
E-mail: blumblum@maui.net

Haikuleana B&B is an 1850s plantation house, set among pineapple fields and pine trees, built for Maui's first doctor, and purchased and fully refurbished by Jeanne and Ralph Blum in 1996. Both are published writers: Jeanne is an Oriental Medicine therapist, and the author of

Woman Heal Thyself; Ralph is an anthropologist and author of *The Book of Runes.* Haikuleana's early Hawaiian architecture is complemented by tropical period pieces, antiques, and designer fabrics. The Hollywood room is decorated with personal photos and memorabilia from the silent screen years, when Ralph's mother was a leading movie star. Set at 500 feet above sea level, temperatures are comfortable year-round. Breakfast, served 8:30–9:30 A.M. at guests' choice of large tables or small, includes tropical juices, homemade banana bread with macadamia nuts, specialty hot entrees, and Kona coffee. Picnic breakfasts are available for trips to see the Haleakala Crater at sunrise; the guest refrigerator is kept stocked with complimentary soda, juice and beer.

"Jeanne and Ralph are fascinating and delightful hosts. Breakfast began with a freshly made fruit smoothie of guava, orange, passion fruit, and banana, followed by a parfait of granola, strawberry yogurt, and kiwi, strawberries, and bananas. The second course was grilled turkey ham and freshly baked peach-pear cobbler with coconut topping, accompanied by Kona coffee." *(Linda Goldberg)* "Inviting and pleasant atmosphere." *(Gail Davis)* "This B&B is located in the quiet countryside, near Mt. Haleakala National Park, with nightly showers, evening rainbows, and clear, pleasant, tropical days." *(Mr. & Mrs. Wallace McTammany)* "The area is full of restaurants; Ho'okipa Beach is for swimming and surfing." *(Doris Evans)* "Most evenings, we sat on the front porch or in the living room with the other guests, enjoying a glass of wine or beer and lively conversation, but privacy was easily available if preferred. A tranquil, nontouristy area, yet convenient to many activities." *(Diana Chang)*

Open All year.
Rooms 4 doubles—all with private shower bath, telephone, clock, hair dryer, ceiling fan.
Facilities Dining room, living room with TV/VCR, books, video library, stereo, games; guest refrigerator; porch; beach towels, mats, ice chests. Fax service. Massage therapy by reservation. 2 acres with swimming pool, hot tub, gardens. Ho'okipa Beach nearby for windsurfing, surfing, swimming; golf, tennis nearby.
Location N central coast. 11 m from town. From airport follow signs to Hana Hwy, Rte. 36. Pass through Paia along coast, past Ho'okipa Beach. Turn right at mile marker 11, onto Haiku Rd. Go 1 m to inn.
Restrictions No smoking inside. Children over 6.
Credit cards None accepted.
Rates B&B, $95–115 double, $85–100 single. Extra person, $15.
Extras French, German, Italian, Russian, Spanish spoken.

HANA, MAUI

Reader tip: "Get the feel of Hana by staying for a few days—not a few hours. It's pretty spread out, and a car is a necessity if you want to visit Wai'anapanapa State Park with its gorgeous scenery and beautiful lava rock formations and caves, black sand beach, and the seven pools at 'Ohe'o Gulch located at Haleakala National Park. Affordable meals can be found at the Hana Ranch Restaurant, serving good inexpensive fast-food take-out all day, as well as a full buffet lunch in the restaurant, plus dinners on Wednesdays, Fridays, and Saturdays. The Gardenland Cafe, on the Hana Highway before the airport, specializes in breakfasts, vegetarian salads and sandwiches, and light, healthy meals. Hana is wetter than much of Hawaii; mosquitoes can be annoying, so bring repellant." *(Linda Goldberg)*

Also recommended: Peaceful, relaxing and beautiful describe **The Hana Kai-Maui Resort** (1533 Uakea Road, P.O. Box 38; 808–248–8426 or 800–346–2772) an 18-unit condominium hotel set in a lush tropical cove. Each unit has a fully equipped kitchen and private bath; most have a private lanai with spectacular water views. Rates range from $110–125. "Beautiful location, just a short drive from Hana. Our unit had a private lanai offering spectacular views of Hana Bay and Popolana Beach, a rocky lava beach just a few steps from the complex. There was also an attractive spring-fed pool and adjacent beachside luau/barbeque area. We enjoyed the attractive bamboo furnishings, and put the kitchen to good use. Plenty of closet space. One night was not enough." *(LG)*

An economical option are the **Hana Plantation Houses** (P.O. Box 249; (800) 228-HANA or 808–248–7868 on Maui), several local homes located in and near the center of town. Prices range from $70–$80 for the smallest studio units up to $160 for a solar electric house accommodating up to five guests on acreage overlooking Hana Bay. Most have color TV, hot tub access, and kitchenette.

Yet another choice is the **Heavenly Hana Inn** (P.O. Box 146, 96713; 808–248–8442), a Japanese-style inn remodeled in 1994. It is decorated with Australian eucalyptus wood floors, spruce and pine beams and paneling, plus skylights. The three suites are simply furnished with Japanese futon platform beds accented with Japanese throw pillows; bathrooms are elegant with black tile and brass fixtures. Each unit has a private bath, a screened lanai, and separate TV sitting area. Breakfast includes sweet breads, juices, coffee, or tea. B&B rates are $175 for two, $235 for four. *(LG)*

The **Hotel Hana-Maui** (P.O. Box 9, 96713; 808–248–8211 or 800–321–HANA) is now under the management of Amana Resorts. One of Hawaii's oldest and best-known luxury hotels, it offers 96 guest accommodations in a variety of cottages, most with a private patio and Jacuzzi tub, at double rates of $395–795; meal plans cost $65 and $85 per person, and extended stay discounts are available. The garden cottages are fairly close together,; the Sea Ranch cottages are a little more spread out along the coast. The decor is luxurious, with hardwood floors, wood-beamed ceilings with ceiling fans, and bamboo four-poster beds with Hawaiian quilt comforters. The perfectly manicured landscaping added to the peaceful, serene setting. The Hawaiian-American cuisine, served in the poolside pavilion or the restaurant, is supplemented by cookouts, clambakes, and luaus. Although many guests choose to relax and do nothing, others prefer to sign up for daily activities ranging from beachside cookouts to guided nature hikes, aqua-aerobics to jeep tours; these are not included in the room rate.

A find for budget travelers are the state-owned, rustic plantation-style **Waianapanapa Cabins** (Department of Land and Natural Resources, Division of State Parks, 54 South High Street, Room 101, Wailuku, Maui, 96793; 808–243–5354), furnished with two bunk beds in the bedroom, two single beds in the living room, and a fully equipped kitchen. Double rates begin at $50.

KULA, MAUI

Head inland to the peaceful mountain quiet of Maui's upcountry, just 35 minutes from the Kahului Airport. About 3000 feet above sea level is the sleepy town of Kula, with views of the ocean below and Mount Haleakala above. Make Kula your base for hikes on Haleakala's trails, and visits to the botanical gardens and the Tedeschi Winery.

Information please: The **Silver Cloud Ranch** (Thompson Road, RR2, Box 201, Kula 96790; 808–878–6101) offers 12 doubles, suites, apartments, and a cottage in buildings dating back to the early 1900s. Double rates range from $85–150 and include a full breakfast, served in the garden sunroom. "With its unsurpassed views of Maui's shoreline, peaceful, remote setting, and proximity to Haleakala crater, it's no wonder that the Silver Cloud Ranch is a favorite escape of Hawaiian islanders. Mainlanders who visit Maui will be impressed by the large, comfortable rooms with appealing decor, and the breathtaking beauty of the nightly displays of twinkling lights from the coastal towns below and the unobstructed views of the stars above. In the daytime, we watched as horses, pigs, cows, and chickens meandered lazily about the property." *(Gail Davis)*

LAHAINA, MAUI

Old Lahaina Town plays a distinguished part in the history of Hawaii; as the first capital of the Hawaiian Kingdom, it was the center of Maui's cultural and social life. Later it became the whaling capital of the Pacific in the 1860s, with all the diverse personalities of that era.

Reader tips: "Although touristy, we enjoyed Lahaina and used it as a base for touring Maui. The Banyan Tree Park leads to charming renovated 1800s buildings. The Court House and two art galleries in the old prison have crafts not found elsewhere; admission is free." *(Michael & Dina Miller)* "Lahaina serves as headquarters for whale-watching cruises, snorkeling tours, shopping, and nightlife." *(SHW)* "It's not hard to find surviving landmarks from the days of whalers and missionaries." *(PG)*

Also recommended: Imagine waking up to breathtaking views of the Pacific, with Lana'i and Moloka'i in the distance. The **House of Fountains** (1579 Lokia Street, 96761; 808–667–2121 or 800–789–6865) enhances this view with an inviting swimming pool, hot tub, and barbecue area. This recently remodeled home has six guest rooms, furnished with island-style white rattan, floral fabrics, private baths, and all modern conveniences. Laundry facilities and beach towels are also available. The B&B double rates range from $85–125, and include a full buffet breakfast, with fresh fruit and juice, cheese and salami, home-baked bread, rolls, and croissants. "German-born Daniela and Thomas Clement are gracious, charming innkeepers. Their elegant home has high ceilings in the living room, lots of windows and white marble floors; the spacious, immaculate guest rooms are well equipped but un-cluttered." *(Linda Goldberg)* Comments welcome.

Information please: Built in 1987, **The Plantation Inn** (174 La-hainaluna Road, 96761; 808–667–9225 or 800–433–6815) is an elegant gray and white woodframe building, decorated with stained-glass win-dows, brass and four-poster beds, flowered fabrics and wallpapers, and oak flooring; the baths have Victorian pedestal sinks and chain-pull toilets. The inn's restaurant, Gerard's, is well established and reputed to be one of Maui's best, specializing in French cuisine. B&B double rates for its 20 guest rooms range from $110–225, and include early morning coffee and a breakfast of fresh fruit, French toast, Kona coffee, and hot chocolate. Reports welcome.

For additional area accommodations, see **Napili.**

The GuestHouse ¢
1620 Ainakea Road, 96761

Tel: 808–661–8085
800–621–8942
Fax: 808–661–1896
E-mail: 76725,3473@compuserve.com

Although clean comfortable rooms and good food are important in any B&B, the GuestHouse also offers another essential ingredient—hos-pitable innkeepers who really enjoy their guests. As owners Tanna Swanson, Raphael and Tammy Djoa note: "Because we are a very small business, it doesn't take long to establish a personal relationship with our guests." They go on to explain that "when we have a group of scuba divers, we pack a big picnic and our gear and head out to catch our din-ner. We usually videotape all the above- and below-water action. In the evening, we edit the dive videos while eating fresh-caught lobster." The GuestHouse was built in 1964, and has been under the current owner-ship since 1988. Rooms have contemporary decor, and the rates in-clude a family-style breakfast of Hawaiian coffee, tropical juice, fruit platter, banana pancakes or French toast, and cereal.

"Lovely rooms, welcoming hosts. The owners encourage questions and offer ideas on all activities. Fresh-made bread daily; we used the kitchen to prepare dinner several nights." *(Helen Pelikan)* "Delightful guests from all over the world." *(Charles Leonard)* "Dad loved the bar-becue, Mom loved the kitchen, my brothers loved the pool, but my fa-vorite thing was the hot tub in our room. Plenty to do and lots of space so we didn't get in each others' face too much." *(Gloria Berkey)*

"A delightful surprise to find this attractive, relaxing, informal B&B hidden behind a high weathered wooden fence. Pleasantly decorated, well equipped, and an excellent value. I stayed in the Bamboo Suite, with a bamboo four-poster queen-size bed, color TV, mini-refrigerator, and complimentary chocolates. At breakfast, I helped myself to juice from the fridge, picked up silverware and cereal from the counter, and asked Tammy to cook my choice of banana pancakes (delicious) or French toast. A nice platter of fresh fruit was set at the table. The pool and hammock on the deck were great places to relax and had wonderful ocean views." *(Linda Goldberg)*

Open All year.

Rooms 5 doubles—4 with private bath, screened patio, Jacuzzi or hot tub. 1 shares bath with hosts. All with air-conditioning, ceiling fan, TV/VCR, refrigerator, telephone.

Facilities Dining room, living room with books, family room with TV/VCR, fully stocked kitchen/laundry; beach mats, coolers, towels, boogie boards. Limited off-street parking, swimming pool. 1½ blocks from beach.

Location 1½ m N of town, 1 ½ m S of Kaanapali Beach. From Lahaina town, take Honoapiilania Hwy N to Charthouse restaurant. Go right on Fleming Rd., left on Ainakea Rd to inn 2 ½ blocks on right.

Restrictions No smoking. Prefer children over 12.

Credit cards Amex, Discover, MC, Visa.

Rates B&B, $59–89 double, $55–85 single. Extra person, $15. AAA, senior discount.

Extras German, French, Dutch, Indonesian spoken.

Lahaina Hotel ¢ ✕
127 Lahainaluna Road, 96761–1502

Tel: 808–661–0577
800–669–3444
Fax: 808–667–9480

The Lahaina Hotel was constructed in 1938 as a general merchandise store and became a popular U.S. Army gathering spot in WWII. The post-war era saw it lapse into general disrepair, until it was purchased in 1986 by Rick Ralston, a successful entrepreneur and historic preservationist who embarked on a year-long restoration of the building. Dick Sargent is the manager.

Keeping its "Frontier Storefront" facade, the new Lahaina Hotel is a re-creation of a Hawaiian Victorian hotel, with walnut banisters, cast iron chandeliers, period antiques, and oil paintings of women in "shockingly little attire"—by Victorian standards, that is. The guest room furnishings include antique brass, iron, and carved walnut beds, Laura Ashley and Ralph Lauren fabrics, and lace curtains. On the ground floor is David Paul's Lahaina Grill, specializing in New American cuisine.Breakfast is set out on a sideboard in the hallway from 7 to 9:30 A.M., so guests can take their choice of Kona coffee or tea, fresh fruit and juice, muffins and croissant back to their room or private veranda to enjoy; robes are provided so there's no rush to get dressed.

"The inn is only a half block from Front Street, the main shopping street along the Lahaina waterfront, in a neighborhood of art galleries and restaurants. Real quality is evident, with carved walnut staircases in the lobby, and pine staircases in the rest of the building. The well-lit hallways have green Laura Ashley–style papers and wood panelling. The Lahainaluna Suite at the rear of the hotel has a king-sized bed, made from two antique twins, with Victorian tables, dresser, and huge mirrored armoire to match the bed. Bold floral paper is complemented by Oriental rugs, ferns, stained glass lamps, and crocheted lace table covers. This suite has a bay window, and thus the smallest lanai. The suites have white hexagonal tiles, tub baths, pedestal sinks, and old-fashioned chain-pull toilets. The medium-sized standard rooms are all similar, with Victorian decor, connecting but partitioned lanais, and antique double beds." *(SHW)* "Fabulous location in the heart of the town and across from the ocean. I particularly enjoyed relaxing on the lanai during the day, where I could view the tourists, mountains, and ocean from my streetside room." *(Gail Davis)* Reports welcome.

Open All year.
Rooms 3 suites, 9 doubles—all with private shower bath, telephone, radio, desk, air-conditioning, fan, balcony.
Facilities Restaurant, lobby. Off-steet parking, $5 daily. 5-min. walk to Lahaina harbor.
Location Historic Lahaina Town. ½ block from Front St. toward ocean.
Restrictions Children over 14. No smoking inside.
Credit cards Amex, Discover, MC, Visa.
Rates B&B, $140 suite, $89–99 double. No tipping.

NAPILI BAY, MAUI

Napili Bay is just eight miles north of Lahaina, and many of its resorts have a Lahaina address.

Also recommended: On the gorgeous sand beaches of the Napili Bay is the **Mauian** (5441 Lower Honoapiilani Road, 96761–9050; 808–669–6205 or 800–367–5034). All 44 units have ocean views from the lanai, and are furnished with a queen-size bed and pull-out sofa, and fully equipped kitchen. Furnishings in the renovated units include 19th-century Hawaiian reproductions, Pacific arts and crafts; many units are designed in the 1950s architectural style of Herbert Bauer. B&B double rates are $100–150. "Relaxed and friendly atmosphere with lots of returning guests. Swimming pool, lush grounds, and deserted beaches to explore, with good restaurants, tennis, and golf nearby. No in-room telephones or TVs to disturb the tranquility. There are barbecues and tables so we cooked dinner outside while watching the sun set. An excellent value." *(Wendi Van Exan)*

Located on ten secluded acres on Napili Bay is the **Napili Kai Beach Club** (5900 Honoapiilani Road, 96761; 808–669–6271 or 800–367–5030). Magnificent ocean views abound from the private lanais of the 162 well-equipped studios and suites, with double rates of $160–250, suites $290–500; many have kitchenettes, and package rates are available. The resort claims to have the largest hot tub in Maui, plus four swimming pools and two 18-hole putting greens. Championship golf and tennis is nearby. "My newly renovated deluxe seaview studio unit had a kitchen and a large bedroom with a king-size bed, cable TV, air conditioning, ceiling fan, Japanese screens, a large covered terrace, and a spacious bathroom. Gorgeous view of one of the swimming pools and the white sand beach, excellent for swimming and snorkeling." *(Linda Gold-*

berg) "A great place for families, with a kids' vacation program; a far better choice than the area's tacky condos, and a much better value than the fancy big-name resorts." *(HAS)*

PAIA, MAUI

Also recommended: Located on the north shore of Maui, a half-block from Highway 36, and six miles east of Kahului Airport, is the **Kuau Cove Plantation** (2 Wa'a Place, Paia 96779; 808–579–8988). This renovated 1939 home has two B&B guest rooms in the main house, and two studio apartments with kitchenettes and private entrances. Rates range from $85–110, and include a breakfast of fresh local fruit and home-baked goods. "Great location, close to the wonderful Mama's Fish House restaurant and Ho'okipa, a world-class surfing and windsurfing beach. The B&B is shaded by two giant monkey pod trees and a rubber tree, with a private walkway leading to a picturesque secluded ocean cove lined with palms. Lovely rooms. An excellent place to overnight if you're going to see the sunrise at the Haleakala Crater or are enroute to Hana. Owner Fred Fox is an experienced and delightful innkeeper." *(Linda Goldberg)*

Information please: On Huelo Point about a quarter-mile from the ocean cliffs of Waipio Bay and 15 minutes from Ho'okipa Beach is **Huelo Pt. Lookout B&B** (P.O. Box 117, Paia 96779; 808–573–0914), with one suite and two cottages, comfortably decorated in Hawaiian decor, all with private baths and kitchens. Exquisite views of the lush greens, rolling pastures, and ocean await guests, as well as a hot tub and swimming pool. B&B rates range from $85–125 cottage. Comments welcome.

For an additional area inn, see **Haiku.**

MOLOKAI

Diehard get-away-from-the-crowd types head directly for Molokai, once known as the Forgotten Isle (renamed the Friendly Isle), for empty beaches and hiking trails, deep-sea fishing, hidden coves, and dramatic sea cliffs and waterfalls. Molokai has a limited number of beaches; several are too rough for swimming in the winter months; another, at Kaunakakai, is just mud and rocks. The island is only 38 miles long and 10 miles wide, with a population of less than 7,000.

Reader tips: "Since the Maui Princess Ferry is no longer operational, the only way to Molokai is to fly one of the local commuter planes, either from Honolulu or Maui, but the views from the air are spectacular. Most visitor shops, restaurants, and services are located in Kaunakakai. The main highway runs from the west end town of Maunaloa to the scenic Halawa Valley in the east. Other roads lead north past coffee and macadamia nut plantations, past the restored 1878 R. W. Meyer Sugar Mill, past Palaau State Park, ending at the Kalaupapa Lookout, where an easy stroll takes you to a panoramic view of the leper settlement. Miles of spectacular, practically deserted, white-sand beaches are at the west end of the island just past the Kaluakoi Resort, about 25 minutes from the airport. Visit the exotic animals at the Molokai Ranch Wildlife Conservation Park Safari; don't forget your camera, and wear old, washable clothes—the red dirt is hard to wash out." *(Linda Goldberg)*

Also recommended: "My one-bedroom unit (#2242) at the Kaluakoi Resort, located on Molokai's west coast on Kepuhi Beach, had an incomparable view of the golf course and palm-fringed beach. It had a high-beamed ceilings with a ceiling fan, as well as a color TV/VCR, stereo, large terrace, and fully appointed kitchen with cooking utensils. The terrace was an ideal place to enjoy a cool drink while watching the most spectacular palm-fringed sunsets of my Hawaiian trip. All the units are just steps away from the pool, restaurant and lounge, and snack bar. The food was good and reasonably priced." *(Linda Goldberg)* Book through **Blair's Original Hana Plantation Houses** (2957 Kalakaua Avenue, Honolulu, 96815; 800–228–HANA); rates range from $89–109, with weekly rates available.

OAHU

Hawaii's most crowded island, Oahu is still a must-see for first-time visitors. Explore Waikiki and climb up Diamond Head for a fabulous view, then visit Honolulu's downtown, with its fine museums and Chinatown markets. Get a car and discover Oahu's magnificent beaches, many ideal for mile-long walks, unspoiled by development.

HONOLULU, OAHU

Overcrowded, overbuilt, overwhelming, Honolulu is both a big city and a major resort area—an unusual combination. It is perhaps the one place in Hawaii where man-made attractions outnumber those of nature. Go to spiffed-up Waikiki to do your souvenir shopping, then to Diamond Head and Ala Moana Beach Park to clear your head. Visit Iolani Palace to understand a bit about Hawaii's monarchy, and the Bishop Museum for a look at the island's Polynesian heritage. Chinatown will give you a taste of the East, and Pearl Harbor's Arizona Memorial pays homage to America's entry into World War II.

Also recommended: Although a 456-room hotel,the **Halekulani** (2199 Kalia Road, Honolulu 96815; 808–923–2311 or 800–367–2343) is worth mentioning: "Built in 1917, this institution is a sanctuary amid Waikiki's high-rises. A tropical paradise of palms, fountain pools, flowing water and marble. Every detail—valet parking, shoe-polishing, bathroom amenities, evening turndown, morning paper—was accomplished without fail. Highlights of the lavish breakfast buffet in the poolside restaurant included custom omelets, poi pancakes with coconut syrup, endless fruit, almond croissants, and macadamia muffins.

Our room and bath were lovely and completely quiet. The swimming pool floor has an enormous blue orchid, made up of 1 million mosaic tiles." (*SHW*) Rates range from $295–$520 for a double and $700–1,720 for a suite.

In one of Waikiki's best neighborhoods, a 12-minute walk from Sans Souci Beach and Kapiloani Park is the **Diamond Head B&B** (book through Hawaii's Best B&Bs, P.O. Box 563, Kamuela, HI 96743; 808–885–4550 or 800–262–9912), located on the west slope of Diamond Head. B&B double rates for the three guest rooms, each with private bath and lanai range from $100–125. "A lovely 50-year-old island home handsomely decorated with heirloom Hawaiian furniture, including a huge four-poster koa wood bed which belonged to Hawaiian Princess Ruth. Breakfast one morning was a complete luau; the next we had bagels and cream cheese with smoked salmon caught and smoked by our hostess. Beach mats, towels, and coolers were supplied for a picnic. Beautiful grounds with tropical flowers and huge trees." (*Barbara-Ann Andersen, also LG*)

Information please: For a low-rise setting of tropical flora and old-style atmosphere about a block from the beach try the **Breakers** (250 Beach Walk, 96815; 808–923–3181 or 800–426–0494). Double rates range $93–99, and each of the 65 units have a fully equipped kitchenette.

New Otani Kaimana Beach Hotel 🛉 ✗
2863 Kalakaua Avenue, 96815

Tel: 808–923–1555
In U.S./Canada: 800–35–OTANI
Fax: 808–922–9404
E-mail: kaimana@pixi.com

The Kaimana was built in 1964, and is ideally located in the center of Kapiolani Park, adjacent to Waikiki's central hotel and shopping area. It overlooks Sans Souci beach, one of the best swimming beaches on Oahu, according to longtime general manager Stephen Boyle.

"A favorite haunt of Robert Louis Stevenson. Today the area includes the hotel, the beach and ocean, 500-acre Kapiolani Park, and Diamond Head. The hotel has one of the few outdoor restaurants in Waikiki, the Hau Tree Lanai, plus an excellent Japanese restaurant, Miyako. A short walk away are the Honolulu Zoo, Waikiki Aquarium, the Waikiki Shell, and bus stops." (*Michael Virgintino*)

"Friendly staff with positive attitudes; each one seemed to appreciate my being a guest—most refreshing." (*Geary Southard*) "Excellent atmosphere, ambiance, service, housekeeping, and hospitality. Quiet, convenient location." (*J. Shukla*) "Our charming, immaculate room had a full view of Waikiki and the Royal Hawaiian Hotel, and opened to the fourth-floor rock garden. Pleasantly remote from cars and noise. Dinner in the Hau Tree Lanai was outstanding." (*KLH*)

"From our small but private lanai we could sit and watch the sunset and enjoy the island breezes. Diamond Head overshadows the hotel and makes for a very picturesque setting. We joined the New Otani Club (it's free), and were given a $6.50 breakfast credit." (*Michael Miller*) "The Kaimana has a wonderful open-air tiled lobby with flowers, ferns, and mosaic paintings. Excellent dinner at the Hau Tree Lanai of papaya mint soup, shrimp curry, and Midori cheesecake. Standard guest rooms are not large, but all are pleasantly decorated in pastel shades of lavender, aqua, and beige; most popular are the ocean-view studios." *(SHW)*

Open All year.

Rooms 30 suites, 94 doubles—all with full private bath, TV, telephone, radio, desk, air-conditioning, balcony, mini-bar. Some with kitchenette, hair dryer, coffee maker, microwave, large-screen TV.

Facilities 2 restaurants, room service, beach. Concierge service. Swimming, windsurfing, golf, tennis, kayaking, hiking, jogging, bicycling nearby.

Location 1 m S of Waikiki, at Diamond Head. 10-min. walk to main Waikiki strip.

Restrictions Rooms on the corner next to the Sans Souci condominium are quite close.

Credit cards Amex, CB, DC, Discover, JCB, MC, Visa.

Rates Room only, $170–600 suite, $110–250 double. Extra person, $15; no charge for children under 12. 10% AARP, NARFE discount. "Room & Car," 5-night minimum stay, Dec. 20–Jan. 5.

Extras Crib, babysitting. Japanese, Korean, Spanish, German, Tagalog, Ilokano spoken.

We Want to Hear from You!

As you know, this book is effective only with your help. We really need to know about your experiences and discoveries. If you stayed at an inn or hotel listed here, we want to know how it was. Did it live up to our description? Exceed it? Was it what you expected? Did you like it? Were you disappointed? Delighted? Have you discovered new establishments that we should add to the next edition?

Tear out one of the report forms at the back of this book (or use your own stationery if you prefer) and write today. *Even if you write only "Fully endorse existing entry" you will have been most helpful.*

Thank You!

Oregon

The Oval Door, Eugene

Oregon has incorporated the best of the late 1960s, making it the most mellow and relaxing state in the country. Along with a less hurried pace and spectacular scenery, you will find a variety of cottage industries, aging hippies, and a legislature that takes social concerns and the environment seriously.

Coastal Oregon: Rich coastal diversity can be sampled by visiting some of the 66 state parks that provide virtually unlimited access to the shore. The southern coast, from the California border to Bandon, has few visitors. It features quiet beaches and cranberry fields and the wild Rogue River. The midcoast area, from Coos Bay to Lincoln City, can get crowded, especially in summer, but there is good reason—here are beaches up to 500 feet wide and 10 miles long, 300-foot sand dunes, sea lion caves, high bluffs with exquisite views (Otter Crest), and inviting rocky shores. Don't miss Devil's Punchbowl, north of Newport, where the ocean bursts through the rock in "spouting horns." The northern coast, from Lincoln City to the Columbia River, boasts summer sand castle contests, Tillamook's renowned cheddar cheese factory, forested headlands, and Cannon Beach's famous monolith, Haystack Rock. A visit to the coast during winter can be particularly romantic with its misty fog, huge storms, totally isolated beaches, and migrating whales.

Central Oregon: Leaving the coast, you'll find the gentle Coast Range mountains and the fertile southwestern area, with its famous wineries and Shakespeare festival at Ashland. More centrally, the lush Willamette River Valley holds most of the state's population from Eugene to Portland, while still retaining large expanses of rich farmland and forest. East of the Willamette are the Cascades, with 10,000-foot-high mountains. A recommended introduction to this part of the state is Route 126, east of Eugene up the rambling McKenzie River Valley, then Route 242 through one of the most bleak, unusual, and unvisited lava areas in the country. Nearby Bend provides excellent skiing and more unusual sites: Lava River Caves, Lava Coast Forest, and, 90 miles south, Crater Lake National Park.

Eastern Oregon: Sparsely populated, the southeastern part is dominated by the dramatic Steens Mountains, wide expanses of desert and dry lakes that still display the wheel ruts of the pioneer wagons. By contrast, the northeastern corner has the heavily forested Blue and Wallowa mountains, a destination for gold miners in the 1860s and for backpackers today. The Columbia River divides the states of Oregon and Washington, descending past dry, striped cliffs, the narrow Columbia River Gorge, Portland, and Astoria, to the Pacific. While the trip down I-84 along the Columbia is attractive, we recommend driving on the Washington side for better views and a more leisurely pace.

A word on the weather: It doesn't rain as much as you have heard. The winters are mild and although west of the Cascades it does often rain from November to mid-April, there are few downpours—just a goodly amount of the (in)famous "Oregon mist."

Rates are generally lowest midweek, from October to May.

ARCH CAPE

St. Bernards—A Bed & Breakfast   *Tel:* 503–436–2800
#3 East Ocean Road, P.O. Box 102, 97102   800–436–2848
                  Fax: 503–436–2800

Deanna and Don Bernard created their own storybook chateau when they built St. Bernards in 1995, a large shingled home complete with tower and gabled windows, set above the white sand beach. Classical music fills the air, and the tile floors, rough plastered walls, French doors, and European antiques are reminiscent of a French country house. Guest rooms have queen- and king-size beds, imported fabrics and wallpapers, comfortable seating areas, and most with ocean views. At 5 P.M., wine and appetizers are served in the comfortable living room. A leisurely breakfast is served at 9 A.M. at two large tables in the sun-filled conservatory; the meal begins with fresh squeezed orange juice, followed by homemade pastry, poached or baked fruit, yogurt, and such entrees as quiche, omelets, or frittata.

"Guest rooms are elegantly furnished with antiques, and plush carpets feel great to bare feet; windows open to fresh sea breezes and the sound of the waves. The Bernards are friendly hosts who make you feel welcome and special, helping with arrangements for dinner and fishing trips." *(Terri Dunford)* "Beautiful, newly-built inn with comfortable, well-appointed rooms and wonderful homemade breakfasts; worth the price." *(Jon May)* "Spacious, airy rooms. Ours had a sleeping nook with a stained-glass ceiling made by the Bernards, and an antique dollhouse concealing the TV. Don and Deanna are gracious and lively, good at keeping the conversation going." *(Joan Tanabe)* "Don showed us all the rooms, built at angles and various levels, and explained the history of their antiques. We walked along the secluded, rugged shoreline, enjoyed an early-morning cup of coffee, and returned for Deanna's breakfast of home-baked muffins, broiled grapefruit, and pastry cups filled with scrambled eggs, goat cheese and sun-dried tomatoes." *(Jill Mulry)*

Open All year.

Rooms 1 suite, 6 doubles—all with private shower and/or tub, telephone, clock/radio, TV/VCR, table, gas fireplace, refrigerator. 4 with ceiling fan. 1 with whirlpool tub.

Facilities Dining room, living room with stereo, books; deck; workout room with sauna. 1½ acres with gazebo. Ocean, fishing nearby.

Location NW OR. 84 m W of Portland; approx. 4 m S of Cannon Beach. From Hwy 101 at Arch Cape sign, go S 1 m & turn left on E. Ocean Rd. to inn.

Restrictions Absolutely no smoking. Children over 12.

Credit cards Amex, Visa, MC.

Rates B&B, $129–189 double. Extra person, $35.

Extras Wheelchair access; 1 room equipped for disabled.

ASHLAND

Ashland is a small mountain town, set in the foothills of the Siskiyou Mountains near the Oregon/California border. It is particularly well known as the home of the 50-year-old Oregon Shakespeare Festival, held annually from late February through October. Over 350,000 people come from all over the Northwest every year to watch first-class professional repertory performances of Shakespeare and other classic and contemporary playwrights, performed in three different indoor and outdoor theaters. (Call 541–482–4331 for ticket information; July and August performances usually sell out soon after the tickets go on sale in the winter.)

To accommodate and entertain all these theatergoers, Ashland offers a wide variety of boutiques and galleries, concerts and ballets, restaurants for every taste, and dozen of B&Bs, yet remains an attractive small town. It's full of visitors in July and August, so make your reservations early, or visit during June or September. Rates tend to be highest on summer weekends and lowest midweek in winter, and do not include city tax. Outdoor activities include hiking in Lithia Park or along the Pacific Crest Trail, rafting, windsurfing, waterskiing, and sailing on nearby rivers and lakes; and skiing ½ hour away at Mt. Ashland. Crater Lake is a reasonable drive, and the area also has several wineries worth visiting.

If you're trying to find a room during a peak period, call the Ashland Area Association of the Oregon B&B Guild at 800–983–4667 for reservations at member inns in Ashland and nearby Jacksonville.

Ashland is in southwestern Oregon, in the Rogue Valley, 350 miles north of San Francisco and 290 miles south of Portland. From the north, take I-5 to Ashland; from San Francisco, take I-80 east to I-505, then north on I-5.

Also recommended: Offering spectacular views in all directions, **Daniel's Roost** (1920 East Main Street, 97520; 541–482–0121 or 800–215–9031) is a contemporary house furnished with Chippendale antiques. Two guest rooms are available, and the $90–110 rates include a full breakfast. "Beautiful grounds with extensive lawns and flower beds. The attractive guest rooms have private baths and comfortable queen-size beds. Delicious breakfasts." *(Jim & Marilyn Russell)*

Two blocks from the Shakespeare festival is the **Winchester Country Inn** (35 South Second Street, 97520; 541–488–1113 or 800–972–4991) with a well-known restaurant and 18 guest rooms. B&B double rates range from $100–180, including a full breakfast. "Much improved in recent years, with beautifully renovated rooms. Our spacious room had two easy chairs, king-size bed, excellent lighting and a large bath. Excellent breakfasts with such choices as pancakes with Grand Marnier sauce, omelets, and more. Off-season packages a great value." *(Carolyn Alexander)*

Information please: When you bathe at the **Lithia Springs Inn** (2165 West Jackson Road, 97520; 541–482–7128 or 800–482–7128), you're relaxing in warm mineral waters from their natural hot springs. Of course, all eleven guest rooms also have private baths, most with whirlpool tubs. The rooms are in four Colonial-style buildings constructed in 1992 about a mile from downtown. The double rates of $75–165 include an expanded continental breakfast. Guests can relax in the living room, help themselves to the cookie jar, or browse through the books in the library.

Built in the 1880s **The Morical House** (668 North Main Street, 97520; 541–482–2254 or 800–208–0960) was restored 100 years later with particular care given to its stained glass windows and detailed woodwork. Owners Gary and Sandye Moore have added two luxurious guest rooms in the garden cottage, each with fireplace, double whirlpool tub, vaulted ceiling, wet bar with microwave, and a king-size bed; in the main house are five comfortable guest rooms, all with private bath and queen- or twin-size beds. B&B double rates are $110–160. "Beautifully decorated in Victorian style. The garden is well-maintained and inviting, and a deck overlooks the valley below. Tasty breakfast of peach smoothies, followed by freshly picked blackberries and scrumptious blueberry pancakes." *(June Sullivan)*

Sixteen miles south of Ashland is the **Mt. Ashland Inn** (550 Mt. Ashland Road, P.O. Box 944, 97520; 541–482–8707 or 800–830–8707) combines the cozy comfort of a rustic mountain lodge with conveniences like a private bath and in-room thermostats. Built in 1987, the Mt. Ashland Inn has such distinctive touches as log arched doorways, a log slab circular staircase, and beds made from black oak and madrona. B&B

rates range from $85–130 for the two doubles and three suites (one with rock waterfall). In winter, go cross-country skiing from the door or downhill a few miles away at Mt. Ashland.

The **Oak Hill Country B&B** (2190 Siskiyou Boulevard, 97520; 541–482–1554 or 800–888–7434) is a 1910 Craftsman-style farmhouse converted to an inn in 1987. Most of the five guest rooms, each with private bath, have a view of the mountains, and bicycles are provided for touring Ashland. Included in the B&B double rate of $60–95 is a family-style country breakfast.

Country Willows B&B ♿	*Tel:* 541–488–1590
1313 Clay Street, 97520	800–WILLOWS
	Fax: 541–488–1611
	E-mail: willows@willowsinn.com

Those who prefer to combine Ashland's theatrical attractions with a peaceful rural setting will especially enjoy Country Willows, a restored 1890s farmhouse that has been an inn since 1984. Dan Durant purchased Country Willows in 1993 and has worked hard to upgrade the rooms and amenities, most recently redecorating the farmhouse rooms and adding a new telephone system. The guest suites are in a restored barn, and the Pine Ridge, the most luxurious, has an open beam ceiling, skylights, lodge pole pine king-size bed, private patio, and a slate bathroom with double Jacuzzi. Guest rooms in the farmhouse are more modest, with floral fabrics and wallpapers, and views of mountains or pasture. Breakfast is served 8:30 to 9:30 A.M. in the porch or sun room, overlooking the willows and the brook; favorite entrees include ricotta cheese blintzes with plum sauce, blue corn crepes with eggs and pepper jack cheese, or pumpkin pancakes with maple pecan butter. Well-fueled, you can take an energizing hike into the hills, visit the curious llamas in the pasture, or just relax on the inn porches, where the country quiet is disturbed only by the occasional honking of the inn's ducks and geese.

"The food was wonderful, with a delicious quiche one morning, and banana pancakes the next. The immaculate Sunrise Suite had a huge bathtub and a two-person shower." *(Cherilyn Phillips)* "The property was lovely, the rooms spacious, and our cottage charming." *(JMB)* "Ideal location, surrounded by a meadow, with a creek and wooded trails. Dan has made this a first-rate inn; attention to guests' comfort is typified by the blankets provided for the outdoor theater. He and David made us feel that innkeeping was a joy for them." *(PH)*

Open All year.

Rooms 1 cottage, 3 suites, 5 doubles—all with private bath and/or shower, telephone with data port, clock, air-conditioning, robes. 5 with radio, desk. 3 suites with refrigerator, microwave; 2 with gas fireplace, deck, whirlpool tub. Suites, 1 double in restored barn.

Facilities Dining room, living room, family room, library with fireplace, guest refrigerator, porches. 5 acres with heated swimming pool, hot tub, lawn games, bicycles, pasture with llamas, geese, ducks.

Location 2 m from center. From I-5, take Exit 14 & go W on Rte. 66. Turn left

on Tolman Creek Rd., then right on Rte. 99. Turn left on Clay St. to inn on right.
Restrictions No smoking. Children 12 and up.
Credit cards Amex, Discover, MC, Visa.
Rates B&B, $140 cottage, $108–185 suite, $72–140 double. Extra person, $30. 2-night weekend minimum, mid-June to mid-Oct. Off-season event packages.
Extras Wheelchair access; 1 room equipped for disabled.

Cowslip's Belle Bed & Breakfast ¢
159 North Main Street, 97520
E-mail: stay@cowslip.com

Tel: 541–488–2901
800–888–6819
Fax: 541–482–6138

Longtime owners Carmen and Jon Reinhardt describe their B&B as "a 1913 Craftsman home, with down comforters, fresh flowers, Victorian and Mission-style antiques, stained glass, Maxfield Parrish prints, and a rose garden." Cheese blintz souffle with blueberry sauce, walnut-wheat germ pancakes with blackberry sauce, shrimp turnovers with sherry sauce, or dill crepes with scrambled eggs and smoked salmon might be the breakfast entree. Afternoon treats include biscotti, shortbread and chocolate-dipped macaroons; a chocolate truffle is left on the pillow next to a cozily tucked-in teddy bear every night.

"Carriage house rooms are large and comfortable, with a lovely long porch for enjoying the summer evenings. Jon and Carmen are knowledgeable and helpful, but not overbearing." *(Jan & Gary Hammerstrom)* "Everything is spotless; the meals tasty and well prepared; attractive antique furnishings and Victorian-style accessories. The teddy bear theme is attractive but not fussy or cute. The Reinhardt's make improvements every year, all in good taste." *(Sharon Chasko)* "Wonderful warmth and family feeling here. Stimulating breakfast conversations." *(Jeff Gold)* "The beds are high and queen-size, with down comforters and fine quality white linens; the baths have extra thick towels and rubber duckies." *(MW)*

"Rooms vary in size from cozy to spacious. Our favorites are at the back with private entrances and outdoor seating. Delicious breakfasts; coffee and tea are always available. Immaculate, with lots of fluffy white towels." *(NI)* "Jon and Carmen's breakfasts are varied, sumptuous, and beautifully served; they visit with their guests without being intrusive." *(Deanna Duvall)* "We were treated like family yet our privacy was respected. The country garden setting is appealing, and we can walk to downtown and Lithia Park." *(Jim & Pam Carlson)* "Although on a main street, noise level is minimal. Even the front suite is surprisingly quiet and the rest of the rooms face the garden." *(Jean Kavanagh)* "Jon and Carmen prepared a delightful vegetarian breakfast of fresh strawberries, blueberry muffins, and buckwheat pancakes with blackberry sauce. We enjoyed the garden, and especially the Reinhardt's cute little dog." *(Gail Davis)*

Open All year. Closed Dec. 24, 25.
Rooms 1 suite, 3 doubles—all with full private bath, deck, air-conditioning, individual thermostat, refrigerator. 3 with private entrance. 2 rooms in main house, 2 in carriage house.

Facilities Dining room, living room with library, fireplace; porch. Rose garden, patio, deck. Paved off-street parking. Fitness club privileges.
Location 3 blocks to theater and plaza. On North Main St. between Laurel and Bush.
Restrictions No smoking. No children under 10.
Credit cards None.
Rates B&B, $95–130 suite or double, $90–125 single. Extra person, $35.

Hersey House	*Tel:* 541–482–4563
451 North Main Street, 97520	800–482–4563
	Fax: 541–488–9317
	E-mail: herseybb@mind.net

A turn-of-the-century home surrounded by beautiful flower beds, the Hersey House is an easy walk to downtown. Each guest room has a different flavor, from country French to Eastlake, with period and reproduction furnishings. In 1996 Paul and Terri Mensch purchased the inn and have make such improvements as the new telephone system with voice mail for each room. Rates include a full breakfast, afternoon refreshments, and evening turndown service.

"An ideal place to relax between plays. Cozy and comfortable with friendly, charming hosts; the two sweet golden retrievers are an extra bonus." *(David & Audrey Huchitel)* "Iced tea and cookies are served at 4 P.M., and can be enjoyed on the huge front porch or the lovely English garden. Terry and Paul are excellent, relaxed hosts who enhanced our stay with sumptuous, leisurely breakfasts." *(Scrub & Vicki Hubner)* "Moderately sized guest rooms, nicely appointed with antiques. Since the innkeepers' quarters are separate, you feel as if you have the house to yourself." *(Carl & Jo Meisel)* "We were welcomed with cookies and lemonade. When we returned after an evening of theater, our bed was turned down and a tiny silver basket of chocolate kisses rested on the pillow." *(Joan Schloetter)* "We love the privacy of the cottage." *(Maureen Feldman)* "Wonderful, honest restaurant recommendations; knowledgeable innkeepers. Beautifully decorated, with excellent lighting and very comfortable beds. Great breakfasts, especially the peach cobbler." *(Gail Hanlon)* "Stunning gardens, with bursts of color everywhere you look. The charming Wildflower Room is done in French country pine with a floral theme. Delicious breakfast of freshly squeezed orange juice, melon with mint, homemade oatmeal, onion and potato frittata, and blueberry muffins." *(Shawna Stephens)* "Terri kept a perfect balance of gracious hospitality with a restrained, professional manner; she and Paul kept a perfect balance of attentiveness with respect for guests' privacy." *(Carol Shelby)* "Breakfasts were varied and imaginative, and concern was shown for guests' schedules. Our hosts were eager to please and interested in solving any problems." *(Robert Dohmer)*

Open All year.
Rooms 1 2-bedroom cottage, 4 doubles—all with private bath and/or shower, air-conditioning, individual thermostat, telephone with voice mail. 1 with desk, balcony. Cottage with TV, fully equipped kitchen.

Facilities Dining room, parlor with books, games; porch, deck.
Location 15 m from Medford Airport. ⁹⁄₁₀ m from center. From I-5 S take Exit 19 to inn at corner of N. Main and Nursery Sts. From I-5 N, take Exit 11. Proceed along Siskiyou and Lithia Way to N. Main.
Restrictions Air-conditioning, insulation minimizes traffic noise in front rooms. No smoking. Children over 11.
Credit cards MC, Visa.
Rates B&B, $130–195 cottage (for up to 6 people); $110–120 double. Extra person, $20. 2-night minimum some weekends.

Pedigrift House B&B   *Tel:* 541–482–1888
407 Scenic Drive, 97520   800–262–4073
        Fax: 541–482–8867

In 1887, a "golden spike" was driven to complete the rail lines connecting the entire Pacific Coast. Ashland grew by leaps and bounds, and in 1888, amid the orchards northwest of the plaza, successful contractor S. Pedigrift built his family home in high Victorian style, complete with twin bay windows, decorative shingles, and ten-foot ceilings. Gently cared for by its numerous owners, the Pedigrift House was renovated as a B&B in 1995 by Dorothy and Richard Davis. The original woodwork, windows and doors have been restored; the nine-foot-tall pocket doors between the living and dining rooms glide on their original sliding mechanism. Antiques and traditional furnishings decorate the light and airy spaces, and the patio provides panoramic views of the southern Rogue Valley. Afternoon beverages, cheese and fruit are available buffet-style in the dining room, and guests gather at tables for four for breakfast from 8 to 9 A.M. A typical menu includes freshly squeezed orange juice, blueberries with creme fraiche, creamy eggs with smoked salmon and a tomato-basil garnish, plus hot biscuits or croissants with butter and jam.

"Antiques and comfy green leather couches grace the living room. All is well maintained, and the guest bathrooms are brand new. Breakfasts are superb, and a guest refrigerator holds wine, soft drinks and snacks. Dorothy and Richard are jovial hosts realizing their dream of innkeeping after respective careers in nursing and engineering." *(Frank Annia)* "Beautiful, clean, and cozy. Dorothy is a warm, relaxed, and natural host, who facilitated enjoyable conversations all around. Our after-theater treat was just-baked cobbler and sherry." *(Richard Scott)* "Friendly yet not overly communal. Tastefully restored house; not cluttered with Victoriana. Nice garden and a garage to store bikes." *(Lynn Anderson)* "The charming innkeeper, comfortable rooms, and delicious food bring me back." *(Alison Kent)*

Open All year.
Rooms 4 doubles—all with private bath and/or shower, clock/radio, air-conditioning, fan. 2 with desk.
Facilities Dining room, living room with fireplace, books; guest refrigerator, porch. ⅓ acre with off-street parking.
Location In historic district. Go N on Rte. 99 (N. Main St.), turn left on Wimer St. Turn right at end to inn on corner of Wimer & Scenic Dr.
Restrictions No smoking. Children 12 and older.

Credit cards MC, Visa.
Rates B&B, $85–120 double. Extra person, $20. 2-night weekend minimum, June-Sept.

The Peerless Hotel	*Tel:* 541–488–1082
243 Fourth Street, 97520	800–460–8758
	Fax: 541–482–1012
	E-mail: peerless@open door.com

Dramatic refers not only to the activities on stage in Ashland during the Shakespeare festival, but also to the decor of the Peerless Hotel with its decoratively hand-painted ceilings and eclectic mixture of antiques from places as varied as New Orleans and Hawaii. Built as a hotel in 1900, the two-story red-brick commercial building was purchased by Chrissy Barnett in 1994; today it is listed on the National Register of Historic Places. Guest rooms have antique iron or wood beds, mostly queen-size, and are fitted with luxurious Italian linens; Room #1 has an exposed brick wall behind a Victorian inlaid walnut bureau and on the adjoining wall, a faux painting of a garden scene. The smallest room, #6, has an iron bed, honey-colored walls, elaborate swag curtains, and dark green beaded board wainscotting in the bathroom. Breakfast is served on the enclosed back porch from 8:45 to 10:30 A.M., and from May through October, may include a granola-baked apple, an asparagus frittata and sausage kebabs, plus glazed poppy seed bread, cereals, and yogurt. Off season, a continental breakfast is available.

"A charming small hotel lovingly restored, with a sophisticated decor of Victorian antiques. Our suite was an architectural feast, with a hand carved four-poster bed swagged with white fabric, deep green walls, and an Oriental rug on the polished hardwood floor. Warm and helpful staff; immaculately clean; no detail is overlooked." (*Karen Parsagian*)

Open All year.
Rooms 2 suites, 4 doubles—all with private shower and/or tub, telephone, clock/radio, air-conditioning, fan. 2 doubles with Jacuzzi tub. 1 suite with gas fireplace, 1 suite with balcony, double Jacuzzi tub. 5 with mini-bar. TV available.
Facilities Dining room, living room with fireplace. Courtyard with lighted off-street parking. Bicycles. Health club privileges.
Location In historic district. 3 blocks from center. On 4th St. between A & B Sts.
Restrictions No smoking. Children 14 and up.
Credit cards Amex, MC, Visa.
Rates B&B, $125–175 suite, $65–135 double. Extra person, $30. Senior/AAA discounts available. Prix fixe dinner, by reservation, $30.
Extras Limited wheelchair access; one room equipped for disabled.

| **Shrew's House B&B** ¢ | *Tel:* 541–482–9214 |
| 570 Siskiyou Boulevard, 97520 | 800–482–9214 |

What to name an inn in a town with a noted Shakespearean festival, and innkeepers named Shrewsbury? The Shrew's House, of course, and that's what Laurence and Laura Shrewsbury did when they opened their B&B in 1990. They report that "guests can enjoy all the privacy they want, breakfasting in their rooms, if desired, or choosing to relax in the common areas." The health-conscious Shrewsburys have a fitness room for guest use; Laura's low-fat breakfasts, served at 9 A.M., feature the best of Oregon's seasonal fruits and grains. A typical menu includes whole grain breads, fresh fruit, an egg entree, a hot beverage and juice.

"Laura and Lawrence are wonderfully warm innkeepers, full of helpful ideas about the area and knowledgeable of its history. The rooms are well kept, with king-size beds, Victorian antiques and traditional furnishings. Sumptuous breakfasts." *(Hank Keeton)* "Comfortable king-size bed; the stone fireplace and porch were nice features, as were the toaster, refrigerator and coffee maker. Good value, convenient location." *(Stuart & Linda Biesnick)* "Our large room was in the garden cottage next to the small swimming pool; we enjoyed privacy and comfort, yet were within walking distance of theaters. The bath was also large, with a Jacuzzi tub. Our breakfast in the dining room was delicious and table conversation was stimulating." *(Barbara Porter)*

Open All year.
Rooms 4 doubles—all with private bath and/or shower, telephone, clock/radio, cable TV, desk, air-conditioning, patio, private entrance, coffee maker, toaster, refrigerator. 2 with whirlpool tub, fireplace. 1 with steam shower. Rooms in 2 houses.
Facilities Dining room, living room with piano, fireplace; fitness room, deck, dining patio. ½ acre with off-street parking, swimming pool.
Location 2 blocks to historic district. Turn on Sherman, right at the first alleyway, parking indicated behind 115 Sherman.
Restrictions No smoking. Children 12 and over.
Credit cards Discover, MC, Visa.
Rates B&B, $55–105 double, $45–95 single. Extra person, $15. 2-night minimum on holidays, high season weekends.
Extras Local airport pickup.

The Woods House ¢
333 North Main Street, 97520

Tel: 541–488–1598
800–435–8260
E-mail: woodshse@mind.net
Fax: 541–482–8027

This 1908 Craftsman-style home was built by Dr. Woods, a prominent Ashland physician; the Woods family lived here through the 1950s; Françoise and Lester Roddy bought this B&B in 1991. Using old photographs, the terraced backyard was restored to its original design; the gardens feature almost 90 rose bushes, a white and black Concord grape arbor, and various fruit and nut trees. The Roddys' lovable Newfoundland, Jasmine, lives in the backyard as well (she's not allowed in the house), and is the favorite of many guests. The guest rooms are simply furnished with antiques and period pieces, lace and floral fabrics, original watercolors, and good bedside lamps and tables. A thoughtful approach is taken to breakfast; by 8 P.M. the night before, guests are asked to give their preferences—either a full or "heart healthy" meal in the dining room at 9 A.M., or a light breakfast brought to the room between 7:45 and 8:30 A.M. A typical menu might include fresh fruit, buttermilk scones or cinnamon-cranberry biscuits, blueberry oatmeal pancakes with turkey ham, or tomato asparagus pie with bacon.

"Breakfasts were delicious and filling. Françoise and her daughter were delightful hosts." *(Jim & Mary White)* "Bright, homey, cheerful, and well maintained." *(Evelyn Fisher)* "Our charming room in the Carriage House was decorated in beautiful lace and rose prints, with a comfortable bed. Breakfast was garnished with edible flowers from their well-tended gardens." *(Bette Shields)* "We chatted in the kitchen, relaxed in the library, enjoyed music from the CDs provided, and lounged on the porch." *(Miriam & Reg Bell)* "Close to the theater and shops, yet set off the street. The sitting room is ample, with books, newspapers, homemade cookies, coffee and sherry. Lester and Françoise are attentive, witty, and warm, but not intrusive." *(Roberta Recken)* "The back garden is marvelous for reading, napping or visiting." *(Diana Gerding)* "The lovely brass canopy bed made me feel like a princess, with pretty, freshly cut flowers and chocolate mints at bedside." *(Gail Davis)*

Open All year.
Rooms 6 doubles—all with private bath, air-conditioning. 1 with desk, fan. 2 share balcony. 2 rooms in carriage house.
Facilities Dining room, living room with fireplace, stereo, books. Porch with swing. ½ acre with gardens, gazebo, picnic area. 30 min. to skiing.
Location 4 blocks to downtown. From I-5, take Exit 19, go W on Valley View Rd. Follow signs to downtown. At 1st traffic light, go left on N. Main St. Watch for signs to Shakespeare Information Center. Inn is 1 m S, on right.
Restrictions No smoking. Street noise on porch.
Credit cards MC, Visa.
Rates B&B, $75–120 double, $75–115 single. 2-night minimum weekends.

ASTORIA

About 15 miles north of Seaside, on the Columbia River, is the town of **Astoria**, with beautiful Victorian mansions, and an outstanding maritime museum.

Also recommended: *Dotti Russo* recommends the **Franklin Street Station B&B** (1140 Franklin Street, Astoria 97103; 503–325–4314 or 800–448–1098), with five guest rooms, each with private bath: "Charming Victorian B&B, with pleasant period floral decor. Breakfasts were delicious; spinach quiche, waffles, fresh strawberries. Great view of the Columbia River from the bedrooms facing downtown." B&B double rates of $68–120 include a full breakfast.

BANDON

Also recommended: Set on a fifty-foot bluff at ocean's edge, the **Bandon Beach House** (2866 Beach Loop, 97411; 541–347–1196) has two guest suites, each with a river rock fireplace, private bath, antique and contemporary furnishings, king-size bed, and lounge chairs for watching the surf crash onto the massive rock formations below. The $125 double rate includes a full breakfast served in the Great Room or brought to your suite. "Wonderful, huge suites with elegant but comfortable furnishings. Incredible ocean views. Delightful innkeepers; scrumptious breakfast." *(Francine Williams)*

For an additional area entries, see **Coquille** and **Port Orford**.

Lighthouse B&B booked 7/31   *Tel:* 541–347–9316
650 Jetty Road, P.O. Box 24, 97411

Just across the Coquille River from the Lighthouse B&B is the real thing, standing sentinel duty, just as it has for the past century. The inn is a spacious contemporary home with large windows and long decks for watching sunsets or sternwheeler cruises on the river or admiring the ocean and lighthouse. Owner Shirley Chalupa sends guests off to a good start with a breakfast of fruit, breads or muffins, an egg entree, juice, and coffee. Complimentary wine is served in the evenings.

"Two guest rooms have views of the ocean and lighthouse, another has a private deck overlooking the river, and the loft room has views of all three. Cozy and comfortable, with wonderful hospitality and a great breakfast of egg-chili casserole with sour cream and salsa, and fried potatoes." *(Nancy Sinclair)* "Shirley is funny and nice. She served a delicious strata for breakfast, and recommended an excellent restaurant for dinner." *(Betsy Immergut)* "Great place for walking. The rooms are clean, with comfortable beds, modern baths, and all the amenities. The lighthouse is nonfunctional, so you don't have a blinding beam in the windows, but a soulful foghorn completes the ambience." *(Don Marioni)* "We'd return for the view and the little town of Bandon. When the tide is out, people go out looking for agates." *(LSW)* "Our greenhouse room was pleasant, and Bandon and its environment provide happy exploring." *(Lee Todd)*

Open All year.
Rooms 5 doubles—all with private bath and/or shower, telephone. 2 with double whirlpool tub, fireplace, TV. 1 with deck.
Facilities Dining room, living room with stereo, TV/VCR. Unscreened porch, deck. On the beach with picnic area. Tennis, golf, fishing, boating, crabbing, clamming nearby.
Location Coos County, 25 m S of Coos Bay on Oregon Coast. Walking distance to "Old Town."
Restrictions Summer foghorn might disturb light sleepers in west rooms. No smoking. Children under 12 by pre-arrangement.
Credit cards MC, Visa.
Rates B&B, $90–145 double, $80–135 single. Extra person, $15. Winter discount for multinight stay, except holidays.

BEND

On the eastern edge of the Oregon Cascade Mountains in central Oregon, Bend is host to many sporting and cultural events throughout the year. The Deschutes River runs through town and is noted for its fly-fishing and white-water rafting. Golf courses, picnic and boating areas, and hiking trails can all be found nearby; downhill skiing is only 20 minutes away at Mt. Bachelor.

Reader tip: "Kayo's Restaurant (61363 South Highway 97; 503–389–1400) was one of our favorite places for dinner, and is popular with the locals. Extensive menu, excellent food, presentation, and service: the Oregon three-berry cobbler and ahi tuna were outstanding." *(Carol Moritz)*

Information please: Although Bend is home to several major resorts and innumerable motels, we need current reports on its inns or B&Bs. For an inviting area inn, see **Sisters.**

BROOKINGS

Brookings is located in the southwestern corner of Oregon, on the coast, just north of the California border.

Also recommended: On the ocean, where the Winchuck River enters the Pacific, is **Lowden's Beachfront B&B** (14626 Wollam Road, 97415; 541–469–7045 or 800–453–4768). Guests enjoy watching the migrating pelicans, seals, whales, and salmon. Each guest room in this contemporary, split-level building has an outside entrance, private bath, refrigerator, microwave, and coffee pot; the $75–90 double rates include a continental breakfast delivered to your room the night before. "Wonderful room right on the river and ocean; a super bathtub for soaking. Host Barbara Lowden made fabulous muffins." *(Dianne Crawford)*

Information please: Just across Pelican Bay from Brookings is the **Oceancrest House** (15510 Pedrioli Drive, Harbor 97415; 541–469–9200 or 800–769–9200), an oceanfront property with beach access via a sturdy staircase; its strategically placed benches are perfect for viewing (and resting on the way up). An equally fine view can be had from the hot tub. The large guest rooms have views of the bay, private entrances and baths, queen-size beds, a stocked refrigerator, microwave, coffeemaker, and TV/VCR. The B&B rates of $99 include a continental breakfast basket delivered to your room the evening before.

Chetco River Inn ¢   *Tel:* 541–670–1645
21202 High Prairie Road, 97415

"Staying at the Chetco River Inn is really getting away from it all, surrounded by nothing but pure, quiet beauty. Driving here you travel quite a distance on a gravel road, occasionally rugged due to flooding. The inn was built in 1987, in a simple contemporary style with many large windows, with the forest in its back and the river practically in the front yard. Innkeeper Sandra Brugger is relaxed and down-to-earth, congenial and conversational, and her two West Highland terriers are equally good natured. We sat around a bonfire in the evening sharing travel stories. Rooms are simply furnished and pristine. There's a nice library on the second floor and we borrowed some good books to read before bed. Breakfast was a hearty affair of eggs, sausage, potatoes, and fruit. " *(Judy Dawson)* "Remote, beautiful and peaceful. It sits on the bend of a scenic river, so we spent time strolling and enjoying the scenery and solitude. Very clean with large guest rooms. One of the things that attracted us to the inn was its reliance on alternative energy sources. There was no compromise in comfort as a result. Next time I will bring my fishing tackle!" *(Gayle Leader)*

Sandra reports "the Chetco River is rated as one of the cleanest in the U.S. Walking, fishing, mushrooming, birding (hummingbirds especially in summer) and star-gazing are the major activities." Herb and vegetable gardens provide many ingredients for the Pacific Northwest cuisine she prepares for special dinners; a recent breakfast, served from 9–10 A.M. featured Dutch baby pancakes, locally made English sausage, browned potatoes with cheese and herbs, a baked apple with brandy-raisin sauce, and orange or cranberry juice.

Open All year.
Rooms 5 doubles—all with private shower and/or tub.
Facilities Dining room, living room with fireplace, TV/VCR, games, books; library with books, deck. 39 acres with hammocks, seating areas, gardens. On river for swimming, fishing; forest for hiking.
Location 18 m E of Brookings. Go 16 m on North Bank Rd. & turn left immediately after crossing the South Fork Bridge. Turn in at 1st gravel driveway on left. Look for the sign.
Restrictions No smoking. Children 12 and over.
Credit cards MC, Visa.
Rates B&B, $95–105 double. Prix fixe dinners by reservation, $20–25.

BURNS

Information please: Burns is located between the mountains and high desert of eastern Oregon, 140 miles east of Bend, and about 120 miles west of the Idaho border. The Malheur Wildlife Refuge lies to the south, and quail are frequently seen among the lilacs at the **Sage Country Inn** (351½ West Monroe, P.O. Box 227; 541–573–SAGE). A restored 1907 Colonial Revival cottage, it offers four guest rooms, with private and shared baths; afternoon refreshments and a hearty country breakfast are included in the $50–75 double rate.

CANNON BEACH

Cannon Beach is a very popular Oregon beach resort, named for the cannon that washed ashore here in 1846. It's also known for Haystack Rock, which sits just offshore at 235 feet, and is the world's third largest monolith. With seven miles of beach, ideal for beachcombing, swimming, surfing, and surf casting, and a location just a 1½ hour drive west of Portland, finding a room here in peak season can be very difficult; early bookings are strongly advised.

Also recommended: "Great views at Ecola State Park just north of

Cannon Beach; a small sign said this was Lewis and Clark's choice of top vistas. I agree." *(Christopher Hart Johnston)*

Also recommended: Built in 1993, the oceanfront **Stephanie Inn** (2740 South Pacific, P.O. Box 219, 97110; 503–436–2221 or 800–633–3466) has massive pine beams, rock fireplaces, and large windows opening to views of Haystack Rock; wicker and leather seating areas provide spots for reading or watching the fog roll in. The 46 well-equipped guest rooms have country and wicker furniture, lush fabrics, whirl-pool tubs, TV/VCRs, refrigerators, gas fireplaces, and balconies. B&B rates of $139–289 include the morning newspaper, a breakfast buffet, and afternoon wine in the chart room. By reservation the inn's chef prepares a four-course dinner of Pacific Northwest cuisine. "Dinners are delicious, and the staff is super. Beautiful for beach walking and visiting the nice little shops in town. Many lovely amenities." *(Lee Todd)*

Information please: Right on the seawall, **The Waves** (224 North Larch Street, P.O. Box 3, 97110; 503–436–2205 or 800–822–2468) includes both modern condo-style motel units with enormous windows and old-fashioned beach cottages. The shops, restaurants, and galleries of Cannon Beach are an easy walk away. There are 35 suites and doubles, all with private bath, and many have a kitchen, fireplace and deck; the rates range from $69 to 275, with minimum stays required in summer. Also under the same management are **The Argonauta Inn** (P.O. Box 3, 97110; 503–436–2601) and **White Heron Lodge** (P.O. Box 3, 97110; 503–436–2205). The Argonauta is a collection of two 2–3 bedroom homes and three studio apartments, with convenient access to either the ocean or to the village; rates are $60–275. Right on the beach in a residential area away from downtown traffic, the White Heron Lodge consists of a Victorian-style fourplex and a contemporary duplex unit, with rates of $125–165.

For an additional area inn, see **Arch Cape.**

CLOVERDALE

Cloverdale is located in Tillamook County, in northwestern Oregon, two hours west of Portland. Cloverdale offers easy access to bay and ocean beaches, lots of flat roads for bicycling, a pioneer museum, and several cheese factories to visit.

Sandlake Country Inn ¢   *Tel: 503–965–6745*
8505 Galloway Road, 97112

On Christmas morning 1890, Ezra Chamberlain received an unusual gift—1 million board feet of red fir bridge timbers dumped onto his beach by a storm-wrecked ship. His neighbor dragged some of it to his homestead to build a sturdy farmhouse and for over 80 years the house remained in the same family; it was renovated as a small but luxurious inn in 1988. Femke and David Durham purchased the Sandlake in 1995 and have added such amenities as double whirlpool tubs. The Rose

Garden room has a canopied king-size bed and is done in summery shades of evergreen, wild rose, and alabaster; the Timbers is a large room at the back of the original 1894 farmhouse, with three by twelve-foot exposed bridge timbers, and deep green and burgundy plaid wallpaper. Breakfast is brought to your room, and might include freshly squeezed orange juice, baked apple oatmeal, fresh fruit parfaits, an artichoke baked omelet, muffins and hazelnut toast.

"Our sweetly decorated cottage had an idyllic setting, with deer and birds outside the French doors in the early morning. Behind its unassuming exterior is a treasure, with a CD player, especially nice linens and towels, a kitchen and eating nook, and a sofa bed by the fireplace. The scrumptious breakfast was delivered in a basket with lovely fine china, linens, and silver, and included fruit and yogurt parfait, chocolate chip muffins, shirred eggs, and lemon bread, assorted teas and gourmet coffee. We loved the inn cat—so friendly we had to scoot it out the cottage door at night!" *(Judy Dawson)* "Femke is a perfectionist, so everything is absolutely pristine and unbelievably comfortable and romantic. A delicious, bountiful breakfast." *(Gene & Roberta Altshuler)* "Femke is warm and friendly, yet respectful of guests' privacy." *(Virginia Swanson)* "Fabulous hiking nearby." *(Stephanie Bric)* "An expansive cedar deck overlooked a rose garden and apple trees where whitetail deer come to eat." *(Bill Norman)* "A nice drive here past forests, coastal views, and winding roads." *(John McLean)*

Open All year.

Rooms 1 suite, 2 doubles, 1 cottage—all with private bath and/or shower, whirlpool tub, radio, TV, mini-refrigerator, deck. 3 with fireplace, double whirlpool tub, TV/VCR, vintage videos.

Facilities Dining room, living room with fireplace, library, games, guest telephone. 2⅓ acres with croquet, bicycles. 1 m to beach.

Location 9 m N of Pacific City. From Pacific City turn left over bridge and continue 8½ m N on Scenic Loop to Sandlake Grocery. Turn left on Galloway Rd. to inn on left ½ m.

Restrictions No smoking. No children under 15 in main house.

Credit cards Amex, Discover, MC, Visa.

Rates B&B, $125 cottage, $110 suite, $80–110 double. Extra person, $10. 2–3 night weekend/holiday minimum. Gourmet picnic basket, $25.

Extras Wheelchair access.

COQUILLE

A river town that has served as Coos County seat since 1896, locals refer to Coquille as the place where the deer and the salmon play; following the river westward will take you to Bandon and its seaside resort attractions 17 miles away.

Information please: The **Barton House B&B** (715 East First Street, 97423; 541–396–5306 or 800–972–7948) was built in 1920 and sits among towering cedar and fir trees in a quiet residential area. Tony and Lauretta Spenader have furnished it with comfortable antique and reproduction pieces, original artwork, and their collection of autographed and first edition books. A typical breakfast might include oatmeal, honey-roasted fruit, coffee cake fruit squares, an egg casserole, and locally made sausage. "Our room was the only one of four with a private bath, but all were well decorated, clean, quiet, and well-lit. The delicious breakfast, served in front of a roaring fire in the dining room." *(Dianne Crawford)*

CORVALLIS

Located on the Willamette River between the Coastal Mountain and the Cascades, Corvallis is the home of Oregon State University, and also one of Oregon's major cultural and commercial centers.

Information please: Listed on the Oregon Historic Register is the **Harrison House** (2310 NW Harrison Boulevard, Corvallis 97330; 541–752–6248 or 800–233–6248), a 1939 Dutch Colonial home with four guest rooms, each comfortably decorated with Williamsburg-style family antiques. Most have a private bath, and the double rates of $60–80 include a full breakfast. Afternoon refreshments include Oregon wines, Northwest micro-brewed beer, and soft drinks.

CRATER LAKE

Crater Lake is the deepest lake in the U.S., with a depth of 1,932 feet, and formed when Mt. Mazama erupted some 7,700 years ago and collapsed. Noted for its deep blue color, the lake has miles of shoreline surrounded by lava cliffs. The National Park Service maintains more than 90 miles of trails, including the Castle Crest Wildflower Trail, so there's plenty of hiking plus fishing and boat tours; two visitor centers offer natural history displays and information on conducted trips. Crater Lake is located in southwest Oregon, 80 northeast of Medford.

Also recommended: Reopened in 1995 after a five-year, $15 million rebuilding, is the only hotel in the park, **Crater Lake Lodge** (Rim Village, mailing address, 1211 Avenue C, White City, 97503; 541–830–8700). This spreading shingle and stone structure dates to 1915; the Great Hall's massive stone fireplace and polished wood floors are warmed with Craftsman-style decor and Stickley oak furniture and reproduction period lighting fixtures. The original 150 guest rooms has been reduced to 71, each with a modern private bath. The double rates range from $100–130; loft rooms which sleep four are $190. Book up to a year ahead for lake-view rooms in July and August. "Totally remodeled, soundproofed, modernized. The view is unsurpassed, especially on the lake side; rooms are small, and a few are tiny, as are some of the bathrooms; service can be uneven. The dining room is good but pricey—$65 per couple would be a normal dinner, and reservations can be hard to come by." *(DR, also SD)*

Surrounded by the Rogue River National Forest and the beautiful Oregon countryside, the **Union Creek Resort** (56484 Highway 62,

Prospect, 97536; 541–560–3565 or 541–560–3339) was built at the turn-of-the-century on the Crater Lake trail used by the pioneers as they crossed the Cascade Mountains. Listed on the National Register of Historic Places, there is a lodge with nine guest rooms, 5 cottages, and 10 housekeeping cabins; its restaurant, Beckie's Cafe, is well known for delicious pies and home-style cooking. It is open year-round for outdoor recreation and adventure, and is located on the road to Crater Lake, 23 miles to the west. Double rates are $38–90.

CRESWELL

Also recommended: Eighteen miles southwest of Eugene, and just five miles from the Creswell exit off I-5 is the **Country House** (30930 Camas Swale Road, Creswell, 97426; 541–895–3924). A contemporary home built in 1985 by Michael and Susie Hanner, it provides ideal lodging for people who prefer a quiet forest setting. The two guest bedrooms each have a king-size bed and a private bath with a tiled shower. A full breakfast is included in the $85 double rates. "The bathrooms are tiled in gorgeous designs, and the dining room is very lovely with a long teak table and Japanese lanterns." *(Barbara Abele)* "A wonderful, private, serene setting where sounds from the woods can be heard at night." *(Beverly Freliche Davis)* "Elegantly served and prepared meals; flexible timing, too." *(Diane Vincent)* "Mike is an architect and designed and built the whole place, from cornice trim to the window sills." *(Tim Hardy)* "The recreation room has a billiard table, exercise bikes, a nordic track and extensive video library. Excellent english croquet too." *(Judy & C.P. Smallwood)* "Wonderful balance of privacy and hospitality. The private hot tub looks out over a tree-filled valley." *(Theresa Gill)* "A reader's paradise, with many places to curl up and thousands of books to choose from." *(Robert & Martha Strand)*

DAYTON

For additional area inns, see **McMinnville** and **Newberg**.

Wine Country Farm ¢   *Tel:* 503–864–3446
6855 Breyman Orchards Road, 97114   800–261–3446
                                   Fax: 503–864–3446 (call first)

In the heart of Oregon's wine country is aptly named Wine Country Farm, a restored 1910 farmhouse surrounded by acres of vineyards. Joan Davenport bought the property in 1990 and opened the inn in 1991; her vineyard's first wine crush was in 1994, and products of the five varieties of grapes can be sampled in the tasting room. Joan also raises Arabian horses, one of whom struts its stuff pulling a buggy for picnics.

"Surrounded by vineyards—Perrier, Domaine Drouhin, Trappist

Abbey—and hazelnut orchards. The inn sits atop a hill with magnificent views of Mount Hood and Mount Rainer and the adjacent fog-
shrouded lowlands. When I returned from an early-morning walk,
Joan was emerging from the barn, carrying a basket of large brown eggs.
Breakfast consisted fresh-ground coffee, blackberries and cream; an
egg casserole with mushrooms and sliced black olives; Mexican salsa;
scones; jam from Joan's own Pinot Noir grapes; bacon and homemade
sausage; sauteed potato chunks; and blended orange/banana juice.
She is urbane, yet conversational, a businesswoman and an attentive,
unobtrusive innkeeper. The lawns, woods, and vineyards are immaculately manicured. One lovable dog and cat complete the domestic
mix." *(Bill Norman)* "Joan's generous French-American breakfasts are
up to Parisian five-star hotel standards while satisfying the caloric requirements of an Oregon lumberjacks. Except for the occasional shriek
of a lovelorn batchelor peacock, the bedrooms are quiet around the
clock." *(Clint Hall)*

Open All year.

Rooms 1 suite, 6 doubles—all with private bath and/or shower, clock, fan,
desk. 3 with air-conditioning, balcony. 2 with fireplace. Suite, in wine-tasting
building, has TV/VCR.

Facilities Dining room; living room and family room with fireplace, TV/VCR;
screened porch, deck, guest refrigerator. Tasting room. 13 acres with gazebo,
lawn games, vineyard, hiking trails. Horse buggy rides. Golf, river sports
nearby.

Location NW OR. Yamhill Cty Wine Country. 30 m SW of Portland, between
Newberg & McMinnville. From Portland, take Rte. 99W through Dundee. Bear
right on Rte. 18, & go right onto Breyman Orchards Rd. to farm.

Restrictions No smoking. Children over 12.

Credit cards MC, Visa.

Rates B&B, $125 suite, $75–115 double, $70–110 single. Extra person, $20.

Extras Limited wheelchair access. Airport/station pickup, $20. Horse boarding.

DEPOE BAY

Information please: Depoe Bay is known as the "world's smallest
harbor," and all thirteen rooms at **Gracie's Landing** (235 SE Bay View
Ave., P.O. Box 29, 97341; 541–765–2322 or 800–228–0448) have a view
of it. The inn, with a Cape Cod exterior and traditional interior, opened
in 1989; the guest rooms have fireplaces, private baths (some with
whirlpool tub), and TV/VCRs. A typical breakfast might include fresh
melon wedges, eggs Jonah (an English muffin topped with fresh baby
shrimp, poached egg, and Hollandaise sauce), and sweet buns or rolls,
finished off with a special "dessert." B&B double rates range from
$85–110.

We'd also like currents reports on the **Channel House** (35 Ellingson
Street, P.O. Box 56, 97431; 541–765–2140 or 800–447–2140), with wonderful views of the harbor channel and ocean. Some of the 12 guest
rooms have private decks with hot tubs overlooking the channel or the
ocean, perfect for those seeking a romantic, private getaway with little

or no guest interaction. Double rates range from $75–225, and include a hearty breakfast.

DIAMOND

"Located in Oregon's high desert, the town of Diamond peaked with a population of 50 people; now the stone ruins of the original store and some stately poplars are all that's left. From here you can visit Malheur National Wildlife Refuge, where millions of birds—pelicans, trumpeter swans, Canada geese, game and song birds—rest in their annual migration." *(SC)*

Information please: "The **Hotel Diamond** (HC–72, Box 10, 97722; 541–493–1898), built in 1898, has six guest rooms with shared and private baths ($45–65 double). Inside are sitting areas on the first and second floors, a deli/wine shop; and the local post office. Meals are served family-style at long tables in the dining room and include generous choices of homemade fare at reasonable prices. Our air-conditioned little room had a comfortable double bed in a white-painted iron bedstead." *(Suzanne Carmichael)*

About 25 miles to the southwest, on the other side of the Malheur National Wildlife Refuge, is the **Frenchglen Hotel** (Highway 205, Frenchglen 97736; 541–493–2825), set along Donner and Blitzen Creek (yes, that's really the name). This small white-frame building is owned by the Oregon State Parks system, and is open from mid-March to mid-November. The eight guest rooms are small, simply furnished with double beds, and share two baths; rates are $48–50. The restaurant, which seats only 20 people, is open for three meals a day, with hearty meats, fresh vegetables, and fruit cobblers as specialties. Dinner is served family-style at 6:30 P.M. sharp, by advance reservation.

The **McCoy Creek Inn** (HC 72, Box 11, 97722; 541–493–2131 or 541–493–2440) is a fifth-generation working ranch; built in 1918, the ranch house was renovated in 1990. Children are always welcome, and there is one bunkhouse and three doubles; double rates are $75 and include a full breakfast, with dinners available. "Peaceful rural setting. Our room had a sloped ceiling, queen-size bed with carved headboard, marble-top side table, two comfortable wicker chairs, and an Oriental rug. From our porch we watched children floating on the creek in rubber tubes, and after dinner, one of the cowboys joined us and shared his thoughts about cattle and the cowboy life." *(SC)*

ELMIRA

Also recommended: *Judy Dawson* recommends **McGillivray's Log Home B&B** (88680 Evers Road, 97437; 541–935–3564) as a "relaxing, homey place with a country decor and two inviting guest rooms. Owner Evelyn McGillivray treated us like family, chatting in the comfortable living room while our son watched TV. Our upstairs room adjoined the loft and had a king-size bed, two twin beds, a game table, a pump organ, tons of magazines, and a lovely private bathroom with a skylight. A door led to a balcony where we played cards and enjoyed the lovely wooded grounds. Delicious country breakfast; sometimes in winter Evelyn cooks pancakes on the old griddle woodstove. Elmira is a small town, so plan to eat dinner in Eugene!" B&B double rates are $70–80. Elmira is 14 miles west of Eugene.

EUGENE

Located located halfway between Seattle, Washington, and San Francisco, California, in west central Oregon, Eugene is the home of the University of Oregon and a major center for lumber and wood products.

Information please: A good choice for business travelers may be the newly renovated **Excelsior Inn** (754 East 13th, 97401; 541–342–6963 or 800–321–6963), built in 1912 as a fraternity house. Now housing a restaurant downstairs, the upper floors have 14 guest rooms, each with a private phone with data port, queen- or king-size bed, private bath, TV/VCR, air-conditioning, and desk. The individually decorated rooms vary in size and are named for classical composers from Bach to Vivaldi. Rates of $70–180 include a full breakfast; corporate rates available.

On a wooded hillside near Hendricks Park is **Maryellen's Guest House** (1583 Fircrest, 97403; 541–342–7375 or 800–736–1475), a contemporary home close to the university. The two guest rooms, each with private bath, open onto cedar decks overlooking a swimming pool and hot tub; the double rates of $82–96 include a full breakfast served at guest's convenience. "Looking into the fir trees from our private deck added to our relaxation. A spacious, warm and friendly place." *(George Rozsa)*

For additional area B&Bs, see **Creswell** and **Elmira.**

Campbell House, A City Inn 👫 ✕ ♿
252 Pearl Street, 97401

Tel: 541–343–1119
800–264–2519
Fax: 541–343–2258
E-mail: campbellhouse@campbellhouse.com

After many tries, Myra Plant succeeded in buying this ramshackle and overgrown 1892 mansion; after a year-long restoration, her elegant inn opened in 1993. Completely renovated, the woodwork gleams, the comfortable seating areas have big sunny windows, upholstered couches, and Queen Anne reproduction chairs. Breakfast is available from 7:00 A.M. until 10:00 A.M. Favorite entrees include malted mini-waffles, crepes, or egg casseroles; their homemade granola is served with a variety of toppings.

"Amazing attention to detail; excellent breakfasts; warm and delightful service. Each room has uncluttered Victorian decor, with a view of the beautifully landscaped grounds." *(Elaine Baskin)* "Just a five-minute walk from downtown shops." *(Pilar Awad)* "The needs of business travelers are well attended to, in a comfortable and relaxing environment, especially appealing when travelling alone." *(Judith*

Sterling) "Highlights include the evening wine and snacks by the fire, and the early morning coffee delivered to our room." *(Jane Duerr)*

"Thoughtful touches include chocolates, extra pillows, soothing music, clean and fluffy white robes." *(Clare Ellis & Kip Webb)* "Updated Victorian home in the nicest part of Eugene—overlooking the city, its parks and the river bike/hike system." *(James Powell & Joan Procter)* "Lovely Waverly comforters and curtains; old-fashioned clawfoot tubs. Fascinating photo albums of the restoration." *(Margala Woods)*

Open All year.

Rooms 12 doubles—all with private bath and/or shower, telephone, data ports, TV/VCR, refrigerator. 10 with air-conditioning, 3 with fan, 2 with gas fireplace, 1 with whirlpool tub.

Facilities Dining room, living room with fireplace, library with books, videotape collection, piano; laundry facilities. 1½ acres with gazebo, lawn games.

Location Skinner Butte historic district, 4 blocks to city center. From I-5, take I-105W. Follow Eugene City Ctr. Mall signs to East Third to Pearl St.

Restrictions No smoking.

Credit cards Amex, Discover, MC, Visa.

Rates B&B, $80–275 double. Extra person, $15. 2–3 night minimum for some rooms. 2–4 night special event weekend/holiday minimum.

Extras Wheelchair access; 1 room equipped for disabled.

The Oval Door ¢
988 Lawrence Street, 97401

Tel: 541–683–3160
800–882–3160
Fax: 541–485–5339

A 1920s Craftsman-style home, the Oval Door was built as a B&B in 1990, and was purchased by Judith McLane and Dianne Feist in 1993. Breakfast, served over a two-hour period, includes a choice of juices, fruit compote, an egg dish such as egg fajitas, and Judy's specialty sweet rolls, breads or muffins—maybe peach upside-down muffins, orange bow knots, or whole wheat bread.

"Great place, great location. Spotless, warm, and cozy; Judy is a wonderfully informative and genuinely nice host. Annie's Room has a beautiful slim desk and an elegant wood rocking chair. The bed was adorned with a white lace cover over a comforter and lots of pillows—great for relaxing during the day too. Our bathroom was large and spotless with a small window looking out at the huge old tree in the front. Breakfasts were delicious—my favorites were the glazed fruit, French toast, and Judy's sweet bread. Conversation at the table was always interesting, with folks coming to visit their kids at the university. Walking back to the inn after dinner we always found a delightful homemade dessert waiting." *(Heather Allen)*

"Judy helped arrange canoeing one day and bike rentals the next; the trails along the Willamette are an ideal summer escape. From the beautiful flowers in our room, to the cookies in the sitting room at night, everything was ideal." *(Sue & Al McDonald)* "Cold drinks upon arrival, thick terry robes, and a sitting area with a variety of books and an assortment of menus made for a terrific stay. Wonderful porch swing." *(Karla Kummer)* "Our reward for a long drive was an incredible whirlpool soak, complete with bubble bath, music, books, candles, and towel warmer." *(Annette Katsaros)* "Elegant without being ostentatious. Impeccably clean and well cared for." *(Alan & Myra Erwin)* "Very good breakfast, great coffee." *(Mr. & Mrs. James Powell)* "The house sits on a corner on a quiet, residential street." *(Eileen O'Reilly)* "Live plants and flowers everywhere." *(Joyanne Barret & Helmut Scholz)* "There's an intimate library complete with a rolling ladder to reach the ceiling-high shelves." *(Janis Baker)*

Open All year.

Rooms 4 doubles—all with private bath, data port/telephone jack, clock/radio, ceiling fan, hair dryer. 2 with desk. Guest phone.

Facilities Dining room, living room with fireplace, library with books, TV/VCR, unscreened porch with swing. Jacuzzi room. Off-street parking.

Location 2 blocks to center; approx. 15 blocks to U of O. From I-5, take exit 194B W to end of freeway (Jefferson St.). Go straight, through traffic light, for 3 blocks. Turn left on 10th. Go 1¾ blocks. Inn on left.

Restrictions May be light traffic noise on one side. No smoking. Children by arrangement.

Credit cards Amex, DC, MC, Visa.

Rates B&B, $70–95 double, $60–85 single. Extra person, $15. 2-night minimum special events, University functions. Discount for 5-night stay.

Extras Port-a-crib.

FLORENCE

Information please: The **Edwin K B&B** (1155 Bay Street, P.O. Box 2687, 97439; 541–997–8360 or 800–8EDWINK), built in 1914, offers six guest rooms named and decorated for the seasons. Most have a queen-size bed, and all have a private bath with either a clawfoot tub, shower, or whirlpool bath. Breakfast, included in the $85–125 rate, is served in the dining room in a formal setting with fine china, crystal, and flatware. "A delicious breakfast was artfully presented and served around an antique table; I felt like part of a large family with everyone freely talking about their activities. Innkeepers Sid and Bob were gracious, friendly and helpful. I stayed in the Fall Room, with its antique queen-size bed, and it was wonderful falling asleep to the sound of the waterfall in the courtyard just outside our door." *(Lee Haworth)*

Ron and Jayne Fraese restored the **Johnson House B&B Inn** (216 Maple Street, P.O. Box 1892, 97439; 541–997–8000), an Italianate Victorian home in 1982, and have decorated it in shades of blue and ivory, with period furniture, prints, photographs, and collectibles. Early morning coffee is available at 7 A.M., and a full breakfast is served at 8:30. B&B double rates for the five guest rooms range from $95–125.

For additional area inns, see **Winchester Bay** and **Yachats**.

GLENEDEN BEACH

Reader tip: "Delightful dinner at Chez Jeannette; comfortable surroundings. Ask for a table near the fireplace." *(Christopher Johnston)*

Information please: Under new ownership in 1996 and recently renovated is the well-known **Salishan Lodge** (Highway 101, 97388; 541–764–2371 or 888–SALISHAN) a 205-room resort, set on a bluff overlooking Siletz Bay. Salishan is a spread-out complex of two-story contemporary buildings, finished in natural wood and connected by covered bridges and walkways. In addition to three restaurants, the 700-acre grounds of this full-service resort provide ample space for an 18-hole golf course, beach, swimming pool, fitness center, tennis courts, and more. Although reader reports over the years have been quite positive—"Spacious room with a fireplace and great view; nice staff." (*Ruth Hurley*)—one reader who visited while renovations were going on was less than enthused about her experience. Reports please.

GOLD BEACH

Set on the southern coast, Gold Beach was named for the deposits obtained by placer mining, which lasted until the 1860s when a flood washed all the remaining gold out to sea. It's a popular resort area, and visitors enjoy exploring the beaches and hiking trails as well as the highly recommended jet boat trips up the Rogue River. Fishing, golf, and horseback riding are other favorite diversions. Gold Beach is on Highway 101 in southeastern Oregon, 35 miles from the California border.

Reader tip: "The Rogue River Hell Gate jet boat excursions are worth the money and crowds. Four-hour dinner and Sunday brunch cruises are available, along with shorter trips without meals. It's fun, it's exciting, and the food is great. Be prepared to get wet!" (*Carol Moritz*) "The all-day jet boat trip was a highlight of our family vacation." (*Judy Dawson*)

Also recommended: For an inexpensive Gold Beach alternative, readers are pleased with the clean, comfortable, simply furnished lodge units and motel rooms at **Ireland's Rustic Lodges** (P.O. Box 774, 97444; 541–247–7718.) Double rates for the 40 rooms are $45–81. "Ask for cabin #18 or 19, which are not attached to any of the others." (*Sharon Bielski*) "For $75, we had a large nonsmoking motel room on the beach, with a balcony and woodburning fireplace. No traffic noise, only the rumbling of the surf. Helpful office staff suggested a good breakfast place." (*Gail de Sciose*)

For additional area inns, see **Brookings** and **Port Orford.**

Inn at Nesika Beach ~~booked~~ Tel: 541–247–6434
33026 Nesika Road, 97444

Reminiscent of a New England Victorian summer cottage, the Inn at Nesika Beach sits a continent away, on a bluff overlooking the Pacific Ocean, and was built in 1992 by innkeeper Ann Arsenault. The comfy family room has inviting seating areas for reading, whale watching, or socializing, and the dining room, where breakfast is served, has a great ocean view. From the inn, guests can explore eight miles of remote sandy beach. Ann notes: "I hope that guests relax and enjoy the comfort of our B&B and the glorious setting; the inn is meant to be a home away from home." If you're planning to take a morning jet boat trip, she will serve your breakfast at 7 A.M., otherwise 8:30 or 9 A.M. is customary. A typical morning starts with fresh fruit, juices, and coffee, followed by crepes with strawberries, coddled eggs with scones, or smoked salmon with bagels and cream cheese.

"Sparkling clean. Wonderful views of the Oregon coast." *(Erin Walstead)* "Sophisticated yet casual with modern Victorian decor. Quiet, away from general traffic." *(Janet Pittenge)* "Our walks along the beach were great, and good for burning off the great breakfasts—each morning was a different treat; eggs Benedict, stuffed French toast, soufflé omelet with Gruyère cheese sauce." *(Vanessa Eisenhauer, also MW)* "The inn complements the beauty of the area. Ann has taken great pains to see to guest comfort with feather beds, wicker rockers on porches and a wonderful breakfast. Spotlessly clean, well-appointed rooms; lovely breakfasts with beautiful linens, tablecloths, and silver all made the atmosphere perfect." *(Helen Grove)*

Open All year.
Rooms 4 suites—all with private bath, whirlpool tub. 3 with fireplace, 2 with balcony, 1 with ceiling fan.
Facilities Dining room, family room with fireplace, piano, TV/VCR, stereo, books; guest refrigerator, porches. 1 acre on ocean.
Location 6 m N of town. Go N on Hwy. 101 & cross Rogue River Bridge. Go 5½ m & turn left at flashing yellow light onto Nesika Rd. Go ⁹⁄₁₀ m & look left for sign & driveway.
Restrictions No smoking. Older teenagers only.
Credit cards None accepted.
Rates B&B, $100–130 suite. Extra person, $20.
Extras Airport pickup.

Tu Tu' Tun Lodge ✕ க்.

96550 North Bank Rogue, Route 1, Box 365, 97444

Tel: 541–247–6664
800–864–6357
Fax: 541–247–0672
E-mail: TuTuTun@aol.com

This lodge takes its name from the Tu Tu' Tun Indians, whose name means the "people close to the river;" it's pronounced "toot-tootin,'" as in "tootin' a horn." Designed by owner Dirk Van Zante's architect parents, the Tu Tu' Tun Lodge is built in a rustic but contemporary style, overlooking the Rogue River. A typical dinner from the set menu might include scallop soup; blue cheese and apple salad; smoked turkey with sage, roasted potatoes with onion rings, popovers, steamed asparagus with mustard; and apple cranberry pie with ice cream. A longtime reader favorite, the Tu Tu' Tun gets consistently high marks for its fine food, comfortable accommodations, and excellent service.

"Perfectly maintained, well planned, and guest oriented. Gourmet dinners, served at large tables, at 7 P.M." *(Sally Ducot)* "The architecture and furnishings are exceptionally tasteful, consistent and beautiful; the rooms, both public and private, are elegant, warm, and comfortable. The meals are excellent and while there is little choice, the food is so good you look forward to each new experience. Service is impeccable and friendly; the innkeepers are skilled at making everyone feel welcome." *(James McCowan)* "Exceptional personal attention, with staff knowing you on a first name basis and catering to almost every whim. Rustically elegant, with a Pacific Northwest flavor. The Frank Lloyd Wright–inspired lighting on the grounds was awesome—the two firepits, lit every evening on the patio, were a cozy, romantic place to have a glass of wine. Highlights included the wonderfully comfortable beds, fluffy throw rugs in the bathroom, waffle-weave robes, quality amenities, excellent cuisine and the old-time player piano for sing-alongs." *(Judy Dawson)*

"Guest rooms are decorated in neutral tones, with fabrics in plaids or Native American designs, Mission-style furniture, and tile. Thoughtful details include comfortable chairs, effective lighting, top quality soaps, midday towel changes, fresh flowers, and evening turn-down with bedside cookies." *(Susan Lane)* "Glorious setting by the Rogue River. Wonderful reading material throughout the inn." *(Jack & Harriet Oppenheimer)* "Every thoughtful touch, from morning newspapers to magnifying mirrors in the bathrooms. Communal dining, to our surprise, turned out to be a plus, due in part to the thoughtful placement of guests by Dirk and Laurie." *(Ruth & Derek Tilsley)* "Our room was large and well decorated, with a beautiful view from the back porch. The helpful staff arranged babysitting, so we could have dinner without the kids. Would return in a heartbeat." *(Ruth Hurley)*

Open April 29–Oct. 30. Suites/cottage open all year.

Rooms 2 cottages, 2 suites, 16 doubles—all with private bath, balcony/patio, hairdryer. Suites with air-conditioning. Some with fireplace, soaking tubs.

Facilities Restaurant, bar, lounge with fireplace, player piano, billiards; library, gift shop. Heated swimming pool, boat dock and ramp, fishing, horseshoes, pitch and putt, children's play equipment. Hiking, golf, horseback riding nearby. Jet boat rides nearby.

Location 7 m E of town on N bank of Rogue River. From Hwy. 101, at N end of bridge, follow North Bank Rd. to inn. 7 m from ocean.

Restrictions Smoking in guest rooms only.

Credit cards MC, Visa.

Rates Room only, $125–310 cottage, $125–185 suite, $85–165 double. Extra person, $10. MAP $38 additional per person. 10% service charge. Outside guests: breakfast, $11; dinner, $33. Box lunch, $9.50.

Extras Wheelchair access. Airport, excursion boat pickup. Crib, babysitting. Spanish spoken.

GOVERNMENT CAMP

For an additional area entry, see listing for **Timberline Lodge** in **Timberline**.

Falcon's Crest Country Inn 👫 ✕
87287 Government Camp Loop Highway
P.O. Box 185, 97028

Tel: 503–272–3403
800–624–7384
Fax: 503–272–3454

From quarrying the rock for the woodstove hearth and exercise room floor to the installation of the cedar ceilings and walls, Melody and Bob

Johnson had their hands full with the design and construction of this chalet-style inn. Their work has paid off: the home fits in perfectly with the natural surroundings of the Cascades, although upgrading the inn is a continuing process. Guest rooms are individually decorated around a theme—the Cat Ballou has a lace comforter, brass bed, and red velvet chairs, the Safari has rattan pieces accented with animal-print fabrics, and the Master Suite has a French country look with an antique high four-poster bed and a Victorian settee.

"Genuine friendliness and little extra touches, such as early morning coffee and hot mini-muffins at our door, at the time we requested. Excellent six-course dinners by advance reservations; favorite entrees were saltimbocca, apricot-stuffed Cornish game hens, and chicken breast stuffed with Pacific baby shrimp." (Leslie Haid, and many others) "Impressive living room, with two-story windows. The Safari room was fun, with lions, tigers, and bears (stuffed, of course)." (Judy Fliagle) "Superb hosts who made us feel pampered." (Daniel Yates) "Loved the firm bed." (Pat Schwinn) "Super mix of great food and warm hospitality." (Melissa Gilley) "We felt pampered and welcome, and especially liked the Christmas tree in every guest room to celebrate the season, and the carolers who entertained at dinner." (LJS) "Immaculate rooms, beautifully maintained. Quality soaps and lotions in the bathroom." (Linda Gorrill) "B.J. is a chef who obviously enjoys his work and is also a great storyteller." (Frederick Teed) "Prompt response to all requests. A serene atmosphere in the woods." (Mark Nugen) "Located on Mt. Hood and surrounded by national forest. The inn itself has wildlife of several kinds eating bread off the decks." (Linda Hunter)

Open All year.
Rooms 2 suites, 3 doubles—all with private bath and/or shower, telephone, desk, balcony/deck. 1 with double whirlpool tub.
Facilities Dining room, breakfast room, living room with woodstove, TV/VCR, books; hot tub. Downhill, cross-country skiing; golf nearby.
Location 54 m E of Portland. Take Hwy 26 E to town.
Restrictions No smoking. Older children welcomed, toddlers discouraged.
Credit cards Amex, Discover, MC, Visa.
Rates B&B, $95–179 suite, double. 2–3 night holiday minimum. Prix fixe dinner, by reservation, $40. Ski, holiday, monthly entertainment packages. Multiple night discount.
Extras Station pickup. Limited babysitting.

GRANTS PASS

Grants Pass is located in southwestern Oregon, two hours south of Eugene, and a departure point for many raft trips on the Rogue River. Other activities include hiking, fishing, and jet boat rides.

Reader tip: "Highway 199, from Grants Pass to the coast is a scenic, forested highway following the river west to Jedediah Smith Redwoods State Park, connecting with Highway 101 in northern California. If you go south from Grants Pass on Highway 238 you come to the tiny town of Williams, with its 100-year-old general store complete with rough cut benches around a potbelly stove, mounted caribou on the wall, and lots of local flavor." *(Carol Moritz)*

Also recommended: A tree-lined, white-fenced drive leads to the **Home Farm** (157 Savage Creek Road, 97527; 541–582–0980 or 800–522–7967), a homey, comfortable B&B within walking distance of the Savage Rapids Park and the Rogue River. Furnishings include hand-stitched quilts, country crafts and collectibles. Shady trees, porches and decks provide quiet spots for relaxing. A hearty breakfast with fresh eggs from the hen house and berries from the garden is served family style around the handmade trestle table in the breakfast room. B&B double rates for the four guest rooms, each with private bath, are $65–85.

A small fishing lodge built in the 1940s, **Morrison's Rogue River Lodge** (8500 Galice Road, Merlin 97532; 541–476–3825 or 800–826–1963) sits on the scenic forested banks of the Rogue River in Merlin, 16 miles northwest of Grants Pass. The lodge offers accommodations in the main lodge or in 1- or 2-bedroom cabins (thirteen rooms in total), all with private bath. Fishing is the main attraction here, with an Orvis fly shop on the grounds, plus fly fishing packages and guided fishing trips. A heated swimming pool, hot tub, two tennis courts, and a putting green will keep the nonfishing members of your family happy. Everyone will appreciate the dining room which is well known for its blend of country and gourmet cuisine, all prepared from scratch in the kitchen and utilizing local products. The double rates of $160–300 include a full country breakfast and a four-course prix fixe dinner; during the fall fishing season picnic lunches are included in the rates.

Specialty painting techniques, lavish lace canopy beds, and creative use of country and European antiques accent the four romantically decorated guest rooms at the **Flery Manor** (2000 Jumpoff Joe Creek Road, 97526; 541–476–3591), built in 1991, and conveniently located just two miles from Exit 66 off I-5. Both the living room, with its cathedral ceiling, large Palladian-style window, and a two-story stone fireplace, and the large wraparound deck offer comfortable spots for viewing the forest-covered mountains. Breakfast is included in the $75–125 double rates, and may feature broiled grapefruit, a breakfast pudding, fresh herb and veggie frittata, and homemade breads. Comments?

Pine Meadow Inn	*Tel:* 541–471–6277
1000 Crow Road, Merlin 97532	800–554–0806
	Fax: 541–471–6277
	E-mail: pmi@cpros.com

Former San Francisco residents Maloy and Nancy Murdock report that "after a long search, we built this inn in 1991, working alongside our crew, doing the landscaping and decorating ourselves." Breakfast is served at the lace-draped dining room table, using organic, natural, and cholesterol-free ingredients as much as possible. Menus vary daily, starting with juice, yogurt and granola, followed by a fruit dish, and such entrees as Granny Smith waffles, German apple pancakes, or dilled frittata. Guests who prefer a light meal can enjoy a parfait of yogurt, fresh fruit, and granola served with muffins or breads. Guest rooms are charmingly decorated with country Victorian pieces, soft florals, and quilts in a color scheme of white, pink, and blue or green. The inn's grounds feature an English cutting garden, plus herb, fruit, and vegetable gardens, enjoyed by guests for their lovely fragrance, appearance, and at breakfast most mornings. In 1997, the inn was awarded three diamonds from AAA, unusual in a small B&B.

"Warm hospitality, pampering experience." *(Carolee Freedman)* "Spotlessly maintained with state-of-the-art plumbing and lighting." *(Donn & Margaret Wells)* "Gracious hospitality—friendly, caring, and efficient hosts, dedicated to having their guests relax, enjoy, and be comfortable." *(Richard Starr)* "Rooms are quiet; we could not hear other guests. The porch with wicker rockers was a favorite." *(Cheryl Clark)* "The outstanding feature was the peace, beauty and serenity of the woods." *(Robert & Catherine Fox)*

"Exceptionally clean and well kept; good lighting throughout. The roomy Willow had a foldout sofa, window seat, queen-size bed, and double sink in the bath; the Heather room is smaller but also lovely. The breakfast table was set with fresh flowers, linens and silver; delicious pecan orange French toast one day and mushroom zucchini frittata the next." *(GR)* "Crisp cotton sheets, supremely comfortable bed and fluffy pillows. Welcoming touches included chocolate chip cookies and chocolates. Breakfast was pleasing to the eye and palate, with herb and flower garnishes. Enjoyed both the pond and the hot tub." (MLV) "Excellent meals, presented in a timely and friendly way. Nancy and Maloy are nice people who obviously enjoy innkeeping." *(MCC)*

Open All year.
Rooms 4 doubles—all with full private bath, telephone, air-conditioning, fan.
Facilities Dining room, living room with fireplace, stereo, books; wrap-around porch. 9 acres with hot tub, gardens, koi pond, hiking. 1 m to Rogue River rafting, fishing, boating. 1 hour to downhill skiing.
Location SW OR. 45 m N of Ashland, 10 m N of Grants Pass. 2 m from town. From I-5, take Exit 61. Go W on Merlin/Galice Rd. for 5 m & turn right on Crow Rd. Go 1 m to inn on left.
Restrictions No smoking. Children over 8 accommodated.
Credit cards Discover, MC, Visa.
Rates B&B, $80–110 double.

HOOD RIVER

Reader tips: "Hood River is a world class center for wind surfing, and several shops in town rent and sell boards. A drive up Mt. Hood to the Timberline Lodge makes a nice trip; another is a ride on the Hood River Railroad in an open-air railroad car the base of Mt. Hood. Other options include visits to the Bonneville Dam, the Maryhill Museum (on the Washington side), and excursions up the Columbia Gorge Highway." *(Allen Dietz)*

Information please: We need current reports on the well-known **Columbia Gorge Hotel** (4000 West Cliff Drive, 97031; 541–386–5566 or 800–345–1921), a 46-room hotel and restaurant built in 1921. Its dining room has a good reputation and features food of the Pacific Northwest. Fast for a week before attempting the trademarked World Famous Farm Breakfast. The hotel's setting is dramatic, perched at the edge of a cliff 200 feet above the Columbia River Gorge, with Washington on one side, and Mt. Hood towering over the hotel on the Oregon side. Some rooms have fantastic waterfall views; others overlook the attractive grounds; some have less appealing sound effects compliments of I-84. B&B double rates range from $150–270, with suites to $365. "Accommodating front desk staff. The restaurant and the farm breakfast are delightful. Gorgeous grounds, setting of unparalleled beauty." *(Pam Phillips)* "Although our room was waterfront as requested, it was broom closet in size and broiling hot. We renegotiated with the front desk, and were given a lovely, large corner room overlooking the waterfall. The elevator was not working, so climbing the three flights of stairs to our room helped to work off the breakfast." *(NPS)*

Overlooking the river, the **Hood River Hotel** (102 Oak Avenue, 97031; 541–386–1900 or 800–386–1859) is a restored turn-of-the-century hotel with 41 suites and doubles, each individually decorated and furnished with reproduction four-poster beds. The hotel has a popular lobby bar and a restaurant which serves traditional and Mediterranean-style meals. "Lovely rooms and wonderful restaurant." *(Norma & Bob Simon)* B&B rates range from $69–145. Reports please.

High on the cliff above the Columbia River, is the **Lakecliff Estate** (3820 Westcliff Drive, 97031; 541–386–7000), a grand summer home built in 1908 by a well-known Portland architect, Albert Doyle. Each of the four guest rooms have fireplaces and river views, and the B&B double rates of $85–110 include a full breakfast. "Surrounded by woods and flower gardens; charming decor. Delightful conversation and breakfast on the deck, with views of the river and its windsurfers." *(Sue Lane)*

For additional area inns, see **Stevenson, Washington** and **White Salmon, Washington**.

JACKSONVILLE

Jacksonville was founded in 1851, following the discovery of gold in Rich Gulch. Today the town is a National Historic Landmark, with over 75 restored pioneer buildings to see and visit. Music also lures people to Jacksonville for the Peter Britt Festivals held every summer, featuring a wide variety of music and dance, from classical to bluegrass. Jacksonville is located in southwestern Oregon, 5 miles north of Medford and 21 miles northwest of Ashland.

Reader tips: "Pick up a copy of a 'Walk through Time' from the gift shop at the Jacksonville Inn, thoroughly describing the important homes and commercial buildings of the town. The Bella Union restaurant, housed in an 1870s building, is excellent for lunch or dinner, with an informal atmosphere, good desserts and a full bar." *(William Novack)* Also: "A delightful little town with restored old buildings. Heartily endorse the recommendation of the Bella Union. Highway 238 is a delightful alternative to the freeway between Grant's Pass and Medford, winding through farm and ranch country, picturesque valleys and rivers." *(Carol Moritz)* "This little town gets quite busy when the Britt Festival is going on; parking is tight, so ask for details." *(MW)* Several readers also commented on the fine meals at the **McCully House Inn**, open daily for dinner in summer and brunch on Sunday. This restored 1861 mansion is located on the edge of the shopping and restaurant district.

Information please: Twenty miles to the west is the **Applegate Lodge** (Box 3282, Applegate 97530; 541–846–6690) with newly built rooms and suites adjacent to its popular restaurant. Guest room balconies overlook the Applegate River, and the rates range from $125–170.

Also recommended: In nearby Medford is the historic **Under the Greenwood Tree** (3045 Bellinger Lane, Medford 97501; 541–776–0000), surrounded by ancient oaks and farm buildings dating back to the 1860s. The four guest rooms, all with private bath, are named after the region's famous pears, and are furnished with Persian rugs, fine quilts, and European and American antiques. "A lush garden, fountains, romantic swing, make this excellent for honeymooners. Renata Ellam, a native of Germany, is a Cordon Bleu chef and her hospitality is exceptional." *(Debbie King)* Rates of $95–125 include a full breakfast.

Jacksonville Inn ✕
175 East California Street, P.O. Box 359, 97530

Tel: 541–899–1900
800–321–9344
Fax: 541–899–1373
E-mail: jvinn@mind.net

The Jacksonville Inn, owned by Jerry and Linda Evans since 1976, is housed in one of Jacksonville's earliest permanent structures. Built in 1861, the walls of the dining area and lounge were built of sandstone quarried locally; specks of gold are scattered throughout the mortar. The breakfast menu offers such choices as omelets, Belgian waffles, and brioche French toast, and is served in the dining room. Lunch options range from sandwiches and salads to pasta dishes. Favorite dinner entrees include veal scallopini, chicken with apple-hazelnut stuffing, fettuccine with tomatoes and garlic, and shrimp scampi.

"The upstairs guest rooms are done in casual frontier style with exposed brick walls and country antiques." *(Pam Phillips)* "The dining areas include a breakfast/lunch section with red Victorian decor, a downstairs dining room and bistro, and a delightful courtyard. Food is well prepared and graciously served." *(Elinor McGrew, and others)* "I loved the soft pastel wallpaper, coordinating carpet, canopy bed, and the well-chosen mahogany furniture in cottage #10. Wonderful selection of teas in our tiny kitchen." *(Susan Vuylsteke)* "Energetic, enthusiastic staff, dressed in period costume. We never saw the cleaning crew—but their thoroughness was apparent." *(Alec & Janie Bodenweiser)* "Our charming cottage had a canopied king-size bed, fantastic sound system, double Jacuzzi, a three-sided fireplace that lit with the flick of a switch, champagne in the refrigerator, fresh strawberries in a basket, and chocolate-almond bars on our pillow. First-rate fresh coffee and freshly squeezed orange juice at our breakfast on the patio amongst flowers and greenery." *(M. Jeanne Kennedy)* "Hearty, simple and fresh approach to cooking." *(R.B. Montaigue)* "Our cottage was quiet, with dimmer switches on most lights." *(Karen Carroll)* "The Peter Britt room had an antique canopy bed, comfy robes, good lighting and plumbing; it was quiet, too." *(Lee Roger)* "Excellent, professional staff who were pleasant and efficient." *(George Baucom)* "Extensive wine list, and a selection of fine cigars." *(Donald Miller)*

Open All year.
Rooms 3 cottages, 8 doubles—all with private bath and/or shower, TV, radio, air-conditioning, refrigerator. 1 double with in-room Jacuzzi, 1 with steam shower. Cottages with Jacuzzi, steam shower, TV/VCR/stereo, fireplace, microwave, refrigerator.
Facilities Dining room, breakfast room, bar/lounge. Off-street parking.
Location In center of town at intersection.
Restrictions No smoking in guest rooms, dining rooms. Fire station next door.
Credit cards Amex, CB, DC, Discover, MC, Visa.
Rates B&B, $195–225 cottage, $90–139 double, $80–129 single. Extra person, $10. Alc lunch, $7–10; alc dinner, $20. Children's menu.
Extras Airport/station pickup.

LA GRANDE

Stang Manor Inn ¢
1612 Walnut Street, 97850

Tel: 541–963–2400
888–286–9463
Fax: 541–963–2400
E-mail: stang@eoni.com

The town of La Grande was named for the beauty of the area—grand! It sits between the Blue and Wallowa mountains, at the western edge of the Grande Ronde Valley, with lumber a major component of its economy. In 1926 timber baron August Stang spared no expense to construct this Georgian Colonial mansion, as can been seen in its extraordinary woodwork. Renovated as an inn in 1987, it was purchased by Marjorie and Patrick McClure in 1992. From 7 to 9 A.M. breakfast is served in the formal dining room, with crystal, fine china and sterling silver; French toast or perhaps strata is offered with homemade breads, muffins, and fresh fruit. In the late afternoon tea is served in the garden or by the living room fireplace.

"A beautiful two-story, columned white house with a pristine lawn and huge trees. My lavish breakfast began with homemade muffins, followed by egg soufflé and sausage and finished off with a berry crumble. Cookies await in the upstairs hall for snacking. Uncluttered rooms; the suite is particularly appealing with a sitting room with a fireplace, and adjoining bedrooms." *(Ellen Clark)* "Ann's room was lovely with a four-poster bed draped with organza. Delicious breakfast, especially the cinnamon apple sausage." *(Kelly Johnson)* "Beautiful gardens, in a scenic neighborhood. Stimulating conversation." *(Lis & Sean Walton)* "Lots of reading material, including some great old magazines dating to the 1940s." *(Pegge Aquilar)* "Spacious rooms, good beds, immaculately clean. Gracious, interesting, helpful hosts." *(Ruth Hoover)*

Open All year.
Rooms 2 suites, 2 doubles—all with private shower and/or tub, telephone, clock/radio, ceiling fan. 1 with TV, fireplace, desk.
Facilities Dining room, living room with fireplace, TV/VCR, organ, books; sun room. 1 acre with rose gardens, 3 off-street parking spaces. 45 min. from skiing.
Location NE OR. 150 m E of Portland. 8 blocks from center. Take I-84 E to Exit 259. Go S on Hwy. 30 to Walnut St. & turn right to inn on right.
Restrictions No smoking. Children 10 and older.
Credit cards MC, Visa.
Rates B&B, $90 suite, $75 double, $70 single. Extra person, $15.
Extras Local airport/station pickups.

McMINNVILLE

Information please: Fifteen miles southwest of McMinnville is the **Middle Creek Run** (25400 Harmony Road, Sheridan 97378; 503–843–7606), a restored Victorian home with four guest rooms, two with private bath. Named for the creek running through the center of their 97 acres of fields and woodland, John Tallerino and Marc Randall opened their inn in 1996. "Five-course breakfasts are served with out-of-the-ordinary style and taste; the menu each day is different and always an experience to savor. Wondrous coffee cakes, rolls, and muffins, special omelets, and the fruit soups are my favorites. The grounds are beautifully landscaped, and the Victorian rose garden is a favorite for weddings and parties. John's cooking talent is top notch, the buffet meals outstanding." *(Tina Clayton)* B&B double rates are $75.

For additional area inns, see **Dayton** and **Newberg**.

Youngberg Hill Vineyard B&B   *Tel:* 503–472–2727
10660 Youngberg Hill Road, 97128   *Fax:* 503–472–1313
                                E-mail: martin@youngberghill.com

A contemporary farmhouse built in 1989, the Youngberg Hill Farm Inn was purchased by Jane and Martin Wright in 1996. A working farm and vineyard, the activities flow with the seasons—lambing in March, blackberry picking in August and September, the grape harvest in October—but all year long guests can enjoy the beauty of the Willamette Valley. A country breakfast is served from 8:30–9:30 A.M. at the large dining room table; a typical menu might include ginger scones and fruit compote, followed by scrambled eggs in puff pastry or baked apple pancakes with turkey sun-dried tomato sausage.

"The soft, rolling countryside, good food and lodging at Youngberg Hill satisfies mind, body, and soul. The Willamette Valley is home to the best pinot noir grapes outside of France; the Wrights are experts on the valley wine producers and have their own wine cellar with hard-to-find local vintages and reasonable prices. Their living room has comfortable seating areas, and the large dining table makes for pleasant breakfast conversation. The spacious bedrooms have large, comfortable beds, ample dresser and closet space, and great views. Delicious breakfasts of eggs Benedict, orange-ginger muffins, kiwi jelly, black currant scones, and freshly squeezed orange juice." *(Ray Sundstrom)*

"Inspiring hilltop location overlooking the Willamette Valley and Oregon wine country, with views of snow-capped Cascades in the distance. The wraparound deck offers comfortable seating, sunny or shade, a perfect place for morning coffee or a sip of local wine in the evening while enjoying the pastoral farm scene below. The fireplace in my room offered a cozy blaze, welcome on a cool July night. Jane and Martin are congenial hosts, who make guests feel at home and are helpful in every way." *(Carole Lee Smith)* "Our queen-size bed was covered with a duvet and a quilt, comfortable as cool breezes swept in our open windows. The sound of birds awoke us for a day of cycling and we returned to fresh, large towels laid out in our bath." *(Sal & Liz LoVecchio)* "In the evening cheese and crackers or fruit is laid out. A small refrigerator is stocked with iced tea and lemonade, and an honor bar has wine. Guest rooms have beautiful replica antique beds and bureaus; a hall closet is filled with amenities often forgotten—shampoo, iron, rubbing alcohol, and more." *(MW)*

Open All year.

Rooms 5 doubles—all with private bath and/or shower, clock, air-conditioning. 2 with fireplace.

Facilities Dining room with refrigerator, living room with fireplace, porch. 50 acres with vineyard, wine cellar, hiking trails. Golf nearby.

Location NW OR. 40 m SW of Portland. 10 m from town. From Rte. 18, take second McMinnville exit, marked 99W McMinnville, Corvallis. Go right, past Texaco station, to traffic signal. Go straight onto Old Sheridan Rd. for 1 m to Peavine Rd. Turn right, then go 2 m to Youngberg Hill Rd. Turn left & go 1 m to inn's sign & entry. Wherever a choice, go up hill. Enter through gate & close behind you.

Restrictions No smoking. Children over 10 preferred because of machinery & electric farm fence.

Credit cards MC, Visa.

Rates B&B, $130–150 double. Extra person, $25. 2-night special event weekend/holiday minimum.

NEWBERG

For additional area inns, see **Dayton** and **McMinnville**.

Springbrook Hazelnut Farm　　　　　　*Tel:* 503–538–4606
30295 North Highway 99 West, 97132　　　　　　800–793–8528
　　　　　　　　　　　　　　　　　Fax: 503–537–4004
　　　　　　　　　　E-mail: springbr@sprynet.com

"A working hazelnut farm; hazelnuts in the succulent cookies awaiting you in your room; local yogurt, fresh raspberries, asparagus frittata, homemade hazelnut granola, and croissants for breakfast. A Craftsman-style farmhouse jazzed up with color (vivid yellow and greens), a dazzling selection of contemporary art—this is no ordinary homestay farm, and owners Chuck and Ellen McClure no ordinary farmers or innkeepers. They are kind, generous-spirited people who genuinely find other people interesting, and are warm hosts and great storytellers. Sophisticated and well-travelled, they know to leave you alone when you need it—or be right there. Total comfort, spectacular food including a grilled veggie-burger brushed with jalapeño jelly, instead of breakfast meat, for a vegetarian. The Carriage House is private and spacious, and its full kitchen was even stocked with a premium hot chocolate. And those rows of trees, serene and orderly, just outside the window." *(Crescent Dragonwagon)*

Anything but ordinary is how you would describe the interior of this 1912 bungalow—instead of the dark woodwork popular in Craftsman-style houses, Ellen has painted the elaborate woodwork in the grand hallway a bright shade of yellow and wallpapered it with a lattice-patchwork motif. Its background is special enough too, so that the house has been listed on the National Register of Historic Places. Guest rooms feature the same eclectic and lively spirit, with a mix of country antiques, stenciled floors, and English floral fabrics. Breakfast is served at 9 A.M. in the wicker-filled sunroom that runs across the front of the house, with favorite entrees of chicken-apple sausage and a frittata or ham crepes with asparagus.

"You enter the shaded, winding driveway and are met by the two official greeters, Ghillie and Duffy (two playful and fun-loving springer spaniels) who will be your new best friends during your stay." *(Mr. & Mrs. Adams)* "Creatively decorated, clean, and comfortable way to enjoy the wine country." *(Bruce Blocher)* "The home is stylish, like Chuck and Ellen; elegant antiques blend with lovely art pieces. Lighting, plumbing, parking are well-designed and safe." *(Tricia Volk)* "Complete privacy in the cottage, always immaculate and appealing. Chuck and Ellen are gracious, friendly and helpful—the perfect hosts. We enjoyed bicycling on the country roads and returning to swim in the pool." *(Jayne Fasady)*

Open Main house open Apr.–Nov.; cottage & carriage house open all year.

Rooms 1 cottage, 1 2-bedroom carriage house suite, 3 doubles—all with private bath and/or shower, clock, fan. 3 with air-conditioning, desk, refrigerator. 1 with telephone, TV/VCR, fireplace.

Facilities Main house: dining room, living room with fireplace, piano, TV, stereo, books, deck. 10 acres of garden, 60 acres of orchard with swimming pool, tennis court, swing, gazebo, croquet, small lake with canoe. 2 hrs. to skiing, hiking.

Location 20 m SW of Portland. From Portland, take I-5 S to Tigard exit. Go W on Hwy. 99W about 14 m to milepost 21. The farm is at the bottom of Rex Hill on the right.

Restrictions No smoking. Some highway noise in front rooms. Infants or over age 18.

Credit cards None.

Rates B&B, $140–200 cottage, carriage house, suite; $95 double, $80 single. Extra person, $25. Weekly, winter rates available.

Extras Local airport pickup. Port-a-crib. Spanish, some Italian, French spoken.

NEWPORT

Newport, on the central Oregon coast about 120 miles southwest of Portland, has been a popular resort and fishing town for over 100 years. Visitor attractions include the Devil's Punchbowl, a rock formation that fills with a roar at high tide; the OSU Science Center and Aquarium; and the restored Yaquina Bay lighthouse.

Also recommended: The **Sylvia Beach Hotel** (267 N.W. Cliff Street, 97365; 541–265–5428), aptly described as a cliffhanger by its literary nonresident owners, is named for Sylvia Beach, owner of the legendary Paris bookstore Shakespeare and Company, and first publisher of James Joyce's *Ulysses*. Guest rooms, named for different writers, are decorated either in period style or inspired by the author's books; many have queen-size beds and ocean views. Tea, coffee, and wine are served in the library at 10 P.M. Dinners in the "Tables of Content" restaurant are served at tables of eight, with one seating at 7 P.M. Sunday through Thursday, and two seatings (at 6 and 8:30 P.M.) on weekends. Readers are generally enthused about the generous buffet breakfasts, the convivial, outstanding seafood dinners, the friendly, eager-to-please staff, and the literary charms of the library and the small but evocative rooms. One frequent contributor was disappointed, and felt that the inn was overdue for a deep cleaning; he also found the well-stocked library to be authentically quiet. B&B double rates range from 21 guest rooms range from $60–150, depending on size of room and view.

Oar House B&B	*Tel:* 541–265–9571
520 Southwest Second Street, 97365	800–252–2358

Constructed in 1900 from timber washed ashore from an abandoned lumber schooner, this Craftsman-style house was large enough to become a boarding house (after all, the wood was free). It had cubicles with cots and washstand for 30 boarders; this arrangement was perfect for its next life as a bordello. Times change, and so did the house, becoming a B&B in 1987 after major renovations (many fewer rooms, for starters), and the addition of a lighthouse tower with widow's walk. In 1992 Jan LeBrun purchased the inn, expanding and improving every room, and decorating with Persian carpets, international art, nautical paraphernalia, and her eclectic collections; exposed beams and timber panelling highlight the decor throughout. Today guests have a choice of seating areas, from the commodious living room to a wind-sheltered deck. The more energetic can climb the ship's ladder on the third floor to enter the cupola with its 360-degree view of the ocean, Yaquina Head, lighthouses, picturesque Nye Beach, and magnificent sunsets. The dining room, where a breakfast of juice, fresh fruit, and a hot entree is served from 8:30–9:30 A.M., has an appealing display of Thai birdcages and china above the sideboard, a cathedral ceiling, and a long pine table surrounded by ladderback chairs.

"Jan was pleasant and informative, welcoming but unobtrusive; her sense of style throughout the house matched the historical seaside feeling of Newport. Soft music playing in the living room enhanced the welcoming atmosphere of big, cushy sofas and throw blankets. We stayed in the Library room and Jan's collection of magazines led to a relaxing evening of reading; the bed was luxuriously comfortable. The bathroom, although tucked in a small space with an interesting slanted ceiling, was clean and well decorated; the wallpaper was reproduction 1900s Sears catalog pages and the clawfoot tub had a strong-flowing hand-held shower attachment. Our breakfast of fresh, homemade blueberry pancakes was delicious and the conversation informative and delightful. The location is great—a comfortable walk from both the beach and the main section of town." *(Marissa Favorite)*

Open All year.
Rooms 1 suite, 4 doubles—all with private shower and/or tub, clock/radio. 2 with desk, 1 with fan.
Facilities Dining room, living room with TV, guest refrigerator; sitting room with fireplace; cupola, porch. Off-street parking.
Location From Hwy 101 S, turn right on Hwy 20. At Olive, turn left & go to inn on right corner of S.W. 2nd St.
Restrictions No smoking. No children.
Credit cards Discover, MC, Visa.
Rates B&B, $100–120 suite, $90–110 double, $85–105 single. Extra person, $30. 2-night off-season midweek discount.
Extras Some Spanish spoken.

Tyee Lodge   *Tel:* 541–265–8953
4925 N.W. Woody Way, 97365   888–553–TYEE
                                              E-mail: mcconn@teleport.com

Centuries ago, the Yaquina, a Native American people, fished this area in summer, and caught many salmon, called *Tyee* in the Chinook language. Today the Tyee Lodge, built in the 1940s, enjoys a park-like setting overlooking the Pacific as its legacy as part of a family estate; another benefit is the trail leading down to the beach. Mark and Cindy McConnell purchased the property in 1995 and have remodelled the house as a B&B, offering crisply contemporary accommodations with large windows to take in the ever-changing ocean view. Mark is the breakfast chef; he strives to keep meals low in fat and cholesterol, and is happy to meet special diet restrictions (with advance notice). Breakfast is served family-style at 9 A.M. and a typical menu includes fresh fruit and juice, freshly baked muffins or cinnamon rolls, and such entrees as pumpkin pancakes, vegetable frittata, or smoked salmon quiche. A beverage bar is available throughout the day, with hot drinks, soda and wine, and plenty of popcorn. "Nice, clean, and new; while rooms are not large, they're adequate and comfortable. Good breakfasts every day. Yaquina Head is adjacent to the inn with a beautiful lighthouse at the end of the cape." *(Terry Busby)* "Our Chinook room was attractive and comfortable, with the decor tied in with Chinook salmon. The inviting guest living room had a cozy fire, binoculars, and a fascinating collection of books and magazines. Breakfast was presented on a beautifully set table, with flowers and candles, and included French toast stuffed with cream cheese and apricot jam, topped with blackberries. Because Cindy teaches full-time, Mark is the innkeeper, but both were delightful, easy-to-talk-to hosts; we also enjoyed peaceful, quiet times listening to the roar of the ocean. Parking is handy, and we took the steep path to the beach; steps and handrails made it safe. The beach was lively and sheltered from the wind by Yaquina Head." *(Sherrie Kuhl)*

Open All year.
Rooms 5 doubles—all with private shower/tub, clock/radio, desk. 1 with fireplace.
Facilities Dining room, living room with fireplace, family room with TV, guest refrigerator, microwave & laundry. ½ acre with fire pit, beach access, lawn games, off-street parking.
Location 3 m from center. From Newport, go N on Hwy. 101. Turn left on N.W. Woody Way, at public parking lot/beach access, just past BP station on right. Bear left, to inn on right.
Restrictions No smoking. Children over 16.
Credit cards Discover/Novus, MC, Visa.
Rates B&B, $90–120 double, $80–100 single. AAA discount; senior discount in winter. 2-night holiday, special event minimum.
Extras Station pickup. Spanish, German, French spoken.

PORTLAND

Oregon's largest city, Portland straddles both sides of the Willamette River near its confluence with the Columbia. A friendly, manageable city, Portland is known for its parks and its lively arts scene. Over 160 parks and public gardens dot the area, including the 5,000-acre Forest Park, the largest wilderness preserve located within the limits of any U.S. city. Portland's vigorous public arts program includes the Saturday market that brings over 300 quality craftsmen and performers together every weekend from April through Christmas. In September you can visit "Artquake," when downtown streets are closed for lively displays by artists and entertainers. Don't miss the March kite-flying contest, the antique shops lining N.E. 13th Avenue in Old Sellwood, or the Skidmore/Old Town Historical District with its mix of people, ethnic restaurants, and funky shops.

From Portland, it's about a 1½-hour drive west to the ocean and a 1-hour drive to the east for skiing. The Columbia and Willamette River recreation areas are about 15 minutes away for swimming, fishing, sailboarding, and tennis courts and golf courses are in ample supply.

Reader tips: "Jake's Crawfish, a Portland institution since 1862, is a fabulous place to eat." *(Judy Dawson)* And: "We find Jake's vastly overrated." *(RS)* "Portland has a high rate of car theft; park defensively." *(Christopher Hart Johnston)*

Also recommended—B&B: The **Heron Haus B&B** (2545 N.W. Westover Road, 97210; 503–274–1846), has a quiet hilltop location, yet is only blocks from the restaurants and shops of northwest Portland. The common rooms of this English Tudor built in 1904 are ample and spacious, most done with contemporary flair. The six guest rooms have Hawaiian names and decorative touches, and the suite with private inside hot tub has fabulous views of the city below and Mt. Hood in the distance. Outside, guests may enjoy a swim in the pool. A continental breakfast is included in the $125–250 double rates; single corporate rate, $85. "We had a large room with two sitting areas and a huge bathroom-dressing area. Walking distance to great shops and restaurants." *(Margaret Sievers)* "Peaceful and relaxing atmosphere. Breakfast is served when you like, at individual tables, ideal for folks who don't want to chat early in the morning. Julie Keppeler is a charming but discrete innkeeper; we saw her briefly at breakfast." *(Wendy Kameda)*

Also recommended—hotels: Listed on the National Register of Historic Places, the Seward Hotel was built in 1909 at the height of the Arts and Crafts movement. After a $15 million renovation joined it with the equally historic Princeton Building next door, the hotel re-opened in 1992 as **The Governor Hotel** (611 S.W. Tenth at Alder, 97205; 503–224–3400 or 800–554–3456). The decor in the public rooms incorporates original details with newer Art Deco and Art Modern flourishes; wall sconces are replicas of a 1940s mica-and-bronze light fixture. The guest rooms range in size from tiny to spacious, and furnishings here are simpler and more traditional in style. The 32 suites and 68 doubles have rates of $210–500 suite and $185–200 double; each has terry-cloth robes, a morning paper delivered to the door, and an honor bar while the more expensive have a fireplace, whirlpool tub, or terrace overlooking the city.

The elegant **The Heathman Hotel** (1001 S.W. Broadway at Salmon Street, 97205; 503–241–4100 or 800–551–0011) was built in the late 1920s and is listed on the National Register of Historic Places. It was almost completely gutted and rebuilt in 1984. Now a full-service luxury hotel, its amenities include terry bathrobes and thrice daily maid service; the 151 rooms are furnished in warm earth tones, highlighted by original artwork. Its highly acclaimed restaurant serves three meals daily, specializing in northwestern cuisine. "Rooms are understated but comfortable with lots of amenities, prompt room service, and helpful staff. There's a library, and afternoon tea, giving a 1920s ambience. The lounge has nightly jazz or piano performances." *(Russ Stratton)* "Liked the Far Eastern decor in our cozy room. Convenient location next to the Performing Arts Center." *(B.J. Hensley)* The double rates range from $180–225 midweek, with weekend rates starting at $140.

The **Hotel Vintage Plaza** (422 S.W. Broadway, 97205; 800–243–0555 or 503–228–1212) offers 107 guest rooms in a luxury environment. Rates of $170–245 include morning coffee and muffins; the Concierge Level rooms have soaking tubs or conservatory windows and additional amenities such as a private lounge with evening cocktails and hors d'oeuvres, and a continental breakfast. "Provided comfort with fine architectural design; tasteful furniture and fabric; attentive service." *(Christopher Hart Johnston)* "My courtyard room was small; my street-side room was noisy." *(EA)*

The renovated **Imperial Hotel** (400 Southwest Broadway at Stark, 97205; 503–223–7221 or 800–452–2323) has state-of-the-art amenities including refrigerators, computer/modem hook-ups and a daily newspaper at your door, plus vanity mirror/hairdryers and fluffy thick towels. B&B double rates for the 136 rooms range from $85–100. "Sharing the same street facade with the Vintage Court next door, I thought the remodeled rooms at the Imperial as comfortable as the Vintage Court at half the price." *(CHJ)*

A longtime reader favorite, the **Mallory Hotel** (729 S.W. 15th Avenue at Yamhill, 97205; 503–223–6311 or 800–228–8657) is known for its old-fashioned, unglitzy charm, ongoing improvements, and pleasant, personable staff. Double rates for the 136 guest rooms and suites range from $75–110. "A bargain, yet we were treated like royalty. Consistently a good value, clean, and secure. Convenient, yet away from the noise of downtown—we used Portland's great transit system to get around. Much of the staff has been there for years, and know many of the repeat guests. While the hallways had not yet been updated, the lobby was inviting, with beautiful arrangements of fresh flowers and gleaming chandeliers. Food and service were superb. Our room had old-fashioned charm; everything was in working order and the bed was comfy." *(Judy Dawson)*

Another equally good budget choice is the **Mark Spencer Hotel** (409 Southwest 11th Avenue, 97205; 503–224–3293 or 800–548–3934), two blocks away, with B&B rates from $75–115. "Friendly staff and practically across street from that Portland institution, Jake's Crawfish, and nearby the stupendous Powell's Books—there couldn't be a better location." *(CHJ)*

An elegantly furnished luxury hotel with 84 guest rooms, the **Riverplace** (1510 S.W. Harbor Way, 97201; 503–228–3233 or 800–227–1333) is part of Portland's Riverplace Esplanade. Hotel amenities include continental breakfast, terry bathrobes, overnight shoe shine, and morning newspapers. "Lovely river views, off the main street." *(Russ Stratton)* "On the river, with esplanade between the hotel and the river. Small marina; lovely restaurant; helpful staff; quiet." *(Mrs. Ward Johnson)* Double rates are $215–220.

Information please: A restored historic hotel of note is **The Benson** (309 Southwest Broadway, 97205; 503–228–2000 or 800–426–0670), built in 1913 in the French Baroque style. Observing the maxim, "if it's not baroque, don't fix it," the hotel was renovated in 1993 at a cost of $20 million. The common areas are elegant once again, and the 286 suites and doubles comfortable with traditional decor. Double rates range from $130–210. "Grand old hotel setting, with London Grill that never disappoints, heir to much of the James Beard school of cooking. The menu is not pricey and there's a spectacular Sunday brunch." *(Russ Stratton)* Reports on the rooms appreciated.

For additional area accommodations, see **Troutdale,** 20 miles east of Portland.

The Lion and the Rose   *Tel:* 503–287–9245
1810 N.E. 15th Street   800–955–1647
Mailing address: 1517 N.E. Schuyler, 97212   *Fax:* 503–287–9245
                          E-mail: lionrose@ix.netcom.com

The Freiwald estate occupied three-quarters of a city block in 1906; Gustav Freidwald, then owner of the Star Brewery, built the complex with a stable for his Clydesdale draft horses, a playground for his children, a garage for his "horseless" carriages, and its most distinctive building, the elaborate, Queen Anne–style home that now houses the Lion and the Rose. Kay Peffer, Kevin Spanier, and Sharon Weil bought this Victorian fantasy in 1993; it's now listed on the National Register of Historic Places, and incorporates ornate decorative plaster work and medieval elements popularized by William Morris, such as oriel windows and a tower. Kay, the innkeeper, serves breakfast from 8:30–10 A.M. at the dining room table; early coffee is ready at 6:30 A.M. A typical breakfast includes strawberry-banana French toast or perhaps baked eggs and potatoes, plus freshly baked muffins, fresh fruit, coffee and juice.

"Beautiful, ornate, 10,000-square-foot Victorian mansion, with authentic period furnishings and elegant decor. Everything is large—the living room, the dining room, and the veranda where we enjoyed a complimentary glass of sherry in the evening. Each guest room is distinctive, but all seemed equal in size and value. Our room had antique carved oak furniture, beautiful rich-looking linens and comforter on the bed, with numerous pillows and shams; the color scheme was dark greens and rose pinks. The Lavonna, the most elegant, has an inviting seating area in the tower portion of the room, plus leaded glass windows, and a king-size iron bed. Service is good, the innkeepers friendly, knowledgeable and helpful. It's located in a historic neighborhood surrounded by other lovely homes; we drove or took public transit to downtown Portland across the river." *(Wendy Kameda)* "The Starina room was most handsome with dark color tones, elegant furnishings, and steps for easy access to the high mattress on the antique Edwardian bed." *(WN)*

Open All year.
Rooms 6 doubles—all with private shower and/or bath, telephone, data port, clock/radio, desk, air-conditioning.
Facilities Dining room, living room with fireplace, parlor with fireplace, porch. Large city lot with gazebo. On-street parking. ½ block to Tri-Met Transit stop.
Location Irvington historic district. 6 min. to downtown by public transit.
Restrictions No smoking. Children over 6.
Credit cards Amex, MC, Visa.
Rates B&B, $85–120 double. Extra person, $15. Visitor breakfast, $8.50, by prior arrangement.

MacMaster House ¢
1041 S.W. Vista Avenue, 97205

Tel: 503–223–7362
800–774–9523
Fax: 503–224–8808
E-mail: cmurphy656@aol.com

Located in the historic King's Hill neighborhood—one of Portland's wealthiest at the turn of the century—the MacMaster House was built in the 1880s in the Queen Anne style. Some 20 years later the house was remodeled as a Colonial Revival, with the addition of a colossal portico with Doric columns and Palladian windows with leaded glass. Owner Cecilia Murphy has furnished her B&B with an unusual mix of European antiques, African furnishings, Asian wicker, and works by Oregon artists. Sourdough French toast with powdered sugar and fresh blueberries are among the many breakfast specialties.

"The decor is eclectic—mildly wild and great fun—with fascinating accessories; books abound in every room. The guest refrigerator is filled with wine, microbrews, soft drinks and mineral water for guests to help themselves." *(Eileen O'Reilly)* "Light, airy, and inviting guest rooms. Cecilia is relaxed, friendly and genuine; she was helpful with information and insights on Portland." *(Madeline Wu, also James Polak)* "I felt at home, sitting by the fire, enjoying a glass of wine, and reading. Breakfast was both tasty and healthy—not always an easy combination to find." *(Karen Fredericks)* "Calming and comfortable from the beautiful bed linens, the special arrangements of antiques to the large, soft bath towels. Close to a wonderful walking path and great shopping; the bus stops right in front." *(Gail Pearson)* "The ever-changing breakfasts feature wonderful local fruits, nuts and berries." *(Debbie Chung)* "Cecilia is accommodating and gregarious, creating a convivial atmosphere." *(Adam Platt)* "Eclectic is the best way to describe the decor of the main sitting room, which has an animal skin rug under a desk, chairs with faux fur covers, an old settee and chairs with black on black fabric, and a little table and chair set that looks like it belongs in an ice cream parlor." *(SC)*

Open All year.
Rooms 2 suites, 3 doubles, 2 singles—2 with full private bath, 5 with maximum of 4 people sharing bath. All with TV, air-conditioning; some with fireplace, desk, balcony.
Facilities Living room, dining room, library, guest refrigerator, veranda, patio. 2 blocks from Washington Park for jogging, tennis.
Location King's Hill. 16 blocks from center.
Restrictions No smoking. Children 14 and over.
Credit cards Amex, Discover, DC, MC, Visa.
Rates B&B, $120 suite, $85 double, $75 single. Extra person, $30.

PORT ORFORD

Information please: While small, with only two guest rooms, the **Home by the Sea B&B** (444 Jackson Street, P.O. Box 606, Port Orford 97465; 541–332–2855) has a view as large as the southern coast of Oregon. This contemporary home has a cliffside location, overlooking port orford's harbor and beach, and is just a two-block walk to town. A full breakfast is included in the $95 double rates; the rooms have private baths, telephones, queen-size beds, and cable TV. "Nice, large, private rooms with wonderful ocean views. Breakfast included local products and thick, light waffles. Innkeeper Alan Mitchell knows the area well." *(Ruth Beal)*

For additional area inns, see **Bandon** and **Gold Beach**.

SALEM

Information please: A charming English cottage–style home built in 1924, the **Cottonwood Cottage** (960 E. Street, 97301; 503–362–3979 or 800–349–3979) is within walking distance of state offices, the capitol, Willamette University and downtown shopping. Each of the two guest rooms offer queen- or twin-size beds, air-conditioning, and TV, and bathrobes are provided for the shared bathroom. B&B double rates of $55–60 include a full breakfast. Well travelled hosts Bill and Donna Wickman report "Willyum and Merry, our resident cats, allow us to live at Cottonwood and welcome your visit."

SEASIDE

Oregon's largest and oldest ocean resort, Seaside offers numerous activities, including beachcombing; deep-sea, stream, and lake fishing; clamming and crabbing; plus tennis, golf, bicycling, and horseback riding. Seaside is on Oregon's north coast about 80 miles northwest of Portland (via Route 26) and 17 miles south of the Columbia River. Seattle lies 170 miles to the northeast.

Reader tip: "Bicycle, rollerblade, or stroll all along the Prom for breathtaking views." *(EVL)* "The Promenade is a fascinating place for a stroll, even in cool, gray weather." *(Carol Worth)* "Unlike the busy, noisy town of Seaside in summer, the beach itself is lovely." *(JM)*

Also recommended: Built in 1898, **Anderson's Boarding House** (208 North Holladay Drive, 97138; 503–738–9055 or 800–995–4013) was restored as a B&B in 1983. Modern insulation, plumbing, and wiring add modern comfort; white gingerbread trim and an inviting wraparound porch add a touch of yesterday. The six guest rooms have private baths and TVs; B&B double rates of $75–90 include a full breakfast. "Close to Seaside's attractions, yet quiet and peaceful." *(Mary Kay Santore)* "Longtime owner Barb Edwards offered a friendly welcome and tasty breakfasts. Our cozy room had a down featherbed, quilt, and antiques, plus a spacious bathroom." *(Laura Dirks)* "Each room has a small decoration reflecting Barb's affection for cats. Delightful homemade granola with a lovely fruit garnish." *(Kirsten Bailey)*

Information please: You can sleep in modern comfort in rooms decorated with a touch of local history at **The Guest House B&B** (486 Necanicum Drive, 97138; 503–717–0495 or 800–340–8150), a contemporary cottage with four guest rooms, each with private bath and TV. The spacious living room has a cozy fireplace, a piano for sing-a-longs, and a game table; a soak in the hot tub is inviting after a day on the go. The double rates of $75–95 include evening snacks, early morning coffee and newspaper and a full breakfast.

If you ever wanted to sleep in a round bed, the **Sea Side Inn** (581 South Promenade, 97138; 503–738–6403 or 800–772–PROM) has one in its Clock Tower room. A contemporary four-story building on the southern, quieter end of the promenade, the Sea Side was built in 1994 and has 14 guest rooms, each with a theme: the Art Deco has a neon ceiling fan, and an ocean-view deck, Granny's House has a double feather bed and a bay window; and the Rock n'Roll has the bed inside a '59 Oldmobile. B&B rates of $90–199 include full breakfasts served in the oceanfront gathering room. "A beachfront B&B. Inviting great room, plus a pleasant garden area in front for watching the kite-flying on the beach and the Prom strollers. Delightful breakfasts, with the chef taking personal orders. Walking distance to shops, yet a quiet, restful atmosphere." *(Vicki Pollitt)*

For additional area inns, see **Cannon Beach.**

Gilbert Inn ¢ ♦♦
341 Beach Drive, 97138

Tel: 503–738–9770
800–410–9770
Fax: 503–717–1070

Alexander Gilbert, one of Seaside's founding fathers, donated land for the first South Promenade and built several buildings on Broadway including this Queen Anne–style home. Owners Carole and Dick Rees have put in a lot of work—painting, redoing the bathrooms, adding queen-size beds, and sprucing up the decor throughout. Adjacent to the inn are four luxury condo units, called Gilbert Gardens.

"An excellent value. The Gilbert Inn is a quiet haven within a busy tourist town, and Carole and Dick are extremely pleasant, helpful and unobtrusive. Both the bedrooms and the public space is comfortable and nicely furnished. Simple, tasty breakfasts." *(James McCowan)* "Lovely decor. The ample common areas allowed a family to enjoy a game in one common room, while we read quietly in the lovely, large, living room. Close to town and the Promenade, yet quiet. Pleasant hosts; interesting fellow guests. Gilbert the cat is as serene as his beautiful surroundings; he kindly provided great photo-ops." *(Carol Worth)*

"The Garret Room, an attic transformed into a splendid country-style suite, had adorable small twig chairs under the eaves, and comfortable hand-hewn fir beds covered with beautiful quilts. Andrew's Room is decorated in black and white, accented with burgundy and forest green floral accents. Stuffed French toast is my favorite for breakfast." *(Denise Weston)* "Beautiful 1880s Victorian with the original tongue-in-groove paneling. The inn has a wood-paneled sitting room; an airy plant-filled sun porch; and a parlor with full-length lace curtains, country French furnishings, and a fireplace." *(Mary Robinson)* "Superior cleanliness. The inn's setting is such that a quiet night's sleep is easy. Great location for walking or bicycling on the promenade. Beautiful Victorian landscaping." *(Ann Brookshe)*

Open Feb. 1–Dec. 31.
Rooms 4 2-bedroom condos, 2 suites, 8 doubles—all with full private bath, telephone, radio, TV. 3 with desk.
Facilities Breakfast room, parlor with fireplace, sitting room with organ, sun porch. Off-street parking. Beach with 3 m promenade for skating, bicycles, surreys nearby.
Location 1 block from ocean. From S, on Hwy. 101, turn left at "City Center"

sign, left at "A" St. to inn on left. From N on Hwy. 101, turn right on Ave. "B" (2 blocks S of light), go straight to ocean, inn on left.
Restrictions No smoking. "We ask Mom and Dad to decide if children will fit in our setting; in Garret Room, no children under 12."
Credit cards Amex, Discover, MC, Visa.
Rates B&B, $110 condo, $95–105 suite, $79–105 double, $74–100 single. Extra person, $10. 2–3 night weekend/holiday summer minimum. Weekly rates.
Extras Local airport/station pickup. Crib, babysitting.

SISTERS

Although its population is only 820 people, the town of Sisters is at the center of a major recreational area, at the crossroads of Highway 20 and 242. It's situated just north of the Sister Mountains (North, South, and Middle) at an elevation of 3,200 feet, where the high desert meets the pine woods, close to the Black Butte Ranch recreation area and to down-hill skiing at Mt. Bachelor and Hoodoo.

Cascade Country Inn   ♿
P.O. Box 834
15870 Barclay Drive, 97759

Tel: 541–549–4666
800–316–0089

Judy Tolonen, an avid pilot, built the Colonial-style Cascade Country Inn in 1994, right next door to a tiny private airport, giving new meaning to the expression, "taxi right to the door." Of course, guests arriving by car are equally welcome to enjoy the beautifully sunny weather found on the eastern side of the Cascades, as well as the myriad opportunities for outdoor recreation this area affords.

Judy and her daughter Victoria have furnished the inviting family room with overstuffed sofas, antiques and country pieces. The sun-filled guest rooms have hand-painted murals and tiles, delicate stencils, and stained glass transom windows, all created by Judy, Victoria, and other family members. Breakfast, served 9–10 A.M., includes such favorites as poached eggs with tortillas, cheese, refried beans, and salsa, stuffed French toast, apple cinnamon oatmeal, and seafood salad English muffins. Rates also include evening refreshments.

The spacious Lifestyles of the Fish and Famous room has a tropical theme; it's perfect for a family, with a queen-size bed, and three day beds. Granny's Garden has a queen-size bed, an antique bureau, and a window seat looking out to the snow-capped beaks of the Three Sisters and Broken Top mountains. Located a short stroll away in the airplane hanger is the Wild Blue Yonder suite with a WWII–aviation theme. The sitting room has a library of aviation books and a glass-topped table crafted from an aircraft radial engine; up a spiral staircase is the queen-size bed and bath.

"Our room had beautiful antiques, lovely stained glass, plush towels, and comfy bathrobes. Very good breakfast, friendly atmosphere." *(Connie Freeman)* "Each room has a spectacular view of the surrounding mountains. Furnishings are fresh and comfortable. The location is extremely quiet and peaceful, yet within walking distance of the quaint town of Sisters. Judy is cheerful and knowledgeable about the area." *(Dean Billing)*

Open All year.

Rooms 1 suite, 6 doubles—all with private bath/shower, clock/radio, air-conditioning, ceiling fan. 1 with fireplace, whirlpool tub. 2 with TV, desk. Suite in airplane hangar.

Facilities Family room with fireplace, guest refrigerator, guest laundry, porch. 4 acres with 2 gazebos. Mountain bikes. Lakes nearby with paddleboats. Hiking, fishing, golf, tennis, rafting, horseback riding, bicycling, snowmobiling, skiing nearby. Deschutes, Willamette Nat'l. Forests nearby.

Location Central OR. 20 m NW of Bend. ½ m E of town. From Hwy. 20 in Sisters go N on Camp Polk Rd. Turn left on Barclay Dr. to inn on left.

Restrictions No smoking.

Credit cards MC, Visa.

Rates B&B, $85–125 suite, double. Extra person, $10. Children under 6 free.

Extras Wheelchair access, one room specially equipped. Small pets allowed by prior arrangement. Adjacent to private airport.

STAYTON

Information please: If you go four miles south from Sublimity do you get to Ridiculous? No, you're in Stayton, where you'll find **A Place in the Country** (9297 Boedigheimer Road, Stayton 97383; 503–769–4555), a 1911 farmhouse lovingly restored to its original charm. You can choose from king-, queen-, or twin-size beds in the four guest rooms, all with private bath and air-conditioning. Outside your door each morning you'll find juice and coffee; a full breakfast is served in the large country kitchen or on the old-fashioned porch. The B&B double rates of $65–95 also include evening refreshments and use of the barbecue grill and laundry facilities. Stayton is in northwest Oregon, 17 miles east of Salem, and local activities include golf, tours of wineries, biking and hiking.

STEAMBOAT

Steamboat Inn ✕ ♿   *Tel:* 800–840–8825
42705 North Umpqua Highway, 97447-9703   *Fax:* 541–498–2411

The Steamboat Inn offers fine cuisine, elegantly rustic accommodations, and world-famous steelhead trout fly-fishing. This section of the North Umpqua River has long been the favorite fishing spot of such notable sportsmen as Zane Grey and Jack Hemingway. Owners Jim and Sharon Van Loan note that "while many of our guests do come for the challenging fishing, others enjoy the wilderness beauty, comfortable accommodations, and the inn's acclaimed food." Dinner is served at 7:00 P.M. in winter, and 30 minutes after sundown (approximately 8:30 P.M.) in summer, after anglers have made that last cast. A recent meal began with an aperitif and spicy chicken wings, followed by red snapper with lime marinade, tomato salad with basil vinaigrette, green chili and corn soufflé, broccoli with sesame butter, herb cheese bread, and ended with rhubarb upside-down cake. Accommodations include pine-paneled cabins with gas fireplaces and a common veranda, hideaway cottages a half-mile upstream from the lodge, and the luxurious River Suites with soaking tubs with a wilderness view. Also available are ranch-style houses, perfect for a family or three couples.

"A fine, remote but accessible retreat. Everything speaks to the Van Loan's pride of ownership." *(Ray & Marilyn Williams)* "Total relaxation at a leisurely pace; the owners and staff are very pleasant, and you are never a stranger here again." *(Kimberly Faulhaber)* "My room was well appointed, with art work, coordinated towels and bedspreads. The lovely long deck, with ample places to sit, affords an awesome view of the river. All meticulously maintained. Garden-fresh herbs and edible flowers were used in the fabulous meals." *(Alicia Bonesteele)* "Our stream side cabin had a freestanding fireplace that you turned on with the flick of a switch; we left the sliding glass door open in order to hear the river 25 feet below, and later followed a rugged trail down to the river's edge. At 7 P.M. we joined other guests for hors d'oeuvres and Oregon wine. The family-style dinner included platters of seared pork tenderloin with a sesame-ginger sauce, accompanied by light potato pancakes and stir-fried vegetables. Irresistible dessert of blueberries layered with puff pastry and topped with dollops of whipped cream. Immaculate rooms, amiable dinner conversations, great hosts, delicious food, and no telephones (there's a pay phone in the dining area)—everything you need to de-stress." *(Joan Merrill)*

Open Mar. 1–Dec. 31. Restaurant closed midweek in winter.

Rooms 8 cabins, 5 cottages, 4 3-bedroom houses, 2 suites—all with private bath and/or shower, deck. Suites with air-conditioning, others with fan. Suites, cottages with fireplace, soaking tub, kitchenette. Cabins with gas fireplace. Houses with washer/dryer.

Facilities Dining room with fireplace, library with videos, books on tape; porch. 2 acres on North Umpqua River for fishing. Fly-fishing equipment shop, guided fishing excursions, mountain bike rentals. Hiking, creeks for swimming, winery tours nearby.

Location SW OR, Umpqua National Forest, foothills of Cascade Mts. 105 S of Eugene, 38 m E of Roseburg, 70 m NW of Crater Lake. From Roseburg take Hwy. 138 E 38 m to inn.

Restrictions No smoking. Traffic noise in some rooms.

Credit cards MC, Visa.

Rates Room only, $235 suite, $160 cottage/house, $125 cabin. Extra person, $20; children over age 4, $10. Prix fixe dinner, $35 (with wine).

Extras Limited wheelchair access. Crib, babysitting.

TIMBERLINE

For an additional area entry, see listing for **Falcon's Crest** in Government Camp.

Also recommended: The **Timberline Lodge** (Timberline Ski Area, 97028; 503–231–5400 or 800–547–1406) is a famous historic lodge dating back to the 1930s. Set at an altitude of 6,000 feet, it sits in the shadow of Mt. Hood, Oregon's tallest peak (11,235 feet). A WPA project, it provided jobs for dozens of unemployed janitors, blacksmiths, and carpenters. The hand-forged iron chandeliers and gates, hooked rugs and draperies, hand-carved wooden newel posts, and stained glass windows remain an impressive testimony to their skills. Built on a massive scale, the lobby is highlighted by a stone chimney over 100 feet high. After considerable restoration work and renovation of both the guest rooms and common areas, the lodge appears today much as it was when Franklin Delano Roosevelt dedicated it in 1937. Double rates range from $95–170 for the 60 suites and doubles. Facilities range skiing in winter to hiking and water sports in summer. "All the grandeur of the Ahwahnee or El Tovar but on a more intimate scale and much better run, too. The dining room was excellent." *(Gene & Roberta Altshuler)*

TROUTDALE

Information please: Edgefield Manor was established in 1911 as the county poor farm, with housing, orchards, vegetable fields, poultry and hog barns, a dairy, cannery, laundry, and meat packing plant; by 1982 the property was abandoned. Now listed on the National Register of Historic Places, Michael McMenamins purchased the complex in 1991, and created a winery, brewery, restaurant, theater in the various buildings on the remaining 25 acres. In 1993 **McMenamins Edgefield** (2126 S.W. Halsey, Troutdale 97060; 503–669–8610 or 800–669–8610) opened with 59 simply furnished guest rooms, in the Georgian Revival–style Main Lodge, the Power Station, and the Craftsman-style Administrators' House. Some have been redone with lovely hand-painted faux plants and draperies, with Mission-style reproduction furnishings. The $80–125 double rates include a breakfast voucher for the restaurant; there are also an additional 40 basic hostel-style accommodations, in men's and women's sleeping quarters, at $18 per person. Although a few rooms have private baths, the majority share central dorm-style bathrooms down the hall. "Comfortable, relaxing hotel. Extremely helpful staff. Huge guest room with a firm mattress. The restaurant offers appealing choices, good food, and ample portions, if a little pricy at dinner." *(Sydney Downs)* Troutdale is 20 miles east of Portland, in the Columbia River Valley.

WINCHESTER BAY

Information please: If you enjoy being on the water, try the **Salmon Harbor Belle B&B** (P.O. Box 1208, 97467; 541–271–1137 or 800–348–1922), a newly built, 97-foot, 100-ton sternwheel riverboat. Its six handsomely furnished staterooms come in queen- and king-size versions, each with its own shower; breakfast is served from 8:00–9:30 in the main salon. B&B double rates are $125–145. "Simple, tasteful decor, exceptionally clean. Each room has large windows and comfortable beds, and the common area has a homey feel with a woodstove burning." *(Mary Woods)*

YACHATS

Pronounced "YAH-hots," this central Oregon coast resort village (140 miles southwest of Portland and halfway between Newport and Florence) offers miles of rocky shoreline and dense forest. Its uncrowded beaches are a favorite with rockhounds (looking for agates, jasper, and petrified wood), beachcombers, fishermen, and clamdiggers. Perhaps best of all is watching the surf pound against the rocky cliffs, especially dramatic during winter storms. South of town, walk to the stone lookout on Cape Perpetua, highest point on the Oregon coast, or follow the hiking trails into the rain forest or along the coast to the sea lion caves, 13 miles to the south.

Also recommended: The **Adobe Resort Motel** (1555 Highway 101 North, P.O. Box 219, 97498; 541–547–3141 or 800–522–3623) offers 93 rooms done in the original adobe as well as more modern ones, plus a handsome restaurant of adobe brick and rough-hewn cedar beams, known for its romantic setting and excellent seafood. Most rooms have picture windows to take in the gorgeous ocean views, perfect for whale and storm watching. Double rates are $61–180; some units have a balcony, fireplace or whirlpool tub. "A clean, neat motel in a great location with friendly service, excellent catch-of-the-day fish dinner." *(Ruth Tilsley)* "Efficiently run, lovely stay." *(B.J. Hensley)*

The **Fireside Motel** (1881 Highway 101 North, P.O. Box 313, 97498; 541–547–3636 or 800–336–3573), a 42-room motel situated in a geologically spectacular area, has two wings: Ocean View West rooms with direct views of the surf crashing on the basalt ledge; second-floor Ocean View Northwest rooms look up the coastline, while the downstairs units have little or no view. The rooms (double rates of $60–130) are spacious and attractive, with amenities such as refrigerators and coffee pots, and are set well away from the highway. A friendly staff and easy access to several restaurants earns this motel high marks from respondents, especially pet lovers, since dogs are welcome. "In addition to recommending a good diner featuring local fish, the proprietors told us where to get bagels for breakfast, which we took out on the balcony so we could hear as well as see the waves breaking on the rocks. The price was also right for one of the best motels we've visited." *(Carol & George Worth)*

Information please: "Just yards from the breaking waves of the Pacific, and just five minutes from Strawberry Point where hundreds of seals hang out, is the contemporary **Kittiwake** (95368 Highway 101 S, 97498; 541–547–4470). This three guest-room B&B was designed and decorated by Joseph and Brigitte Szewc, and reflects their impeccable taste. Our room had a huge bath with beautiful tiling, a window wall facing the ocean, and a Jacuzzi. Delightful, gracious hosts; Brigitte was born in Germany and her mouth-watering breakfasts reflect her native cuisine." *(Beverly Davis)* Each guest room has a queen-size bed, down comforter, private bath, and access to the beach from a private entrance. The $100–140 rates include always-available refreshments and a continental breakfast delivered to your door, or full meal in the dining room.

Information please: Located halfway between Yachats and Florence, is the renovated 1893 Victorian lightkeeper's house at the **Heceta Head Lightstation** (access: Devils Elbow State Park; reservations: 541–547–3696). Open for B&B ($95–125 double) Thursdays through Mondays, it has three simply furnished guest rooms, with private and shared baths, queen or double beds; the Mariner's Room has a magnificent ocean view. The house is managed by the U.S. Forest Service, and serves as an interpretive center during the summer, with activities typical to the lightkeeper's duties. Tours of the lighthouse itself are operated by the Oregon State Parks and Recreation Department (541–997–3851). "Staying here is like going to Grandma's, complete with chickens, goats, cats, and a dog in the yard. While in need of sprucing up, it's definitely a unique experience. Outstanding seven-course breakfast. It was fun to walk the trail to the lighthouse after dark." *(Judy Dawson)*

For additional area inns, see **Florence** and **Newport**.

The Oregon House ¢   *Tel:* 541–547–3329
94288 Highway 101, 97498   *E-mail:* orehouse@aol.com

The slogan, "Don't leave home without it," takes on new meaning at the Oregon House—the main house, an exact duplicate of one in southern California, was built in the 1950s as a wedding present for a bride reluctant to leave her home behind. Nestled on a cliff high above the Pacific, this estate complex was in great disrepair when Bob and Joyce Freeman purchased it in 1987. Today the five restored buildings and cottages house the guest accommodations, and no two are alike, except they all have a country decor, accented with wicker and collectibles, and queen- or king-size beds.

"Solitary, peaceful location; clean, well-maintained grounds. The three units we've stayed in were unusually clean, with more than adequate cooking facilities; the baths had good pressure, no dripping faucets, and easy-to-control water temperature. Just right for a tranquil and quiet stay." *(Thomas & Ann Bommarito)* "A grouping of cottages with a terrific ocean view and private beach. Our Blue Moon cottage, right near the entrance, was spacious and had a balcony with barbecue grill, a full kitchen, and a woodburning fireplace, enjoyable on a chilly night. The grounds were lovely, with lawn chairs placed on a bluff. The beach is private, unspoiled, and uncrowded beach. Cape Perpetua is nearby for great hiking." *(Judy Dawson)*

"A retreat from the chaos and noise of the world. No TVs or phones interrupt your peaceful reverie; at night the roar of the surf below lulls you to sleep." *(Dyan McClure)* "The isolated beach provides a background for glorious, romantic sunsets." *(Jean Rees)* "Joyce and Bob suggested interesting activities. Our kids loved the inn's friendly cats." *(Dawn Hayden)* "The main building and some of the cottages are constructed of white painted concrete block; others are wood framed. The cliff is dotted with windswept cedars; on one side a creek tumbles down a rock path toward the ocean. A lighted path leads down the bank to a beach studded with driftwood and rocks." *(SC)* "Love looking for agates and exploring the tide pools on the beach." *(Cheryl Duncan)*

Open All year.

Rooms 5 buildings, each with 1–3 housekeeping suites or doubles—all with private bath and/or shower, ceiling fan. Most with kitchen, deck, barbecue grill. 5 with fireplace, 3 with Jacuzzi tub. 1 B&B double with Jacuzzi bath, balcony, use of living room with fireplace. 1 cabin with hot tub, fireplace.

Facilities 3½ acres, picnic area. 1½ m of private ocean beach with tidepools, caves. Tennis, golf, fishing nearby.

Location 8 m S of Yachats, 18 m N of Florence on Hwy. 101.

Restrictions No smoking. Well-behaved children of any age permitted in some cottages; under age 12 must be supervised at all times while outdoors. Outside guests only with advance notification.

Credit cards DC, Discover, MC, Visa.

Rates Room only, $70–110 suite, $45–70 double. B&B room, $90 double. 2–3 night minimum weekends/holidays. Outside guests, $5 per person daily.

Extras Limited wheelchair access.

Sea Quest B&B
95354 Highway 101, P.O. Box 448, 97498

Tel: 503–547–3782
800–341–4878
Fax: 541–547–3719

Elaine and George bought this contemporary, weathered cedar house in 1990 and renovated it to provide comfortable guest rooms with unobstructed views of the crashing surf. An eclectic decor fills the house—antiques, comfy sofas and chairs, leafy plants. Breakfast is served buffet-style at a choice of tables, and usually two hot entrees are offered along with homemade granola, large platters of fruit, coffee cakes, muffins, juices and coffee.

"The food was creative, fresh, beautifully presented and absolutely delicious. There are huge windows in the Great Room to view the ocean, and there is a wonderful deck. Elaine's decorating is not standard—she does the unexpected and pulls it off wonderfully. My room had a comfortable bed, lovely sheets, soft chairs for reading, and a private entrance to the deck; the bath had a full-size mirror, large towels, and was spotless. Adorable and well-behaved are Sebastian and Murphy, the dogs, and Clouseau, the cat. The inn is way off the highway so there is no traffic noise whatsoever." *(Kathy John)* "An elegant yet unpretentious gem. It sits on a quiet stretch of beach that is one of Oregon's best spots for collecting agates. The view from the living room and second floor is so fine we had a hard time pushing ourselves out the door to explore the coast. Inside, the rooms are playfully but not preciously decorated with seaside and country knick-knacks. The bottled spring water was a welcome touch." *(George Landau)*

"The second-floor living room has a fireplace covering an entire wall, and games, books, and collectibles. Soft music played and we were always welcome to sit and read or talk. Our downstairs room was cozy yet roomy; we melted into our comfortable bed, and a toasty comforter kept us warm as we listened to the crashing surf through the open sliding glass door. Elaine puts the coffee on at 6 A.M. for early risers; breakfast was delicious. George and Elaine made us feel right at home; terrific restaurant recommendations and suggestions for shopping and sightseeing." *(Rebecca Pfeifer & Bill Gibson)* "Bathrooms display George's wonderful, colorful tilework. The location is convenient to hiking trails, sea lion caves, parks, and miles of ocean sand." *(Cheri Larson)*

Open All year.
Rooms 5 doubles—all with private bath and/or shower, private entrance. 4 with double whirlpool tubs.
Facilities Dining room, living room with fireplace, stereo, games, books; deck. 2½ acres with lawn games. On bluff above beach.
Location 6 m S of Yachats. On Hwy. 101 between mile markers 171–172.
Restrictions No smoking. Children over 14 preferred.
Credit cards MC, Visa.
Rates B&B, $150–250 double. 2–3 night weekend, holiday minimum.

We Want to Hear from You!

As you know, this book is effective only with your help. We really need to know about your experiences and discoveries. If you stayed at an inn or hotel listed here, we want to know how it was. Did it live up to our description? Exceed it? Was it what you expected? Did you like it? Were you disappointed? Delighted? Have you discovered new establishments that we should add to the next edition?

Tear out one of the report forms at the back of this book (or use your own stationery if you prefer) and write today. *Even if you write only "Fully endorse existing entry" you will have been most helpful.*

Thank You!

Washington

Roberta's B&B, Seattle

About the only things eastern and western Washington have in common are a governor and a shared border, the Cascade mountain range. Western Washington, dominated by water and mountains, includes most of the state's population and scenic highlights: the Olympic Peninsula, Puget Sound, the San Juan Islands, and the Cascade Mountains and volcanoes.

The Olympic Peninsula   The large central core of this peninsula is a vast wilderness incorporating the world's only temperate rain forest and the glaciers, peaks, and rugged terrain of the Olympic Mountains. Going west, toward the Pacific Ocean, a national wildlife refuge, four Indian reservations and delicate archaeological digs make public access to the ocean difficult. The north side of the peninsula faces the Strait of Juan de Fuca and is known for the Victorian Port Townsend, the Manis Mastodon Site, and six-mile Dungeness Sandspit, home to over 250 species of birds. Hood Canal and its nearby parks form the eastern edge of this varied peninsula. Access to the Pacific is found southeast of the peninsula between Ilwaco and Pacific Beach. Here you can walk the 28-mile Long Beach, dig for clams, go deep-sea fishing, or fly kites. Virtually the only road on the peninsula is Route 101, often referred to as the Olympic Loop.

Puget Sound   Puget Sound extends like a giant thumb into the center of western Washington. Most of the state's population lives along its eastern shore, from Olympia north to Seattle and Everett. In Tacoma visit 698-acre Point Defiance Park to survey its extensive flower gardens, forest roads, and outstanding views. From Seattle take a round trip on one of the ferries linking urban Washington to nearby commuter islands.

Board the Mukilteo-Clinton ferry to Whidbey Island and there drive north through rolling farmlands, past sandy beaches, to impressive Deception Pass. In the spring be sure to see the acres of blooming daffodils and tulips in Skagit Valley north of Everett. If you're heading up to British Columbia, get off the freeway at Burlington and take scenic Route 11 to Bellingham. The road hugs the coast and provides gorgeous views of the San Juan Islands. The San Juan Islands themselves are a highlight of any Washington trip: small resort towns, stands of virgin timber inhabited only by eagles and other wild critters, miles of rugged shore, and picturesque small coves.

The Cascades and Volcanoes   Every bit the equal of the Colorado Rockies, the rugged, snowcapped Northern Cascade Mountains (Route 20 from Marblemount to Winthrop) are at their best during the fall, when the leaves change color. In the central Cascades you can ski, hike, fish, see 268-foot high Snoqualmie Falls, and visit Leavenworth, a "Bavarian" village. To the south the Cascades are interrupted by 14,410-foot Mt. Rainier, offering rock and glacier climbing, cross-country skiing, spring wildflower bonanzas, and summer hiking. Also plan to visit Mt. St. Helens National Volcanic Monument to witness the devastation that occurred there in 1980. Call 360–274–2103 for a recorded message about days/hours the Monument is open; or call 360–247–5473 to speak to the Forest Service for additional information.

  Reader tip: "Be sure to visit Mt. St. Helens, just an hour north of Portland. The information center just off Interstate 5 makes the experience especially memorable. The untouched devastation seen in the last few miles of the approach shows the enormity of what happened there ten years ago." (*Christopher Hart Johnston*)

Eastern Washington   Although it includes two-thirds of the state, most of eastern Washington offers little to tourists. The exceptions are the Yakima Valley, center of Washington's wine country; Spokane, a lively city centered around a refurbished riverfront park; the resort areas surrounding 55-mile-long Lake Chelan, and rolling hills and lush vegetation of the Palouse country along Route 195 between Spokane and Colfax. In between these points, visitors will find miles of apple orchards, wheat farms, and desert. Worth stopping to see are the waterfalls in Palouse Falls State Park located south of Washtucna; Okanogan Valley ghost towns; the Ginkgo Petrified Forest east of Ellensburg; and, near Coulee City, the unusual Dry Falls that, in prehistoric times, was the site of a 3½-mile-wide, 400-foot waterfall. More recommendations for this area would be especially welcome.

  Note: Summer is very much peak season in western Washington, especially in the San Juans; make reservations two to three months ahead to avoid disappointment.

ANACORTES

Gateway to the San Juan Islands, Anacortes is on Fidalgo Island, 2 hours south of Vancouver, British Columbia and 1½ hours north of Seattle via I-5 and Highway 20. From I-5 take Exit 230 to Anacortes and the San Juan Ferry.

Also recommended: Guests are delighted with their stay at **The Blue Rose B&B** (1811-9th Street, 98221; 360–293–5175 or 888–293–5175), a Craftsman-style home built in 1910. Each of its two guest rooms has a private bath, and the B&B double rates of $79–91 include a full breakfast and assistance with ferry connections. "A lovely home with beautiful antiques and a lovely rose garden. The innkeepers are hospitable and helpful. Breakfast included griddle cakes with fresh raspberries and strawberries, but delicious ferry pack breakfasts for early morning departures are also available. Enjoyed cookies on the porch and the fresh roses in our room." *(RC, also K. Letterman and others)*

Albatross Bed and Breakfast ¢   *Tel:* 360–293–0677
5708 Kingsway West, 98221   800–622–8864
              E-mail: albatros@cnw.com

People who like boats will especially enjoy the Albatross; just across the street is a marina and a charter boat company. A 1927 Cape Cod–style home with views south to Whidbey Island, the inn still has some of its original cedar walls and woodwork, accented with simple furnishings. Ken Arasim and Barbie Guay have owned the inn since 1992, and serve a hearty breakfast of Belgian waffles or omelets, accompanied with bacon or sausage, juice, and fresh fruit.

"A large home at the commercial edge of a quiet, pleasant neighborhood. Our large room had plenty of lighting, a king-size bed and a sparkling clean bathroom tucked into the original large closets; space to hang clothes and store luggage fit neatly along the wall. In the evening Barbie asked about any dietary restrictions, and took them into account when preparing breakfast. After touring Ken's garage of classic cars, and Barbie's collection of—you guessed it—Barbie dolls—we found that Ken had slipped out and wiped the morning dew off our car windows. They are warm, friendly people who make you feel instantly at ease." *(Dale Johnson)* "We stayed in the Scarlett O'Hara room with an 1860 southern-style canopy bed, and enjoyed a scenic cruise on their sailboat." *(Angele Schunken & Brian Vandenberg)* "Our attractive room had a view of the deer grazing outside." *(Don & Dolores Coleman)*

Open All year.
Rooms 4 doubles—all with private shower, radio, clock. TV available.
Facilities Living room with fireplace, TV/VCR, stereo; dining room, library, guest refrigerator, porch. ¾ acre with off-street parking, lawn games. 46' sailboat for sightseeing, crabbing; bicycle rentals. Tennis, hiking, golf, fishing, boating, scuba diving, beach for swimming nearby.
Location NW WA. ½ m from International Ferry Landing. Enter Anacortes,

turn left onto 12th St. Go past Washington State Ferry Terminal (to San Juan Is.).
Turn left on Skyline Way. Turn left again onto Kingsway to inn on left.
Restrictions No smoking. Children over 4 preferred.
Credit cards MC, Visa.
Rates B&B, $69–90 double, $65–85 single. Extra person, $15. Senior, AAA discount.
Extras Limited wheelchair access. Ferry/airport/bus station pickup. Pets by prior arrangement.

The Channel House ¢
2902 Oakes Avenue, 98221

Tel: 360–293–9382
800–238–4353
Fax: 360–299–9208
E-mail: beds@sos.net

A Victorian home built for an Italian count in 1902, The Channel House is set on the Guemes Channel, and has been owned by Dennis and Pat McIntyre since 1986. An early morning coffee basket is delivered to your door, and breakfast is served in the dining room. In the evening, guests enjoy soaking in the outdoor hot tub, watching the boats and the sunset over Puget Sound.

"Outstanding, cheerful service from Pat and Dennis. Wonderful ocean views; delicious stuffed French toast." *(Lanny Sawchuk)* "Careful attention to detail, from the big, fluffy towels to use after a soak in the hot tub, to the ready-to-light fireplace." *(Patti Sutter & Jim Houston)* "Great coffee and cookies." (Neil & Sandy Klockziem) "The Victorian Rose Cottage has a fireplace, wonderful four-poster bed, whirlpool tub, and robes for going to and from the hot tub." *(Christine & Greg Tyler, also Dean Braddock)* "Excellent value. The cottage rooms are most convenient to the outdoor hot tub. Our Country Rose room had an outside screened sitting area, and inside, goosedown duvets, plus wine glasses and corkscrew on a silver tray." *(ACR)* "The first-floor living room has old-fashioned, well-used, comfortable furniture; the library has a fainting couch, books, and games. Our spacious third-floor room had a sloping attic ceiling, a comfortable king-size bed, and a large bath with clawfoot tub and a gorgeous view of the San Juans. On the landing was a charming sitting area with a wheelbarrow filled with teddy bears, an old-fashioned dollhouse and a baby buggy." *(Suzanne Carmichael)* "Grandma's room has an antique brass bed and log cabin quilt; the bath was tiny but adequate." *(BA)*

Open All year.
Rooms 6 doubles—all with private bath and/or shower, clock/radio. 2 in cottage have fireplace, whirlpool tub; 1 with deck.
Facilities Living room, library, dining room, all with fireplace. Hot tub. Boating, fishing, hiking, golf, swimming beaches nearby.
Location NW WA. Enter Anacortes, continue right on Commercial Ave. to 12th St. (Chevron station on corner). Turn left to inn 1½m on the right.
Restrictions Light sleepers may be disturbed by early ferry traffic. No smoking.
Credit cards Amex, Discover, MC, Visa.
Rates B&B, $69–105 double, $59–89 single. Extra person, $20. Off-season rates.
Extras Local airport/station pickups.

ASHFORD

Also recommended: Dating back to 1912, **Alexander's Country Inn** (37515 State Road 706 East, Ashford 98304; 360–569–2300 or 800–654–7615) is the oldest structure in the Mt. Rainier area; the 13-foot waterwheel out front is a local landmark. The restaurant specializes in salmon fresh from the Tacoma docks, rainbow trout from the inn's ponds, homemade breads, and wild blackberry pies. The fourteen guest rooms have private and shared baths, and the B&B rates range from $75–145. "The rooms are nice but the best part was the dining room at night, especially the strawberry shortcake." *(Dean Braddock)*

For additional area accommodation, see **Mt. Rainier National Park.**

BAINBRIDGE ISLAND

Bombay House ¢
8490 Beck Road, 98110

Tel: 206–842–3926
800–598–3926

Overlooking Rich Passage, Bombay House is a turn-of-the-century home, set high on sloping lawns and encircled with porches and flowers; Bunny Cameron and Roger Kanchuk are the owners. Most guest rooms have a queen- or king-size bed. Breakfast is served between 8:20–9:30 A.M. in the large country kitchen with a view through the trees to the water beyond. The meal may include coffee cakes, bread pudding, pastries, cheese, homemade cereal, toasting and quick breads, fresh fruit, baked apples, jams, jellies, and the house speciality, orange butter.

"The aroma of brewing coffee and muffins baking is followed by a tempting breakfast. We watched the birds, and glimpsed the ferry as it winds through nearby Rich Passage. The rooms are neat, clean, and comfortably furnished. Bunny, Roger, and their daughter, Cameron, were friendly, polite, and helpful in guiding us to great local restaurants, activities, and the charming shops in the little town of Winslow." *(Johnnie & Donna Schell)* "Perched on a hill on this slow-paced country island with forests and open spaces—seemingly a million miles away from Seattle's hubbub. Our spacious second-floor suite, with woodstove, claw-foot tub, and comfortable sitting areas, covered the whole front of the house." *(MB)* "Friendly innkeepers; peaceful, relaxing atmosphere; enjoyed the cupola, wraparound porch, and gazebo." *(Kathleen Muldoon)*

Open All year.
Rooms 1 suite; 4 doubles—3 with private bath and/or shower, 2 with maximum of 4 sharing bath. All with desk, air-conditioning; 1 with fan, fireplace.
Facilities Living room with fireplace, piano; kitchen/breakfast room, porches. ½ acre with flower gardens. Swimming, fishing, boating, clamming, hiking, tennis, golf, bicycling nearby.
Location W WA. Puget Sound, 35 min ferry ride W of Seattle. 4 m SW of Winslow. From downtown Seattle, take Winslow ferry. Go left on Winslow Way, right on Madison, left on Wyatt, right at the "Y" in the rd., 0.4 m past elemen-

tary school, take sharp right on W. Blakely & go right on Beck. Inn at corner of Beck and West Blakely. Agate Pass Bridge (Rte. 305) links island to Poulsbo, Bremerton, Olympic Peninsula.

Restrictions No smoking. Children over 8.
Credit cards Amex, MC, Visa.
Rates B&B, $149 suite, $59–89 double, $55–85 single. Extra person, $15.

BELLINGHAM

Snuggled along the northwest shore of Puget Sound, Bellingham is definitely worth a stop on the way from Seattle to Vancouver. Getting to this midsize town with a Victorian flavor and a smattering of counterculture shops and eateries is half the fun: Route 11 between Burlington and Bellingham winds prettily along the wooded shore, providing outstanding views of the San Juan Islands. The town is home to Western Washington State University. Recommended stops include a stroll among the contemporary sculptures scattered about the University campus, a self-guided tour of its Victorian homes (call 360–733–2900 for a brochure), and a browse through the Old Town antique shops.

Bellingham is located in the northwest corner of Washington, 40 miles south of Vancouver, BC, and 90 miles north of Seattle, easily accessible via Interstate 95.

Also recommended: A dramatic contemporary home overlooking Lake Whatcom, **Schnauzer Crossing** (4421 Lakeway Drive, 98226; 360–733–0055 or 800–562–2808) offers a cottage, a suite, and a double room, in addition to a private tennis court, hot tub, and use of a canoe. Donna McAllister, owner since 1986, includes a full breakfast in the B&B double rates of $110–115. "Friendly, professional service. Relaxing location, removed from town, yet close to good restaurants and shops. The dogs are delightful but not intrusive." *(Gerald O'Driscoll)* "Our suite was decorated in Danish modern furnishings, and had a mini-kitchen with a microwave, refrigerator, coffee maker and a nice selection of snacks. There was a goosedown comforter on the bed, and terry robes to wear to the hot tub. Wonderful breakfast with French toast, Black Forest ham, fresh fruit parfait, blueberry bran muffins, lime scones." *(Georgia & William Hoover)* "Spectacular house and gardens; deliciously healthy breakfasts. Excellent library of books and videos." *(Barbara Babcock Canada)*

Stratford Manor B&B
1416 Van Wyck Road, 98226

Tel: 360–715–8441
Fax: 360–671–0840

Built in 1979, this Tudor-style home was renovated as an inn by Leslie and Jim Loshe in 1996. Rooms are traditionally furnished, each with a queen- or king-size bed. Wake-up coffee is delivered to your door, and breakfast is served at 9 A.M. at the dining room table; the menu changes daily, but typically includes fresh fruit and juice, cinnamon rolls or muffins, and such entrees as Dutch Babies, Mexican quiche, or perhaps French toast.

"A small basket of fruit and homemade cookies awaited us in the room, along with an inviting selection of classical CDs and books. Luxurious robes. A tap on the door in the morning announced the delivery of a tray of coffee and sweet breads an hour before the beautiful breakfast was served." *(Judith & James Frank)* "Beautiful accommodations, spotlessly clean. The food was delicious and abundant. Rural, peaceful grounds." *(Bayla Greenspan)* "Exceptionally hospitable, attentive, helpful innkeepers. Careful attention to detail included the fresh flowers in our room." *(Grace Lander)* "Leslie and Jim saw to every need." *(Larry & Fran Bohall)*

Open All year.

Rooms 1 suite, 3 doubles—all with full private bath, clock/radio, CD player, hair dryer, robes. 3 with whirlpool, air-conditioning, gas fireplace.

Facilities Dining room, living room with fireplace, TV room with video library, refrigerator; library, solarium with hot tub; exercise room. 30 acres, 5 acres landscaped with pond, 3 golf holes. 3 golf courses within 15 minutes.

Location 15 min. from Bellingham. Take I-5 to Sunset Dr. Exit. Go E on Sunset, then left (N) on Hannegan Rd. Take Hannegan to Van Wyck. Go E on Van Wyck to "flood area" sign on right, & watch for inn on left.

Restrictions No children. No smoking.

Credit cards MC, Visa.

Rates B&B, $165–175 suite, $125–135 double. Extra person, $15.

Extras Airport/station pick up.

BLAINE

Also recommended: Set on a spit of land surrounded by water on three sides, **The Inn at Semi-Ah-Moo** (9565 Semiahmoo Parkway, 98230; 360–371–2000 or 800–770–7992) is a resort hotel, opened in 1987 on the site of the Alaska Packers Association's Semiahmoo Cannery. The simple four-story buildings are reminiscent of the straightforward style of the original cannery, a theme continued inside with the pine floors and exposed beams. Semi-Ah-Moo means either "half-moon bay" or "he who sits beside the shore eating oysters," (not half a cow, silly). The resort has 196 guest rooms, plus all facilities: indoor tennis, racquetball, squash courts, health club, indoor/outdoor swimming pool, golf, marina, and a bicycle path. Rates range from $129–319 double, with suites from $209–499. "Manicured luxury, dramatic setting. My huge room was well-equipped, and had a small patio overlooking the lawn, pebble beach, and water beyond. Outstanding seafood in the restaurant; fresh, delicious and well-served." *(June Horn)*

KALALOCH

Information please: About seven miles west of Forks is the **Manitou Lodge** (P.O. Box 600, Kalaloch 98331; 360–374–6295), in the heart of the Olympic Peninsula rain forest. "With only a few guest rooms, it straddles the line between being a rustic B&B and an upscale fishing lodge. The gorgeous, isolated stony beaches of Olympia National Park's coastal area are only a few miles away. First-class hospitality." *(James & Pamela Burr)* Current reports welcome.

Information please: Perched on a bluff, overlooking the Pacific ocean, is **Kalaloch Lodge** (157151 Highway 101, 98331–9396; 360–962–2271), located 35 miles south of Forks, on the western coast of the Olympic Peninsula. Meaning "land of many clams," the lodge was built in 1953, and has 60 guest rooms, some in the main lodge, most in 40 log cabins, sleeping two-to-nine people. Most have kitchens, and many have woodstoves; wood is provided, cooking utensils are not. While isolated and rustic, advance reservations are essential in season. Rates range from $68–110 for lodge doubles, $100–200 for suites, and $99–199 for cabins. Ask about package rates midweek off-season. The lodge has a full service restaurant, open for three meals daily. Menus are reasonably creative for a National park concessionaire (ARAMARK), and feature seafood dishes (carnivores and vegetarians also accommodated). Activities include hiking, beachcombing, and guided tours. "Our one-room Bluff Cabin overlooked the beach below and the ocean beyond, and had a small sitting area, mini-refrigerator, and wood-burning stove [units 1–10]. Some of the cabins are in rows behind the bluff units [units 19–35], but none are very far from the ocean. We enjoyed delightful meals in the restaurant; an Elderhostel was in progress while we were there, so no common area was available for guests. The intimate restaurant overlooks the ocean and was a delightful surprise in terms of food, service, and atmosphere. We much preferred it to Lake Quinault, although the management is the same." *(AK)* In contrast: "Having stayed at both Kalaloch and Quinault, we much preferred the latter." *(EOR) Reports welcome.*

For additional accommodation, see **Quinault.**

LA CONNER/MT. VERNON

La Conner is a picturesque fishing town with many historic homes, set on Skagit Bay at the Swinomish Channel. The area is particularly popular in April, when thousands of tulips are in bloom in the nearby fields, and also from July to September. Advance reservations are essential. Some feel that La Conner's historic qualities are overwhelmed by the number of tourists visiting during these peak times; as usual, we recommend an off-season visit if possible.

La Conner is located in northwestern Washington, about 60 miles north of Seattle, and 80 miles south of Vancouver; Mt. Vernon is six miles east of La Conner.

Reader tips: "A great base of operations from which to explore the San Juans, as the Anacortes ferry is only 20 minutes away." *(Craig Davison)* "La Conner's main street has lots of charming upscale galleries, gift and craft shops, and I picked up a few gifts to bring home." *(JH)*

Information please: For an in-town historic property, a good choice may be the **Hotel Planter** (715 First Street, 98257; 360–466–4710 or 800–488–5409), built in 1907, and extensively renovated in 1987. Rates for the 12 guest rooms range from $75–125. "Front rooms look across the street to the water beyond, and have floral decor with reproduction furnishings. At the back is an attractive garden courtyard with a gazebo-covered hot tub." *(SC)*

Another in-town option is the **La Conner Channel Lodge** (205 North First Street, P.O. Box 573, 98257; 360–466–1500), a 40-room property with B&B double rates of $120–245. "Contemporary cedar-shingled lodging overlooking the Swinomish Channel. Pleasant sitting areas, plus a breakfast room where a continental breakfast is offered. Be sure to get a room with a balcony overlooking the channel; some have fireplaces and double Jacuzzi tubs." *(SC)*

The Wild Iris Inn (121 Maple Avenue, P.O. Box 696, 98257; 360–466–1400 or in WA/BC, 800–466–1400) was built in 1991 to resemble a Victorian farmhouse. Wraparound porches offer inviting spots to sit, and the cozy living room has a stone fireplace and Queen Anne reproduction furnishings. A breakfast buffet is served in the dining room, and dinner is offered on weekends. B&B rates for the 20 guest rooms range from $90–190. "We loved the private outdoor hot tub, from which we could see mountains and watch bald eagles. Our room was comfortable and nicely furnished, and we enjoyed both breakfast and dinner in the inn's restaurant." *(James & Pamela Burr)* Current reports appreciated.

Ridgeway Farm Bed & Breakfast　　　　　　*Tel:* 360–428–8068
1292 McLean Road, Mount Vernon　　　　　　　800–428–8068
Mailing address: P.O. Box 475　　　　　　　*Fax:* 360–428–8880
La Conner, 98257　　　　　*E-mail:* ridgeway@halcyon.com

Built in 1928, the Ridgeway Farm B&B is a large Dutch Colonial brick home, owned by John and Louise Kelly. In addition to the guest rooms in the main house, the Kellys have restored a historic farmhouse which they moved onto the property in 1995, as well as an old laundry/fruit-house/woodshed building, rebuilt with a Jacuzzi suite. Rooms are traditionally furnished, with floral fabrics and wallpapers in the guest rooms. At the rear of the property is a historic barn, surrounded by tulip fields—probably the area's most photographed barn. "Wonderful accommodations, hospitality, and food." *(Chuck & Lou Crandall)* "Beautiful decor, lots of fresh flowers, and comfortable atmosphere. Early bird coffee followed by breakfasts of whole wheat pancakes, fruit compote, homemade granola and yogurt. All beautifully presented with edible fruit garnishes. In the evening we were greeted by scrumptious strawberry pie or apple tart with tea, coffee, and hot chocolate. Great cats, friendly but unobtrusive. Wonderful location." *(Catherine LaCroix)* "Warm atmosphere; unparalleled hospitality; delicious breakfast; beautiful rooms, decorated with quilts and antiques; exceptional cleanliness." *(Shelley Pritchard)*

"Magazines and books line the shelves of the comfortably furnished living room; menus from local restaurants helped us decide where to eat. Our hosts were there when we needed them and disappeared when privacy was appreciated. John can even take you on a scenic plane ride. Flowers were in every room as were tempting chocolate truffles; stuffed bunnies and kittens accented the decor, including a real live feline who remained downstairs. Guest rooms are named for the Kellys' daughters and granddaughters—the Cynthia was spacious, with comfy bed, floral down comforter, matching drapes and an in-room clawfoot tub. Breakfast, at the lovely dining room table, included baked apples, bacon, link sausage, omelets, fresh muffins and homemade jam, warm fruit compote, and light-as-a-feather oatmeal pancakes." *(Nancy & Robert Andes)* "Louise and John suggested interesting adventures—a walk on the dike, cycling the islands, hiking at Deception Pass." *(Sharon Weibe)*

Open All year.
Rooms 8 doubles—5 with private bath and/or shower, 3 sharing 2 baths. All rooms have sink. 2 rooms in cottage, with kitchen; restored fruit house with Jacuzzi suite.
Facilities Dining room, living room with fireplace, piano, TV/VCR, stereo, books; porches. 2¼ acres with croquet and orchard.
Location 4 m E of La Conner, 4 m W of Mt. Vernon.
Restrictions No smoking. Children over 11 preferred.
Credit cards Amex, Discover, MC, Visa.
Rates B&B, $75–155 double, $70–150 single. 2-day minimum stay during Tulip Festival.

The White Swan Guest House ⊄   *Tel:* 360–445–6805
1388 Moore Road, Mt. Vernon 98273

The White Swan, on Fir Island overlooking the Skagit River, was built in 1898 by a Norwegian ferryboat captain who used the turret to observe the river traffic (including its swans—hence the inn's name). Restored in 1986 by innkeeper Peter Goldfarb, the White Swan's clear, sunny color scheme and tasteful country-style floral fabrics reflect his years in Manhattan as an interior designer; the queen- and king-size beds ensure guest comfort. Peter reports that "the White Swan is a small, one-person operation; nothing grand or pretentious, just like 'Granny's' house. Guests are encouraged to enter through the kitchen door, where they'll find freshly baked cookies and lively conversation." Breakfast includes homemade muffins, fruit, juice, coffee and tea.

"Set in the green fields of the Skagit River farming delta, enormous poplar trees line the drive to the house. The house is beautiful and the surrounding lawns are green and lush and filled with bed after bed of flowers. Peter Goldfarb is warm, welcoming, and yet respectful of guests' privacy. The interior is beautiful and each room is filled with fresh flowers, beautiful quilts, and have garden views. The evening cups of tea and cookies are delightful. Guests are roused from sleep by birdsong and breakfast aromas. Breakfast is served around a large dining room table and includes fresh fruit, homemade muffins, and French toast." *(Josephine Valdez)* "Worth a visit for the chocolate chip cookies alone." *(MW)*

337

"Breathtakingly beautiful gardens. Peter is an accommodating host who pays attention to small details. Wonderfully thick bath towels; immaculate bathroom." *(Yvonne Stoner)* "Set within a grove of trees, bordered by farmland and the river. The house is comfortable and warm, with reading nooks and crannies. Guests' comfort is paramount, from the comfortable mattresses and massive pillows on the beds to the large bathtub, perfect for soaking after a long day of bike riding. Great cookies. Peter's breakfasts always include fresh fruit, and delicious just-baked pastries. Beautiful garden with an amazing variety of flowers, and seating for one to enjoy a book or watch the birds. I heard only crickets at night." *(Craig Davison)*

Open All year.

Rooms 3 doubles in main house share 2 baths. 1 cottage with private bath, kitchen, deck.

Facilities Dining room, parlor with woodstove, porch. 1 acre with patio, English gardens.

Location NW WA, 60 m N of Seattle, 6 m S of La Conner. From I-5, take Exit 221 to Fir Island Rd. Go to yellow blinking light, straight to Moore Rd.

Restrictions No smoking. Children in cottage only.

Credit cards MC, Visa.

Rates B&B. Double $80, single $65. Cottage, $135. Extra person in cottage, $20.

Extras Member, WBBG.

LEAVENWORTH

Surrounded by the Cascade Mountains, Leavenworth is a Bavarian-style village offering outdoor recreation in all seasons—fishing, hiking, and rafting, and golf in the warmer months; downhill and cross-country skiing, sleigh rides, sledding, and snowshoeing in the colder months. Leavenworth is in central Washington, 120 miles east of Seattle and 150 miles west of Spokane. Take I-90 to Ellensburg, go north on Route 97 to Route 2, then east on Route 2 to Leavenworth.

Reader tip: "An old mining town fallen on hard times, Leavenworth re-invented itself as an ersatz Bavarian village. Most appealing is the lovely riverside park and promenade; it's clean, graffiti free, and very European with meandering paths, and lots of benches to sit and enjoy the views. Don't come here to shop—the town stores sell what appears to be wall-to-wall kitsch." *(SC)*

Information please: Built in 1994 is the Austrian-style **Abendblume Pension** (12570 Ranger Road, P.O. Box 981, 98826; 509–548–4059 or 800–669–7634). Private balconies with mountain views, archways and hand-carved ceilings reflect alpine architecture. The seven guest rooms have queen-size pencil post beds, European bedding, heated tile floors, fireplaces, whirlpool tubs, and TV/VCR's. B&B double rates of $80–160 include a hearty German breakfast buffet with pastries, a hot entree, and assorted meats and cheeses.

For a real getaway, consider the **Mountain Home Lodge** (Mountain Home Road, P.O. Box 687, 98826; 509–548–7077 or 800–414–2378), secluded in its own alpine valley. In summer, car access is via a 2½-mile dirt road; in winter you'll be transported via the lodge's heated Sno-Cat. Despite the isolation, the lodge is far from primitive—modern amenities range from the VCR to the outdoor hot tub. Dinner is served by candlelight and the three course meal begins with fine wines and appetizers. B&B rates for the ten guest rooms range from $90–175 in summer; the winter rate of $185–305 includes all meals. Comments welcome.

Run of the River B&B   *Tel:* 509–548–7171
9308 East Leavenworth Road, P.O. Box 285, 98826   800–288–6491
Fax: 509–548–7547
E-mail: rofther@rightathome

"The name Run of the River comes from a John McPhee short story about small water turbines and reflects owners Monty and Karen Turner's intention to adjust to the flow of life's events. I would say that the effect of the Turner's wonderful place is to smooth the torrents of the outside world to a gentle, vibrant flow to which no adjustment is necessary. This feeling stems as much from their unobtrusive, friendly nature as the rustic charm of the log building, itself something of a work of art with extensive details added by a local craftsman." *(John Morgan & Barbara House)*

Monty and Karen Turner, innkeepers since 1986, offer hot beverages in the lounge each afternoon, and serve a family-style breakfast of juice, yogurt, fruit, and a hot entree. Typical of their thoughtfulness and thoroughness are their helpful hiking, bicycling, and motoring guides to assist guests in area explorations.

"As close to perfect as a B&B can be. An oasis of perfect taste, surrounded by river and mountain views, and vibrant bird life. The comfortable Rose Room has a hand-hewn peeled-log queen-size bed and puffy down comforter. A small loft in the room reached by a log ladder—a little carpeted hideaway with a soft pillow. Every little detail has been provided: comfortable reading chairs, fresh flowers, wood branch bedside tables, a light on each side of the bed, binoculars and bird books, wine glasses and regular glasses, a TV with remote control, a small fridge hidden in an oak cabinet. Even the wastebasket has class—it's made of birch bark, lined with blue tissue paper. We relaxed on the swing, watched the river flow by, and explored the grounds, with several tranquil sitting areas. Delightful fellow guests gather for bountiful breakfasts of fresh fruit, yogurt, granola, pancakes and syrup, eggs with sausages, cilantro, pine nuts, and cheese." *(Suzanne Carmichael)*

"Exceptionally well designed and decorated rooms; many fixtures, including the towel racks and hooks were handcrafted out of birch. Guest rooms have sliding glass doors leading out to the porch and downstairs to the hot tub." *(Dan Winter)* "Monty greets you as you pull into the driveway, where you may also see a deer grazing in the yard. Each room has a log frame bed, mounds of pillows, robes for the hot tub, and even a jar of bubbles to blow—you can be a kid again. Breakfast is ready at 8:30 A.M., and is served family-style around a large oval oak dining table. Monty makes something different each day—perhaps quiche with homemade salsa and oven-fried potatoes with sausage, or waffles with hot maple syrup." *(Sheri Solwold)* "Karen and Monty go the extra mile for their guests whether this is your first stay or your 15th; they are warm, helpful and caring." *(Peg Fenton)* "Gorgeous and secluded location; breathtaking views. Breakfast included thick slices of cinnamon swirl French toast, freshly blended yogurt fruit shakes, and warm apple casserole. Superb service; wonderful memories." *(Jodi Wagner)* "At the top of the stairs is a basket of toiletries, in case you've forgotten something." *(Karin & Jack Armstrong)*

Open All year.
Rooms 2 suites, 4 doubles—all with private bath and/or shower. All with TV, fan, deck, fireplace, robes. Suite with 2 woodstoves; 3 with Jacuzzi tub.
Facilities Breakfast room with stereo, library with TV, phone; deck. 2 acres with hot tub, picnic area, mountain bikes, fishing, hiking trails.
Location 1 m E of Leavenworth. From Hwy. 2, go 1 m E on E. Leavenworth Rd. to inn on right.
Restrictions "Smoke-free inn & grounds." No children.
Credit cards Amex, Discover, MC, Visa.
Rates B&B, $150 suite, $95–130 double, $85–120 single. 2-night weekend/holiday minimum.
Extras Station pickup. Spanish spoken.

LONG BEACH

Long Beach is located at the southern end of the Long Beach peninsula, in southwestern Washington. It's 110 miles west of Portland, Oregon, and 130 miles southwest of Seattle. Area activities include swimming, boating, surf- and deep-sea fishing, as well as golf and tennis. A 2000-foot-long boardwalk is inviting for strolling, as are the peninsula's 28 miles of uninterrupted beach, excellent for long walks. Long Beach is famous for kite flying and hosts three major competitions annually; advance reservations essential. Canoeing and kayaking can be enjoyed on nearby Willapa Bay.

Information please: The **Edgewood Inn** (112 8th St. NE, 98631; 360–642–8227 or 800–460–7196) is a 1904 Craftsman-style bungalow, offering four guest rooms, two with private bath. B&B double rates of $85–99 include a continental breakfast. Children are welcome and the beach and shops are an easy walk away. "Attractive decor, great innkeepers, good food, priced right." *(Russell Anderson)* Reports welcome.

For additional area inns, see **Ocean Park** and **Seaview**.

Boreas Bed & Breakfast ¢
607 North Boulevard, P.O. Box 1344, 98631

Tel: 360–642–8069
888–642–8069
Fax: 360–642–5353
E-mail: boreas@aone.com

Boreas, in Greek mythology, was god of the north wind, which brings crisp clear weather. That's the favorite climate of Susie Goldsmith and

Bill Verner, owners of Boreas, who have remodeled in an eclectic style which mixes art, antiques and the contemporary with casual comfort. From their B&B, nothing obstructs the view of the Pacific except an expanse of sand dunes and seagrass. Recent additions include a heated cedar-and-glass gazebo by the dunes, housing a therapeutic spa, as well as the Dunes Suite, with a jetted tub in the bath, and an Impressionist-style mural of the local dunes and North Head lighthouse.

Breakfast is usually served at the dining room table by the fireplace, or in guests' rooms for special occasions; one day's menu might be butter-roasted bananas and apricots, blueberry cake, citrus muffins, and smoked salmon omelets with shiitake mushrooms, and home fries; followed the next morning by fresh fruit compote, chocolate chip muffins, cranberry coffee cake, and gingerbread pancakes with lemon sauce. "An easy walk to the beach." *(Steve Broderick)* "Delightful owners; delicious, generous breakfast; extremely clean; home to the world's sweetest dog." *(Jacqueline Davis)* "The rooms are beautifully decorated with antiques, lace, and fresh flowers. A warm and relaxing atmosphere. Susie and Bill were helpful with local information." *(Denise Walsh)* "A warm and cozy dining room with a wonderful fireplace; a bright and cheery living room; exceptional hospitality. Although we were on the first floor, we heard no noise from the rooms above." *(Meggan Scott)* "Immaculately clean, comfortably furnished. The hot tub was wonderful for an evening dip after a long day. Enjoyed our off-season visit." *(Mary Grant)*

Open All year.
Rooms 3 suites, 2 doubles—3 with private bath and/or shower, 2 with maximum of 4 people sharing bath. All with radio, clock, cassette player. 2 with desk, 2 with deck, 1 with jetted bathtub.
Facilities Dining room, living room with fireplace, baby grand piano; family room with games, piano, stereo, books, audio library. ½ acre with enclosed gazebo with spa, lawn games. 5-min. walk to beach. 9 miles to kayaking on bay.
Location 6 blocks N of downtown. Go right on Pacific Hwy. at Bolstad Light, left on 6th St. North. Go 1 block to North Blvd. & inn on right. (NW corner of 6th St. & North Blvd.)
Restrictions No smoking. Children by arrangement.
Credit cards Amex, Discover, DC, MC, Visa.
Rates B&B, $105–125 suite, $95 double. Extra person, $15. 2–3 night weekend/holiday minimum.
Extras Local airport/station pickup.

Scandinavian Gardens Inn B&B

1610 California Avenue, 98631

Tel: 360–642–8877
800–988–9277
Fax: 360–642–8764
E-mail: RDAKAN@AONE.COM

A contemporary natural-wood home built in 1977, Scandinavian Gardens has been owned by Rod and Marilyn Dakan since 1993. Marilyn notes that our guests come to be "relaxed, refreshed and renewed by the ocean; at night, you can fall asleep listening to the waves." The decor reflects the inn's Scandinavian theme with white Berber carpeting, bright and cheery colors, contemporary and antique furnishings, colorful throw rugs and wall hangings by local Finnish artisans, queen-size beds imported from Swedish, and traditional Scandinavian rose-maling artwork on the door of each room. The spacious honeymoon suite has a double soaking tub surrounded by plants and seashells, with a skylight above.

Breakfast is served at 9 A.M. at the dining room table, and includes fresh fruit, the inn's signature creamed rice and fruit soup, homemade sorbet, pastries, and such entrees as shrimp in a cloud, smoked salmon omelets, quiche, or blueberry French toast. Rates also include afternoon tea and cookies.

"Marilyn and Rob cook an elegant breakfast starting with sorbet and just-baked breads. The luxurious suite is clean, comfortable, well decorated, with more than enough space." *(Debra Mensik)* "A comfortable atmosphere; friendly and helpful owners; delicious breakfast." *(Jen Distler)* "The whole house was immaculate and beautiful." *(Julie & Michael Hansen)*

Open All year.
Rooms 1 suite, 4 doubles—all with full private bath, clock. 3 with desk, suite with double soaking tub, refrigerator.
Facilities Dining room, living room with fireplace, piano, books, stereo, games. Off-street parking, sauna, hot tub, gardens.
Location At the junction of Hwys. 101 & 103 go N on Hwy 103 (Pacific Hwy). Go left on 16th (at McDonalds). Go 1 block to California & go left to inn.
Restrictions No smoking. Children over 2 welcome.
Credit cards Discover, MC, Visa.
Rates B&B, $125–140 suite, $105–115 double, $95–105 single. Extra person, $15. 10% AAA, senior discount.
Extras Airport/station pickups. Crib.

MAZAMA

Mazama is located in the Northern Cascades region of north central Washington, on the North Cascades Highway (Highway 20), three to five hours drive east of Seattle and Vancouver, depending on road conditions. The closest town is Winthrop, 15 miles south.

Information please: In the heart of the Methow Valley, overlooking Freestone Lake, is the **Freestone Inn** (17798 Highway 20, 98823; 509–996–3906 or 800–639–3809). The inn includes the recently built log lodge, with 12 handsome guest rooms, each with stone fireplace (gas log), plus additional accommodations in eight lodges and restored cabins. Plans call for the construction in 1998 of more guest rooms in the main lodge, plus additional cabins. Most rooms have balconies, porches, or patios, and queen- or king-size beds; some have double whirlpool tubs or vaulted ceilings. The lodge restaurant is open for breakfast and dinner, and specializes in Northwest cuisine, using local suppliers whenever possible. Double rates range from $105–250, cabins and lodges from $65–300. Miles of trails lead from the front door, for hiking in summer, cross-country skiing in winter, although some find it hard to leave the soaring stone fireplace in the vaulted great room.

For an additional area inn, see **Winthrop**.

Mazama Country Inn ¢ ✗ ♿
P.O. Box 223, 98833

Tel: 509–996–2681
800–843–7951
Fax: 509–996–2646
E-mail: mazama@methow.com

At the edge of the Pasayten Wilderness, and only a short distance from North Cascades National Park is the Mazama Country Inn, built in 1986 and owned by George Turner. In summer, when all roads are clear of snow, guests have the option of enjoying the fine meals served at the inn, doing their own cooking in the housekeeping cabins, or visiting an area restaurant. Winter rates include a hearty country breakfast, served 7–10 A.M., with omelets, waffles, or French toast, with fruit, yogurt, and granola. After breakfast, guests prepare a pack lunch of sandwiches, fruit, and cookies to take on whatever adventure the day brings. Dinner entrees include such choices as sockeye salmon with wild rice cakes; local lamb chops with thyme, sage roasted chicken, or barbecue ribs with Yukon gold potatoes.

"Charming, comfortable accommodations; friendly, helpful, attentive staff." *(Ursula Potter)* "You can smell cookies or bread baking while you relax by the fireplace. As homey as grandma's house, yet I'm treated like a queen. Soaking in the hot tub or relaxing in the sauna is perfect after long day of skiing. The inn is clean, cozy and quiet." *(Denise Rabius)* "Wonderful dining room and service, beautiful setting, and numerous outdoor activities." *(Sandra Schooley)* "The food is wonderful and plentiful, the rooms comfortable, and the cross-country skiing amazing." *(Bobbe Gordon)* "No phones, TV, or radios in the rooms—the quiet was wonderful. Lovely decor and casual atmosphere; beautiful setting; fine value. The kitchen staff was good enough make us coffee for an early departure." *(Jeff Smith)*

"There is a horse corral and a wide bubbly river, lots of fir trees and mountain views. Our duplex room had a single bed, bath, and sitting area below, and a double bed in a sleeping loft above; also a little porch. Partly paneled, it was simply but tastefully decorated with a frieze of game birds. The handsome dining room is two stories high with a huge stone fireplace; there's a patio where one can eat breakfast in the sun." *(Carolyn Mathiasen)*

Open All year.
Rooms 6 2–5 bedroom cabins, 3 loft rooms, 11 doubles—all with private bath and/or shower. Cabins with woodstove, kitchens, some with TV.
Facilities Restaurant, living room with fireplace, game room with piano, patio. Hot tub, sauna, lawn games, mountain bike rentals, horseback riding, fishing, flower walks, birding, whitewater rafting, rock climbing, kayaking. 120 m cross-country ski trails, ski rentals, lessons; heli-skiing, sleigh rides. Pasayten Wilderness, North Cascades National Park for hiking, fishing.
Location N central WA, 14 m N of Winthrop on Hwy 20 (Cascade Loop).
Restrictions No smoking. Children welcome; no children under 13 in inn rooms from Christmas through Presidents Day weekend if specified.

Credit cards Discover, MC, Visa.

Rates Summer, room only, $95–130 cabin; $80–95 double. Extra person, $15. Winter, three meals daily, $150–185. Extra person, $50. Packages available. Midweek four-night discounts, off-season specials. Alc breakfast, $6; lunch, $6; dinner, $25.

Extras Wheelchair access.

MOUNT RAINIER NATIONAL PARK

Also recommended: Approximately 20 miles east of Ashford, at an elevation of 5,000 feet, is the **Paradise Inn** (c/o Mount Rainier Guest Services, P.O. Box 108, Ashford 98304; 360–569–2275). The lodge is open from late May to early October, and the 126 simply furnished guest rooms, some with private bath, cost $70–130. "At the timberline on Mt. Rainer, in acres of meadows filled with wildflowers and the snowy mountain above, is this 1917 mountain lodge, built from cedar tree trunks, with huge fireplaces. Although the lobby was filled with tourists during the day, the balcony is reserved for overnight guests; free afternoon tea is served here. All around the lobby and balcony are cedar log alcoves with benches and tables for writing. Our room was small but comfortable, with private bath and mountain view. Helpful, dignified service. Good food, unhurried service in the dining room. Advance reservations are essential, but we lucked out on a last minute cancellation." *(Constance Gardner)*

Information please: Also inside the park is the **National Park Inn at Longmire** (P.O. Box 108, Mt. Rainer National Park, 98397; 360–569–2275), open year-round. Set at an elevation of 2,700 feet, the inn was originally built in 1916 and was extensively remodeled in 1990. Eight of the 25 guest rooms have private baths; the rest share baths. Double rates range from $70–130; breakfast is included off-season. The restaurant is open for three meals daily, and a lounge with stone fireplace is reserved for overnight guests. Hiking and cross-country ski trails are available from the front door, with ski rentals in winter. The inn is located in the Longmire Historic District, six miles from the southwest entrance to the park.

For an additional area inn, see **Ashford.**

OCEAN PARK

For additional area inns, see **Long Beach** and **Seaview.**

Caswell's on the Bay	*Tel:* 360–665–6535
25204 Sandridge Road, 98640	888–553–2319
	Fax: 360–665–6500

Having vacationed for years in the Long Beach area, Bob and Marilyn Caswell originally purchased property for a retirement home on Willapa Bay because, according to Marilyn, "the bay side is ten degrees warmer than the beach, and we can grow flowers here." Inside of retiring, though, they decided to build a 6,000 square-foot B&B instead. Surrounded by pine trees, this neo-Victorian Queen Anne home has a turret, gables, a wraparound porch and was completed in 1995. It's painted yellow with white trim, accented in deep red. The Caswells spent the previous five years collecting antiques, finding Victorian, American, and French antiques dating back to the early 1800s to furnish the rooms—most with lovely views across peaceful Willapa Bay to the coastal mountains beyond. The spacious guest rooms have reading lamps and bedside tables on both sides of the bed, Victorian bedroom suites, floral comforters and fabrics.

Breakfast is served at the dining room table or on the veranda at 9 A.M. (earlier if requested for business or bird-watching) and includes fresh fruit and juice, just-baked muffins or scones, a breakfast meat, and such entrees as waffles, pancakes, or egg dishes. Coffee, tea, and cocoa are available all day.

"Marilyn's warm welcome extends from the delicious breakfast to afternoon tea and cookies. Each guest room is different, but all are lovely." *(Lee Todd)* "Beautiful, peaceful setting, away from the tourist bustle, with lovely flower beds and rock gardens. The Caswells are friendly, helpful, and unobtrusive. Breakfasts taste as good as they look." *(Charles & Madeleine Bowerman)* "The food was excellent, the beds comfortable, the towels luxurious, the gardens beautiful, and innkeepers helpful." *(Zelda Baron)* "Outstanding atmosphere and ambience; spacious and beautifully decorated public rooms." *(Dr. Hans E. Lilienthal)* "Our delightful room had a TV/VCR with a large selections of videos. Sweeping bay views from our deck. The location is both convenient and quiet. I enjoyed relaxing with a cup of cocoa and a book from the extensive library. Breakfast was good and generous; Marilyn and Bob were friendly and helpful." *(Marlaina M. Wall)*

Open All year.

Rooms 2 suites, 3 doubles—all with full private bath, clock/radio, ceiling fan. TV/VCR on request. 1 with deck.

Facilities Dining room, living room with fireplace, library. 3.5 acres with off-street parking, flower gardens. On Willipa Bay; 1 m to ocean beach. Fishing, boating nearby.

Location SW WA, Long Beach peninsula. 2½ hrs. NW of Portland; 3¼ hrs. SW of Seattle. 1 m to Ocean Park, 4 m N of Long Beach. Take Hwy. 101 across Astoria Bridge. Go left to Ilwaco, then N 12 m on Hwy 103 to Ocean Park.

Restrictions No smoking. Children over 11.

Credit cards MC, Visa.

Rates B&B, $120–150 suite, $95–150 double. 2nd night half-price. Extra person, $15. AAA discount.

PORT ANGELES

Port Angeles is located in northwestern Washington, midway up the northern end of the Olympic Peninsula, along the Strait of Juan de Fuca. It's a popular place to overnight for those traveling the Olympic Loop Highway (Rte. 101) and for those taking the ferry to or from Victoria, on Vancouver Island, British Columbia.

Nearby attractions include Hurricane Ridge, just 17 miles from town. At 5,000 feet, it offers a beautiful view of the surrounding valleys, mountains, and sea. Other area attractions include Lake Crescent, the Dungeness Spit Wildlife Refuge, the Sole Duc Hot Springs, charter fishing and boating in the straits or the Pacific, hiking and backpacking, and cross-country skiing in the winter.

Also recommended: For comfortable cabins and excellent food, the **Sol Duc Hot Springs Resort** (Olympic National Park, P.O. Box 2169, 98362; 360–327–3583) may be a good choice. A famous resort at the turn of the century, Teddy Roosevelt was among Sol Duc's many prominent visitors; it was recently rebuilt by the National Park Service. There are 32 cabins, 6 in duplex units with cooking facilities; rates for two people are $88–98. "Well-maintained cabins, welcoming staff and management. The mineral pools are kept immaculately clean. Beautiful hiking trails for all levels of ability. So quiet at night you can hear the pine needles drop." *(James Ball)*

Information please: Current reports are needed on the **Lake Crescent Lodge** (416 Lake Crescent Road, 98363–8672; 360–928–3211), offering breathtaking vistas of Lake Crescent and mountains beyond, set between the rain forest to the south and the Strait of Juan de Fuca to the north. The buildings include the early 1900s-era wooden main lodge, with its huge wraparound porch and fireplace; the more modern Pyramid Mountain Lodge, with lake and mountain views; 17 cabins; and two motel-type buildings. "The best rooms are in the four large cabins with fireplaces; book early, everybody wants them. The rooms in the lodge on the north side are worth the view over the lake, even with shared baths." *(Suzanne Carmichael)* Open late April through October, the lodge has 17 cabins ($99–150) and 35 double rooms ($69–109). National Park Concessions, Inc., is the National Park concessionaire for this property.

For additional area accommodations, see **Port Townsend** and **Sequim.**

Domaine Madeleine B&B, on Finn Hall Road   *Tel:* 360–457–4174
146 Wildflower Lane, 98362   *Fax:* 360–457–3037
                                         E-mail: domm@olypen.com

Innkeepers Madeleine Lanham and John Chambers welcome those who like books, gardens, wildlife, spectacular views of water and mountains, and stimulating conversation. But if quiet is your desire, they will "provide a sound level in which you could hear an oyster yawn!" Leisurely multicourse breakfasts begin at 9 A.M. and end around 10:30, and might include French baguettes and cheese, fresh fruit and juice, such entrees as French toast stuffed with fruit; shrimp crepes; or pecan apple soufflé pancakes; with a dessert of fruit tarts, or chocolate mousse. Coffee and tea is available around the clock in the dining room, and three guest rooms have a refreshment area stocked with hot beverage makings and popcorn.

"Guests' comfort is of prime importance to John and Madeleine." *(S. Faulkner)* "Elegant, peaceful and comfortable. We enjoyed quiet chats with our hosts. Rooms have incredible water views. The delightful

Rendezvous Room has a remote-control gas fireplace, TV/VCR, CD player, candlelit Jacuzzi, and a wonderful garden view. Unbelievable breakfasts: fresh croissants with three kinds of jam, poached pears, salmon with spinach, sorbet and cream puffs; the next morning we were treated to fresh baked rolls, scones, fruit platters, ratatouille omelets, turkey sausage, cheesecake with caramel sauce." *(Jane Plank Thiemens)* "We appreciated the option of eating breakfast in the privacy of our room. A charming, romantic experience." *(Joan Johnson)* "Fine attention to detail in amenities and cleanliness. Delighted with the Ming Room. Excellent food, ample privacy." *(Robert Herman)*

"From the back this contemporary house has a view of Victoria, British Columbia, and the Strait; to the front are the Olympia Mountains. We even saw whales spouting." *(Elizabeth Baxin)* "Furnished with Asian and European antiques. Both downstairs rooms, the Monet (complete with replica garden) and the Renoir have beautiful views. The Ming, upstairs, has a 30-foot balcony, tiled Jacuzzi, and mirrored bath with designer robes and French perfumes." *(Marie Harris)* "Welcoming touches included a filled ice bucket, fresh fruit, current magazines, and intriguing books." *(Shale Baskin)* "Helpful hosts; they do everything and want it to be perfect." *(Betsy Immergut)*

Open All year.

Rooms 3 suites, 2 doubles—all with private bath and/or shower, telephone, radio, TV/VCR, air-conditioning, deck. 5 with fireplace, 4 with Jacuzzi tub, 3 with refrigerator, microwave, coffee pot.

Facilities Dining room with fireplace; living room with TV/VCR, video library, stereo, books, harpsichord, games; porch, deck, laundry facilities. 5 acres with gardens, badminton, croquet, volleyball. Nature tours.

Location NW WA. 7 m E of town center. Take Hwy 101 E 7 m. Go left onto Old Olympic Hwy; go 1.4 m. Go left onto Gehrke, go 3 m. Go right on Finn Hall & go $^2/_{10}$ m to inn's sign.

Restrictions No smoking. Children over 12 welcome.

Credit cards MC, Visa.

Rates B&B, $145–165 suite, $99–160 double, $79–89 single. Extra person, $25.

Extras Local airport pickup. French, Spanish, German, Farsi spoken.

Tudor Inn B&B *Tel:* 360–452–3138
1108 South Oak Street, 98362 *E-mail:* tudorinfo@aol.com

Transplanted Texan Jane Glass moved to the Olympic Peninsula after 10 years in England and Norway. While abroad, she made plans to open an English-style B&B and started visiting inns in England, buying antiques and collectibles. In 1983 she and her late husband Jerry purchased the historic Butler home, a Tudor-style, half-timbered house built in 1910. In 1995, the inn was renovated, with private baths added and rooms enlarged; Jane's daughter Katy Stansifer joined her as innkeeper. Handsomely furnished with beautiful antiques (some for sale) and brass and canopy queen- and king-size beds, the inn is presided over by their elegant white Persian cat. A new room added in the renovation is the delightful Country Room, with a cathedral ceiling, fireplace, and French doors opening to a balcony with mountain views. Lots of windows and charming pastoral scenes painted on two walls and on the folding screen that surrounds the antique claw-foot tub make this room an especially inviting hideaway.

Breakfast, served 8:30–9 A.M. at the dining room table, includes fruit compote, biscuits or muffins, bacon or sausage, and such entrees as buttermilk waffles with homemade blackberry syrup, smoked salmon egg soufflés, or apple caramel French toast. Take-along breakfasts can be arranged for early morning ferries.

"Elegant decor, fabulous antiques, warm and inviting, with afternoon tea and cookies served by a toasty fire. Jane is an open, warm, and charming host. A short walk away is a scenic panoramic view of the Straits of Juan de Fuca and Victoria, BC. Immaculate housekeeping; delicious breakfast." *(Jamie Reis)* "Our room was large and comfortable with a spacious bathroom. The sitting room was comfortable and well decorated, and we enjoyed the company of their friendly cat. Good advice on dining options." *(Catherine LaCroix)* "Comfortable, inviting home in a quiet residential neighborhood. Inviting place for the travel-weary to curl up with a good book." *(James & Pamela Burr)*

Open All year.
Rooms 5 rooms—all with private bath and/or shower, clock, fan, individual thermostats. 2 with desk, 1 with fireplace, balcony,
Facilities Dining room, living room with fireplace, piano; library with fireplace, TV/VCR, books; guest refrigerator; porch/deck.
Location From Hwy. 101 (Front St.), turn S (left) onto Lincoln St. Continue on Lincoln to 11th. Go 2 blocks to Oak St. to inn on corner of 11th & Oak. 10–15 min. walk downtown; 5-min. drive to Victoria Ferry.
Restrictions No smoking. Children over 12 welcome.
Credit cards Amex, MC, Visa.
Rates B&B $75–125 double, $70–110 single. Tips welcome for housekeepers. Off-season senior, AAA discount.

PORT LUDLOW

For additional area inns, see **Port Townsend** and **Poulsbo**.

Inn at Ludlow Bay 🏃 ✕ ♿   *Tel: 360–437–0411*
One Heron Road, 98365   *Fax: 360–437–0310*

Everyone enjoys a relaxing soak in a double Jacuzzi tub, but the experience is even more delightful when accompanied by views of Ludlow Bay and the Olympic and Cascade Mountains. Add a toasty fireplace and comfortable queen- or king-size bed, topped by a down comforter and lots of pillows, and it's no surprise that guests of the Inn at Ludlow Bay don't always do as much sightseeing as they had planned. Located on a spit of land jutting out into the bay, the inn was built in 1994; it's owned by Paul and Pam Schell and partners; David Holt is the innkeeper. The inn's popular waterfront dining room features fresh, seasonal seafood blending Northwest and Asian cuisine, with such entrees as lemon grass–crusted salmon, rack of lamb with dried cherry port reduction; or sweet potato, parsnip and gruyere ravioli.

"Spectacular service, decor, scenery, and location. The exterior has clapboard siding and cedar shingles, while the interior is done in reproduction Mission style. The lobby area is small but quaint with a registration desk and a small nook with a built-in wooden bench by the fireplace. A long hallway, done in cherry wood, leads to two eating areas, a sun room and a formal dining room. The sun room is surrounded by glass walls looking over the grounds and bay. Casual round wood tables and chairs are topped by small flower vases. A continental breakfast buffet is available here each morning from 7 to 10 A.M. The guest rooms are on the second and third floors, and most have a four-poster Mission-style bed, writing table or desk, and Mission-style chairs set next to a tiled gas fireplace. The large bathrooms have granite counters, modern fixtures, shower, and large Jacuzzi tub; the doors open from one side of the tub, giving a view out the window to the water and mountains beyond. High quality linens and towels. Although not all rooms have a balcony, each has a magnificent view. During the day we went kayaking in the bay out to some rocks where seals played; the kayak rental place is only a few steps from the inn. At night, we enjoyed glasses of wine on the large veranda which runs along one side of the building, facing the marina. In addition to the overnight guests, the restaurant is popular with people arriving by both boat and car, and reservations are essential. Our outstanding dinner included salads of mixed greens with goat cheese puffs, chicken with cranberry sauce, and lavender flower ice cream. All was presented beautifully; service was prompt and attentive." (*Wendy Kameda*)

Note: Under the same ownership is the Friday Harbor House in San Juan Island and the Inn at Langley in Whidbey Island; see entries.

Open All year.
Rooms 3 suites, 34 doubles—all with full private bath with double whirlpool tub, telephone, radio, clock, TV/VCR, video library, desk, gas fireplace, refrigerator, coffee maker, robes; some with fan, balcony/deck.
Facilities Restaurant, bar/lounge, sun room, library/den with books, fireplace; porches. Off-street parking, rose, herb garden, lawn games. On marina for water sports; boat moorings; kayak rentals. Priority rates & tee times at 27-hole golf course. Tennis, hiking nearby.
Location Olympic Peninsula, 90 min. W of Seattle. After crossing Hood Canal Bridge (St. Hwy. 104), follow signs to Port Ludlow. Turn right on St. Hwy. 12 (Beaver Valley Rd.). Go turn right on Oak Bay Rd. Inn at end of Heron Rd., adjacent to marina.
Restrictions No smoking.
Credit cards Amex, MC, Visa.
Rates B&B, $300–450 suite, $150–200 double, $135–200 single. Extra person, $35. Alc dinner, $35–45.
Extras Wheelchair access; room specially equipped. Cribs. Pets allowed.

PORT ROBERTS

Also recommended: If we gave awards for B&Bs in unlikely locations, we'd have to add the **Maple Meadow B&B** (101 Goodman Road, 98291; 360–945–5536) to the list! Port Roberts is found at the tip of a small peninsula of southwestern British Columbia, Canada. Because it goes south of the 49th parallel, it's Washington, not BC. Built in 1910, this restored farmhouse has three guest rooms (one with private bath), and B&B double rates of $75–100. Guests can relax in the hot tub, or head down to the bay for wonderful views. It's 15 minutes to the Tsawwassen ferry terminal, and 40 minutes to downtown Vancouver. "Gracious, perky, generous, friendly innkeeper, Terri LaPorte. We were welcomed with cheese and crackers, coffee, and cake. Our room had beautiful antiques, a comfortable king-size bed, chocolates, fresh flowers, and homemade blackberry liqueur. A delightful experience." *(Lori Murray Sampson)*

PORT TOWNSEND

Port Townsend has been designated a National Historic District and is considered to be the best example of a Victorian seacoast town north of San Francisco. Nearly 70 Victorian buildings can be seen, along with the town's many appealing craft shops, art galleries, and restaurants. Good salmon fishing is available, along with beaches for crabbing, clamming, and oystering. The town offers public golf courses and tennis courts and is within a short drive of the Olympic National Park. Because of the protection of the Olympic Mountains, the climate is fairly mild, with more than 200 sunny days a year and about 20 inches of rainfall (less than half of Seattle's).

Port Townsend is located on northwest Washington's Olympic Peninsula, on Puget Sound. It's less than 60 miles from both Seattle and Victoria and is 13 miles north, via Route 20, off the scenic Olympic Loop, Highway 101.

Reader tip: "We visited the point to watch the sun set; it was breathtaking watching it sink behind the San Juans. A 'don't miss' experience." *(BJ Hensley)*

Also recommended: A Colonial Revival–style home built in 1934, the **Commander's Guest House** (400 Hudson Street, 98368; 360–385–1778 or 800–826–3854) was originally the residence of the Commanding Medical Officer of the U.S. Quarantine Station at Point Hudson, and offers 2,000 feet of frontage on scenic, unspoiled Admiralty Inlet beach. Longtime owners Ray and Pattie Ferschke restored their home as a B&B in 1996, with three inviting guest rooms, each with private bath. B&B rates of $85–125 include creative full breakfasts, served between 8:30–9:30 A.M. "Warm and helpful hosts; tasty breakfast. Incredible water views. Falling asleep to the sound of a clanging buoy was a special treat." *(Frank Reeder)*

The **Ravenscroft Inn** (533 Quincy Street, 98368; 360–385–2784 or 800–782–2691) is set on a bluff overlooking Admiralty Inlet and is a Colonial re-creation of an early American seaport inn. Some of the eight lovely guest rooms have beamed ceilings, French doors opening to balconies, floral comforters, and period furniture. The B&B rate of $69–165 includes a full breakfast. "Charming rooms, delicious breakfast, warm hospitality." *(BJ Hensley)*

Information please: Situated on the bluff overlooking the mountains and Puget Sound is the **Ann Starrett Mansion** (744 Clay Street, 98368; 360–385–3205 or 800–321–0644), a striking example of classic Victorian architecture, with frescoed ceilings and a three-tiered spiral staircase, leading to an unusual domed ceiling. Built in 1889 by George Starrett as a wedding present for his wife Ann, the inn has magnificent formal public rooms, and eleven guest rooms furnished with authentic period antiques; the least expensive ones are at ground level, a floor below the common rooms. Additional accommodations are found in two cottages with fireplaces and Jacuzzi tubs. A full breakfast, served at 8:30A.M., is included in the B&B double rates of $125–225.

Built in 1872, the **Holly Hill House** (611 Polk, 98368; 360–385–5619 or 800–435–1454) is located in uptown Port Townshend, and is distinguished by its fine woodwork and authentic Victorian plantings, including a Camperdown elm tree, and towering holly trees. B&B double rates for the five guest rooms, each with private bath, range from $80–150, including a full breakfast. "Friendly innkeeper, great breakfast, beautiful home." *(Sally Ducot)*

Listed in past editions, we need current reports on **The James House** (1238 Washington Street, 98368; 360–385–1238 or 800–385–1238), built in 1891 and listed on the National Register of Historic Places. Set on a bluff with sweeping views of Port Townsend, the Olympic and Cascade ranges, and Puget Sound, the inn has nine guest rooms, with B&B rates ranging from $75–175, including a full breakfast, afternoon tea and cookies, and evening sherry.

Built in 1892 and designed to resemble a European medieval castle, **Manresa Castle** (7th and Sheridan, P.O. Box 564, 98368; 360–385–5750 or 800–732–1281) is an elegant mansion, highlighted with European antiques and elegant hand-painted wallcoverings. Its location on Castle Hill affords views of the town, shipping lanes, and mountains beyond. "A bit out of town. A magical dining room, looking out on a charming garden, with a cook unexpected in such a small town." *(Russ Stratton)* "Although other rooms were more modest, we were pleased with the Tower Suite and its marvelous views. Breakfast is a modest continental affair, served on the basement level." *(SC)* B&B double rates for the forty guest rooms range from $75–$175, with a $159 package including two nights accommodation plus dinner one night, available midweek in season, daily off-season. By the way, if you've always wanted a castle to call your own, this one was for sale at press time.

For additional area inns, see **Port Ludlow** and **Sequim.**

The English Inn ¢
718 "F" Street, 98368

Tel: 360–385–5302
800–254–5302
Fax: 360–385–5302
E-mail: NANCY@macaid.com

Built on a hill overlooking a valley with the Olympic range in the distance, the English Inn is an Italianate Victorian home built in 1885, and was purchased by Nancy and Dave Borino in 1995.

In addition to the original cast hardware and ceiling moldings, the inn is decorated with a rich color palette, complementing its antiques and period furnishings. Guest rooms are named for English poets, and one handsome room has a king-size bed, terra-cotta walls, and matching comforter, drapes, and wallpaper border in coordinating terra-cotta florals and dark green, while another is more feminine in pink and blue with wicker furnishings and a quilt-topped queen-size bed. Breakfast is served in the dining room or can be enjoyed in bed. Menus vary daily: in addition to granola, a summer morning might bring passion fruit juice with strawberries, fruit pinwheels, ginger pancakes with raspberry sauce, herbed hash-brown potatoes, and orange yogurt muffins; a winter menu might consist of cranberry-raspberry juice with star fruit, broiled grapefruit with Triple Sec, eggnog cheese French toast, sauteed mushrooms, and English tea muffins. After a day exploring the town, guests enjoy watching the sunset in the garden gazebo, or relaxing in the hot tub.

"Warm hospitality, delicious breakfasts. Lovely fresh flowers inside the house, wonderful gardens outside." *(GR)* "Beautifully decorated for Christmas." *(MW)*

Open All year.

Rooms 5 doubles—all with private bath and/or shower. 2 with clock, desk, 1 with radio.

Facilities Dining room, living room with stereo, TV/VCR, piano. Off-street parking, garden, patio, hot tub, gazebo, bicycles. Golf, ocean nearby.

Location 10-min. walk to Uptown district; 5 min. drive to historic downtown. From Hwy. 20 (Sims Way), go through light at Kearney. Half-left up hill on Washington. Go 2 blocks. Go left onto Walker (becomes Cherry). Go right onto "F" St. Go 2 blocks.

Restrictions No smoking. Children over 14.

Credit cards Amex, DC, Discover, MC, Visa.

Rates B&B, $75–105 double. Extra person, $25.

POULSBO

Information please: Listed in past editions, we need recent comments on the well-known **Manor Farm Inn** (26069 Big Valley Road N.E., 98370; 360–779–4628), a century-old farmhouse restored and expanded as an inn in 1984. The light and airy decor has antique French country furnishings in both the common areas and the nine guest rooms. May through October, and weekends year round, the B&B double rate ranges from $110–160, and includes afternoon tea, evening cake, morning room tray of coffee and scones, and full farm breakfast. Midweek off-season, all rooms are $100, including a 9:00 A.M. tray of juice, scones, and coffee. Dinner is served on Fridays and Saturdays, March through December; the prix fixe menu is $30 ($55 for the December Christmas feast). "Pleasant staff, comfortable room, excellent breakfast, superb dinner, delightful farm atmosphere." *(Catherine LaCroix)* Current reports needed.

QUINAULT

Olympic National Park, with an average annual rainfall of almost 150 inches, offers many sights of interest, including the Hoh Rain Forest, filled with massive Douglas firs that are covered with shaggy green moss. The area was set aside as a forest reserve in 1898 by Grover Cleveland and was declared a National Monument by Teddy Roosevelt in 1909. In 1938 it was toured by Franklin Roosevelt, who declared it a national park.

Also recommended: Built in 1926, the **Lake Quinault Lodge** (South Shore Road, Box 7, 98575; 360–288–2900 or in WA/OR, 800–562–6672) is the best-known lodge in Olympia National Park, and advance reservations are essential; ARAMARK is the concessionaire. If possible, try to book one of the recently renovated or newly built rooms. Ask about the 36 lakeside rooms, decorated with wicker furniture in typical motel layouts: "Our lakeside room was attractive with a private balcony and good light for reading." *(Tom Wilbanks)* Readers have been less pleased with some other rooms: "A small wooden chair at the desk was the only seating in our room. The bathroom was awkward and shabby, the plumbing noisy." *(MJ)* A total of 92 guest rooms are found in several buildings; double rates range from $65–140, suites from $125–270. Food seems to be about average, sometimes better than other national parks, and service seems to be the usual friendly but uneven sort found in most of our parks. There's no dispute about the setting: "Quinault's strength is the ease of access to a beautiful environment. Rain forest trails are across the road, the beautiful seashore a short drive away." *(James McCowan)*

For additional area accommodation, see **Kalaloch.**

SAN JUAN ISLANDS

If you can visit only one part of Washington State, choose the San Juans. Depending on the tide, between 175 and 300 rock-cliffed islands dot the area between Puget Sound and Canada. Here you will find secluded bays and densely forested ridges inhabited by eagles. From Anacortes on the mainland, ferries travel to Victoria, Canada, stopping at four of the more populous islands. The largest is Orcas, where you can climb Mt. Constitution for spectacular views of the other islands, Canada, and the Olympic and Cascade mountain ranges. Lopez is perfect for cyclists;

and Shaw is known for the nuns who operate its ferry dock. On San Juan Island (namesake for the whole chain) visit the site of the infamous "Pig War" between the U.S. and England; relax in remote Roche Harbor or join the summer crowds in Friday Harbor.

By ferry the islands are three hours north of Seattle and the same distance south of Vancouver, B.C., and east of Victoria. The ferry from Anacortes takes about an hour. One warning: If you're traveling in the summer, advance reservations for accommodations and ferry passage are *essential.*

Reader tip: "From Memorial Day to Labor Day, don't expect to get the first ferry you try for; they fill up quickly, and you may end up waiting several hours. Don't schedule tight connections." *(Adam Platt)*

SAN JUAN ISLANDS—LOPEZ ISLAND

Just 80 miles north of Seattle, Lopez Island has few places to stay (or even eat), making it a haven for those who want to get away from crowds. Most visitors to this island are fishermen and women and cyclists who peddle the relatively flat back roads.

Also recommended: An elegant Victorian-style country inn built in 1990, the **Edenwild Inn** (P.O. Box 271, Lopez Island, 98261; 360–468–3238) was purchased in 1996 by Lauren and Jamie Stephens. The eight guest rooms, all with private bath, overlook Fisherman's Bay, the San Juan Channel, or wooded garden; one room is family friendly and another is fully equipped for the disabled. "Wonderful innkeepers working hard to make their inn even more delightful. Family-style breakfast served in a lovely dining room overlooking the garden. The common area has a big fireplace and comfy chairs and sofa. Wicker chairs on the porch invite you to read or relax. Convenient village location for walking, bicycling, and kayaking. The views of Fisherman Bay are beautiful, and a log to sit on and watch the sunsets is only a stroll away." *(Pam Phillips)* B&B double rates range from $100–160 and include a full breakfast and afternoon aperitif.

Information please: Overlooking Aleck Bay is the eponymous **Aleck Bay Inn** (Aleck Bay Road, Rte. 1, Box 1920, Lopez Island 98261; 360–468–3535), named for the captain of the first sidewheeler steamboat in the Pacific Northwest, and the builder of this waterfront house. B&B rates for the four guest rooms, each with private bath, range from $80–150, including a full breakfast. Children are welcome in the family suite.

Under new ownership in 1997 is the **Inn at Swifts Bay** (Port Stanley Road, Route 2, Box 3402, Lopez Island 98261; 360–468–3636). Although a past reader favorite for its exquisite decor, marvelous attention to detail, excellent breakfasts, and welcoming ambiance, current reports are requested. Five guest rooms are available; two smaller ones share a bath and cost $85–95; three larger rooms have private baths and fireplaces, with rates of $145–175; a full breakfast is included.

Lopez Farm Cottages (Fisherman Bay Road, P.O. Box 610, Lopez Island 98261; 360–468–3555) is a series of four cottages surrounded by cedar trees and a large meadow, set on 30 acres. Decorated in a Scandinavian style with light hardwood floors, tasteful and comfortable furnishings, each cottage has a fireplace, fully equipped kitchen, deck and private bath with shower. Breakfast is delivered to your door and includes juice, fruit, muffins, coffee and tea. The cottages are conveniently located across the road from Lopez Vineyards, 1½ miles from the village and 2½ miles to the ferry. "Privacy and serenity. We enjoyed eating at a small table overlooking the meadow. Every convenience was thought of—corkscrew, wine glasses, candles, matches. The bathroom was beautiful with a two person shower and large plush towels. The bed was so comfortable, I pulled up the high-quality sheets to get the brand name of the mattress. Owner John Warsen plans to add more cottages and restore the original farmhouse to provide more accommodations." *(Pam Phillips)*

SAN JUAN ISLANDS—ORCAS ISLAND

Orcas Island combines a lively arts community with outdoor recreation opportunities and pampered resort life. It's possible to spend the morning hiking Mt. Constitution, pop into a trendy cafe for lunch, browse in small galleries and bookstores, then while away the rest of the afternoon beachcombing, fishing, or having a spa treatment.

Also recommended: Within walking distance of Eastsound village is the **Kangaroo House** (P.O. Box 334, Eastsound 98245; 360–376–2175), a charming Craftsman-style cottage, built in 1907, and named for the pet kangaroo which made her home in its yard back in the 1950s. Guests can cuddle up by the stone fireplace in winter, or relax on the deck in summer. B&B double rates for the five guest rooms range from $75–125, including a full breakfast; children are welcome. "Friendly innkeepers, delightful stay." *(Elisa O. Shostok, also PP)*

Overlooking a small trout pond, **The Old Trout Inn** (Route 1, Box 45A, Eastsound 98245; 360–376–8282) is a contemporary cedar lodge with five different decks and patios where you can watch island sunsets reflected in the water. B&B rates of $125–185 include a full breakfast and afternoon wine. Two of the guest rooms have private hot tubs and in-room fireplaces; there's another hot tub for all to enjoy. "Articulate, knowledgeable, pleasant innkeeper; exceptional library; spotless, comfortable accommodations; tasty breakfast, mercifully served at individual tables." *(Gene & Robert Altshuler)*

The **Orcas Hotel** (P.O. Box 155, Orcas 98280; 360–376–4300), was built as a hotel in 1904, and sits on a knoll overlooking the ferry dock in Orcas Harbor. Many of the twelve guest rooms have water views, and peak season rates include a full breakfast in the hotel's well-regarded restaurant; the deluxe rooms range from $110–170 in price, the more modest ones (with garden views) are $79–89. Off-season rates (except holidays), are an affordable $50–85 (no breakfast). "Wonderful location. The inn is run by a friendly, laid-back family. The rooms have views of the water or lovely gardens, and each is furnished with taste and individuality. Only a few have private baths, but the shared ones are immaculate and there are several. The restaurant was closed when we visited, but the Espresso-Bakery Cafe served simple but good meals and seemed to be popular with locals." *(Elisabeth Ring)* "Breathtaking views from the second-floor balcony; wonderful flower gardens." *(Sharon Bielski)* "Spacious rooms with good reading lights and comfortable queen-size beds. Helpful, attentive, friendly staff. Wonderful front veranda. An ideal base for exploring the islands." *(Pam Phillips)*

Turtleback Farm Inn ♿   *Tel:* 360–376–4914
Crow Valley Road, Route 1, Box 650,   800–376–4914
Eastsound, 98245   *Fax:* 360–376–5329

"The Turtleback Farm Inn is the place to experience the three R's—rest, relaxation, and romance—not necessarily in that order." *(Rikki Rothenberg-Klein)* Owned by Bill and Susan Fletcher since 1985, the inn has recently been expanded by the construction of the Orchard House, a cedar-sided Shaker-style barn set in the inn's apple orchard. Each of its four spacious king-bedded rooms have an individual deck, fireplace, sitting areas, full bath, and refrigerator; guests can opt for breakfast in their room or at the inn.

"This restored 1800s farmhouse is shaded by a 300-year-old elm in a serene, pastoral setting overlooking rolling meadows where sheep graze and chickens wander about. The house is meticulously maintained, including fresh flowers every day. Superb breakfasts, different each day." *(Patricia Scoville)* "The wonderful breakfasts are hearty as well as interesting; the comfortable guest rooms have cozy wool comforters, great vistas, and modern bathrooms." *(Corinne Ruokangas)* "Our room was beautifully appointed with a combination of old and new, blending antiques with comfortable furniture." *(Melvyn Greenberg & Carole Malone)* "Beds are wonderfully comfortable. Breakfasts are nourishing and delicious, fueling us for a day's bicycling." *(Elizabeth Shaw)*

"Bill got us situated, recommended a restaurant for dinner, suggested several activities for the next day, and laid wood for a fire. The Fletchers live in a separate house, so guests are free to make themselves at home throughout the inn. Never intrusive, Bill and Susan were attentive to our every need, and entertained us with tales of island lore. We relaxed in the evening in front of a roaring fire sipping sherry. Served in the dining room or on the valley-view deck, breakfast was wonderful; my favorite was the egg, cheese, and herb bake. The inn combines attention to detail with a country simplicity that is the perfect accompaniment to the island's slow, calm beauty." *(Scott & Katie King)*

Open All year.
Rooms 11 doubles—all with private bath and/or shower. 10 with radio, 6 with deck, 4 with fireplace, refrigerator.
Facilities Dining room with wet bar, refrigerator. Living room with fireplace, game table. 80 acres with 6 ponds. Tennis, swimming, hiking, boating, kayaking, sailing, whalewatching nearby.

Location 2.4 m from West Sound Marina, 4 m from Eastsound, 6 m from ferry landing. From ferry, take Horseshoe Hwy.; take first left, then right onto Crow Valley Rd.; inn on right.

Restrictions No smoking. Children 8 and over by arrangement.

Credit cards MC, Visa.

Rates B&B, $80–185 double, $70–185 single. Extra person, $25. Tipping "not expected." 2-night minimum May 1–Oct. 31; also holidays, weekends. Midweek rates, Nov. 1–April 1. Picnic lunches, special occasion dinners.

Extras Wheelchair access; 1 room fully accessible.

SAN JUAN ISLANDS—SAN JUAN ISLAND

San Juan Island is the westernmost island in the archipelago. Although its main town, Friday Harbor, is the county seat, it is still a sleepy small town with a few shops and galleries, a busy waterfront, the Whale Museum, and a newly opened performing arts center. From Friday Harbor, take a drive around the craggy western end of the island for superb views, or better yet, follow the popular bike route. Continue on to the site of the "Pig War," which started when an American farmer killed a British pig as part of a general dispute about the western boundary of the U.S. While here, watch out for the hundreds of wild rabbits that live in this area! Be sure to stop at Lime Kiln Park on the west side of the island, the only whale-watching park in the continental U.S. Area activities include bicycling, bird watching, diving, fishing, hiking, golf, and kayaking.

Reader tip: "The casual Springtree Cafe is located in the heart of downtown with a lovely outdoor patio. Exceptional salmon, fabulous chef, excellent service. A relaxing and thoroughly enjoyable evening." *(KMB)*

Also recommended: Only two blocks from downtown Friday Harbor is the **Argyle House** (685 Argyle, P.O. Box 2569, Friday Harbor 98250; 360–378–4084 or 800–624–3459), a 1910 Craftsman home surrounded by flower gardens and fruit trees. Each of the three guest rooms has a private bath, and the cottage is just steps from the hot tub. B&B double rates range from $75–125. "Owners Bill and Chris Carli have lived on the island for years; Bill is a licensed Coast Guard captain, and can arrange boat charters and cruises. Beautifully decorated rooms; lovely antiques. The cottage is decorated in crisp green and white colors. Its high ceilings and large windows create a light and comfortable feel." *(KMB)*

The **Mariella Inn & Cottages** (630 Turn Point Road, Friday Harbor 98250; 360–378–6868) has a beautiful location overlooking the sea, just a few blocks from the ferry landing. The eleven rooms and ten cottages, furnished with antiques, have lovely views of the bay or gardens; some have Jacuzzi tubs, fireplaces, and/or decks. You can relax on the porch overlooking the water, or curl up with a book before the fireplace in the sitting room. A full breakfast is served in the nicely restored dining room with a sweeping view of the bay. Other amenities include kayaks, badminton, and classic wooden rowboats for the pond. B&B double rates range from $100–275; cottages from $140–380; prix fixe dinners from $25–35, plus service, tax, and wine. Readers have been delighted with the breathtaking setting, and satisfied with the meals, service, and accommodations. "The wraparound porch was a wonderful place to relax and enjoy the breathtaking views of the bay." *(PP)* Reports welcome.

Two couples traveling together, an adult family, or those who don't mind sharing a bath will be delighted with the guest house at **The Meadows** (1980 Cattle Point Road, Friday Harbor 98250; 360–378–4004). Two spacious guest rooms share a large bath, entered directly from each guest room. B&B double rates of $85 include a continental breakfast. "Excellent beds, good lighting. Tasty breakfast, wonderful hosts." *(Rita Moore)* "Longtime owners Burr and Dodie Henion were helpful and hospitable, and shared island stories." *(Ken & Tina Holzapfel)* "Wonderful views of Puget Sound. Great granola." *(Phyllis Clancy)* "Beautiful grounds, comfortable and clean." *(Violette Shantz)*

A gracious Queen Anne–style home, complete with turret and welcoming veranda, the **Towerhouse** (1230 Little Road, 98250; 360–378–5464 or 800–858–4276) has two guest rooms, each with private bath and queen-size bed. The B&B double rate includes a full breakfast. Guests can explore the grounds with the aid of owners Chris and Joe Luma's friendly guide cat, then return to the kitchen for a hot cup of tea or coffee. "Warm, gracious innkeepers who care about their guests. Excellent meals, careful attention to detail in both decor and comfort." *(Susan Winner)*

Information please: Set in a valley with views of the snow-capped Olympic Mountains is the **Trumpeter Inn** (420 Trumpeter Way, 98250; 360–378–3884), named for the swans which can often be seen on area ponds. An unassuming contemporary structure built as a B&B, the inn has six guest rooms, each with a private bath. After a day of exploration, guests can relax on the hammock or in the hot tub. B&B double rates of $90–115 include a full breakfast. "Beautiful meadow setting; relaxing atmosphere." *(KMB)*

The Duffy House B&B ¢
760 Pear Point Road, Friday Harbor 98250

Tel: 360–378–5604
800–972–2089
Fax: 360–378–6535

What could be better than an inn with water views? An inn with water views *and* bald eagles, that's what. Although there are no guarantees when it comes to wild creatures, several eagles maintain nests on the grounds of Duffy House, and the aptly named Eagle's Nest room has a direct view of a nest. Owned by Arthur and Mary Miller since l992, this 1920s Tudor-style farmhouse was carefully restored and eclectically decorated with antiques, chintz fabrics, earthen pots, and Navajo rugs, and quilted accent pieces. Most rooms have lovely views of Griffin Bay and the snow-capped Olympic Mountains. Breakfast menus change daily: in addition to fresh-squeezed orange juice and fresh fruit, the meal might include home-baked cinnamon rolls and pancakes with strawberries and ham; or perhaps oatmeal coffee cake, cheese strata, and bacon.

"Accommodating, friendly, flexible, unobtrusive innkeepers. Outstanding breakfasts." *(Ruth Wheaton)* "Mary and Arthur are gifted innkeepers who make guests feel right at home. Beautiful home, graciously appointed. The breakfasts are masterpieces and the views of the bay are magnificent." *(Catherine Monserrat)* "Personable hostess; beautifully decorated inn; relaxing atmosphere." *(KMB)*

Open All year.
Rooms 5 doubles—all with private shower and/or bath, clock/radio, fan. 1 with desk.
Facilities Dining room, living room with stereo, books, fireplace; guest refrigerator. 5 acres with off-street parking, swings, gardens, orchard. Private beach with mooring, kayak access.
Location 1¾ m from Friday Harbor; 3 m from ferry. From ferry landing, go SW along Spring St. for about 2 blocks. Go left on Argyle Ave. & go 1 m to Pear Point Rd. Turn left & go ¾ m to inn on left.
Restrictions No smoking. Children over 8.
Credit cards MC, Visa.
Rates B&B, $70–105 double, $65–100 single. Extra person, $20.
Extras Airport/ferry pickup. Limited Spanish.

Friday Harbor House ✕ 🚶 ♿ *Tel:* 360–378–8455
130 West Street *Fax:* 360–378–8453
P.O. Box 1385, Friday Harbor 98250 *E-mail:* fhhouse@msn.com

You could join the ranks of bicyclers exploring the island hills. You could paddle the waters in a kayak or a canoe. Later, that is. For now, it's enough to sit on your peaceful balcony overlooking the San Juan Channel, Friday Harbor marina, and Mt. Constitution, and watch a float plane take off, or the ferry arrive. For a private, luxurious getaway, the Friday Harbor House is an excellent choice. Built in 1994, it's located on a quiet street on a bluff overlooking the marina, and has been simply but elegantly decorated in reproduction Mission-style furnishings, with queen-size beds and Northwest and nautical decorative accents. Paul and Pamela Schell are among the partners; Jim Skoog is the innkeeper. Rates include continental breakfast, served 7:30–9:30 A.M. The inn's restaurant overlooks the harbor, and the menu changes with the seasons; winter entrees might include pan-roasted mussels with black bean sauce, lamb or shrimp satays with cucumber peanut dipping sauce, or pork with apple chutney and root vegetables.

"Breathtaking view of the water and mountains from my room. Delightful location, quiet and private, yet within walking distance of all shops and restaurants. Jim Skoog is very personable and helpful." *(KMB)* "The decor is simple but elegant, modern and tasteful." *(Keith Miller)* "Comfy and well-equipped; immaculately clean; wonderful fresh flowers; amazing food. The helpful staff provided us with binoculars for bird-watching, and umbrellas for a rainy day. Blissful Jacuzzi. A perfect honeymoon spot." *(Patty Postweilar-Pyrz)* "Wonderful decor; comfortable bed; excellent view of the harbor and ferry traffic. We enjoyed watching the sun set from the lounge chairs on the lawn. Both breakfast and dinner were delicious. Gracious, pleasant, friendly innkeeper and staff." *(Hope Sherman)*

Note: Under the same ownership is the Inn at Ludlow Bay in Port Ludlow and the Inn at Langley in Whidbey Island; see entries.

Open All year.

Rooms 1 suite, 19 doubles—all with full private bath with double whirlpool soaking tub, telephone, clock/radio, TV, gas fireplace, refrigerator, coffee maker, robes. 10 with balcony. 2 rooms in courtyard building.

Facilities Restaurant with fireplace, stereo. Lawn overlooks harbor for boating, fishing.

Location From ferry dock follow traffic up Front St. which turns left up Spring St. Turn right at 1st St., right again on West St. to inn at end of the block overlooking harbor.

Restrictions No smoking.

Credit cards Amex, DC, MC, Visa.

Rates B&B, $257–277 suite, $167–197 double. Extra person, $35. No charge for children under 17. Alc dinner $20.

Extras Wheelchair access; room specially equipped. Airport/ferry pickup. Pets with approval. Crib, babysitting.

Hillside House B&B   *Tel:* 360–378–4730
365 Carter Ave, Friday Harbor 98250   800–232–4730
       Fax: 360–378–4715
       E-mail: rsr@sanjuaninfo.com

Hillside House is a B&B&B—in addition to delightful accommodations (the first "B"), tasty breakfasts (the second "B"), longtime owners Dick, Cathy and Meghan Robinson have added a third "B"—for the birds which occupy their two-story 10,000-square-foot aviary, complete with a pond. Four of the guest rooms have window seats looking into the aviary, so you can enjoy bird-watching while still in your pajamas. The Robinsons are also pleased to share information on the 200 resident and migratory birds which are found in the San Juans. One could even add a fourth "B" for boat: the Robinsons are avid sailors, having spent three years aboard their 46-foot-long trawler *Vixen*. This 4,000-square-foot contemporary home sits on a hillside among pine trees and gardens, overlooking Mount Baker and the harbor entrance. The decor combines traditional and contemporary pieces, and most rooms have queen-size beds. The Eagle's Nest is popular for special occasions, and is isolated on the third floor, with a king-size bed, sitting area, private balcony overlooking the harbor, and a spacious bathroom with both a shower and separate double Jacuzzi tub. Breakfast, served 8:30–10A.M. changes daily; printed on the menu is the entree recipe, a thoughtful touch. Fresh fruit and juice, breads or muffins, and homemade granola are always available, followed by cornmeal waffles or perhaps spinach-cheese strata. Other favorite dishes include blackberry cobbler, cloud biscuits, and potato casserole.

"I had my hearty breakfast on the sunny deck, listening to the wind chimes and the sounds of a small fountain in the garden. Combined with the views of the bay, it was a great way to start the day." *(KMB)* "Delightful inn; Dick and Cathy are the best!" *(Paula Montgomery)*

Open All year.
Rooms 1 suite, 6 doubles—all with private bath and/or shower, clock. Some with radio, desk. Suite with TV, wet bar, telephone, double whirlpool tub.
Facilities Dining room, living room, guest refrigerator, decks. 1 acre with gardens, off-street parking.
Location ¾ m to town. Taxi, $5. From ferry terminal, go 1 block on Front St. & turn left on Spring St. Take second right onto 2nd St. Go to end, then go left onto Guard St. Turn right on Carter Ave., to inn on left.
Restrictions No smoking. Children 10 and over.
Credit cards Amex, Discover, MC, Visa.
Rates B&B, $145–165 suite, $65–120 double. Extra person, $25. Off-season discount. Mystery weekends.
Extras Spanish spoken.

SEATTLE

Snuggled on six steep hills between Puget Sound and Lake Washington, Seattle is both sophisticated and friendly. It's known as a "city of neighborhoods." Visitors can sample the unusual restaurants and shops in the International District, home to Seattle's Asian population, or stroll through Ballard, the Scandinavian enclave.

On the southern end of downtown Seattle, Pioneer Square Historic District boasts unusual boutiques, the Seattle Children's Museum, and sidewalk cafes. Pike Place Market, in the middle of the business district overlooking Elliot Bay, opened as a farmer's market in 1907. Here you will find fishmongers and fresh produce stands, street musicians and handicrafts, ethnic markets and superb eateries. A few blocks north is Seattle Center, the site of the 1962 World's Fair. Take a ride up the center's 605-foot Space Needle for wonderful views, and take your kids to the excellent exhibits at the Pacific Science Center. Stop by the Center House for a variety of ethnic fast-food choices.

Tour the waterfront by boarding one of the vintage 1927 Australian trolley cars. Be sure to visit the Seattle Aquarium, where an underwater viewing area provides fish-eye views of Puget Sound's sea life. For something really different, take the underground Seattle tour to see nineteenth-century sidewalks and storefronts left underground when the streets were raised to avoid the spring mud. In the evening visit jazz clubs in the University District or the lively restaurants and nightclubs on Capitol Hill.

Seattle has outstanding public art collections, starting with the 18 works displayed at the airport. Excellent theater can be found at Seattle Repertory Theater, A Contemporary Theater, or The Empty Space. Also worth attending are the Pacific Northwest Ballet and the Seattle Opera's Wagner Festival. The best of Seattle's various festivals include the Seafair Festival in late July, the Bumbershoot street art festival around Labor Day, and the Christmas cruise in December.

Reader tip: "Excellent dinner at Pirosmani in the Queen Anne Hill area." *(Stephanie Roberts)* **Also recommended—hotels:** Readers are delighted with the service, accommodations, food, and pet-friendly policy at the luxurious **Alexis Hotel** (1007 First Avenue, 98104; 206–624–4844 or 800–426–7033). Extensively renovated, refurbished, and expanded, the hotel has 109 well-equipped and elegant guest rooms, including 44 suites; in addition to the usual amenities, each room has a two-line phone with dataport/fax modem and voice mail. "Friendly, helpful and accommodating staff. Appreciated the no-tipping policy. Attractive room with French and Italian designer fabrics, comfortable bed. Also recommended are the Painted Table restaurant and The Bookstore bar and cafe." *(Kathy Banak)* "Wonderful staff; gracious and welcoming. Lovely, remodeled old building, with live plants and flowers everywhere. Spacious, well-equipped guest room." *(Steve Holman)* B&B double rates of $175–380 include continental breakfast, morning paper, shoeshine service, and evening turndown with chocolates. The Alexis is a member of the Kimpton Hotel Group.

Marie Harris recommends **The Claremont Hotel** (2000-2004 Fourth Avenue at Virginia, 98121; 206–448–8600 or 800–448–8601) as "an ideal compromise between a B&B and an expensive hotel. Located on a quiet street, right on the edge of downtown, an easy walk to shops, museums, galleries, and the Pike Place Market. There's a comfortable lobby and a friendly helpful staff. Many of the suites have kitchens and washer/dryers, so you can save by cooking your own breakfast and doing your own laundry. Extra-long, old-fashioned bathtub, great for soaking. Excellent Italian restaurant in the building. A charming hotel, with friendly, accommodating staff." Rates for the 110 rooms and suites range from $129–189, with the popular kitchen suites at $169; children under 18 stay free.

Seattle's only waterfront hotel is **The Edgewater** (Pier 67, 2411 Alaskan Way, 98121–1398; 206–728–7000 or 800–624–0670). Double rates for the 238 guest rooms range from $129–230, with AAA discounts available. Views of Puget Sound and the Olympic Mountains can be had from most guest rooms, the inviting lodge-like lobby and its restaurant, Ernie's Bar and Grill. "Breathtaking views; friendly, helpful staff; good dinner, reasonably priced." *(Maryellen Forde)* Current reports appreciated.

Restored by the Kimpton Group, well known for its boutique hotels (including the Alexis described earlier) is the 1920s-era **Hotel Vintage Park** (1100 Fifth Avenue, 98101; 206–624–8000 or 800–624–4433). Each of the 129 guest rooms are named for a winery or vineyard; rich colors predominate in the decor—burgundy (of course), rose, and dark greens. Standard hotel amenities abound, and Tulio's Restaurant features Italian cuisine. Rates range from $135–220, with government and corporate rates available. "Quiet, comfortable luxury, with a handsome lobby reminiscent of a private club. While tiny, my rooms was decorated with rich fabrics, good lighting, comfortable bed, desk, reading chair, and entertainment center, plus every conceivable hotel amenity." *(Mark Mendenhall)* "Delicious lunch at Tulio's, popular with both business people and tourists." *(KMB)*

Although somewhat noisy and expensive, readers remain delighted with the popular **Inn at the Market** (86 Pine Street, 98101; 206–443–3600 or 800–446–4484), in the heart of Pike's Place. Rates for the 68 luxurious, well-equipped guest rooms range from $130–325. "Situated on the incline between busy 1st Avenue, and bustling Pike Place, this inviting European-style hotel and restaurant provides a charming retreat from the constant activity just outside the door. Guest rooms on the Market side provide terrific views of the market, Puget Sound, and the Olympic Mountains. The staff is unobtrusive and efficient. Our room was quiet, clean and comfortable; elegant and understated. Comfort, charm, and pampering, in a location ideally suited for taking in Seattle's attractions." *(Ray Sundstrom, also Elizabeth Ring)*

The **Pioneer Square Hotel** (77 Yesler Way, 98104; 206–340–1234 or 800–800–5514) is a renovated turn-of-the-century hotel with reproduction period decor, located in the restored Pioneer Square historic district, within blocks of the Aquarium, train station, ferry terminal and other waterfront attractions. B&B double rates for the 75 rooms and suites are $89–129, including a light continental breakfast. "Helpful staff; comfortable accommodations." *(Barry Chukerman)* "Great ambiance; outstanding historic location." *(Pamela Gross)* "Convenient location, only five minutes from the train station. Our room was spacious, well furnished, and quiet; ask for a room on the north or east side." *(Duane Roller)*

A convenient choice for convention-goers is the **Plaza Park Suites** (1011 Pike Street, 98101; 206–682–8282 or 800–426–0670), a 194-room all-suite hotel. The $125–340 rates include a continental breakfast and downtown shuttle. "Small but comfortable two-room suite with spacious bathroom and well-equipped kitchen; excellent convention rate and family-friendly too. Attentive staff; excellent restaurant advice. Efficient downtown shuttle service." *(Diane Wolf)*

Built in 1909, **The Sorrento Hotel** (900 Madison Street, 98104; 206–622–6400 or 800–426–1265) derives its name from its grand facade, in the tradition of the houses of Sorrento, Italy, with terra-cotta trim and an Italian fountain. The 76 luxurious guest rooms have all the luxuries one expects in a hotel of this type—antiques, fresh flowers, goose-down pillows, bathrobes and oversized towels, turndown service, bed-warmers for chilly nights, and afternoon tea. Ask for a room above the third floor, on the west side, for a fine view of the city and Puget Sound. The hotel restaurant prepares innovative Pacific Northwest cuisine as well as traditional American. "Lovely suite, though no view; excellent service." *(Yvonne Stoner)* Double rates are $200–220, with suites from $240–425; various packages are available.

On the shores of Lake Washington and minutes to downtown Belleuve is **The Woodmark Hotel at Carillon Point** (1200 Carillon Point, 98033; 425–822–3700 or 800–822–3700). A lakeside promenade, park, restaurants, boutiques and art galleries complement the marina and public pier. This top-rated luxury hotel has a comfortable bar and lakefront restaurant featuring Northwest cuisine. The hotel offers 100 luxurious guest rooms complete with an honor bar, refrigerator, TV/VCR with free tapes, coffee maker, and bathrobe, morning paper; most have lake and Olympic Mountain views. Rates range from $180–230 double, with suites from $250–1,250. Comments welcome.

Also recommended—B&Bs: Located in Seattle's North End between the Fremont neighborhood and Woodland Park, **Chelsea Station on the Park** (4915 Linden Avenue North, 98103; 206–547–6077 or 800–400–6077), is a red-brick 1929 Federal Colonial house with eight guest rooms, each with queen- or king-size bed, private bath, and telephone. B&B double rates of $69–119 include breakfasts of fresh fruit and juice, vegetable frittata, ginger pancakes with lemon sauce, or perhaps Brie-and-apple stuffed French toast; also included is afternoon tea and cookies. John Griffin has owned the inn since 1994; Karen Carbonneau is his longtime innkeeper. "Great breakfasts." *(Sally Doucet)* "Impeccable housekeeping; convivial fellow guests; appealing location across from the rose garden and zoo." *(JB Jackson)* "Karen is caring, warm, hospitable, professional, and service oriented." *(Jeff Warren)* Comments welcome.

Located in the Queen Anne neighborhood is the **Green Gables** (1503 Second Avenue West, 98119; 206–282–6863), a two-story American Foursquare Prairie-style house. The interior shows handsome Craftsman influences, with natural wood wainscotting and broad ceiling beams. Two of its four guest rooms have private baths; the decor includes stained glass windows, and queen- and king-size beds. B&B double rates of $65–125 include a full breakfast. "Warm, gracious hospitality." *(Susan Winner)* Reports appreciated.

Conveniently located in the Capitol Hill district is the **Hill House B&B** (1113 East John Street, 98102; 206–720–7161 or 800–720–7161), a Victorian home built in 1903. B&B double rates for the five guest rooms range from $70–115, including a creative full breakfast. "Elegantly yet comfortably decorated; convenient location to shops and restaurants." *(KMB)*

If you'd like to have your own darling cottage as your Seattle base, contact the **Holly Hedge House** (908 Grant Avenue South, Renton 98055; 425–226–2555 or 888–226–2555), just ten minutes east of Sea-Tac airport and 20 minutes southeast of downtown Seattle. Built in 1900, this restored house has a charming sun room, fully equipped kitchen, bedroom with queen-size bed, private bath with whirlpool tub, cedar deck with hot tub, and a lovely garden with a swimming pool and hammock. Your choice of a full or continental breakfast is delivered at your convenience. The double rate is $85–130, depending on length of stay and type of breakfast requested. Guests are delighted with the relaxed, homey atmosphere, delicious breakfasts, immaculate housekeeping, wonderful innkeepers, Marian and Lynn Thrasher.

For additional area inns, see **Tacoma.**

B.D. Williams House
1505 Fourth Avenue North, 98109

Tel: 206–285–0810
800–880–0810
Fax: 206–285–8526
E-mail: innkeepr@wolfenet.com

A turn-of-the-century home at the top of Queen Anne hill, the Williams House has been owned by Susan and Doug Williams since 1984. Rates include a full breakfast, with a continental breakfast available for early departures, as well as 24-hour access to coffee, tea, and cookies.

"The Brass and Satin room was pretty, clean, and comfortable, and looked right down on the Space Needle. Sue and Doug were very helpful, giving us many suggestions on what to do in Seattle. Hot tea and fresh chocolate chip cookies awaited us after dinner. Pleasant, well-run B&B." *(Stephanie Roberts)* "Ideal place to stay while I attended a conference in downtown Seattle. Returning to the Williams House each evening was like coming home to family. The rooms were quiet and the beds comfortable. The owners made a special effort to prepare early breakfasts for conference-goers. The food was delicious and fortified me for a full day of action. Terrific location, with great views of Seattle and a beautiful neighborhood for walking and exploring. Friendly cat, too." *(Susanne Ban)*

"Magnificent view of the city lights and the Space Needle. Inside, rich dark wood leads to cozy corners to sit and read or look out onto roses and flowers everywhere. Other little touches include the phone booth on the stairwell landing (no change needed), the robes and slippers in the bathroom, and, of course, the smell of home-baked muffins wafting its way upstairs each morning." *(Kris Kegg)* "Beds are comfortable, breakfasts are excellent—always lots of fresh fruit and a great variety of breakfast dishes." *(Marilyn Bommer)* "Located in Queen Anne Hill—a beautiful place; parking was easy. Our light, airy room had a bed with lace awning, a good mattress and comforter, and a large futon on which to sit and read." *(Marsi Fein & Todd Miller)* "Sue was accommodating and helpful, the inn well run and spotless." *(VLK)* "The decor is a pleasant mixture of antiques and functional pieces; my favorite was the Bay Room." *(SHW)*

Open All year.
Rooms 5 doubles—all with private bath and/or shower. Some with desk.
Facilities Parlor, sun porch, dining room, TV room; fax/copier service; gardens.
Location Queen Anne district, 1 m from downtown. From I-5, take Mercer St./Seattle Center exit, follow signs to Seattle Center. Turn right at sign to Opera House & Space Needle, right onto 5th Ave. Go left on Highland, right on 3rd Ave., right on Galer St. Inn is at corner of Galer and 4th Ave.
Restrictions Smoking on porch only.
Credit cards Amex, DC, MC, Visa.
Rates B&B, $79–150 double. Extra person, $25. Discount for 5-night stay Oct.–April.

Chambered Nautilus ¢
5005 22nd Avenue Northeast, 98105

Tel: 206–522–2536
800–545–8459
Fax: 206–528–0898
E-mail: chamberednautilus@msn.com

Like the seashell it is named for, the Chambered Nautilus offers guests "a home of beauty, warmth, and security." Perched on a hill in the University District, this handsome Georgian Colonial mansion was built in 1915 by one of the early faculty members at the University of Washington; it was bought in 1996 by longtime Seattle residents Joyce Schulte and Steven Poole. The inn's landscaped gardens create an impressive display of flowers with lovely views of the Cascade Mountains in the distance. Served in the dining room or on the sun porch, a typical breakfast might include pineapple-mango fruit juice, maple pecan granola, poached pears, breakfast pie with salmon, egg, and cheese, rosemary buttermilk muffins, and fresh-ground coffee; stuffed French toast and apple quiche are also favorite entrees. Afternoon tea and cookies are also served.

"Relaxed, warm, gracious and inviting atmosphere; spacious, comfortable rooms. Delicious pancakes with hot cinnamon raisin syrup." *(Robert Summers)* "Wonderful location, close to the university, great restaurants, and fabulous shopping. The windows and balconies open to lush gardens. Rocking chairs, down comforters, and tons of books; tea and cookies always available. Delightful sun room; I love to curl up by the living room fireplace with a book or the newspaper. Steve and Joyce are helpful but not intrusive, offering good restaurant recommendations." *(Teri Mathis)* "Ideal for visiting the University of Washington." *(Sherryl Gundelhoefor)* "Pretty grounds, attractive, immaculate, and well-decorated house. Interesting breakfast conversation with personable fellow guests, mostly academics; classical music plays softly in the background." *(Audrey Foote, also MW)* "Comfortable bed, wonderful pillows, friendly teddy bear; matching robes, bottled water, windows that open, and a better closet than at home. We had to leave early one morning so Joyce and Steve fixed us breakfast to go. Special diets accommodated with a smile (and advance notice)." *(Alice & William McNamara)*

Open All year.
Rooms 6 doubles—all with private bath and/or shower, clock/radio, desk, fan, robes, hair dryer. 4 with porch.
Facilities Living room with fireplace, Victrola, books; dining room with fireplace, sun porch, open porches. ½ acre with landscaped gardens, sitting areas. On-street parking. Burke-Gilman Trail, Green Lake, Ravenna Park nearby for jogging, walking, bicycling. Boating, fishing, golf, tennis nearby.
Location University district. 10 min. from downtown Seattle, walking distance to U. of WA. Take exit 169 off I-5 N. Go right (E) on NE 50th St. to stop sign at 20th Ave. NE & turn left. Go 4 blocks to NE 54th St. Turn right, go 2 blocks to 22nd Ave. NE. Turn right to inn at #5005.
Restrictions No smoking. Children under 12 by prior arrangement. 27 steps up to front door. On-street parking.
Credit cards Amex, MC, Visa.
Rates B&B, $79–109 double. $72–104 single. Extra person, $15. Long-term, winter rates. 2–3 night weekend/holiday minimum
Extras French spoken. Bus stop nearby.

Roberta's B&B ¢
1147 16th Avenue East, 98112

Tel: 206–329–3326
Fax: 206–324–2149
E-mail: robertasbb@aol.com

A classic turn-of-the-century home, Roberta's B&B has been owned by (surprise) Roberta Barry since 1968; she opened her home to B&B guests in 1984, but improvements to enhance guests' comfort are ongoing—most recently she added central air-conditioning "for those hot August days." She also notes that "one of the neatest things about my B&B is that it's in a nice old neighborhood, convenient to almost every place in town." Breakfast starts with a fruit dish, such as peach cobbler or baked apples; next comes juice, freshly baked muffins (maybe apricot walnut or zucchini walnut) or breads, homemade jam, and a hot entree—perhaps omelet, cheese strata, Dutch babies, French toast, or ginger pancakes with lemon sauce.

"Clean, comfortable, and convenient. Wonderful hospitality. Delicious breakfast with low-fat recipes." *(Olga Vargas de Lester)* "Quiet residential area. Charming, comfy rooms with antiques. Roberta is the female Will Rogers: warm, funny, outspoken and knowledgeable. Neat guests from all over. Healthy breakfasts; yummy Dutch babies. " *(NT)* "Roberta's sits among massive Edwardian clapboard homes in Seattle's fashionable and centrally located Capitol Hill area. Simply decorated with period pieces and oak furnishings, this appealing B&B is filled with an eclectic collection of books, a reflection of Roberta's wide-ranging tastes and interests, as well as up-to-date guidebooks; the *New York Times* appears daily in the sitting room." *(Esther Magathan)*

"The Hideaway suite fills the third floor with its charming nooks, crannies, and angled ceiling. Roberta's generous breakfasts will keep you fueled until late afternoon." *(Abby Humphrey)* "Near the Broadway district which is a little like Greenwich Village with a wide assortment of people. If you're going to explore the area shops and restaurants, go on foot—parking is difficult." *(SC)* "Although our room was small, it had ample closet and drawer space, and two good bedside reading lamps." *(Lillian Koltnow)*

Open All year.

Rooms 1 suite, 4 doubles—all with private bath and/or shower, air-conditioning. 3 with desk; telephone on request.

Facilities Dining room with pot-belly stove, living room with fireplace, piano, books. Tennis in Volunteer Park, 1 block away. Golf nearby. 1½ m from Lake Washington for swimming and canoeing.

Location Capitol Hill area, 1 block E of Volunteer Park, 1½ m E of downtown. From I-5 N, take Exit 166 (Olive Way). Follow to 15th Ave. E. Turn left on 15th Ave. E to Prospect. Turn right on Prospect, then left on 16th Ave. E. Turn left to inn.

Restrictions Smoking on porch only. No children under 12.

Credit cards DC, MC, Visa.

Rates B&B, $86–125 double, $80–110 single.

SEAVIEW

Seaview is located on the Long Beach peninsula of southwestern Washington, between the Columbia River and the Pacific Ocean. It's two hours north of Portland, three hours south of Seattle. Endless walks await on 28 miles of beach; the area is also good for sport fishing.

For additional area inns, see **Long Beach** and **Ocean Park**.

Shelburne Inn ✕ &.
4415 Pacific Highway, P.O. Box 250, 98644

Tel: 360–642–2442
Fax: 360–642–8904
E-mail: shelinn@aone.com

Built as a hotel in 1896, the Shelburne Inn was purchased in 1977 by Laurie Anderson and David Campiche, who have been fixing it up ever since, adding and refurbishing guest rooms, and enhancing the restaurant and pub with Art Nouveau stained glass windows salvaged from a church in England. The inn is also home to the Shoalwater restaurant, specializing in fresh, locally harvested foods and regional wines. Readers are delighted with the inn's breakfasts, served at a large table in the lobby, with such choices as corn, spinach, and bacon frittata, scrambled eggs with salmon, or razor clam fritters, accompanied by fruit, juice, and just-baked pastries.

"The breakfast here never disappoints." *(Pat Van Orman Price)* "Outstanding breakfast; beautifully decorated; friendly and welcoming innkeeper; charming antiques." *(Julie Johnson)* "We were welcomed warmly by the innkeepers; wonderful aromas wafted from the kitchen. The fantastic breakfast was shared at a large dining table in the lobby before a crackling fire." *(James Sheasley)* "Rooms are furnished with Victorian era antiques, with modern amenities." *(Michael & Joyce Larkins)* "We spent time relaxing on the large leather sofa in front of the fireplace in the lobby." *(Joel Martin & Lori Jenkins)* "A first-class experience, exceptional food. Long beach walks in the evening and morning." *(James Burr)* "Our clean, cozy room had a heavy wooden bed with handmade quilt. Breakfast was delicious, the portions enormous." *(Sharon Bielski)* "Rooms are in three sections: above the restaurant, above the lobby, and in the new section. The oldest ones have considerable charm, albeit uneven floors. The new section, overlooking the herb garden is appealing, with larger rooms. The pub is lively, but not noisy. The beach is a few blocks to your right going out the front door." *(DCB)*

Open All year.
Rooms 2 suites, 14 doubles—all with private bath and/or shower.
Facilities Lobby, restaurant, pub. ½ acre with gardens, off-street parking. 3 blocks to beach.
Location Follow Hwy. 101 to Seaview. In Seaview, go N ½ m on Hwy. 103 to inn on left at 45th St.
Restrictions No smoking. "Quiet, well-supervised children welcome." Limited soundproofing in older rooms.
Credit cards Amex, MC, Visa.
Rates B&B, $169 suite, $99–139 double, $93–133 single. Extra person, $10. Midweek, off-season packages. Alc dinner, $25–40.
Extras Wheelchair access; 1 room specially equipped. Crib.

SEQUIM

Often overlooked between the well-known towns of Port Townsend and Port Angeles, the sleepy Sequim/Dungeness Valley offers peaceful farmland and lovely water views. Birdwatching is a highlight at the Dungeness National Wildlife refuge, a six-mile sandspit reaching into the Strait of Juan de Fuca; animal lovers will enjoy the Olympic Game Farm, where the buffalo roam (over to your car for a handout). The climate is dry and sunny, with an annual rainfall of only 16 inches (less than half of Seattle's). Sequim (pronounced "Skwim") is located on the Olympic peninsula, 80 miles northwest of Seattle.

Sequim makes an ideal base from which to explore Hurricane Ridge, the Hoh Rain Forest, and other Olympic National Park attractions. Also available are two year-round golf courses, an aquatic recreation center, casino, and the nearby ferry to Victoria, BC.

Reader tip: "Excellent dinner at the Oyster House; the Three Crabs Diner was just OK." *(Michelle Butler)*

Also recommended: Four miles north of Sequim is **Brigadoon** (62 Balmoral Court, 98382; 360–683–2255 or 800–397–2256) a 1920 farmhouse decorated with English antiques. Each of the three guest rooms have a private bath, and B&B double rates range from $65–120. "Our room was decorated in soothing shades of green with coordinating floral patterns. Beautifully landscaped grounds with an apple orchard. Owners helpful with dinner recommendations. Wonderful three-course breakfast with outstanding oatmeal." *(Michelle Butler)*

Greywolf Inn ¢
395 Keeler Road, 98382

Tel: 360–683–5889
800–914–WOLF
Fax: 360–683–1487

Named for the fast-running Greywolf River, the Greywolf was built in 1976, and was renovated as an inn in 1990 by Peggy and Bill Melang, North Carolina retirees. Most of the spacious guest rooms have queen-size four-poster or canopy beds, and each has a different decorating theme. A favorite is the luxurious Marguerite room, with a king-size French country sleigh bed, fireplace, and book-lined wall. Breakfast is served from 8–9:30; menus change daily, but include fruit juice, creative fresh fruit plates, hot breads and muffins, and such entrees as eggs scrambled with smoked salmon and chives; wild rice quiche with Parmesan potatoes and stewed apples; or North Carolina country ham with red eye gravy and hot biscuits with scrambled eggs. Breakfast is enhanced by sweeping valley views that often include a passing herd of Roosevelt elk.

"Nancy's room has a comfortable Asian-style four-poster bed and beautiful Oriental art. Fabulous views; generous, beautifully served breakfast. Lots of books. Refined, reserved, yet friendly proprietor. Easy drive to restaurants." *(Walter & Joan Stevenson)* "Lovely, comfortable, immaculate room." *(Wayne Doerr)* "We enjoyed the hot tub, in a separate building off the patio, and exploring the property. Peggy is an excellent cook and a gracious innkeeper." *(Norma Simon)* "We were especially impressed by the Melang's attention to detail: thick towels, several robes to choose from, flip-flops for the spa, and interesting, diverse reading material. Excellent breakfast—elegant, light, and satisfying." *(Teri Hein)* "Wonderful breakfast of sausage quiche and strawberry sherbert for dessert. Loved the view of their sheep, Hazel, and cows grazing in the meadow. Their two labs made us feel even more welcome." *(Mr. & Mrs. William Cayford)* "Comfortable rooms with firm beds. Easy drive to the National Park, marina, seashore, mountains, animal park, and downtown; owners helpful with area information." *(Joseph Dziados)*

Open All year.

Rooms 1 suite, 4 doubles—all with private bath and/or shower, clock/radio/cassette player, fan, robes, hair dryer. 4 with desk, 1 with telephone, 1 with TV/VCR, 1 with fireplace, deck.

Facilities Dining room, living room with fireplace, TV/VCR; library with books, games; decks, courtyard. 5 acres with Japanese hut with hot tub, exercise equipment; lawn games, walking trail. Boating, fishing, golf, hiking nearby.

Location 1 m E of town. From Seattle, exit Hwy 101 at Keeler Rd. Turn right at Keeler. Drive ½ m to bottom of hill. Turn left into driveway.

Restrictions No smoking. Children over 12 preferred.

Credit cards Amex, Discover, MC, Visa, .

Rates B&B, $180 suite, $65–120 double. Extra person, $20. Senior, AAA discount.

Extras Airport pickup, $25.

Juan de Fuca Cottages 👫
182 Marine Drive, 98382

Tel: 360–683–4433

The Juan de Fuca Cottages have been owned by Sheila Ramus since 1983. All have views of Dungeness Bay, the National Wildlife Refuge, the Dungeness Spit, the Strait of Juan de Fuca, and Victoria, 18 miles across the water, and are equipped with a queen-size and a double bed. Rates include free videotapes and complimentary tea and coffee.

"Spotlessly clean, well-equipped cottages. Excellent setting, right on the water with a view of the Dungeness Spit." *(Ron Ridgely)* "Fantastic ambiance, housekeeping, and hospitality." *(MJ Brauner)* "Sheila is a friendly, attentive, and unobtrusive hostess. The cottage was charmingly designed, attractively furnished, complete with fluffy towels, microwave popcorn, coffee and tea, and movies for the VCR. I enjoyed sitting in the glassed-in gazebo in the garden with the view of the water on one side and the mountains on the other." *(Marcy Weinbeck)* "Cozy, comfortable cottage, with adequate kitchen utensils and such extras as a pretty tea pot and current magazines." *(Breta Malcorm)* "Spectacular views of the Straits of Juan de Fuca and Canada from the large picture window. Beautiful stone fireplace, Jacuzzi tub with skylight, and lovely furniture." *(Michael & Linda Gooch)* "Outstanding location. Plenty of hiking and beachcombing nearby. Our proprietor was kind and friendly—never intrusive." *(John Marshall)* "Our dog was welcomed as a part of our family." *(Shawna Willan)* "Great book and video library. Plenty of wood for the fireplace." *(Jennifer Hicks & Thomas Johnson)*

Open All year.

Rooms 5 cottages, 1 suite—all with private bath (whirlpool tub), radio, clock,

TV/VCR, fan, refrigerator, fully equipped kitchen, deck. 1 with fireplace, double Jacuzzi.

Facilities Lobby with video library. 6 acres with off-street parking, gazebo, lawn games, private beach, clamming.

Location From Hwy. 101 in Sequim, go N on N. Sequim Ave. Bear left at Sequim Dungeness Way, right on Marine Dr. to inn on right. (Follows scenic loop tour.)

Credit cards MC, Novus, Visa.

Rates Room only, $135–200 two-bedroom unit, $100–115 one-bedroom cottage. Extra person, $7. 2-night minimum July–Aug. & weekends.

Extras Limited wheelchair access; 1 step into cottage. Airport, bus station pickup. Pets with permission. Crib.

SNOQUALMIE

Reader tips: "The primary reasons to visit Snoqualmie are the falls, the winery, and the great scenery. Everyone we met in the area was most pleasant and friendly." *(KW)* "Be sure to visit the Snoqualmie Winery, about a half-mile from the interstate exit in the opposite direction from the town. It's located in a peaceful mountain meadow setting with panoramic views of the snow-capped mountains. Nice wine-tasting too, plus a lovely shop." *(Susan Schwemm)*

   Also recommended: The **Salish Lodge** (37807 SE Fall City/Snoqualmie Falls Road, P.O. Box 1109, 98065; 206–888–2556 or 800–826–6124) sits at the top of 268-foot Snoqualmie Falls, close to Highway 202. The restaurant offers game, beef, lamb and seafood dishes, accompanied by an extensive wine list. Double rates for the 91 guest rooms range from $165–225, with suites from $250–500. "Beautiful lobby, with exposed beams and stone floor. Guest rooms have elegant lodge-style decor in honey-colored wood, two queen-size beds or one king-size bed with goosedown comforters, a wood-burning fireplace, padded window seat, TV, and coffee maker. Lovely bathrooms with a double Jacuzzi and terry-cloth robes, cleverly designed so you can see the fireplace from the Jacuzzi. Since it's only 30 miles from Seattle, Snoqualmie Falls State Park is popular with daytrippers, many of whom jammed the lobby, gift shop, and restaurant on the beautiful day I visited. As far as I could determine, from the inside of the hotel, the falls can be seen only from the suites and the bar. Helpful concierge." *(SHW)*

   Information please: Set among the fields is the **Old Honey Farm Country Inn** (9050 384th Avenue SE, 98065; 206–888–9399), with ten guest rooms, each with private bath, and furnished with antiques and collectibles; some have Jacuzzi tubs. "Comfortable inn with pleasant public areas., located on a quiet country road. Our quiet room was clean and comfortable, with good lighting. Appreciated having a choice at breakfast; enjoyed buckwheat waffles with fresh fruit." *(Karl Wiegers)* B&B double rates are $75–125.

SOAP LAKE

Information please: Halfway between Seattle and Spokane is the **Notaras Lodge** (236 East Main Street, Highway 17, P.O. Box 987, 98851; 509–246–0462), an unusual motel with 16 guest rooms, and rates of $55 double, $100–125 suite. "Handcrafted decor, from the tooled leather light switches to the horseshoe door handles to the unusual rustic furniture. The John Wayne room has a gun, a swing, and a caribou head, among other Western memorabilia. Spacious guest rooms, some with Jacuzzi, with both regular and mineral water for the bath. Lighting was a bit dim at night, and we couldn't find much in the way of a restaurant for dinner." *(MW)* "Soap Lake is a good jumping-off place to explore the gorgeous Grand Coulee area. Notaras was constructed in 1983 of spruce logs from 20 to 65 feet long; the largest are 42 inches in diameter." *(SC)*

SPOKANE

Washington's second largest city, Spokane is located in western Washington, about 25 miles east of the Idaho border.

Information please: Listed on the National Register of Historic Places, **Angelica's** (West 13321 Ninth Avenue, 99204; 509–624–5598 or 800–987–0053) is a 1907 Craftsman-style brick home with four guest rooms, each with private bath. B&B double rates of $85–125 early morning coffee and a full breakfast.

The **Fotheringham House** (2128 West Second Avenue, 99204; 509–838–1891) was built in 1891 by Spokane's first mayor; he also built the Patsy Clark Mansion (now a restaurant) across the street. Located in Browne's Addition, a National Historic District, the house is an eclectic Stick-style Victorian mansion. "Wonderful gardens; impressively restored turret. Delicious chocolate truffles at night; tasty breakfast of huckleberry juice, broiled grapefruit, waffles, and applesauce." *(Marie Wilson)* B&B double rates are $75–90.

The **Marianna Stoltz House** (East 427 Indiana Avenue, 99207; 509–483–4316 or 800–978–6587) is a classic American four-square home built in 1908. The original fir woodwork, high ceilings and leaded glass are enhanced by Oriental rugs, period antiques and reproductions. B&B double rates for the four guest rooms, range from $65–80, including a full breakfast.

Facing Corbin Park is **Waverly Place** (West 709 Waverly Place, 99205; 509–328–1856) a Queen Anne Victorian house built in 1899. B&B double rates of $70–95 include a full breakfast and afternoon tea and cookies.

STEHEKIN

Information please: The **Silver Bay Inn** (10 Silver Bay Road, 98852; 509–682–2212 or 800–555–7781) is located at the headwaters of Lake

Chelan in the heart of the North Cascades National Park. The inn consists of a main house with two guest rooms for B&B guests, plus two charming cabins. The B&B double rate of $85–135 includes a continental breakfast; the cabins ($95–155) have kitchens for guests to do their own cooking. All are welcome to enjoy the private swimming area on the lake, as well as the gazebo and a hot tub. The inn can be reached by boat or float plane; pickups provided. "Charming home, delicious breakfasts. We relaxed on the sun porch, watching the blue herons with the wonderful Cascades as a backdrop. Although we loved the spacious, well-decorated master suite, doing your own cooking in the cabins might provide more variety than having dinner at the North Cascades Inn each night, about a mile and a half away." *(Barbara Porter)*

STEVENSON

Information please: The **Skamania Lodge** (P.O. Box 189, Stevenson, 98648; 509–427–7700 or 800–221–7117) was constructed in 1992 as a joint project of the U.S. Forest Service, Skamania County, the Columbia River Gorge Commission, and Salishan Lodge (see listing, Gleneden Beach, Oregon). Opened in 1993, Skamania sits on 175 wooded acres, with an 18-hole golf course, horseback riding, tennis, indoor swimming pool, fitness and conference centers, and restaurant. The 195 guest rooms are housed in the four-story wood lodge designed with heavy timbers, board-and-batten siding, and stone. Double rates range from $110–240; children under 12 stay free, and off-season, midweek packages are available. "Courteous, polite, well-trained staff; outstanding food; immaculately clean; child friendly; and great walks in woods." *(Betsy Immurgut)* "Popular as a conference center." *(MW)* "Designed to look like a turn-of-the-century rustic lodge, the woodwork, lighting fixtures, and fabrics were all custom designed and handsomely executed. The Pacific Northwest art displayed on the walls is special—everything from paintings to Navajo rugs to fine carvings to rubbings of the petroglyphs found on the walls of the Columbia Gorge. Many rooms offer spectacular views of the Gorge." *(Lee Todd)*

TACOMA

Information please: Perched on a hill overlooking Puget Sound, the **Chinaberry Hill** (302 Tacoma Avenue North, 98403; 253–272–1282) is an 1889 Queen Anne Victorian inn with six guest rooms, at B&B rates of $85–125, including a full breakfast. Each has a private bath, and some have a double Jacuzzi tub, sitting room, fireplace, or harbor view. Families are welcome in the carriage house suite. Located in Tacoma's Stadium Historical District, it's close to museums, galleries, antique shops, waterfront restaurants and several parks. Comments welcome.

The Villa ¢   *Tel:* 253–572–1157
705 North Fifth Street, 98403   *Toll-free:* 888–572–1157
                                                   Fax: 253–572–1805
                                             E-mail: VillaBB@aol.com

Whether you're traveling on business, looking for a close-to-home romantic getaway, or are visiting friends and relatives, Becky and Greg Anglemyer promise you a warm welcome and a delightful stay at The Villa. A 7,000-square-foot mansion built in 1925, it offers the style of an Italian palazzo, from its elegant, formal entrance to its beautiful gardens. The extensive common areas have cozy nooks and light-filled spaces, with ample room for guests who wish to socialize as well as those who prefer privacy. Breakfast, served 7–10 A.M. includes fresh fruit and juice, muffins and breads, and omelets, waffles, or Dutch baby pancakes.

"Exceptionally spacious accommodations and living areas in a truly gracious house with warm, friendly, flexible hosts. We were welcomed with hot tea and served a hearty breakfast the next morning." (*Norma P. Simon*) "Really lovely B&B. The living room is a lovely peach color with hardwood floors, with a fireplace and games; the grand dining room is large yet homey. Our breakfast included broiled grapefruit with coconut, tiny muffins, and individual egg casseroles with cheese and mushrooms. Their cat was barely noticeable and the house so clean that she didn't even bother my allergies. The sun room was the perfect place to read, chat, or just relax. Although all the guest rooms are quite lovely, our favorite was the huge Bay View Suite, with a comfortable king-size bed piled high with pillows, a large sitting area, and good-sized balcony where we watched the sun set over the Olympic Mountains." (*Suzanne Carmichael*)

Open All year.
Rooms 2 suites, 2 doubles—all with private bath and/or shower, clock/radio, fan. Some with desk, fireplace, balcony.
Facilities Dining room, living room with stereo, family room, library, sun room with TV, books, games; guest refrigerator, laundry, porch. ½ acre with gardens, off-street parking. Hiking, Puget Sound nearby.
Location 30 m S of Seattle. From I-5 take I-705 to City Center Exit 133, Tacoma. Follow signs for Shuster Pkwy., then take Stadium Way Exit. At stop sign turn right on Stadium Way. Curve left at N First; continue to light. Turn right onto Tacoma Ave. N; go left onto N 5th St. Go 1 block to inn on right.
Restrictions No smoking.
Credit cards Amex, MC, Visa.
Rates B&B, $110–135, $79–89 double. Extra person, $15. Senior, AAA discounts.
Extras Station pickup. A little Spanish, German, French, Italian, Korean spoken.

WHIDBEY ISLAND

Whidbey Island parallels the upper Puget Sound mainland from Everett north to La Conner. The largest of the many islands which dot the Sound, Whidbey is close enough to Seattle for an easy weekend getaway, yet offers quiet island ambience and small, friendly towns. Scattered between the pleasant hamlets are loganberry farms. The country's main source for this tart-sweet fruit, some of the farms also produce a delightful loganberry liqueur.

Coupeville, just past the center of the island, is one of the state's oldest towns. Nearby is scenic Madrona Drive which follows the outline of Penn Cove. Langley, on the east side of the southern part of Whidbey Island, is a tiny town suspended in the 19th century. It has a charming (and short) main street lined with antique shops and friendly restaurants. From First Street, you can look across Saratoga Passage to the mainland, the Northern Cascade Range, and volcanic Mt. Baker. To reach Whidbey Island, take Interstate 5 or 405 north from Seattle approximately 25 miles to the Mukilteo exit 182. Take State Highway 525 west to Mukilteo. Take ferry to Clinton, then follow 525 to the various small towns. **Reader tip:** "Langley is one of those beautiful hamlets on Puget Sound and is a charming place to visit. Lots of great little shops and galleries to while away the time." *(Pam Phillips)* "Giuseppe's Trattoria in Langley has the atmosphere of a small Italian village, with a warm and welcoming owner. Outstanding salmon." *(KMB)*

Also recommended: The well-known **Captain Whidbey Inn** (2072 West Captain Whidbey Inn Road, Coupeville 98239; 360–678–4097 or 800–366–4097), overlooking Penn Cove, offers rooms with antique charm—and shared baths—in the original inn, along with more modern rooms overlooking the lagoon. Although you can no longer arrive directly by steamer from Seattle at the inn's private dock, the charming, old-fashioned atmosphere here has changed little. The inn's restaurant features such favorites as basil steamed mussels and house-smoked roasted turkey with an apple relish. B&B double rates include a continental breakfast, and range from $95–155 for inn suites and doubles with shared baths; $160–205 for the cabins; a three-course dinner will cost about $35, plus wine, tip, and taxes. Guests are thrilled with the lovely setting, gorgeous bay views, peaceful atmosphere, warm and friendly service, and delicious food; rooms are generally satisfactory.

Just a short walk to the village are two cottages, the **Chanutecleer House and Dove House** (3557 Saratoga Road, Langley 98260; 360–221–5494 or 800–637–4436), owned by Bunny and Bob Meals. The charming Dove House has Southwestern decor, a full kitchen, two bedrooms, and a fireplace. The elegant Chanutecleer House is furnished with pine antiques and has a kitchen with bay window, living room with fireplace, large bedroom and private deck for viewing the sunsets. B&B double rates of $150–175 include a full breakfast. "Exquisitely decorated. Bunny is extremely personable and did all of the decorating herself. Comfortable and relaxing atmosphere." *(KMB)* Guest rooms at the **Saratoga Inn** (201 Cascade Avenue, P.O. Box 428, Langley 98260; 360–221–5801) overlook either the Saratoga Passage and the Cascades, or the charming town of Langley. Each has a gas fireplace, private bathroom with oversized shower, phone, and TV; the B&B double rates of $125–275 include a full breakfast. "Perfect location at the south end of town. You can walk to shops and restaurants, or take in the beauty of the bay while sitting on one of the porch rocking chairs. The rooms and common areas are decorated in elegant yet comfortable country decor." *(KMB)*

Eagle's Nest Inn   *Tel:* 360–221–5331
4680 Saratoga Road, Langley, 98260   *Fax:* 360–221–5331
*E-mail:*eaglnest@whidbey.com

Although historic inns have a flavor that can't be duplicated, new homes constructed as B&Bs often have a comfort level that's hard to beat. Years of thought and planning went into Eagle's Nest, built by Dale and Nancy Bowman in 1987, and purchased by Joanne and Jerry Lechner in 1994. Breakfasts include kiwi sorbet, pecan praline toast with wild blackberry syrup, and garden scrambled eggs with sausage; or sliced melon, blueberry walnut muffins, and smoked salmon soufflé the next.

"Wonderful amenities and such special treats as the thick robes, scented soaps, lotions, and the bottomless cookie jar!" *(GLH)* "The inn is set high on a hill with spectacular views of the Saratoga Passage; guest rooms are furnished with queen- or king-size beds." *(Caroline & Jim Lloyd)* "The building's octagonal shape was designed with numerous windows to offer mountain and water views from every one." *(Darla Blake-Ilson)* "Our room was the Eagle's Nest, reached by a private stairway, with windows all around." *(SC)* "After a day of seeing the sights, we relaxed in the hot tub on the spacious deck." *(Bill & Eileen Youngdahl)* "Our immaculate ground-level room was decorated with a flower theme, from the couch pillows to the dried flower arrangement hanging over the bed. Our bathroom was outfitted with shower cap, hairdryer, bathrobes, and lemon-scented shampoo and soap. Breakfast was served at a long table in the kitchen, and talking with the guests from all over the country was a pleasure." *(Sylvia Ann & Del Anorbes)* "After dinner we met friends from Seattle and sat in the living room late into the night by a cozy fire." *(Gerri Yarborough)*

Open All year.
Rooms 4 doubles—all with private shower, radio, TV/VCR. 3 with deck, air-conditioning.
Facilities Breakfast room, living room with woodstove, piano; library with games, video library; decks, hot tub. 2½ acres with walking paths, lawn games, canoe. Beach across street. Tennis nearby.
Location Whidbey Is. From ferry at Clinton, go N 2.7 m on Hwy. 525. Turn right on Langley Rd., go 3.7 m to Langley. Turn left on 2nd St. (becomes Saratoga Rd.), go 1.5 m to inn on left.
Restrictions No smoking. No children under 12. No shoes in house.
Credit cards Discover, MC, Visa.
Rates B&B, $95–115 double, $75–105 single. Extra person, $25. No tipping necessary. 2-night holiday/weekend minimum.
Extras Airport/ferry pickup. Member, WBBG.

Guest House Cottages   *Tel:* 360–678–3115
3366 South Highway 525, Greenbank, 98253

At this most unusual B&B, which has long been awarded a four-diamond rating from AAA, Don and Mary Jane Creger invite guests to a private getaway. Their romantic cottages, built for two, are scattered about the 25 acres. No one is asked to "rough it" in the woods; each log or frame home is decorated with country antiques and equipped with everything from fireplaces, to featherbeds, to microwave ovens, to "instant hot water" to VCRs.

"From the massive stone fireplace to the Jacuzzi, just steps from your bed, all needs are met with exquisite care and comfort. You can enjoy your morning coffee sitting on the white cedar deck, or feed the resident geese and ducks that live on the pond. Wonderful breakfast, too." *(David & Kelly Hill)* "Even lovelier than your writeup indicated. I could hardly tear myself away. Perfect honeymoon spot." *(Merryl Woodard)* "Gracious welcome, immaculate cottages. Fresh fruit on the table, candies, sachets, soap in quilted flowery baskets on the bedside table. Terry robes in the ample closets." *(Juanita Dooston)* "Our breakfasts were set up attractively on trays in the refrigerator." *(Mr. & Mrs. C.G. Breeding)* "A fireplace warmed our cozy cabin, and sunlight streamed in through the skylights. Our bed had heaps of fluffy pillows." *(Joy & Sean Hildebrandt)* "A peaceful, quiet, private sanctuary in the woods. We stayed in the Lodge, with a Jacuzzi in the bedroom, set on a platform so you can gaze down at fireplace or out over the pond." *(Gene Baker)* "Fresh eggs from the resident chickens, and ham and cheese croissants are just a portion of the delicious breakfast." *(Gary Freudenberger)* "No need to lock your doors or even draw your shades." *(Boyce & Tracey Sharf)*

Open All year.

Rooms 1 suite, 6 cottages—all with full private bath, radio, TV/VCR, movie library, kitchen, fireplace, Jacuzzi tub. 3 with desk, 1 with air-conditioning.

Facilities 25 acres with exercise room, heated swimming pool, hot tub, badminton, horseshoes. Ocean, lakes, parks nearby.

Location NW WA. Central Whidbey Island, 10 m S of Coupeville, 1 m S of Greenbank. On the island, follow State Hwy. 525 16 m N of ferry to 3366. Office is at 3366 S. Hwy. 525 in farmhouse, lower level.

Restrictions No smoking. No children. No pets.

Credit cards Amex, Discover, MC, Visa.

Rates B&B, $125–295 cottage, $110 suite. 2-night weekend minimum.

The Inn at Langley ✕ ♿

400 First Street, Langley, 98260

Tel: 360–221–3033
Fax: 360–221–3033

Of course you know that the sun rises in the east and sets in the west, but in case you wanted to be really sure, we can't think of a better place to check than from your private porch at the Inn at Langley. You can watch the sun rise above the Cascade Mountains on the mainland to the east, and set over the Saratoga Passage to the west. In between, you sit by the river rock fireplace in the dining room for a breakfast of fresh fruit, muesli, muffins, cereals, juice and coffee, served 8–10 A.M., or enjoy a weekend four-course dinner at 7 P.M. The menu changes frequently, but might include mussels in black bean soup, duck with logan berries or salmon with leeks, salad with Gorgonzola and walnuts, and pear torte with chocolate and whipped cream. Room decor is simple but elegant with oversized Jacuzzi soaking tubs facing the water view and fireplace, plus queen-size beds with down comforters. Built in 1989, the inn is owned by Paul and Pam Schell; Stephen Nogal is the longtime manager and chef.

"A beautiful place to unwind and enjoy the beauty of the Passage. Simple but lovely decor." *(KMB)* "Comfortable atmosphere. Wonderful thick robes and towels. Great video selection." *(Anne Weaver)* "Serene and classy interiors, fabulous Jacuzzi overlooking wonderful views. Impressive wine cellar, wonderful dinner." *(Judith Barr)*

Note: Under the same ownership is the Inn at Ludlow Bay in Port Ludlow and the Friday Harbor House in San Juan Island; see entries.

Open All year. Restaurant open Fri, Sat year-round; also open Sun May–Oct.
Rooms 2 suites, 22 doubles—all with full private bath with whirlpool tub, telephone, clock/radio, TV/VCR, fireplace, refrigerator, coffee maker, balcony/deck.
Facilities Dining room with fireplace, lobby with fireplace; 2 acres with off-street parking, herb garden. Water sports, tennis nearby.
Location Follow St. Hwy. 525 to Langley Rd. Turn right at 1st stop sign. Go through 2 more stop signs on First St. to inn at #400.
Restrictions No smoking. Children over 12.
Credit cards AMEX, MC, Visa.
Rates B&B, $269–289 suite, $189–199 double. Extra person, $35. Prix fixe dinner, $125 for two; reservations required. 2–3 night weekend/holiday minimum.
Extras Wheelchair accessible. Spanish spoken.

Log Castle B&B   *Tel:* 360–221–5483
4693 Saratoga Road, Langley 98260   *Fax:* 360–221–6249
                              E-mail: innkeepr@whidbey.com

This is the house that Jack built. No ordinary house, mind you, but a stunning log home designed by Norma Metcalf and built by her husband, Congressman Jack Metcalf. Highlights include the cathedral-ceilinged common room with fieldstone fireplace, leaded glass windows, a wormwood stairway, and the third-story turret bedroom overlooking the water, beach, mountains, and pasture. Karen and Phil Holdsworth manage the inn for the Metcalfs.

"Wonderful rooms, fantastic views, great food; exceptionally relaxing and comfortable, hospitable yet private. Karen was warm, witty, accommodating, cheerful, and knowledgeable, always ready with glasses of lemonade and a plate of cookies. The inn is whimsical and charming—much like walking into a Tolkien novel like *The Hobbit*. We breakfasted on eggs in scallop shells, watching bald eagles hunt for their morning meal outside. You eat at a table made from a huge slab of cedar wood about eight feet in diameter." *(Allen Hay)* "The innkeepers and owners welcomed us warmly, creating a homey atmosphere. Our fellow guests were pleasant and interesting, a good mix." *(G.H. Lynum)* "Ann's Room on the top floor has a private tower magnificently surrounded by log luxury—woodstove, white iron bed amid the five windows forming the octagon, tiny but well-stocked private bath, private balcony with wonderful view of the Cascade Mountains and the water." *(SC, also KMB)* "We fell asleep to the sound of waves lapping at the shore, and awakened in the morning to a 180-degree view of Puget

Sound. Delicious home-baked cinnamon rolls and just-picked berries for breakfast. At night, we brought sandwiches back and had an indoor picnic in front of a roaring fire." *(Nancy Clifford)*

"We sat on our secluded deck, and watched the sea, amid beautiful gardens with hummingbirds, eagles, bunnies, chipmunks; the Pachebel Canon played softly in the background. Enjoyed a healthy bowl of oatmeal for breakfast, accompanied by delightful conversation." *(Carole Mitchell)* "Guest rooms are supplied with fresh fruit, nuts, and mints; bottomless cookie jar downstairs." *(Rich & Maggie Verlinde)* "We watched the sunset from our private deck and the sunrise from our bed." *(Sandra Silva)* "When the tide is out, walking the beach to Langley is possible." *(Margaret Orth)* "Our king-size bed had the softest sheets; the room's many extras included binoculars, a basket of fresh fruit, fresh flowers, and a variety of reading material. The large bathroom had two sinks, a shower/tub, and plush dark green towels. Karen, and her husband, Phil, are delightful; their soft voices lend to the restful feeling that permeates the inn." *(Elaine Leslie)*

Open All year except Christmas.
Rooms 1 suite, 3 doubles—all with private shower and/or bath. 1 with desk, 2 with woodstove, 3 with balcony, 1 with porch..
Facilities Common room with fireplace. Balcony with hammock. 2½ acres with 500 ft. of waterfront on Saratoga Passage. Canoe, rowboat for fishing. Walking trails.
Location 1½ m to village. From Langley, follow Saratoga Rd. to inn on right.
Restrictions No smoking. No alcohol. No children under 10.
Credit cards Discover, MC, Visa.
Rates B&B, $95–120 suite, double. Extra person, $25.

WHITE SALMON

For additional area inns, see **Stevenson** and also **Hood River,** Oregon.

Inn of the White Salmon ¢ 🏃   *Tel:* 509–493–2335
172 West Jewett, P.O. Box 1549, 98672   800–972–5226
E-mail: innkeeper@gorge.net

If breakfast is your favorite meal of the day, the Inn of the White Salmon is the place for you. Built in 1937, the inn has been owned by Janet and Roger Holen since 1990. Breakfast, served 8–10 A.M. weekdays, 8–11 A.M. weekends, is a highlight of most guests' stay. Choices include artichoke frittata, broccoli quiche, or scrambled eggs with ham and cheese, with a selection of over twenty pastries, tarts, and cakes, plus fresh fruit and juice, coffee and tea. "The inn is decorated with antiques and old photographs. Our room was clean and comfortable; the staff efficient and helpful, and we had a view of Mt. Hood from our window. I could get used to chocolate cheesecake for breakfast." *(Nancy Sinclair)*

Open All year.
Rooms 5 suites, 11 doubles—all with private shower bath, telephone, TV, air-conditioning. 2 with desk, refrigerator.

Facilities Dining room, living room, hot tub. Near Columbia River Gorge National Scenic area for windsurfing, fishing, white-water rafting. Hiking, golf, skiing nearby.

Location SW WA. 65 m E of Portland, OR; NE of Hood River, OR. From Portland, take I-84 E to Exit 64, Hood River. Cross Columbia River. Go E on Hwy. 14, N on Hwy. 141 to inn in center of town.

Restrictions Light sleepers should ask for a quiet room. No smoking in public rooms; in guest room by arrangement.

Credit cards Amex, CB, DC, Visa.

Rates B&B, $105 suite, $89 double, $75 single. Extra person, $20. Children 12 & under charged $1 per year of age. 3rd night free off-season. Breakfast (outside guests), $13.

Extras Crib. French, German, Spanish, Tagalog spoken.

WINTHROP

Reader tip: "Winthrop is great for casual restaurants, some shopping. It is a small village with a Western theme, charming and fun to visit." *(Pam Phillips)* "Winthrop redid itself as a western town, and did a good job—fun, not too cutesy. Local handmade pottery and an ironworks had quality work for sale." *(June Horn)*

For additional area inns, see **Mazama**.

Sun Mountain Lodge 🛏 ✕ 🐾 ♿   *Tel:* 509–996–2211
Highway 20, P.O. Box 1000   800–572–0493
                                Fax: 509–996–3133
            E-mail: smtnsale@methow.com

On a private mountain top, 3,000 feet above the Methow Valley, is Sun Mountain Lodge, combining luxury accommodations (a four-diamond rating from AAA), a magnificent setting, and environmental sensitivity. Originally built in 1968, this full-service resort was renovated at a cost of $21 million in 1990; Brian Charlton is the longtime manager. The restaurant serves three meals daily; menus highlight Northwestern cuisine. Breakfast favorites are blueberry buttermilk pancakes, apple raisin oatmeal, crab crepes, grilled vegetable omelets, and vanilla-almond French toast. Lunch selections include chicken curry soup, foccacia bread pizzas, salads and sandwiches; dinner entrees highlight grilled Ellensburg lamb with rosemary, Southwest red chili chicken, and roasted vegetables in phyllo with couscous.

"Casual, quiet sophistication. Fabulous views of wildlife and the snow-capped mountains from every window. The spacious, inviting lobby has lots of comfortable seating, and two large stone fireplaces. We selected volumes from the lodge's extensive library of nature books, and curled up near the toasty fire. Our room was done in quiet earth tones; the bathroom was large. The restaurant sits near the edge of the mountain, and has a wide-ranging menu of upscale dining selections. Dinners are long and leisurely, with good wine selections and a variety of Northwest inspired dishes. Breakfasts are especially tasty. Fab-

ulous cross-country skiing." *(Pam Phillips)* "Wildflowers were blooming everywhere during my early summer visit; snow still topped the
high peaks. We took a nature walk down the mountainside with a naturalist and a float trip on the Methow River. Impressive lodge construction with two-story lobby, lodgepole beams and floor-to-ceiling
river rock fireplaces. I enjoyed meals from the pub menu in the lounge.
My lovely room was well furnished with wall sconces of pierced tin or
copper, a seating area with sofa, club chair, coffee table, a handmade
quilt on the bed, and had a magnificent view of snow-capped peaks.
Spacious bathroom with step-up bathtub, terry robes, and thick towels; quality toiletries were set in a miniature clawfoot tub." *(June Horn)*

Open All year.
Rooms 8 suites, 94 doubles, 13 cottages—all with full private bath, telephone,
clock/radio, desk, air-conditioning, robes. Some with whirlpool tub, fireplace,
refrigerator, balcony. Rooms in 3 buildings plus cabins.
Facilities Restaurant with evening pianist, bar/lounge, library with fireplace,
gift shop, exercise room, laundry facility. 3,000 acres with 2 swimming pools (1
heated), 3 hot tubs, 4 tennis courts, swing sets, lawn games. Hiking, nature
walks, horseback riding, river rafting, mt. biking. Lake for sailing, swimming,
kayaking, boating, fly fishing; children's program. 175 km cross-country skiing
trails; ski school; ice skating, sleigh rides. Golf, downhill & heli-skiing nearby.
Location N central WA. N Cascades. 185 mi NE of Seattle; 9 mi to Winthrop.
From Seattle, take North Cascades Hwy (Hwy. 20) or Stevens Pass (Hwy. 2) or
Snoqualmie Pass (Hwy. 90). Hwy. 20 generally closed late Nov.–mid-April.
Restrictions No smoking.
Credit cards Amex, MC, Visa.
Rates Room only, $185–280 suite, $100–215 double. Extra person, $18. Children
under 12 years free in parents' room. 10% senior, AAA discount. Alc lunch, $10;
dinner, $30.
Extras Wheelchair accessible; rooms specially equipped. Local airstrip pickup.
Cribs; babysitting. German, French spoken.

YAKIMA

Information please: Ten miles west of Yakima, in south central Washington, is **Mystery Manor** (3109 South Wiley Road, Wiley City 98903;
509–966–9971), originally built in 1886 as a cowboy hotel, and restored
as a B&B in 1996 by Charlie and Toniya Cornelius. B&B double rates
for the four simply furnished guest rooms range from $45–55, includ-
ing breakfast of fresh fruit and juice, toast and cheese, and oatmeal waffles. Guests can relax in the indoor swimming pool, and Toniya, a
stress-reduction therapist, offers a free foot massage to overnight guests.
The first weekend of each month, from April to November, they also
offer a murder mystery show. "Homey atmosphere, beautiful grounds
and pool." *(Julia K. Sherman)* "Clean, comfortable old-fashioned rooms;
extensive gardens; friendly, attentive owners." *(Dr. Hans Van De Vosse)*
"Excellent value." *(James Shober)*

Western Canada

Destiny Bay Resort, Boswell

Canada is a huge and beautiful country with a number of wonderful places to visit, from the exciting, cosmopolitan cities to the peaceful countryside and rugged interior. Far from a carbon copy of the United States, Canada offers visitors subtle "foreign" experiences from French Quebec in the east to the very British city of Victoria, in British Columbia, to the west.

Although most of Canada's population is located in metropolitan areas not far from the U.S. border, it's worth wandering further afield to sample some of the country's most scenic and remote areas. In the west, this means sampling the Gulf Islands, Vancouver Island beyond Victoria, and Alberta's fabled Canadian Rockies. In the east, explore the Gaspe Peninsula, Nova Scotia's Cape Breton Island, the Laurentides Mountains north of Montreal, and Ontario's shores along Lake Superior and Georgian Bay.

A few notes for first-time visitors to Canada: Radar detectors are illegal and seat belts are mandatory. When consulting maps and speed limits remember that Canada is metric. Ask your auto insurance company for a free "Canadian Non-Resident Inter-Provincial Motor Vehicle Liability Insurance Card"—it will speed up immeasurably any procedures if you are involved in an accident. Finally, it is often advantageous to purchase Canadian currency in the U.S.—make some comparison calls first (the rate varies from bank to bank).

Rates quoted in this section are noted in Canadian, not U.S., dollars. U.S. $1 = Canadian $.73; exchange rates are subject to constant fluctuations.

In 1991, a federal Goods and Services Tax (GST) of 7% went into effect, which also applies to accommodation and restaurant meals, *in addition* to existing sales taxes. Nonresidents are eligible for refunds on most goods and accommodations but not meals, alcohol, or fuel; inquire to obtain appropriate forms or call 800–66VISIT (in Canada) or 613–991–3346. Explanatory GST booklets are available at border crossings, shops, and hotels. Original (not photocopied) bills must accompany your claim for a refund. Refunds can be obtained by mail, or on the spot at Canadian Land Border Duty Free Shops.

Reader tip: "I must emphasize how much a bargain Canada is with the weakened dollar. The exchange rate provides superb prices for those visiting from the U.S." *(Bradley Lockner)*

Note: The GST and provincial sales taxes do not currently apply to some B&Bs with three guest rooms or less, a significant savings.

Alberta

Alberta is home to the Canadian Rockies; Banff, Jasper, and Lake Louise are the major resorts where most visitors go for hiking and fishing in summer and skiing in winter. This province's key cities are Edmonton and Calgary. Though Edmonton is the capital, its major claim to fame seems to be the West Edmonton Mall, a mile-long indoor shopping and recreation complex containing about every imaginable shop and recreation facility, even a 360-room hotel, the Fantasyland, with a selection of theme rooms devoted to different countries and periods (403–444–3000). Calgary is a center for agriculture and oil production. Its most famous event is the annual Stampede, a combination rodeo and state fair; it is also home to a fine collection of museums devoted to telecommunications and energy, along with more traditional subjects of art and history.

All rates quoted in Canadian dollars, and do not include taxes.

Note: Despite Alberta mailing addresses, entries for **Emerald Lake Lodge** and **Lake O'Hara Lodge**, both located in British Columbia's Yoho National Park, are in fact listed under the town of *Field* in the British Columbia chapter. Similarly, see under **Kootenay National Park** in British Columbia for the **Kootenay Park Lodge**.

BANFF

Reader tip: "Be sure to visit Canada House and Najinska in the Banff Springs Hotel complex. These stores have authentic Native American painting and crafts—not little tom-toms with dyed chicken feathers. A treat to browse amid such high quality merchandise." *(Bill MacGowan)*

Also recommended: Although there's nothing little about the **Banff**

Springs Hotel (Box 960, Banff T0L 0C0; 403–762–2211 or 800–441–1414), many consider it one of Alberta's finest hotels. A $80 million renovation has updated all the guest rooms and public areas, and another $12 million has created a popular spa with a super-heated indoor mineral water pool. Built by the Canadian Pacific Railroad, it was modelled after a castle in Scotland. "Huge halls and fireplaces with Elizabethan furniture. Our attractive room faced the river valley. A visit to the Upper Hot Springs pool nearby is very special; go at night when the stars are out, or when it is snowing." *(Marilyn Parker)* A reader who visited during the peak summer seas was less pleased: "The harried hotel personnel are swamped daily by hundreds of busloads of tourists who trample everyone and everything in sight." Double rates for the 770 rooms (we said it was big) start at $135 and go over $1000, depending on size, view, and season; standard rooms have little or no view. The complex also includes numerous shops, restaurants, and a conference center.

"**The Rimrock Resort Hotel** (Mountain Avenue, P.O. Box 1110, Banff T0L 0C0; 403–762–3356 or 800–661–1587) is built into the side of the mountain at the base of the Sulphur Mountain gondola. Huge windows in the lounge overlook the mountains, valley, and the grounds of the Banff Springs Hotel in the distance. From the deck you see mule deer grazing in Rimrock's courtyard with pond; there are also two restaurants, shops, indoor pool, outdoor hot pool, fitness center with whirlpool, meeting rooms, and a squash courts. The 346 rooms are comfortable in size, with lots of extras and large closets; prices vary according to view and season. Spotlessly clean. It's a great value for the area, at rates close to one-half that of Banff Springs Hotel." *(Perri & Michael Rappel)* Double rates are $135–325, and include scheduled shuttle bus service into town.

Information please: Under the same management as the Emerald Lake Lodge (see the British Columbia chapter) is the **Buffalo Mountain Lodge** (Tunnel Mountain Road, P.O. Box 1326, Banff T0L 0C0; 403–762–2400 or 800–661–1367). It's within walking distance of The Banff Centre and the Whyte Museum of the Canadian Rockies. The mountain-style main lodge has hand-hewn timbers and a huge field-stone fireplace; outside is a 14-foot hot tub. With guest rooms in 85 chalets, accommodations range from doubles to two-bedroom suites, most with fireplace and balcony—many have a kitchenette; decor includes custom-made cherry, pine, and bent-willow furniture, and handmade copper and glass light fixtures. Rates are $155–265 double occupancy, and children under age 13 stay free.

In 1911 explorer and photographer Mary Schaffer Warren wrote a humorous account about roughing it in the remote Canadian Rockies and helped establish the region's value as a place for wilderness journeys and scientific study. Her wood and stone bungalow, built in 1913, is now the **Tarry-a-While B&B** (117 Grizzly Street, Box 2782, T0L 0C0; 403–762–0462), and its natural fir interior is furnished with antiques and handmade Canadian pine furniture. Double rates for the three guest rooms, all with private bath, start at $135, and include a continental breakfast; coffee, tea and hot chocolate are available throughout the day in the upstairs sitting room.

For additional area inns, see **Canmore** and **Kootenay National Park.**

CALGARY

Reader tip: "Calgary is a clean, exciting, and satisfying city. Downtown, south of the river, is laid out in a grid pattern, so places are easy to find. For an inexpensive, memorable meal, try Savoir Faire on 17th Avenue S.W., where old-fashioned diner food is superbly prepared. One block west is an artists' cooperative, Provenance, with paintings and works in wood, ceramics, and textiles." *(Bill MacGowan)*

Big Springs B&B   *Tel:* 403–948–5264
R.R. 1, Airdrie T4B 2A3   *Fax:* 403–948–5851
          E-mail: whittake@cadvision

In the rolling foothills of the Canadian Rockies is the Big Springs B&B, a contemporary home built in 1976 by Earle and Carol Whittaker. After retiring as teachers, they renovated their home as a B&B in 1995. Guests have their own sitting room—the English Garden—with comfortable seating, good lighting, Queen Anne reproduction furniture, with a cheerful color scheme of hunter green, rose, and ivory. Breakfast is served at 8 A.M., either in the dining room or on the deck, and includes fresh fruit and juice, biscuits or perhaps banana bread, and the daily entree: pancakes, French toast, frittatta, sausage strata, or possibly breakfast lasagna; special diet considerations are cheerfully accommodated. Rates also include evening beverages and goodies, and bedtime chocolates.

"A quiet location while visiting the Stampede—it was an easy drive to the outskirts of Calgary and then a switch to the LRT train. Earle and Carol created a homey, relaxing atmosphere yet respected our privacy. The Bridal Room was decorated with a wrought iron queen-size canopy bed, maple bureau and bookcase, pastel floral fabrics, and soft lighting. White tulle decorated the windows and bed canopy, and photographs of brides and grooms were displayed. Breakfast included delicious rhubarb sour cream coffee cake with rhubarb sauce, sausage rolls, a baked egg dish, and plenty of coffee." *(Todd & Debbie McLean)* "Friendly, cordial hosts. Beautifully set table, with fine china and linens." *(Margaret & Fred Davis)* "We were greeted with a warm welcome and a cold glass of iced tea. Charming sitting room, with hot beverages and snacks in the evening." *(Nadine & Chris Krystkowiak)* "Meticulously clean. Carol and Earle are gracious, delightful people." *(Dr. & Mrs. Richard Adicks)* "Sensitive to our needs. Our schedule conflicted with breakfast so the Whittakers packed us a picnic, and got up early to see us off." *(Murray & Dianne Brookman)*

Open All year.
Rooms 4 doubles—all with private bath and/or shower, clock. 3 with desk.

Facilities Dining room, guest sitting room, family room with TV, porch. 10 acres with hot tub, patio, deck. Desk area with access to facsimile, computer, modem.
Location SW Alberta. 20 min. NW of Calgary. From airport, go N on Hwy. 2 10 km to Balzac. Turn left on Rte. 566. Go 12 km to Rt. 772 & turn right. Go 6 km & turn left on Rte. 567. Go 7 km to inn on right.
Restrictions No smoking.
Credit cards Visa.
Rates B&B, $85–100 double. Extra person, $15.
Extras Horses boarded.

Inglewood B&B	*Tel:* 403–262–6570
1006 8th Avenue S.E., T2G 0M4	*Fax:* 403–262–6570

Built in 1992 as a B&B, this neo-Victorian home is located in one of Calgary's oldest neighborhoods. Owners Valinda Larson and Helmut Schoderbock have furnished the guest rooms with pleasing European simplicity, with queen-size beds, lace curtains, and floral comforters. Breakfast is served in the sitting room at 8:30 A.M.; a menu is provided for guests to choose their meal, from a simple muffin, fruit and cheese, to eggs Benedict.

"Comfortable and immaculate, reasonably priced. Next to the Bow River, where there is a walking/bicycling path to downtown or to the zoo." *(Jerry & Michele Choate)* "Established Victorian neighborhood. Reasonable restaurants within walking distance. Well-presented breakfast, with choices of eggs, bagel with cream cheese, muffin with cheddar cheese, cinnamon French toast, or homemade granola with fruit and yogurt. Very friendly, helpful hosts." *(Amber Frost)*

Open All year.
Rooms 3 doubles—all with private shower bath, radio, clock. 1 with TV.
Facilities Dining/sitting room with TV/VCR, books, porch, guest refrigerator. Off-street parking. 50 yds. to Bow River for fly fishing.
Location 25 min. walk to downtown. From Trans-Canada Hwy, exit on Centre St. & go S to 9th Ave. (Calgary Tower). Turn left & continue to 8th St. SE. Turn right on 8th Ave. SE to inn on left.
Restrictions No smoking. Children over 4.
Credit cards MC, Visa.
Rates B&B, $75–125 double, $65–90 single.
Extras German spoken.

CANMORE

Located at the eastern gateway to Banff National Park, Canmore was a down-on-its-luck mining town that struck gold at the 1988 Winter Olympics—being chosen as the venue for the nordic ski events. Today it is considered a less-touristy alternative to Banff, located 26 miles to the northwest, and business is booming with visitors from all over world.

Reader tip: "We enjoyed a fabulous, reasonably priced dinner at The Peppermill restaurant; the atmosphere is casual and the service friendly." *(Perri & Michael Rappel)*

Also recommended: While too small for a full write-up, with only two guest rooms, we have received enthusiastic reports on the **Wedgewood Mountain Inn** (1004 Larch Place, Box 3035, T1W 1S7; 403–678–4494), a spacious alpine-style cedar home built in 1980. Floor-to-ceiling windows in the living room offer views of the Rockies; a network of walking trails meanders along the Bow River, adjacent to the inn, and links most of Canmore. "For reasonably priced accommodations, wonderful comfort and hospitality, look no further than this inn and hosts Kathie and Frankie Claxton." *(Chris Weiz)* "Country decor; fresh towels, coffee and hot chocolate in our room." *(Jill Tocws)* "Beautiful walking path. Loved the Wedgewood room with its deep rose and blue decor, king-size bed, and large whirlpool tub." *(C.L. Marsh-Williams)* Both rooms have private baths, and the B&B rates of $85–140 include a full breakfast, possibly a poached egg on a croissant, stuffed French toast, or blueberry pancakes with sausage.

Information please: Hiking trails in Cougar Canyon lead from the back door of **Cougar Canyon B&B** (3 Canyon Road, T1W 1G3; 403–678–6636 or 800–289–9731), a contemporary home built in 1994. B&B double rates of $80–100 include a full breakfast, and well-behaved children are welcome. Two guest rooms are available, each with private bath, and guests are welcome to relax in the guest loft with a fireplace and TV.

The **Kiska Inn B&B** (110 1st Avenue, Deadman's Flats, T1W 2W4; 403–678–4041), a contemporary chalet-style home, reflects different facets of Canadian history. Each of the six guest rooms has a different theme —exploration and the fur trade in the Voyageur room, local history and native crafts in the Green room, and prints of historic Canadian ships in the Marine room. All have private baths, queen-size beds, and individual thermostats. Rates of $80–125 include a continental breakfast.

Georgetown Inn   *Tel:* 403–678–3439
1101 Bow Valley Trail, Box 3327, T0L 0M0   *Fax:* 403–678–3630

Named in memory of an Alberta mining town even smaller than Canmore, the English Tudor–style Georgetown Inn was built in 1993 by Doreen and Barry Jones. Originally from England, they have decorated the inn with memorabilia from the old mining days, plus antiques, down comforters, plush towels, and queen- or twin-size beds. The lounge, The Miner's Lamp, is reminiscent of an English pub, and a favorite item on the menu is a Cornish pastry. Guests are served a traditional English breakfast each morning in the dining room from 7:30 to 9 A.M.

"Relaxed and comfortable, with family photographs here and there. Plenty of variety in the decor—not everything is flowers and lace—plus all have a mountain view." *(MW)* "Our room had a queen-size bed, really great mattress and pillows, good reading lights on either side, a comforter that coordinated with the soft country floral wallpaper, and a shelf with hooks below instead of a closet. The tiny bathroom had a large tub with shower; the sink was in the bedroom. The water pressure was exceptional and hot water was plentiful. Everything was sparkling clean and the entire inn is well maintained. The sound-proofing is good—with the windows closed we heard neither the road traffic or the train. Friendly and accommodating innkeepers; good, hearty breakfast. Comfy seating in the pub, where soda is complimentary for inn guests. All in all, a good lodging value, about half the cost of staying in Banff." *(Perri & Michael Rappel)*

Open All year.
Rooms 14 doubles—all with private bath and/or shower. Some with whirlpool tub.
Facilities Dining room with fireplace, pub with fireplace.
Location SW Alberta. 95 m W of Calgary. On Hwy 1A, via Canmore exit from Trans-Canada Hwy.
Restrictions Traffic noise might disturb light sleepers. No smoking in some guest rooms.
Credit cards Amex, MC, Visa.
Rates B&B, $79–129 double. Extra person, $10–20. Children under 6 free in parents' room.
Extras Wheelchair access; room specially equipped. Winter plug-ins.

EDMONTON

Capital of Alberta, Edmonton offers science at the Edmonton Space and Science Centre, history at the Fort Edmonton Park, and shopping (and more) at the West Edmonton Mall, with over 800 shops, an indoor water park, ice skating rink, dolphin show, and deep sea adventure.

Also recommended: Conveniently located to downtown Edmonton, is the **Alberta Setting Sun B&B** (7911-98th Ave, T6A 0B5; 403–468–3217), a renovated 1950s home with a guest suite with a kitchen and living room. There's a lovely yard and patio surrounded by flowering plants, and a friendly cat named Babykins to greet you. B&B double rates of $55 include a country breakfast. "Quiet and spotless. Friendly hosts, Paul and Peggy Martel." *(Don & Jean Meldrum)* "Super comfortable beds, loads of towels and magazines, wonderful food. Caring service." *(B.G. English)* "Exceptionally clean suite. Hosts are generous with treats and little extras." *(Lynn McEachern)* "Everything is thought of right down to make-up remover pads. Perfect spot for running along Edmonton's beautiful riverbank, in a safe and accessible neighborhood." *(Sheila Manning Artus)*

"A stately mansion built in 1912 by Bidwell Holgate, the **Holgate House** (6201 Ada Boulevard; 403–448–0901) is a historic property recently restored as a stunning B&B, by architect Richard Venderwell and his wife, Jeannie. In the quiet Highlands neighborhood not far from trendy Strathcona, the Holgate House offers two guest rooms, both with private bath. The common areas have charming details like Oriental rugs, oak paneling, beveled glass, marble fireplaces, a large veranda for afternoon tea, a cozy library with a self-service coffee bar, and a resident cat. Lovely parkland along Ada Boulevard are perfect for strolling. Breakfast includes piping hot croissants, scones, muffins, homemade preserves and French toast or a baked pancake dish. Jeanne took extra special care of us!" *(Dawn Austin)* B&B double rates are $85–125.

For an additional area inn, see **Wetaskewin**.

JASPER

Also recommended: Too large for a full entry at 442 rooms, is the well-known **Jasper Park Lodge** (Box 40, T0E 1E0; 403–852–3301 or 800–441–1414), set on the shores of Lake Beauvert. Dating back to 1927, it now ranks as a world-class resort, with a full complement of activities, set amid spectacular scenery. Though it caters primarily to tour groups, readers continue to be reasonably pleased with the views, cabins, and facilities. Double rates range from $125–620; inquire about B&B and MAP rates when you reserve.

Alpine Village 🏃 ¢   *Tel:* 403–852–3285
Box 610, T0E 1E0   *Fax:* 403–852–1955

Built in 1946, this cluster of log cabins on the shores of the Athabasca River was purchased in 1986 by Chris and Rena Allin. It is surrounded by a natural pine forest and boasts a panoramic view of the river valley with Mt. Edith Cavell towering in the background. Guest cabins have log interiors, river stone fireplaces, carpeting, and comfortable upholstered sofas and chairs. "The grounds and individual cabins are very attractive, neat, clean, and modern. A popular place to stay in season, so reserve well in advance." *(Marilyn Parker)*

Open May 1st thru Oct. 15th.
Rooms 42 1–2 bedroom cabins—all with full private bath, TV, desk. 36 with radio/clock, 29 with fireplace. Most with kitchen, porch, barbecue grill.
Facilities 11 wooded acres with hot tub, children's playground, lawn games, hiking. On river for fishing.
Location 2.5 km S of Jasper on Hwy 93. Turn E on Hwy 93A.
Restrictions No smoking in 7 cabins.
Credit cards MC, Visa.
Rates Room only, $70–190 double. Extra person, $10. Children under 7 free in parents' cabin. 3-night minimum, high season. Weekly, off-season rates.
Extras Cribs, babysitting facilities. German spoken.

LAKE LOUISE

Also recommended: Although too large for a full entry at 511 rooms, the **Chateau Lake Louise** (403–522–3511 or 800–441–1414) is a must for those who don't mind paying a premium to be right on the lake. "Our small room faced the lake for an incredible mountain view. We enjoyed breakfast in the Poppy room and dinner in the Wine Bar. We were there the week before Christmas; it wasn't crowded and it was great to walk out the door to skate on the lake or cross-country ski along its edge." *(Marilyn Parker)*

Also recommended: The **Deer Lodge** (109 Lake Louise Drive, Box 100, T0L 1E0; 403–522–3747 or 800–661–1595), was built in 1921 as a log and stone teahouse; the first of 73 guest rooms were added in 1925. The handsome, rustic log-beamed restaurant in the original building features hearty soups, homemade breads, and fish, veal, and beef entrees. Room rates, varying by season, are $90–$195 for double occupancy; children under 13 stay free. A rooftop hot tub provides a breath-taking spot for viewing Victoria Glacier. "A quieter, reasonably priced alternative to Chateau Lake Louise. A ten-minute walk will bring you to the lake and the admiring throngs. Excellent food, and if you don't mind creaky floorboards, a good place to stay." *(Bill MacGowan)* One reader noted that the guest rooms in the new addition were "standard motel," but a good value; the breakfast buffet is recommended.

The **Post Hotel** (200 Pipestone Road, Box 69, T0L 1E0; 403–522–3989 or 800–661–1586) is comprised of a log building, constructed in 1952, which houses the hotel's acclaimed restaurant; a handsomely built yellow cedar and field stone addition which houses the luxurious guest rooms and duplex suites; and a separate conference facility. "The comfortable furnishings and impressive staircase made the lobby feel warm and inviting. The lawn and patio were great places to view the surrounding mountains. The pool, steam room, and hot tub were welcome after a long day of hiking." *(Ronald & Linda Craddock)* There are 96 rooms and two luxury cabins, ranging in size, decor, view, and price from modest to top-of-the-line; double rates are $120–455.

Information please: The **Baker Creek Chalets** (Highway 1A, Bow Valley Parkway, Box 66, T0L 1E0; 403–522–3761) offer eight suites in the main lodge (two with Jacuzzi tub), plus 25 cedar log chalets dotting the wooded grounds beside Baker Creek. The cabins have a double bed in an alcove, carpeting, and a combination sink/stove/refrigerator unit; some also have a loft with twin beds. The restaurant is open for three meals daily in summer. Double rates range from $90–205 suite; during the winter season a complimentary continental breakfast buffet is included. "Located off the old highway between Banff and Lake Louise, so there's little road traffic; we sat up one night to watch the evening train go by. Our attractive log cabin was clean, compact, and well equipped. Great view of Castle Mountain at dinner. Delicious dinner of trout, salad, whole wheat rolls and raspberry sorbet." *(Marilyn Parker)* Reports needed.

Moraine Lake Lodge ✗ ♿ *Tel:* 403–522–3733
Box 70, T0L 1E0 *Fax:* 604–985–7479
E-mail: info@morainelake.com

The Moraine Lake Lodge dates back to 1908, when a tea house was built to cater to hikers willing to make the twelve kilometer trek from Lake Louise to Moraine Lake. From a tent camp in the 1920s to log cabins and lodge, it was expanded over the years to accommodate guests enamored of the azure blue waters and the breathtakingly rugged beauty of the valley. In 1990, under new ownership, the resort was totally redesigned and rebuilt, to blend with the environment and accommodate day visitors while respecting the privacy of overnight guests. It opened in 1991 under the management of David Hutton. Lodge rooms and cabins are decorated with custom-made furniture, and all have magnificent views of the lake, mountains, and glaciers. Complimentary coffee, tea, and freshly baked pastries are served in the library each afternoon; after dinner you can treat yourself to a brandy or sherry while relaxing in front of the library fireplace.

"Lodge is cleanly and neatly decorated, with some antiques to give it flavor, plus the best gift shop in the area. We hiked to Sentinel Pass, returned for tea and cookies, and then went canoeing on the lake. The dining room is intimate, the menu limited but good, especially our hearts of palm salad and the Alberta beef." *(Marilyn Parker)* "Stunningly designed cabins, with vaulted ceilings, massive log-hewn beds, and fireplace nooks with built-in sofa. The wooded property provides privacy from hikers at the lake. Service friendly, front desk staff quite good. Well prepared food. Spectacular setting." *(AP, also Tom Wilbanks)*

Open June 1–Sept. 30.

Rooms 18 cabins, 1 suite, 14 doubles—all with full private bath, deck. 25 with woodburning fireplace. 8 rooms in lodge.

Facilities Dining room, library, lobby—all with woodburning fireplace; cafe, gift shop. Park naturalist lectures Tues. & Fri. evening. 5 acres with canoes, hiking guide service.

Location 12 km S of Lake Louise. Go left off Lake Louise Rd. to inn.

Restrictions Children age 16 and over preferred.

Credit cards Amex, MC, Visa.

Rates Room only, $195–$415 double. Alc lunch, $10–12; alc dinner, $35–45.

Extras 1 room wheelchair accessible, equipped for disabled. Train station pickup. Cribs. French, German, Japanese spoken. spoken.

PRIDDIS

Information please: Want to experience the beauty of the Rocky Mountain foothills from the back of a horse? **The Homeplace Ranch** (Site 2, Box 6, RR 1, Priddis, T0L 1W0; 403–931–3245) assigns you a horse for the duration of your stay, and the wranglers determine your skill level before taking you on daily rides. There are accommodations in the lodge (at 4900′ elevation) for twelve guests, in private rooms with bath, or on their south ranch one hour away (at 6000′ elevation), in three-person tent-cabins with bunks. All meals are served family style, staff and guests together; after a hard day in the saddle, you can relax in the Jacuzzi or splash in the creek. Rates for the three-night minimum stay, including accommodations, riding, all meals, snacks, and activities, are $542 per person, double occupancy. Priddis is located between Calgary and Banff, about 25 miles southwest of Calgary and bordered by the Kananaskis Forest Reserve.

WATERTON PARK

Waterton Lake National Park was established on the international boundary between Canada and the United States in 1895; in 1932, in connection with Glacier National Park, it was designated the world's first International Peace Park. Attractions include Upper Waterton Lake, the deepest lake in the Canadian Rockies; high alpine meadows filled with wildflowers during the early summer; a wide variety of fish and wildlife; and such natural attractions as Red Rock Canyon and Cameron Falls.

Reader tip: "We drove to Red Rock Canyon and hiked to the falls, where we had three bear sightings. The road to Cameron Lake is a canyon drive with rivers and snowy peaks. The all-day hike from the end of the road back to town is a favorite, with lakes and vistas not visible from the road. The boat excursion to Goat Haunt features a knowledgeable narrator who explains geology, wildlife, and history during the two-hour trip; we spotted a bald eagle, mountain goats, and elk. It can be cold and windy, even in July. When the clouds finally lifted, we had glorious views of the snow-capped mountains. Returning to Vancouver we followed Highway 3 for gorgeous scenery, interesting little towns, fruit stands, and wildlife galore. The road east of Hope is spectacular—wild country with lots of lakes, gushing waterfalls and dense forests." *(Carol Moritz)*

Also recommended: We've had generally good reports on the **Prince of Wales Hotel** (June–Sept: Waterton Park, T0K 2M0; 406–226–5551 or out-of-season: Glacier Park Inc., Greyhound Tower, Station 5510, Phoenix, AZ, 85077; 602–207–6000), an historic 1920s-era hotel designed in Alpine style, overlooking Waterton Lake. The 82 guest rooms have private baths, and double rates range from $130–175 double. "The most gorgeous setting imaginable, on a high bluff overlooking the lake, mountains, and glaciers. Be sure to ask for a room with a lake view, preferably one with a balcony; some of the other rooms are very small with miniscule showers. Beautiful views through the floor-to-ceiling windows of the spacious lobby." *(SC)* "Adequately furnished, clean rooms. Enjoyable afternoon tea." *(Nanci & Norm Cairns)* "The charming appearance of the hotel, the imposing lobby, and the lake view make this place special. The kilt-clad staff were all polite and friendly; we hated to bother them to run the elevator for us." *(CM)*

Kilmorey Lodge 👤 ✕
117 Evergreen Avenue, Box 100, T0K 2M0

Tel: 403–859–2334
Fax: 403–859–2342
E-mail: travel@watertoninfo.ab.ca

The Kilmorey is a gabled log-style structure, built in the early 1900s. The interior is paneled in knotty pine and is furnished with antiques and country furniture.

"More personal than area hotels. Guest rooms are beautifully decorated with antiques. Excellent dining room with outstanding Caesar salad, Quebec-style baked onion soup, wild Saskatoonberry jam, and a mouthwatering appetizer with artichoke hearts, spinach, and mushrooms in Hollandaise sauce, caribou, terrific lamb, and great beef filet." *(Carol Moritz)* "Friendly, informative staff. Convenient location a ten-minute walk from the boat dock, town, Cameron Falls, and theater. Make dinner reservations; the restaurant is popular. During the summer, drinks and sandwiches are also served in the gazebo. Quiet at night—I was awakened only by the smell of bread baking and coffee brewing." *(Shirley Lieb)* "Our bathroom sparkled, towels were fluffy; a down quilt was on our bed. The owners, Leslie and Gerry Muza, are sincere and hospitable." *(Mavis & Eric Roland)* "Where else can you find mountain sheep lying content at the back door, sheltered from the wind and oblivious to the humans watching them? At breakfast one morning, as we ate our meal, a deer was peering through the window, munching away at his." *(Carol Breakell)* "Our motel-style room on the first floor was clean and comfortable, with a headboard attached to the wall, and a pretty flowered comforter. Service in the restaurant was fine, the food adequate. The town itself is small and manageable, and the area surprisingly untouristy, even in August." *(SC)*

Open All year.

Rooms 4 suites, 19 doubles—all with private bath and/or shower, desk, fan.

Facilities Restaurant, bar/lounge with fireplace, TV; library/game room with fireplace; heated gazebo. Picnic tables. Fishing, boating, bicycling, hiking, trail rides, stream fishing, tennis, 18-hole golf course nearby.

Location SW AB, near provincial border with British Columbia and close to US border at Montana. 80 m SW of Lethbridge via Hwy. 5; 145 m S of Calgary via Hwys. 2, 3, & 6. From Glacier National Park, take Hwy. 6N from Chief Mt. Customs; Waterton is 40 m from St. Mary, MT. Lodge faces Emerald Bay on Upper Waterton Lake.

Restrictions No smoking in some guest rooms.

Credit cards Amex, DC, Enroute, MC, Visa; personal checks for advance deposit only.

Rates Room only, $165–171 suite, $86–133 double, single. Extra person, $10. Children under 16 free in parents' room. Cot or playpen, $10. Ski, golf, mystery, romance packages. Alc dinner, $32.

Extras Wheelchair access; 2 rooms specially equipped. Crib, babysitting. French, Spanish spoken.

WETASKEWIN

Also recommended: 70 miles southeast of Edmonton is the **Karriage House 1908 B&B** (5215 47th Street, Wetaskewin; 403–352–5996). "Breakfasts are awesome, the facilities comfortable and well-appointed with a good feel of history. The inn's curio shop is an enticing blend of collectibles and antiques that represent great value. Tom and Sue are caring people, and knowledgeable about the community and area." *(Dave & Carol Anderson)* B&B double rates range from $65–85.

British Columbia

Bordering Washington, Idaho, and part of Montana, British Columbia stretches north to the Yukon and Northwest Territories and west to the Pacific. Although British Columbia is 50% larger than Texas, more than 75% of its population (of only 3,282,000) lives near the two principal cities, Vancouver and Victoria. Since British Columbia is something of a mouthful to say, just about everyone in Canada and the northwestern U.S. refers to the province as "BC," which is just what we're going to do here.

Summer is very much peak season in BC; we'd strongly recommend making your reservations two to three months ahead.

Vancouver Island is located 40 miles away from the city of Vancouver on the mainland. To get here, take a ferry from Anacortes, Washington, through the beautiful San Juan Islands; from Port Angeles, on Washington's Olympic Peninsula; or from the city of Vancouver. Victoria, the very British capital of BC, sits at the southern tip of Vancouver Island and is the starting point for island explorations. Near Victoria, scattered like jewels off the southeastern coast, are the 100 Gulf Islands, known as bucolic getaways with all the amenities of island life.

Be sure to travel beyond Victoria when visiting Vancouver Island. There are no continuous roads on the west shore of the island, so you must take Route 1 up the east coast. Turn inland near Parksville, then either stop in Port Alberni to board the MV *Lady Rose* for a romantic cruise to Bamfield or visit Pacific Rim National Park, between Tofino and Ucluelet, for beachcombing and scuba diving. For more adventure, take Route 1 to Campbell River, Route 28 to Gold River, and board the MV *Uchuck III,* which sails the remote fjords of the northwest part of the island.

Mainland BC Plan to spend several days in the city of Vancouver and the surrounding area. For one good side trip, take Route 99 north past a long inlet, then into the Coast Range Mountains, ending at Whistler, an excellent ski area near Garibaldi Provincial Park. For another, follow picturesque Route 101 up the "Sunshine Coast" from Vancouver to Powell River. This route includes crossings on tiny ferries at both Horseshoe Bay and Earls Cove.

Routes 1 and 3, east of Vancouver, lead you to the most interesting interior spots in the province. On Route 7, stop first at historic Harrison Hot Springs (worth a look but not an overnight), then drop south at Agassiz to Route 1 and the multilayered Bridal Veil Falls. From here you begin seeing the sharply sculptured, snowcapped Cascade Mountains rising directly behind the Fraser River Valley. At Hope you have a choice. Route 3 winds through the mountains and past the apple orchards of the Okanagan Valley to Penticton and Lake Okanagan, a popular but overcrowded resort area. Alternatively, Route 1 follows the Fraser River Canyon past dramatic Hell's Gate (take the tram across the narrow canyon) into the dry, high plains near Kamloops. From there you enter remote forested back country until you reach the spectacular Mt. Revelstroke and Glacier national parks, with their massive sharp peaks, rolling alpine meadows, and hundreds of glaciers. To the north, the remaining two-thirds of interior BC is sparsely populated; with extreme distances between towns and rustic accommodations in the towns, it's not high on our must-see list.

All rates are quoted in Canadian dollars, and do not include taxes.

Reader tip: "Washington ferries require you to arrive 90 minutes before departure for the trip from Sydney, BC, to Anacortes, Washington. Leaving from Salt Spring Island and going to Tsawwassen via the BC ferry system requires arrival only 30 minutes before departure—and the ferries are cleaner and better appointed."

BOSWELL

Destiny Bay Resort ¢ ✕ ♿	*Tel:* 250–223–8234
Highway 3A, V0B 1A0	800–818–6633
	Fax: 250–223–8515
	E-mail: destinyb@kootenay.awinc.com

Hanna and Rolf Langerfeld bought this small resort on the shores of Kootenay Lake in 1977 and have been renovating it ever since. "Excellent service; I caught a few fish and the chef prepared them that evening." *(Silvio Dobrio)* "Outstanding cleanliness; friendly innkeepers and staff—the inn dog Buffy is delightful and well-behaved. Awesome food with good variety; veranda dining was a pleasure." *(Jeanmarie Brill)* "Very private lakeside cottages, meticulously equipped and maintained." *(Bill & Eleanor Hooson)* "Magnificent, totally unspoiled environment with an abundance of wildlife. Freshly baked muffins are delivered to your door at 7 A.M., and there's a small fridge and coffee maker in the room; Rolf and Hanna easily accommodated a special diet." *(Trish Thomasser)* "Well situated, away from an little-traveled highway, with rustic log cabins with sod roofs growing wildflowers. Quiet, restful place." *(Mary & Richard Coe)*

"Hanna's food is extraordinary and Rolf is a master at spending just enough time chatting to make you feel personally welcome and then leaving you to enjoy the peace they have created. The greatest disturbance we encountered was the squabbling among the hummingbirds who dine along with you on the porch of the main lodge." *(Mrs. P. W. Warren)* "We drove a short distance to a beautiful hiking trail up Lockhart Creek, then explored the Kootenay Forge blacksmith and gift shop with handcrafted native gifts. You can take the free ferry across to Nelson for a day trip." *(Nancy Lindberg, and others)* "Everything is clean and neat, European both in atmosphere and cuisine." *(Penn Fix)* "Delicious meals—Mediterranean lamb stew was my favorite." *(Bill & Kathy Cole)* "Our immaculate private cabin had cedar panelling, attractive wallpaper, cathedral ceiling, and a birchwood fire ready to light. Parking in front; flower boxes line the windows." *(Katie Lawler)* "Firm mattresses, adjustable heat, large bath towels, and big bars of soap." *(Rose-Marie & Bob Beasley)* "The decanter of sherry at fireside was doubly warming." *(Maurice Twomey)*

Open April–Oct.

Rooms 3 suites, 5 cottages—all with full private bath, desk, porch, refrigerator, patio, coffee maker. 1 suite has fireplace, double whirlpool tub. 3 cottages with fireplace.

Facilities Dining room, sitting room, library. 3 acres with flower gardens, oversized chess game. Private beach with fireplace, sauna, rowboats. Swimming, fishing, hiking. Heli-hiking, golf nearby.

Location SE BC. 30 m N of Creston on Hwy. 3A, 3 hrs. N of Spokane, WA.

Restrictions "We are an adult-oriented resort; children must be properly supervised."

Credit cards MC, Visa.

Rates MAP, $150–190 suite or cottage (double), $110–150 single. Extra person, $40. 2-night minimum. Prix fixe dinner, $24–30.

Extras Wheelchair access. German spoken.

COURTENAY

Also recommended: At **Greystone Manor** (4014 Haas Road, RR 6, Site 684-C2, Courtenay V9N 8H9; 250–338–1422) you can see glorious English gardens created by true English gardeners, innkeepers Mike and Mo Shipley. "Fabulous flowers, interesting area, charming but unobtrusive innkeepings, pleasant breakfast. Furnishings adequate." (*SC*) "Comfortable beds, ample hot water, relaxing atmosphere. Innkeepers knowledgeable about the area, helpful with suggestions." (*Bradley Lockner*) B&B double rates for the three guest rooms are $70–75.

FAIRMONT HOT SPRINGS

Information please: "The waters at **Fairmont Hot Springs Resort** (Box 10, Fairmont Hot Springs V0B 1l0; 250–345–6311 or 800–663–4979) are not sulphurous; there are five different pools, indoor and outdoor, at temperatures between 90 and 100 degrees. These are the main attraction, and many folks, locals and guests alike, enjoy them immensely—just sitting and soaking or watching those diving off the high and low boards—it's good for the soul (and muscles). The resort is pleasant, beautifully landscaped, with lots of families from all over and the extra amenities of a golf course and tennis courts. Excellent modern rooms, with good views. Large, tasty breakfast buffet with lots of choices. For dinner, a second restaurant has a children's menu and less expensive fare. Helpful staff." (*Bill MacGowan*) There are 140 rooms (some 2-bedroom units with kitchenette); the double rates are $80–150, and rates for the hot pools are $6–9 daily. In winter, the resort has its own alpine ski center with lifts and ski programs; in spring it can be one of the few places where you can ski and golf in the same day! Fairmont is located in southeastern BC.

For an additional area inns, see **Fort Steele** and **Kootenay National Park**.

FIELD

Yoho National Park stretches along the border of Alberta and British Columbia, in the Canadian Rockies just west of the Continental Divide and the resort city of Banff. "Yoho" is the Kootenay Indian exclamation for wonder or astonishment.

Also recommended: Built by the Canadian Pacific Railway in 1902 of hand-hewn logs with massive stone fireplaces, **Emerald Lake Lodge** (P.O. Box 10, Field, V0A 1G0; 250–343–6321 or 800–663–6336) was expanded in the 1920s and was totally renovated in 1986. The 85 guest rooms (in 24 cabin-style buildings) are decorated in pastel colors with natural pine or oak furnishings, and each has a fieldstone fireplace and private balcony. "To avoid the peak season tour groups, we planned our hiking, rafting, or riding trips for midday. By late afternoon all was peaceful, and we rewarded ourselves with a relaxing soak in the hot tub, surrounded by mountain flowers, with a spectacular view of the lake and surrounding mountains." *(Mary Beth O'Reilly)* "Tasty dinner of salmon on wild rice and spinach, berry pie for dessert. Healthy buffet breakfast—orange and cranberry juice, cereal with fruit and yogurt, bran muffins and poppy seed cake." *(Marilyn Parker)* Double rates are $155–325, and include use of the Club House, with large outdoor hot tub, exercise room and sauna.

Information please: On the opposite side of Victoria Glacier from Lake Louise is the **Lake O'Hara Lodge** (P.O. Box 55, Lake O'Hara Lodge, Ltd. Lake Louise Alberta T0l 1E0; 250–343–6418 or 403–687–4110), a two-story wooden lodge built by the Canadian Pacific Railroad in 1926. At 6,700 feet, it is the highest resort in the Canadian Rockies and the blissful setting entices guests to return year after year—the blue waters of Lake O'Hara are ringed by dark evergreens and golden larches, with a background of 11,000-foot snowcapped peaks. Access is limited, and it's hard to believe that bustling Lake Louise lies just on the other side of the mountains. There are fifteen cabins plus seven guest rooms in the lodge; all are furnished simply but comfortably, and those in the lodge have shared bathrooms. The food is surprisingly sophisticated: a typical set dinner might consist of a goat cheese tart, tomato salad with basil, prime rib with Yorkshire pudding, and apple tart. Rates also include afternoon tea and cookies or gluhwein. "The public can visit the lodge between 9 A.M. and 3 P.M., and for afternoon tea, which also included lemonade and at least six varieties of home-baked cookies and cakes to sample. A really beautiful area with lots of trails to hike; to take the bus in just for hiking you reserve a month ahead. Overnight accommodations also require advance planning." *(Marilyn Parker)*

Information please: Not far from Emerald Lake lies **Kicking Horse Lodge** (Box 174, V0A 1G0; 250–343–6303 or 800–659–4944), a contemporary two-story ranch-style structure. The fourteen rooms have queen-size beds, TVs, and full private baths; 7 have a porch. A large family unit is available with a kitchenette and whirlpool tub. The restaurant serves three meals daily; dinner entrees include Coho salmon with spiced butter and dried fruit; grilled steak with pepper-corn sauce; and spinach manicotti. Double rates range from $60–160; no charge for children under 6. "Fresh linens, ironed sheets and pillow cases, and nice fluffy white towels." *(Bertha Krepps)* "Appealing with flowers and hanging plants on the porch. Our clean and well-maintained unit had attractive pine furniture, adequate lighting, and a well-supplied kitchenette. Good food, prompt service." *(Dorothy Russon)*

FORT STEELE

Reader tip: About ten miles southwest of Fort Steele is Cranbrook and The Canadian Pacific Railroad Museum. "Definitely worth a stop, with many restored opulent old railroad cars. After the tour visitors can treat themselves to scones and coffee or tea inside the restored dining car." *(Carol Moritz)*

Emery's Mountain View B&B   *Tel:* 250–426–4756
183 Wardner-Fort Steele Road, P.O. Box 60, V0B 1N0

John and Joanna Emery's Mountain View B&B is a modern ranch home situated on a ridge above the Wild Horse River and some interesting marshland. All around is BC–owned property, so there are panoramic views of the Kootenay Valley mountains—and no close neighbors. Built in 1993, the decor of the house is eclectic, with modern, antique and "re-found" furniture; oil and watercolor art, stained glass, and Oriental rugs on polished wood floors. Guests enjoy the large porches, and the gardens provide fresh flowers and vegetables. Breakfast, served at the dining room table from 8:30 to 9:30 A.M., includes home-baked breads and muffins, homemade jams, locally grown fruits, cheese and yogurt, scrambled eggs, sausage or bacon. "John and Joanna retired from careers in civil engineering and nurse administration, respectively, and wholeheartedly enjoy meeting and visiting with people. They have built a lovely home, nicely furnished and scrupulously clean, on acreage that is very quiet and secluded with beautiful scenery, a panoramic view of the mountains." *(OT)* "Warm hospitality, relaxing setting, great berry picking. Excellent food, comfortable rooms, outstanding scenery." *(GR)*

Open All year.
Rooms 1 cabin, 2 doubles—all with private bath and/or shower, radio, clock, fan, deck. Cabin with woodstove, refrigerator, barbecue.
Facilities Dining room, living room, den with TV/VCR, stereo; refrigerator, guest laundry, porch, patios, lawn furniture. 37 acres with creek, birding, children's swing set. Fly fishing nearby in Wild Horse River. 10–30 min. to skiing, hiking.
Location SE BC. 3 hrs. SW of Banff, Alberta. 5 min from historic Fort Steele. Turn at Esso Station in Fort Steele, go down hill to small bridge over Wild Horse Creek (on Wardner-Fort Steele Rd). Inn is 1 km on right.

Restrictions No smoking. Parents must be responsible for children.
Credit cards Visa.
Rates B&B, $95 cabin, $65–95 double, $55–85 single. Extra person, $20. Children under 2, free.
Extras Airport/station pickup. Crib. Some French spoken.

GOLD BRIDGE

TYAX Mountain Lake Resort 🏃 🎿 ♿
Tyaughton Lake Road, V0K 1P0

Tel: 250–238–2221
Fax: 250–238–2528
E-mail: Tyax@XL.ca

Located in the southern Chilcotin mountains, TYAX Mountain Lake Resort is the largest modern log-built lodge in western Canada, and was built in 1986. The resort's restaurant boasts a 30-foot-high freestanding stone fireplace, and overlooks the lake and mountains, as do the guest rooms. Each chalet is situated right on the lake, with a section of beach, and is surrounded by two acres of wooded land for privacy. "The lodge sits above lawns that sweep down to a crystal clear, glacier-fed lake. In the background is a circle of tall, craggy mountain peaks dusted with snow even in August. Our large room was done in pine, with a large, comfortable sofa, a firm double-size platform bed with an eiderdown quilt and lights on both sides; clean bathroom, and a wonderful porch overlooking the lake. Simple meals are served buffet-style. When we left, we took the 'back route' which came out above Whistler ski area. This was great fun but I'd recommend it only for experienced, hardy drivers." *(SC)* "To my kids' delight, the horses roam freely and graze on the lawn at night; booking our horseback rides when we make our reservations was a good idea. Our nonriders enjoyed fishing and sailing." *(MW)*

Open All year.
Rooms 5 3–6 bedroom chalets, 29 doubles—all with private bath and/or shower, desk, balcony. Some with TV. Chalets with kitchen, fireplace, canoe, private beach.
Facilities Dining room with fireplace, lobby, lounge with occasional weekend entertainment; children's playroom & bicycles; porch. 275 acres; 6000' on lake with beach, fishing, canoes, sailboat, windsurfer, paddle, motor boats. Tennis, hot tub, sauna, fitness center, playground, gazebo, horseshoes, volleyball, hiking, horseback riding, cross-country & heli-skiing, snowmobiling, ice-fishing, sleigh rides. Float-plane trips. 2 hrs to white-water rafting.
Location Central BC. 200 m N of Vancouver, 58 m W of Lillooet.
Restrictions No smoking in restaurant, on 3rd floor.
Credit cards Amex, MC, Visa.
Rates Room only, $140–400 chalet, $70–80 double, $60–70 single. Extra person, $20; no charge for children under 12 in parents' room. Crib or cot, $10 per day. Tipping encouraged. Weekly, package rates, also B&B, MAP rates. 2–3 night minimum. Alc lunch, $9; alc dinner, $15–25. *Rates in US dollars.*
Extras Limited wheelchair access. Pickups: rail, $70 per person.

GULF ISLANDS

Sitting like giant stepping stones between the mainland and Vancouver Island, the Gulf Islands are wooded hideaways that offer the very best of island life: tiny villages, deserted beaches, sweeping views of the Strait of Georgia and distant snowcapped mountains. Easily accessible by a web of ferry routes, the islands offer a pleasant contrast to the bustling cities of Vancouver and Victoria. Take your choice between northernmost Denman Island and those islands that are only minutes away from Victoria.

GULF ISLANDS—GALIANO ISLAND

Galiano Island rests almost in the middle of the Strait of Georgia, between Vancouver Island and the city of Vancouver.

Reader tip: "Galiano Island is shaped like a very long cigar. Although little of the coast is accessible (there's a steep cliff along its western side, almost no public access on the east), there is one superb area at the northern tip called Coon Bay, where sandstone has been carved into areas that look like Swiss cheese and other areas that look like huge gaping lions' mouths."

Information please: A short walk from the ferry is **The Bellhouse Inn** (Box 16, Site 4, Galiano Island V0N 1P0; 250–539–5667 or 800–970–7464), an 1890s farmhouse renovated in 1995 to provide such modern amenities as private balconies, and whirlpool or deep soaker tubs in the private baths; the decor is highlighted with antiques. Guests can relax in a hammock, play croquet, or just sit and enjoy the spectacular views from the quiet six-acre grounds. There are four guest rooms in the main house, and the B&B double rates of $110–150 include a full breakfast often served on the deck. Families enjoy the two housekeeping cabins on the waterfront, each with two bedrooms and full kitchens, with rates of $125 daily.

The **Woodstone Country Inn** (Georgeson Bay Road, R.R. #1, Galiano Island, V0N 1P0; 250–539–2022) was built in 1989, and seeks to offer guests a relaxed atmosphere in which to enjoy the island's natural beauty; boots, binoculars, and guidebooks are available for birding. To provide sustenance for these fresh-air endeavors, creative, four-course dinners are served. Twelve guest rooms are available, and B&B double rates range from $100–195, including a full breakfast and afternoon tea. Rooms overlook the valley or forest. "A pleasant place, overlooking a deer-filled meadow. Our room had a glass wall overlooking the meadow, plus a Jacuzzi." *(CH)* Reports welcome.

GULF ISLANDS—MAYNE ISLAND

Mayne Island is in the Gulf Islands of southwestern British Columbia and is approximately 30 miles from both Victoria and Vancouver. It can be reached by ferry from either Tsawwassen (just south of Vancouver) or from Vancouver Island. Heavily wooded, with rolling hills and a tiny village center, Mayne offers a variety of beaches from pebbled ones to small sandy coves surrounded by soft sandstone ledges that jut out into the Strait and have been so scoured by other stones that they resemble lace.

Oceanwood Country Inn ✗
630 Dinner Bay Road, V0N 2J0

Tel: 250–539–5074
Fax: 250–539–3002
E-mail: oceanwood@gulfislands.com

Owners Marilyn and Jonathan Chilvers, former residents of Vancouver, summered on Mayne Island for years; in 1990, they began offering their favorite things—good books, good music, good company, and good food and wine—to paying guests. Major renovation in 1995 increased the number of rooms to twelve and relocated the restaurant so that it now overlooks the water. The inn's dining room specializes in Northwest food and wine and has received widespread acclaim; the inn's gardens provide many of the vegetables which appear on the menu. Breakfasts include juice, yogurt, cereal, home-baked goods, and such entrees as poached eggs with salmon and a dilled hollandaise sauce, or blueberry buckwheat pancakes with homemade veal and pork sausage. Dinner menus change daily: a recent one included smoked tomato-cheddar cheese soup, a pancetta-spinach flan, entrees of broiled wild Coho salmon or braised lamb shank with thyme, and a dessert of Grand Marnier creme caramel.

"Warm hospitality from Marilyn and Johathan. A secluded oasis designed for quiet walks, evening hot tubs, wine and a good book in the common area or in front of a fireplace in your own room." *(Luann Cefola)* "Quiet seclusion; surrounded by woods and colorful gardens at the water's edge. Charming atmosphere, from the well-stocked library, to the pretty garden room, to the cozy living room." *(Miriam Myllymaki)* "Outstanding cuisine and good Canadian wines." *(Robin & Carol Malim)* "Warm hospitality; helpful innkeepers. Elegant afternoon tea with classical background music." *(Donna & John Ferrara-Kerr)* "The spacious Geranium Room has a view of the water from the private balcony, with handsome, simple Victorian-style furniture, and a comfortable bed. The main house has four common rooms, comfortably furnished with such details as telescopes for birdwatching, plus binoculars and bird guides." *(Susan Bliss)*

"Fresh flowers everywhere. In our bath, thick large towels and luxurious terry robes." *(Richard & JoAnn Sheldon)* "Spotlessly clean." *(Dorothy Westcott)* "The island is great for bicycling—hilly but manageable. Lots of space to sit out on decks and patio." *(Judith Shands)* "Marilyn and Jonathan are pleased to offer advice on day trips, or to chat about gardening, decorating, a favorite opera or whatever." *(George Medovoy)*

Open March 1–Nov. 30.
Rooms 12 doubles—all with private bath and/or shower. 8 with whirlpool or soaking tub, 7 with fireplace, 9 with private balcony.

Facilities Living room, dining room, library with fireplaces; garden room, game room. Meeting room. 10 acres on ocean with gardens; bicycles. Swimming, sailing, kayaking, fishing nearby.
Location From ferry, turn right on Dalton Dr. to Dinner Bay Rd.
Restrictions Smoking in library only. No children under 16.
Credit cards MC, Visa.
Rates B&B, $120–295 double, $110–285 single. 2-night weekend/holiday minimum. Prix fixe dinner, $35.
Extras Limited wheelchair access. French spoken.

GULF ISLANDS—NORTH PENDER ISLAND

Also recommended: For incredible water views, consider **Cliffside On-the-Sea** (Box 50, V0N2M0; 250–629–6691), with four guest rooms and B&B double rates of $135–185. "Our room looked over the water, the islands, and Mt. Baker; the hot tub is on a deck off the beautiful glass-walled dining room. The Garden Suite has a queen-size bed and a fireplace while the Channel View suite has a king-size bed and a living room with fireplace. Owner Penny Tomlin likes to help guests with all those little details that make a pleasant stay; her cooking is excellent, and the staff is charming and gracious. In the afternoon, tea and fresh cookies await in the lounge. A lovely island, with lots of artists and galleries to browse, walks to take and whales to watch." *(Norma & Bob Simon)*

GULF ISLANDS—SALT SPRING ISLAND

Largest of the Gulf Islands; people come to relax and enjoy the pretty, rustic setting. Activities include all water sports—both ocean and lake—as well as hiking, tennis, horseback riding, and golf.

Salt Spring Island is 20 m north of Victoria and is accessible via ferry from Victoria or Vancouver or float plane from Vancouver or Seattle.

Information please: Current reports are needed on the well-known **Hastings House** (160 Upper Ganges Road, V8K 2S2; 250–537–2362 or 800–661–9255), an elegant seaside farm estate, composed of five restored buildings—the Manor House, the Farmhouse, Cliffside, the Post, and the Barn. The Tudor-style Manor House contains the inn's dining and common rooms, while the eight guest rooms and suites are spread out among the inn's buildings. Known for its food, the five-course dinners feature fresh produce and herbs from the inn's gardens, eggs from its hen house, and local lamb and seafood. B&B double rates range from $255–490, including breakfast and afternoon tea. Ouch.

For peace and serenity, and magnificent views of Sansum Narrows, call the **Summerhill Guest House** (209 Chu-An Drive, V8K 1H9; 250–537–2727). The three tastefully decorated guest rooms have private baths, cozy duvets, bathrobes, and excellent reading lights at bedside. Guests can relax in front of the fire in the oceanside sitting room; the double rates of $95–115 include a full breakfast served in quiet, casual surroundings overlooking the water. Reports welcome.

KELOWNA

Also recommended: "Appropriately named, **A View To Remember B&B** (1090 Trevor Drive, V1Z 2J8; 250–769–4028) has a spectacular view of Okanagan Lake and the vineyards. Lovely home, with friendly innkeeper and gourmet breakfasts." *(WVE)* There are three rooms, all with private bath and double or queen-size beds; guests can stroll through the gardens or relax on the sunny patio. Double rates range from $70–80 and include a full breakfast.

"An impressive home in an exclusive neighborhood, the **Augusta View B&B** (998 Augusta Court, V1Y 7T9; 250–763–0969) has three guest rooms. Ours had a double bed, single bed, and a lovely sitting area all cozily decorated with antiques. There's a private guest entrance and lounge. Hosts Kurt and Edith Grube were friendly and treated you as one of the family. Wide choice of food for breakfast, and it varied daily." *(WVE)* The B&B double rates are $60–85.

Kelowna is located in south central BC. For an additional area inn, see **Vernon.**

KOOTENAY NATIONAL PARK

For additional area inns, see **Fairmont Hot Springs** and **Banff,** Alberta.

Kootenay Park Lodge ¢ 👤 ♿
Vermilion Crossing,
Box 1390, Banff Alberta T0L 0C0

Tel: 403–762–9196
Fax: 403–262–5028
E-mail: mntlodge@telusplanet.net

Kootenay National Park was created as part of a 1920s deal to build the first motor road across the Continental Divide in Canada: the provinces ceded the land, the government built the road, and the Canadian Pacific Railway built the tourist accommodations. Known as the Vermilion River Camp when constructed in 1923, it was purchased by Paul Holscher in 1991 and renamed Kootenay Park Lodge. In 1997 he opened the Vermilion Crossing Visitor's Center, offering an expanded general store and an information center to provide backcountry permits, fishing licenses, and maps in a relaxing atmosphere.

The restaurant serves breakfast from 8 to 10 A.M.; in addition to the usual cereal, eggs and bacon, there are fruit-topped crepes, and eggs Benedict. The dinner menu offers traditional favorites with a twist: roast turkey with a whole cranberry and sherry cream sauce; poached rainbow trout with hollandaise; spaghetti with a chunky veggie-tomato meat sauce; plus burgers, salads, and crepes; and for dessert, homemade fruit clafoutis with raspberry sauce.

"Circled by tall firs, the Kootenay Park Lodge consists of a series of log cabins, as well as a main lodge with delightful wraparound porch. The lodge's cozy atmosphere centers around the central stone fireplace, library corner, and calming background music. The restaurant's food was most tasty, and while the menu was not extensive, there was ample variety and a nice wine list. The clean, neat cabins have a main room with queen-size bed, casual chairs, and small bathroom; outside is a porch with chairs for mountain watching. Excellent service, leisurely pace, genuine rusticity, quiet atmosphere, friendly people." *(Bob & Lyn Vivenzio)* "A homey, old-fashioned place. Nobody's in a hurry, nobody is pretentious. A perfect place to read, hike, and enjoy your cabin's fireplace. Reasonably priced for a popular tourist area." *(Bill MacGowan)*

Open Mid-May–late Sept.
Rooms 10 cabins—all with private shower bath, desk, coffee maker, porch. 9 with mini-refrigerator, 7 with fireplace, 6 with hot plate, 1 with kitchen.
Facilities Restaurant with fireplace, lodge with fireplace, library; guest laundry, porch. Visitor center/general store. 5 acres in Kootenay National Park with hiking trails. Near river for fishing, canoeing/kayaking, whitewater rafting.
Location SE BC. 70 km SW of Banff, 200 km W of Calgary. From Banff, go W on Hwy 1 (Trans-Canada Hwy) 30 km to Hwy 93 S. Go 42 km to lodge.
Restrictions Smoking permitted in some cabins.
Credit cards MC, Visa.
Rates Room only, $50–90 double. Extra person, $5. Children under 5 free in parents' cabin. Cot, $10. Kitchen utensils, $7. Alc breakfast, $7; lunch, $10; alc dinner, $18.
Extras Limited wheelchair access. Bus stops at lodge. Pets allowed. Crib. French, Dutch, German spoken.

LADNER

Ladner is a farming community located on the Fraser River delta, fifteen minutes south of Vancouver, convenient to the Tsawwassen ferry.

Information please: "A river runs through it" could describe the floating cottage at the **River Run Cottage & Breakfast** (4551 River Road West, Ladner V4K 1R9; 604–946–7778). In addition, three landbased cottages perch on pilings at the river's edge, and all of them have a private bath (some with Jacuzzi or two-person soaking tub), telephone, TV, refrigerator, microwave, CD player, and fireplace. Breakfast is brought to your door at your choice of time between 8 and 10 A.M., and might include fresh squeezed orange juice, Starbucks coffee, homebaked cinnamon buns, fresh fruit, and eggs Benedict. Double rates range from $95–175, with discounts for multinight stays.

MALAHAT

Information please: Austrians Leo and Maria Schuster were reminded of southern Europe when they saw this mountainside property 30 minutes north of Victoria, and they designed **The Aerie** (600 Ebedora Lane, VOR 2LO; 250–743–7115) as a Mediterranean-style villa that seems to cascade down the hill. Luxuriously and romantically designed with waterfalls, garden paths, gazebos and patios to take in the dramatic views of the Strait of Juan de Fuca and the Olympic Mountains, the inn is especially appealing for weddings and honeymoons. Rates for the twenty guest rooms, all with private bath, are $150–395; a European-style continental breakfast is included. The Aerie's dining room is highly regarded, with the freshest of Northwest cuisine with a French touch; there's also an indoor swimming pool, indoor and outdoor hot tubs, spa services, and a tennis court. The Aerie is affiliated with Relais et Chateaux and has a four-diamond AAA rating.

QUADRA ISLAND

If fishing is your passion, then head for the Inland Passage and Quadra Island where salmon are the game of choice. Quadra is located about 20 miles north of Courtenay, and accessible by ferry from Campbell River.

Information please: You can take a float plane directly to the dock of the **April Point Lodge & Fishing Resort** (P.O. Box 1, Campbell River, V9W 4Z9; 250–285–2222 or 888–334–FISH). This 65-room lodge, on 200 acres, offers heli-fishing as well as heli-hiking, native feasts, and barbecue picnics on the beach; guides can take you salmon fishing, and your catch will be prepared for the journey home. Guests choose between cabins or guest rooms, many with fireplace, kitchenettes, or hot tubs. Rates range from $99–395; 50% discount off-season. Reports welcome.

Set on Cape Mudge, **Tsa-Kwa-Luten Lodge** (P.O. Box 460, Quathiaski Cove, Quadra Island V0P 1N0; 250–285–2042 or 800–665–7745) is the only resort in Canada featuring authentic Pacific Coast native food, art and cultural activities. Guests can partake of the area's legendary fishing; they're also invited to take part in ceremonial dances and feasts as a way of learning about the culture of the Kwagiulth People who own and operate the lodge. "Dramatic lobby with huge timbers and a 45-foot-high ceiling; it's modeled after a traditional native longhouse. Decorations include dramatic carved masks, petroglyph rubbings, a huge carved ceremonial screen, and century-old photos of local villages and ceremonies. Our room, with vaulted ceiling, had tan walls, wine-colored accents, Northwest Indian artwork, and knotty pine furniture." *(SC)* There are 26 suites and four 2-bedroom cabins, all with private bath (some with whirlpool). A vacation package, including breakfast and dinner, is $145 for two; regular rates (no meals) are $115–240; and substantial off-season discounts are available in spring and fall. Reports appreciated.

QUALICUM BEACH

Qualicum Beach is located on Vancouver Island, about two and a half hours north of Victoria. A popular summer resort, it's known for its sunny weather and white sand beaches.

Reader tip: "Qualicum Beach, a major retirement center, is a pleasant little town with some good restaurants, lots of interesting shops, and challenging courses for the golfer. The beach is long, sandy, and reasonably warm. Parksville to the south has an even larger beach, but traffic is terrible in season and the urban sprawl unappealing." *(Bradley Lockner)*

Bahari B&B   *Tel:* 250–752–9278
5101 Island Highway West, V9K 1Z1   *Fax:* 250–752–9038
E-mail: lhooper@macn.bc.ca

A contemporary house built by Yvonne and Len Hooper in 1990, the Bahari B&B overlooks the Georgia Strait and the northern Gulf Islands. Guests enjoy watching sea lions cavort and seals bask in the sun, or shucking oysters on the beach. The Hoopers opened their home to B&B guests in 1992, enhancing the pleasing blend of traditional and modern decor with the finest quality all-cotton bed linens, eiderdown comforters, and queen-, king-, or extra-long twin size beds; most rooms have unobstructed ocean views. Breakfast is served from 7:30 to 9 A.M. at the time chosen the night before and with the entrees selected—perhaps strawberry crepes with cream cheese filling, honey-orange French toast, sauteed shrimp and vegetables with poached egg, or whole wheat hotcakes.

"High-quality amenities and warm hospitality." *(JT)* "The library has an inviting seating area and a great view, as does the balcony. Our room was spotless, and the bath well supplied with robes, hair dryer, and soaps. Quiet spot, nicely landscaped." *(Donald Gow)* "Good-sized rooms, fine service, outstanding homemade meals." *(Wendy Stanhope)*

Open Feb.–Nov.
Rooms 1 2-bedroom apartment, 3 doubles—all with private bath, radio, clock, fan, deck/balcony. 2 with fireplace.
Facilities Dining room, living room, library, guest refrigerator, deck. 7 acres with hot tub, lawn games. Boating, ocean swimming nearby.
Location 8 km N of town on right side of Island Hwy.
Restrictions No smoking. B&B guest rooms not appropriate for children.
Credit cards MC, Visa.
Rates Room only (apartment), $120–180. B&B (guest rooms), $70–120 double.
Extras Airport/station pickups, $15.

Blue Willow B&B ¢ ♦♦   *Tel:* 250–752–9052
524 Quatna Road, V9K 1B4   *Fax:* 250–752–9039

The blue and white china, from which the Blue Willow inn gains its name, highlights the decor of this Tudor-style cottage with leaded glass windows and beamed ceilings, owned by John and Arlene England.

"Guests especially enjoy our English Cottage garden," notes Arlene. She also explains that "warm ocean currents make the Qualicum Beach a popular location for seaside activities. The town has a profusion of flowers, small delightful shops, and an excellent art gallery." Breakfasts, often served on the patio amid Arlene's beautiful gardens, include home-baked treats and a choice of a continental or full English breakfast.

"The Garden Suite was perfect for our family; its decor was pleasant, comfortable, informal. Excellent bathroom with an abundance of towels, good shower, and tub; beds were comfortable and firm. Gorgeous gardens, with a profusion of flowers and mature trees with separate garden areas and paths for contemplation and relaxation. Arlene's breakfasts were elegantly served, most delicious, and thoroughly filling." *(Bradley Lockner)* "Delightful decor, in typical English tradition; picture-perfect bedrooms with furniture, linens, and wallpaper matching and in elegant good taste. Breakfast is served on blue willow china at the dining room table; all guests are courteously introduced and conversation proceeds in an informal, friendly, and relaxed manner. Both John and Arlene are a delight to talk with, enjoy being hosts, and are most accommodating." *(R. L. Sather)* "These lovely people never encroached on our privacy." *(Peggy King)* "Serene setting. Ask about the shortcut for a beautiful walk past some gorgeous property on the beach at Judge's Row. Rooms are exceptionally clean and neat; some have a private bath across the hall." *(Owen Halliday)*

Open All year.
Rooms 1 2-bedroom suite, 3 doubles—all with private bath and/or shower, radio, desk. Suite in separate building.
Facilities Dining/breakfast room, guest lounge with TV/VCR, desk, books. Laundry facility. Off-road parking. Golf, swimming, boat rentals, boat ramps nearby.
Location Vancouver Island. From Victoria or Nanaimo follow Island Hwy. N to Qualicum. Turn left at Qualicum Rd., right on Quatna Rd. to inn.
Restrictions No smoking.
Credit cards MC, Visa.
Rates B&B, $70–95 suite, double. Extra person, $20. Family rates.
Extras Airport/station pickup. French, German spoken.

---

70 MILE HOUSE

It's not a typo—the name of this town is truly 70 Mile House, a rural community five hours north of Vancouver, about 150 kilometers northwest of Kamloops, and 30 miles south of 100 Mile House.

Information please: The **Flying U Ranch** (P.O. Box 69, 70 Mile House V0K 2K0; 250–456–7717) is the oldest guest ranch in Canada, and sits on 40,000 acres on the north shore of Green Lake. Guests can saddle up one of 120 horses from 9 A.M. to 4 P.M. each day with a packed lunch. There are rustic log cabins with woodstoves, hand-hewn log furniture, and electricity. A central shower house provides basic shower and toilet facilities; a co-ed 15-person sauna eases the aches and pains of a day on horseback. Per person rates of $125 daily, $750 weekly (less for kids) include all meals, served family-style.

SOOKE

Sooke sits on a natural harbor formed by the Jordan River; forestry and fishing feature prominently in the economy, and a festival of logging sports is held every July. Located at the southwestern end of Vancouver Island, an especially scenic portion of Highway 14 runs the 27 miles east from Victoria to Sooke.

Also recommended: With only two rooms, the **Richview House** (7031 Richview Drive, RR #4, V0S 1N0; 250–642–5520) is too small for a full entry, but we've received rave reports about its gracious and informative hosts, Joan and Francois Gething; the lovely setting overlooking the Strait of Juan de Fuca and the Olympic Mountains; the comfortable, private rooms; and the delicious three-course breakfasts, included in the $175–195 double rate. "Spacious, private, light, and airy." *(Cathy Bahn & Jeff Flax)* "Hosts were friendly but not intrusive." *(Don & Connie Hall)* "Eggs from their hens for lighter-than-air crepes, homemade French bread toast. The view is enhanced by the lovely gardens." *(T. Drake)* "Timber and stucco-style house. Each guest room has a queen-sized bed, down comforter, Jacuzzi on a private deck, and a wood-burning fireplace. Just a three-minute walk to Sooke Harbour House." *(Stephanie Pietromonaco).* "Expert carpentry, decorating and cooking." *(Margaret Sievers, and others)*

Ocean Wilderness Inn
109 West Coast Road,
RR #2, V0S 1N0

Tel: 250–646–2116
800–323–2116
Fax: 250–646–2317
E-mail: ocean@sookenet.com

To commemorate a special occasion, guests at the Ocean Wilderness can plant a tree; owner Marion Rolston will provide the watering can, shovel, and a Douglas fir seedling. Built in 1930, this log home has a wooded oceanfront setting, and was restored as a B&B in 1989; most guest rooms have lovely ocean views from the deck or picture window. Guests can soak in the private hot tub in the Japanese-style gazebo overlooking the ocean and Olympic Mountains. One-half hour before breakfast, a silver service of coffee or tea, is delivered to each guest door. In addition to muffins, juice and fresh fruit, breakfast might include a spinach roulade with grilled tomatoes.

"Delightful seaside location with private beach." *(Trish Rankin)* "Romantic, rustic yet extremely comfortable and most relaxing. The food and hospitality were superb." *(Steele Jordan)* "Marion and Richard were good sources of information about what to do and where to go." *(Timothy & Jodie Emmons)* "One day we cooked our catch of salmon and Dungeness crabs on the beach, while a couple of seals watched from offshore and a bald eagle flew overhead." *(CH)* "An old log cabin filled with interesting antiques; guest rooms are new, elegant, and luxurious.

My room had a four-poster bed, polished wood floor, beautiful carpets, and a large, spotless bathroom, supplied with fluffy white bathrobes. Marion made us feel right at home. She prepares the food, assisted by her son. On an absolutely beautiful evening, dinner was served on the beach—corn chowder, barbecued salmon, just-caught shrimp and crab; rice pilaf, green salad, fresh fruit, and Marion's wonderful biscuits. The tables were set with white linens, silverware, and fresh flowers. Breakfast was elegantly served in the dining room—endless coffee, fresh fruit, more feather-light biscuits, and individual cheese soufflés." *(Barb Voynovich, and others)*

Open All year.
Rooms 9 doubles—all with full private bath, radio, clock. 8 with refrigerator. 3 with double soaking tub. 2 with deck.
Facilities Dining room, porch, 4 patios. 5 acres with hot tub in gazebo, gardens.
Location 8.5 m from town. From only traffic light in town, go 8.5 m to inn.
Restrictions No smoking.
Credit cards MC, Visa.
Rates B&B, $85–175 double. Extra person, $15–25. Prix fixe dinner by reservation.
Extras One room wheelchair accessible.

Sooke Harbour House ✕ ⚹
1528 Whiffen Spit Road, RR 4, V0S 1N0

Tel: 250–642–3421
800–889–9688
Fax: 250–642–6988
E-mail: shh@islandnet.com

Sooke Harbour House, a small white clapboard farmhouse, sits on a bluff overlooking Whiffen Spit. Originally built in the 1930s, the inn was expanded first in 1986 to provide additional guest rooms, and again in 1996. Rates include breakfast, brought to your room, and lunch in the dining room. Frederique and Sinclair Philip, owners of this inn, describe it as being located on the "edge of the wilderness, with whales, otters, seals, bears, cougars, and bald eagles nearby. Honeymooners love the romantic location, while adventurous diners can try the sea urchins, sea cucumber, pickled kelp, lavender ice cream, edible flower salads, and more." Known as one of Canada's best restaurants, menus change daily and feature the freshest possible local organic foods, creatively prepared. The inn's garden is home to hundreds of edible flowers and herbs, along with summer and winter salad greens, vegetables, fresh fruits, and berries. A spring dinner might include oyster soup with salmon dumplings; roast veal with pepper glaze or ginger-steamed salmon with crab; and a bittersweet chocolate parfait in puff pastry.

"A place to relieve stress, recharge internal batteries, and treat your taste buds." *(Arnold Hobson, Jr.)* "Superb wine list." *(Sally Morgan & Lionel Sandner)* "Friendly, helpful staff." *(Rollin Geppert)* "The Native American art in our spacious room was exquisite, yet comforting." *(John Lane)* "The 'Edible Blossom' Room has a split-level design, and ceramic tiles to match." *(Jack & Sue Lane)* "The Beach Room is one of the smallest, but was most comfortable, with a decanter of port by the bed." *(Lynne Derry)* "A Jacuzzi soak by moonlight was wonderful." *(Ross Thomson)* "Our room had seashells and books of local interest, an unlimited supply of real firewood, plus thick robes, fresh fruit and cookies, freshly ground coffee, and a coffeemaker; the refrigerator held real cream and bottled water. Grounds are well-kept, but informal—an eight-foot rosemary bush was next to our Jacuzzi." *(Kingsley & Sharon Johnson)* "Delectable food with superb awareness of subtle flavors, tremendous variety of regional ingredients." *(Ian Cameron & Maryaleen Trafford)*

Open All year.

Rooms 18 suites, 9 doubles—all with private bath, radio, desk, fireplace, balcony, or terrace. Some with Jacuzzi, stocked wetbar, or hot tub.

Facilities Restaurant, dining/breakfast rooms with fireplace, lounge, library, living room. Musical entertainment some weekends. 3 acres with herb, flower, vegetable gardens; orchard, beach for water sports. Massage therapists by appointment. Hiking nearby. 2½ hrs. to downhill, cross-country skiing.

Location 1 m from town. Take Hwy. 14 for ⅜ m past Otter Point Rd. (at Gulf station), turn onto Whiffen Spit Rd. to inn.

Restrictions No smoking.

Credit cards Amex, Enroute, MC, Visa.

Rates B&B plus lunch (except Aug.), $200–280 double. 15% service. Extra person, $27. Tipping only for meals. Alc dinner, $65.

Extras 3 guest rooms equipped for disabled. Pets by prior arrangement, $20. Crib by prior arrangement. French spoken.

TOFINO

Information please: Favorite travel seasons are usually based on a pleasing climate or appealing activities; at the **Wickaninnish Inn** (Osprey Lane at Chesterman Beach, P.O. Box 250, V0R 2Z0; 250–725–3100 or 800–333–4604) guests come during the Pacific storm season just to watch the 25-foot waves roll in. Built in 1996, the Wickaninnish is a three-story, weathered cedar building perched on a rocky promontory at the westernmost point of Chesterman Beach, on Vancouver Island's rugged west coast. Each of the 46 spacious guest rooms has an ocean view, queen- or king-size bed with down comforter, fireplace, kitchenette, deep soaker tub, terry robes, and a private balcony. The Pointe restaurant showcases fresh seafood and Pacific Northwest wines. Double rates are $140–320; the winter storm package includes use of rain gear!

UCLUELET

A Snug Harbour Inn   *Tel:* 250–726–2686
Box 367, 460 Marine Drive, V0R 3A0   *Toll-free:* 888–936–5222
                                          Fax: 250–726–2685
                                          E-mail: asnughbr@island.net

Set in a private, old-growth forest overlooking the rugged, dramatic west coast of Vancouver Island, Snug Harbour Inn provides an intriguing, romantic experience. From its many decks and windows, guests can look through powerful binoculars, watching for eagles, migrating whales, and distant ships. When it's time to warm up, the huge stone fireplace and inviting conversation pit make the great Room an appealing spot to socialize. Denise and Skip Rowland, who built this contemporary-style inn in 1996, also offer charter helicopter flights for guests wishing to whale watch, picnic lunch on glaciers, go wilderness touring where there are no roads, or just go flight-seeing. A breakfast of muffins, pastry, fruit, and juice is served from 8 to 11 A.M. at tables set around the great room.

"Immaculately clean and tidy; welcoming, courteous hosts." *(Margaret Mann)* "Lots of privacy, yet lots of conversation. Good parking and easy to find." *(Sheron Erickson)* "Skip and Denise share warm laughter and enjoyable conversation with one and all." *(Vicky Gardner)* "The coastal environment has rugged, tranquil beauty." *(Greg & Noriko Smith)* "Our Sawadee room was decorated in Thai style, in rich shades of blue, with beautiful wood carvings and wall hangings. The linens are top-of-the-line. Awesome bathroom with two-person tub, shower and beautiful stained glass window; towels are fluffy and thick." *(MK)* "Nicely set tables, with linen napkins and lovely china." *(Elizabeth Ashbaugh)* "Elegant rooms, with exceptional comfort and class, fine furnishings, and attention to all details. Our bath was a dream come true—fireplace, double Jacuzzi, heated floors, superb cleanliness. The nautical theme and marine charts and equipment in the common room were fascinating, the views terrific. Skip was friendly, warm, and full of wonderful tales of adventure at sea." *(Kerry Dawson)* "The Great Room, focal point of the Inn, overlooks the rocky harbour below; a staircase leads from the deck to the private beach below the cliff." *(Gerald Steele)* "We felt extra special and pampered." *(Cerese Carlstrom)*

Open All year.

Rooms 2 suites, 2 doubles—all with full private bath with whirlpool tub, clock, fireplace, balcony. Cordless phone available.

Facilities Great room with fireplace. 1 acre with hot tub, stairway down cliff to helicopter pad. Private beach with boating, sport fishing. Nearby hiking trails.

Location W coast of Vancouver Island; 175 N of Victoria. 1 m to town center. From Ucluelet, take Peninsula Dr. to right on Marine Dr. to inn at end.

Restrictions No smoking. "Children over 14; those younger not encouraged due to cliff location."

Credit cards MC, Visa.

Rates B&B, $160–280 suite, $120–250 double/single. Extra person, $25.

Extras Airport pickup, $25; free bus pickup. Thai spoken.

VANCOUVER

Dramatically situated on a peninsula where towering mountains sweep down to the sea, Vancouver is Canada's loveliest city. At once cosmopolitan and amiable, Vancouver offers exciting cultural, shopping, and recreational opportunities. The compact heart of the city is located on a tiny peninsula, one-half of which is Stanley Park, known for its gardens, zoo, golf course, bathing beach, and jogging trails. Downtown Vancouver is a wonderful amalgam of apartment houses, hotels, sidewalk cafes, smart shops, galleries, and office buildings. It is lively, clean, and safe, and bubbles with people late into the night.

Vancouver's rich ethnic mix adds to its charm and makes for diverse shopping and dining adventures. Chinatown and nearby Japantown are a jumble of exotic markets, shops, and restaurants. In south Vancouver (near Main and 49th) is a thriving East Indian community where you can buy beautiful silk saris and outrageously colored sweets. The Greeks and Italians have also left their mark on this wonderful city.

Originally a tidal flat known as Mud Island, Granville Island had developed by 1930 into an industrial park. In the late 1970s the island was the focus of a major waterfront redevelopment project, and it is now home to a variety of commercial and artistic endeavors: a public market, selling everything from mussels to bagels; a kids' market and water-play park; a brewery; two theaters; and a variety of trendy cafes and boutiques, restaurants, and art galleries. Although fun for families and shoppers alike, one reader warned that "parking is impossible, so take the False Creek ferry if you do go." She goes on to note that another restored area is Gastown, "a well-conceived redevelopment area with charming restored buildings and an interesting steam clock."

Do *not* miss a trip to the Museum of Anthropology on the campus of the University of British Columbia. In a dramatic building designed by Arthur Erickson, you will see 40-foot totem poles, ancient canoes, and other items emphasizing the artistic diversity of the Northwest Coast Indians.

For a wonderful view of southeastern British Columbia, go up to the top of 3,900-foot Grouse Mountain where you can see the city of Vancouver, the Gulf Islands, the Fraser River, the Strait of Georgia, and, on a clear day, the Olympic Mountains in Washington State. In winter you can ski here in the morning, then lunch in town. Visit Andusen Botanical Gardens for vibrant displays of flowers during the spring and summer.

Vancouver is located in the southwest corner of the mainland of British Columbia.

Reader tip: "We enjoyed dinner at the Shanghai Chinese Bistro downtown and had a great lunch in Chinatown at the Buddhist Vegetarian Restaurant." *(KLH)* "Very few Vancouver inns have air-conditioning—if you're visiting in the summer, ask if fans are available (although they're rarely needed)." *(MW)*

Also recommended—hotels: For a reasonably priced hotel with an excellent West End location consider **The Barclay Hotel** (1348 Robson Street, V6E 1C5; 604–688–8850), built in the 1920s and renovated in 1988. The 85 guest rooms have rates of $59–149. It's modest, simply furnished, but comfortable; no elevator or bellhops.

A 21-story European-style boutique hotel built in 1986, **The Sutton Place Hotel** (845 Burrard Street, V6Z 2K6; 604–682–5511 or 800–961–7555) has 397 luxuriously appointed guest rooms and suites, with amenities that include the daily newspaper, stocked mini-bar, two telephone lines, plush bathrobes, and an umbrella. There's a restaurant, lounge, shops, and a fitness/beauty spa; next door is an 18-story luxury travel apartment complex **La Grande Residence at The Sutton Place Hotel** for stays of seven nights or longer. Rates range from $270–605 suite, $195–455 double; children under 18 stay free. "While a large hotel, the atmosphere is that of an intimate luxury hotel. My room had period reproduction decor, floral fabrics, and soft peach-colored wallpaper." *(SC)* "Elegantly appointed room, with marble bath; both quite compact. Good location. Uninspired breakfast buffet." *(JH)*

A modern 489-room hotel, the **Waterfront Centre Hotel** (900 Canada Place Way, V6C 3L5; 604–691–1991 or 800–441–1414) offers panoramic views of the harbor, and is linked to a concourse of shops and the convention center. Double rates are $190–250. "Our clean, attractive room had curved glass walls with harbor and city views. Quiet, convenient location, just across the street from the cruise terminal, and two blocks from the Gaslamp district." *(KLH)*

Also recommended—B&Bs: With a convenient, quiet West End location, the **English Bay Inn** (1968 Comox Street, V6G 1R4; 604–683–8002) is a traditionally decorated 1939 Tudor-style home. The B&B double rates of $180–275 include a full breakfast and afternoon sherry; the five guest rooms have private baths. "Rooms well decorated in a variety of antique styles. The large, bright breakfast room brought everyone together in the morning, and its gas fireplace provided a welcoming glow throughout my visit. The location is perfect for a weekend in Stanley Park or visiting nearby Denman Street restaurants." *(Christopher Johnston)*

Fifteen minutes from downtown Vancouver is **Laburnum Cottage** (1388 Terrace Avenue, North Vancouver V7R 1B4; 604–988–4877), a Victorian-style home set in a half-acre of beautifully kept English gardens, surrounded by virgin forest. B&B double rates include a full breakfast, and are $160 double, $240 for the garden cottages. "Truly wonderful; great landscaping; good food. Owner Delphine Masterton is a darling, rooted in the community; a super innkeeper who welcomes you warmly, but gives you space." *(Ned Shanks)*

Information please—B&Bs: The **Beachside B&B** (4208 Evergreen Avenue, West Vancouver V7V1H1; 604–922–7773 or 800–563–3311) is a contemporary home located on a tranquil beach, with magnificent views of Lions Gate Bridge, English Bay and Vancouver skyline. Long-time owners Gordon and Joan Gibbs serve a full breakfast, included in the B&B double rates of $120–250. Each of the five guest rooms has a private bath and TV/VCR; some also have a Jacuzzi and fireplace.

A contemporary-style mansion with floor-to-ceiling windows overlooking English Bay, **The Palms Guest House** (3042 Marine Drive, West Vancouver, V7V 1M4; 604–926–1159 or 800–691–4455), was built in 1996 by Heidi Schmidt. The decor throughout reflects Heidi's experience as an interior designer, with antiques tastefully highlighting the light-filled spaces. The four guest rooms have private baths, queen-, king-, or twin beds, down duvets, fine linens, and spectacular ocean and city views from private balconies; the Master Suite has a double Jacuzzi, king-size canopy bed, and a fireplace. The B&B double rates of $150–225 include afternoon tea and a breakfast of fruit, freshly squeezed orange juice, a hot entree, and freshly baked breads.

For additional area inns, convenient to the Tsawwassen Ferry, see **Ladner** and also **Port Roberts, Washington.**

Columbia Cottage Guest House
205 West 14th Avenue, V5Y 1X2

Tel: 604–874–5327
Fax: 604–879–2128

"A small neatly kept Tudor-style cottage devotedly run like a miniature inn. Close to City Hall and a modern shopping complex, it's on a quiet, tree-lined, residential street only blocks from the Cambie Street Bridge. The rooms are well laid out—ours was a charming upstairs back room, comfortably and tastefully furnished with a king-size bed, antiques, and well-chosen artwork on the walls. The bath had a modern shower and an ample supply of luxury towels. A second bedroom was separated from ours by a small, nicely laid out lounge area and a sink and sideboard for making tea and coffee. Coffee and iced tea are offered during the day as well as sherry and nuts in the early evening in the inviting common room on the main floor. Breakfasts include homemade muffins, omelets, French toast, and fresh fruit. The intimate dining room was set with lace tablecloths, beautiful china, and a pleasant view of the front garden. Classical music quietly plays throughout the day and evening. Special little touches were the homemade cookies at bedside and the robes and slippers for lounging." *(Colin & Kay Bailey)* "Innkeepers Susanne Sulzberger and Alisdair Smith are friendly and helpful, the food very good. Immaculately clean. Just three blocks to the bus; excellent location, quiet, with fine restaurants nearby." *(R. Mikel Westwood)* "Cozy, comfortable room; the window fan kept us cool on a warm August night. The two inn dogs were wonderful." *(KO)*

Open All year.
Rooms 1 suite, 4 doubles—all with full private bath.
Facilities Dining room, living room, guest pantry. Garden with patio, fountain. On-street parking.
Location 7 min. from downtown. At corner of W. 14th Ave. & Columbia St.
Restrictions No smoking.
Credit cards MC, Visa.
Rates B&B, $130–160 suite, $80–135 double/single. Extra person, $20.

Johnson House B&B ¢
2278 West 34th Street, V6M 1G6

Tel: 604–266–4175
Fax: 604–266–4175

Innkeeper Sandy Johnson tells us that "after ten years of renovating we have actually finished restoring our Craftsman-style home and decorating it with an eclectic selection of antiques and collectibles. Our bedrooms have antique king- or queen-size beds with comfortable modern mattresses; the plumbing and wiring are all new, although many old fixtures have been refitted. Breakfast includes good strong coffee, juice, homemade jams, homebaked muffins or scones, bacon or sausage, and whole wheat-oatmeal pancakes, French toast, or eggs. Blueberries, strawberries, raspberries, and grapes grown on the property are served in season. The rock and rhododendron gardens create an incredible spring display with hundreds of flowering bulbs, accented with antique Indonesian sculptures."

"Incredibly relaxed environment with careful attention to detail. Breakfasts were original, fresh, and bountiful." *(Chris Peoples)* "The spotless Carousel Room has windows that open, a marvelous bathroom, and comfortable bed." *(Jacqueline Townsend)* "Wonderful collectibles: double-wheeled iron coffee mill, old clocks, tin containers, wind-up gramophones with trumpet horns, and more. The spacious bedrooms have beautiful patchwork quilts, with ample storage space. The bathrooms are supplied with ample towels and a variety of toiletries. Guests can relax in the small but lovely garden; adequate parking on the quiet street." *(Maurice & Carol Murphy)* "Pleasant neighborhood for walking." *(Tim McMulden)* "Convenient location, accessible to city bus stops." *(Philip & Susie Loh)* "Excellent view of the harbor and mountains." *(Susan Izumi)* "Warm hospitality, inviting garden for relaxing and reading. Great mix of people around the breakfast table, combined with a superb breakfast to enhance our stay." *(Phyllis & Dan Pliskow)*

Open All year.
Rooms 1 suite, 3 doubles—all with private bath and/or shower, radio, fan; 2 with desk.
Facilities Dining room; living room with fireplace, TV/VCR, stereo, books; porch, deck. 2 m to ocean, beaches.
Location Kerrisdale district. 10 min. drive from city center. From downtown, go S on Granville, W on 33, S on Vine to inn at corner of 34th & Vine.
Restrictions No smoking. No children under 11.
Credit cards None accepted.
Rates B&B, $120–155 suite, $75–105 double, $65–145 single. 2-night summer minimum.

Kenya Court Ocean Front Guest House
2230 Cornwall Avenue, V6K 1B5

Tel: 604–738–7085

On English Bay, with a rooftop view of Stanley Park, ocean, mountains, and downtown Vancouver, is the Kenya Court Ocean Front Guest House, a three-story heritage apartment building constructed in Art Deco style. Guest rooms have king-, queen- or twin-size beds, and families will appreciate the separate entrance and spacious two-bedroom suites. "Most reasonable rates for a great deal of space. The innkeeper, Dorothy Williams, serves a breakfast of juice, fruit, cereal, fresh breads and croissants." *(KC)* "Our first-floor apartment had a large living room, small dining room, fully equipped kitchen, two bedrooms and a bathroom; all was clean and simply furnished with pieces from the 1950s, with a comfortable king-size bed. Across the street is a great park with views of downtown Vancouver, the soaring mountains north of Vancouver, and the bay. Breakfast was served in the rooftop solarium with view of the bay and mountains. We had grapefruit halves, orange juice and melon, bread and muffins; at our request, Mrs. Williams also prepared eggs and bacon." *(SC)*

Open All year.
Rooms 8 1–2 bedroom suites—all with private bath and/or shower, private entrance, kitchenette.
Facilities Rooftop breakfast solarium. Tennis, saltwater swimming pool, jogging trails across the street. Walking distance to Granville Market, Fourth Avenue.
Location On English Bay, across Burrard Bridge. From bridge, take right fork onto Cornwall Ave. to inn.
Restrictions No smoking.
Credit cards None accepted.
Rates B&B, $85–120 double.
Extras Italian, French, German spoken.

Lonsdale Quay Hotel   *Tel:* 604–986–6111
123 Carrie Cates Court, North Vancouver   800–836–6111
V7M 3K7   *Fax:* 604–986–8782

"This may be the most interesting place to stay in town. This ultra-modern hotel is located on the third floor of the Lonsdale Quay Market, overlooking bustling Burrard Inlet and the skyline of downtown Vancouver. On the first floor of the market complex are rows and rows of fresh fruit, vegetable, fish and other food vendors, plus a slew of ethnic takeout food stands. On the second floor are a variety of boutiques, bookstores and several restaurants. On the third is the hotel. The lobby includes comfortable seating with views over the balcony to the hubbub below. Around the outside of the hotel/market is a huge fountain, with lots of seating on a deck overlooking the harbor. About a half-block away is a passenger-only seabus that whizzes you downtown.

"Our room was contemporary and well decorated, in a soothing gray with tea rose accents; it had a queen-size bed and nice bathroom, and was on the east side where we could look out at the water and down at a tugboat landing. Those on the south face the water and downtown Vancouver, while those on the west look toward a snippet of water and the sail-shaped convention center. The tugs (from small ones to gigantic ocean tugs) puffed in and out and were fascinating to watch. Room service was prompt, and the food good, with excellent soups and salads." *(Suzanne Carmichael)* "Just as appealing on a return visit. The room colors and appointments are in excellent shape, the market is great fun and has lots of ethnic fast food as well as luscious produce." *(SC)*

Open All year.
Rooms 70 suites & doubles—all with full private bath, telephone, TV, mini-bar, hair dryer, coffee maker. Some with whirlpool tub, balcony.
Facilities 2 restaurants, pub, nightclub, meeting rooms, fitness center, whirlpool, sauna, children's playroom, covered parking.
Location N Vancouver, on Burrard Inlet. 12 min. to downtown via Seabus. From Upper Levels Hwy. (Hwy. 1), take Lonsdale exit & go S to end.
Restrictions No smoking in some guest rooms.
Credit cards Amex, CB, DC, Discover, JCB, MC, Visa.
Rates Room only, $150–300 suite, double. Extra person, $25. Children under 12 free in parents' room.

"O Canada" House　　　　　　　　　　　　*Tel:* 604–688–0555
1114 Barclay Street, V6E 1H1　　　　　　　　*Fax:* 604–488–0556

In 1909 Vancouver pioneer and banker Ewing Buchan owned this 1897 Victorian home; it was here that he wrote *"O Canada,"* which became the national anthem of Canada. Jim Britten and Mike Browne bought the house in 1995, and after extensive renovation, opened "O Canada" House as an inn. It has been designated a heritage "A" property for its historical and architectural merit, and is furnished with museum quality lighting, furniture and artwork from the Victorian and Edwardian eras. The common rooms have inviting seating areas; the guest rooms have queen- or king-size beds and modern amenities—such as a telephone and TV—discretely blended into the decor. Sherry is served in the front parlor at 5 P.M.; from 8–9 A.M. on weekdays, 8:30–9:30 A.M. on weekends, guests gather at the dining room table for breakfast, perhaps broiled honey-glazed grapefruit, freshly baked raisin scones, and poached eggs on English muffins, with broiled tomatoes.

"Centrally located within easy walking distance of all Vancouver sights; good off-street parking; quiet and peaceful." *(Mark Chay)* "Outstanding service, ambiance and food." *(WC)* "Spotless, with modern facilities. Thoughtful innkeepers suggested activities and loaned maps. Coffee, cookies, and fruit are always available from the open pantry." *(Susan Moeser)* "Tastefully furnished in period style, both comfortable and interesting; great effort in restoring ambiance along with the decor. Within ten minutes you can walk to the city center, Stanley Park, or a wide variety of restaurants." *(Andrew Clark)*

Open All year.
Rooms 1 cottage, 5 doubles—all with private bath and/or shower, telephone, radio, clock, TV, desk, fan, refrigerator. Some with fireplace, balcony. Cottage with patio.
Facilities Dining room, living room & library with fireplace, stereo, books, TV/VCR; guest kitchen, porch. City lot with croquet, off-street parking.
Location Downtown Vancouver. From Hwy 99, take Seymour to Smithe. Turn NW on Smithe & go to Thurlow. Turn S & go to Barclay. Turn right to inn on left.
Restrictions No smoking. Children over 11.
Credit cards MC, Visa.
Rates B&B, $125–195 double. Extra person, $20. Tipping optional. 10% senior, AAA discount.
Extras Airport/station pickup, $10–15.

Sylvia Hotel　　　　　　　　　　　　　　*Tel:* 604–681–9321
1154 Gilford Street, V6G 2P6

"Imagine a 1940s ocean liner of a hotel anchored on the shores of English Bay in the best residential area of the city, a bit dated but full of the quality of charm and relaxation that we all thought was long gone. Large suites with complete kitchens at especially low prices. The Sylvia is in very high demand and reservations are often taken years in advance." *(Christopher Hart Johnston)*. "Enviably wonderful location, steps from the beach and Stanley Park. While the front desk seemed rushed, it's obviously popular and a superb bargain." *(SC)* "Our seventh-floor room had a wonderful view looking over the bay. Kind, helpful staff." *(GF)*

The hotel restaurant serves three meals daily, from the breakfast standards of eggs and pancakes, to lunches of fish and chips, salads, and burgers, to dinners of prawns with garlic, seafood stew, and grilled lamb chops.

Open All year.
Rooms 22 suites, 98 doubles—all with full private bath, telephone, TV, desk.
Facilities Restaurant, dining room, bar/lounge. Underground parking garage (80 spaces), $5 daily. 3 blocks from Stanley Park for swimming, tennis, golf, playground.
Location 15 minutes from downtown Vancouver. At corner of Gilford & Davie St., on Seawall Promenade.
Restrictions No smoking in some rooms.
Credit cards Amex, DC, EnRoute, MC, Visa.
Rates Room only, $110–170 suite, $65–125 double. Extra person, $10. Children under 18 free in parents' room. Children's menu. Alc breakfast, $4–7; alc lunch, $7; alc dinner, $20. Prix fixe dinner, $15.
Extras Some rooms wheelchair accessible. Cribs, $5. Babysitting facilities. French, Spanish, Italian, Mandarin Chinese spoken.

Wedgewood Hotel ♿ 604–689–7777
845 Hornby Street, V6Z 1V1 800–663–0666
Fax: 604–688–3074
E-mail: Wedgwood@portal.ca

Overlooking charming Robson Square, the Wedgewood Hotel is probably Vancouver's best-known small hotel, and we have received consistently positive reports on the attentive and gracious staff, the attractive rooms, and the excellent location. It's owned and run by sisters Joanna Tsaparas and Eleni Skalbania. The hotel's popular restaurant, Bacchus, features contemporary Northern Italian cuisine at lunch and dinner, with such entrees as halibut with artichoke ragout, baked polenta with grilled rataouille, and osso buco with saffron risotto. From 2 to 4 P.M., the style is British, when tea with scones, Devon cream, and finger sandwiches, are served.

"Fully endorse entry. The doorman always greeted us by name, and the whole staff was friendly and helpful. We enjoyed breakfast and tea in the lovely dining room. The lobby was beautifully decorated for Christmas, and smelled heavenly." *(Lee Todd)* "Exceptionally helpful staff assisted with everything from touring directions to dining recommendations. Our spacious, uncluttered room, was painted blue and had a beautiful city view—but no traffic noise. Thick, apricot-colored towels in the bath. Wonderful location." *(Nina Piccirilli)* "Dinner was superb, from the antipasto with grilled fennel and marinated prawns, to the pasta with smoked salmon and green peppercorns." *(SC)* "China-town is only a few minutes' drive east and Stanley Park is to the west; the harbor is only a 10-minute walk." *(Joni Hiramoto & Mac Master)* "Guest rooms are available in four price categories; all have luxurious appointments and are decorated with a country French motif with dark red and blue colors. Be sure to ask if any promotional or off-season rates are in effect when booking." *(SWS)* "Lovely downstairs lounge. We should have read your description earlier and stayed here." *(RS)* "Delightful stay; highly recommend. Our room was clean, quiet, pretty, comfortable, and overlooked a small shady courtyard. Delightful dinner at Bacchus." *(KLH)*

Open All year.
Rooms 38 suites, 59 doubles—all with private bath and/or shower, dual-line telephone/modem, radio, TV, air-conditioning, mini-bar, in-room safe, hair dryer, coffee maker, balcony. Penthouse suites with fireplace.
Facilities Restaurant, lounge with piano bar, breakfast room, meeting rooms. Business, concierge services. 24-hr. room service. Valet parking. Health club.
Location Downtown. Across from Robson Square & the Law Courts, between Smythe & Robson Sts.
Restrictions No smoking in some guest rooms.
Credit cards All major.
Rates Room only, $400–540 suite, $240–340 double, $220–320 single. Seasonal specials. Weekend, honeymoon, anniversary packages. Afternoon tea, $13; weekend brunch, $12–20. Alc lunch, $15–25; alc dinner, $35–55.
Extras Wheelchair access, one room equipped for disabled. Crib, babysitting. Chinese, French, Greek, Iranian, Japanese, Spanish spoken.

West End Guest House
1362 Haro Street, V6E 1G2

Tel: 604–681–2889
Fax: 604–688–8812

Built in 1906 for the Edwards family, the West End Guest House is constructed entirely of straight grain cedar (meaning it is without knots). The young Edwards men operated the first photography shop in Vancouver and many of their photographs of interior British Columbia and the Yukon hang in the inn. In 1985 it was restored as a B&B, complete with a "Painted Lady" pink, white, and teal color scheme. It was purchased in 1991 by Evan Penner, who has furnished the rooms with Victorian antiques and reproductions. Guest rooms are supplied with terry bathrobes and fine linens; the brass beds are fitted with feather mattresses and goose-down comforters. Breakfast is served at the dining room table from 8–9 A.M., and includes fresh fruit, hot and cold cereal, homemade baked goods, and such entrees as sausage and pepper frittata, orange waffles with apricot sauce, or scallop, shrimp and salmon omelets; in the afternoon tea and cookies are set out, plus sherry from 5–7 P.M..

"Hot chocolate, coffee and tea is always handy in the comfortable parlor. Mountain views from the wraparound porch and front bedrooms. Spotlessly clean." *(Katherine Moore)* "Quiet and restful, yet sophisticated; helpful, friendly owners; excellent preparation and quality of breakfast. Convenient parking." *(W.I. Cameron)* "A personal note of welcome and plate of chocolates and fruit awaited in our room." *(Debbie & Michael Swiatek)* "We had the least expensive room, the small-but-cozy Terra Double on the lower level of the house. The common rooms are a comfortable mix of traditional and Art Nouveau furniture." *(Anita Epler)*

Open All year.

Rooms 2 suites, 6 doubles—all with private bath and/or shower, telephone, radio, TV. Some with desk, ceiling fan, sundeck. Suites with gas fireplace.

Facilities Dining room, living room with books, stereo, games; sun deck, porch. Bicycles. 15-min. walk to beach, marina. Off-street parking.

Location 1 block S of Robson & Broughton Sts. 6 blocks W of Robson Sq. Walking distance to Financial District, Stanley Park.

Restrictions No smoking. No children under 13.

Credit cards Amex, Discover, MC, Visa.

Rates B&B, $175–210 suite, $145–180 double. Extra person, $15. 2-night weekend, holiday minimum.

VERNON

On the eastern side of the Cascades, in southern BC, Vernon sits at the confluence of five valleys and three lakes. "Not overly touristy, Vernon has a few good restaurants and a relaxing downtown park. The climate and terrain make for superb outdoor activities—skiing at Silver Star Mountain in winter, and during the hot, dry summer (pleasantly cool at night), swimming and water sports at Kalamalka or Okanagan lakes, hiking on miles of trails, and visiting wineries and the historic O'Keefe Ranch. Nearby attractions include the historic O'Keefe Ranch, numerous wineries, and incredible fruit in harvest season." *(BL)*

Also recommended: A turn-of-the-century Victorian home, **The Tuck Inn** (3101 Pleasant Valley Road, Vernon, V1T 4L2; 250–545–3252) was restored as a B&B in 1992; the four guest rooms share two baths. "Modern amenities with country Victorian charm; the bedrooms have designer wallpapers, comfortable beds, and air-conditioning (masking any possible traffic noise in the front rooms. The shared bathrooms were spotless. The sitting room is a comfortable spot to watch TV, chat with other guests, or listen to music. Breakfast is served 7:30–9:00 A.M. in the inn's tea room, also open to the public for lunch and tea from 11 A.M. to 4 P.M. The decor is delightful and the service friendly and efficient. Our meals were substantial with walnut waffles and eggs and sausage. Innkeepers Irene and Bill Tullett have created a comfortable small inn; Irene is warm, open, obliging, and her love for the Vernon area is infectious. She is always willing to chat but also allows guests their privacy." *(Brad Lockner)* The B&B double rates are $65–85; children are welcome.

For additional area inns, see **Kelowna.**

VICTORIA

Set at the southeastern tip of Vancouver Island, Victoria is known for its British ambience, combined with a distinctly un-British mild and sunny climate. Among the city's many beautiful gardens and parks, Butchart Gardens is the most famous of all and is well worth the trip

14 miles north of town. On summer evenings the gardens are illuminated until 11 p.m. Other attractions include the Houses of Parliament, a grand edifice built in 1893; and the Provincial Museum, with an excellent Northwest Coast Indian Collection, along with exhibits on natural history and 19th-century development. The city is small, so be sure to wander through Beacon Hill Park, the Old Town area, the now-compact Chinatown, and explore the shops—those specializing in Indian and Eskimo art and handicrafts as well as those offering the best of British imports. Although there are many excellent restaurants, the Indian and Chinese ones offer the most interesting dining at the most reasonable prices.

Reader tips: "Victoria is, of course, the most wonderful city. I even think it has stolen my heart from San Francisco." *(Norma Simon)* On the other hand: "We loved Seattle and Vancouver, but found Victoria less interesting, lacking even its vaunted quaintness." *(SR)* "Victoria is very popular in season; rates double and advance reservations are essential. We thought it was a charming city, with real British flavor." *(MW)*

Also recommended—hotels: Located in the heart of Victoria's Old Town, **The Bedford Regency** (1140 Government Street, V8W 1Y2; 250–384–6835 or 800–665–6500) is an intimate, 40-room hotel close to Parliament and shopping areas. "Spacious lobby, with furniture that adds a South Pacific flavor, and friendly desk staff. Room 38 on the third floor has a view of the Inner Harbor, and has a granite-faced fireplace, comfortable soft chairs, a queen-size bed with down comforter, and a peach and moss color scheme." *(SC)* "My clean and light-filled room had windows that opened and lovely flower-filled window boxes." *(Leigh Robinson)* The double rates are $95–220, depending on room and season.

Victoria's most famous hotel is **The Empress** (721 Government Street, V8W 1W5; 250–384–8111 or 800–441–1414) built in 1908 and overlooking the Inner Harbour. The meticulously restored common rooms are both very grand and very busy; the 483 renovated guest rooms are generally modest in size. "Wonderful location for strolling day or night; the Parliament building is lit up like a Disney castle, and bands, magicians, and comedians entertain tourists along the park. My attractive room had flowered chintz wallpaper, two comfortable chairs, desk, and overlooked the gardens. Outstanding, friendly service everywhere. Excellent breakfast buffet of sausages, smoked and poached salmon, waffles, and omelets made to order." *(June Horn)* "Huge, but a nice, elegant old hotel. Restaurant is pricy, but good. Great shops." *(KLH)* "When in Victoria, afternoon tea at the Empress Hotel is a must." *(Barbara Walsh)* Double rates are $140–315; afternoon tea is $15–25.

"While not a small inn, the **Ocean Pointe Resort Hotel & Spa** (45 Songhees Road, V9A 6T3; 250–360–2999 or 800–667–4677) is a delightful change of pace. Rooms are comfortable and pleasant, the dining room excellent, and the spa/fitness center is handy. It faces the inner harbor and Parliament, and you can walk to downtown in five minutes, or take a beautiful stroll on the harbor waterwalk." *(Norma Simon)* A luxury hotel, built in 1992 in a neo-Victorian Chateau-esque style, the Ocean Pointe has two restaurants, a piano bar, heated indoor swimming pool and whirlpool, a squash/racquetball court, two tennis courts, and extensive health spa facilities. There are 250 guest rooms, with rates of $495–695 suite, $119–279 double; children under age 12 stay free.

The **Olde England Inn** (429 Lampson Street, V9A 5Y9; 250–388–4353) offers not only an antique-filled Tudor-style mansion but also an English village containing replicas of Shakespeare's birthplace, Anne Hathaway's cottage, Harvard House, the Garrick Inn, a Tuck (sweet) Shop, and the Olde Curiosity Shoppe—all, of course, set on Chaucer Lane. Staff is dressed in period clothing, and most of the 50 guest rooms (all with private bath) have canopy beds; rates range from $80–200. Breakfast in the restaurant includes scones or crumpets, while dinner features roast beef and Yorkshire pudding, and steak and kidney pie. "Only the bathroom and TV were modern in our thatched cottage; we felt transported back to the 1600s. Our salmon dinner was delicious; the staff friendly and helpful. An easy 15-minute bus trip takes you right to the Empress, or you can stroll along the Seawalk in about 40 minutes." *(Sharon Bielski, also MW)*

Information please—hotels: Named for the Victorian mansion that once stood on the property, the **Chateau Victoria** (740 Burdett Avenue, V8W 1B2; 604–382–4221 or 800–663–5891) is a luxurious 178-room hotel with an indoor swimming pool and spa, and double rates of $126–260. Its rooftop restaurant, Parrot House, is named for the pet parrot, Louis, who inherited the estate in 1946 when his owner died; only upon his demise at age 115 (in 1985) was this highly desirable property available for development. "Our beautiful, well-equipped suite was immaculately clean and tastefully decorated. Comfortable living room, huge bedroom; matching blue and beige decor. Extremely accommodating, friendly staff. The restaurant has a gorgeous, rooftop view, reasonable prices, and good food." *(Maryellen Forde)*

Suzanne Carmichael suggests the 149-room **Clarion Hotel Grand Pacific** (450 Quebec Street, V8V 1W5; 250–386–0450 or 800–663–7550) for its convenient location, its attractive rooms, its good exercise facilities, and best of all, for the harbor views. "Ask for an even-numbered harborside room on the 7th or 8th floor; you'll be able to see the whole Inner Harbour from your own balcony." Double rates are $95–255 depending upon the season.

A contemporary building in a parklike setting within reasonable walking distance of downtown, the 200-room **Laurel Point Inn** (680 Montreal Street, V8V 1Z8; 250–386–8721 or 800–663–7667) offers resort facilities and atmosphere. You can stroll the flower-lined paths along the harbor, enjoy the Japanese garden, watch the ferries sail by from your bedroom window, or relax in the swimming pool or hot tub. Rates range from $125–650, depending on season and location; rooms in the newer South wing are more expensive but are preferable in terms of decor, amenities, layout, and view.

Also recommended—B&Bs: The **Holland House Inn** (595 Michigan Street, V8V 1S7; 250–384–6644) is a bright and airy 1930s building, decorated with paintings, sculpture, and drawings by Victoria's leading artists. "Perfectly situated for walking to Victoria's Inner Harbor, the British Columbia Museum, and shops. Harry Brock, the innkeeper, helped us plan our trip and took a personal interest in advising us while there. His wife Margaret is responsible for the elegant, outstanding decor in this immaculate inn. The library and solarium are welcoming settings for the luscious full breakfast (eggs with salmon were our favorite), which can also be enjoyed in your room or private deck. Off-street parking." *(Sandy & Chuck Mitchell)* B&B double rates for the ten guest rooms, all with private bath, are $90–225.

Information please—B&Bs: Overlooking the quiet Portage Inlet bird sanctuary, the **Arundel Manor** (980 Arundel Drive, V9A 2C3; 250–385–5442) is just ten minutes drive from downtown. This 1912 Tudor-style home offers stunning sunset views over the water. The three guest rooms, each with private bath, are decorated with a charming mix of antiques, collectibles and family heirlooms. The B&B double rates are $95–150, and include a full breakfast.

For a private, romantic getaway, a good option is the **Humboldt House B&B** (867 Humboldt Street, V8V 2Z6; 604–383–0152), a Victorian home built in 1895. Each of its five guest rooms has a large Jacuzzi tub and wood-burning fireplace, plus a CD player and goosedown comforter. The B&B double rates of $145–185 include welcoming wine and homemade chocolates, plus a breakfast basket delivered to your door. It's two blocks walk to the Empress and the Inner Harbor, and one block to Beacon Hill Park.

Hilarie Morgan reports that the **Palace On Dallas** (1482 Dallas Road, V8S 1A2; 250–361–9551) has "friendly and knowledgeable proprietors to assist with information and reservations. Quiet, beautiful home with antique decor, incredible ocean views, yet just minutes from many activities. Clean, easy to find, lots of parking, good food. Nice walkway for jogging or strolling, just across the street, along the ocean cliffs and beaches." Three guest rooms are available at B&B double rates of $65–110, including a full breakfast.

In 1910, when the King of England's representative to British Columbia needed an appropriately grand home, the **Prior House** (620 St. Charles Street, V8S 3N7; 250–592–8847) was built. The inn has a ballroom and drawing room, stained glass windows, oak paneling, period and antique furnishings, and crystal chandeliers. The six guest rooms have brass and antique beds, down comforters and pillow, and lavish use of fabrics to create romantic canopies; some of the private baths have whirlpool tubs. A full breakfast is served from 8:30–9 A.M., usually in the dining room; tea is served from 4 to 6 P.M. The B&B double rates are $105–270.

The spectacular view of the Strait of Juan de Fuca and the promenade makes **The Sea Rose B&B** (1250 Dallas Road, V8V 1C4; 250–381–7932) ideal for those who long for the ocean. "This 1921 Craftsman-style home has four guest rooms, each with private bath, TV, and wet bar. Ours had an ocean view and felt like a mini-apartment. The owner, Gail Hamhuis, was pleasant and accommodating; good breakfasts, too." *(Susan Doucet)* The B&B double rates of $120–170 include a full breakfast; Dutch apple pancakes are a speciality.

One-half block from the ocean and a short walk through the park to downtown is the **Wellington B&B** (66 Wellington Avenue, V8V 4H5;

250–383–5976), a 1912 Craftsman-style home furnished with many charming pieces and collectibles. There's a guest living room with extensive library, a relaxing garden spot, and a sun porch; the four guest rooms all have private baths. The B&B double rates of $75–110 include a breakfast served from 8 to 9 A.M., with fresh fruit, scones, breads, and a hot entree.

For additional area inns, see **Malahat** and **Sooke.**

Abigail's Hotel   *Tel:* 250–388–5363
906 McClure Street, V8V 3E7   800–561–6565
                    Fax: 250–388–7787
                    E-mail: innkeeper@abigailshotel.com

Built in 1930 as a luxury, English Tudor–style apartment building, Abigail's was totally restored in 1985 as an intimate B&B hotel. In 1995 Daniel and Frauke Behune purchased the inn, extensively redecorating and renovating it. The decor features an elegant European country-style look, with lots of muted colors and flowers, and goosedown comforters on the beds. Guests can enjoy sherry and hors d'oeuvres in the library each evening, and at breakfast, served 7:30–9:30 A.M., dine on fresh baked pastries, fruit, juice, and a choice of a savory or sweet entree.

"Perfect example of what a B&B should be—everything works and is spotless; charming hosts to tend to your needs; rooms tastefully furnished and homey; ready-to-light fireplaces with a good supply of wood; beds with wonderful pillows and luxurious cotton sheets and duvets; and bathrooms with thick fluffy towels. The east-facing breakfast room is cheery, and breakfast well prepared—freshly squeezed orange juice, fruit compote, breads and muffins, and eggs with bacon and hash brown potatoes, or perhaps spicy baked fruit. The library is furnished with comfortable leather sofas and wing chairs, and a selection of games, current magazines and newspapers; pre-breakfast coffee is set out here, as is hot mulled wine and homebaked cookies each afternoon. Promptly at 6 P.M., sherry and hors d'oeuvres, crackers with cheeses, and crisp vegetables with dips are served. Loved the ambiance and quality, convenience to downtown, and the pleasant residential area. Although our room was one of the least expensive, it was comfortable and uncrowded." *(Esther Magathan)* "Delightful owners; wonderful breakfasts. Lots of fireplaces and huge soaking tubs." *(Barbara Walsh)*

Open All year.
Rooms 16 doubles—all with private bath and/or shower, telephone, radio, clock. 8 with fireplace, 5 with whirlpool tub, 4 with refrigerator.
Facilities Dining room, library with fireplace. ¼ acre with limited off-street parking, Victorian gardens. 3 blocks to beach, park.
Location 3 blocks from center. On McClure between Quadra & Vancouver Sts.
Restrictions No smoking. Children over 10 years.
Credit cards Amex, MC, Visa.
Rates B&B, $145–299 double. Extra person, $30.
Extras French, German spoken.

Andersen House B&B
301 Kingston Street, V8V 1V5

Tel: 250–388–4565
Fax: 250–388–4563
E-mail: andersen@islandnet.com

An appealing combination of Victorian architecture and uncluttered, light, airy decor, the Anderson House is a restored 1891 Queen Anne–style painted lady built for a prosperous sea captain, complete with twelve-foot ceilings, numerous fireplaces, stained glass windows, and beautiful hardwood floors. Residents since 1972, Max and Janet Andersen opened their home as a B&B in 1988, and emphasize the eclectic nature of their furnishings—antiques, original modern paintings and sculpture, Peruvian rugs, and Raku ceramics. Guests have their choice of guest rooms in the house, or they can stay on the Andersen's classic 1927 fifty-foot motor yacht, *Mamita*, moored one block away and make the short walk over to breakfast each morning. At 8:30A.M. in summer, and 9 A.M. in winter, breakfast is served at the large dining room table and includes an egg dish or pancakes with sausage or bacon, fruit, homemade scones and jam, toast, and juice. "Fascinating owners who are warm and down-to-earth hosts. Comfortable accommodations, nice breakfasts. In a quiet neighborhood not far from the Empress Hotel and the ferry dock." *(Arleen Keele)*

Open All year.
Rooms In house: 2 suites, 3 doubles—all with private bath and/or shower, telephone, clock/radio/CD player, private entrance. 1 with double Jacuzzi tub. On 50-ft classic motor yacht: bedroom, private shower bath, lounge with skylight, deck with chairs.
Facilities Dining room, porch, decks, patio with fireplace. City lot with on-street parking, croquet. Two blocks to harbor, exercise facility.
Location 3 blocks from center. 1½ blocks W of Parliament buildings.
Restrictions No smoking. Children over 12.
Credit cards MC, Visa.
Rates B&B, $95–195 suite, $85–185 double. Extra person, $35.

The Beaconsfield Inn
998 Humboldt Street, V8V 2Z8

Tel: 250–384–4044
Fax: 250–384–4052
E-mail: beconsfield@islandnet.com

The Beaconsfield is an Edwardian mansion restored as an inn in 1984 and furnished with period antiques in exceptional taste. It was purchased by Con and Judi Sollid in 1993, professionals in the fields of law and dentistry. A recent breakfast, served at individual tables in the dining room, included freshly squeezed orange juice, cheese scones with mango-cranberry preserves, gingerbread pancakes with pear-currant sauce or salmon-spinach soufflé; cereal, granola and muesli are also available. Tea is served in the inviting Victorian library in the afternoon, with sherry and nibbles offered in the early evening.

"The Emily Carr room is decorated in burgundy and green. Tasty breakfast with fresh fruit, just-baked goodies, homemade jam, and an egg entree." *(Mark & Lori Smigel)* "A cozy inn offering warm hospitality and luxurious rooms with many amenities." *(Tim & Lisa Hogan)* "We particularly liked chatting with other guests over tea or sherry.

Nothing was too much trouble for the staff—information and assistance was always available. The menus from local restaurants enabled us to choose where to dine. In a quiet, residential area, just a few minutes walk from the harbor and town center." *(Kathleen Imhof)* "Rooms are clean, bright, and beautifully appointed; excellent lighting and bathroom facilities. Delicious breakfasts." *(J. & E. Gilbert)*

Open All year.

Rooms 1 oceanfront cottage, 3 suites, 6 doubles—all with private bath and shower, desk. 8 with fireplace, whirlpool tub.

Facilities Dining room with fireplace, library with fireplace, sun room. ½ acre with English gardens, off-street parking.

Location Historic district, 4 blocks from center of town. From Port Angeles ferry terminal, go E on Belleville, left on Blanshard, right on Humboldt to inn at corner of Vancouver St. From Swartz Bay/Sidney terminal, follow Hwy. 17 into town. Turn left onto Humboldt.

Restrictions No smoking. "No children please." Some kitchen noise in one room.

Credit cards MC, Visa.

Rates Room only, $395 cottage. B&B, $275–350 suite, $175–325 double. Extra person, $65. 2-night weekend minimum, April–Oct.

Dashwood Seaside Manor 👫

1 Cook Street, V8V 3W6

*Tel:*250–385–5517
800–667–5517
E-mail: reservations@dashwoodmanor.com

The last ice age some 15,000 years ago made way for the Manor's beautiful bluff-top location. Designed by Samuel Maclure, a renowned architect of the Edwardian era, the inn was completed in 1912. Unfortunately, the good times didn't last, and in 1978, Derek Dashwood rescued this architectural gem from impending demolition. Since then, Derek has spent more than $1 million on rebuilding and restoration—an ongoing process. Victoria's only seaside inn, it has guest rooms innovatively designed for the building: one suite has a granite fireplace, beamed ceiling, and a chandelier; another has stained glass inserts above each of the large windows; all have antiques and period pieces. Each suite has a kitchen, so guests make their own breakfast from the ingredients provided (juice, hot and cold cereals, fruits, bread, ham, eggs, coffee and tea); also included in the rates is an evening glass of wine or sherry in the library.

"The location, atmosphere, staff, and Derek's accommodating attitude make this place ideal." *(Diane Tyler)* "Beacon Hill Park on one side and the open waterfront on the other provide fantastic vistas. Marvelous walks and close to downtown Victoria." *(D.M. Hughs)* "A relief not to have to make small talk with strangers at breakfast. Enjoyed evening sherry in the library." *(MW)* Comments appreciated.

Open All year.

Rooms 14 suites—all with private bath, radio, TV, kitchenette. Some with desk, fireplace, balcony.

Facilities Library with fireplace. Laundry facility. 2 city lots with off-street parking. Near public tennis, lawn bowling, golf and other recreation.

Location Next to Beacon Hill Park.
Restrictions No smoking.
Credit cards Amex, MC, Visa.
Rates B&B, $75–285 suite. Extra adult, $45; extra child over 12, $25; extra child under 12, $10. 2-night weekend minimum. 10% senior discount.
Extras Crib, babysitting.

Swans Hotel ¢ 👥
506 Pandora Avenue, V8W 1N6

Tel: 250–361–3310
800–668–7926
Fax: 250–361–3491
E-mail: swans@islandnet.com

Built in 1913 as a granary and feed store, corn was delivered by train through what is now the main entrance of Swans Hotel. In 1987, English-born shepherd-turned-entrepreneur Michael Williams bought this "ugly duckling" warehouse and renovated it into Swans, an all-suite hotel with a pub, cafe, and brewery—Buckerfield's—maintaining a 74-year-old tradition of storing grain. The flavor of Olde Towne Victoria remains, with iron wheels from the original grain elevators displayed in the pub, chandeliers which originally came from the Empress Hotel, and furnishings made by local craftsmen. Guest rooms have contemporary decor with natural oak furniture and original Northwest paintings; most are two-story, with high ceilings, exposed beams, and beds in the loft. Seafood features prominently in the Fowl Fish Cafe and Oyster House menu, with five oyster appetizers; entrees include trout with peach chutney, prawns with Szechuan sauce, chicken fettuccine in ale sauce, and steak with green peppercorns; homemade ale bread is served with every meal. Breakfasts are served in the glass-walled courtyard cafe; contemporary pub cuisine, such as bangers and mash, halibut and chips, salads and burgers, and ten varieties of beer and ale are favorites at Buckerfield's. Janina Ceglarz has been the manager since 1992.

"Excellently run small hotel, with pleasant dining room, English-style pub, and helpful, accommodating staff." (*J. Ward*) "Large, bright, clean rooms with unfancy, uncomplicated, comfortable furnishings." (*Bob Muhalchan, also RM*) "While there is a lively pub and cafe downstairs, the upstairs is quiet. Excellent pub food." (*Mrs. Keith Carkner*) "Convenient central location; I walked to most places of interest on either side of the Inner Harbor; just behind the hotel is Chinatown, and across the street is a good bakery. A wonderful restoration, with a small reception area and spacious guest rooms; those on the top floor in the back are especially quiet. My loft suite was spotless; the bathroom had efficient good plumbing and lots of hot water; the little kitchen was convenient for making breakfast. Cheerful, friendly staff. The main dining room is particularly attractive with fresh floral arrangements and an eclectic art collection. Excellent meals, tasty beer, and delicious ale bread. The early dinner option, available between 5–6 P.M. was especially reasonable." (*Barbara Goodwin*) "The fully equipped kitchen appealed to my restaurant-weary self, and the smoke-free rooms were appreciated." (*Michael Bailey*)

Open All year.

Rooms 29 1-2 bedroom suites—all with full private bath, telephone, radio, clock, TV, desk, kitchen with microwave. Some with fan, balcony.

Facilities Restaurant, pub with midweek musical entertainment, sidewalk cafe, brewery. Off-street parking.

Location Olde Towne, Inner Harbour in the center of Victoria, opposite Market Square.

Restrictions Smoking permitted in some rooms. Street noise in a few rooms.

Credit cards Amex, DC, EnRoute, MC, Visa.

Rates Room only, $99–185 double. Extra person, $20. Two children under 12 free in parents' room. 15% senior, AAA discounts. Alc breakfast, $5–8; alc lunch, $8; alc dinner, $30.

Extras Limited wheelchair accessibility. Cribs. Babysitting referrals. Spanish, French, German spoken.

WELLS

In 1933, when the rest of the world was deep in the Depression, gold was discovered at the Cariboo mine and the town of Wells became a thriving company town. With 4,500 residents, it was the largest town and cultural center in the interior of British Columbia. Today it is home to an art community, hosts visitors on their way to Barkerville, a former mining town and restored ghost town, and is close to the 75-mile canoeing circuit of the Bowron Lakes. Area activities also include mountain biking, hiking, and llama trekking.

The Wells Hotel ¢ ✗ ♦
Box 39, Wells V0K 2R0

Tel: 250–994–3427
800–860–2299
Fax: 250–994–3494
E-mail: whotel@abc.awinc.com

With gold fever creating a boomtown, The Wells Hotel was built in the 1930s to accommodate the newcomers. Now a heritage building, the hotel was remodelled in 1996 by Jim Savage. Mining artifacts and photographs are displayed in the lounge, where guests can enjoy a hot drink in front of a roaring fire. The guest rooms range in size from cozy, European-style with simple furnishings and shared baths, to more spacious ones with full private baths. They all have natural pine furniture and fir floors; the decor features rag rugs, floral comforters, wooden window blinds, and quality linens. The aroma of freshly baked cinnamon buns, muffins and scones will bring you to the breakfast table, which also includes fresh fruit, eggs, bacon and toast. The Poole Street Cafe serves lunch and dinner, and features homemade soups and stews, pastas, and grilled specialties such as rainbow trout with garlic-lemon butter, and pork tenderloin with apricot chutney.

"A little bit of the 1930's in the 90's. The smell of spruce burning in the fireplace, the authentic architecture, and wonderful art throughout our room provided a special experience." *(Chris Hamilton)* "Local history proudly displayed in a tasteful way. Food, service, and hospitality were tops." *(Chris Harris)* "Friendly, helpful staff; welcoming atmosphere." *(JC)* "Superb baking. Excellent selection of food." *(MVH)* Comments welcome.

Open All year
Rooms 16 doubles—7 with full private bath, 9 with a maximum of 4 people sharing bath. All with clock, radio, fan.
Facilities Restaurant, meeting room and lounge all with fireplace. Occasional musical entertainment. Patio, hot tub. On-street parking. 20 min. to canoeing, downhill skiing. Cross-country skiing from door.
Location S central BC, Cariboo Mountains. 475 m N of Vancouver, 1 hr. E of Quesnel. From Quesnel, take Hwy 26 E to Wells, then take 1st left onto Pooley St. to hotel.
Restrictions No smoking. Children welcome.
Credit cards Amex, Interact, MC, Visa.
Rates B&B, $49–115 double, $49–95 single. Extra person, $10–15. Children uner 6 free. Alc lunch, $15; alc dinner, $25.
Extras Local airport/station pickups. Crib.

WHISTLER

The fastest-growing resort in North America in 1995, and consistently rated as one of the best for skiing, Whistler continues to expand and offers year-round sports activities. Its closeness to Vancouver, just 75 miles to the southwest, makes it a popular weekend destination for Vancouverites and an easy reach for tourists.

Durlacher Hof ♿
Box 1125, 7055 Nesters Road, V0N 1B0

Tel: 604–932–1924
Fax: 604–938–1980

"The Durlacher Hof, owned by Austrian-Canadians, Erica and Peter Durlacher, is a fresh alternative to the usual run-of-the-mill ski resort. Located about two minutes from the ski slopes of Whistler, this charming Tyrolean inn is a custom-designed alpine lodge complete with an enormous fireplace and beautiful hardwood floors (slippers are available next to the front door). The fresh, clean guest rooms have plump, comfortable goosedown duvets, twin- or queen-size beds, and antique Tyrolean furniture. The second floor rooms with balconies have good views of the mountains, while those on the top floor are most spacious with sleeping alcoves under the eaves. Erica is a wonderful chef who has organized several theme weekends featuring regional cuisine. Peter and Erica take an active interest in guests' welfare, and both are seasoned hoteliers who make their inn a memorable experience. The inn is also popular with skiers from Germany and the U.S." *(Christopher Johnston)* Rates include afternoon tea, plus a breakfast buffet with home-baked breads and pastries, sliced meats and cheese, egg dishes, fresh fruit and juice.

Open All year.
Rooms 1 suite, 7 doubles—all with private bath. Some with Jacuzzi tub. Most with balcony.

Facilities Family room with woodstove, game room. Sauna, whirlpool tub, badminton court, ski storage. Tennis, golf, skiing nearby.

Location SW BC. 125 km N of Vancouver on Hwy 99. 1.5 km N of Whistler village.

Restrictions No smoking. "Adult environment; children by special arrangement."

Credit cards MC, Visa.

Rates B&B, $255 suite, $115–195 double. 2-night weekend minimum. Ski, golf, adventure packages.

Extras Wheelchair accessible; some rooms specially equipped. Station pickups.

Yukon

The Yukon Territory occupies the northwestern part of Canada, bordered by British Columbia to the south, and Alaska to the west.

WHITEHORSE

Capital of the Yukon Territory, Whitehorse developed during the 1897–98 Yukon gold rush, and grew during World War II when the Alaska Highway was under construction. Today it's a popular stop for overland travelers on the Alaska Highway.

Reader tip: "The *Frantic Follies* at the Westmark Hotel was a bit touristy but nonetheless highly entertaining and well done." *(Marty Wall)*

Also recommended: "A delightful B&B, **Highland Home** (One Eleventh Avenue, Y1A 4H5; 403–633–5804) is owned by Dorothy and Richard Martin, transplants from Wales and Scotland. Located on the top of a hill in the woodsy Porter Creek area, it's a five-minute ride to the center of town. Friendly and gregarious hosts eager to make your stay enjoyable. A breakfast of juice, coffee, tea, fruit, assorted cereals, homemade muffins and breads is served in the sun room; hot entrees are available on request. Tea and quick breads are offered upon arrival. Delightful stay." *(Marty Wall & Kip Goldman)*

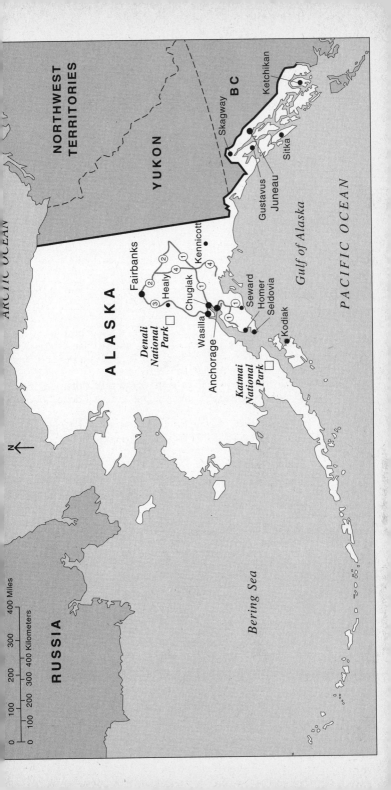

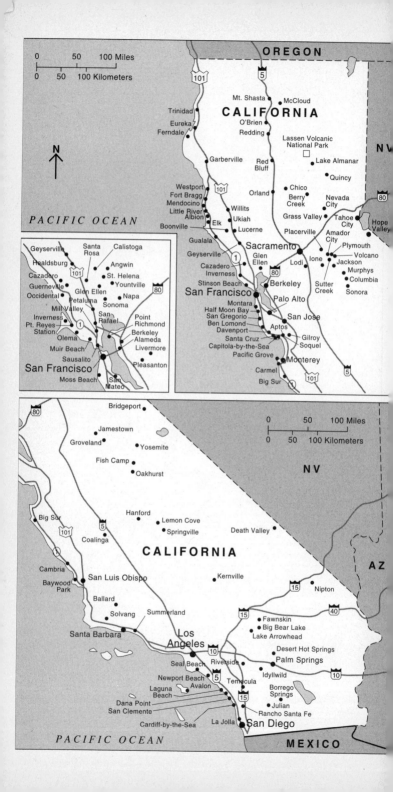

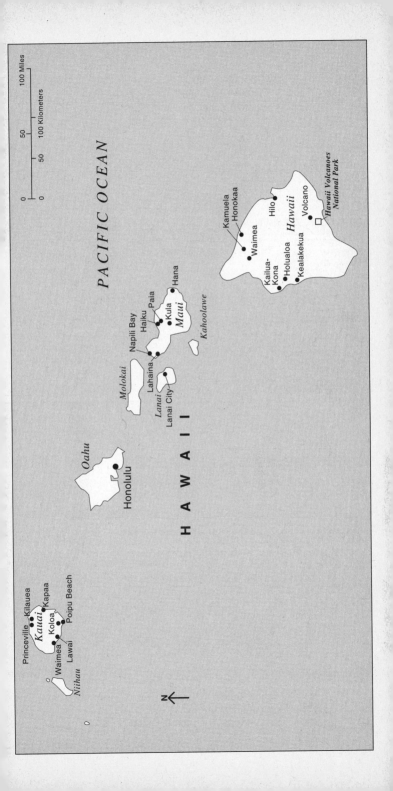

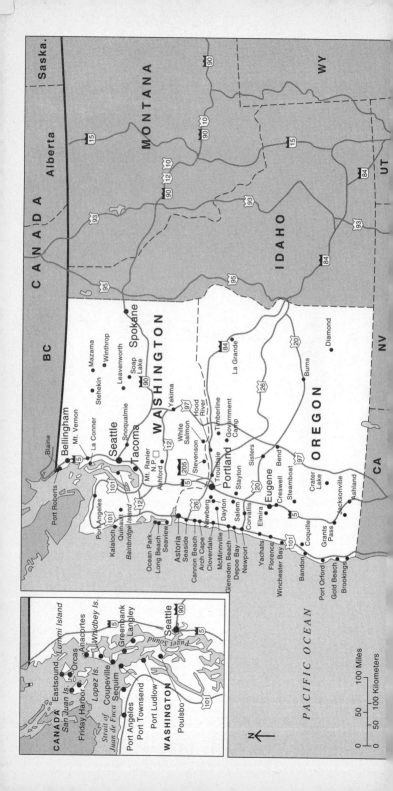

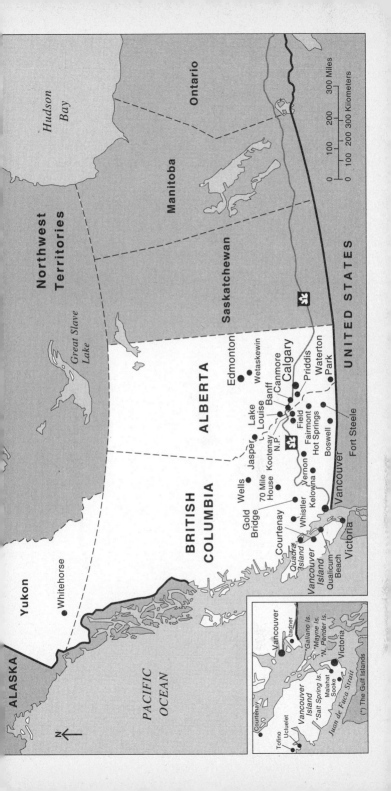

Index of Accommodations

436

Hotel/Inn Report Forms

The report forms on the following pages may be used to endorse or critique an existing entry or to nominate a hotel or inn that you feel deserves inclusion in the next edition. Don't feel you must restrict yourself to the space available; feel free to use your own stationery or e-mail. All nominations (each on a separate piece of paper, if possible) should include your name and address, the name and location of the hotel or inn, when you have stayed there, and for how long. Please report only on establishments you have visited in the last eighteen months, unless you are sure that standards have not dropped since your stay. Please be as specific as possible, and critical where appropriate, about the character of the building, the public rooms, the accommodations, the meals, the service, the nightlife, the grounds, and the general atmosphere of the inn and the attitude of its owners. Comments about area restaurants and sights are also appreciated.

Don't feel you need to write at length. A report that merely verifies the accuracy of existing listings is extremely helpful, i.e., "Visited XYZ Inn and found it just as described." There is no need to bother with prices or with routine information about the number of rooms and facilities, although a sample brochure is very helpful for new recommendations.

On the other hand, don't apologize for writing a long report. Although space does not permit us to quote them in total, the small details provided about furnishings, atmosphere, and cuisine can really make a description come alive, illuminating the special flavor of a particular inn or hotel. Remember that we will again be awarding free copies to our most helpful respondents—last year we mailed over 500 books.

Please note that we print only the names of respondents, never addresses. Those making negative observations are not identified. Although we must always have your full name and address, we will be happy to print your initials, or a pseudonym, if you prefer.

Reports should be sent to P.O. Box 150, Riverside, CT 06878, ssoule@msn.com.

To: *America's Favorite Inns, B&Bs, and Small Hotels,*
    P.O. Box 150, Riverside, CT 06878 or ssoule@msn.com.

Name of hotel _____

Address _____

Telephone _____

Date of most recent visit _____ Duration of visit _____

☐ New recommendation   ☐ Comment on existing entry

Please be as specific as possible about furnishings, atmosphere, service, and cuisine. If reporting on an existing entry, please tell us whether you thought it accurate. Unless you tell us not to, we shall assume that we may publish your name in the next edition. Thank you very much for writing; use your own stationery if preferred:

I am not connected with the management/owners.
I would stay here again if returning to the area.   ☐ yes   ☐ no
Have you written to us before?   ☐ yes   ☐ no

Signed _____

Name _____
                          (Please print)

Address _____
                          (Please print)

_____

WE98/99

FAX TO: 1-801-321-6301

InnPoints Enrollment Application

PERSONAL INFORMATION

Title (Mr/Mrs/Ms etc.) ☐☐☐☐   Code AFI

Last Name ☐☐☐☐☐☐☐☐☐☐☐☐☐☐☐☐☐

First Name ☐☐☐☐☐☐☐☐☐☐☐☐☐ Initial ☐

Company ☐☐☐☐☐☐☐☐☐☐☐☐☐☐☐☐☐

Home Phone ☐☐☐ – ☐☐☐ – ☐☐☐☐

Office Phone ☐☐☐ – ☐☐☐ – ☐☐☐☐

Fax Number ☐☐☐ – ☐☐☐ – ☐☐☐☐

MAILING INFORMATION

Address ☐☐☐☐☐☐☐☐☐☐☐☐☐☐☐☐☐

☐☐☐☐☐☐☐☐☐☐☐☐☐☐☐☐☐

City ☐☐☐☐☐☐☐☐☐☐☐☐ State ☐☐

Zip Code ☐☐☐☐☐ ☐☐☐☐

YOUR P.I.N. NUMBER

(For internal verification purposes only)

Choose a Personal Identification Number (P.I.N.)
that only you will know and remember. ☐☐☐☐☐☐

Mother's Maiden Name –OR– (Use numbers only, please.)

☐☐☐☐☐☐☐☐☐☐☐☐☐☐☐☐

OR MAIL TO: P.O. Box 510605, Dept. AFI
Salt Lake City, UT 84151-0605